Routledge
Taylor & Francis Group

www.routledgesw.com

An authentic breakthrough in social work education . . .

New Directions in Social Work is an innovative, integrated series of texts, website, and interactive case studies for generalist courses in the Social Work curriculum at both undergraduate and graduate levels. Instructors will find everything they need to build a comprehensive course that allows students to meet course outcomes and prepare for effective and ethical social work practice. The New Directions series is distinguished by these unique features:

- All texts, interactive cases, and test materials are **linked to the 2015 CSWE Policy and Accreditation Standards (EPAS)**.
- **One Web portal with easy access** for instructors and students from any computer – no codes, no CDs, no restrictions. Go to **www.routledgesw.com** and discover.
- **The series is flexible and can be easily adapted for use in online distance-learning courses as well as hybrid/blended and traditional format courses.**
- Each text and the website can be used **individually** or as an **entire series** to meet the needs of any social work program.

Research for Effective Social Work Practice, 4th Edition by Judy L. Krysik and Jerry Finn
Social Work and Social Welfare, 5th Edition: An Invitation by Marla Berg-Weger
Human Behavior in the Social Environment, 5th Edition by Anissa Taun Rogers
Social Policy for Effective Practice, 5th Edition: A Strengths Approach by Rosemary Chapin and Melinda Lewis
The Practice of Generalist Social Work, 5th Edition by Marla Berg-Weger and Deborah Adams

For more information about this series, please visit: **www.routledgesw.com**

"In an era of political upheaval and shifting social priorities, Chapin and Lewis provide a strengths-based context for examining social policies and the people served by them. Guided by our NASW Code of Ethics, the authors provide a framework for culturally-sensitive analysis of policy practice."

Claire L. Dente, *Professor of Social Work,*
West Chester University of Pennsylvania

"This textbook is as accessible as it is exhaustive. The writing allows students to understand the rich history of social welfare policy and to see examples of the real-world impact of policy, and all within a strengths-based perspective. An impressive feat, and one which I value greatly as a professor."

Eric Toth, *CEO at CoveCare Center in Carmel, NY*

Social Policy for Effective Practice

The fifth edition of *Social Policy for Effective Practice* offers a rich variety of resources and knowledge foundations to help social work students understand and contend with the continually evolving social policy landscape that surrounds them. The authors have continued their values-based approach and kept the focus on clients' strengths to help students position themselves for effective engagement on new fronts where policy threats and outcomes affect clients' lives in myriad ways.

The new edition comprehensively covers the process of defining need, analyzing social policy, and developing policy, and each chapter builds on the practical knowledge and skills forged from previous ones. New to this edition:

- Thorough examination of new policies, including challenges to the Affordable Care Act, voting rights, immigration, women's rights, and LGBTQ+ rights, as well as situations involving substance use, mental health, and economic inequality.
- Expanded coverage of shifting demographics, including population diversity and aging.
- Increased connections drawn between historical, present, and potential future policy contexts.
- Updated exercises, exhibits, and social media links in-text and an entire suite of web-based tools found through **www.routledgesw.com**, including complementary reading suggestions and teaching tips, a full library of lecture slides and exam questions, and EPAS guidelines.

For use as a resource in generalist social policy courses, either at the baccalaureate or master's levels, the new edition of *Social Policy for Effective Practice* will challenge students to find areas of policy practice that spark their passion and prepare them to think about and use policy practice as a tool that can lead to the changes they care about.

Rosemary Kennedy Chapin is an award-winning teacher and researcher, possessing extensive program development experience in the social policy arena. After receiving her doctorate degree, she worked as a Research/Policy Analyst for the Minnesota Department of Human Services. She established and directs the Center for Research on Aging and Disability Options (CRADO) at the University of Kansas.

Melinda Lewis is an Associate Professor of Practice in the School of Social Welfare at the University of Kansas and Associate Director of the School's Center on Community Engagement and Collaboration. She also has years of experience advising students and field agencies on policy analysis and policy practice.

Social Policy for Effective Practice
A Strengths Approach

Fifth Edition

*Rosemary Kennedy Chapin
and Melinda Lewis*

Routledge
Taylor & Francis Group
NEW YORK AND LONDON

First published 2020
by Routledge
52 Vanderbilt Avenue, New York, NY 10017

and by Routledge
2 Park Square, Milton Park, Abingdon, Oxon, OX14 4RN

Routledge is an imprint of the Taylor & Francis Group, an informa business

© 2020 Taylor & Francis

The right of Rosemary Kennedy Chapin and Melinda Lewis to be identified as authors of this work has been asserted by them in accordance with sections 77 and 78 of the Copyright, Designs and Patents Act 1988.

All rights reserved. No part of this book may be reprinted or reproduced or utilised in any form or by any electronic, mechanical, or other means, now known or hereafter invented, including photocopying and recording, or in any information storage or retrieval system, without permission in writing from the publishers.

Trademark notice: Product or corporate names may be trademarks or registered trademarks, and are used only for identification and explanation without intent to infringe.

Library of Congress Cataloging-in-Publication Data

Names: Chapin, Rosemary Kennedy, author. | Lewis, Melinda K., author.
Title: Social policy for effective practice : a strengths approach / Rosemary Chapin and Melinda Lewis.
Description: Fifth Edition. | New York City : Routledge, 2020. | Series: New directions in social work | Revised edition of Social policy for effective practice, 2017. | Includes bibliographical references and index.
Identifiers: LCCN 2019045057 | ISBN 9780367357054 (hardback) | ISBN 9780367357061 (paperback) | ISBN 9781003001447 (ebk)
Subjects: LCSH: Social service—United States. | United States—Social policy. | Public welfare—United States. | Human services—United States.
Classification: LCC HV95 .C416 2020 | DDC 361.973—dc23
LC record available at https://lccn.loc.gov/2019045057

ISBN: 978-0-367-35705-4 (hbk)
ISBN: 978-0-367-35706-1 (pbk)
ISBN: 978-1-003-00144-7 (ebk)

Typeset in ITC Stone Serif Std
by Apex CoVantage, LLC

Visit the companion website: www.routledgesw.com

Rosemary Kennedy Chapin: This text is dedicated to my husband, Barry, my children, Brett, Bridgett, and Ben, and now my grandchildren, Margaret Rose, Katie Sue, Zacha Rosalia, and Phoebe Lynn. They encourage and support my work. It is also dedicated to my father, Willie B. Kennedy, and to my mother, Dorothy Konovalski Kennedy, who understood the wisdom of building on people's strengths and worked to do just that every day.

Melinda Lewis: I am thankful to Rosemary for her mentoring early in my career and for generously inviting me to continue the work of this text. My husband, Kory, and my four inquisitive, compassionate, and all-around-incredible children, Sam, Ella, Ben, and Evie, help me carve out space to engage in policy change and, now, to share those ideas on these pages.

BRIEF CONTENTS

Preface xxvi

Acknowledgments xxxvii

CHAPTER 1 Social Work and Social Policy: A Strengths Perspective 1

CHAPTER 2 The Historical Context: Basic Concepts and Early Influences 21

CHAPTER 3 The Historical Context: Development of Our Current Welfare System 54

CHAPTER 4 The Economic and Political Contexts 99

CHAPTER 5 Basic Tools for Researching Need and Analyzing Social Policy 141

CHAPTER 6 Social Policy Development 167

CHAPTER 7 Civil Rights 205

CHAPTER 8 Income- and Asset-Based Social Policies and Programs 258

CHAPTER 9 Policies and Programs for Children and Families 309

CHAPTER 10 Health and Mental Health Policies and Programs 353

CHAPTER 11 Policies and Programs for Older Adults 415

CHAPTER 12 The Future 458

Afterword A–1

References R–1

Glossary/Index I–1

DETAILED CONTENTS

Preface xxvi

Acknowledgments xxxvii

CHAPTER 1 *Social Work and Social Policy: A Strengths Perspective* 1

Social Work and Social Policy 3

The Relationship between Social Policy and Social Work Practice 4

Social Work Values and Policy Practice 6

The Social Worker's Responsibility for Policy Practice 6
Connecting Social Policy to Personal Experience 7

Social Work and the Strengths Perspective 8

Policy Practice Infused with the Strengths Perspective 9

Expanding the Clients' Role 10
Claims-Making 10

Principles of Strengths Perspective Policy Practice 11

Integrating a Strengths Perspective: Benefits and Cautions 13

Benefits of the Strengths Perspective: A Summary 13
Cautions Regarding the Strengths Perspective 14

Connecting Social Work Values to Policy Practice 15

Developing Your Policy Practice Abilities 15

Conclusion 17

Main Points 18

Exercises 18

CHAPTER 2 *The Historical Context: Basic Concepts and Early Influences* 21

The Genesis of Social Welfare Policy 22

Religious and Spiritual Traditions 22

Judaism 22

Islam 22
Buddhism 23
Confucianism 23
Native American Spiritual Traditions 23
Christianity 23

Current Implications 23

Conflicting Historical Views Regarding Social Welfare 24

A Framework for Understanding How Historical Approaches Influence Current Policy 25

English Poor Laws 27

Background of the Poor Law 27

Population Growth and Migration 27
Poverty 28

The Poor Law of 1601 28

Poor Law Amendments 28

Analyzing the Poor Laws 29

Influence of the Poor Laws on U.S. Social Policy 30

Social Welfare Policy in the United States from Colonial Times to the Progressive Era 31

The Colonial Era: Adapting the English System, 1600–1775 31

Social Welfare in the English Colonies 31
Almshouses and Workhouses 32
Slavery and Indentured Servitude 32
The American Revolution: Civil Rights in the New Nation, 1775–1800 33
The Constitution and Civil Rights 33
Expanding Public and Private Assistance 34

From Independence to Civil War: Racism, Expansion, and Immigration, 1800–1865 34

Treatment of African Americans 34
Native Americans 36
Latinx Communities in the Southwest 37
Discrimination against Immigrants 38
Growth of Cities and Public Institutions 39
Mental Health Reform 39

The Civil War and Its Aftermath: Reconstruction, Segregation, and Homesteads, 1865–1890s 40

Reconstruction 41

From Reconstruction to Jim Crow   42
The Homestead Act   42

The Origins of Modern Social Work   42

The Child-Saving Movement   42
The Charity Organization Society   44
The Settlement House Movement   44
Building the Social Work Profession   46
African-American Social Workers   47

The Progressive Era and the Expansion of Social Welfare Policy, 1890–1917   47

Maternalistic Approaches and Mothers' Pensions   49
Child Welfare   50
Prohibition and Discriminatory Enforcement   51
The New Immigration   51

Conclusion   51

Main Points   52

Exercises   52

CHAPTER 3   *The Historical Context: Development of Our Current Welfare System*   54

Expanding the Welfare State in War and Depression: 1917–1945   54

The New Deal   56

The Townsend Movement   58
The Social Security Act   58

The Impact of World War II   59

The Evolution of the Modern Welfare State: 1945–1970   62

The Struggle for African-American Civil Rights   63

The Challenge to School Segregation   63
The Challenge to Jim Crow   64
Civil Rights Laws   66

The Struggle for Latinx Civil Rights   66

The Struggle for LGBTQ+ Civil Rights   68

Mental Health and Intellectual Disability Initiatives   68

The War on Poverty   69

New Frontier Anti-Poverty Programs   69
The Great Society and the War on Poverty   70

Medicare and Medicaid 70
The War on Poverty: Successes and Failures 71

Continuity and Change: The 1970s 72

Family Assistance Experiments 72

Social Service Reforms 73

Watergate and After 74

Women and Civil Rights 74

Native Americans and Civil Rights 75

Termination and Relocation 75
Militancy and the Struggle for Sovereignty 75
Child Welfare 76

Affirmative Action 77

Affirmative Action and Employment 77

Changes in Social Work 78

Retrenchment to Imperiled Progress: 1981 to 2016 78

Implementing a Conservative Agenda 80

New Federalism, OBRA, and Devolution 80

OBRA and Block Grants 81
From Reagan to Bush 81

"New Democrats" and Social Welfare Policy 82

Family Leave and People with Disabilities 83
Health Care: The Reform That Did Not Happen 83
The Contract with America and the PRWORA 83

The Contested Election of 2000 84

Privatization and Faith-Based Initiatives 85
Tax Cuts and Reduced Benefits 85

A Turning of the Tide 86

Health Care 88
Immigration 89
Muted Gains in Obama's Second Term 89

The Trump Presidency: Return to Tax Cuts, Unwinding the Administrative State, and New Threats 91

Regulatory Retreat 92

Reshaping the Federal Judiciary 93

A Nationalistic Approach to Immigration 94

Conclusion 95

Main Points 96

Exercises 97

CHAPTER 4   *The Economic and Political Contexts* 99

How Context Affects Social Policy 100

Influence of Regulatory Policy 100

The Impetus for Social Programs 101

Institutional and Residual Approaches to Social Welfare 103

Institutional Approaches 103

Residual Approaches 103

Economic and political Influences on the Social Welfare System 104

Competing Explanations for the Development of the Welfare System 104

The Industrialization-Welfare Hypothesis 105
The Maintenance of Capitalism Hypothesis 105
Social Conscience Hypothesis 106
The Marshall and Titmuss Hypotheses 106
A Critique 106

The Enabling State and the Capacity-Building State 108

Economic and Political Schools of Thought 108

Keynesian Economics 109
Supply-Side Economics 109
Democratic Socialism 110

The Political Continuum 110

Conservatives and Liberals 111
Other Political Influences 112

Implications for Understanding Policy 113

The Three Branches of Government 114

The Impact of Funding Policies 117

The Federal Budget and Spending Policies 117

Mandatory versus Discretionary Spending 117
The Federal Deficit and Federal Debt 119
Budget Allocation Issues 120

State Budgets and Spending Policies 121

Tax Strategies 123

Evaluating Current U.S. Social Welfare Expenditures 126

The Nature of U.S. Social Welfare Spending 126

Adequacy of Current Expenditures for Social Programs 127

Income Distribution 127
Inequality in Wealth 129
U.S. Social Welfare Expenditures Compared to Those of Other Countries 131

The Role of the Private Sector 133

Benefits and Drawbacks of Different Combinations of Funding Strategies 134

The Economy of the Agency 135

The Ramifications of Globalization 135

Globalization and Social Development 137

Conclusion 138

Main Points 138

Exercises 139

CHAPTER 5 *Basic Tools for Researching Need and Analyzing Social Policy* 141

Policy Analysis Fundamentals 141

Social Conditions and Social Problems 142

Alternative Views 143

Defining Needs and Problems: The Social Constructionist Approach 144

The Social Construction of Teenage Pregnancy 144
The Social Construction of Family Violence 145
Understanding Different Views of Reality 145

Using Strengths Perspective Principles to Consider Needs Determination 146

Needs Definition Shapes Policy 146

Analyzing Social Problems from an Expanded Viewpoint 147

Defining and Documenting Problems or Needs 147

Values, Ideologies, and Problem Definition 152

Causal Theories 152

Claims-Making 154

The Various Bases of Claims-Making   154
Assumptions Embedded in Claims-Making   155

A Framework for Policy Analysis   156

Policy Goals and Objectives   157

Locating Goals and Objectives   158
Manifest and Latent Goals   158
Incorporating Clients' Perspectives   159

Benefits or Services Provided   159

Eligibility Rules   160

Service Delivery Systems   161

Financing   163

Cost-Effectiveness and Outcomes   164

Conclusion   164

Main Points   165

Exercises   165

CHAPTER 6   *Social Policy Development*   167

Steps in Policy Development   170

Determining Need and Making Claims   172

Groups Involved in Needs Determination and Claims-Making   173
The Legislative Agenda   174

Crafting Policy Goals   175

Achieving Consensus   176
Utilizing the Strengths Perspective   176

Examining the Feasibility of Policy Alternatives   177

Enacting and Implementing Policy   179

Evaluating Policy Outcomes   180

Social Work Policy Practice and the Ecological Perspective   181

Policy Research and Practice   182

Identifying and Defining the Target Client Population   183

Examining Your Perspective   184

Getting on the Agenda   185

Strategies for Utilizing the Strengths Approach   186

DETAILED CONTENTS

       Working with Others   186
       Identifying Policy Options That Include Client Perspectives   187
       Negotiating Policy Goals   187
       Helping to Get Policy Enacted   188
           Considering Whether a New Law Is Needed   188
           Analyzing Costs   189
       Evaluating Policy Based on Client Outcomes   189
   A Place to Start   191
       Seeking Support   192
       Taking Action   193
           Integrating Other People into Action Plans   194
           Focusing Your Efforts   194
           Interacting with Your Opposition   194
           Supporting Client Groups   195
           Interacting with Policymakers   195
           Facing Limits on Political Activism   196
   Conclusion   197
   Main Points   197
   Exercises   203

CHAPTER 7   *Civil Rights*   205

   Background and History   205
   Civil rights in the united states: promising foundation for ongoing struggles   211
       Disenfranchised Groups: Civil Rights and Social Justice   211
           African Americans   212
           Native Americans   214
           Latinx Communities   216
           Asian Americans   219
           Sexual Orientation and Gender Identity   220
           People with Disabilities   224
           People with Mental Illness   225
           Older Adults   226
           Women and Civil Rights   228
   Major Policies and Programs   232
       The Civil Rights Act of 1964   233

The Voting Rights Act of 1965 234

Affirmative Action 237

The Education for All Handicapped Children Act of 1975 239

The Americans with Disabilities Act of 1990 241

The Reauthorization of the Violence Against Women Act, 2005 and 2013 242

The Lilly Ledbetter Fair Pay Act 2009 243

The Matthew Shepard and James Byrd, Jr. Hate Crimes Prevention Act 2009 243

Ongoing Challenges in Civil Rights 244

Next Steps 247

Reconsidering "Neutral" Policies 248

The Role of Social Workers 249

Conclusion 252

Main Points 252

Exercises 254

CHAPTER 8 *Income- and Asset-Based Social Policies and Programs* 258

Definitions of Poverty 259

The Poverty Line/Poverty Threshold 260

Poverty Guidelines 261

Alternative Poverty Measures 262

Income-Support Policies and Programs 262

Universal Programs 263

Old-Age, Survivors, and Disability Insurance: How It Benefits Both the Young and Old 263

Unemployment Insurance 266

Workers' Compensation 268

Veterans' Benefits 269

Selective Programs 270

Temporary Assistance for Needy Families 271

History and Development of TANF 272

TANF Goals 272

Family Formation Goals 273

TANF Work Requirements and Sanctions 273
Work Instead of Welfare 277

Non-Cash Programs That Assist Low-Income Families 277

The Supplemental Nutrition Assistance Program 278
The Women, Infants, and Children Nutrition Program 280
Public Housing 281
Tenant-Based Rental Assistance Program 282
HOME Investment Partnership Programs 284

Supplemental Security Income 285

General Assistance 286

The Earned Income Tax Credit 287

Evaluation of Income-Support Policies and Programs 290

Positive Impact of Safety Net Programs 290

TANF from the Strengths Perspective 291

Strengths-Based Priorities for TANF Reform 293

OASDI from the Strengths Perspective 294

Women and OASDI 294
People of Color and OASDI 295
Is OASDI Regressive or Progressive? 296
OASDI: Solvency and Reform 296

Promising directions in anti-poverty policy 297

A Roadmap to Ending Child Poverty 297

Asset-Based Approaches 299

Universal Basic Income: Fundamental Reform to End Poverty 301

Conclusion 303

Poverty in the Global Context 303

Anti-Poverty Social Work Practice 303

Main Points 305

Exercises 306

CHAPTER 9 *Policies and Programs for Children and Families* 309

History and Background of Programs Protecting Children and Families 312
Children and Families Today 312

Impact of High Poverty Rates on Child Welfare 315

The Child Welfare System   316

The Juvenile Justice System   317

Major Policies and Programs Affecting Child Welfare and Juvenile Justice   320

The Child Abuse Prevention and Treatment Act   321

The Juvenile Justice and Delinquency Prevention Act   322

The Indian Child Welfare Act   323

Adoption Assistance and Child Welfare Act   326

Family Preservation and Support Services   327

The Multi-Ethnic Placement Act   327

The Adoption and Safe Families Act   329

Family First Prevention Services Act (FFPSA)   331

Independent Living Transition Services   332

The Child Support Enforcement Program   333

Legislation for Children with Special Educational Needs   335

Evaluating Policies and Programs for Children and Families   337

Child Protection Policy from the Strengths Perspective   339

Family Rights and Child Safety   339

Family Reunification   340
Teen Pregnancy   341
Privatization   342
Strategies for Supporting Families More Effectively   343

Juvenile Justice from the Strengths Perspective   345

The Role of Social Workers in the Child Welfare System   348

Conclusion   348

Main Points   348

Exercises   351

CHAPTER 10   *Health and Mental Health Policies and Programs*   353

Health Care in the United States   354

The High Cost of Health Care   359

History and Background of Health Care Programs   360

Growing Federal Involvement in Health Care   360
Medicare, Medicaid, and Civil Rights   361

Background on Approaches to Health Care Finance and Cost Control   361
Health Reform in the 1990s   364

2010 Patient Protection and Affordable Care Act (amended by the Health Care and Education Reconciliation Act)   364

The 2012 Supreme Court Decision   365
Continued Challenges, Regulatory Erosion, and Administrative Undermining   366
Issues Left Unaddressed   368

Major Health Care Policies and Programs   369

Medicaid   369

Mandatory and Optional Coverage   371
Medicaid and PRWORA   371
Medicaid Waivers and Variations among States   372
Medicaid and Managed Care   374
Medicaid and Health Care Access   376

Medicare   377

Medicare Part A, Hospital Insurance (HI)   377
Medicare Part B   378
Medicare Part C, Medicare Advantage   378
Medicare Part D   378

Medicare Financing   380

The Children's Health Insurance Program (CHIP)   382

The 2010 Patient Protection and Affordable Care Act   384

The Affordable Care Act: Financing and Cost-Control Issues   387

Major Mental Health Policies and Programs   388

History and Background of Mental Health Programs   391

Community Mental Health and Deinstitutionalization   391
Incarceration of People with Mental Illness   393

Managed Care and Mental Health   394

The Mental Retardation and Community Mental Health Centers Construction Act   394
The State Comprehensive Mental Health Services Plan Act   394

Substance Use Disorders   395

Evaluating Health and Mental Health Policies and Programs   397

Challenges in the Medicare System   399

Ageism in the Medicare Health Care Cost Debate   400

Mental Health Parity and Concerns for Specific Populations   400

Veterans' Mental Health   401

Growing Concerns Related to Children and Mental Health   401

Substance Use Disorders, Pandemics, and the Health Care System   402

Substance Use Disorders   402

Pandemics   403

Next Steps for Promoting More Effective Health and Mental Health Policies   404

Medicare Reform   405

Mental Health Care   406

Strategies to Promote Health   406

Social Workers and Health Reforms   407

Conclusion   409

Main Points   410

Exercises   412

CHAPTER 11   *Policies and Programs for Older Adults*   415

Policy and Program Responses   419

Economic Security in Later Life   419

Private Retirement Programs   420

Public Retirement Programs   420

Changes to Job-Specific Pension Programs   420

Pensions at Risk   422

Supplemental Security Income for Older Adults   423

Policies to Provide Health Care and Support Social Engagement   424

The National Institute on Aging   424

Mental Health Services   425

Long-Term Care   425

Prescription Drug Policy   427

Shortage of Gerontologically Trained Professionals   427

Demographics and Future Policy Imperatives   427

Poverty and Aging in the Community   431

Voting Patterns of Older Adults   432

Major Policies and Programs for Older Adults   433

The Older Americans Act   433

The Employee Retirement Income Security Act   435

No CLASS: Loss of the Long-Term Care Provisions of the Affordable Care Act   436

The Elder Justice Act and the Patient Safety and Abuse Prevention Act   437

Evaluating Policies and Programs for Older Adults   438

Economic Security   440

Health Care   444

   Long-Term Care   444
   Mental Health   445
   End-of-Life Planning   446

Social Engagement   447

Next Step: Supporting Long, Healthy Lives   448

Next Step: Promoting Economic Security in Later Life   449

Developing a Strengths-Based Agenda   451

Creating Needed Infrastructure   451

Conclusion   452

Main Points   452

Exercises   454

CHAPTER 12   *The Future   458*

Guidelines for Understanding Future Forecasts   460

Analyze the Purpose   461

Assess Underlying Assumptions and the Credibility of Source Information   462

Thinking About the Future Using a Values-Based Lens: The Strengths Approach   466

Factors that Will Shape Future Social Policies   467

Population Growth and Shifts   467

Medical and Technological Advances   470

Occupational Automation   473

Global Political Realignments   475

Climate Change and Environmental Justice   478

The State of the Future Index   480

Future Policy Directions   481

    The Future of Work 482
        Wages, Jobs, and Retirement 484
    Health 485
    Information Technology and Privacy 485
    Devolution and the Geography of Opportunity 486
    Environmental and Climate Justice 487
    Using the Electoral Process 489
The Strengths Perspective in a New Era 490
Charting a New Agenda: Social Work Grand Challenges 491
Conclusion 492
Main Points 492
Exercises 493

Afterword A–1

References R–1

Glossary/Index I–1

PREFACE

MAJOR CHANGES TO THE FIFTH EDITION

Welcome to the fifth edition of *Social Policy for Effective Practice: A Strengths Approach.* This edition contains updated content to help social work students grapple with the evolving social policy landscape and gird themselves for effective engagement on the new fronts where policy threats and opportunities alter clients' lives. We have sought to sort through the high-profile headlines, to help students see what is truly consequential for clients, today and in the future. We have kept a focus on clients' strengths and our social work values at the center of our analysis, in an effort to help students similarly position themselves in an often-contested climate. The text incorporates features that will allow students to immediately begin applying what they learn about policy and programs to improve conditions for their clients. We have also significantly streamlined the material so that busy students can make social policy study part of their developing professional identities. These changes incorporate the feedback that many faculty and students have graciously taken time to share.

Reaction to previous editions has been very positive. Faculty are particularly enthusiastic about content on the social construction of issues and the emphasis on social work values and capacity-building. However, both faculty and students report that the transition of content from classroom to policy practice is still a struggle for many students. To help with this transition and to make social policy approachable for students who urgently seek additional tools with which to help their clients, this fifth edition contains new exercises and exhibits. Students are given practical strategies for combining policy practice with other responsibilities. Chapters have been revised to encourage students to interact even more with the information, and a thorough revision has made this edition the most concise presentation possible.

Far more than just a textbook, this edition is full of resources, including online links to help students engage in policy practice and exercises that prompt critical analysis of current issues and relevant controversies. Like the previous editions, this text provides students with a value-based approach to understanding social policy. The strengths approach to policy analysis and development is grounded in social work values of self-determination, social justice, and respect for diversity. The premise of this text is that a greater focus on the strengths and resources of people and their environments rather than on their problems and pathologies should be integrated into the social policy development process. The past few decades of practice and scholarship have demonstrated the efficacy of strengths approaches, and we believe that this emphasis is particularly crucial in the current context.

In addition to comprehensive coverage of major social policies and programs across fields of practice, the latest information on federal and state policy initiatives and reforms is presented and carefully analyzed for potential impact. This edition provides new information on many policies, including challenges to the Affordable Care Act, the ongoing struggle for voting rights, the political battleground that is today's immigration policies, rights for transgender people, women's rights, criminal justice, juvenile justice reforms, growing attention to substance use and mental health crises, and economic inequality. Changing demographics, including growing population diversity and aging, are presented as both challenges and opportunities, and students are encouraged to critically consider how their social work practice successfully navigates these shifting landscapes. In addition to individual policy contests, themes that reflect the shifts in underlying ideologies motivating policy change are highlighted for students, to help them make connections between, for example, the shifting of risks onto individuals' shoulders in the arenas of retirement, health care, and economic security, or the devolution of responsibility from the federal to state governments in health care and income support. This edition has expanded discussion of policy made outside the legislative process, including the impact of regulatory policymaking in health care and civil rights, and of judicial decisions that have had important consequences for Americans' lives, including far-reaching decisions in immigration, disability rights, and civil liberties. Recent trends in social policy are discussed, including many that have undermined gains made in the previous decade on issues such as health care and LGBTQ+ rights. The text also includes a discussion of some of the shifts in norms, ideologies, and social interactions that are altering social policy and reshaping how people experience policy, including populism, nationalism, and intensifying polarization.

This edition links history and information about future projections to help students build their capacity to understand both historical and likely future policy contexts. Content on potential future policy challenges is integrated throughout the text, including greater emphasis on the natural environment and the imperative of working for climate and other environmental justice. We also call attention to how language frames policy debates and urge students to engage in reframing to, for example, talk about insurance benefits rather than entitlements in discussing OASDI and emphasize the ways older adults contribute to their communities. In several places, the text underscores racial inequity as a defining feature of U.S. social policy and uses disaggregated data to explore how indicators such as wealth, life expectancy, infant mortality, and poverty divide along lines of race.

We have increased the text's incorporation of scholarly literature and trusted analysis. Recent research points the way to promising policy reforms, in areas including the effects of wealth inequality on children's educational outcomes, the ways trauma's effects stay with children throughout their lives, and how greater access to health care improves long-term health outcomes. These discussions and the citations that support them are resources students can draw on for their own inquiries into evidence-based social policy reform. This information is integrated into chapters at the points where students would be curious enough to look up the study—a practice on which they will rely as social workers and policy practitioners.

Beginning with Chapter 1, students are challenged to find areas of policy practice that ignite their passion. They are encouraged to apply the concepts and content of the text to their own practice, and chapters are peppered with actual examples of social work students who engaged in policy practice to improve services for their clients. Once students begin to think about policy practice as a tool that can be used to bring about changes they care about, they have greater motivation to master the content in this text. In addition to learning about the historical, political, and economic context of social policies, they will learn skills needed for policy analysis and policy development. They will then use those skills to become knowledgeable about the major policies and programs that impact their clients.

Supplemental readings, with accompanying discussion questions, offer more breadth and depth to selected topics. Using these readings to complement the texts gives students and instructors opportunities to explore the complexity of the issues most important to them. These readings can also help students pursue self-directed learning and may help instructors who are using the text with students at different levels. For example, an instructor in a graduate-level course may assign more supplemental readings than one teaching at the baccalaureate level; an instructor teaching a course focused on a particular area of policy—such as health care—may use more of the readings related to that content.

For all five books in the *New Directions in Social Work* series, each addressing a foundational course in the social work curriculum, the publisher has created a unique teaching strategy that revolves around the text but offers much more than the traditional text experience. The series website (**www.routledgesw.com**) leads to custom websites coordinated with each text that offer a variety of features to support instructors as they integrate the many facets of an education in social work. In addition to the companion readings, the series website houses six interactive fictional cases with accompanying exercises that bring to life the concepts covered in the book—all extensively revised to incorporate current terminology, relevant issues, and additional emphasis on critical thinking as a core social work competency. The interactive cases can help students not concurrently in a field placement to make connections between the classroom and clients' situations. There are two downloadable cases that instructors can incorporate into class discussions and/or assignments; a bank of exam questions (both objective and open-ended) and PowerPoint presentations; sample syllabi showing how the text can be used in a variety of course structures; and annotated links to a treasure trove of articles, videos, and websites. The rich variety of resources and links provided as part of the *Social Policy for Effective Practice* text and website makes it possible to expand or contract the content to fit the variety of timeframes and levels in which social policy courses are taught, while a master matrix demonstrates how the text and website used together through the course satisfy the Council on Social Work Education (2015) Educational Policy and Accreditation Standards.

ORGANIZATION OF THE BOOK

The chapters reflect social policy topics that are basic for effective social work practice. In Chapters 1–6 we examine different frameworks and contexts for understanding social policy, as as tools for analyzing and influencing social policy. We also consider the influence of history, political alignments, and economics on social policy. Chapters 7–11 provide students with a chance to build their skills in policy analysis. Each of these chapters describes policy developments in key fields of practice: civil rights, income support and asset building, child welfare, health care, and aging. Additionally, connections are made among different policy areas, to illustrate for students how, for example, children's health influences outcomes in later life, and how insufficient investment in family economic well-being affects the child welfare system. Intersectionality is a core theme of the text, and data are disaggregated by race, gender, and other identities that affect people's outcomes. The policy analysis framework presented in earlier chapters is applied to major U.S. social policies in Chapters 7–11, including recent developments in juvenile justice, addictions, and child welfare. In each topic, needed reforms are discussed so that students can consider what it would take for policy to more closely align with social work values of justice and equity. Moreover, each chapter incorporates a strengths approach so that students can begin to consider clients' strengths and resources as well as their needs when evaluating relevant policies. In Chapter 12, the book concludes by looking to the future to consider ideas about how social workers can effectively respond to projected future challenges, including those related to changing demographics, technological advances, the changing nature of work, continued climate change, and strained global cooperation.

The chapter descriptions that follow briefly introduce each of the chapters, with emphasis on the updated content.

Chapter 1

Social Work and Social Policy: A Strengths Perspective provides an overview of social policy and programs and introduces the basic concepts that are the foundation for the rest of the book. We discuss the connections between micro, mezzo, and macro practice and how all three connect to policy practice. Our goal is to help students understand why policy practice is critical to effective social work practice and how their social work practice skills will facilitate effective policy engagement. We discuss the value base of the strengths perspective and explain how a strengths approach and solution-focused strategies change not only the policy product but also the process of policy analysis and development. Students are challenged to find an issue they are passionate about and to begin to build policy practice skills. Integral to this chapter is the concept of dual assessments. Students are encouraged to incorporate an assessment of the specific policy issues that impact their clients into their initial assessment and planning processes. Instructors can use this first chapter to help students consider the use of dual assessments in different practice contexts. By the end of the first chapter, we hope students will be excited about policy practice and interested in acquiring the knowledge and skills necessary to help influence social policies and programs.

Chapter 2

The Historical Context: Basic Concepts and Early Influences presents history as a policy practice tool and provides an analytic framework to support that approach. This chapter examines the historical context for the development of social welfare policies and programs, discusses the genesis of social welfare in early societies, and traces the development of U.S. social policies through the early years of the twentieth century. The chapter discusses the origins of social work, discriminatory health and mental policies during this period, formation of the Democratic and Republican Parties, the importance of policy research and advocacy done by pioneer social workers, and the pivotal role of women in social policy development during the 1800s and 1900s. New to this fifth edition are expanded discussions of slavery, oppression of Native Americans, and the racist origins of many U.S. social policies. Throughout this chapter, we have drawn connections between historical policies and current debates, including those related to work requirements in means-tested programs. As requested by reviewers, exhibits in Chapter 2 are designed to make historical events and people "come alive" for students. The voices and experiences of women and people of color are also highlighted in these history chapters, even if they were seldom centered in policy discussions at the time.

Chapter 3

The Historical Context: Development of Our Current Welfare System begins with World War I and continues through the period following the 2018 mid-term election. These chapters are premised on the idea that history is not merely a prologue to the present. Rather, the ways in which historical social policy approaches are understood and reinterpreted directly and immediately affect the social policy decisions made. Chapter 3 contains an expanded discussion of the Civil Rights Movement and of income support strategies enacted since World War II. The changes that brought us retrenchment and devolution during the Reagan era are examined and connected to policy developments in the present time. This fifth edition has expanded discussion of the effects of the Great Recession, including how different populations were disproportionately impacted and how the lingering effects of the economic downturn are felt by different groups. Other major updates to this edition include analysis of the dynamics that contributed to Donald Trump's 2016 election and the most consequential effects of his presidency, including the erosion of regulatory oversight, the rollback of essential civil rights protections, and the reshaping of the federal judiciary. Social workers are encouraged to focus their attention on these changes and the ways in which they are likely to continue to reverberate, with particular importance for people of color and others often marginalized in U.S. social policy. An effort has been made to avoid redundancies between this chapter and other chapters that address policy developments in specific fields of practice. For example, this chapter now includes only brief mention of judicial rulings that altered affirmative action, since Chapter 7 includes an extensive discussion of the evolution of affirmative action policies.

Chapter 4

The Economic and Political Contexts helps students understand how economic fluctuations and political change interact with shifting social values to shape and reshape social policy. New to this chapter is a much greater emphasis on the international political and economic contexts that increasingly influence our social policy, including the rise of populism and economic nationalism. We added information about income and wealth inequality and how they shape both economic outcomes and political alignments. In addition to core content describing how the branches of government and working of the U.S. economy influence social policy, Chapter 4 has been thoroughly updated so that students and instructors have the most current statistics with which to ground consideration of political dynamics and economic conditions. Key terms are bolded throughout, to help students and instructors draw attention to those foundational concepts that will equip them to analyze policies presented later in the text—and in their practice.

Chapter 5

Basic Tools for Researching Need and Analyzing Social Policy illustrates how to use a policy analysis framework to understand social policy. Students can then apply this framework to do hands-on analysis of legislation that addresses homelessness. Strength principles for policy analysis are explained and their application is discussed. Students' critical thinking is encouraged, with a discussion of social construction of policy issues, to help students reflect on the forces that shape how we think and what we believe. The examples provided in the section "A Framework for Policy Analysis" have been updated and carried throughout the entire section. While we have streamlined this chapter, we added some specific information on how to analyze social policy and additional tools to help students approach the policy analysis task on any issue of interest.

Chapter 6

Social Policy Development examines the process of policy development in detail and then focuses explicitly on the ways in which social workers can intervene in that process. Explanations of policy practice approaches and examples of social workers engaged in strengths-based policy practice have been expanded. New exhibits with examples of social work students doing advocacy work have been added. The Case Study and Sample Action Plan, which lays out how to develop and implement strategies to influence social policies, have been updated and expanded. To augment the text's other discussions of housing policy and the particular challenges facing young adults, the Case Study and Action Plan focus on youth homelessness.

Chapter 7

Civil Rights provides a detailed look at the groups who have experienced discrimination and oppression, throughout U.S. history and still today. While social justice is a theme throughout this edition—in response to 2015 EPAS' emphasis, students' growing commitment to social justice, and our own values—social justice takes center stage in this chapter. This edition includes more information on immigration policy, including the recent debates about refugee admissions, border security, and inclusion efforts. We also added information about crucial civil rights concerns related to police violence, treatment in the criminal justice system, and the rights of individuals with mental illness. While much of Chapter 7 focuses on race as the principal dividing line in American society, we examine other, intersecting, identities that influence people's experiences with social policy, including advances and setbacks in the LGBTQ+ movement, including the struggle for rights for transgender people. While

President Trump's attacks on vulnerable groups and retreats from civil rights gains require careful attention from social workers, we also emphasize the importance of state policy as part of the "front line" on civil rights. We include states' efforts to restrict women's rights, including anti-abortion and anti-contraceptive bills, as well as some states' commitment to ensure that transgender people have nondiscriminatory access to facilities and opportunities. This chapter highlights voting rights as a crucial area of civil rights and an essential foundation of policy practice to expand civil rights in general. Chapter 7 includes substantial and expanded end-of-chapter exercises, so that instructors can direct students to focus on populations or issues of particular interest. To facilitate development of critical thinking skills, this chapter helps students analyze seemingly neutral policies for negative impact on traditionally oppressed groups. Importantly, the experiences and achievements of individuals who have experienced oppression are highlighted throughout, with particular attention to their priorities for policy change in these domains. Beginning in Chapter 7 and continuing through the remainder of the text, we analyze major policies in separate boxes using the simple framework introduced in earlier chapters. This is done so that students can easily grasp the basic policy elements of goals, service delivery, and financing, and then can more readily understand later amendments. Students and instructors have repeatedly told us that this presentation is a valuable study aid, so we have retained it, applying the same framework to the analysis of policies enacted since the last edition.

Chapter 8

Income- and Asset-Based Social Policies and Programs examines the major government policies and programs designed to reduce poverty. This chapter emphasizes means-tested and insurance-based policies and programs that provide cash to clients. However, because SNAP, employment policy, and housing subsidies also directly help ameliorate the effects of poverty, we examine these policies and programs as well. This edition includes expanded discussion of affordable housing as a crucial social problem and a threat to individuals' and families' well-being. There is a thorough overview of income supports available to older adults, including comparative analysis of OASDI and TANF, as well as discussion of the current state of SSDI and Social Security solvency. In response to reviewer feedback, we added content on hunger, a discussion of Universal Basic Income proposals, and more information about asset-based approaches to facilitating upward mobility. We also analyze official definitions of poverty, contrast universal with selective programs, and explore how devolution has increased states' responsibilities in anti-poverty policy, particularly following the institution of TANF in 1996. The significance of the strengths perspective as the lens for analysis is especially prominent in this chapter, which considers how to better invest in people's capacities to meet their needs and reach their goals.

Chapter 9

Policies and Programs for Children and Families focuses on policies and programs dealing with child protection, family preservation, permanency planning, adoption, foster care, and juvenile justice. Programs for children with special needs are also examined. All statistics and policies have been updated throughout the chapter, including recent policy changes in child welfare that have increased the emphasis on preventing maltreatment. This edition also expands the discussion of child support enforcement policies. Information on childcare as a key support for family and child well-being has also been added. Illustrating the interactions among policy areas, this chapter considers how child poverty affects outcomes and how policy can protect children's civil rights. This edition also contains an expanded discussion of how child welfare and family policy can be improved, and includes content on family capacity building. Policies that could help communities identify and prevent childhood trauma are discussed, as is the evolving research base about the harmful effects of trauma. Distinct from other discussions of trauma, ours takes a strengths-based approach, to emphasize resilience and individuals' capacity to thrive, with the right supports.

Chapter 10

Health and Mental Health Policies and Programs has been substantially revised so that instructors and students a have thoroughly updated, well-referenced foundation for their study of policies in this essential area of social work practice. This chapter traces recent developments in health care policy, including efforts to undermine the Affordable Care Act through regulatory action, judicial challenge, and legislative repeal. We analyze Medicaid, Medicare, and CHIP, and provide information about how they have been changed due to the Affordable Care Act, state policy efforts, and the ascendance of managed care. Chapter 10 includes not just access to health care but also policies that affect health more broadly, including those shaping the social determinants of health and those affecting the quality and diversity of the health care workforce. The ecological perspective, presented in earlier chapters, provides the foundation for discussion of how the built environment influences individual and population health, and how changes in the built and natural environment may affect outcomes. Potential future changes to health care policy—including Medicaid waivers and making Medicare a voucher program—are highlighted, and policy practice strategies social workers can use to influence these debates are provided. To help students understand the context for their own social work practice, there is considerable discussion of state-level differences in health policy. The sections on mental health and substance use disorders have been substantially updated to include discussion of the opioid epidemic, changing attitudes and state policies about drugs and addiction, and recent funding increases in response to growing need. Students are provided with resources and discussion to examine pressing topics in health policy, including suicide prevention, mental health and criminal justice, health disparities, and efforts to control health care costs.

Chapter 11

Policies and Programs for Older Adults provides an overview of key policy issues that influence older adults. This chapter was revised to reduce redundancy with other parts of the text, while still acknowledging that policies in other domains affect older adults' outcomes. This edition has expanded discussion of retirement security and how the risks associated with retirement have largely shifted to individuals. The chapter also includes content on elder abuse and legislative efforts to respond to this problem, the reauthorization of the Older Americans Act, long-term care and the imperative for new social policy structures to provide assistance with this need. We analyze voting patterns of older adults and the ways in which generational shifts are reshaping political realities. Students are helped to critically assess the concept of *aging well*, the policies required to facilitate this outcome, and how different populations may experience the redefinition of later life. We conclude this chapter by examining policy strategies to promote economic security, adequate health care, and social engagement, as well as ways to support intergenerational cooperation. The intent of this chapter is to engage students of all ages in thinking about what they want for themselves as they age, what policies would best support older adults, and how policy practice related to aging can be part of their own social work in any field.

Chapter 12

The Future focuses on strategies for dealing with future policy dilemmas. The policy basics covered in earlier chapters provide the foundation for thinking about how we may begin to address future challenges. This edition has expanded content on the biases that can interfere with accurate forecasting; there are examples that illustrate how such predictions can go astray, and students are helped to develop the critical thinking necessary to become informed consumers and crafters of future forecasts. Students are encouraged to synthesize what they have learned and chart their own strategies to apply policy practice content in a rapidly changing political, physical, social, and economic environment. Information on how students can be involved in shaping the future of social policy has been included to assist with this synthesis. For this edition, this chapter was substantially revised, with expanded emphasis on environmental justice, particularly within the context of climate change; emerging technologies that are transforming social work practice and individuals' lives; and the evolving nature of work and what new labor market realities may mean for social workers and their clients. The text closes with a challenge to students to help develop a vision of the future that will energize their efforts and those of the profession to improve policies and, ultimately, future outcomes for our clients.

INTERACTIVE CASES

The website **www.routledgesw.com/cases** presents six unique, in-depth, interactive, fictional cases with dynamic characters and real-life situations to provide opportunities to immediately apply policy knowledge and policy practice skills. As noted above, these cases have been extensively revised since the last edition of this text. While instructors will recognize the individuals, families, and communities used in the cases, there have been considerable updates to the contexts and issues with which they are grappling. Additionally, discussion and reflection questions now emphasize critical thinking to a greater extent; students will develop these imperative capabilities and insights through careful consideration of these in-depth cases. In addition, in response to instructors' feedback, the website now includes two peer-reviewed downloadable cases—one addressing the needs of a transgender youth and one focusing on racial inequity and police violence—so that even students without reliable online access can complement their use of the text with an engaging case study. Each of the interactive cases uses text, graphics, and video to help students learn about engagement, assessment, intervention, and evaluation and termination at multiple levels of social work practice. Some instructors make the cases a centerpiece of their course, requiring students to complete activities and questions as class assignments, engaging students in discussion within class and/or online, and having guest speakers whose work touches on the issues presented in the cases. This book takes full advantage of the interactive element as a unique learning opportunity by including exercises in each chapter that require students to go to the website and use the cases. To maximize the learning experience, you may want to start the course by asking your students to explore each case. The more the students are familiar with the presentation of information and the locations of the individual case files, the case study tools, and the questions and tasks contained within each phase of the case, the better they will be able to integrate the text with the online component.

The Sanchez Family: Systems, Strengths, and Stressors

The ten individuals in this extended Latinx family have numerous strengths but are faced with a variety of challenges. Students will have the opportunity to experience the phases of the social work intervention, grapple with ethical dilemmas, and identify strategies for addressing issues of diversity. In the text, there are numerous connections between current policy issues and the goals and concerns of the Sanchez family. Students are encouraged to begin from a perspective centered on these clients, as they consider policies related to immigration, income support, health care, aging, child welfare, and substance use disorder. These linkages make these issues more relevant for students and allow them to practice starting their policy practice from clients' hopes and needs—a tenet of strengths-based social work.

Riverton: A Community Conundrum

Riverton is a small Midwest city in which the social worker lives and works. The social worker identifies an issue, homelessness, that presents their community with a challenge. Students and instructors can work together to develop strategies for engaging, assessing, and intervening with residents.

Carla Washburn: Loss, Aging, and Social Support

Students will get to know Carla Washburn, an older African-American woman who finds herself living alone after the loss of her grandson. In this case, students apply their growing knowledge of aging and exercise the skills of culturally competent practice. In coordination with this text, students apply an intersectional lens to consider how Mrs. Washburn's identities might affect her experiences with social policies.

RAINN: Rape Incest and Abuse National Network

This interactive case exposes students to practice at the organizational level and gives them a chance to assess an increasingly common human service delivery system: online intervention.

The RAINN case incorporates discussion of the crucial issue of sexual violence, critical ethical dilemmas for student consideration, and the interaction between social policies and organizational innovation. Reflection and analysis questions in the text make connections between RAINN and current issues related to sexual violence and needed policy responses.

Hudson City: An Urban Community Affected by Disaster

This interactive case gives students a chance to learn about disaster relief and crisis intervention. Given the effects of climate change and its disproportionate effects on disadvantaged communities and the greater emphasis on environmental justice in the 2015 EPAS, thinking through the policy issues related to dealing with disasters is becoming increasingly critical for social work competence.

Brickville

A real-estate developer has big plans to redevelop Brickville, a community that has suffered from generations of disinvestment. The redevelopment plans have stirred major controversy among stakeholders. As this case focuses on the community level, with a family case embedded, students will be challenged to think about two levels of client systems and the ways in which they influence one another. This case has substantial real-life significance for many students in parts of the country that are similarly grappling with redevelopment and its consequences. For this edition, the Brickville case has been revised to emphasize strengths inherent in the family and community contexts.

IN SUM

Social Policy for Effective Practice provides an integrated approach to policy-informed social work education. A clear philosophical base and a common theoretical framework underlie the discussion of each component of the policy process. The focus is on understanding how social policy can contribute to effective social work practice across the range of social work settings. Our aim is to spark students' desire to understand and influence social policy. In pursuit of this outcome, we have interwoven four essential themes throughout this book: (1) the importance of thinking critically about social policy; (2) the benefits of using the strengths perspective, a value-based approach, in policy analysis and development; (3) the vital role social policy plays in all areas of practice; and (4) the absolute responsibility of every social worker to engage in policy practice.

This new edition integrates new tools and resources and increases the incorporation of peer-reviewed and high-quality professional literature. The revision also prioritized elimination of any redundancies so that the resulting fifth edition is as short as possible. We know that students need context and nuance to become sophisticated policy analysts and practitioners; we also know that their time is limited and that policy practice must feel accessible if they are to embrace it.

ACKNOWLEDGMENTS

Many people have helped shape this book. This fifth edition builds on the strong foundation of Dr. Chapin's first four editions. Those efforts were aided by faculty colleagues steeped in the strengths perspective at the University of Kansas (KU), as well as colleagues at other universities. The New Directives in Social Work series truly functions as a series. The other authors—Anissa Rogers, Marla Berg-Weger, and Judy Krysik—have helped craft this innovative way of introducing core content to social work students, as did original series editor, Alice Lieberman. At Routledge, Tyler Bay and Charlotte Taylor have provided invaluable production and development support, elicited reviews from social work faculty, and ensured that the final product will be the tool strengths-based social work policy practitioners need for this critical moment. Our thanks also go to Shannon LeMay-Finn, whose copyediting contributed greatly to this edition. We are grateful for the feedback from our peer reviewers, particularly Dr. Kathy Briar-Lawson, whose expertise has made such valuable contributions to editions of this text.

CHAPTER 1

Social Work and Social Policy: A Strengths Perspective

My practicum agency is in a largely immigrant neighborhood, and our programs used to serve people from all over the world. In the past several months, fewer immigrant parents have participated in our family support services, fewer immigrant children are in our after-school program, and fewer nearby residents come to request food and rental assistance. We know the community still has a lot of needs, but we're hearing that people are scared that interacting with an agency—even an immigrant-friendly one like ours—could risk attracting the attention of immigration authorities. How can we help these would-be clients connect to our resources?

I work at a school with adolescents struggling with depression. Some of my clients are LGBTQ+ youth who are suicidal. They often tell me they feel marginalized. I think school policies should affirm transgender students' rights to facilities, require training for teachers to ensure that there are allies for queer students, and protect students from discrimination. These issues are questions of social justice, and they're also important for students' mental well-being.

My placement is working with people discharging from the hospital. Many of my patients are older adults. I'm expected to help get them out of the hospital, but I know many of them will be rehospitalized too quickly because they need community-based services, which face continuous cuts in funding.
—Social Work Student

TODAY, SOCIAL WORKERS FIND OURSELVES STRUGGLING TO FILL the gaps when vital mental health, child welfare, safety net, and disability services are underfunded or eliminated. The current political and economic environments create more uncertainty, as some of the tools social workers rely on seem increasingly precarious. How can social work students facing dilemmas like those described above build the skills they need to tackle these challenges? Perhaps even more importantly for the profession, clients, and society, how can the tremendous assets students bring—commitment to equity, compassion for those in need, and conviction that change is possible—contribute to fundamental improvements in social policy and substantial progress in the march toward justice? In all these cases—and in so much of social work practice—meeting clients' needs and addressing the roots of their challenges will require changing social policy.

Social policy is part of the context in which practice occurs. **Social policies** are the laws, rules, and regulations that govern the benefits and services governmental and private organizations provide to assist people in meeting their needs. Social workers define a **need** as the gap between an existing condition and some societal standard or required condition. For example, our society has developed standards of adequate nutrition for children. When children do not have access to foods to meet those standards, their nutritional needs are not being met. Levels of funding are directly affected by social policies, as are the rules that govern who can receive which services and what hoops a client must jump through to access resources. And social policy practice is not a separate endeavor from other types of practice. As they build alliances and leverage power to improve systems, social work students who engage in policy practice experience the transformative power of relationships that is the foundation of all social work. Your social policy knowledge and skills, then, are additional tools that increase your ability to help your clients.

Social workers also press for social justice to combat unfair conditions. **Social justice** is a core social work value that refers to the equitable distribution of societal resources, including material goods and social benefits, rights, and protections. Social justice also encompasses procedural equity and fairness in the social, economic, and political spheres. While the negative effects of repressive and ineffective social policies are often easy to identify, social policies can also be instruments for promoting social justice and for improving clients' lives.

While changing social policy is indeed difficult, so is all social work. Social work students who envision a career helping people overcome addiction, navigate to mental health, or recover from traumatic loss have no illusion that their work will be easy. Similarly, social workers who embrace policy practice do so with a clear-eyed assessment of the challenges. Indeed, this recognition often strengthens their resolve to understand and influence the policies that shape their practice and their clients' lives. This book will provide you with the knowledge and skills you need to effectively engage in policy practice. Those of you already working on social justice issues will gain new competencies. Others will ignite a desire to develop social policies that better meet clients' needs. Specifically, this text equips social work students to look at social policy through a strengths perspective lens. The **strengths perspective** is a philosophical approach to social work that puts the goals, strengths, and resources of people and their environments, rather than their problems and pathologies, at the center of the helping process (Saleebey, 1992). Evidence suggests that we can improve the outcomes of social policies by focusing on people's strengths and resources in social policy development. You can read more about the strengths perspective, including its origins and its application in social work practice, at the University of Kansas School of Social Welfare strengths website (**http://socwel.ku.edu/strengths-perspective**).

This chapter introduces and critiques some of the basic concepts and frameworks that will be the building blocks of your understanding of social policy. In addition, it explains how the ways we define and understand social problems shape the social policies we develop to address them. **Social problems** are concerns, widely held by broad consensus and/or voiced by social and economic elites, about the quality of life of large groups of people (Chambers & Bonk, 2013). Social workers spend much of their professional careers attempting to reduce social problems and/or helping clients deal with their effects. Addiction, juvenile delinquency, child maltreatment, and homelessness are just a few examples of social problems. You may have been drawn to the social work profession because of concern with these or other social problems. Subsequent chapters detail how social workers can analyze and develop social policies to address these problems. You will also learn about the historical, political, and economic contexts that shape policy and about the major social policies that affect clients' experiences with these problems. Further, this text will consider the strengths and goals of those experiencing social problems, as well as the resources available in their contexts, as part of the examination of policy responses and articulation of proposed reforms.

SOCIAL WORK AND SOCIAL POLICY

Social policies shape the U.S. social welfare system. The term **social welfare** refers to the system of programs, benefits, and services that help meet those social, economic, educational, and health needs fundamental to the maintenance of society. Social policies make it possible for clients to receive benefits and services they need. To a considerable extent, we are all clients of social welfare systems, since we all benefit from investments in health, safety, education, and other social policies (Abramovitz, 2001; Dolgoff & Feldstein, 2013). In this book, however, the term **client** refers to the recipient of the direct service or benefits a social worker provides. The terms **client group** and *service users* also refer to the population that is the primary focus of a social policy or program. While taxpayers and policymakers are important social work constituents, clients are a social worker's main concern.

In 1973, the National Association of Social Workers (NASW) defined **social work** as "the professional activity of helping individuals, groups, or communities to enhance or restore their capacity for social functioning and creating societal conditions favorable to this goal" (p. 4). In 1996, the NASW further delineated the mission of social work, stated as part of the NASW Code of Ethics. This mission was reinforced in the 2017 revision to the Code:

> The primary mission of the social work profession is to enhance human well-being and help meet the basic human needs of all people, with particular attention to the needs and empowerment of people who are vulnerable, oppressed, and living in poverty. An historic and defining feature of social work is the profession's focus on individual well-being in a social context and the well-being of society. Fundamental to social work is attention to the environmental forces that create, contribute to, and address problems in living.
>
> (NASW, 2017a)

Social workers are ethically obligated to combat injustice through policy practice. Section Six of the NASW Code of Ethics speaks to this responsibility:

> Social workers should advocate for living conditions conducive to the fulfillment of basic human needs and should promote social, economic, political, and cultural values and institutions that are compatible with the realization of social justice.
>
> (NASW, 2017a, 6.01)

> Social workers should engage in social and political action that seeks to ensure that all people have equal access to the resources, employment, services, and opportunities they require to meet their basic human needs and to develop fully.
>
> (NASW, 2017a, 6.04)

In addition to these explicit policy practice mandates, it is arguably impossible to fulfill the mission of the profession—to enhance human well-being and meet basic needs—without securing and preserving policies that advance justice. Further, the quality of the services we deliver is influenced by policies that govern delivery systems, staffing ratios, and funding allocations, so social workers' ability to act with integrity and competence—in essence, to do social work—is also affected by social policy constraints and complements. Social workers are ideally positioned to see ways that client concerns could be addressed by social policy changes and to use policy practice skills to achieve these goals. Additionally, we are professionally obligated to do so. Those opposed to needed changes in the service system count on public apathy and professional complicity, but your policy practice can be a powerful tool.

The Relationship between Social Policy and Social Work Practice

The relationship between social policy and social work practice is illustrated in policies, programs, and practice governing social work with different client groups. For example, social policies in child abuse and neglect determine who may remove children from their homes, where the children can be placed, whether they receive specialized counseling services, who can provide those services, and how much providers are paid. Social workers serving children and other client groups cannot hope to help their clients without understanding the parameters social policies set and how those parameters shape practice.

The child in foster care, the older adult in a nursing facility, and the teenager in prison have all experienced the results of social policies in potent ways. Social workers, whether in private practice, public child welfare, health care, schools, or other settings, also experience the consequences of social policy. A basic understanding of how policy influences practice will make you a more effective social worker. These insights can also help you to move beyond understanding how policies work and coping with their implications to begin to proactively shape policies. For example, a social worker with knowledge of the challenges foster children face can educate legislators about the need for social programs to help them successfully transition to adulthood. Further, social workers approaching this policy practice from a strengths perspective can begin by asking youths about their goals and inviting them to advocate for the policies that would best support them.

Both public and private sector entities can develop social policies. Social policies created by federal, state, and local governments are public policies. Although most social policy in the U.S. is public policy, private entities, including businesses and religious organizations, may also develop social policies. For example, policies put in place by program directors influence childcare and elder care programs offered in their private organizations. Social workers can influence these entities' policies as well. Indeed, many students' policy practice begins with efforts to influence policies of their practicum placement or employer. For example, a social work student convinced her agency to remove gender-binary pronouns on its intake forms, while another shared stories of clients' negative experiences with the agency's no-show policy to convince the executive director to alter it. Social workers should recognize the considerable power they have over the policies of their organizations; indeed, in many cases, social worker discretion moderates clients' experiences of social policies (Lipsky, 1980).

Social policies can benefit clients in many ways. They can help clients achieve their goals, as when, for example, a policy mandating equal opportunity in employment helps single mothers secure well-paying jobs. Social policies can also help clients by creating social programs. **Social programs** are specified sets of activities designed to solve social problems and/or meet human needs. For example, public social policies that create childhood nutrition programs and private programs that fill gaps during the summer break both make it possible for children to receive adequate food. Social workers are integral to making the programs created by social policies work. They often deliver program services, help clients navigate program resources, and attempt to overcome program gaps.

Exhibit 1.1 illustrates the relationships between the social welfare system, social policy, and social workers. Here, the social welfare system includes benefits and services to families who, because they have insufficient incomes, cannot adequately nourish their children. The Child Nutrition Act is the social policy that created the Special Supplemental Nutrition Program for Women, Infants, and Children (WIC). Clients who qualify receive food benefits, nutrition and health education, and referrals to other social services. Social workers deliver some of these services. Note that the arrows in Exhibit 1.1 go in both directions. Social workers are both influenced by *and* influence social policy.

Although social policies and programs are often created to assist people, they can also be used to oppress them. For example, public social policies mandated separate schools for students of color. Women and people of color were denied the right to vote. While these policies have been changed, other policies still oppress some groups. For example, public policies that inequitably finance public education still result in inequitable educational opportunities for students of color, while policies restricting ex-offenders' voting rights have disenfranchised millions. In other cases, policies that inequitably advantage some groups may have the effect of oppressing others by increasing inequality (see Katznelson, 2005).

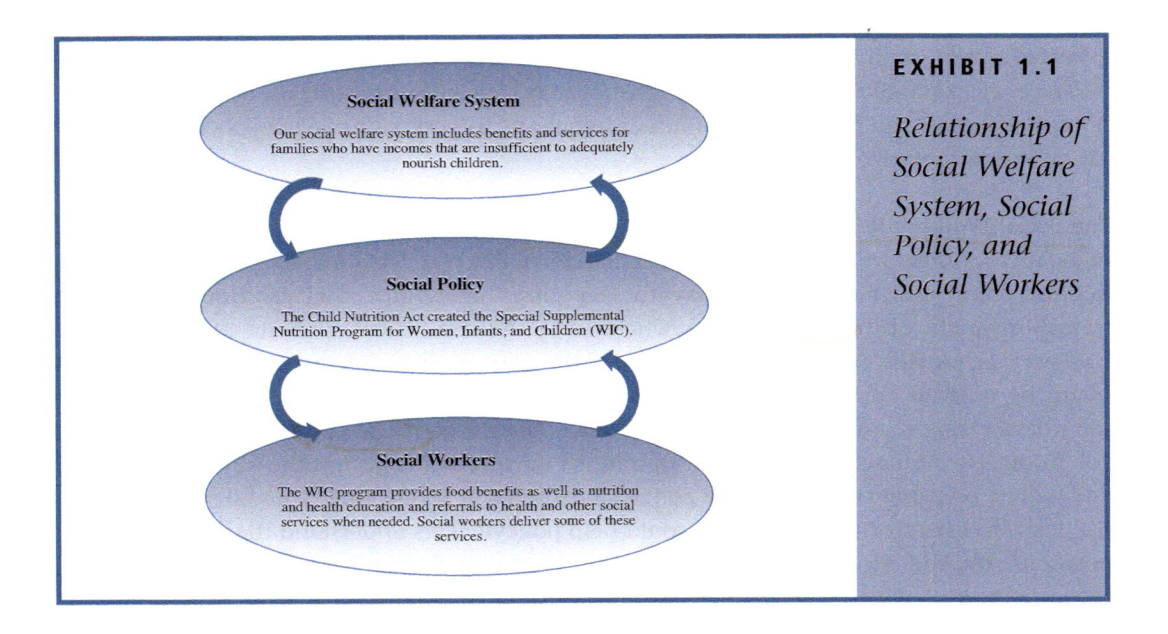

EXHIBIT 1.1

Relationship of Social Welfare System, Social Policy, and Social Workers

Social Welfare System
Our social welfare system includes benefits and services for families who have incomes that are insufficient to adequately nourish children.

Social Policy
The Child Nutrition Act created the Special Supplemental Nutrition Program for Women, Infants, and Children (WIC).

Social Workers
The WIC program provides food benefits as well as nutrition and health education and referrals to health and other social services when needed. Social workers deliver some of these services.

Social workers see first-hand the results of both failed and effective social policies. We are expected to do more than complain about unjust and ineffective policies; we must take action by engaging in policy practice. **Policy practice** "encompasses professional efforts to influence the development, enactment, implementation, modification, or assessment of social policies, primarily to ensure social justice and equal access to basic social goods" (Barker, 2003, p. 330). By engaging in policy practice, you can help craft policies that support effective social work. You will use many of the same skills that serve you in direct practice—assessing, engaging, and communicating. Your social work values will be your guide.

Social Work Values and Policy Practice

Unlike many other approaches to policy analysis, which may claim to be value-neutral, social work policy practice—like all social work practice—is informed by social work values (NASW, 2017a). Two fundamental values that can guide our efforts to shape more effective policy are self-determination and social justice. **Self-determination** refers to people's control over their own destinies. This value is essential to the strengths perspective and influences *how* social workers engage in strengths-based policy practice—by involving clients in all aspects of the work—as well as the types of policies pursued. Recall that social justice involves the fair distribution of societal resources. Valuing self-determination and social justice reinforces the proposition that people who are disadvantaged by the current social order should have equal access to resources, equal opportunities to meet their needs, and power to influence the policies that affect their lives. Indeed, while people's definitions of "equity" sometimes vary, this concept—of everyone getting what they need to succeed, based on where they start and where they want to go—is key (Putnam-Walkerly & Russell, 2016). Obviously, according to this definition, much about the existing social policy landscape is inequitable.

Respect for diversity is also central to social work practice. Therefore, social workers are expected to campaign for societal action on behalf of disadvantaged groups, regardless of gender, race, age, disability, or other characteristics that have been the basis for denying access to resources. Review the NASW Code of Ethics frequently as you continue your social work education (**www.socialworkers.org**).

The Social Worker's Responsibility for Policy Practice Although a desire to help clients and a mandate to comply with the Code of Ethics compel policy practice, some social workers remain hesitant policy practitioners. They may not recognize the resources they can bring to the policymaking arena, or they may feel overwhelmed by the crises clients present. Although social workers can provide valuable perspectives on the consequences of social policies and what might be superior approaches, even social workers passionate about systemic injustices and their devastating consequences may be uncertain about how to proceed. This book can help you bridge the distance between your aspirations for social change and the unjust status quo. You will be prepared to navigate the policy landscape and secure what your clients need. You will learn to listen for the stories that could help policymakers understand the impact of their decisions. You will become a conduit to ensure a better connection between policymakers and those most affected by policy. If you work as a clinician, you may pilot groundbreaking clinical approaches that can lay the foundation for successful new programs. If you work in administration, you may take a promising program to scale. If you are a case manager, you may reframe clients' issues as policy gaps and make the case for increased resources to close them. This book will show you how to make your voice and those of your clients heard in policy arenas.

As you engage and assess your clients, you will also need to evaluate the policies and programs that either facilitate success or create barriers to the achievement of their goals. You can then determine whether and how you may need to put your policy practice skills to use. This **dual assessment** can be used with laws and major programs such as the Child Nutrition Act and with the rules of your own agency. In either case, you're assessing the "fit" between the client's needs and the policy's effects, and you're looking for patterns where several clients are negatively influenced by the same policy. These patterns should alert you to the need for action. The process of making the connection between individuals' needs and the policy issues that affect them and then working to change those policies is referred to as moving from "case to cause." The concept of dual assessment speaks to social workers' simultaneous engagement at the micro, mezzo, and macro levels. **Micro-level practice** involves engaging at the individual level, while **mezzo-level practice** involves work with groups or neighborhoods. **Macro-level practice** involves intervening in large systems and may affect policies and practices at the agency, local, state, national, and global levels. To effectively help your clients, you will need to build practice skills at all levels and understand how they can complement each other.

Advocacy entails helping to make the needs of a group clear to people in decision-making positions in ways that are most effective with the targeted decision-makers. Advocacy efforts may involve helping clients who want to tell their stories, conducting public education campaigns, introducing legislation, helping to bring legal challenges to court, working to change programs so that they are more effective for clients, and/or creating demonstrations or petitions. Advocacy requires an array of skills, including understanding how to help clients become involved in the policy process, providing research and technical information, forging alliances, identifying and cultivating champions, and presenting issues in ways that policymakers can embrace (Jansson, 2013; Reisch, 2000). As an advocate, you will need to be willing to take risks. You must also have realistic expectations, because you will certainly not always succeed. Each time you advocate, you build your skills. You may also develop new relationships that can help in future efforts. Even if you fall short of the ultimate goal, the effort may increase client engagement, improve understanding of issues, or promote awareness.

Connecting Social Policy to Personal Experience You can practice applying your new policy-focused skills using the interactive cases at www.routledgesw.com. You can also reflect on a situation in which you tried to help someone. When you were working with that person, did you give any thought to how social policies may have influenced your ability to help? For example, if you were working for a social service agency, the agency's policies determined who could receive which services, who could offer those services, and how they would be financed. Even if you were trying to offer assistance on a less formal level, such as when friends were getting a divorce or a grandparent was injured, it is likely that policies governing marriage and divorce, child custody, or long-term care significantly influenced your ability to help. Once you understand how to analyze social policies and advocate for change, you can be a more effective helper.

SOCIAL WORK AND THE STRENGTHS PERSPECTIVE

A medical practitioner diagnoses a patient as having a pathological condition such as influenza and then prescribes appropriate treatment. This approach is known as the medical model, in which intervention begins with identifying the individual's problem. Methods of social work intervention and approaches to policymaking have often been based on this model. Like medical practitioners, social workers and policymakers have focused on defining and assessing "problems" that characterize individuals and institutions. Often, this has included a search for deficits or pathology in the people experiencing the problems.

You have probably been taught to always begin with a thorough analysis of a problem. Indeed, careful analysis of social problems is needed to craft and implement effective social policy. However, it is unlikely that you have been taught to couple that problem analysis with a thorough analysis of strengths. Policy analysis approaches seldom give similar attention to identifying the strengths of the people and environments the policy targets (Chapin, 1995). Social problem analysis that focuses on the pathology of the person experiencing the problem often leads to policy strategies that blame the victim. For example, a homeless mother may be deemed unfit and lose custody of her children, even though there is no available housing in the community that she can afford.

Think for a moment about problems such as teen pregnancy and homelessness. In assessing these problems, many people focus immediately and solely on the possible deficits of the people involved. Thus, they assume that a homeless person's circumstances are due to addiction, laziness, or some other personal deficit, and that teenagers become pregnant because they lack self-control. Responsibility for solving the problem is then presumed to rest solely with those experiencing it. Sometimes understanding of a social problem may be so negative that people come to believe the problem is unsolvable. For example, some communities see crime as so entrenched in certain neighborhoods that they essentially "give up" trying to work with residents to increase safety. These communities would benefit from reconsidering their perception of the problem.

In contrast to the medical model, the strengths perspective looks for the strengths, goals, and resources of individuals and their communities as well as for barriers to meeting their needs. For example, social workers who examine homelessness from the strengths perspective begin by looking carefully at those who experience homelessness and exploring their strengths and goals, as well as available community resources. They consider barriers that contribute to the problem, including economic conditions, unaffordability of housing, and availability and quality of job training programs. Identifying and acquiring the resources necessary for people to meet their goals are steps central to the strengths perspective. Similarly, viewing teenage pregnancy through this lens requires focusing not only on the problem but on the teenagers' strengths, goals, and needs. The strengths perspective asserts that homeless people and pregnant teens possess and/or have access to personal and environmental resources (or strengths) that can help them achieve positive outcomes.

Chapters 5 and 6 present a more detailed account of how social workers can use the strengths perspective to redefine and more effectively respond to social problems. Often, this approach helps social workers to arrive at policy solutions that align with values of social justice. Consider, for example, a historically marginalized population: people with disabilities. Based on the deficits approach, this population was labeled "handicapped," and their opportunities to contribute to their communities were minimized. However, employing a strengths-based strategy, people with disabilities and their advocates insisted that these were individuals who could thrive, if equitable access to community resources, rather than their disabilities, became the central focus of relevant social policies. Their activism led to passage of the Americans with Disabilities Act (ADA), a 1990 law that requires accommodations to facilitate full participation of people with disabilities in such areas as employment and transportation. They could not have achieved this result without convincing policymakers to abandon the deficits approach in favor of a more positive focus on strengths and resources. They even worked to change norms around language used to describe the client group, as an essential step in reframing. Crucially, the ADA is also an example of how a strengths approach to policy development changes not just the product, but also the process. People with disabilities played key roles in shaping policy alternatives and advocating for changes, rather than entrusting that work to legislators or professional advocates. People with disabilities helped to craft a very different policy outcome than would have resulted otherwise.

Policy Practice Infused with the Strengths Perspective

When we understand there are alternatives to the view that social problems are rooted in individual or environmental pathology, we can explore new possibilities. In this section, we will consider how policy development could reflect a strengths-based approach. We will begin with the initial stage in the policymaking process, which is defining needs, strengths, and goals. We will then focus on reconceptualizing social problems, involving clients in the process, and convincing decision-makers to allocate resources to meet clients' needs.

Policy analysis and reform begin with an identification of social problems warranting attention. From a strengths perspective, social problems are no longer cast as being rooted in individual pathology. Rather, individual and community strengths are emphasized, and policy analysis incorporates listening to affected populations' experiences, understanding their priorities, and identifying individual and community resources that can be used to remove barriers and meet their goals. For example, when working with people with mental illness, it is important to recognize not only their disability, but also their strengths and any environmental resources that may contribute to their recovery. How have they managed to cope to this point? What brings joy to their lives? What are their goals? Client strengths and goals are legitimate starting places in developing social policy.

Identification of problems to be addressed should be accompanied by discovery of relevant strengths. In addition to clients' own strengths—personal relationships, reservoirs of resilience, accumulated skills and knowledge—there are valuable resources available in all contexts. Perhaps the most fundamental are neighborhood and community institutions such as schools, community centers, health facilities, and self-help organizations. Appropriate social policies can enhance these resources, improve their responsiveness, and increase disadvantaged groups' access to them. When practicing social work, your assessment of which policies and programs can help your clients reach their goals will help you identify resources available to your clients. In turn, your assessment of the barriers and gaps in policies and programs that create stumbling blocks for clients will help focus your policy practice.

Expanding the Clients' Role A strengths-based approach to policy development gives clients an expanded role. According to the strengths approach, the role of the professional helper is not that of expert who develops policy goals alone. Rather, the social worker's role is to encourage policymakers to take clients' perspectives into account, to act as a resource, and to collaborate with clients throughout the policy process. Because any initiative that does not start "where the client is" will be more likely to fail, policymakers must understand policies from the viewpoint of service users. It is crucial, then, that clients be included in the processes whereby needs are identified, problems are defined, and policies are developed. For example, policymakers need to understand that homelessness has many causes and systemic roots, including in the labor and housing markets. Hearing about or speaking with a homeless mother who works hard but cannot find affordable housing can help them see the issue in a new light.

Temporary Aid to Needy Families (TANF), the federal program that provides financial assistance to low-income parents, is one example of how the failure to incorporate clients' perspectives can produce inappropriate policy. One of policymakers' principal goals in developing TANF was to reduce caseloads. Had client perspectives driven policy development, it is likely that the primary goal would have been to reduce child poverty or to support child development. Instead, driven by its articulated goals, TANF imposes strict work requirements but makes inadequate provision for childcare and fails to invest in education to help parents secure well-paying jobs. When clients inevitably struggle to succeed against these odds, they often face sanctions, resulting in loss of benefits—and the accomplishment of policymakers' goal of reducing TANF rolls. Had more policymakers believed that people rely on public assistance not because they are unwilling to work but because they have to care for young children or lack the skills needed to qualify for well-paid jobs, they might have incorporated more funds for childcare subsidies and less emphasis on strict work requirements. When social workers help to give voice to the realities of client groups, policymakers who see recipients as the "other" may begin to perceive the common human needs that they and recipients share (Banerjee, 2002). This can reveal avenues for advocacy. For example, consensus around broad goals such as providing adequate childcare or ensuring that work can move families out of poverty can form the basis for effective policy collaboration.

Claims-Making Recognizing needs, strengths, and goals from the clients' perspective creates a base for policymaking. However, for social policy to be enacted, concerned individuals must make a successful claim that resources should be allocated to meet a recognized need. This process is known as **claims-making**. People base their claims to resources on their values. For example, social workers who help their clients with disabilities often make social justice claims based on the belief that these individuals have the same right as others to access community services. Claims-making that asserts the right to equal opportunity is consistent with the strengths perspective. Moreover, the strengths approach requires that clients themselves be involved in the claims-making process. Chapter 6 examines claims-making in greater detail. For now, be aware that simply recognizing a need will not automatically result in the enactment of social policies to address that need. Concerned parties have to make a successful claim that the need deserves policy attention.

When social workers attempt to engage in claims-making and influence policy formulation, there will be groups that oppose their ideas and others that agree with them. Self-interests and political ideology influence individual views. Chapter 4 examines these economic and political contexts, and the policy practice sections in Chapter 6 explore strategies and tactics for building strengths-based coalitions effective in the conflictual policy environment. The strengths approach, like other empowerment-based helping strategies, seeks to join with client groups to build skills to influence policies and can help awaken latent capacities in these resilient individuals. The work of the LGBTQ+ community to secure equal treatment is a clear example of a group building its capacity to influence social policy, as is the movement-building of undocumented immigrant youth. This text is designed to be an empowerment tool that will help guide your work to combat injustice.

Principles of Strengths Perspective Policy Practice

The most important policy-focused strengths perspective principles are discussed in depth in Chapter 5. Many of these principles are not new to social work nor unique to the strengths perspective. They build on work to incorporate social work values into policy development (see Hill, 2008; Nissen, 2006; Rapp, Pettus, & Goscha, 2006). Exhibit 1.2 presents policy-focused strengths perspective principles.

EXHIBIT 1.2

Strengths Perspective Policy Practice Principles

- Client strengths and goals are legitimate starting points for developing social policy. Problems and deficits are not given center stage.
- Clients' perspectives concerning their problems, strengths, and goals should inform the social construction of needs.
- Social policies and programs should build on individual and community strengths and resources and remove structural barriers that disadvantage the target group. When making claims for benefits and services, social workers should emphasize the structural barriers that create unequal opportunities and impair clients' abilities to meet their needs.
- Claims for benefits and services that allow people to overcome these barriers are made based on the right to equal access to resources and opportunities to meet their needs and reach their goals, regardless of gender, race, age, disability, sexual orientation, gender identity, or other characteristics.
- The role of the social worker is not that of the expert but of the collaborator and resource person who helps draw attention to the perspectives of the target group and supports clients in advocating for policies to improve their lives.
- Social policy goals and design should focus on access, choice, and opportunities that can help empower the target group to meet their needs and goals.
- The target group should be involved in all phases of policy development. The process as well as the product, or outcome, of policy development will be enhanced by their involvement.
- Evaluation should center on assessment of client outcomes.

The strengths perspective can be integrated into many existing frameworks for policy development. Comparing what is emphasized and omitted from the various frameworks will expand your understanding of the diverse lenses through which to view social policies. Quick Guide 1 compares a problem-centered framework with one infused with the strengths perspective. It synthesizes many of the ideas discussed in this chapter and illustrates how those ideas inform the various stages of policy development. The point is not to propose that one formulation of the policy development process is correct. Indeed, some social workers and scholars see the contrast between orientations focused on strengths and problems as an "unnatural dichotomy" (McMillen, Morris, & Sherraden, 2004). Throughout the profession's history, most social workers have tried to build client capacity, and it is a reality that strengths-based social workers still seek to help clients solve their problems. This comparison adds to your critical insights by highlighting the values that underlie each approach, the outcomes you can expect when you use each, and the direction each provides for understanding and developing social policy.

QUICK GUIDE 1 — Comparison of Problem-Centered and Strengths-Based Approaches to Policy Development

PROBLEM-CENTERED APPROACH	STRENGTHS-BASED APPROACH
Define problem.	Define needs, goals, and barriers in partnership with clients.
• A situation is labeled a problem to be corrected.	√ Identify basic needs and barriers to meeting needs. √ Identify client goals.
Analyze the problem, its causes, and consequences.	√ Identify strengths clients currently use to overcome barriers to reaching their goals. √ Identify programs/approaches that can help clients overcome those barriers. √ Focus on solutions.
Inform the public. Engage in claims-making.	Claims-making is based on the right to self-determination and social justice.
Develop policy goals.	In partnership with clients, identify resources and opportunities for clients to meet their goals. √ Formulate policy goals informed by client collaboration.
Legitimize policy goals by building consensus and/or building powerful alliances.	Legitimize policy goals by negotiating consensus and/or building powerful alliances.
Develop and implement policy/program.	Develop and implement policy/program in partnership with clients. √ Program design informed by client collaboration.
Evaluate policy/program effectiveness.	Evaluate outcomes in partnership with clients, emphasizing client outcomes and feedback to improve policy.

Social workers have a responsibility to ensure that policy reflects clients' realities. So, for example, policymakers need to understand that students who fail to graduate from high school are not always making a conscious decision to "drop out." Instead, these students may face significant barriers to continued school progress, which could include inadequate health care, mental illness, poverty, family crisis, or learning disabilities. Further, systemic issues may be involved, including school violence, discrimination or bullying, and/or insufficient education funding that contributes to inadequate staffing levels. Hearing about or talking to these young people can help policymakers see the problem in a new light. Further, asking client groups what solutions they envision can help engender hope and energize the process of formulating new policy or improving existing policy and programs.

Once a policy has been negotiated and formulated, the strengths perspective mandates that clients be involved in implementing and evaluating the resulting policy and programs.

It follows that benefits and services, financing, and the service delivery system should be evaluated according to how effectively they help clients achieve their goals, rather than solely on cost or ease of administration. A policymaking process that includes the strengths approach strongly emphasizes clients' involvement throughout all phases. It also recasts claims-making and the role of the social worker.

Integrating a Strengths Perspective: Benefits and Cautions

A major goal of social work education is to foster critical thinking skills. With this precept in mind, you should adopt a healthy skepticism concerning the advantages of integrating a strengths perspective into your policy practice. You should also weigh the potential benefits and drawbacks of the strengths perspective. The sections that follow can serve as a starting point.

Benefits of the Strengths Perspective: A Summary The strengths perspective requires social workers to assertively look for strengths and resources in clients and their environments. Clients are not seen as problems. While social work students trained in a pathology-centered approach may be initially reluctant to ask people about their strengths and goals, they can typically develop skills in identifying strengths quickly. Further, the strengths perspective is not just ideologically appealing but promising in terms of impact. Inviting people to envision their own solutions and collaborate in developing strategies to attain those goals often improves outcomes.

Second, the strengths perspective gives voice to populations whose views previously have been ignored. Listening to traditionally oppressed groups explain how they have managed to survive and even flourish can help students elevate core social work values such as social justice and respect for the individual. Further, the insights gained from this approach can inform claims-making based on rights to equal access. This approach to claims-making advances equity and therefore has the potential to result in positive outcomes for the broader society, as well as for client groups.

Third, once students move beyond the model of a professional expert, they generally become enthusiastic about working collaboratively toward common aims. Similarly, when policymakers have a sense of the strengths in the target population, it may make them more motivated to take action. Recent advances in criminal justice reform were hard-fought and would be difficult to imagine without the advocacy and leadership of individuals currently involved in the system, ex-offenders, family members, and communities impacted by harsh sentences and disproportionate police contact. Centering claims on people's right to opportunities and access to services changed the narrative around punishment and created space for strengths-based progress.

Students from historically oppressed groups particularly seem to warm to the strengths approach. For example, one Native American student who was also a tribal leader developed a strategy for using gambling proceeds to build a health and social services infrastructure. She began by educating tribal leadership on how to use a strengths perspective to determine where tribal resources should be targeted. She conducted an assessment that identified healthy children and older adults as major strengths and then pressed for the use of gambling proceeds to build an infrastructure to help keep children and older adults on the reservation healthy, including childcare facilities and assisted living. She also collaborated with potential users of these services and with tribal policymakers. The strengths perspective was used as a catalyst to improve community outcomes.

Cautions Regarding the Strengths Perspective   Although the strengths perspective has many important benefits, there are some concerns to consider when applying it to social policy. First, when focus is on clients' strengths as well as needs, the public may lose some sense of urgency that an exclusive focus on the helpless hungry child or bereft older person may convey. Social workers and clients must find ways to portray strengths as well as needs in a manner that can garner resources while avoiding **victim blaming**. Indeed, this has been the approach of the movement to increase investment in early childhood education, a push that has relied more on highlighting the potential gains from seizing critical moments in early brain development than on portraying children without access to early childhood education as uniformly needy.

A second concern is that, although there is extensive anecdotal evidence that the strengths perspective is a useful tool, insufficient formal research has been conducted to provide evidence of the specific mechanisms by which practice grounded in the strengths perspective influences client outcomes (Dunkle, Ingersoll-Dayton, & Chadiha, 2015; Fukui et al., 2012; Oko, 2006; Roose, Roets, & Schiettecat, 2014; Saleebey, 2013). There is even less established knowledge about the outcomes of strengths-based policy development. Research is needed to show how the strengths approach operates in comparison to other strategies, including in the domain of policy practice.

It is therefore critical that you scrutinize the benefits and drawbacks of all the conceptual tools you will be exposed to throughout your social work education, including those that integrate a strengths perspective. Each conceptual tool illuminates some aspects of a situation and blinds us to others. Think about what you might miss using a strengths perspective, as well as what you might notice that you otherwise could have overlooked. We examine social policies through the lens of the strengths perspective because this approach centers on clients' priorities, aligns with social work values, and provides a valuable counterpoint to many of the assumptions on which policy rests. As you will see throughout this text and in your own social work practice, outcomes of social policies developed without sufficient attention to clients' strengths provide ample evidence of the need for their careful consideration.

Connecting Social Work Values to Policy Practice

We challenge you to consider how you can incorporate the strengths perspective and the social work values we have discussed, such as client self-determination and commitment to social justice, into your policy practice. What kinds of policy practice initiatives could help the frightened immigrants, LGBTQ+ teens, and people discharging from hospitals whose concerns we considered at the beginning of this chapter? How might you use a dual assessment to approach your work? What strengths might these individuals and groups possess—within themselves and in their environments—that you could incorporate into your strategies?

DEVELOPING YOUR POLICY PRACTICE ABILITIES

Recognizing that your clients possess expertise and can share stories of strength and resilience broadens the perspective you bring to policy examination. Exploring your own strengths, resources, and areas of expertise can lay the groundwork for discovering your clients' strengths. While your skills will continue to evolve, even brand-new social work students can leverage their own strengths to advance policy consistent with social work values. For example, one group of students met with elder advocates and decided to help develop a home-sharing program for students and older adults. The older adults indicated they had large homes and were willing to have someone live with them but needed help with upkeep. The students knew others who would be willing to help older adults with upkeep in exchange for housing. Class members were encouraged to see themselves as competent and to look for strengths in the person (students/older adults) and the environment. Their project culminated with the presentation of a program that was then modified and implemented with the support of the local senior center. The students also helped the center develop policies governing home sharing. Their work provided the class with a hands-on example of policy and program development that included careful attention to populations' perceptions of their needs and goals, recognition of strengths and resources, and a search for "evidence-guided" models.

No doubt there are many people in your community who can help you build policy practice skills. Perhaps someone in your agency or university interprets rules and regulations, or someone is assigned to lobby the legislature or make presentations at public hearings. Or you might have a friend or social work colleague who is passionate about a certain aspect of social policy and has become an advocate. If you cannot identify anyone, begin by considering your interest area. For example, if your primary interest is working with older adults or children, find advocacy groups in your area. If you have time, volunteer to help with one of their initiatives. Observe what they do. Ask questions. See if they will talk with you about the ideas presented in this book, how these ideas might apply to their work, and how you might implement them. You can contribute a fresh perspective, help translate into practice the theories you are learning, conduct background research, engage stakeholders, and help build coalitions among students, practitioners, and advocates (Carey, 2007; Sherraden, Slosar, & Sherraden, 2002). You will cement your policy knowledge more readily if you can apply it to actual policy practice efforts.

Remember that other students can be valuable resources in your policy practice explorations. The social work profession today is invigorated by the efforts of students, many of whom are active in movements for environmental justice, anti-poverty, racial equity, queer organizing, and immigrant rights. These efforts require students to utilize policy practice skills and root their work in social work values. You can build your own competency through work on the causes that most resonate with your emerging identity as a professional. As a student, you can join the National Association of Social Workers for a reduced rate; this can be a valuable place to connect with colleagues, learn about evolving policy, and continue your development.

While some social workers have jobs in which policy advocacy is a primary job function, many of you will provide counseling or case management. However, in all social work roles, a practitioner who is alert to policy implications will be able to carve out some time to help shape policy. You can begin by speaking up when clients are stereotyped. You can apply **solution-focused approaches** that ask people to identify the outcomes they want. Hopefully, thinking about potential solutions will help you develop fresh insights that will spur involvement in policy practice. You can also contact your state legislator or members of Congress when you feel that policies are not working for your clients. You can use social media and letters to the editor to shape public perceptions of issues that matter to you. You can engage your clients as voters and invite policymakers to learn about your social work agency. If you brainstorm with other students, all sorts of ideas for influencing policy will emerge, many of which do not require great amounts of time or expertise.

You are not expected to craft new laws and get them passed single-handedly. Most policy changes happen incrementally and with contributions from multiple allies. Further, many meaningful changes can be made at the organizational level, by influencing public and private agencies' policies regarding eligibility, service delivery, and staff training. Social workers grappling with the results of misguided policies may feel powerless, but the effective involvement of a wider group of social workers can change that dynamic. The NASW Code of Ethics does not require that we make policy practice our full-time job, but it also does not excuse those who are "busy" from this responsibility. Exhibit 1.3 describes steps students can take to change policy. You will find additional examples of how students engaged in policy practice throughout this book. Start now to identify and develop your own strengths, which will help you make a real difference in the lives of your clients.

EXHIBIT 1.3

Students Take Action

Policy students at a Midwestern university knew that their state legislature was planning to cut funding for mental health centers in their state. They engaged in policy practice to help prevent the cuts. Students identified their strengths, including experience with family members with mental illness, familiarity with social media, and membership in their church outreach program to people with mental illness who were homeless. They also identified community strengths, which included key people and organizations with whom they could collaborate. They developed a plan that emphasized accountability of each student. To implement their plan:

1. They talked to their local legislator so that they understood in detail what was being proposed. They identified themselves as her constituents. Their legislator put them in touch with legislative research staff who were examining the proposed legislation.
2. They researched whether other states had introduced or passed similar legislation. They looked for information on outcomes if the legislation passed and information on strategies used by opponents where legislation was successfully blocked.
3. They strategized with local members of the National Alliance on Mental Illness (NAMI) to share ideas and prevent duplication of effort.
4. They arranged for a reporter to do a story in a local paper that featured a family member who was willing to talk about what the cuts would mean personally.
5. They worked with NAMI to organize a social media campaign encouraging people to contact their legislators. They provided an outline of talking points based on their research and meetings with key stakeholders.
6. The funding cuts that were ultimately enacted were much smaller than those originally proposed.
7. The students personally thanked the legislators who opposed deep cuts. They savored their success, evaluated what had worked well, and considered what they would do differently.

CONCLUSION

As a future social worker, your commitment to help shape policies and programs that can provide resources, support, and opportunities for clients is vital. Integrating the strengths perspective into your understanding of social policy can help clarify your role, provide concrete guidance on how you can help to craft effective policy, and reinforce your responsibility to view your clients as collaborators. Each time you begin to assess new clients, you also need to assess the policies and programs that either facilitate or impede achievement of their goals. This kind of dual assessment is basic to effective social work. The chapters that follow are designed to equip you with new tools for conceptualizing social needs and analyzing policy, a more inclusive approach to policy formulation, and an expanded array of policy options. You will discover how historical, political, and economic contexts affect social policy. You will learn about specific policies and programs in areas including child welfare, mental health, and aging, as well as how these policies and programs influence social work practice. The text closes with a focus on the future. We invite you to share in the excitement of learning to shape social policies and programs that can help your clients and potentially thousands of others.

MAIN POINTS

- To be effective practitioners, social workers need to engage in policy practice. Students can and should develop their policy practice skills.
- Social work values, including self-determination and social justice, are the foundation for policy practice and are integral to the strengths approach.
- Social policies can be tools for achieving social justice but may serve to perpetuate inequity, particularly when designed without adequate consideration of clients' needs.
- A dual assessment examines clients' goals as well as the policies and programs that either facilitate or create barriers to the achievement of their goals.
- Social workers engage in practice at the micro, mezzo, and macro levels.
- Problem-focused models for defining issues and developing policy can limit the social worker's ability to craft effective policies that build on clients' strengths.
- The strengths perspective can be used to reconceptualize the policymaking process. In fact, it is the change to a process emphasizing clients' strengths and collaboration that is likely to produce a more effective policy.
- The role of a social worker using the strengths perspective shifts from one of expert to one of collaborator and resource person. Identification of potential solutions and goals from the clients' perspective is key.
- There are benefits to using a strengths perspective as well as cautions that critical thinkers should keep in mind.
- Begin to build your policy practice skills now. Becoming involved in policy practice will enable you to try out the ideas presented in this book.

EXERCISES

1. Go to **www.routledgesw.com/cases** and get to know the Sanchez family. After exploring the Sanchez family case, respond to the following questions:
    a. Reflecting on your social work practice skills and experiences building rapport with diverse communities, do you feel you have cultural competence in working with Latinx[1]

families? If not, how can you build that competence? How is cultural competence essential for building a working relationship with the Sanchez family? How is cultural competence important for engaging in effective policy practice alongside clients?

b. Complete a dual assessment of Alejandro Sanchez. Identify his needs, strengths, and goals. Identify three social policies that would influence social work practice with Alejandro. Try to include one federal, one state, and one agency policy. What are the policies and how do they influence practice?

c. Do you think Alejandro would consider the policies you have identified effective? What improvements to the policies you identified can you suggest?

d. What persons or groups do you think made these policies? If you could talk to these people, what would you tell them about the results of their decision? How might you ensure that policymakers consider the voices of the people affected by these policies, such as members of the Sanchez family, as they develop new policy approaches?

2. Go to www.routledgesw.com/cases and become familiar with Riverton. Imagine you are a social worker in Riverton. Your work with the community will undoubtedly involve policy practice. You will need to understand current city policies related to the homeless shelter and the policies of the shelter itself, as well as how different groups in the community want these policies to change.

a. Thinking about what you have learned thus far about policy practice using the strengths perspective, where would you start?

b. Who would you talk to and what would you ask them?

c. What patterns do you see in terms of policies that are helping or hindering homeless individuals as they seek temporary shelter and, ultimately, permanent homes?

d. How do you think social workers using the strengths approach would differ from those using a problem-centered approach in their work in Riverton?

3. Go to www.routledgesw.com/cases and review the Carla Washburn interactive case.

a. How might a social worker assess Mrs. Washburn's major needs? How would you, as a social worker, engage her to determine how she sees her needs?

b. Identify at least three strengths Mrs. Washburn has that could help her meet these needs and at least three resources in the community that can potentially help her meet her needs.

c. What policies and programs are already helping her meet her needs?

d. Can you identify any policies that are making it more difficult for her to meet her needs?

4. Go to www.routledgesw.com/cases and become familiar with Brickville and the people who live there.

a. Can you identify policies that are helping or hindering the people of Brickville as they seek the resources they need? How might different Brickville residents experience the same policy differently?

b. How do you think a social worker using a strengths approach might begin to help people in Brickville to address policy issues that impact their community?

5. Go to www.routledgesw.com/cases and complete the exercises that introduce you to the RAINN interactive case. RAINN is a private, nonprofit organization. How do you think engaging in policy practice to influence programs within an organization such as RAINN would be different from working to change policies in the public sector?

6. Visit the NASW website to review some of the profession's policy statements (**www.socialworkers.org**, then search for Advocacy and Policy Issues). How do these statements compare with what you expect to see from the profession? How might these statements influence how others—policymakers, client groups, and potential allies—view the profession and its role in the policy process?
7. Review the downloadable case "Willow's Transition." How would you use the NASW Code of Ethics to navigate your policy involvement in this case? What parts of the Code compel your advocacy on behalf of Willow and her family? What ethical guidelines should inform your consideration of your approach?

NOTE

1. We use the term "Latinx" as a gender-inclusive term that is in other ways largely synonymous with "Hispanic" or "Latino."

CHAPTER 2

The Historical Context: Basic Concepts and Early Influences

The less that is given, the better for everyone, the giver and the receiver.
Josephine Shaw Lowell, 1890

We don't want to turn the safety net into a hammock that lulls able-bodied people to lives of dependency and complacency.
Congressman Paul Ryan, 2012

THESE QUOTES, MORE THAN A CENTURY APART, illustrate crucial truths students of social policy need to understand: today's policies have historical roots, and values and assumptions that underlie our policy approaches reverberate. Here, an early leader of the Charity Organization Society—an organization that strongly influenced the development of social work—and a powerful contemporary U.S. politician both express a theme of social welfare throughout history: the tension between providing assistance and fearing that such help will lead to moral decay. These concerns reflect a belief that, perhaps, many individuals are poor due to their own failings. As we survey persistent gaps in social policy systems and their effects on clients' lives, we should consider options for change with an understanding of the influence of these beliefs. Toward that end, in this chapter, we provide historical background on social policies, the social welfare system, and the social work profession.

Our current social welfare policies are the product of decades or, in some cases, centuries of debate and struggle. Religious and spiritual teachings introduced thousands of years ago continue to shape people's orientations to policy responses and the parameters that drive current debates, including the idea that some individuals are more deserving of assistance than others. Your study of this historical context will be more useful for your practice if you link what you learn about history to the policies that shape social work today. Further, knowing that the policies that form the backdrop of our current social welfare system were often hotly contested during their development underscores the potential for change. To engage in effective policy practice, it is crucial to understand factors that influenced social policy in the past and those likely to influence policy in the future.

THE GENESIS OF SOCIAL WELFARE POLICY

Social work clients often live in poverty. Further, anti-poverty policy is a potent example of the relationship between beliefs about the origins of problems and the nature of responses to them. For these reasons, this chapter begins with an exploration of practices in pre-industrial societies that gave rise to current programs for people who have low incomes. The major religions and spiritual practices of these societies require their adherents to care for people who are poor. Later, these individual obligations gave rise to increasingly sophisticated institutions and systems of relief. At the same time, powerful members of the ruling elite were careful to maintain the social and economic barriers that oppressed poor people and protected their own privilege. Thus, the social welfare structures that evolved to address poverty also served as a means of social control. This dynamic continues today.

Religious and Spiritual Traditions

We begin our discussion of the early historical mandates that shaped social policy by examining selected religious traditions from around the world. Throughout history, these religious traditions and systems often developed in parallel in different communities around the globe; therefore, they are presented here without intention to construct a chronology or, certainly, a hierarchy. Further, as dynamic movements, these religious and spiritual traditions have evolved over the centuries, influencing each other and responding to their social contexts. We encourage you to examine early religious writings for additional examples of attitudes and practices related to social welfare and to consider how they relate to current social policy.

Judaism   Basic Jewish teachings and laws, known as the Torah, mandate that Jews provide for people living in poverty, within the context of the agrarian society of the period in which they were written. For example, Leviticus 19:9–10 instructs:

> And when ye reap the harvest of your land, thou shalt not wholly reap the corners of thy field, neither shalt thou gather the gleanings of thy harvest. And thou shalt not glean thy vineyard, neither shalt thou gather the fallen fruit of thy vineyard; thou shalt leave them for the poor and for the stranger: I am the Lord your God.

Overall, the Torah instructs that justice be extended even to the most vulnerable members of society (Anderson, 1986). Significantly, the Torah also dictates that justice be extended to "strangers" who are not of the community.

Islam   All branches of Islam accept the fundamental tenet that the faithful must provide charity to people in need. The Koran (Qur'an) teaches the faithful to give up part of their wealth for the benefit of poor people and people with disabilities. This annual almsgiving is called *zakat*. According to the Koran, when you give away part of your possessions, Allah will bless whatever is left. "Piety does not lie in turning your face East or West. Piety lies in … disbursing your wealth ... among your kin and the orphans, the wayfarers and mendicants, freeing the slaves ... and in paying *zakat*" (Koran, 2:177).

Buddhism According to Buddhist teachings, doing good deeds toward others may help lead to rebirth as a more prosperous and wiser individual. Followers are instructed to feel compassion for and to assist those whose burdens are hardest. Buddhism focuses on the individual doer of good; the belief is that giving enriches the giver. A core Buddhist text, the *Dhammapada*, says of Buddhist monks that: "They are true disciples who have trained their hands, feet, and speech to serve others" (Hays, 1989, p. 195).

Confucianism The religious practice of Confucianism developed around 500 bce. Mostly viewed today as a moral philosophy, Confucianism has been highly influential in China, Korea, Japan, and Vietnam. At the core of Confucianism is the virtue Ren, which is often translated to benevolence, humanity, humanness, or goodness (Canda, 2002). For Confucians, this and other principles guide all levels and relationships in society.

Native American Spiritual Traditions Native American tribes have diverse spiritual traditions. The social structures of Native American groups often reflect a collective approach to the use of resources. Taking care of others is understood as a way of building new relationships while maintaining and reinforcing old ones. A key value is appreciating the reciprocal nature of relationships. Native Americans and many other cultures recognize that working together as a group helps the entire community prosper.

Christianity Christian religious teachings instruct that people serve God by caring for one another. The New Testament of the Bible contains a parable in which God indicates to the righteous that they will be allowed into heaven because they have cared for the poor: "For I was hungry and you gave me something to eat, I was thirsty and you gave me something to drink, I was a stranger and you invited me in, I needed clothes and you clothed me, I was sick and you looked after me, I was in prison and you came to visit me." God further instructs, "Truly, I say to you, as you did it to one of the least of these my brothers, you did it to me" (Matthew 25:35–36).

The biblical concept of charity refers to unconditional love and benevolence. Themes in early Christian teachings include elevation of the importance of charity and the portrayal of poor people as just as worthy in the eyes of God as rich people—or perhaps worthier—to enter the Kingdom of Heaven.

Current Implications

Several elements of these teachings and practices have implications for the U.S. social welfare system. First, caring for others was defined as a religious duty, and a righteous person shared at least a portion of their wealth with people in need. This promoted the development of social welfare. Second, in many cases religious beliefs promoted the development of an institutionalized method to provide for the welfare of less fortunate people. Third, charitable actions were historically directed primarily toward *neighbors* in need, which contributed to localized responses and restrictions on aid to foreigners and newcomers. Finally, historically, accepting charity was relatively non-stigmatizing. The recipient was not typically portrayed as inferior or at fault. However, even some early religious leaders expressed strong beliefs about the necessity of work (Dolgoff & Feldstein, 2013), which contributed to subsequent distinctions among groups in need. While in all societies, actual practices may vary for many reasons, examining historical records provides insight into the guiding principles of the period.

Conflicting Historical Views Regarding Social Welfare

An examination of the history of social welfare shows that earlier cultures struggled to reconcile conflicting attitudes. These debates continue today. For example, although ancient Greek and Roman societies developed social welfare systems, philosophers warned against rewarding paupers for begging. Similarly, by the thirteenth century, Christians clearly differentiated between the "worthy poor" and those who were unwilling to work, and they questioned whether it was appropriate to help strangers. Social policies and programs today similarly exhibit a tension between the mandate to help people and a willingness to help only those who adhere to a certain moral code or are otherwise deemed "worthy." For example, sanctions in welfare policies can deny housing and income assistance to those with drug or other convictions, while work requirements are increasingly prevalent and strict.

In the United States in the 1800s, the wedding of Social Darwinism and the Protestant work ethic created further support for stigmatizing the poor as unworthy. **Social Darwinism** is a philosophy that applies Darwin's theory of evolution (Darwin, 1859) to human societies (Day, 2009). Social Darwinists proposed that poverty was part of natural selection; in a competitive society, those who were most capable and worked hardest would succeed, and the rest would fail. Therefore, helping people in poverty would only enable survival of the unfit. People who amassed great wealth were seen as living testaments to the correctness of these beliefs. The Protestant work ethic, a sociological concept denoting the view that hard work and thrift are signs of a person's worthiness for eternal salvation, also lent support to this view of poverty and to the policies that reinforced it.

Not all Americans, however, embraced this harsh philosophy, and countervailing beliefs developed within the religious communities themselves. For example, in the late 1800s and early 1900s, some Protestant and Catholic denominations began espousing a "Social Gospel" that called for social justice. They preached that fair wages and profit sharing were necessary to alleviate the ills of poverty, overwork, and underpayment. They spoke out against laissez-faire (characterized by minimal government regulation) capitalism, concentration of wealth, and unrestrained competition (Swatos, 1998; Trattner, 1999).

Human societies have attempted to deal with poverty and inequality since the earliest times. Unfortunately, although people in many societies have called for social justice, these calls have often been disregarded as, at various points, societies have found ways to justify inequality. Think about how these same dynamics manifest today. For example, how are tax cuts for wealthy people described as rewards for superior talent or effort? How do advocates for workers' rights appeal to policymakers' own moral and religious values to convince them to champion protections? As you read about historic and current social welfare practices, consider what future students might identify as the guiding principles of our current programs for assisting people in poverty.

A FRAMEWORK FOR UNDERSTANDING HOW HISTORICAL APPROACHES INFLUENCE CURRENT POLICY

The questions in Quick Guide 2 provide a framework for understanding the implications of historical events for current social policy and social work practice (Chambers & Bonk, 2013; Chapin, 1995; Spano, 2000). You can use these questions to examine the historical development of different social programs. The example below uses them to consider faith-based policy initiatives. These initiatives give public funds to religious organizations that provide social services. Some proponents assert that if such faith-based approaches are implemented more widely, religious organizations will do a better job of providing social programs than public entities and, further, that private funding of social welfare programs may save taxpayer dollars.

How do historical policy approaches to this social problem/need shape current policy?

Religious and faith-based approaches to poverty continue to influence social policy today. Current social policies reflect historical themes of support for social justice and aid to people in poverty, differentiation between the worthy and unworthy poor, and ambivalence toward strangers and immigrants. Today, religious organizations continue to administer to needs but lack sufficient resources to do so adequately.

What was the cultural context at the time these historical approaches were taken? In what ways are the current political and economic contexts the same or different?

Early approaches to social welfare developed in largely agrarian societies with rather homogeneous populations. Religious institutions typically played a major role in providing social

---

QUICK GUIDE 2 A Framework for Linking History and Current Social Policy

- How do historical policy approaches to this social problem/need shape current policy?
- What was the cultural context at the time these historical approaches were taken? In what ways are the current political and economic contexts the same or different?
- Who were the key players involved in developing these historical policies? Which groups' interests were the policies intended to serve?
- Is there any reason to think that these historical policy approaches would work better or worse today?
- Did these historical policy approaches build on the strengths of target populations? How?
- Alternatively, were these policy approaches predicated on a pathology or deficit view of people in need?
- How have definitions of this social problem/need and related policy approaches to address these needs changed over time?

welfare. As societies became more diverse, the issue of how to treat people who were considered different became highly divisive. This issue is prominent in the United States today, where the population reflects a variety of backgrounds, and immigrants are often targeted for particularly restrictive policies. Further, when considering the relevance of a faith-based approach today, it is important to consider that people with different religious backgrounds or those who do not identify with any religion may be wary of faith-based social services.

Who were the key players involved in developing these historical policies? What groups' interests were the policies intended to serve?

In very early cultures, particularly in desert societies in which many of the major religions first developed, it was clear that even those members who had relatively more resources would not survive without the help of the group. People were tied together through "status relationships" such as relative, lord, or serf. Powerful people like tribal leaders, lords, and family heads used their status to develop systems that favored and maintained their positions. These leaders often influenced the systems of charity that religious institutions developed. The absolute necessity of mutual aid as well as powerful elites' desire to maintain social control motivated social welfare.

Is there any reason to think that these historical policy approaches would work better or worse today?

Contemporary U.S. society is highly complex, diverse, industrialized, and technologically advanced. Although religious institutions still play an important role in providing social welfare, many people do not belong to organized religions. Additionally, many church-based welfare services already receive funding from federal and state governments and do not have sufficient funds to take on more roles. For example, religiously affiliated nursing facilities often receive more than half of their funding from Medicaid, a program jointly funded by federal and state governments. Further, certain segments of the population, for example, the LGBTQ+ community, have reasons to be wary of the transfer of authority for social services to faith-based communities that might not fully support their needs.

Did these historical policy approaches build on the strengths of target populations? How? Alternatively, were these policy approaches predicated on a pathology or deficit view of people in need? How have definitions of this social problem/need and related policy approaches to address these needs changed over time?

In societies in which many people lived at subsistence levels, it appears that poverty held little stigma. People provided help to those in need through religious organizations with the knowledge that they themselves could require aid if poor crops or sickness depleted their resources. However, as the gap between rich and poor members of society widened, the belief that people in poverty were somehow different gained greater acceptance. Although religiously affiliated organizations may do an excellent job caring for members of their own community, critics of policies that allow more public funds for social services to go to religious organizations express concern that these organizations may not provide culturally competent services to people of differing backgrounds. Additionally, the scale and scope of faith-based organizations' capacities are limited compared to the significant social problems faced today.

This short exploration illustrates the impact a variety of cultures have had on social welfare policy. We now turn to a set of specific historical governmental approaches to caring for people in poverty that are recognized as directly influencing current U.S. social policy. Because many specific policy elements can be traced to social policies initially developed in England during the Middle Ages, this examination begins with the English Poor Laws.

ENGLISH POOR LAWS

The feudal system of the Early Middle Ages was based on a hierarchy in which a lord protected the serfs who farmed his land. In general, treatment of serfs and peasants was at the lord's discretion and varied greatly based on available resources and the lord's temperament. This agrarian economy produced very little surplus. Lords took a portion of the produce of their lands as payment for the protection they offered, and famine was common. Canon Law—the law directing church activities—demanded that each parish provide for the poor. Anyone who had extra resources was exhorted to share. Consistent with widespread condemnation of those believed responsible for their poverty, however, the "willfully idle" were not to be assisted (Quigley, 1996a).

Before the Middle Ages, church teachings had long supported begging and giving. However, after the thirteenth century, the church began to view begging in a more negative light (Quigley, 1996a). During the Middle Ages, guilds—associations of merchants and artisans—provided mutual aid and disaster insurance for their members. Private foundations and hospitals also contributed to the welfare infrastructure.

Background of the Poor Law

By 1500, English society was experiencing a dramatic economic, political, and social transformation. The feudal system had declined, and feudal relationships that bound serfs and lords were giving way (Reid, 1995). Although most people continued to make their living in agriculture, many small industries were beginning to develop, concentrated in towns throughout the country. A stratum of society made up of tradesmen and merchants was emerging in which position was based on profession rather than birth. Contracts that specified the number of hours to be worked or the product to be delivered increasingly defined relationships. England, then, was undergoing the initial stages of industrialization that came to characterize economic relationships in much of the world.

Population Growth and Migration Starting in 1348, a series of outbreaks of plague, known as the "Black Death," claimed the lives of between one-third and one-half of England's overall population. As these epidemics subsided, the population began to rebound. During the period 1500–1700 the number of inhabitants nearly doubled (Clark & Slack, 1976). In many villages, the number of residents was increasing, and land was becoming scarcer. To raise sheep to supply wool for the expanding textile industry, landowners were closing off areas that had formerly been accessible to the community. In addition, many agricultural families continued to practice primogeniture, a system whereby the eldest son inherited his family's entire estate. As a result of these developments, many villagers were forced to acquire land or seek employment elsewhere (Cannon, 1997).

One major result of rural overpopulation was a massive migration, as people from farming villages moved to towns seeking work or some type of charitable relief. Unfortunately, towns also lacked sufficient jobs and housing. This led to subsistence migration, in which poor migrants moved from town to town, looking for work or begging for charity. By 1600, the number of beggars in England may have soared as high as 20,000. Complaints of criminal behaviors grew. Many concerned people began to associate vagrancy with an "underworld culture" that threatened the social and economic order (Singman, 1995, p. 17).

Poverty Many workers who were able to secure jobs contended with seasonal unemployment or periods of economic downturn. A series of poor harvests from 1594 to 1597 led to shortages that drove up grain prices, generating popular discontent. In many towns, at least 20 percent of residents were unable to meet their basic needs (Singman, 1995). Increases in poverty and unemployment spurred greater demand for relief (Clark & Slack, 1976; Rowse, 1950).

The Poor Law of 1601

As poverty increased, towns were unable to meet the growing demand for assistance. Many wealthy taxpayers became disgruntled with the heavy tax burden of caring for the poor. At the turn of the seventeenth century, "poverty was the major concern of all urban governors," and local officials looked to the central government in London for support (Clark & Slack, 1976, p. 121). In 1597, Parliament agreed to consider the issue, and in 1601 the government passed the Act for the Relief of the Poor, more commonly called the Poor Law of 1601. This law created a uniform system for addressing poverty and unemployment. Justices of the peace in every parish were empowered to appoint officials known as overseers of the poor to supervise relief programs. The law further authorized a tax to raise funds for relief.

This system of relief served as the foundation for poor relief in England for many years. A subsequent law, the Act of Settlement of 1662, restricted assistance to people who were born in the parish or who were long-term residents. Others had to return to the parish in which they were born to receive aid (Cannon, 1997; Olsen, 1999; Rowse, 1950). This law embodied the principle of **local responsibility**, which mandated that each locality was responsible for helping only its own residents.

Poor Law Amendments

In the late eighteenth century, England was experiencing wars and inflation. Many people were living in poverty. The plight of poor agricultural workers became even more dire when grain prices increased. The Speenhamland System of 1795, which amended the Poor Law of 1601, sought to aid these workers by providing relief based on a sliding scale. The cost of bread and the number of persons in a family determined the amount of aid received. At the time, many heavily criticized this system. Some felt this new aid would increase dependency and encourage poor people to have larger families. Others argued that basing relief on this bread scale provided a subsidy to rich farmers who profited from increased prices of goods while refusing to increase wages for their workers. The Poor Law Amendment Act of 1834 ended the

Speenhamland System. However, the idea that government policy should supplement wages to make low-wage work more profitable and to keep people employed—rather than receiving other forms of welfare—still echoes in U.S. welfare policy. Indeed, this is the rationale for policies such as the Earned Income Tax Credit (EITC), discussed in Chapter 8.

The Poor Law Amendment Act of 1834, widely known as the New Poor Law, was a sweeping reform. It established a central commission to make regulations for the administration of relief. Persons needing relief were sent to live and work in a **workhouse**. People who lived in workhouses were issued uniforms and required to relinquish their personal possessions. The physical structures were reconfigured to segregate "inmates" by gender and age. Exhibit 2.1 depicts an artist's rendering of a London workhouse. Note the presence of children and people with disabilities, as well as the apparent prosperity of the overseer.

Analyzing the Poor Laws

The Poor Law of 1601 codified traditional distinctions between the "worthy" and "unworthy" poor—a demarcation that continues to characterize much social welfare policy. For the "worthy poor," the law instructed towns to raise "competent sums of money for and toward the

EXHIBIT 2.1

Poor people coming to a workhouse for food, c. 1840

Credit: Wellcome Collection. CC BY

necessary relief of the lame, impotent, old, blind, and such other among them, being poor and not able to work" (Axinn & Stern, 2001, p. 10). Towns could also use tax monies to assist unemployed people who were capable of working, but only by "setting to work all such persons" (Axinn & Stern, 2001, p. 10). In other words, all able-bodied people seeking aid, including children whose parents were unable to support them, were expected to work.

Relief took different forms. Under the Speenhamland System of 1795, people received **outdoor relief**; that is, aid provided in their homes or other non-institutional settings. Although workhouses and almshouses had long been in existence, the New Poor Law of 1834 encouraged the building of new workhouses and pressed people to enter workhouses to receive public relief. Although residents were better off than unemployed beggars, workhouse conditions were sufficiently harsh to deter anyone who could secure employment from applying for public charity. By contrast, **almshouses** were supported by private funds and reserved for the "worthy poor," particularly the elderly. However, the distinctions between workhouses and almshouses became blurred, particularly as elderly people and unmarried mothers sought refuge in workhouses as the only shelter available.

Influence of the Poor Laws on U.S. Social Policy

Because the United States based many of its laws on the systems in place in England, it is not surprising that our policies dealing with poor people reflect many principles of the Poor Laws. For example, we can see philosophies that designate older adults, people with disabilities, widows, and orphans as the "worthy poor" at work today if we contrast benefits provided by two current social welfare programs: Old Age, Survivors, and Disability Insurance (OASDI), popularly known as Social Security, and Temporary Assistance for Needy Families (TANF). Social Security is intended for "worthy" recipients such as retired workers and families of deceased and disabled workers. In contrast, TANF provides assistance to low-income families with children. These parents are often depicted as unworthy of help. Understanding the historical distinctions between those seen as "worthy" and "unworthy" brings differences between OASDI and TANF into sharper relief. In 2019, the estimated average monthly benefit for retired workers covered by OASDI was $1,467 (Social Security Administration, 2019a), whereas in 18 states the monthly TANF payment for a family of three or less was at or below *20 percent* of the poverty line—$346 per month (Burnside & Floyd, 2019). In addition, TANF imposes strict work requirements and time limits, and recipients can be sanctioned for a variety of infractions, while the Social Security Administration provides online, in-person, and telephone assistance to help retired workers navigate their benefits. Further emphasizing the framing of TANF recipients as "unworthy" and the emphasis on work, many people oppose cash assistance programs that would raise incomes enough that low-wage workers could escape poverty, out of fear that such benefits discourage work—an outcome seen as worse than child poverty. Finally, proposals to further cut TANF, which provides at least minimal "outdoor relief," harken back to the distaste for subsidizing poor families that led to passage of the New Poor Law of 1834.

As we shift our focus to the history of social welfare in the United States, consider how principles established by the English Poor Laws continue to shape approaches to social policy in this country, and how these principles have influenced the profession of social work.

SOCIAL WELFARE POLICY IN THE UNITED STATES FROM COLONIAL TIMES TO THE PROGRESSIVE ERA

The remainder of this chapter chronicles the development of U.S. social policies through the early years of the twentieth century. You will see that, as our population grew and became more diverse, our economy more industrialized, and our society more urban, some of the responsibility for helping people in need gradually shifted from private institutions and local governments to the federal government. Examination of milestones in the development of our current welfare system will help you understand the confluence of factors that shape social policy. This should spur you to think about how you can use this knowledge to influence the development and implementation of more effective policies.

The Colonial Era: Adapting the English System, 1600–1775

Native Americans, living in North America when the colonists arrived, were the first people to provide European immigrants with charity in what would become the United States. In contrast, White settlers' struggle to control the land was marked by bloodshed, broken treaties, and oppression of Native peoples. Colonialism in the United States began along the eastern shore in the 1600s when Dutch and English settlers and merchants began supplanting established Native American communities. Spain established settlements and missions in Florida during the late 1500s and 1600s. In the Southwest, Catholic missionaries, who numbered over 3,000 by the 1600s, accompanied Spanish invaders (Day, 2000). Although the missions became a major welfare system that provided hospitals, hospice care, alms, and shelters for homeless people, the elderly, and people with disabilities, they were often oppressive forces in the lives of Native Americans. Native Americans were used as forced labor at some missions, and diseases brought by Spanish soldiers devastated Native populations (Gumbel, 2015).

Social Welfare in the English Colonies English colonists along the eastern seaboard categorized poor people in much the same way they had in England, distinguishing between those deemed "worthy" and "unworthy." Emphasizing self-sufficiency, the colonies passed laws that required families to take in relatives in need. Local government, churches, and philanthropy offered aid only when families could not provide it themselves.

Public relief at the time was based strictly on a **residual approach**; that is, the government provided relief only to people who could not work and whose families were unable to provide for their basic needs. The residual approach is often contrasted with the **institutional approach**, which asserts that government should ensure that everyone's basic needs are met as a right of membership in advanced economies. Not only did the values of colonial society align with a residual approach, further, the fledgling colonies had neither the money nor the infrastructure to sustain an institutional approach.

Towns in the colonies developed their own policies for helping poor people. Whatever assistance they offered was funded using local resources. Reflecting the philosophy that underlay the English Act of Settlement, some towns instituted eligibility rules that restricted poor relief to people who owned property or had been local residents for a number of years.

Almshouses and Workhouses The first workhouse in this country opened in 1658 in Plymouth Colony (Quigley, 1996b). As the numbers of people needing assistance increased, the quest to find less costly means of providing help fueled the growth of institutions for the poor (Quigley, 1996a). Workhouses were also called "houses of correction" because they housed people who violated colonial laws and required people to work (Quigley, 1996b). Many times, these institutions were not segregated by gender, age, or disability; further, criminals and poor people were often housed together. Mortality rates were high. Almshouses and workhouses were the forerunners of hospitals, penitentiaries, and reform schools (Day, 2009). Some almshouses began to segregate people with mental illness from other residents and were, then, the forerunners of asylums for people with mental illness.

As in England, colonial policies governing the treatment of poor people were designed to ensure that everyone who could potentially work would be motivated to do so, even for meager or no wages. Although these policies helped provide a continuous supply of labor for farms and industry, efforts to reduce the costs of assisting poor people continued. As is often true today, many colonial residents were dissatisfied with whatever system of poor support was used (Dolgoff & Feldstein, 2013; Quigley, 1996b). Considering echoes of these policies in our current policy landscape, strengths-based social workers critically analyze the focus on encouraging work. Although supporting economic independence can be characterized as building on strengths, many policies that emphasize the necessity of work were not designed to facilitate economic well-being, then or now.

Slavery and Indentured Servitude Slavery is the most extreme and inhumane example of the control of human labor to benefit the ruling class. Colonial and later American law defined slaves as property. The first African slaves were brought to the colony of Jamestown, Virginia, in 1619. Importation of African slaves continued until 1808. Mortality among slaves was excessively high due to the brutal conditions they endured (Steckel, 1979, 1986). Nonetheless, the slave population grew to approximately 3.9 million by 1860 (Bailey, 1994). Slave labor helped build the economic foundations of the nation and enriched the fortunes of many of its founders. For those forcibly transported from their homelands to a life of servitude, however, the founding of the United States meant only injustice. Frederick Douglass, abolitionist and escaped slave, spoke eloquently to the contradictions between the professed values of the new nation and the evils of slavery:

> What, to the American slave, is your Fourth of July? I answer: a day that reveals to him, more than all other days in the year, the gross injustice and cruelty to which he is the constant victim. To him, your celebration is a sham; your boasted liberty, an unholy license; your national greatness, swelling vanity; your sounds of rejoicing are empty and heartless; your denunciation of tyrants, brass-fronted impudence; your shouts of liberty and equality, hollow mockery; your prayers and hymns, your sermons and thanksgivings, with all your religious parade and solemnity, mere bombast, fraud, deception, impiety, and hypocrisy—a thin veil to cover up crimes which would disgrace a nation of savages.
>
> (in Foner, 1950)

As study of social policy reveals, the horrific consequences of policies that allowed and facilitated slavery still reverberate today.

While the injustice inflicted on African slaves was unique in its scope and depravity, colonial societies also included a large population of indentured servants—people who were required to work for someone to pay off a debt. In fact, almost half of White immigrants to early colonies were indentured. The typical term of indenture was five to seven years, although it doubled for political dissenters (Faragher, 1990). Many people agreed to be indentured to pay for their passage to America. In addition, England sent dependent children, beggars, convicts, and political dissenters to the colonies as indentured servants (Hymowitz & Weissman, 1980). Overall, approximately 350,000 indentured people came to America prior to 1775, predominantly boys and young men between the ages of 15 and 25. Although indentured servants were supposed to receive remuneration when they completed their indenture, such payment was often meager, if it was provided at all.

The American Revolution: Civil Rights in the New Nation, 1775–1800 The American Revolution ushered in a new system of government in the colonies but largely continued existing approaches to social welfare provision. Much of the social policy developed in the late eighteenth century reflected the influence of the classic liberal construct, which stressed individualism, the moral importance of work, personal responsibility, and distrust of collectivism and centralized government (Reid, 1995).

The Constitution and Civil Rights The U.S. Constitution was intended to increase the power of our central government while protecting state and individual rights. The democratic political system it instituted specified that elected representatives would make policy decisions. However, until the twentieth century, voters were almost exclusively White men. Rights for women were ignored. People of color were not even considered citizens; as such, they were denied access to democratic participation. Instead, the new nation developed social policies that entrenched White men's control of political power and economic resources. To gain insight into women's struggle for civil rights during the colonial era, read the letter Abigail Adams sent to her husband John Adams in 1776, imploring him to "remember the ladies," and his rebuke, "Letter from John Adams to Abigail Adams, 14 April, 1776," at the Massachusetts Historical Society website (**www.masshist.org**).

Although the Constitution initially protected only the rights of White, landowning males, it did establish the basis for broader civil rights. Many of the framers of the Constitution believed that voters' ability to choose their leaders would not be enough to protect their rights. Thomas Jefferson organized the Democratic Republican Party, which became the current Democratic Party, to press for a "bill of rights" to outline exactly which freedoms were guaranteed to citizens. Appended to the Constitution in 1791, The Bill of Rights comprises the first ten amendments and addresses such issues as freedom of speech and of the press, the right to trial by jury, and protection against unreasonable searches and seizures. Subsequent amendments and numerous judicial rulings have expanded and ensured the constitutional rights that underpin the civil rights standard in the United States today. Civil rights protection is a cornerstone of social welfare. Without it, public benefits and opportunities can be arbitrarily withheld from certain groups, who are then left without legal recourse. Chapter 7 deals with the relationship between civil rights and social welfare in greater detail.

Although the newly established federal government was unwilling to address the plight of most categories of people in need, they created policies explicitly to assist men who had fought for their country. In 1790, Congress provided financial support for disabled veterans and for widows and orphans of veterans (Axinn & Stern, 2001). Similarly, even in today's fractured political climate and preference for limited social welfare investments, veterans and their families are widely considered deserving of help. Further, some of the policy structures developed to aid veterans—including provision of cash pensions and construction of mental health systems—have paved the way for interventions with other client groups.

Expanding Public and Private Assistance The Constitution laid the groundwork for a system that held states primarily responsible for social welfare. However, in 1798, the federal government did establish the U.S. Public Health Service (Barker, 1999) to provide health care for merchant seamen. In the nineteenth century, the agency's responsibilities expanded to include medical examination and the quarantine of immigrants. Currently, this agency has a broad mandate to protect, promote, and advance U.S. health and safety.

Still, at the turn of the nineteenth century, much of the assistance individuals received was in the form of voluntary charitable giving. In their analysis of U.S. social welfare from the strengths perspective, Tice and Perkins (2002) point out that this tradition of private philanthropy helped support educational programs, libraries, and community organizations such as emergency services and firefighting. There was growing awareness in both the public and private sectors of this period that lack of education and health care was linked to poverty and that communities needed to develop health and social service systems in order to thrive.

From Independence to Civil War: Racism, Expansion, and Immigration, 1800–1865

During the first half of the nineteenth century, the territory of the new nation expanded dramatically. Its population also grew as large numbers of immigrants arrived from Europe, especially from Ireland, Germany, and Scandinavia. From the late 1800s to the early 1900s, more than 19 million immigrants entered the United States (Day, 2009). Abundant natural resources provided many immigrants with opportunities to escape poverty. However, for slaves and Native Americans, national economic growth and development meant greater oppression.

Treatment of African Americans By the early nineteenth century, the South was relying on the labor of increasing numbers of slaves to build its economic infrastructure. In 1857, in *Dred Scott v. Sandford*, the U.S. Supreme Court ruled that no person of African ancestry, whether slave or free, could be granted U.S. citizenship; therefore, African Americans could not sue in the federal courts. Dred Scott was a slave who had sued for his freedom because he had moved from a slave state to a free state. The *Dred Scott* ruling undermined rights for African Americans by denying them the protection of the courts, essentially placing them beyond the reach of the Constitution.

Because slaves were considered property and not people, they were ignored by the formal social service system. The rudimentary types of physical and mental health care available during this period were usually denied to African Americans, particularly in the South.

For example, before 1861 mental asylums in the South seldom admitted African Americans. This clearly inequitable policy was justified by the assertion that African Americans exhibited milder forms of mental disorders. Some went so far as to suggest that the structured life of a slave helped guard against mental illness (Lowe, 2006). In this institutional vacuum, African Americans developed informal methods of support. Strong self-help organizations emerged and continue to flourish in many Black communities. Seen through the lens of the strengths perspective, support for self-help organizations in the Black community is a legacy of resistance and resilience. So, too, is mistrust of the formal social service system. Social workers and policymakers need to understand the ramifications of this history of discrimination in order to develop and implement effective programs in partnership with Black communities.

During this period, both Black and White abolitionists campaigned for an official end to slavery. Among these were escaped slaves like Frederick Douglass and Harriet Tubman. Exhibit 2.2 tells the story of Tubman's life. You can learn more about these early abolitionists at the Library of Congress website (**www.loc.gov**). Search "Influence of Prominent Abolitionists."

EXHIBIT 2.2

Harriet Tubman

> **EXHIBIT 2.2**
>
> *Continued*
>
> Harriet Tubman was born a slave c. 1820 in Dorchester County, Maryland. Her parents named her Araminta Harriet Ross and called her "Minty." As a child growing up in slavery, Araminta endured a hard life and suffered repeated beatings. During early adolescence, a White overseer struck her in the head with a heavy weight. This injury left her with painful headaches and episodes of narcolepsy that lasted the rest of her life. Despite this cruelty, Araminta remained unflappable.
>
> In 1844, Araminta married John Tubman and changed her name to Harriet Tubman. Although married to a free man, she was not free, and her marriage was short-lived. Tubman remained enslaved until about 1849, when she fled to Philadelphia. Having finally found freedom, Tubman returned to the South many times to free slaves by leading them North via the Underground Railroad, an elaborate network of routes and safe "stations" including homes, churches, and other safe stops. Tubman became one of the most successful conductors of the Underground Railroad, earning the nickname "Moses." Tubman also took part in the Civil War, aiding the Union as a cook, nurse, armed scout, and spy.
>
> After the Civil War, Tubman continued her mission to help people, aiding elders and supporting the Women's Rights Movement. In 1869, she married Nelson Davis, a Civil War veteran. The two later adopted a baby girl, naming her Gertie Davis. The injuries Tubman sustained as a child increasingly troubled her as she aged, and she underwent brain surgery to help alleviate the pain. Harriet Tubman died on March 10, 1913, of pneumonia. She was given full military honors and buried at Fort Hill Cemetery in Auburn, New York.
>
> *Source:* Library of Congress

It was also during this period that the present-day Republican Party, or Grand Old Party (GOP), began to develop. The party first came to power in 1860 with the election of Abraham Lincoln. The party started as a coalition of anti-slavery activists and other groups pressing for the free distribution of frontier lands, protective tariffs, and the construction of a transcontinental railroad, all under the broad theme of a commitment to liberty. Business and libertarian interests were also part of the initial coalition. They contributed to the later evolution of the Republican Party from its original roots to its philosophical opposition to "big government."

Native Americans Native Americans were driven from their traditional homelands as White settlers made their way westward. The U.S. government regularly violated treaties made with Native Americans. Seizure of tribal lands, decimation of Native cultures, and genocide marked this period of American history. In 1824, the federal government created the Bureau of Indian Affairs, assumed legal responsibility for Native Americans, and promised them material assistance. However, oppression and cultural decimation continued. In 1830, Congress passed the Indian Removal Act, which ultimately forced many tribes to move to reservations located west of the Mississippi (Hine & Faragher, 2000). Some tribes attempted to use the courts to protect their territory. For example, the Cherokee Nation, under the leadership of Chief John Ross, asked the U.S. Supreme Court to intervene to protect Cherokee lands in a case involving Georgia state laws that violated their sovereignty. However, in the 1831 Supreme Court decision *Cherokee Nation v. Georgia*, Chief Justice John Marshall denied the Cherokee Nation's claim that they constituted a sovereign foreign nation. Although conceding that tribes should exercise some control over their lands, Marshall ruled that all Native Americans were "completely under the sovereignty and dominion of the U.S." He compared their relationship to the government to "that of a ward to his guardian" (Commager, 1958, pp. 256–257).

In 1838 and 1839, as part of President Andrew Jackson's Indian removal policy, the Cherokee Nation was forced to migrate to an area in present-day Oklahoma. This journey became known as the "Trail of Tears." The Cherokees faced hunger, disease, and exhaustion, and more than 4,000 died on the forced march (Hine & Faragher, 2000). By 1850, the removal was largely complete, and White settlers had appropriated what had been Indian lands (Kutler, 2003). In 1851, Congress passed the Indian Appropriation Act, which declared the lands to which the Indians had relocated to be official reservations (Nabokov, 1993). Then, in 1871, Congress officially terminated the practice of executing treaties with Native American tribes. The Dawes Act, passed in 1887, eliminated the traditional system of tribal land ownership by allotting specific parcels of land to individual tribe members and families, thereby confining Native Americans to smaller regions and eroding their communal ways of life (Nabokov, 1993).

Brutality toward Native Americans was not limited to the seizure of land. In 1860, the Bureau of Indian Affairs established the first boarding school for Native children on the Yakima reservation. Justified as an investment in Native children's education, the policy of Native boarding schools removed thousands of children from their homes, often forcibly, for socialization into the values and practices of the dominant culture (Evans-Campbell & Campbell, 2011). Exhibit 2.3 illustrates the effects of the government policy of removing Native children to boarding schools. This practice resulted in devastating theft of cultural identity, language, and family bonds, and these traumas had long-lasting effects (Evans-Campbell et al., 2012). Native Americans' distrust of the government responsible for years of mistreatment may contribute to reluctance to access government-provided services. Disproportionate mental and physical health disparities and high rates of unemployment, poverty, and child welfare involvement are legacies of government policies toward Native American communities.

Latinx Communities in the Southwest In 1845, the United States officially annexed Texas after it had achieved independence from Mexico. A resulting conflict regarding the border led to war between the United States and Mexico. The United States was focused on gaining new territory to accommodate westward expansion.

In 1848, after two years of fighting, the two countries signed the Treaty of Guadalupe Hidalgo. Under the treaty, the United States took a vast territory that was formerly part of Mexico, including present-day Arizona, California, New Mexico, and Texas and parts of Colorado, Nevada, and Utah. The treaty also specified that Mexican nationals living within the new border would be granted U.S. citizenship and protection of property and civil rights.

> **EXHIBIT 2.3**
>
> *U.S. Government Policies Attempted to Systematically Decimate Native American Culture and Resources*
>
> Wounded Yellow Robe, Henry Standing Bear, and Timber Yellow Robe before and after their Pennsylvania boarding school gave them "proper" clothes and haircuts.
>
> *Credit*: John N. Choate/Dickinson College Archives & Special Collections

However, conflicts between American settlers and Mexican landowners frequently resulted in Mexicans losing their lands in legal disputes. The United States acquired even more land from Mexico with the Gadsden Purchase of 1853. These actions dramatically increased the size of the Latinx population in the United States. Think about how this history may shape attitudes toward Latinx immigrants today, assertions about what policies should be enacted to limit the entry of workers from Mexico and other Latin American countries, and the reactions of Latinx communities to these proposals. This history and the evolving political and demographic realities in this region will undoubtedly influence future social policy, particularly regarding workers' rights, health care, education, and social services.

Discrimination against Immigrants Six million people, mostly poor people from Europe, emigrated to the United States between 1820 and 1860 (Coll, 1972). Many of these immigrants were relatively unskilled. Most faced stereotyping and discrimination in the labor market and in communities, and many lived in crowded slums. When work was available, parents and children often toiled long hours under harsh conditions. Immigrant families who managed to acquire the resources necessary to move west also faced a daunting struggle to establish new homesteads, learn English, and find ways of making a living.

Some people who were themselves descendants of earlier waves of immigrants were prejudiced against new arrivals and made the transitions even more difficult. For example, some earlier immigrants claimed that new Irish immigrants were lazy. Such derogatory stereotypes are similar to those African Americans often face, and they live on in the anti-immigrant attitudes sometimes leveled at immigrant groups today. Despite these obstacles, some immigrants who arrived in the United States in the mid-nineteenth century managed to achieve financial success, although many remained in poverty. Underscoring the role of race as a crucial determinant altering individuals' experiences and outcomes, the ability of Irish and other light-skinned European immigrants to change their names, lose their accents, and assimilate contributed to their subsequent prosperity. However, people of color could not blend into a predominantly White culture; instead, for these communities, individual and institutional racism pose substantial barriers to upward mobility—historically and currently.

Growth of Cities and Public Institutions   Cities on the east coast were unable to keep up with the rapid growth during this period, as waves of poor immigrants sought places to live and work. Municipalities failed to develop adequate sanitation or safety standards. By the 1820s, the United States was searching for reforms to improve living conditions and help those in need. People who considered poverty to be the result of individual failings tended to view poor communities as teeming with people who exerted negative influences that perpetuated poverty. Increasingly, people viewed institutional care for those who were impoverished or dependent as the best solution to all manner of social ills, including misbehaving children, destitute elders, people with disabilities, and unwanted infants. During this period, states began to enact social policies to regulate local government provision of social services and institutions, while the federal government continued to reject a more active role in social welfare.

Mental Health Reform   Although mental illness was a recognized problem in colonial America, it became a public concern only when it jeopardized public safety. Treatment varied depending on the cause to which mental illness was attributed. If sin was thought to be the root, prayer or even exorcism might be in order. Great misfortune, physiological afflictions such as digestive dysfunction, or even the alignment of the stars were also suggested as potential causes. By the late eighteenth century, growing interest in curing mental illness led to the establishment of institutions. Private hospitals, where the emphasis was on creating a curative environment, were available for the affluent. In contrast, people without financial resources often went to prison without receiving mental health care.

The federal response to efforts to expand services for people with mental illness, led by social reformers such as Dorothea Dix, underscored the government's continuing reluctance to become involved in providing for health and social welfare. Depicted in Exhibit 2.4, Dorothea Dix was instrumental in the establishment of state mental institutions. She found that many states were either unwilling or unable to fund adequate care and concluded that the federal government needed to take responsibility. Dix submitted a proposal to Congress for funding the care of the indigent mentally ill (Day, 2009). In response, Congress passed a bill in 1854 providing for institutions, not only for people with mental illnesses, but also for people who were blind and deaf. However, President Franklin Pierce vetoed the bill, reaffirming that states,

EXHIBIT 2.4

Dorothea Dix

"In a world where there is so much to be done, I felt strongly impressed that there must be something for me to do." —*Dorothea Dix*

Source: Library of Congress

and not the federal government, were responsible for social welfare. Pierce feared that earmarking provisions for the care of people who were mentally ill would imply that the government eventually had to care for all needy persons (Trattner, 1999).

The Civil War and Its Aftermath: Reconstruction, Segregation, and Homesteads, 1865–1890s

Opposition to slavery, disagreement over states' rights, and determination to preserve the Union led to the long and bloody Civil War (1861–1865). In 1863, President Lincoln issued the Emancipation Proclamation. This executive order, issued to the armed forces, directed the U.S. government to treat as free those enslaved in the Confederacy. Thus, emancipation followed the slow progress of the Union Army across the South, reaching the remaining enslaved people in Texas on June 19, 1865. Following the Union victory, congressional action abolished slave labor throughout the United States and enacted new policies regarding the treatment of African Americans. However, newly freed former slaves struggled to survive. Policies put in place to address their plight were undermined by ongoing racial hostility and were ultimately woefully inadequate.

Reconstruction The period immediately following the Civil War, known as Reconstruction, was one of meaningful, if temporary, progress toward racial justice. The Freedman's Bureau, operated by the War Department, provided emancipated African Americans opportunities to own land, vote, receive an education, and begin to accumulate assets. The Freedmen's Bureau established schools, provided food, educated former slaves regarding land ownership, and acted as an employment agency. The Bureau lasted only seven years and did not accomplish all its intended goals. Nevertheless, it assisted many African Americans, while also outlining a potential role for the federal government in providing social services in situations where localities were unable or unwilling to do so.

Perhaps the most significant development during Reconstruction was the ratification of three constitutional amendments, beginning with the 13th Amendment, in 1865, which prohibited slavery. In 1868, the 14th Amendment guaranteed citizenship for "all persons born or naturalized in the U.S." and guaranteed all citizens "due process of law" and "equal protection of the laws." Significantly, in 1884, the Supreme Court ruled in *Elk v. Wilkins* that the 14th Amendment did not cover Native Americans because they were not citizens. Citing, among other cases, *Cherokee Nation v. Georgia*, the Court affirmed that tribes, although not technically "foreign states," nevertheless were "alien nations" whose members "owed immediate allegiance to their several tribes" and "were in a dependent condition" to the U.S. government. Because tribal members were not U.S. citizens by birth, only those Native Americans who completed the naturalization process were entitled to the protections of the 14th Amendment (*Elk v. Wilkins*, 112 US 94, 1884). The 15th Amendment, ratified in 1870, guaranteed voting rights for all male citizens, including former slaves. Although women abolitionists had hoped otherwise, the 15th Amendment did not extend suffrage to women.

Opposition to Black suffrage quickly emerged. Vigilante groups such as the Ku Klux Klan, organized in Tennessee in 1866, employed violence and intimidation to prevent newly enfranchised voters from exercising their rights. In response, the federal government issued a series of Force Acts from 1870 to 1871 that authorized the government to use military force if necessary to enforce the 15th Amendment. Aided by these enforcement efforts, freed men voted in large numbers, and African Americans filled many elected positions in the South and even won a handful of seats in Congress. However, the period of Reconstruction was brief, cut short by resistance from White Southerners and ambivalence of other White people about racial equity (Reisch, 2017a). In 1876, Northern Republicans compromised with Southern Democrats to elect their presidential candidate, Rutherford B. Hayes, in exchange for an end to the Northern military presence in the South. Without military oversight, southern politicians enacted policies to counteract advances achieved during Reconstruction. Federal retreat from the Reconstruction effort allowed for the reemergence of legal, economic, and political marginalization and oppression of African Americans.

From Reconstruction to Jim Crow After Reconstruction ended, conditions for African Americans in the South deteriorated. By imposing a system of poll taxes and literacy tests, intimidating would-be voters, and simply blocking voting booths, White southerners denied African Americans their rights as citizens. This process, whereby most of the reforms instituted during Reconstruction were overturned, continued throughout the last decades of the nineteenth century. A critical step occurred in 1896, when the Supreme Court ruled in *Plessy v. Ferguson* that separate accommodations for African Americans were constitutional as long as they were judged to be "equal." In the wake of this decision, states and municipalities passed numerous **Jim Crow laws** that legally separated Blacks and Whites in public areas and institutions, including schools, restaurants, theaters, hospitals, and parks (Knappman, Christianson, & Paddock, 2002). In addition to social, residential, and educational segregation, African Americans experienced discrimination in employment that often forced them into the least skilled, lowest-paying jobs. In this way, Jim Crow laws worked to keep African Americans in poverty while allowing those in power to profit at their expense. Jim Crow laws are a classic example of social policies that perpetuate rather than alleviate poverty and oppression.

The Homestead Act Although the federal government did not enable most former slaves to become landowners, it did help White settlers acquire homesteads. In 1862, Congress passed the Homestead Act, which allowed families to assume ownership of land—generally in the West—after they had lived on it for five years (Hine & Faragher, 2000). This enabled thousands of Americans, including veterans and their widows, to become landowners. Indeed, many Americans can trace the origins of their families' property ownership to this policy (Williams, 2000). However, these early capital opportunities redistributed wealth unjustly, particularly for recently emancipated African Americans (Williams, 2003). By making available to settlers what was originally communal Native American land, the government facilitated plunder of Native lands. This policy thus perpetuated continued inequality by unfairly privileging White Americans' positions over those of people of color.

The Origins of Modern Social Work

In the years following the Civil War, the United States experienced massive increases in immigration and urbanization, which magnified the need for social services. However, as the federal government continued to leave social reform to states, local governments, and private charities, the quality and availability of services provided was uneven. Programs for people in dire need overburdened city, county, and state budgets. The modern social work profession emerged as one response to these developments. Social work pioneers worked to change the ways in which the needs of poor people were met. Social work traces its roots to privately organized and financed movements, including the child-saving movement, Charity Organization Society (COS), and the Settlement House Movement (Trattner, 1999).

The Child-Saving Movement The child-saving movement developed in response to the growing numbers of children who were overcrowding institutions and living on city streets. Because there was very little assistance of any kind for impoverished families, their children suffered. Despite the widespread belief that the state should not interfere with the family, there was some popular support for interventions to support children's safety and development. Children had long been included among the "worthy poor." Also, many people were concerned that failing to intervene with poor children would lead to higher rates of crime and other social problems (Day, 2009).

As described in Exhibit 2.5, Charles Loring Brace founded the first Children's Aid Society in New York in 1853. Similar child-saving societies were established in other cities during this period (Day, 2009). Brace organized the famous "orphan trains" that carried thousands of children west to be placed with families across the United States between 1853 and 1929. Largely reacting to the

EXHIBIT 2.5

The Children's Aid Society

Charles Loring Brace, a minister and social reformer, worked with other individuals interested in social reform to found the Children's Aid Society (CAS) in 1853. The CAS focused on homeless, delinquent, and neglected children. Brace believed that if children were taken off the streets or away from parents who could not provide for them, raised in a loving family home, and given appropriate work and educational opportunities, they would turn into productive members of society. While Brace and the CAS may be most well-known for starting the orphan train movement, CAS also used funds from wealthy donors to open houses that lodged homeless youth and to establish schools to teach disadvantaged youth trades such as cobbling and sewing. With the Progressive Era shift to family-saving rather than child-saving policies, the goals of the CAS also shifted. One of the central goals of CAS in the early twentieth century was the preservation of high-risk families.

Source: The Social Welfare History Project; retrieved from www.socialwelfarehistory.com/organizations/childrens-aid-society-of-new-york

conditions children experienced as laborers, Brace argued vehemently that children should be in a home environment that could demonstrate adequate family life. This approach directly conflicted with the prevailing ideal of saving children through correctional methods. However, orphan trains did not necessarily deliver children to homes that were more benevolent than institutions. Some were treated well in their new homes, but others were abused and forced into hard labor. Further, these children were not necessarily orphans; some were children of single parents or immigrants too poor to support them. Taking these children from their communities engendered anger and resentment, especially among Catholic immigrants, whose families were often targeted.

Other child-saving efforts were initiated during this period, including the first Society for the Prevention of Cruelty to Children, which was founded in New York in 1875. Other cities soon established similar organizations to prevent child maltreatment. While the modern child protection system as we know it today did not emerge until much later, these organizations were its forerunners.

The Charity Organization Society The Charity Organization Society (COS) emerged in the United States in the late 1870s. The COS developed the idea of "scientific charity," which used systematic procedures to assess needs and determine the most effective and efficient strategies to address them. The COS tried to organize philanthropic groups to reduce the possibility that people were receiving assistance from multiple entities and to provide "friendly visitors" to people in need. In addition to Social Darwinism, the writings of Thomas Malthus, a British economist who predicted that populations would multiply faster than the production of goods to meet their needs, influenced early COS workers, who largely believed that poor people caused their own problems through spending thoughtlessly, neglecting responsibility, and drinking excessively. Many of these workers held that providing direct financial assistance to the poor would reinforce negative behaviors (Day, 2009). For this reason, early COS workers identified moral reform as the most effective anti-poverty policy. When a contributor asked Josephine Shaw Lowell of the COS how much money would go directly to people in poverty, she proudly replied, "Not one cent!" (Trattner, 1999, p. 90). However, as workers learned about the conditions of poor people first-hand, their appreciation of people's struggles grew. The COS engaged in social research to broaden views of how science could inform charity, helped sustain and organize charitable giving, organized record keeping, and developed training programs. Emphasizing individual intervention rather than social reform, they were pioneers in social casework. By the 1890s, COS workers sought to establish themselves as professionals.

The Settlement House Movement The Settlement House Movement began in England in 1884 with the founding of Toynbee Hall in East London. Young professionals "settled" in this house in an impoverished area and worked as volunteers to contribute to neighborhood development. After living in Toynbee Hall, Stanton Coit started the first settlement house in the United States in New York in 1886. Similarly inspired, social reformers Jane Addams and Helen Gates Starr founded the famous Hull House in Chicago in 1889 and were followed by others in other cities. Workers established settlement houses in working-class neighborhoods and strove to improve living conditions. With the houses often sustained by wealthy donors, settlement house workers lived side by side with those they served, on a permanent basis. Jane Addams, social work pioneer, is profiled in Exhibit 2.6.

EXHIBIT 2.6

Jane Addams

Jane Addams was born September 6, 1860, into a wealthy family in Cedarville, Illinois. Her father worked as a miller and served as a U.S. senator. In 1881, Addams graduated as valedictorian from Rockford Female Seminary. For six years following graduation, she studied medicine, but she experienced health issues and was hospitalized intermittently. During these years she also spent time traveling in Europe. During one of her trips, Addams and her close friend, Ellen G. Starr, visited London's Toynbee Hall, a settlement house in London's East End that provided services to people living in poverty.

After the visit to London's settlement house, Addams and Starr returned to Illinois and opened a settlement house in a low-income neighborhood on the West Side of Chicago. The women leased a large home and moved in with a goal to improve the lives of those living in poverty in the community, particularly a growing number of immigrant families. This was the beginning of the famous Hull House. Staff at Hull House provided an array of support and services including clubs, childcare, and classes for children and adults. Hull House was also a meeting place for groups pressing for political and community change. The founders knew the power of community and organization. They raised money, gave speeches on deplorable working and living conditions, and recruited wealthy families to finance the work. Ultimately, their organizing helped to bring about significant improvement in living conditions for impoverished immigrant families in Chicago.

Addams' work has been praised locally, nationally, and internationally. Most notably, in 1931 she was the first American woman to be awarded the Nobel Peace Prize. Jane Addams died on May 21, 1935. Her work changed society, and she will be forever remembered as a pioneer of social work and social justice.

Image Credit: Swarthmore College Peace Collection; text: www.nobelprize.org/nobel_prizes/peace/laureates/1931/addams-bio.html

Settlement house reformers documented the deplorable conditions in immigrant neighborhoods and worked to influence public opinion and elected officials. The Settlement House Movement was both influenced by and had a profound impact upon the Progressive Era, a time of widespread social action and political reform, which began in the late 1800s (Davis, 1984). Settlement house workers fought for child labor laws, occupational health and safety, safe housing, fair wages, and decent sanitation. They combated prostitution and, concerned about effects of excessive drinking on families, campaigned for Prohibition. Settlement house workers were also researchers. They investigated working conditions in factories and sweatshops where new immigrants and their children labored and used their findings to fight for fair labor practices. For example, when Florence Kelley, who moved to Hull House in 1891, was later appointed to the Illinois State Bureau of Labor Statistics, she involved the women of Hull House in her investigation of labor conditions (Day, 2009).

Settlement house workers put into practice many of the tenets now associated with the strengths perspective. Work in settlement houses was premised on the belief that poverty arose from economic, educational, and political exclusion rather than from individual deficiencies. Consequently, while settlement house workers believed that both social justice and social control were worthy goals, in contrast to COS workers, they focused much of their attention on social reform rather than on individual casework. These early reformers sought to meet needs by identifying and marshaling individual and community resources. They were instrumental in starting preschools and the juvenile court system, and in creating jobs for people in their communities. However, while they often focused on helping immigrants, here as in other strands of social reform, the needs of African Americans were largely ignored, and racism was evident (Tice & Perkins, 2002).

Building the Social Work Profession By the end of the nineteenth century, the social work profession was starting to gain public recognition. In 1896, the New York Charity Organization Society offered training courses to charity workers and settlement house workers, first called "social workers" by educator Simon N. Patten in 1900 (Barker, 2003). While the work of the COS, settlement houses, and orphan trains was all privately funded and governed, during the late nineteenth and early twentieth centuries, Progressive Era reformers pushed for publicly financed social services. As social workers were needed to provide these services, the Progressive Era thus created an environment conducive to the growth of social work.

Despite distinct origins of the Settlement House Movement and charity organizations, the groups began to cooperate and even merge by the turn of the century (Trattner, 1999). In 1909, Jane Addams was elected president of the National Conference of Charities and Correction, an organization that was instrumental in establishing casework as a distinct field within the social services. In 1917, Mary Richmond published *Social Diagnosis*, which became a primary text for social workers. Richmond applied the medical model to social work and prescribed investigation, diagnosis, prognosis, and treatment focused on the individual. Casework began to overshadow social reform (Tice & Perkins, 2002). Also in 1917, social workers formed their first professional organization, the National Social Work Exchange (now NASW).

By the 1920s, COS training programs began to develop into schools of social work. Although these programs recognized that human problems also arose from deficiencies in social structure, communities, and families, they focused on the individual and taught social workers to provide social services rather than to advocate social reform. They primarily concentrated on **case advocacy**, which focuses on helping a particular client navigate existing systems, rather than class advocacy. Although workers skilled in **class advocacy**, which focuses on helping groups of clients who have similar needs, had helped bring about reforms in arenas such as child labor and sanitation, the drive for professionalization and wider recognition of the profession was characterized by an emphasis on clinical skills focused on working with the individual, rather than on policy practice.

African-American Social Workers African-American social work pioneers recognized that racism was the major barrier that prevented African Americans from meeting their needs. Significantly, they focused on both helping individuals within their communities *and* addressing larger societal issues. Their work included promoting the education of women and children, improving family conditions, and countering racism. The National Association of Colored Women's Clubs (NACWC) was formed in 1896 and enhanced solidarity between women's groups. African-American reformers built a multifaceted system of social services that paralleled the White-dominated social service system. Their work continues to be a model for service delivery focusing on mutual aid, racial solidarity, and self-help efforts (Carlton-LaNey, 1999) and an inspiration to social workers seeking to integrate micro and macro approaches.

As part of the tradition of teaching Black communities to advocate for themselves, many of these early social change advocates taught at educational institutions for students of color. By the first quarter of the twentieth century, some universities were offering courses of social work study specifically for and about African Americans. Black social work pioneers played an important role in improving life for African Americans and shaping social work scholarship and education. Exhibit 2.7 outlines the life of Dr. E. Franklin Frazier, an influential teacher and author who directed early social work programs at historically Black colleges and universities.

The Progressive Era and the Expansion of Social Welfare Policy, 1890–1917

The Progressive Era spanned the years from the late 1800s through the first decades of the 1900s. Following a period of strife between industrialists and laborers, progressive leaders advocated an activist, morally responsible government to limit the negative economic and environmental impacts of unrestrained industrial capitalism (Hofstadter, 1963). As captains of industry were creating monopolies in business sectors including railroads and steel, progressive leaders backed reforms they believed would return the country to the democratic ideals that had helped to shape the nation. Consequently, the government engaged in several cases of "trust busting," aimed at breaking up monopolies. In 1914, Congress passed the Clayton Antitrust Act to limit the size and power of large corporations. As an extension of the belief that government should protect its citizens, progressives advocated on behalf of farmers and small businessmen. They also were interested in developing the concept of social insurance, whereby society recognized the normal risks of living, and people and the government pooled money to help when misfortune, such as unemployment or injury, struck. This signaled a shift away from blaming the individual for being unable to avoid or manage these risks unaided.

During the Progressive Era, the federal government started to assume responsibility for child protection, workplace regulation, and consumer protection. During President Theodore

EXHIBIT 2.7

Dr. E. Franklin Frazier

Edward Franklin Frazier was born in Baltimore, Maryland, in 1894. After graduating from a segregated high school in Baltimore, he received a scholarship to attend Howard University, where he earned his undergraduate degree. After completing a master's degree in sociology at Clark University, Dr. Frazier taught sociology at Morehouse College, a historically Black institution in Atlanta, Georgia, and directed the Atlanta University School of Social Work. He earned a PhD in sociology at the University of Chicago and later became the director of the Department of Sociology at Howard University.

Dr. Frazier was a leading scholar in the field of race relations. During his career, he wrote widely on the Black experience in America and the nature of prejudice. He published a critical examination of middle-class African Americans and asserted that many had adopted subservient conservatism (Frazier, 1962). He also wrote that prejudice was abnormal behavior and that otherwise law-abiding White Southerners, driven mad by their hatred for Black people, committed terrible acts of cruelty. Dr. Frazier's writings were controversial. Threats following the publication of "The Pathology of Race Prejudice" led to his departure from his position at Morehouse College.

While at Howard University, Dr. Frazier was also a strong advocate for social work education. He was a pioneer in championing standards and proper training for social workers and directed the first basic social work curriculum offered through the sociology department.

Source: image: BlackPastor; text: E. Franklin Frazier (2000). Howard University, Social Work Library. Available at: **www.howard.edu/library/social_work_library/Franklin_Frazier.htm**

Roosevelt's administration, Congress passed the Meat Inspection Act (1906) and the Pure Food and Drug Act (1906) to protect consumers against unsafe products. At the same time, African-American groups and women's groups organized to improve their political and economic status. Two organizations that emerged during the Progressive Era—the National Association for the Advancement of Colored People (NAACP) and the National Urban League—have played a major role in the African-American struggle for civil rights and economic opportunities. In 1920, women's suffrage advocates finally achieved their goal with the ratification of the 19th Amendment, which extended to women the right to vote. Even before the victory on suffrage, women were at the forefront of reform movements, demanding policies to support and protect women and children. Their efforts laid the groundwork for modern social welfare policy and provided role models for activist women social workers today.

Progressive reformers pressed for a federal income tax, and in 1913 the 16th Amendment to the Constitution, which gave Congress legal authority to tax income, was ratified. The income tax was a progressive tax; that is, the greater people's income, the greater the percentage of their income they paid in taxes. Today, the federal government uses income tax revenues not only to fund programs for people in need, but also to fund national defense and many other priorities.

Maternalistic Approaches and Mothers' Pensions   Women activists pressed for public programs to provide cash assistance for poor mothers and children at the state level. In 1911, the Illinois legislature passed the first statewide mothers' pension law in the United States. Progressive pressure for mothers' pensions led to the establishment of programs to support mothers and children in most states between 1911 and 1919 and set the stage for the federal government to assume responsibility for funding many social welfare programs in the 1930s. The establishment of state programs meant that public, rather than private, organizations set the rules that determined access to assistance. Notably, assistance was no longer doled out as charity (Reid, 1995).

Leaders of the mothers' pension movement asserted that mothers should be allowed to devote full-time effort to child-rearing (Tice & Perkins, 2002). Unfortunately, states never adequately funded these pensions, and they reached only a small proportion of eligible women. Applicants had to not only demonstrate financial need but also pass a morals test. For the most part, only mothers who were judged not to have violated the moral codes of the community received pensions. Therefore, most pensions were awarded to widows rather than single mothers. Latinas, Native Americans, African Americans, and immigrants also faced discrimination when applying for these pensions. When benefits were not summarily denied to them, the arbitrary nature of the morals tests opened the door for all kinds of capricious actions against "undesirable" applicants. For example, workers could take issue with the work schedules (as excessive or inadequate), associations with men, and/or "housekeeping" standards of mothers of color as an excuse to deny them pensions. The few women of color who did collect benefits typically received much lower subsidies, which ensured that they would continue to work as domestics and field laborers (Neubeck & Cazenave, 2001).

Overall, the proportion of women receiving pensions was minimal compared to the level of need. Even for those mothers who did qualify, pensions were so small that many recipients still had to work (Gordon, 1998). In other cases, pensions were inadequate to keep children out of institutions. Few jobs were open to women, and what jobs were available typically were poorly paid. Nonetheless, critics feared that putting money into the hands of poor women would encourage more men to abandon their families (Tice & Perkins, 2002).

Historians such as Theda Skocpol (1993) have defined the mothers' pension movement as an effort to establish a maternalistic, as opposed to a paternalistic, approach to family support. That is, this initiative focused on mothers, in contrast to the later Social Security program, which reflected the male breadwinner model. Supporters lauded this maternalistic approach for recognizing the importance of helping women provide for their children. However, state mothers' pensions declined and eventually collapsed during the Great Depression of the 1930s, when it became clear that only the federal government had a sufficient tax base to support impoverished families during widespread economic downturns (Tice & Perkins, 2002).

Child Welfare   From the mid-nineteenth century through the early twentieth century, reformers pressed vigorously for improved care for orphans, child labor laws, and programs to enhance children's health. Pioneer settlement house workers were leaders in this effort (Tice & Perkins, 2002). Their work bore fruit in 1912 when Congress passed a bill establishing the Children's Bureau within the Department of Labor. Significantly, the Bureau was not endowed with regulatory authority. However, it was empowered to investigate and publicize the working and living conditions of the nation's children. As such, the Bureau represented the first federal agency to focus exclusively on child welfare (Trattner, 1999). Pioneer social workers had pressed for this government recognition of the importance of child welfare. Julia Lathrop, a Hull House alumna, was the first head of the Children's Bureau.

The Children's Bureau's investigations drew attention to many issues, including child labor. In the second half of the nineteenth century, many very young children toiled long hours under appalling conditions. Exhibit 2.8 depicts some of these child laborers, whose work

EXHIBIT 2.8

Child Labor

Source: Library of Congress

tasks and conditions threatened their health and development. In 1916, Congress enacted the Keating–Owen Child Labor Act to regulate child labor. Two years later, the Supreme Court declared the bill an unconstitutional overreach of federal power. Although some condemned the bill as a threat to families' authority over children, it served as a model for subsequent state regulations. By 1930, every state, as well as Washington, DC, had enacted child protection laws (Day, 2009; Link & Catton, 1967). Social workers' commitment to child welfare, which continues to this day, helped build the public's perception that social workers are leaders in child advocacy and the experts in this field (Briar-Lawson, 2014).

Prohibition and Discriminatory Enforcement Although the consumption and manufacture of alcoholic beverages were well-established in American culture, alcoholism was seen as a social problem. Many of the crusaders against alcohol considered drinking a sin. Concerns about alcohol consumption increased following the Civil War, as an unprecedented number of Americans who had been exposed to horrific violence struggled with the physical and mental wounds of war (Faust, 2009). Although surviving evidence is scant, historians believe that returning soldiers may have coped with what we now understand as post-traumatic stress disorder (PTSD) by self-medicating with alcohol. As Americans who grew up in this context grappled with responses to problems whose origins they did not understand, their activism swelled the ranks of the Temperance Movement in the 1880s. These converging forces culminated in the 1919 ratification of the 18th Amendment, which prohibited the manufacture, sale, or transportation of intoxicating liquors, and the Volstead Act, which provided for the amendment's enforcement. Successful reform initiatives, then as now, are propelled by a variety of supporters. Women's groups and some early social workers took up temperance as one of their many causes, while, in the South, the Ku Klux Klan supported Prohibition out of fear of alcohol-fueled behavior among people of color. Racism not only motivated some supporters' enthusiasm, it was also evident in Prohibition's discriminatory enforcement, which some have compared to harsh and inequitable enforcement of drug laws today (Provine, 2007). In 1933, the 18th Amendment became the only amendment to the U.S. Constitution to ever be repealed.

The New Immigration Although Progressive Era advocates achieved some success in establishing more humane social welfare policies, racism and discrimination against certain groups increased during this period. Immigration patterns were beginning to change. Whereas the majority of "old immigrants," such as Germans and Scandinavians, were Protestant, many of the "new immigrants" were Catholic or Jewish. As in earlier periods, fear of greater competition for jobs was combined with a general mistrust of people who spoke foreign languages and who came from different cultures. Nascent social work initiatives facilitated integration but could help only a small portion of new immigrants. In the 1920s, the government passed legislation that severely curtailed immigration to the United States.

CONCLUSION

This chapter has explored social welfare approaches from early cultures to the beginning of the twentieth century. Understanding history will help you identify and critique the values and ideologies that drive current policies and programs. It will also enable you to identify similar policies that were implemented in the past and to evaluate their results. This chapter drew attention to our legacy of policy and service disparities based on race. We must own this history and work to eliminate these injustices. It is vital that social workers speak up when subjects critical to their clients' well-being are debated. The examination of historical policy initiatives provides valuable insights that can help social workers and policymakers develop more effective policies and programs.

MAIN POINTS

- History has a direct influence on current social policies and programs and must be understood to effectively craft future policy.

- The framework provided in Quick Guide 2 can help you explore relationships between current social policies and historical approaches.

- Because social workers' clients often live in poverty, understanding the history of poverty laws is foundational to effective policy practice.

- Poor Laws passed in the 1600s in England—which established public responsibility for paupers, categorized "worthy" and "unworthy" poor, and established residency rules—influence many of our current social policies.

- Oppression of people of color throughout U.S. history continues to influence social policies and programs.

- The social work profession traces its roots to the child-saving movement; the Charity Organization Society, which stressed casework and individual causality of poverty; and the Settlement House Movement, which advocated for structural change, including changes in sanitation and child labor laws.

- Progressive Era legislation laid the foundation for many social reforms of the later nineteenth and early twentieth centuries. Women were at the forefront of Progressive reform movements, including women's suffrage and mothers' pensions.

- Historically, social workers have been leaders and advocates for child welfare policies and programs and have become widely recognized as experts in this field.

EXERCISES

1. Go to **www.routledgesw.com/cases** and continue learning about Carla Washburn. How do you think Mrs. Washburn's experiences as a person of color in the United States may contribute to her reluctance to accept social services, including those designed to help older adults continue to live in the community?
2. As you become familiar with the Sanchez family, you will find that their church is an important source of support. Review the discussion of the role of religious institutions in the provision of social welfare.

BASIC CONCEPTS AND EARLY INFLUENCES   53

    a. What historic and cultural factors might contribute to the Sanchez family being more willing to receive help through their church than through public agencies?
    b. What are the potential benefits and drawbacks for the Sanchez family when public policy allows for the provision of publicly funded social services through their church?
3. Residents of Riverton are concerned about homelessness in their city. Review how the English Poor Laws dealt with homelessness and vagrancy.
    a. How are the causes of contemporary homelessness similar to or different from the causes of homelessness in England at the time the Poor Laws were enacted?
    b. What similarities and differences do you see between Riverton's attempts to deal with homelessness and policies created by the Poor Laws?
4. Consider examples of the influence of historical social welfare policies on today's policy debates. For example, have any states attempted to insert residency requirements into their welfare policies so that people who move to the state are ineligible for assistance? How do policymakers and others talk about work requirements for food assistance, childcare, and income assistance? What do these statements suggest about assumptions regarding people who rely on these supports?
5. Browse the biographies of social work pioneers provided by the NASW Foundation (**www.naswfoundation.org/Our-Work/NASW-Social-Work-Pioneers/NASW-Social-Workers-Pioneers-Bio-Index**). Select at least two biographies of social workers you have heard of and at least two with whom you are not familiar. What were these social workers' primary contributions to the profession and to social policy?
6. What similarities and differences do you see when you compare current approaches to providing for children in need of care to the approaches originally developed by Charles Loring Brace and the Children's Aid Society? After identifying similarities and differences, determine probable reasons why some elements have remained the same while others have shifted. What are the implications for future policy development? Do you think these early approaches were strengths-based? Why or why not?
7. Throughout history and to the present day, addressing poverty has been a major focus of social policy. Disagreements over the causes of poverty—whether poverty is primarily the result of individual failings or unjust social and economic structures—have complicated efforts to develop effective policies to reduce poverty. At the same time, limited and incomplete understanding of what constitutes "poverty" has also constrained these efforts. To help you make the connection between what you are learning about poverty in this text and issues of poverty in your community, go to **http://livingwage.mit.edu** and select your location. Compare various family sizes, the cost of living, and the average incomes for persons in your community. Contrast the living wage, minimum wage, and poverty wage for various family sizes in your community.
    a. How might someone analyzing poverty in your community trace the causes of poverty? What could serve as evidence for more individual explanations? What supports the idea that the environmental context shapes who is poor?
    b. How have historical policies defined poverty, and how have these definitions limited the capacity to address poverty?
    c. What policies do you think would need to be implemented to help families in your community become financially secure?

CHAPTER 3

The Historical Context: Development of Our Current Welfare System

Let us never forget that government is ourselves and not an alien power over us.
Franklin D. Roosevelt, 1938

In this present crisis, government is not the solution to our problem; government is the problem.
Ronald Reagan, 1981

The danger of too much government is matched by the perils of too little.
Barack Obama, 2009

THIS CHAPTER CHRONICLES MAJOR POLICY INITIATIVES FROM World War I through the first part of the twenty-first century. As the quotes above illustrate, people who shaped social policy during this period have had widely varying views of government. This chapter examines how such opinions have influenced American social welfare policy and, ultimately, well-being. The nation made important yet insufficient strides during this period in helping people meet their basic needs and lead long and productive lives. Life expectancy increased dramatically, and poverty and child mortality rates decreased as improved public sanitation, health care, labor regulations, and pensions provided greater protection. However, there is more work to do. Millions of Americans still struggle to fulfill their needs. Inequality strains our national bonds. Growing numbers of our children lack adequate food, shelter, and educational opportunities. And securing civil rights for all is a continuing battle.

EXPANDING THE WELFARE STATE IN WAR AND DEPRESSION: 1917–1945

As we saw in Chapter 2, progressive reformers left a valuable legacy of public sanitation and health, child labor, and state-level mothers' pension laws. Although the U.S. entry into World War I in 1917 distracted attention from domestic reform efforts, war and its aftermath increased the need for social services. Mary Richmond and many of her colleagues were actively involved in efforts by the American Red Cross to provide casework services to displaced veterans and their families. Social workers were also involved in the peace movement. Jane Addams and other prominent social reformers of the day opposed World War I.

After a long struggle, women finally secured the right to vote shortly after the end of World War I. A major milestone took place in 1848, when Elizabeth Cady Stanton and Lucretia Mott organized the first women's rights conference at Seneca Falls, New York. In the ensuing years, several women's rights groups formed, such as the National American Woman Suffrage Association (NAWSA). As early as 1878, these groups called for a constitutional amendment to guarantee full voting rights for women. Several states, particularly in the West, did grant women suffrage. In fact, women in Wyoming and several other territories had the right to vote even before statehood. Montana elected the first woman to Congress in 1916—social worker Jeanette Rankin. However, many other states either restricted women's votes to certain elections or outlawed them completely.

During World War I, the NAWSA, under the leadership of Carrie Chapman Catt, led the final push for suffrage. This movement gained the support of President Woodrow Wilson, in part because of women's contribution to the war effort. As depicted in Exhibit 3.1, women used direct action to keep suffrage in the public consciousness and build popular support. The 19th Amendment, which mandated that "the right of citizens of the U.S. to vote shall not be denied or abridged by the U.S. or by any State on account of sex," was finally ratified in 1920. Having secured full citizenship, some women's groups struggled for a broader guarantee of rights and opportunities. In 1923, the Equal Rights Amendment (ERA) was introduced in Congress. The ERA states that equality of rights under the law will not be denied on the basis of gender and gives Congress the authority to enforce the provisions of the amendment. Congress initially defeated the ERA, but it was subsequently reintroduced every year until 1972, when it was

EXHIBIT 3.1

Women's Suffragettes at the New York Fair

Source: Library of Congress

finally passed. However, the ERA has never been ratified by enough states to become part of the Constitution, although many national and local organizations are still advocating for it. The struggle over the ERA illustrates the degree to which women's rights continue to be a battleground in U.S. politics, a century after women won full voting equality. Despite winning a record number of elected offices at the federal and state levels in the 2018 midterm elections, women's political power trails their demographic and economic significance.

Beginning in 1916, Margaret Sanger, an activist who worked to secure women's reproductive rights, opened the first family planning clinics in this country. Sanger was a pioneer in an arena that continues to be controversial, a fact illustrated in debates over requirements that contraception be included in health insurance plans, congressional Republicans' repeated attempts to defund Planned Parenthood, and Senate confirmation battles centering on judges' positions on abortion rights.

The New Deal

The decade following World War I was a time of prosperity for many Americans, and the needs of those who did not share in that prosperity were largely ignored. Voters elected three successive Republican presidents unwilling to engage in large-scale social reform: Warren G. Harding, Calvin Coolidge, and Herbert Hoover.

The stock market crash of 1929 and the dire economic conditions that followed during the Great Depression changed the federal government's historic reluctance to provide aid to people in need. The plight of millions of Americans who were now without jobs could not be denied. More than 25 percent of the workforce was unemployed, with unofficial reports of joblessness as high as 80 percent in some major cities (Reisch, 2017a). Wages fell, city and state aid budgets were overwhelmed, and social unrest increased pressure on the federal government to act (Reisch, 2017a). As in social work practice with individuals, a crisis can also be an opportunity for change. In response to the Great Depression, U.S. social policy changed in significant ways. In 1932, voters elected President Franklin D. Roosevelt, a Democrat, who held the office until his death in 1945. The Roosevelt Administration implemented a series of economic policies that reflected the theories of British economist John Maynard Keynes (1936), who advocated increased government spending and manipulation of interest rates to dampen inflation and manage recessions.

During the Roosevelt Administration, the federal government initiated work relief programs and other forms of aid to help people in need. Designed to align with traditional values that emphasize work as a path out of poverty and to avoid upsetting existing racial and gender hierarchies (Reisch, 2017a), these programs were nonetheless dramatic turning points in the history of the U.S. social welfare system. Collectively, these innovations are referred to as the New Deal. The Works Progress Administration (WPA), Civilian Conservation Corps (CCC), and Civil Works Administration (CWA) were among the most prominent New Deal programs. These programs employed millions of people in such diverse activities as building roads, bridges, and other public infrastructure; planting trees and preserving forests; performing plays; and painting murals. The Great Depression and the New Deal marked a fundamental change in the way many people thought about the government's responsibility to address needs. Because even robust state efforts were inadequate to meet needs during the Great Depression, federal aid was considered vital. The conviction that the federal government must assume some responsibility for people who are in need through no fault of their own replaced the principle that social welfare was largely a local and state responsibility.

Social workers were leaders in the development of several New Deal programs. For example, Harry Hopkins, director of the Federal Emergency Relief Administration (FERA), Frances Perkins, secretary of labor, and Martha Eliot, director of the Children's Bureau, helped develop and administer the new social policies of the era (Tice & Perkins, 2002). Charlotte Towle wrote *Common Human Needs*, a manual intended to instruct workers involved in administering the Social Security Act of 1935 (Towle, 1945/1987). Towle's monograph, based on the premise that people have common human needs, helped articulate a more compassionate view of people who could not provide for themselves. Social work was distinguishing itself as a profession that addressed not only individual needs but also policy reforms at the state and national levels. Exhibit 3.2 profiles one of the most prominent social workers who helped shaped the federal government's policy response to the Great Depression.

EXHIBIT 3.2

Harry Hopkins

Harry Hopkins was born in Sioux City, Iowa, in 1890. In 1912, Hopkins graduated from Grinnell College, where the curriculum was strongly influenced by the values of the Social Gospel Reform Movement. After graduation, Hopkins began his social work career, working with the poor in New York as a "friendly visitor." Hopkins eventually moved into a management position, and in 1923 he was elected president of the American Association of Social Workers (AASW). Then the governor of New York, Franklin D. Roosevelt, asked Hopkins to head the Temporary Emergency Relief Administration, the first state-run relief program in the country. The partnership between Hopkins and Roosevelt continued once Roosevelt became president, and Hopkins was a principal developer of the collection of policies and programs designed to stimulate the economy and get people back to work—known as the New Deal. Although some New Deal programs were terminated, many of the programs for people with disabilities, children, families, and older adults created by the Social Security Act are still in existence.

Source: Library of Congress

The Townsend Movement In the years leading up to the Depression, people were living longer, yet there were fewer jobs, particularly for older adults. Researchers estimated that three out of four people over the age of 65 were unable to support themselves. Also, due to societal changes, many families could not support their elder members in the ways previously expected.

In 1933, out-of-work 66-year-old American physician Francis Everett Townsend, frustrated with the plight of growing numbers of impoverished elders, outlined a plan for income security in older age in numerous letters to the editor of his local newspaper. Particularly popular in California, the Townsend Movement had a strong national following among older adults and is credited with influencing President Roosevelt and Congress to pass the Social Security Act in 1935. The Townsend Movement helped make clear that some sort of support for elders had become politically and economically necessary.

The Social Security Act This law encompassed major social insurance and public assistance programs that have become integral to our social welfare system. The original Act made provisions for old-age benefits, financial assistance for aged and blind persons and dependent and disabled children, maternal and child welfare, public health measures, and unemployment compensation. Crucially, it provided benefits to retired workers through a system of social insurance, which replaced the more stigmatizing practice of public assistance.

The Old Age, Survivors, and Disability Insurance (OASDI) program, established by the Social Security Act and subsequent amendments, is a social insurance program based on the proposition that "worthy" workers and their employers can pool money to provide for retirement, disability, and surviving family members after a worker's death. This approach has important implications for OASDI's political fortunes. The middle class is often more supportive of initiatives built on an insurance model than of measures in which the government uses general tax revenues to provide for people in need. OASDI changed the traditional paradigm whereby dependent groups like impoverished children and elders were expected to rely on their families or on private charity for economic support. By paying OASDI insurance premiums—unfortunately labeled "payroll taxes," a term that overlooks the purpose of the payments—workers and their employers could now ensure that they had an income even when they could no longer work. However, linking eligibility to paid work in industries predominated by men reinforced the role of the male breadwinner and built on historic ideals of willingness to work as a precondition for assistance. Because many jobs, such as farm worker and housekeeper, were not initially included in OASDI, people of color, unmarried women, and their children often were segregated into separate, less generous, needs-based public assistance programs (Katznelson, 2005).

Perhaps the most important public assistance program the Social Security Act established was Aid to Dependent Children (ADC), which provided cash assistance for impoverished children and replaced the mothers' pensions provided by many states. The law defined a "dependent child" as "a child under the age of 16 who has been deprived of parental support or care by reason of the death, continued absence from the home, or physical or mental incapacity of a parent," and who was living with the other parent or another relative. Initially, payments were made only for the care of children. Later, grants for parents of dependent children were added, and the name of the program was changed to Aid to Families with Dependent Children

(AFDC). In general, public assistance programs have been much more controversial, more punitive, and less generously funded than social insurance benefits for "worthy" retirees. Not surprisingly, then, these programs have also been less successful in meeting the needs of their target populations. OASDI is quite effective in reducing poverty among older adult retirees, while poverty and deprivation among children whose families receive public assistance has increased, especially in recent years.

The provisions for retired workers contained in the Social Security Act were originally called Old Age Insurance (OAI). As its name implies, the program initially provided benefits only to retired workers. However, amendments adopted in 1939 extended coverage to two additional categories of people: (1) the spouse and children of a retired worker, and (2) the survivors of a deceased covered worker. At this point, the name was changed to Old Age and Survivors' Insurance (OASI) (DeWitt, 2003). In 1956, disability insurance benefits were added for workers aged 50 to 64 who have disabilities and for adult children of retired or deceased workers, if they have permanent and total disabilities. The program then became known as Old Age, Survivors, and Disability Insurance (OASDI). In 1960, workers of all ages and their dependents were made eligible for disability insurance benefits (Social Security Administration, 2007). To learn more about the fascinating history of the Social Security Act and its components, visit the Social Security Administration website and search for Social Security History (**www.ssa.gov/**).

The discussion in Chapter 8 provides critiques and analysis of the Social Security Act. For now, it is important to recognize its passage represented a milestone in public social welfare. Significantly, those parts that provide social insurance were premised on recognition of common human needs. Pooling resources in social insurance programs so that people have sufficient funds when faced with retirement or disability is in keeping with the strengths perspective, emphasizing collective responsibility and vesting individuals with resources with which to pursue their goals. However, eligibility for these programs often hinged on one's status as among the "worthy" poor. At the same time, the public assistance programs the Act established were means-tested and failed to address the structural barriers that keep people in poverty, such as lack of access to employment, education, and health care. The disparities in these two approaches also served to amplify inequality by elevating the position of those already privileged (Katznelson, 2005). In total, then, while the Act provided some relief, it also reinforced the gender, class, and racial divisions in U.S. social policy. Exhibit 3.3 profiles one of the women whose advocacy and policymaking aimed to counter some of these inequities.

The Impact of World War II

Just as World War I had diverted the nation's attention from the Progressive Movement, the attack on Pearl Harbor in December 1941 drew national attention away from the social reforms of the New Deal. The nation's entry into World War II had a profound effect on the economy. The federal government dramatically increased spending, creating jobs for millions of Americans in the armed services and war-related industries, and pulling the United States from the Great Depression. U.S. involvement in World War II also had social implications. As millions of men joined the military, women entered the workforce and often moved into traditionally male-only areas, such as manufacturing jobs in shipyards and aircraft factories. Exhibit 3.4

EXHIBIT 3.3

Frances Perkins

Frances Perkins was born Fannie Coralie Perkins in 1880. She obtained her undergraduate degree from Mount Holyoke College in 1902. As part of her studies, she visited factories and became interested in working conditions and labor law. She went on to earn her master's degree in economics and sociology from Columbia University. After witnessing the Triangle Shirtwaist Factory fire in 1911, Frances sat on several committees established to determine what had caused the fire and how to prevent such fires from occurring again. During this time Perkins became even more committed to labor rights reform. In the late 1920s, Governor Franklin D. Roosevelt asked Perkins to serve as commissioner of labor for the State of New York. In this role, Perkins implemented policies that reduced the work week for women to 48 hours and fostered the development of minimum wage laws. Once Roosevelt became president in 1932, he asked Perkins to be his secretary of labor. With this appointment, Perkins became the first female cabinet secretary. She was instrumental in the development of New Deal legislation, the abolition of child labor, the implementation of maximum-hour laws, and, through the enactment of the National Labor Relations Act of 1935, the establishment of workers' right to organize and collectively bargain. Perkins' efforts to nationalize social insurance also contributed to passage of the Social Security Act in 1935. Frances Perkins was a dedicated advocate for workers' rights and played a key role in instituting social reforms that are cornerstones for current policy.

Source: Library of Congress

EXHIBIT 3.4

Images of Strong Women like Rosie the Riveter Were Used to Recruit Women into the Workforce during World War II

Credit: National Archives; Library of Congress

shows some of the posters used to recruit women into the workforce. Note that these posters illustrate the evolutionary nature of social norms, as permission from one's husband is still included in one of the images. This undercurrent of patriarchy still influences women's experiences in the workforce.

When the war was over, job opportunities and support for working women, such as worksite childcare, largely disappeared. Women were once again bombarded with messages extolling the virtues of traditional gender roles. You can learn more about how women were drawn into new kinds of jobs and the dilemmas they faced by visiting the National Park Service site for Rosie the Riveter WWII Homefront (**www.nps.gov/rori/index.htm**).

African Americans were also able to join the industrial workforce in increasing numbers during the war. Initially, they faced opposition to their employment in the defense industry. In response, in 1941, A. Philip Randolph, a prominent Black labor and civil rights leader who was pressing for fair employment practices as well as integration of the military, threatened to mobilize thousands of African Americans in a March on Washington. Organizers called off the march when President Roosevelt issued Executive Order 8802 on June 25, 1941, which prohibited discrimination in employment in defense industries and created the Fair Employment Practices Commission (FEPC) to monitor compliance. Despite discrimination, Black employment in industry more than doubled during the war. However, when the war was over, many of these jobs disappeared. Instead, job preference was given to returning veterans, most of whom were White.

During World War II, the United States again enacted racist policy when it enforced President Roosevelt's executive order to detain and then transport to internment camps without trial nearly 120,000 Japanese Americans. While survivors of this Japanese internment would not receive reparations until 1988, when Ronald Reagan authorized $20,000 each, the horrors of the Holocaust led many Americans to begin to reexamine beliefs that supported prejudice and discrimination. These lessons contributed to the Civil Rights Movement of the 1950s and 1960s.

THE EVOLUTION OF THE MODERN WELFARE STATE: 1945–1970

With the end of World War II in 1945, the federal government developed programs to provide support for returning veterans. For example, in 1944, Congress passed the Servicemen's Readjustment Act, commonly referred to as the GI Bill of Rights, to help returning soldiers build assets. The GI Bill provided loans for veterans to purchase a home or establish a business and grants for college tuition. While the rationale for the bill was to restore to veterans the opportunities they lost by serving in the military, millions of veterans took advantage of the GI Bill and were able to improve their status beyond what would likely have been possible otherwise. The legislation opened the doors to colleges to many more people, including children of immigrants, Catholics and Jews, people from working- and middle-class backgrounds, and those from rural areas. Many of these veterans were the first generation in their families to attend college. Some universities that had previously educated few students of color began diversifying their student bodies.

However, continuing segregation in both housing and education limited the utility of the GI Bill for Black veterans and hindered African Americans' accumulation of assets. In this way, although the education and training veterans received through the GI Bill upgraded the overall quality of the workforce, the policy also ensured the perpetuation of racial inequities in human capital and, especially, wealth (Katznelson, 2005). Housing segregation was particularly stark, with deed restrictions and racial covenants and other unjust exclusions resulting in what some have called "American apartheid" (Reisch, 2017a). Although marred by institutional racism, the GI Bill reflects a strengths perspective in that it focuses on overcoming structural barriers by enhancing economic and educational opportunities. It is, therefore, a good example of a policy that reflects a **capacity-building approach**.

In addition to focusing on the economic needs of returning veterans, the federal government addressed the mental health needs of World War II draftees by passing the Mental Health Act of 1946, which created the National Institute of Mental Health (NIMH) and ultimately helped move public treatment of mental illness out of state institutions and into community-based programs (Reid, 1995). With the GI Bill and the Mental Health Act, the federal government took a more activist role in social welfare. These initiatives improved opportunities for many people. However, discrimination and segregation continued to limit access, and poverty remained widespread for many traditionally oppressed groups.

The Struggle for African-American Civil Rights

During the postwar years, individuals and institutions could legally discriminate based on skin color. However, African Americans who had served in the war brought home more egalitarian ideas about racial justice and an expectation of greater respect and opportunity in exchange for their military service. In addition, throughout the 1940s and 1950s, large-scale migration of African Americans to Northern cities, where they could vote, increased their political power. Over the next two decades, these demographic and cultural shifts contributed to substantial changes in race relations and policy structures in the domain of civil rights.

The Challenge to School Segregation In a milestone event, the National Association for the Advancement of Colored People (NAACP) challenged the "separate but equal" doctrine. In 1954, the Supreme Court ruled in *Brown v. Board of Education of Topeka* that in "public education the doctrine of 'separate but equal' has no place." It further asserted that "separate educational facilities are inherently unequal" and therefore violate the 14th Amendment's guarantee of equal protection of the law (Knappman et al., 2002). The *Brown* decision is an excellent example of how the judiciary generates social policy. Throughout modern history and still today, social workers should consider how the judicial branch can be used to change unjust policies, as well as how others may use the courts to attempt to roll back policies that promote social justice.

The *Brown* ruling, which overturned the 1896 *Plessy v. Ferguson* ruling, helped bring an end to Jim Crow laws. It is considered one of the most important civil rights rulings of the twentieth century. However, resistance movements and legal challenges arose across the country and limited the immediate power of *Brown*. That it took several years for many states to even begin implementing the *Brown* ruling's requirements highlights the limits of the judiciary's social policymaking. The legacy of *Brown* also underscores the entrenched nature of racism in the United States. Even more than 60 years later, most Black children are still educated in schools in which most students are students of color (Geiger, 2017). To learn more about the *Brown* ruling and its aftermath, you can visit the *Brown v. Board of Education* National Historic Site (**www.nps.gov/brvb/index.htm**).

The Challenge to Jim Crow Beginning in the 1950s, African-American civil rights activists and their allies initiated a campaign of direct action to challenge the nation's system of racial subordination. On December 1, 1955, in Montgomery, Alabama, an African-American woman named Rosa Parks refused to surrender her seat on a bus to a White person, in violation of local segregation laws. Her arrest, depicted in Exhibit 3.5, led to Black residents of Montgomery boycotting the city's bus system. They demanded an end to segregated seating, better treatment for Black riders, and the hiring of Black drivers. The boycott continued for almost a year until the Supreme Court ruled that Montgomery's segregation law violated the 14th Amendment. The boycott was a landmark victory for advocates of social justice, and it also brought attention to a new civil rights leader, Dr. Martin Luther King, Jr., and a new organization, the Southern Christian Leadership Conference (SCLC), both of whom were willing to directly challenge the South's oppressive racial system (Patterson, 1996).

Civil rights protests intensified in the 1960s. On February 1, 1960, four Black college students in Greensboro, North Carolina, sat down at a lunch counter that was designated "Whites Only."

EXHIBIT 3.5

Rosa Parks

Source: Underwood Archives/Getty Images Associated Press

They were not served, but their sit-in continued until closing time. Similar sit-ins to protest segregation in schools, colleges, theaters, churches, swimming pools, and stores occurred across the South, bringing the issue of segregation to the consciousness of more Americans and politicizing a generation of Black youth.

During John F. Kennedy's presidency from 1960 to 1963, the Civil Rights Movement intensified. In the first years of his presidency, Kennedy moved cautiously, but the civil rights demonstrations and crises of 1963 compelled him to introduce comprehensive legislation before his assassination on November 22, 1963. Civil rights advocates in this era worked hard for reform and faced violent opposition. In 1961, Freedom Riders seeking to integrate interstate travel were brutally attacked in Alabama. Law enforcement was complicit and even participated in the attacks. In 1964, Mississippi segregationists murdered three civil rights workers: social worker Michael Schwerner, James Chaney, and Andrew Goodman. In 1965, 25-year-old Student Nonviolent Coordinating Committee leader and future U.S. Congressman John Lewis, pictured in Exhibit 3.6, was nearly killed when he was attacked by Alabama State Troopers during a voting rights march in Selma, Alabama.

Black leadership in the South mobilized to press for civil rights. In May 1963, King and the SCLC led a major protest in Birmingham, Alabama, to demand an end to segregation and employment discrimination in the city. The Birmingham police eventually arrested more than a thousand demonstrators—including hundreds of young children—and aimed water hoses and police dogs at them as a stunned nation watched the events unfold on television. Dr. King wrote his "Letter from a Birmingham Jail" in response to criticism from White leaders who called protests against segregation "extreme measures." In his response, King laid out his philosophy of nonviolence, explained the use of civil disobedience in pursuit of social change, and critiqued those he saw as "more devoted to order than to justice." You can read the text

EXHIBIT 3.6

John Lewis

Credit: Library of Congress

of Dr. King's letter and listen to him read it in the King Institute's archives (**https://kinginstitute.stanford.edu/king-papers/documents/letter-birmingham-jail**).

While the Civil Rights Movement was certainly not led by social workers, they did play a role in the struggle. For example, Dr. Dorothy I. Height, an African-American social worker, was the only woman in the United Civil Rights Leadership, which included Dr. Martin Luther King, Jr., Whitney Young, A. Philip Randolph, James Farmer, Roy Wilkins, and John Lewis. She also helped found the National Women's Political Caucus in 1971. She viewed the fights for equality for women and for African Americans as part of the same larger struggle and worked to unite these two historically separate movements, efforts that were particularly critical given evident sexism in the Civil Rights Movement and pervasive racism in many women's rights organizations. A civil rights legend, Height was a lifelong advocate for the rights for women and people of color (NASW, 2016).

Civil Rights Laws Civil rights activists campaigned for the enactment of a comprehensive national law to protect the civil rights of African Americans. They achieved this objective with the passage of the Civil Rights Act of 1964, which prohibited employment discrimination on the basis of race, sex, or ethnicity; banned federal funding for institutions that practiced discrimination; and mandated equal access to public accommodations. By banning discrimination based on race as well as gender, this legislation incorporated **intersectionality**, which focuses on the interrelation of dimensions of oppression such as racism and gender inequality. Chapter 7 will examine the Civil Rights Act of 1964 in greater detail.

In 1964, Congress also ratified the 24th Amendment to the Constitution, which prohibited the use of poll taxes or any other taxes to deny voting rights in federal elections. The following year, Congress passed the Voting Rights Act of 1965, which suspended requirements that voters pass literacy tests and assigned federal registrars to enroll voters. Civil rights advocates used these new policies to launch a successful assault on the Jim Crow system. Still, full and equal political participation for people of color continues to be elusive more than 50 years after the passage of this landmark civil rights legislation. Indeed, as we will discuss in Chapter 7, voting rights face intensified threats in today's political landscape.

The Struggle for Latinx Civil Rights

The annexation of Texas and the Treaty of Guadalupe Hidalgo that concluded the Mexican War significantly increased the Latinx population of the United States. Throughout the Southwest, Whites exploited native-born and immigrant Latinx to meet the demand for cheap farm labor. These laborers worked for low wages under dangerous and unsanitary conditions. Throughout U.S. history, policies concerning immigrant workers have often fluctuated with changing economic and political conditions. Beginning in 1942, the Bracero Program (roughly translated, *bracero* means "strong arm" in Spanish) brought Mexican men to the United States to replace field workers who had been deployed in World War II. Like most women, who were pressed to return to the home after World War II ended, these bracero workers faced discrimination and even deportation after the war. This same pattern was also seen during the Depression, when thousands of people of Mexican origin were deported, regardless of their citizenship status (Nash et al., 2004). Employment was not the only domain in which Latinx were oppressed. Jim Crow-type laws segregated schools and public accommodations, restricted property holding, and prohibited intermarriage.

Some Latinx workers organized to demand decent wages and working conditions. In 1962, Cesar Chavez and Dolores Huerta co-founded the National Farm Workers Association to press for fairer treatment. Three years later, that group evolved into the United Farm Workers (UFW) and initiated La Huelga, a major strike of agricultural workers in California, depicted in Exhibit 3.7 (Patterson, 1996). The struggle to improve conditions continues today, as agricultural workers receive among the lowest wages and have the fewest protections of workers in any industry in the country.

Today, the Latinx population in the United States includes immigrants from Central and South America, Cuba, Mexico, and Spain and their descendants, along with people whose ancestors were indigenous to the Southwest when the United States annexed that territory. This ethnic group is diverse, comprising individuals who identify as White, Black, or multiracial, as well as those who see their central identity as indigenous. Some still speak primarily Spanish, while others speak English and/or various indigenous languages. Latinx have achieved considerable gains and carved out positions of power within government and commerce. However, indicators such as high poverty rates reveal continued disadvantage. As the percentage of the U.S. population who identify as Latinx continues to grow, initiatives to increase opportunities and address discrimination are increasingly important.

EXHIBIT 3.7

Dolores Huerta, September 24, 1965, Delano, CA, Grape Strike

Source: Paul Richards, Harvey Richards Media Archive

The Struggle for LGBTQ+ Civil Rights

Although it was not as visible as other civil rights movements until the late 1960s, the struggle for LGBTQ+ civil rights in the United States was building decades earlier. In 1948, Alfred Kinsey published *Sexual Behavior in the Human Male*. Here, Kinsey published the results of interviews with 5,300 American men, 10 percent of whom reported identifying primarily as homosexual. This often-cited publication increased public awareness of the prevalence of homosexuality, but it did not end policies that stigmatized and even criminalized same-sex activities and relationships. Sodomy laws, which were common across the United States, directly persecuted the LGBTQ+ community. In 1952, the American Psychiatric Association (APA) released the *Diagnostic and Statistical Manual (DSM) of Mental Disorders*, which described homosexuality as a mental illness and led to people being institutionalized for homosexuality.

In 1950, Harry Hay co-founded one of the first gay activist groups, the Mattachine Society. The goal of the organization was "to liberate the homosexual minority from the oppression of the majority and to call on other minorities to fight with them against the oppression" (Cain, 1993, pp. 1558–1559). Although the Mattachine Society was able to organize large numbers in the Los Angeles area, they did much of their early work in secret. In 1955, the Daughters of Bilitis, a lesbian activist group, formed in San Francisco. Both groups worked to reach more people, formed chapters across the country, and published magazines to highlight issues and provide resources to their communities (Faderman, 2015).

In 1954, the California Post Office refused to mail one of these publications, claiming its content was obscene (Cain, 1993; Faderman, 2015). The publisher sued the postmaster, citing First Amendment protection. The suit was unsuccessful in both the federal trial and appellate courts, but these decisions were reversed by the U.S. Supreme Court in 1958 (Cain, 1993). Freedom of speech prevailed, and this case was a major victory for the LGBTQ+ community.

The Stonewall Riot of 1969 was a turning point in the struggle for gay rights. When New York police raided the Stonewall Inn, a gay bar in Greenwich Village, patrons resisted. Inspired by this activism, gay and lesbian groups around the country coalesced to organize for their civil rights. The anniversary of the Stonewall Riots has been the date for gay pride parades across the nation, and the Stonewall Inn was listed as a National Historical Landmark in 1999.

Mental Health and Intellectual Disability Initiatives

During the early 1960s, advocates for people with developmental disabilities and mental illness pressured the federal government to allocate greater resources for their treatment and community-based care. They found a powerful ally in President Kennedy, who had a sister with intellectual disabilities. Their efforts culminated in the passage of the Mental Retardation Facilities[1] and Community Mental Health Centers Construction Act of 1963. This Act provided money to construct and staff community mental health centers and facilities for people with intellectual disabilities. Although Congress never provided sufficient funding to meet the need for community-based services, this Act helped usher in an era of deinstitutionalization in which people with mental illness were integrated into the community rather than confined to hospitals (Trattner, 1999). Where mental illness had been something to be hidden, work was underway to establish the expectation that better mental health should be considered an attainable goal for all.

The War on Poverty

Closely associated with the Civil Rights Movement were a variety of initiatives by the federal government to address the problem of poverty. The administrations of Presidents Kennedy (1961–1963) and Johnson (1963–1968) implemented several programs to create jobs, improve education, and provide financial assistance to people in need. Political scientist Michael Harrington's 1962 book *The Other America* was a particularly strong influence on Kennedy's views on poverty. It helped to expose the reality of structural poverty, which arose from lack of opportunities rather than individual deficits. *The Other America* is often credited with renewing concerns about poverty after the relative affluence of the 1950s.

New Frontier Anti-Poverty Programs Kennedy's domestic agenda, known as the New Frontier, included several measures to help move people out of poverty. The Area Redevelopment Act of 1961 allocated federal monies to disadvantaged areas such as Appalachia. The following year, Congress approved the Manpower Development Training Act to train or retrain workers who lacked the skills necessary to succeed in a changing economy. The Equal Pay Act of 1963 attempted to address gender-based wage discrimination by promoting the concept that women should receive equal wages for performing the same work as men. Although these initiatives were limited in scope, they symbolized a growing belief that the federal government should take action against poverty even during relatively prosperous periods (Patterson, 1996).

Of special significance for social workers were the 1962 Public Welfare Amendments to the Social Security Act, referred to as the Social Service Amendments. These amendments allocated federal support to the states so that local welfare departments could provide recipients of public assistance with case management and other social services. Growing attention to psychiatric social work fueled support for this approach. Social workers who proposed ideas for addressing dependency and family breakdown among public welfare recipients indicated that these interventions would promote motivation and family unity, which in turn would reduce the welfare rolls significantly (Day, 2009). Instead, welfare participation increased by nearly 50 percent between 1962 and 1967 (Moffitt, 1993).

Illustrating how policy changes, demographic shifts, and social transformations can combine to produce outcomes, there were a variety of reasons for this increase. During the 1960s, large numbers of African-American mothers began to claim AFDC benefits. Formerly reluctant to claim benefits and strongly discouraged by racist interpretations of welfare rules, Black women now pressed for needed assistance (Tice & Perkins, 2002). A burgeoning Welfare Rights Movement organized recipients to protest unfair treatment, and these mothers used direct action to draw attention to the challenges facing low-income single parents. At the same time, eligibility rules were relaxed, sometimes through Supreme Court decisions, so that more people could receive help. However, political tensions, public ambivalence, and inadequate resources compromised AFDC's effectiveness (Bertram, 2011). Problematically, public assistance seldom provided clients with sufficient support to take advantage of expanded educational and social services (Reisch, 2000). For example, without transportation and childcare, parents could not attend job training and parenting classes. These limitations undermined the potency of the social services provided.

Most social workers knew that offering social services to individuals in poverty without addressing underlying social conditions would not significantly reduce welfare participation. Ameliorating poverty requires addressing not only the personal problems of poor people, but also the structural barriers they confront. However, to secure funding for programs that can help individuals, advocates often feel they must promise unrealistic outcomes. Because social workers had advocated for the Social Service Amendments, when these programs failed to reduce welfare participation, many people became skeptical of the effectiveness of social services. Unfortunately, unrealized promises accumulate and contribute to public cynicism.

The Great Society and the War on Poverty The assassination of President Kennedy in November 1963 ushered in the presidency of Lyndon Johnson. As president, Johnson was able to work with Congress to pass civil rights, health, and anti-poverty legislation. These policies and the programs they created were core initiatives of Johnson's Great Society, which included his War on Poverty. Whitney Young, Jr., an African-American social worker and a leader in the Urban League, developed proposals for reform that are widely credited as being the inspiration for the War on Poverty.

The centerpiece of the War on Poverty was the Economic Opportunity Act of 1964. This landmark law focused on community organizing, increasing economic opportunities, and empowering, rather than "fixing," the poor. Some of the programs and agencies the Economic Opportunity Act established are still in existence. These include Volunteers in Service to America (VISTA), a program in which volunteers directly assist people in need; Head Start, which provides preschool, parent engagement opportunities, and social services to low-income families; and Community Action Programs (CAPs), which provide economic development and social services to poor communities while encouraging residents' "maximum feasible participation."

The Economic Opportunity Act reflected the belief that ending poverty would require major changes in the provision of educational and employment opportunities. These changes, in turn, could take place only as people in poverty and from traditionally oppressed groups began to exercise political power, beginning with their vote. The Economic Opportunity Act, then, reflected a strengths-based approach. Because the goal was to rely less heavily on professionals and instead position target populations as experts on how to escape poverty, anti-poverty programs created in the War on Poverty initially did not incorporate social workers. However, programs soon brought in social workers to help with community organizing, administration, and direct service provision (Popple, 1995).

Medicare and Medicaid Another feature of the War on Poverty was federal legislation to assist older adults and those with low incomes with their medical expenses. In 1965, three decades of lobbying to incorporate health care into the Social Security Act finally resulted in the passage of Title XVIII, which established Medicare, and Title XIX, which established Medicaid. Although these programs did not provide universal health care, they did ensure basic medical care for certain categories of individuals. They also laid the foundation of government responsibility for health care.

Medicare is a national health insurance program for people aged 65 and older who are eligible for Social Security, and for certain categories of younger people with disabilities. Medicare focuses primarily on acute care and provides little coverage for long-term care. Medicare Part A provides hospital insurance, and Part B is an optional program that allows people aged 65 and over to purchase coverage for Medicare-eligible physician services, outpatient hospital services, certain home health services, and durable medical equipment. Medicare Part D, which went into effect in 2006, provides subsidies to make prescription drug coverage more affordable for older adults. The Medicare program is federally funded through payroll taxes. Medicare Part C (also called Medicare Advantage) allows private health insurance companies to offer Medicare benefits using a managed care model.

Medicaid provides health care for certain categories of people with very low incomes. Medicaid is a **means-tested** program, which means eligibility is based on financial need. It is financed jointly by federal and state dollars and is typically thought of as a program that benefits poor families with children. Indeed, Medicaid has greatly increased children's access to health care. However, Medicaid is also the primary payer of nursing home care (Kaiser Family Foundation, 2017), as many older people are impoverished by the costs of long-term care and thus become eligible for Medicaid. Many younger people with disabilities also qualify for Medicaid. Although states can use Medicaid to make home- and community-based services available for some older adults and young people with disabilities, there are often long waiting lists for these services.

The War on Poverty: Successes and Failures   As with most major reforms, the War on Poverty experienced both successes and failures. Although programs promised too much and were inadequately funded, they nonetheless generated some positive outcomes. Certainly, the civil rights legislation of the period made some progress in addressing the structural problems created by discrimination. The national poverty rate dropped from 22 percent in 1960 to 11 percent in 1974. Although economic growth was the major cause of this decline, anti-poverty programs contributed as well. The full effects of these investments are only visible when using a more sophisticated poverty measure than the official government calculation. These analyses show that anti-poverty programs are particularly crucial for reducing child poverty, deep poverty, and poverty during economic downturns (Fox et al., 2015).

War on Poverty policies and programs incorporate many strengths-based policy tenets, such as involving clients in developing and providing services. Further, several of the anti-poverty policies and programs implemented during this period have enduring legacies. In addition to Medicare and Medicaid, War on Poverty initiatives still serving low-income Americans include the Food Stamp Act of 1964 and the Older Americans Act of 1965. The Food Stamp Act, now known as the Supplemental Nutrition Assistance Program (SNAP), provides subsidies to low-income families for the purchase of nutritious food. The Older Americans Act contains provisions designed to promote social interaction and enhance independent living for older adults, including funding for congregate meals and transportation.

Despite meaningful accomplishments, the major anti-poverty programs generally received inadequate funding, and most failed to address the social, economic, and demographic forces that contributed to growing need. In particular, more low-income families were migrating from the South to urban areas in the North, where they found insufficient jobs, inadequate housing, and ineffective transportation systems. Rather than pushing for structural reforms, critics who were not mindful of these underlying dynamics classified the War on Poverty as a failure when poverty continued.

Other critics contended that the War on Poverty did not go far enough and was ultimately undone by its multiple and sometimes conflicting objectives. In their book *Regulating the Poor*, Frances Piven and social worker Richard Cloward contend that the expansion of programs providing economic support was used as a tool for controlling unrest, particularly in cities (Piven & Cloward, 1971). They assert that the government provided temporary aid to suppress dissent, without addressing structural problems that limited opportunity. Although their assertions are open to debate, their critical analysis underscores the multiple goals of many anti-poverty initiatives.

Decreased funding for anti-poverty programs led Martin Luther King, Jr., to wonder whether social and economic justice would ever become a reality for people of color. Other Black leaders, such as Malcolm X and Stokely Carmichael, openly rejected the premise that nonviolence and integration would produce racial equality. They rallied their followers with calls for "Black power" and "Black separatism." However, a multiracial coalition opposed their ideas in part because they felt that African Americans did not control sufficient resources to establish a separate economy. Also, many people strongly supported nonviolent action on moral grounds, even when frustrated with the slow pace of change. Despite continued resistance, there were many gains for civil and economic justice in the 1960s. However, the White backlash that emerged intensified in the wake of urban riots, such as the one in the Watts section of Los Angeles in 1965. This dynamic fueled a political turn to the right that contributed to the election of a Republican president, Richard Nixon, in 1968.

CONTINUITY AND CHANGE: THE 1970S

Richard Nixon presided over the tumultuous first years of the 1970s, including the controversy that culminated in his own resignation. However, during his administration, spending on anti-poverty programs almost doubled (Tice & Perkins, 2002). The discussion that follows highlights experiments with a different approach to providing cash assistance to low-income people, the negative income tax, and considers the continuing push for greater civil rights, including among women and Native Americans.

Family Assistance Experiments

Nixon presidential adviser Daniel Patrick Moynihan proposed a major social welfare initiative—the Family Assistance Plan (FAP). The FAP would have established a minimum income by providing cash to all families whose incomes fell below a certain level. This policy is sometimes referred to as a "negative income tax." Reflecting a philosophy that dates at least to the English Poor Laws, the FAP also would have required all able-bodied recipients to work or to participate in a job-training program. If enacted, this plan would have replaced AFDC.

The FAP quickly became the target of criticism from across the political spectrum. Liberals pointed out that the minimum income was less than the established poverty line. Moreover, they objected to the work requirements, in part because the "able-bodied" poor included mothers with children over three years of age. Meanwhile, many conservatives argued that the FAP would significantly increase federal spending on welfare, especially if other assistance programs, such as food stamps, were not eliminated (Moynihan, 1973; Trattner, 1999). Although Congress did not pass the FAP, many countries in Western Europe have long had some form of child or family allowance. Indeed, many observers see these diverging approaches as driving differences in family poverty rates between those countries and the United States. Examining the debates around the FAP in the context of policy considerations today illustrates how political and economic environments shape which policy alternatives are considered "acceptable." Today, some of the provisions that were objectionable within the FAP when it was proposed are, for example, accepted components of Temporary Assistance to Needy Families (TANF), while, as described in Chapter 8, proposals such as Universal Basic Income have gained some traction.

Although unsuccessful, the negative income tax proposal heightened interest in using the tax system to aid low-income families. In 1975, Congress passed legislation that established the Earned Income Tax Credit (EITC). The EITC provides a refundable tax credit to working families whose incomes fall below the federal poverty line. While this tax credit was initially modest and did not significantly reduce poverty, it established the principle of using the tax system to provide resources to low-income families, an approach that parallels tax incentives for wealthy and middle-class families. Today, the value of the EITC, at the federal level and in many states, is such that it does lift millions of Americans out of poverty. Additionally, because it is administered by the Internal Revenue Service and does not require a separate application, the EITC can reduce the stigma of assistance.

Social Service Reforms

Although the 1970s are not considered a period of major social service reform, several measures introduced during the administrations of Richard Nixon and his successor, Gerald Ford, contributed to social welfare. In 1972, Congress enacted legislation creating the federal Supplemental Security Income (SSI) program. Prior to 1972, states had a patchwork of programs to aid elderly people, those who are blind, and low-income people with disabilities. SSI replaced this arrangement with a uniform national system for very low-income people in these categories. Importantly, Social Security and SSI benefits are also indexed through an automatic cost-of-living adjustment, which made them more adequate for meeting people's needs.

Proposals to provide a demogrant—"a uniform payment to certain categories of persons, identified only by demographic (usually age) characteristics" (Burns, 1965, p. 88)—were considered as a way to create a universal safety net, but the idea was never sufficiently popular to be implemented nationally. The overwhelming preference in the United States is to link benefits to workforce participation whenever possible and to provide only minimal means-tested benefits to people not attached to the workforce, even those who fall into the category deemed "worthy." The Social Service Amendments of 1974, specifically Title XX, did make grants available to states to provide social services to welfare recipients as well as to people above the poverty line. Although the amount of money available for these programs was capped, these amendments gave states a great deal of latitude in determining how to provide services.

Also in 1974, Congress passed the Child Abuse Prevention and Treatment Act, following intense lobbying by child welfare advocates. This law established a national standard for child protection and enabled child advocates to document trends in child abuse to highlight the need for protective services. Notably, however, private, voluntary organizations continued to play crucial roles in child welfare, including in the investigation of maltreatment and arrangement of out-of-home placements.

Watergate and After The Watergate scandal, which led to Nixon's resignation in August 1974, undermined the public's belief in the positive power of government. The next two presidents, Gerald Ford and Jimmy Carter, focused on controlling the budget deficit, taming inflation, and dealing with foreign policy crises. President Carter did propose a guaranteed annual income plan that would have created a safety net for all Americans, but it was not enacted (Tice & Perkins, 2002). In 1978, President Carter signed the Full Employment and Balanced Growth Act. This legislation mandated that federal policies be directed toward achieving a zero-unemployment rate. The Act harkened back to the New Deal, when President Roosevelt proposed that citizens should have the "right to a useful and remunerative job in the industries or shops or farms or mines of the nation" (Sunstein, 2004, p. 13). While asserting that the federal government should commit to promoting economic conditions that would reduce unemployment, the law stipulated that if the private sector does not yield full employment, the public sector must provide the missing jobs. Clearly this goal of full employment has not been achieved. However, this legislation continues to be a tool for advocates who believe the public sector should be tasked with job creation.

Women and Civil Rights

In 1966, a group of activists founded the National Organization for Women (NOW) to press for equal rights and opportunities for women across a broad spectrum of arenas, including employment, education, and athletics. NOW's first president, Betty Friedan, was the author of the landmark 1963 book *The Feminine Mystique*. This book helped increase awareness of societal stereotypes that limited women's roles.

While, as described earlier, the Equal Rights Amendment—passed by Congress in 1972—never gained the approval of 38 states needed for ratification, other policies affecting women's lives have been more successful. For example, Title IX of the Education Amendments of 1972 banned discrimination and exclusion in schools on the basis of sex in both academics and sports, greatly expanding opportunities for women. The following year, the Supreme Court decision in *Roe v. Wade* legalized abortion. Activism by women continues to shape health, welfare, and civil rights policy. However, despite the activist environment of the time and the preponderance of women in the social work profession, the NASW did not elect a woman president until 1980 (Hooyman, 1994).

Native Americans and Civil Rights

In the twentieth century, Native American activists and their allies worked on multiple fronts to challenge unjust arrangements. In 1934, as part of the New Deal, Congress passed the Indian Reorganization Act, which abolished the Dawes Act allotment policy and returned certain expropriated lands to various tribes. Moreover, it authorized the tribes to establish governments or councils that would exercise some degree of sovereignty (DeLoria, 1993).

Termination and Relocation Compared to the harshly oppressive history, the New Deal reforms demonstrated greater sensitivity toward Native American autonomy and culture. However, in the conservative political atmosphere of the 1950s, the government's approach emphasized incorporating Native peoples into "mainstream" culture. To accomplish this objective, it pursued policies of termination and relocation. Formally implemented by two congressional actions of 1953, termination involved abolishing the special status of tribes as wards of the federal government and authorizing states to assume some of the functions of tribal governments. One objective of this policy was "to cut off public aid to Indians and to get them to fend for themselves" (Patterson, 1996, p. 376). Importantly, because the government failed to provide transition supports or compensate tribes for past losses, many Native Americans suffered yet again. For example, when Native Americans were billed for property taxes they were unable to pay, they lost their homes, which in turn left them unable to support schools, sanitation systems, and highways in their communities. Groups like the National Congress of American Indians vigorously opposed termination and argued that Native Americans should exercise a dual identity as members of a tribe and citizens of the United States. However, by the time President Nixon ended termination in 1969, several dozen tribes had been terminated (DeLoria, 1993; Patterson, 1996).

A related policy, relocation, encouraged Native Americans to move from their reservations to cities. The purpose of this policy was not only to provide greater economic opportunity, but also to promote assimilation. Again, Native Americans were pressed to abandon their cultural roots. In practice, relocation "frequently involved nothing more than a trade of rural for urban poverty" (DeLoria, 1993, p. 427). Consequently, many disillusioned young people returned to reservations, where they faced systemic and entrenched barriers.

Militancy and the Struggle for Sovereignty Like other marginalized groups, Native Americans adopted the direct-action strategies of the African-American Civil Rights Movement during the late 1960s and 1970s. In 1968, activists organized the American Indian Movement. As depicted in Exhibit 3.8, activists from several tribes occupied Alcatraz Island, California, the following year, asserting that the land should be returned to them according to treaties that stipulated that out-of-use federal lands should be returned to Native people. Alcatraz Penitentiary had been closed in 1963 and declared surplus federal property in 1964. In 1972, activists organized the "Trail of Broken Treaties" caravan to Washington, DC, where a group of militants took over the headquarters of the Bureau of Indian Affairs (BIA). Activists also used the courts to press historical land claims that were supported by treaties but not honored and to assert traditional water rights and fishing rights. These actions led to frequent confrontations

EXHIBIT 3.8

Occupation of Alcatraz

Source: U.S. National Library of Medicine

with non-Natives, who claimed that Native Americans were receiving special treatment from the government (DeLoria, 1993; Nash et al., 2004).

Child Welfare Another target of Native American activism was government policy regarding child welfare. Continuing patterns of Native boarding schools, courts removed many Native American children from their homes during the 1960s and 1970s. By 1978, almost 30 percent of American Indian children were no longer being raised in Native American homes (Tice & Perkins, 2002). Racist child welfare policies and practices led to the wide-scale adoption and out-of-home placement of these children with little regard for preserving their Native heritage. Leah Katherine Hicks Manning, a social worker who was a member of the Shoshone-Paiute tribe and a staff development specialist at the BIA in the 1960s, believed that adoption and foster care policies for Native American children should emphasize keeping them on their reservations or near their families (Mizrahi & Davis, 2008).

Manning, who is profiled in Exhibit 3.9, played a prominent role in developing and advocating for the Indian Child Welfare Act (ICWA), which Congress passed in 1978. The goal of the

> **EXHIBIT 3.9**
>
> *Leah Katherine Hicks Manning*
>
> Leah Katherine Hicks Manning was born on the Nixon Reservation in Nevada in 1917. As a member of the Shoshone-Paiute tribe, Manning played a key role in bringing the needs of Native American families to the attention of Congress. She taught at a Native American primary school and in the early 1960s worked at the Bureau of Indian Affairs, educating social workers on Native American culture and traditions. Manning began her social work studies at the University of Chicago before taking time off to marry Arthur Manning, a chairman of the Shoshone-Paiute tribe who advocated for treaty rights. After raising her family, Manning earned her master's in social work from the University of Utah in 1968.
>
> Manning is responsible for creating what many consider to be the first program that provided social services to Native Americans in Nevada. Manning was the director of this program and supervised Native American professionals who provided substance use prevention, family counseling, public health services, and financial assistance. Manning was a lifetime member at the National Congress of American Indians, and in 1974 the Nevada chapter of NASW named her Social Worker of the Year. On February 12, 1979, Manning, her daughter Tina, and Tina's three children were killed in a fire in her husband's home while they were all sleeping.
>
> *Source*: Indian child welfare act is her legacy (1998). NASW NEWS. Retrieved November 13, 2012, from **www.socialworkers.org/profession/centennial/manning.htm**

Act was to strengthen and preserve Native American families and culture. It reestablished tribal authority over the adoption of Native American children. The ICWA also requires "active" efforts rather than "reasonable" efforts to avoid out-of-home placement for Native American children, a distinction that holds the system to higher standards. To learn more about the history of ICWA, go to the website of the National Indian Child Welfare Association (**www.nicwa.org**).

Affirmative Action

The policy transition from nondiscrimination to affirmative action was a major development that affected opportunities and economic status for oppressed groups. **Affirmative action** is a general term that refers to policies and programs designed to compensate for discrimination. To redress losses to groups that suffered discrimination and to ameliorate current discriminatory practices, affirmative action policies establish criteria that give these groups preferential access to opportunities, most importantly in education and employment.

Affirmative Action and Employment Title VII of the Civil Rights Act of 1964 prohibits employment discrimination based on race, color, religion, or national origin and empowers the federal courts to "order such affirmative action as may be appropriate" to remedy past injustices. While affirmative action was initially limited to such actions as reinstating employees who had been unjustly terminated, the concept was broadened in the ensuing years. For example, Executive Order 11246, issued September 24, 1965, required all government contractors to submit written "Compliance Reports" that specify the number and percentage of women and workers of color on their projects (Weiss, 1997).

In 1969, the so-called "Philadelphia Plan" went even further, mandating that government contractors submit numerical goals and timetables for hiring women and workers of color. It also empowered the government to cancel the contracts of employers who failed to comply with these regulations and to prohibit them from receiving future contracts. Opponents contended that these policies resulted in fixed quotas and reverse discrimination (Weiss, 1997). **Reverse discrimination** is defined as discrimination against the dominant group due to policies designed to redress discrimination against minority groups. As we will discuss in Chapter 7, affirmative action battles have played out in disputes and legal decisions related not only to hiring but also to university admissions.

Changes in Social Work

The social service sector continued to grow in the 1970s as the for-profit and voluntary sectors expanded (Reid, 1995). As social workers lobbied for legislation that would require practitioners to be licensed at the state level, some have asserted that the profession moved away from involvement with policy and large-scale social change (Tice & Perkins, 2002). Licensure proponents argued that licensure would protect the public, raise the status of the profession, shield social workers from competition, and enable social workers to receive direct payments. However, because licensure requirements can reduce the ability of low-income people and people of color to practice social work and can deny some populations and regions adequate access to social work services, these moves have led some to charge that social work is an elitist profession. Specht and Courtney (1994) expanded on factors that influenced the shift in professional emphasis. In their book, *Unfaithful Angels: How Social Work Has Abandoned Its Mission*, they state that: "Social workers have been socialized for more than seventy years to believe that psychiatry, psychoanalysis, and humanistic psychology are appropriate means for dealing with social problems" (p. 28). However, as the NASW Code of Ethics, the profession's statements on a wide range of policy issues, and the activist orientations of many social workers attest, the profession's historic emphasis on collective responsibility for poor and oppressed populations has not been extinguished.

RETRENCHMENT TO IMPERILED PROGRESS: 1981 TO 2016

Ronald Reagan's inauguration in 1981 ushered in an era of conservative politics reminiscent of earlier periods when there was little support for a federal social safety net. Reagan did not cut spending on all social programs, however. Instead, his administration primarily targeted social welfare programs directed toward low-income people and other marginalized groups. While Medicare expenditures increased during his tenure, the administration used a portrayal of the welfare state as a failed social experiment to rationalize curtailing funding for programs that meet the basic needs of those in and near poverty (Reid, 1995). These decisions were not isolated policy changes or responses to economic cycles. Instead, they reflected an ideological shift.

During the last decades of the twentieth century and the beginning of the twenty-first, the locus of responsibility for assuring individual and social well-being shifted away from the federal government. It fell instead to states and localities, which have less capacity to confront significant challenges, and onto the shoulders of individuals in need themselves. This marked a dramatic departure from the policy orientation reflected in New Deal initiatives, when policy moved away from blaming those unemployed and/or poor for their own plights. In the Reagan era, conservative policymakers and pundits realized that dismantling the social safety net would require reshaping the **social contract** that governs people's expectations of what core benefits government will provide as part of societal membership. Therefore, they sought to locate responsibility for hardship within the behaviors and attributes of people in poverty. According to this worldview, reducing or even eliminating housing, nutrition, and cash assistance is not an inexcusable assault on poor families. Rather, these cuts are an act of charity that rescues people from the trap of government assistance and dependency (Pear, 1986) or, at least, a fair outcome of families' own failings. Some have also justified cuts in social welfare spending as reinvestments in the private sector, believed to fuel economic growth. In this framing, government itself is often seen as part of the problem.

An increased focus on individual responsibility rather than on shared risk is not limited to the welfare policy arena. You may see the effects of this change in your own life or that of your family, perhaps in the shift from corporate pensions that guaranteed retired workers a given benefit in later life to defined contribution plans, where the value of one's retirement benefits depends largely on individual initiative. Students may recognize this trend in tuition increases and cuts in need-based student financial aid—erosions of public commitment to higher education that have contributed to a dramatic increase in student borrowing.

Consistent with this social policy approach, Reagan pressed for **devolution**, whereby responsibility for social welfare increasingly was transferred from the federal government to the states. He also sought to increase reliance on the private sector to provide social welfare services, often through arrangements of **privatization**, where ownership or control is transferred from government to private enterprise. Typically, in the United States, privatization has meant allocating public funds to private entities that then provide the benefits or services. Conservative politicians have claimed that these policies "give every American a stake in the promise and future of our country" and "build an ownership society" (Bush, 2005). Underscoring the insecurity that accompanies the fraying of the safety net, political scientist Jacob Hacker characterizes these policy changes as emphasizing individual responsibility rather than collective well-being. Hacker has termed the result "the great risk shift"—more *on your ownership* than authentically empowering (Hacker, 2006).

Different in scope but not entirely novel, policies that complement individual initiative are not necessarily unhelpful to disadvantaged Americans. Indeed, in the past, government policies such as the Homestead Act and the GI Bill required considerable individual sacrifice *and* helped many poor families build assets. Policies to promote ownership are often premised on the underlying ideology that increasing people's ability to control their own lives and wealth, rather than relying on government transfers, best promotes their well-being. This belief aligns with social work values of self-determination, dignity, and autonomy. In practice, however, the resulting policies have seldom catalyzed new approaches to social intervention. Instead, this approach has served more to excuse retrenchment, retreat from collective commitment, and position people as responsible for their own difficulties.

Implementing a Conservative Agenda

In addition to curtailing spending on social programs for low-income Americans and couching this retreat as consistent with American values of self-reliance, Reagan successfully lobbied Congress to reduce taxes, especially on higher earners, and to increase defense spending. Reagan's approach of decreasing taxes on the wealthy people and corporations, dubbed "supply-side economics," was supposed to dampen inflation, spur economic growth, and revive the sluggish economy. However, economic growth continued to lag during the 1980s supply-side era compared to the non-supply-side era of the 1990s (Ettlinger & Linden, 2012). In combination, then, these policies increased the national debt. This allowed Reagan to justify cuts in social welfare spending as necessary to hold the debt in check. This was highly strategic, as endorsing tax cuts can garner taxpayer support for benefit cuts without having to directly attack programs for those living in poverty.

Social policies championed by President Reagan emphasized individual pathology as the reason that people could not meet their needs. Even those with disabilities were not spared. New rules defining disability restricted access for many people with addictions and mental illnesses, and program administrators turned away unprecedented numbers of applicants. Many people already receiving disability were afraid to pursue any sort of rehabilitation for fear that they would lose their benefits.

While the net effect of policies in the Reagan administration was to remove supports for low-income and vulnerable Americans, President Reagan did institute a significant policy change that meant millions of children and adults with serious disabilities, who had formerly only been able to receive Medicaid long-term care services in institutions, could begin receiving these services in their homes. In 1981, he approved legislation creating Medicaid Home- and Community-Based Waivers. Now, states could apply for a waiver that allowed Medicaid funds to pay for long-term supports and services in the community. This program helped end the practice of institutionalizing children with disabilities.

The combination of tax cuts and reduced social welfare spending was supposed to encourage wealthy households to donate more money to charity. Thus, there would be less need for federal government involvement in social welfare. In fact, it was asserted that some traditional public social programs could be privatized and their functions assumed by nonprofit entities financed by charitable contributions. However, leaders from major charities knew they could never garner sufficient private resources to replace public social programs. In reality, a shift from public to private funding often leads to cuts in services and benefits.

New Federalism, OBRA, and Devolution

The changes in the social contract during this period were not confined to just public/private relationships. The Reagan Administration also sought to restructure the relationship between the federal and state governments. The administration's policy, labeled "New Federalism," transferred more social welfare responsibility to the states. Specifically, Reagan proposed that states assume all costs for the Food Stamp Program, SSI, and AFDC. The federal government would take full responsibility for Medicaid.

OBRA and Block Grants Although the Reagan Administration was unable to convert this vision into reality, it did preside over passage of the Omnibus Budget Reconciliation Act (OBRA) of 1981, which reduced funding for and access to social programs. For example, OBRA reduced funding for food stamps by 19 percent and for AFDC by 11 percent and also tightened eligibility requirements for AFDC.

OBRA also transformed the nature of federal assistance to the states. Specifically, it consolidated dozens of **categorical grants**—in which the federal government strictly regulated how the monies were spent for programs such as community development, mental health, addiction treatment, social services, and maternal and child health services—into a much smaller number of **block grants**, which allocated much of the decision-making authority to the states (Kenney, 1981). Under the changed funding structure, states no longer had to provide matching funds to receive federal funds. The block grants allowed state and local governments greater latitude to direct federal funds toward specific social problems. However, this increased flexibility came at a cost. OBRA reduced federal funding for each block by between 25 and 30 percent (Walker, 1987). Additionally, the loss of state matching funds resulted in funding decreases as great as 50 percent. By 1984, the poverty rate had risen to 15 percent, its highest level since the 1960s (Tice & Perkins, 2002).

Funding for community mental health centers was collapsed into block grants that could be used for a variety of mental health services. This diminished centers' ability to provide the services necessary to enable people with serious mental illness to successfully live in the community. States were attempting to deinstitutionalize more people who had lived in state mental hospitals, and community mental health centers were unable to fulfill the promise of community treatment for all these people as state hospitals closed. In this vacuum, other institutions, such as prisons and nursing facilities, began to house increasing numbers of people with serious mental illness. This shift continues; although recent efforts to combat homelessness and increase law enforcement's competence to deal with people with mental illness have resulted in some progress, record numbers of people with mental illness are in our prisons and on our streets.

From Reagan to Bush George H. W. Bush took office in 1989, vowing to follow in Reagan's footsteps by holding the line on domestic spending, avoiding a tax increase, promoting a conservative social agenda, and maintaining a strong national defense. However, circumstances and activism on the part of some marginalized groups sometimes pressured him to change course. For example, in 1991, mounting racial tension exploded into race riots in Los Angeles, following the acquittal of four White police officers who were videotaped beating Rodney King, an African American, after a high-speed car chase. In November of that year, after two years of debates, vetoes, and threatened vetoes, President Bush reversed himself and signed the Civil Rights Act of 1991. This Act strengthened existing civil rights laws and provided for damages in cases of intentional employment discrimination. However, not all groups experiencing discrimination were included. Two years later, almost one million people participated in the third National March on Washington to demand equal rights for LGBTQ+ Americans and an end to discrimination based on sexual orientation.

One group achieved a major breakthrough during the Bush years. In 1990, Congress passed the Americans with Disabilities Act (ADA), which prohibited discrimination against people with disabilities in employment, public accommodations, and transportation. Exhibit 3.10

EXHIBIT 3.10

President George H. W. Bush Signing the ADA

Source: George Bush Presidential Library and Museum

commemorates President Bush's signing of this landmark legislation. The ADA provides a clear example of how legislation that builds on strengths can be passed in a conservative era. The Act had dedicated support from the disability advocacy community. The Disability Rights Movement had a long legacy of activism and demanded active participation in drafting any legislation that impacted them. Advocates worked tirelessly and shrewdly to see this legislation passed. Additionally, the ADA's emphasis on work and opportunity spoke to traditional American values and therefore attracted the endorsement of many conservatives.

Advocates for people in need had hoped that the collapse of the Soviet Union and the fall of communism throughout Eastern Europe would lead the United States to cut defense spending and direct greater attention to domestic issues. However, with few exceptions, Bush generally maintained the priorities of the Reagan era. In a sluggish economy, Bush was not reelected.

"New Democrats" and Social Welfare Policy

Bill Clinton, who identified with the then-ascendant moderate wing of the Democratic Party, was elected in 1992. In 1985, Clinton had helped co-found the Democratic Leadership Council, which sought to establish middle ground between more liberal Democrats, who championed income redistribution, civil rights protections, and reductions in defense spending, and "new Democrats," who focused on a narrower range of economic reforms such as job training, infrastructure improvement, free trade, and balanced budgets. "New Democrats" emphasized the needs of the middle class, in part because they feared that Democrats were losing voters who believed that the party was putting the interests of low-income groups and racial minorities over those of the majority of Americans (Tice & Perkins, 2002). Some of the policy initiatives of the Clinton Administration provided much-needed help for diverse constituencies. At the same time, replacing AFDC with TANF was a giant step backward in the effort to provide economic security for the nation's children.

While President Clinton's actions on social welfare, particularly cash assistance, were remarkably aligned with the Republicans who preceded and followed him, his approach to tax policy diverged substantially. The 1993 Clinton tax increases meant high earners and corporations had to pay higher rates. Other tax changes included increasing the taxable portion of Social Security benefits and raising transportation fuel taxes. In the ensuing years, the national debt decreased.

Family Leave and People with Disabilities The Clinton Administration advanced reforms that assisted families and people with disabilities. In 1993, Congress passed the Family and Medical Leave Act (FMLA). This law required larger employers to guarantee a 12-week unpaid leave period for workers following births or adoptions or if the employee or an immediate family member has a serious health condition. In 1999, Congress passed the Ticket to Work and Work Incentives Improvement Act. This legislation allowed millions of Americans with disabilities to remain eligible for Medicaid or Medicare if they became employed. Prior to its passage, many people with disabilities were reluctant to work out of fear of losing their health care coverage. The law also provided vouchers to pay for vocational rehabilitation and enabled more Americans with disabilities to lessen their dependence on public benefits (Social Security Administration, 2007).

Health Care: The Reform That Did Not Happen The Clinton Administration's efforts to reform health care were far less successful. In 1994, Clinton supported the Health Security Act, which proposed extending medical coverage to 95 percent of Americans by 2000 and establishing a commission to devise a strategy to reach the remaining 5 percent. The plan would have required many employers to assume some of the costs of coverage. The effort failed, and in 1994, voters elected a Republican Congress, ushering in the Contract with America.

The Contract with America and the PRWORA The Contract with America was a series of conservative proposals sponsored by the Speaker of the House, Republican Newt Gingrich. A major focus of the Contract was to further decrease the role of the federal government in providing for social welfare. Among other initiatives, it included reducing taxes on capital gains and imposing a "gag rule" that prohibited medical practitioners who receive Medicaid payments from discussing abortion as an option with their patients (Drew, 1996).

Supporters of the Contract helped propel the passage of the Personal Responsibility and Work Opportunity Reconciliation Act of 1996 (PRWORA). On August 22, 1996, after vetoing two earlier versions, President Clinton, who campaigned on a promise to "reform welfare as we know it," signed PRWORA into law (Carcasson, 2006). This law replaced AFDC with Temporary Assistance for Needy Families (TANF), thereby canceling the 1935 Social Security Act's federal guarantee of support for poor children. As a block grant, TANF varies considerably from state to state; further, if a state runs out of money, it can terminate TANF payments. Supporters of this legislation carefully orchestrated the debate to focus attention on women's morality (childbearing outside of marriage) and work, rather than on the needs of poor children or the impossibilities of the labor market for mothers with young children and few skills. TANF limited recipients to five years of lifetime support and imposed stringent work requirements. TANF also sought to promote marriage by removing some barriers to welfare in two-parent households and funding marriage classes (Horn, 2001).

TANF echoed colonial Poor Laws in its return to an emphasis on local responsibility. PRWORA limited food stamps and SSI benefits for legal immigrants and left provision of Medicaid, TANF, and Title XX benefits for legal immigrants up to the discretion of each state. Indeed, these were the principal ways TANF supporters were able to tout the law's financial savings. Soon after the passage of the PRWORA, benefits were reinstated for legal immigrants who had resided in the United States prior to the passage of the Act. However, it still denied benefits to new immigrants for their first five years of lawful permanent residency. These actions signaled reduced national responsibility for "strangers" entering the country, as the immigration debate increasingly centered on concerns that large-scale immigration would drive up the costs of public education and aid.

Because of economic prosperity during the second Clinton Administration, more low-income people were able to find jobs, which somewhat obscured the harsh effects of the adverse policies. However, policy changes had severely weakened the safety net for low-income families, leaving them extraordinarily vulnerable in economic downturns. Many of these families were headed by single women. Although most single mothers support their children without TANF benefits, most families receiving TANF are headed by single women. The lack of adequate childcare and few job options beyond minimum wage leave children in these families at great risk of negative outcomes.

The 1997 passage of federal legislation establishing the State Children's Health Insurance Program (SCHIP) provided some help regarding children's health. SCHIP, a successful reform that resulted from the Clinton Administration's work to increase access to health care, authorizes states to offer health insurance to children, up to the age of 19, who are not already insured. This program, covered in detail in Chapter 10, made health insurance for children much more widely available.

The Contested Election of 2000

George W. Bush became the first president of the twenty-first century. Bush lost the popular vote but, after intervention by the U.S. Supreme Court to halt vote recounting, he won a narrow Electoral College victory. Some observers see the roots of today's intensifying partisan divides, increasing politicization of the courts, and growing mistrust of the integrity of U.S. election systems in the chaotic 2000 election and the Supreme Court's 5–4 decision in *Bush v. Gore* (Semet, Persily, & Ansolabehere, 2014). With the election marred by voting irregularities in Florida, including technical failures and racially disproportionate voter purges, the spectacle of a presidential election that hinged on just 537 votes hung over the new administration. However, relatively shortly after the Bush presidency began, the terrorist attacks on September 11,

2001 turned attention to global threats. George W. Bush's tenure was wracked by economic and political turmoil as the economy slumped and the United States went to war in Afghanistan and Iraq. Changing policies toward torture and concern about eroding civil rights, particularly for Muslims or those presumed to be Muslim, marked this period. With Republicans in control of the White House and both houses of Congress and the public occupied with security concerns, resources and services for vulnerable Americans were scaled back in many areas.

Privatization and Faith-Based Initiatives Like the Reagan and first Bush Administrations, George W. Bush sought to increase reliance on and funding for faith-based initiatives, even as the percentage of Americans with no religious affiliation was increasing (Pew Research Center, 2015). Proposals to strengthen faith-based social services received both support and criticism from religious institutions, many of which were interested in expanding their ministry but wary of assuming financial and organizational responsibilities they could not meet. State experiments with turning over adoption and foster care services to religiously based organizations had already driven some of these entities into bankruptcy (Kansas Action for Children, 2001). As we saw in our examination of the Great Depression, relying solely on nongovernmental institutions for social services, particularly during economic downturns, is not economically viable or morally defensible social policy.

Medicare Part D, which began in 2006, uses a private sector strategy to provide prescription drug benefits for people receiving Medicare. For-profit pharmaceutical and insurance companies lobbied hard for this legislation. In contrast to traditional Medicare, in which the government generally chooses benefits and sets prices, for Medicare Part D, elders and people with disabilities must choose their plans from a large variety of often-confusing private options. There is no question that this benefit has helped many people afford costly prescription drugs; however, making it more cost-effective and sustainable remains a challenge.

Tax Cuts and Reduced Benefits In keeping with supply-side economic policy, George W. Bush reversed many of Clinton's tax policies. By combining tax cuts with increased defense spending, George W. Bush followed the Reagan playbook to limit the money available for social services without directly attacking popular programs. Growth in the federal debt, illustrated in Exhibit 3.11, eroded the nation's capacity for future investments in shared prosperity (Linden & Ettlinger, 2011). Hundreds of thousands of Americans who qualified for assistance were put on waiting lists or were turned away from public agencies when they applied for help with childcare, meals, utility bills, and housing (Claxton & Hansen, 2004), while those with higher incomes benefited from lower taxes. Further, because federal and state tax codes are often linked, diminished tax revenues also necessitated cuts at the state level. Essentially, this was a reverse government redistribution of wealth.

As a result, structural barriers that keep people in poverty were reinforced, and the distance between the haves and the have-nots increased. In 2008, the last full year of the Bush presidency, the increased poverty rate was accompanied by a decline in real median household income, from $52,163 to $50,303 (U.S. Census Bureau, 2009). In the face of worldwide economic crisis brought on by the collapse of U.S. financial markets, surging home foreclosure rates, declining property values, and high unemployment, many began to question the

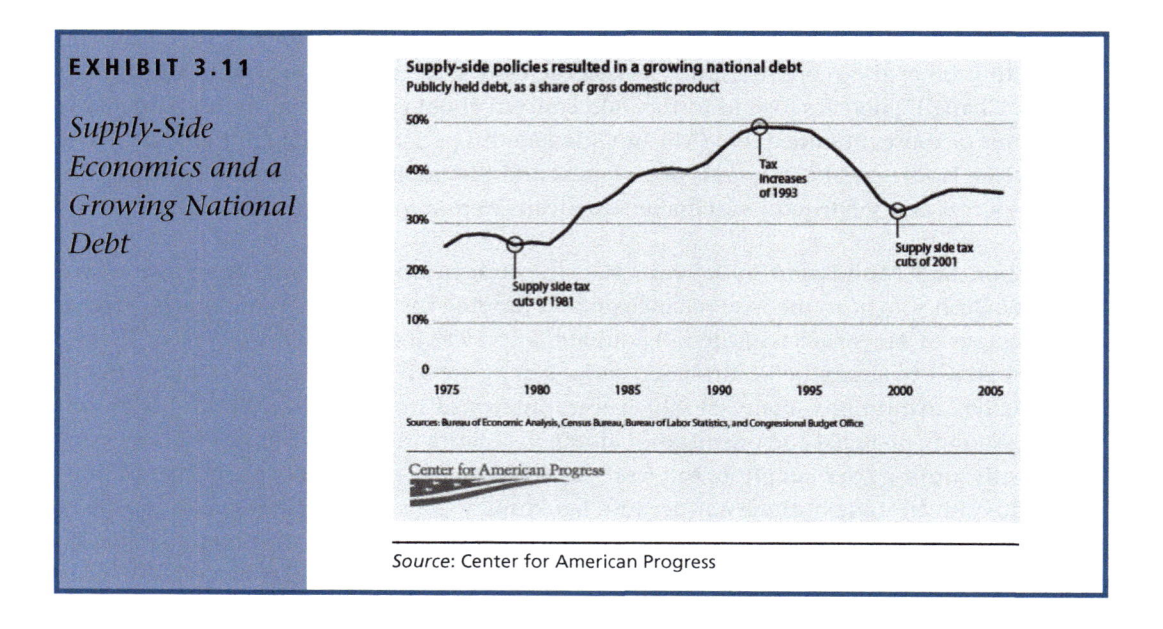

EXHIBIT 3.11

Supply-Side Economics and a Growing National Debt

Supply-side policies resulted in a growing national debt
Publicly held debt, as a share of gross domestic product

- Supply side tax cuts of 1981
- Tax increases of 1993
- Supply side tax cuts of 2001

Sources: Bureau of Economic Analysis, Census Bureau, Bureau of Labor Statistics, and Congressional Budget Office

Center for American Progress

Source: Center for American Progress

---

free-market ideology and lack of regulation that had characterized the Bush presidency. Beset by growing economic turmoil and two ongoing wars, voters in 2008 elected Barack Obama, a Democrat and the first African-American president of the United States.

A Turning of the Tide

Barack Obama won 52 percent of the popular vote and took office with Democratic majorities in both houses of Congress. Although his campaign centered on the need for change in the regulation of financial markets, health care reform, and action to address climate change, economic crises became the focus of the election and the first part of his presidency. After bringing unprecedented numbers of young people and voters of color into a coalition that advanced a message of hope for the future, Obama promised a "new foundation" that would provide for economic growth and greater security. Repudiating the conservative belief that public programs somehow harm the social order, Obama saw government as part of the solution: adequate, publicly funded income security and health care programs not only make it possible for citizens to weather economic downturns, they also keep money flowing in the economy when unemployment is high. Competent government employees are crucial to the administration of public programs and the effective enforcement of regulations such as those that might have prevented the disastrous 2010 British Petroleum (BP) oil spill or the risky financial arrangements that contributed to the housing market collapse that began in 2007.

As many middle-class families in the United States lost jobs, health insurance, and stable housing in what became known as the Great Recession, more people realized that public supports were inadequate. The resulting tumult helped catalyze reforms. However, as during the Great Depression, reform initiatives sparked fierce debate. Many people opposed strengthening the public health and welfare safety net. Concern about rising national debt and its effects on overall economic stability remained a central issue. Nonetheless, the scope and scale of the Great Recession prompted substantial policy change. Foreclosure rates quadrupled, and housing values collapsed (Ellen & Dastrup, 2012). The economy lost almost nine million jobs and the unemployment rate rose to 10 percent, with unemployed people staying jobless for long periods and many becoming discouraged and leaving the labor market altogether (CBPP, 2018a). In 2010, three in four people were either laid off or had a close friend or relative out of work (Godofsky, van Horn, & Zukin, 2010). In some industries, the losses of the Great Recession approached those of the Depression of the 1930s. One in three construction workers and one in four manufacturing workers lost their jobs. State income tax receipts fell 27 percent between 2008 and 2009, and sales taxes fell 17 percent (Gordon, 2012). The U.S. economy appeared to be in a free fall. Many economists were talking about the likelihood of another global depression.

Before leaving office, the Bush Administration convinced Congress to provide $700 billion in additional funding to shore up failing financial markets. Then, the new Congress hurriedly passed the American Recovery and Reinvestment Act (ARRA), which provided $787 billion in economic stimulus, shortly after Obama became president. Some of these dollars went directly to low-income and otherwise vulnerable households, in the form of targeted tax relief and expansions of Medicaid, SNAP, and other means-tested programs, while other funds went to stabilize local and state government budgets. Although most analysts conclude that the economy grew more quickly than it would have without any stimulus (Carlino, 2017), recovery has been slow, uneven, and, like so much of the U.S. economy, unequal (Pfeffer, Danziger, & Schoeni, 2013; Smeeding, 2012). The effects of the Great Recession on households' labor market prospects and wealth holdings have been long-lasting (Greenstone & Looney, 2013; Irons, 2009), and declining tax revenues and increased expenditures combined to increase the national debt.

Even as the Great Recession has largely faded from public discussion, then, its scars remain. Companies replaced workers without advanced degrees with higher-skilled workers who had lost their jobs, "contractors" who worked in informal arrangements without job security or a workplace safety net, or machines that never need a day off to care for a sick child (Foote & Ryan, 2015; Hershbein & Kahn, 2018; Yagan, 2018). As robots play ever-larger roles in some industries, these effects may be permanent. Housing recovery has been far stronger in already-wealthy areas than disadvantaged ones, which further exacerbates wealth inequality. As has been true in previous downturns, households of color suffered more in the recession, as they were more likely to be victims of predatory lenders and live in communities hardest hit by lost property value (Burd-Sharps & Rasch, 2015). The prolonged unemployment and financial stress of the Great Recession have dire health consequences that will continue, potentially for generations (Garfield, McLanahan, & Wimer, 2016). And, critically, the Great Recession's intensification of inequality—and the fact that few of the powerful interests culpable for its creation were publicly held accountable—are believed to have contributed to today's political mood, as those who feel justifiably wronged by existing arrangements were eager to support politicians who promised dramatic change and claimed to be earnest defenders of a lost era and the "forgotten" American worker (Bradlee, 2018). Social workers have been on the frontlines and have seen how the recession accelerated declines in upward mobility and erosion of the middle class. Social work advocates have a responsibility to ensure that policymakers learn the lessons of this dark time in recent history and build policy structures that are more recession-proof than is the case today.

Health Care President Obama's strategy was to promote economic recovery by investing in infrastructure and job creation, particularly "green" jobs that would help produce cleaner energy. Obama also moved aggressively to enact health care reform. The United States spends much more on health care per person than any other country and evidences poorer outcomes than other advanced economies in many areas (Papanicolas, Woskie, & Jha, 2018). Because many business and health care leaders, as well as most Americans, were dissatisfied with the existing system, it appeared that the time might be right to overhaul health care policy. Unlike the proposals of the Clinton Administration, however, Obama did not advocate direct government provision of health care. Rather, he pressed for a pluralistic system that included the private sector. The government's role would be to ensure all citizens had health insurance and to regulate features of the health care plans that covered them. Although single-payer health care systems, where the government collects health care funding and pays for services, are favored globally because they can help control costs, it was clear there was insufficient support to implement such a system in the United States. Indeed, even a public insurance option that would have provided more choice for consumers and more competition for insurance companies could not garner congressional majorities. Negotiating within these political constraints, President Obama signed a comprehensive health reform law (Exhibit 3.12), the Patient Protection and Affordable Care Act of 2010 (Public Law 111-148) as modified by the Health Care and Education Affordability Reconciliation Act (H. R. 4872) (Gorin, 2010). This Act was a major victory for his administration and an important step toward ensuring health care for all Americans. This legislation and its implications are discussed in detail in Chapter 10.

EXHIBIT 3.12

President Obama Signs the Affordable Care Act

Source: Whitehouse.gov

Immigration Buoyed by strong support and unprecedented voter turnout among the growing Latinx and Asian American electorates in 2008, then-candidate Obama promised to address the nation's broken immigration system. However, the struggling economy, battles over health care reform, continued anti-immigrant sentiment, and congressional reluctance to take up the complex and controversial legislation stymied his plans for an immigration overhaul. As the 2012 election loomed, immigrants and their advocates expressed dismay that President Obama had deported more people than any previous chief executive, while failing to deliver the reforms so badly needed. At least partly in response, the Department of Homeland Security, in June 2012, used its existing authority to grant deferred action for some immigrants who arrived in the United States as children, thus protecting them from deportation and making them eligible for legal work.

Building on this limited victory, the Obama Administration proposed deferred action for a broader group of immigrant adults. However, that measure was immediately enjoined as an overreach of executive authority. In 2016, the eight-member Supreme Court (after the death of Justice Scalia) deadlocked on the ruling. This left the lower court's ruling to stand and thus prevented implementation of the policy. High-profile events, such as the arrival of unaccompanied children fleeing violence in Latin America in the summer of 2014 and actions in many states in 2015 to resist refugee resettlement from some majority-Muslim nations, sparked greater attention to immigration, particularly among those strongly opposed to or in favor of immigrant rights.

Muted Gains in Obama's Second Term The economy failed to improve dramatically during President Obama's first term, and many conservative Republicans swept into Congress in 2010. Although most of the individual components of health reform legislation were quite popular, repeal of the Affordable Care Act was a cornerstone of the Republican agenda. In 2012, the Supreme Court upheld key provisions of the Affordable Care Act, including the mandate that everyone have insurance. However, somewhat surprisingly, the Court struck down penalties for states that do not expand Medicaid to provide health care for all nonelderly people with incomes below 133 percent of the poverty line (Kaiser Family Foundation, 2012). This left governors who were ideologically opposed to this approach or politically committed to thwarting President Obama with a choice between improving the health of their populations, at little cost to the state, and rejecting significant federal dollars in order to stand on principle against the ACA. In Chapter 10, we will see how this decision has constrained the ACA's impact on reducing the size of the uninsured population.

The 2012 presidential election, the first following the U.S. Supreme Court decision in *Citizens United v. Federal Election Commission* (2010) that essentially negated limits on campaign spending, broke all previous expenditure records. The status of the economic recovery was the driving issue in the election, in which Obama again successfully organized a wide coalition of voters, including people of color, young people, and women. In total, President Obama brought 15 million new voters into the electoral process, 69 percent of whom voted for him, reshaping the political landscape as the nation grew more diverse (Anderson, 2018). The early part of President Obama's second term continued to focus on economic growth, although critical incidents and pent-up frustration over congressional failures vaulted other priorities to the agenda as well. Several horrific mass shootings sparked a push for gun control, changing demographics helped to drive renewed emphasis on immigration reform, and social issues such as same-sex marriage and access to birth control continued to be contentious.

Large Bush Administration tax cuts in 2001 and 2003, the collapse of the financial markets in 2008, and the cost of two wars have increased the country's debt dramatically. President Obama faced the daunting challenge of reducing debt while sustaining the educational, economic, health, and welfare infrastructure. Additionally, as climate change intensified the dangers of hurricanes and other natural disasters (Reed et al., 2018), these events became increasingly damaging and costly (U.S. Global Change Research Group, 2018). Disasters also kept the climate threat in the public consciousness. Obama, who had promised to prioritize environmental issues, signed a historic international climate accord in Paris in 2015. Terrorism and the tradeoffs between privacy and security also demanded attention. In the face of congressional gridlock, Obama, like many Republican and Democratic presidents before him, used Executive Orders to act on some fronts. For example, in 2013, Defense Secretary Leon Panetta signed a memorandum lifting a ban on women serving in combat. In 2016, the military officially recognized transgender individuals serving in the military and committed to paying for gender transition surgery for service members. The Obama Administration also used Executive Orders to respond to gun violence and protect public lands and natural resources. These pieces of Obama's legacy would prove fleeting, however, as the 2016 election of Donald Trump sparked a rash of executive activity and regulatory retreat.

President Obama worked on many fronts to ensure that his presidency would be significant for reasons other than his identity as the first African-American elected to this high office. He attracted significant percentages of White voters and consistently referenced themes of American democracy, opportunity, and equality. On his election night in 2008, Obama said, "If there is anyone out there who still doubts that America is a place where all things are possible; who still wonders if the dream of our founders is alive in our time; who still questions the power of our democracy, tonight is your answer."

However, political fractures remained, and Obama faced unprecedented allegations questioning his citizenship, faith, and patriotism. Further, a significant portion of the electorate felt their needs were largely ignored. Crucially, while previous elections have often centered on economic concerns, alienation and loss of dignity and cultural identity are especially salient for some demographics today (Cramer, 2016; Hochschild, 2018). While the nation continues to grapple with how our political landscape is changing, evidence suggests that at least some of the 2016 election outcome can be attributed to racial animosity, fear of losing privileged status, and backlash against the election of a Black president (Mutz, 2018). Sexism clearly played a role in the 2016 outcome as well. Analysis has shown that some voters—both men and women—still hold sexist beliefs about women that influenced their preference for a male candidate (Maxwell & Shields, 2017). Further, while Donald Trump relied on a predominantly White electorate, Democratic activists struggled to activate Obama's multiracial coalition without him on the ballot, particularly after states' voter suppression efforts had locked millions of Americans out of the electoral process. Ultimately, Hillary Clinton, the 2016 Democratic candidate, was unable to break the final "glass ceiling" to become the first woman president of the United States.

THE TRUMP PRESIDENCY: RETURN TO TAX CUTS, UNWINDING THE ADMINISTRATIVE STATE, AND NEW THREATS

Having promised to "Make America Great Again," Donald Trump rode his personal celebrity and a surge of nationalist and protectionist impulses to victory in the 2016 election. Before the end of his first year in office, Trump had subverted norms that have long governed U.S. politics. He used Twitter to announce personnel changes and major policy initiatives, defended and befriended foreign leaders with reputations for human rights abuses and interference in American political affairs, and frequently contradicted himself. Where other presidents—both Republican and Democrat—have at least made attempts at bipartisan collaboration, Trump's large public rallies abandoned all pretense of national unity. He personally attacked Democrats and even members of his own party who opposed or criticized him, refused to cooperate with congressional inquiries, sought foreign involvement in U.S. political matters, and vowed legal action against those who threaten his interests. In what many see as a damaging attempt to undermine free expression, Trump is particularly critical of news media, repeatedly calling the press "the enemy of the people." He describes the United States as under siege and in need of a strong defender, and he has positioned himself in this powerful role. Notably, many Republicans have proven willing to condone or at least tolerate behavior from Trump they would otherwise denounce.

It is not yet known what the long-term effects of Trump's presidency will be. Certainly, he has changed perceptions about the highest office, rewritten assumptions about how federal policy change happens, and intensified polarization. In other respects, however, his tenure echoes that of other conservative presidents. The sizable tax cuts he championed through Congress in December 2017—the Tax Cuts and Jobs Act (TCJA)—cut the maximum corporate income tax rate, provided a deduction for pass-through income, and increased the estate tax exemption, all changes that primarily benefit households in the upper income and wealth brackets (Gale et al., 2018). As with the tax cuts of the Reagan and George W. Bush eras, the TCJA not only makes after-tax income more unequal, it also reduces overall federal revenues. As was anticipated before TCJA passed, analysis has found that TCJA reduced projected revenues by $275 billion in 2018 (Gale & Krupkin, 2019). These reductions may now be used as justification for spending cuts to avoid increases in the federal deficit.

Today, Donald Trump looms large in all policy developments and conversations. Even though he was not on the ballot, more than two-thirds of voters said that Trump motivated their vote in the 2018 midterms—among both those who support and oppose him (Agiesta, Luhby, & Sparks, 2018). The political storm of his impeachment proceedings overshadowed even the large Democratic presidential field in 2020. Perhaps more even than other presidents, both his style and substance are the center of national attention. While it can be difficult to avoid getting caught up in the vortex that swirls around the president, his statements, and the churning of his staff, social workers must remain focused on the effects of policy changes on those we serve.

In late 2018, when the dispute between President Trump's insistence on funding for a border wall between the United States and Mexico led to the longest government shutdown in U.S. history, much of the media coverage focused on the potential political fallout.

Pundits debated whether American voters primarily held President Trump or congressional Democrats responsible and argued about whether a physical barrier other than a wall would appease the president's demands.

Social workers, however, focused on the human consequences, including the 800,000 federal workers, many of whom were thrown into economic crisis when they abruptly missed two paychecks. The NASW issued a statement shortly before the government reopened, citing the "heavy toll on many NASW members and the often financially fragile clients they serve" (2019). For social workers whose clients were affected by the lapse in subsidized housing contracts, delays in processing long-awaited tax refunds, interruptions in Violence Against Women Act grants, or worries about loss of essential food assistance, the 35-day shutdown illustrated an imperative but often-forgotten truth: the federal government and the resources it expends are crucial to Americans' lives. During the shutdown, many essential government functions stopped, including not only direct financial benefits but also key activities in oversight, data collection and analysis, and communication. These functions are often invisible and unappreciated; however, as is often the case, they were missed in their absence. More than one in five Americans reported being personally inconvenienced by the shutdown, as many people realized only after the fact just how much the federal government matters. The Congressional Budget Office estimated that the five-week government shutdown cost $11 billion (2019a). However, measured in terms of increased anxiety, damage to public lands, plummeting federal worker morale, and escalated safety risks, the total cost was far greater. When Congress and the president struggled to reach a budget agreement just weeks later, the public mood was so decisively against a shutdown that Trump ultimately signed a bill that pushed federal spending beyond what he had wanted, gave federal workers a pay raise, and omitted his preferences on contentious issues such as gun policy and abortion.

Making people's lives the center of policy analysis points to three domains where the actions and inactions of the Trump Administration are especially likely to leave a lasting legacy: use of regulatory levers to retreat from social policy advances, reshaping of the federal judiciary, and the attempt to redefine what it means to be an "American" and the social contract that comes with this belonging. We conclude this chapter with discussion of evolving action in each of these areas.

Regulatory Retreat

Immediately after his inauguration, President Trump used his executive authority to undermine the Affordable Care Act by signing an executive order allowing federal agencies to not enforce regulations deemed to impose a financial burden on a company, state, or individual. Having pledged to repeal at least two regulations for every new regulation issued, other executive actions followed. By July 2017, the administration had announced a list of 860 pending regulations to be suspended or eliminated. Many undid policy made during the Obama Administration, although others dated back further.

By reducing consumer and worker protections, rolling back environmental standards, and increasing corporate power, most of these regulatory changes are predicted to have negative effects on client groups. For example, the Treasury Department has worked to revise rules that require financial institutions to lend to low-income borrowers. The Consumer Financial Protection Bureau gutted new regulations on payday loans that would have required lenders to verify that borrowers could pay back their loans on time while still covering basic living expenses. The Education Department withdrew a rule that aimed to forgive student debt for defrauded borrowers and increased the standard of proof required to discipline college students accused of sexual assault (*Wall Street Journal*, 2018).

While some of the regulatory retreat could be reversed just as quickly in a subsequent administration, other changes will likely be difficult or even impossible to completely rewind. For example, relaxing environmental rules could cause irrevocable damage to air, water, or endangered species. The administration withdrew a rule limiting carbon emissions—a major contributor to climate change—from coal-powered power plants in 2018 and replaced Obama's Clean Power Plan in 2019. While the long-term effects are still uncertain, Environmental Protection Agency data released in June 2019 revealed a recent decline in air quality in the United States, after years of improvement (Borenstein & Forster, 2019). President Trump also overturned a ban on the use of insecticides—shown to cause brain damage in children—on food crops (*Wall Street Journal*, 2018). Even where rules remain, diminished enforcement compounds the reduction of the federal government's regulatory reach. In the first two years of the Trump Administration, Environmental Protection Agency penalties were 85 percent below the average over the previous two decades (Elperin & Dennis, 2019). This retreat not only hobbles future enforcement by reducing available funds, it also potentially sends a message that environmental damage will be treated leniently.

Civil rights protections have also suffered from deregulation. As history has demonstrated, preserving the rights of those marginalized requires a willingness to not only enact protective policies but also to use government authority to enforce them. The Trump Administration withdrew guidelines that allowed transgender students to use restrooms that correspond to their gender identity and pushed back the Department of Housing and Urban Development rule requiring local governments to submit plans to counter housing segregation. The nonpartisan Brookings Institution maintains a deregulatory tracker to monitor delayed, revoked, and new regulations in key policy domains. To explore the most recent activity, visit **www.brookings.edu/interactives/brookings-deregulatory-tracker/**. In total, these changes underscore the substantial policymaking that occurs outside the legislative process and the need for advocacy not only with elected officials but also the appointed bureaucrats and career civil servants who interpret, implement, and enforce policy.

Reshaping the Federal Judiciary

Judicial appointments are some of the most significant powers of the president. By the midpoint in his presidency, Trump had already had two U.S. Supreme Court nominees confirmed to lifetime appointments. One took the place that would have gone to Barack Obama's nominee, had Senate Majority Leader Mitch McConnell not refused to hold hearings during the final year of Obama's term. The other—Brett Kavanaugh—was almost derailed by sexual assault allegations and an extraordinarily contentious Senate fight. He was ultimately confirmed and, importantly, replaced a moderate "swing" vote. At the levels of district and appeals courts, nominations and confirmations attract less media and public attention. However, these judges have tremendous power to decide cases with far-reaching policy impact. By August 2018, a Republican-controlled Senate had confirmed Trump nominees to occupy 15 percent of the nation's circuit court judgeships, while Trump's confirmations to the court of appeals outpace his predecessors (Wheeler, 2018). Although many of these judges may appear to merely substitute one Republican appointment for another, Trump's nominees are ideologically to the right of many Republican-nominated judges. In fulfillment of a long-range goal of conservative policymakers, these judges identify as strict "originalists" (Zengerle, 2018) who tend to oppose expansions of civil rights and government authority to curb corporate power. By securing so many confirmations to the federal judiciary, the Trump Administration has ensured that its views will continue to influence social policymaking for years, even decades, to come.

A Nationalistic Approach to Immigration

Social workers who work with immigrants and refugees were among those most concerned when Donald Trump became president. Trump has long made statements and alliances that align him with immigration "hardliners" and those who espouse White nationalist views. At his campaign announcement in June 2015, Trump said of Mexican immigrants, "They're bringing drugs. They're bringing crime. They're rapists. And some, I assume, are good people." This set the anti-immigrant tone for his campaign, which became a policy direction after he took office. Vital to the nation's society and economy, immigrants and refugees were nonetheless adversely affected by many Trump Administration policies in health, education, taxes, and social services. They are also frequent targets of harsh rhetoric and policy attacks. For example, in September 2017, President Trump issued an executive order ending the Deferred Action for Childhood Arrivals (DACA) program for immigrants who came to the United States as children. He also used executive authority to deploy military personnel at the U.S. border with Mexico, separate parents and children detained at the border, and ban travel to the United States from majority-Muslim countries.

Immigrant rights advocates have used the courts, regulatory mechanisms, and public pressure to resist many of these actions. However, even victories are often partial and bitter for immigrants and their allies. After the first version of the travel ban was enjoined by federal courts, the Trump Administration revised it, with devastating consequences for the families of those denied admission. When the courts forbade indefinite detention of those seeking asylum, the Department of Homeland Security began limiting the number of people who can apply for asylum in a given day, requiring those fleeing their home countries to instead await processing in ports outside the United States. Advocates succeeded in convincing the U.S. Supreme Court that the rationale provided for adding a citizenship question to the 2020 Census was insufficient; however, many fear that the prolonged controversy may suppress immigrants' participation in the essential count, nonetheless.

Despite the advocacy of immigrants and their allies, the period since the 2016 election has largely been one of growing nationalistic fervor and increasing restrictions on entry and integration of newcomers. As described in more detail in Chapter 7, hate crimes against immigrants and those perceived to be immigrants have increased. Although strong majorities of Americans believe that immigrants' contributions strengthen the nation (Jones, 2019), national policies mostly run counter to this strengths-based view. Led by Trump's portrayals of foreign-born individuals as threats, elected officials are increasingly willing to demonize immigrants for political gain. Particularly after President Trump set refugee admission limits to their lowest in history in 2019, the United States has largely ceased to be a place of refuge and welcome for those fleeing persecution and seeking opportunity. Social workers working in immigrant communities have reasons to worry that it will continue to grow more difficult for them to meet the needs of those they serve.

CONCLUSION

Students of social policy understandably feel that these are unprecedented times with unique challenges for those committed to our profession's values of service and social justice. Policies proposed today seldom evidence respect for the dignity and worth of individuals, particularly those disadvantaged by race, ethnicity, gender, class, sexual orientation, nationality, and/or disability status. However, a review of social policy history reveals the obstacles that have long confronted these communities and the social workers who serve them. As you contemplate new social policies and social problems, take time to consider their historical precedents. Look back at the framework (Quick Guide 2) for linking historical and current policy, introduced in Chapter 2. This framework can guide your investigation of new policy.

History directly shapes social policy today. So, too, the strategies and struggles of our social work predecessors can inform our current work. There are also tremendous strengths to be marshalled in these moments of difficulty. For example, in the past, African-American activists used multiracial coalitions, strong connections to faith institutions, and strategic deployment of civil disobedience to upend racial hierarchies and establish a foundation of legal rights. Women secured their own right to vote and leveraged this political power to advance causes of economic and social justice. Today, young people are turning tragic mass shootings into a rallying cry for gun reform and civic participation. Activists concerned about climate change are using scientific research, social media, and consumer action to mobilize public opinion and increase corporate accountability. And Americans from all walks of life are resisting moves that erode social policy protections and threaten our collective well-being. Students—including social work students—have crucial roles to play in this work. Armed with historical insight and knowledge of policy precedents that built on the strengths of client groups, you will be better able to understand policy, think through how current and likely future conditions resemble earlier periods, and advocate for needed changes.

MAIN POINTS

- The twentieth century ushered in important social policy initiatives, including child labor laws, women's right to vote, anti-discrimination laws, Social Security, Medicaid and Medicare, and public health and sanitation laws. However, many Americans still struggle to meet basic needs for food, shelter, and health care.

- The Old Age, Survivors, and Disability Insurance (OASDI) program changed the traditional paradigm whereby impoverished children and elders were expected to rely on their families for economic support. The program is based on an insurance model; workers and employers pay OASDI insurance premiums so that workers and their families have income in retirement or if they are or become disabled.

- The War on Poverty yielded both successes—including significant investments in anti-poverty and human development programs that persist today—and failures.

- Oppressed groups, aided by allies including social workers, have struggled to eliminate discrimination based on race, gender, disability, and sexual orientation. Despite victories in the passage of important policies such as the Civil Rights Act, Title IX of the Education Act, and the Indian Child Welfare Act, discrimination persists.

- Although the widespread poverty of the Great Depression of the 1930s spurred establishment of many major health and social service programs, and the Civil Rights Movements of the 1960s and 1970s led to expanded access to benefits and services, years since have seen retreats on these fronts.

- Certain policies, such as the GI Bill of Rights and the Americans with Disabilities Act, reflect the premise that people have strengths and will take advantage of opportunities if structural barriers are removed.

- Other policies, such as the Personal Responsibility and Work Opportunity Reconciliation Act of 1996, are based on the premise that people must be made to work, and that social policy should therefore focus on strict work requirements and time limits rather than on removing structural barriers such as lack of access to education and training.

- The United States has a long history of public–private partnership in social welfare. The late twentieth-century push to privatize social welfare reflected a renewed reluctance on the part of the federal government to take responsibility for the welfare of its people.

- In 2010, President Obama signed the Affordable Care Act into law. This comprehensive health reform legislation was a major victory for his administration and an important step toward ensuring health care for all Americans.

- Although the Supreme Court has been an important lever for social change in the past century, President Trump's confirmed justices have contributed to a Supreme Court increasingly skeptical of civil rights, workers' protections, and social investments.

- Social workers and social work students have crucial roles to play in building on the successes of our social welfare history, preserving crucial investments, and preparing for continued progress.

EXERCISES

1. Go to the Sanchez case at **www.routledgesw.com/cases**. How would members of the family be affected by some of the policies pursued by the Trump Administration? For example, how might they experience a requirement to provide their citizenship on the U.S. Census form? What about changes to the rule surrounding "public charge," which expands the list of public benefits that count against an aspiring immigrant's application for permanent residency? Research these issues and reflect on what they might mean for the Sanchez family.
2. Considering the Carla Washburn case, how might Mrs. Washburn's life be different if she was aging without the resources provided by the Social Security Act? What about prior to passage of Medicare? Why do you think Mrs. Washburn might find Medicare and Social Security acceptable but be reluctant to accept other public social services?
3. Go to the Riverton case at **www.routledgesw.com/cases**. Homelessness often increases dramatically in periods of recession.
    a. How would you expect attitudes toward homeless people in Riverton to change during economic downturns? Do you believe the people of Riverton might be more willing to fund homeless shelters during economic downturns? Why or why not?
    b. Contact a homeless shelter in your community and find out how they are funded. Is the funding public or private, state or federal, increasing or decreasing? Can they suggest one or two policy changes that would improve conditions for people who are homeless in your community?
4. How do you think knowing about the history of Brickville—including demographic shifts, changes in the economy, and political cycles—could help you work more effectively with this community?
5. Review the Hudson City case at **www.routledgesw.com/cases**. The Economic Opportunity Act of 1964 established several programs and services that are still in existence that could be utilized to help the residents of Hudson City. Make a list of these programs and discuss how these programs could be utilized for the residents.
    a. What roles do the government and private sectors play in helping this community?
    b. When government services are cut, what do you expect the impact would be on private service providers?
6. Interview someone who remembers the Great Depression of the 1930s, World War II, and/or the Civil Rights Movement.
    a. Ask for their recollections about what it was like to experience these events.
    b. Ask if this person thinks the social policies that arose because of these events, such as the New Deal, the GI Bill, and school desegregation, were effective or not.
    c. Based on your study of history, do you agree or disagree? Why or why not?

7. One of the lessons of history is the power of language. Examine news coverage of the debate surrounding President Trump's immigration policy proposals. What terms are used to describe immigrants who will be impacted? How does the language lead audiences to view the policy proposal in a positive or a negative light? Watch for other examples of how language is used to produce negative or positive portrayals of people, policies, and programs with which social workers are involved. What influence do you think this use of language has on efforts to develop strengths-based social welfare policies and programs?
8. The Equal Justice Initiative has mapped reported lynchings of African Americans in U.S. history as part of an effort to trace the ongoing and painful legacy of this campaign of racial terror. While many lynchings occurred in the nineteenth century, the twentieth century was a time of racial terror in many communities. You can review the map at the Equal Justice Initiative website (**https://lynchinginamerica.eji.org/explore**). Were there lynchings where you were born? What about where you go to school? What patterns do you see? How might this history continue to influence attitudes, experiences, politics, and policies in different parts of the country?

NOTE

1. Although most people now consider it offensive, "mental retardation" was the term often used during this period to refer to intellectual and developmental disabilities.

CHAPTER 4

The Economic and Political Contexts

SOCIAL WORKERS HELP PEOPLE IN NEED. In many cases, this need has economic dimensions. The economy determines what people pay to secure basic goods, the opportunities they find in the labor market, and the distance that separates them from others. In a society, however, dollars and cents are not the only calculations that matter. The political environment shapes the policy outcomes considered acceptable and the resources available to meet people's needs. For example, politics are at work in outlining the social welfare programs voters are willing to support and the requirements imposed on those seeking assistance. Effective policy practice requires understanding how economic and political contexts influence U.S. social policy and, therefore, our ability to help our clients.

Examination of the historical context of social work made clear that economic fluctuations and political change interact with shifting social values and changing demographics to determine U.S. social policy. Developing the critical-thinking skills to analyze how these elements are woven together is vital for you to become an effective social work policy practitioner. The ability to scan and navigate political and economic landscapes is an essential part of promoting **economic justice**, where all members of a society have sufficient opportunities to obtain the material resources necessary to survive and to fulfill their human potential (Barker, 2014).

The process of developing and implementing social policy is strongly influenced by political and economic interests. The **economic context** of social policy focuses on the production, distribution, and use of resources, while the **political context** focuses on the pursuit and exercise of power in public affairs. Although these terms have distinct meanings, they are often enmeshed. Competition and conflict, inherent in both economic and political processes, influence how, when, and what types of social policies and programs are developed and implemented. Political decisions also influence the health of the economy, another factor that contributes to diverging policy outcomes. And, of course, economic conditions have political implications, as when high unemployment, rising prices, or widening economic disparities influence how voters feel about policymakers and the nation's political direction. Political choices and their economic consequences may promote social justice, preserve the status quo, or intensify economic insecurity and inequality.

HOW CONTEXT AFFECTS SOCIAL POLICY

The United States has a **marketplace economy**, which means that people exchange goods and services to meet their needs. In addition to working for wages, people may earn income from assets such as stocks and property. These sources generate the money to purchase goods and services. However, many people find that their labors do not produce enough income to meet their needs. In the labor market, the balance of power is generally with the employer. There are often many workers competing for jobs unless the pay is very low, working conditions are adverse, or the necessary skill level is very high. When the marketplace is the primary driver of public policy, non-monetized work is undervalued, marginalized, or even ignored. For example, there is no policy to compensate individuals for caregiving or other labor provided informally. Further, many people cannot participate in the labor market due to obstacles such as disability or discrimination, or to gaps in our social policy infrastructure, such as inadequate childcare or poor-quality education. Critically, the market system contains no mechanisms to provide for the needs of those who cannot work or whose work does not produce adequate rewards.

Basing our economy on the workings of the marketplace intensifies inequality, the detrimental effects of which damage the overall fabric of society. Analysts Richard Wilkinson and Kate Pickett examined a range of negative outcomes—reduced life expectancy, low educational attainment, crime, high rates of mental illness—and found that the gap between the rich and poor, rather than the absolute poverty of those at the bottom, explained most of the incidence of social problems (Wilkinson & Pickett, 2009). Importantly, inequality also perpetuates itself by solidifying an economic and political aristocracy that crafts and maintains policies that uphold structural barriers to equal opportunity (Bartels, 2002). Research has demonstrated that, when people even *feel* that their economic positions are superior to others, their willingness to share economic resources and political power equitably declines (Brown-Iannuzzi et al., 2015).

While typically described as a capitalist country, where the means of production (facilities and resources used to produce goods and services) are privately owned, the United States in fact has a mixed system. Federal, state, and local governments make massive investments in infrastructure, such as highways, transportation, sanitation, technology, public safety and education—all resources vital to the survival and profitability of businesses. Further, some major industries, such as utilities, may be government-owned, and markets are publicly regulated. The American marketplace is not absolute, then, or entirely unfettered. Governments are often called on to regulate private commerce to protect citizens from harm. Such regulatory actions often gain support after a man-made disaster, such as a coalmine collapse, the housing crises that precipitated the Great Recession, or a nuclear facility meltdown. As further illustration of the connections between the economic and political contexts, powerful actors can wield regulatory power—and its absence—as a tool to improve their own economic positions.

Influence of Regulatory Policy

Laws that require employers to pay overtime wages and that mandate workplace safety requirements are examples of regulatory policy. Others include laws that limit how much pollution companies can create or require vehicles to meet certain safety standards. As described in

Chapter 3, the political context has important implications for the government's stance on regulatory policy. While some elected officials and bureaucrats favor a more activist government role in regulating market activities, others prefer to allow market forces to operate without much intervention. Regulatory policy mediates marketplace effects on people's lives. For example, children living in poverty can benefit from child-support enforcement rules that require employers to withhold support payments from wages. Regulations that require that businesses be accessible to people with disabilities facilitate their access to needed goods and services. Civil rights advocates have used regulatory policy to prescribe remedies for voting infringement and employment discrimination, and reformers reshaped the health insurance marketplace with regulations that compel coverage. Other regulations serve as gatekeepers to restrict individuals' access to opportunities. For example, the Trump Administration's expansion of public benefits that can imperil an immigrant's application for adjustment of status is a regulatory provision that will make it harder for families to secure both immigration status and essential safety-net supports. Social workers should critically examine not only the claims being made for or against regulatory policy, but also the intended purpose and actual effect of regulations. While regulatory policies do not appropriate tangible resources directly to individuals or communities, they are not without cost. The private sector often incurs the cost of complying with regulations, and there are public costs associated with enforcement and monitoring.

Thinking beyond social welfare policies, recent history has illustrated the need for more effective regulation and oversight, particularly of financial institutions and technology and energy companies. While public opinion about government intervention in the marketplace tends to fluctuate in response to external events, polls find that beliefs about the appropriate level and role of government regulation tend to correlate to political affiliation (Smith, 2017). This means that regulation will continue to be contested, as groups vie to exalt or constrain regulatory authority. The economic devastation wrought by the collapse of financial markets, personal upheaval stemming from data breaches by technology companies, and environmental disasters related to energy production have had negative effects on the well-being of many Americans. These consequences could possibly have been avoided had the enterprises involved been more closely regulated. At the same time, when regulations are not updated to keep pace with evolving technology or correctly calibrated with an eye to economic objectives, there are potential harms there, as well (Cass, 2018).

The Impetus for Social Programs

Faced with a gap between existing policy responses and people's needs, social workers ask, "How should our society respond?" Not surprisingly, there is no consensus on this question. Political support for government policies to assist people who are unable to meet their needs through the marketplace waxes and wanes. In general, when the economy is doing well, people may place increased emphasis on individual responsibility. When the economy is failing, people may be more likely to turn to the government for relief. However, economic forces are not the only influences on policy development. Political ideology matters too. Even core U.S. values sometimes conflict. Reflecting opposing values of individual and social responsibility, the United States has developed a social welfare system to attempt to balance the mandates of the marketplace with the reality that individual circumstances and economic cycles contribute to needs that the market cannot accommodate.

Because of our market economy, two conditions must generally exist for a public social program to be developed. First, there must be a clear indication of a social problem, or what some economists have termed a "market failure." A **market failure** is a "circumstance in which the pursuit of private interest does not lead to an efficient use of society's resources or a fair distribution of society's goods" (Weimer & Vining, 1999, p. 41). That is, the free market, the family, and other private entities are not providing for basic needs—education, housing, health care, or retirement income—for a sizable segment of the population. Then, people in power and their constituencies must recognize the problem and support intervention to solve it. They must also be convinced that government action will not do more harm than good (Waldfogel, 2000). The development of the federal Old Age, Survivors, and Disability Insurance program (OASDI) is one example of government intervening to respond to a market failure—in this case the inability of many older Americans to adequately sustain themselves in retirement, particularly in the aftermath of the Great Depression.

Some economists suggest that transaction costs should be included in determining when the government should intervene in cases of market failure (Zerbe & McCurdy, 2000). **Transaction costs** refer to all costs incurred during government intervention, including financial, personal, and environmental costs. For example, publicly funded low-income housing may have a financial impact on people who own low-cost rentals because they may have to compete for tenants. People who are concerned about a social problem should weigh the transaction costs against the expected benefits to determine whether intervention is appropriate or desirable, and, if so, what type of intervention is preferable. At the same time, social workers should include the costs of *inaction* in our accounting. Without any intervention, social problems are likely to continue, with consequences for client groups and all of society.

Groups and individuals who examine options for intervention generally consider both economic efficiency and equity in their assessment of the best course of action. The principle of economic efficiency focuses on three interrelated issues:

1. The probable effect of the intervention on the overall economy.
2. The relative merits of spending on one intervention rather than another.
3. The ways in which the incentives and/or disincentives the intervention will create are likely to influence individual behavior.

To understand how principles of economic efficiency can be applied to social policy, consider the debate over "free college"—a topic probably of personal interest to you. While free college has gained political momentum as more Americans become frustrated with the high cost of tuition, these policies have been criticized as inefficient. Making college tuition-free is expensive, would subsidize large numbers of students from high-income families who do not necessarily need help to access higher education (Zinshteyn, 2017), and may not help low-income students much, since their tuition is largely paid through existing financial aid (Poutre, Rorrison, & Voight, 2017). Alternatives to free college, including more generous need-based aid, investments in subsidized child savings accounts, and better policies to help students cope with debt, may prove more efficient ways to respond to the problem of college unaffordability.

The principle of equity revolves around two underlying questions: will the policy treat all people with a particular need equally, a concept referred to as **horizontal equity**, or will it redistribute resources to those who possess fewer resources and/or have greater need and thus exhibit **vertical equity** (Waldfogel, 2000)? For example, regarding the provision of services for people with mental illness, horizontal equity would extend equal access to services to all people with mental illness, irrespective of demographics, location, severity of diagnosis, or socioeconomic status. In contrast, social policy based on vertical equity might provide services to people with low incomes at no charge while requiring those with higher incomes to pay a fee or prioritize services to those with the most compromised functioning. Of course, many public policies are neither horizontally nor vertically equitable. This is particularly true in the economic sphere, where resources are often redistributed to those who already have more. For example, families who save for their children's college educations can receive sizable tax benefits while those taking out loans on their children's behalf receive no comparable subsidy. Benefits awarded to the privileged reduce the nation's fiscal capacity to invest in policies that serve those who are disadvantaged. They also further solidify the advantage others enjoy.

INSTITUTIONAL AND RESIDUAL APPROACHES TO SOCIAL WELFARE

There are two competing approaches to social welfare in the United States: institutional and residual. To determine which programs—and which approach—to support, policymakers and social workers must consider their respective outcomes and evaluate claims about equity and efficiency.

Institutional Approaches

The **institutional approach** to social welfare asserts that the government should ensure that the basic needs of all people are adequately met. Advocates of the institutional approach focus on creating universal programs to address common human needs. As their name suggests, **universal programs** serve everyone within a broad category. For example, our public-school system is a universal program because it makes education broadly available to all children.

Most agree that universal programs determine eligibility more efficiently than **selective programs**, which base eligibility on the satisfaction of parameters such as income, diagnosis, or geographic residence. When everyone in a broad category is automatically eligible for a service, the eligibility determination process is simple and administrative costs are low. Because universal programs typically attempt to treat all recipients equally, they align with the concept of horizontal equity.

Residual Approaches

In contrast to the institutional approach, the **residual approach** posits that the government should intervene only when the family, marketplace, and other private entities are unable to meet needs adequately. Residual policies tend to create selective programs. When employing a residual approach, the government uses revenue collected from a broad spectrum of taxpayers to provide assistance that is narrowly targeted to those who possess the fewest resources, meet specific priority criteria, and/or have the greatest needs. Thus, the residual approach reflects the principle of vertical equity. However, there is sometimes a danger that selective programs will "cream" participants to choose those deemed most likely to succeed, since they are not expected to serve everyone. Such practices undermine the principle of vertical equity. Further, residual programs are often inadequately funded, such that some eligible individuals are unable to receive needed assistance. For example, whereas public education is a universal program available to all children, Head Start is a residual program because it is designed specifically for low-income students. Because funding is insufficient to meet the full need, Head Start often has waiting lists.

Although eligibility can be based on criteria other than financial need, the residual approach often employs **means tests**, which base eligibility on financial circumstances. This process reduces overall spending by ensuring that the program supports only people who are unable to assist themselves. However, administrative costs of residual programs are often greater because of the expenses associated with verifying that individuals meet eligibility guidelines.

ECONOMIC AND POLITICAL INFLUENCES ON THE SOCIAL WELFARE SYSTEM

Over the centuries, our economy has evolved from one based on agriculture and small business to a post-industrial economy. When the United States was founded, independent farmers made up 80 percent of the labor force (Bell, 1987). The other 20 percent were primarily independent craftsmen. Most women did not work outside the home. Today, most of the labor force is composed of wage-earning and salaried workers, many of whom are employed in service occupations and information technologies. Most working-age women now participate in the labor force. These shifts reflect broader economic changes. Increased global competition, the erosion of a U.S. manufacturing base, and stagnant wages, particularly for American males, have held down average family incomes, necessitated two-income households, and increased the financial insecurity with which many people contend. These dynamics underscore the challenges U.S. social welfare policy must meet, if Americans are to succeed in the economic realities of today and of the future. Further, policymakers and social work advocates must grapple with the political implications of many Americans' sense that the economy is not meeting their needs, particularly as even extended periods of economic growth fail to bring real prosperity to millions of individuals and families.

Competing Explanations for the Development of the Welfare System

Informed by the work of James Midgley (2009, 2014), a social worker and policy scholar, the discussion that follows examines theories that explain the relationship between the economy and social welfare policy development.

The Industrialization-Welfare Hypothesis One explanation of the origins and functions of the welfare system, termed the **industrialization-welfare hypothesis**, emphasizes industrialization as a significant factor in the development of the welfare state. This hypothesis proposes that, in industrial and post-industrial societies, the government assumes the welfare functions that in a pre-industrial society would be performed by institutions like the family, church, and community—for example, caring for elderly parents. The government's motivation is not primarily humanitarian but pragmatic. Industrialization necessitates a more collective response. When families are uprooted as people relocate in search of opportunities, deprivation, insecurity, and need increase. In response, the government establishes social programs designed to substitute for the informal welfare "system."

The Maintenance of Capitalism Hypothesis A second explanation, termed the **maintenance of capitalism hypothesis**, also emphasizes the role of capitalist industrialization in the creation of the welfare state. However, this theory also contends that the welfare state specifically encourages capitalism by providing some assistance in order to reduce the pressure for radical political and economic restructuring. In this way, welfare spending can be seen as sustaining the very system responsible for perpetuating the inequities (Piven & Cloward, 1971). This view postulates that a "power elite" from the government and private sectors exerts control on policymaking to maintain their positions and wealth. Notably, there is evidence that many Americans, across the political spectrum, ascribe to this view of U.S. economic and political structures; in 2019, a majority of Americans see the economy (62 percent) and the political system (72 percent) primarily working to benefit those already in power, not all people (*Washington Post*-ABC News, 2019).

One variation of this hypothesis argues that these powerful interests use social welfare policy to control women's lives (Abramovitz, 1996). For example, the type of caring work that women have traditionally done is not defined as "work" for Social Security eligibility. Consequently, to secure public retirement benefits, women must either marry a person eligible for Social Security or enter the paid workforce in addition to their caregiving responsibilities. Further, when programs are not in place to make it financially possible for mothers to stay at home and care for their children, these mothers must often take any job they can fit into their mothering responsibilities. This ensures a ready supply of low-paid workers. Throughout history, there have been numerous examples of social policies instituted both to assist people in need and to promote social control. Due to inequities located at the intersections of identities such as race, class, and gender, the social control functions of social welfare policies have particularly affected disadvantaged groups.

A related explanation of the relationship between social welfare and industrial capitalism posits that the government introduces welfare programs to promote both accumulation of capital by businesses and popular acceptance of the capitalist system (O'Connor, 1973). Seen through this lens, the government's role is to introduce and sustain social programs that create an efficient yet inexpensive labor force. Public education is one example of a popular social program that improves workforce capabilities. Additionally, the public sector often shoulders costs for health and environmental problems caused by industry. When taxpayers assume these expenses, businesses' costs go down and their profits go up. Programs such as Social Security retirement can enhance social contentment and stability and create an environment conducive to business growth.

To some extent, the accumulation and legitimization functions of welfare capitalism benefit both the recipients and the capitalist system. However, when the state's resources for providing the services that maintain the system are exhausted or when the public objects to assuming responsibility for maintaining a ready pool of workers, a crisis ensues. This is particularly true when private enterprises unwilling to fund public social welfare programs have the political power to undercut them. Changes in the global economy and in the opportunities available in the U.S. labor market exacerbate these strains. In particular, as more corporations shift from manufacturing to finance and information technology and convert job functions to automated and mechanized systems, their need for low-wage, low-skill workers is reduced. This may contribute to the decreased willingness to pay taxes for social programs that support low-wage workers. Additionally, globalization has reduced the extent to which companies feel tied to particular geographic communities and, then, willing to pay taxes to support local investments. As these forces converge, the political consensus supporting capitalism may be faltering. Americans prefer a dramatically more equal distribution of wealth than our capitalistic system currently delivers (Norton & Ariely, 2011). With many Americans living paycheck to paycheck and increasingly dismayed at the lack of supports to help them thrive, growing support for an expanded social safety net will create political pressures to which leaders will need to respond.

Social Conscience Hypothesis According to the **social conscience hypothesis**, human beings' innate, altruistic concerns for others have led to the creation of the welfare state. These explanations trace the roots of the modern welfare state to the charitable activities of ancient religious groups. Proponents of social conscience theory also argue that industrialization, globalization, urbanization, the disruption of traditional social ties, and increased competitiveness have all weakened people's desire to help others. Therefore, it is now much harder to garner support for the expansion of the welfare state, even as these forces have created additional social problems that cannot be resolved by humanitarian aid alone.

The Marshall and Titmuss Hypotheses British theorists T. H. Marshall and Richard Titmuss further developed arguments focused on legitimizing the social welfare function. Marshall (1950) argued that rights to adequate education, housing, and income are part of the evolution of citizenship. Additionally, people in a democracy are more capable of fulfilling the responsibilities of citizenship when these basic rights are legally protected. Further, Marshall described the development of the welfare state as the subordination of the market to social justice and asserted that social rights should not be dependent on work status.

Richard Titmuss (1974) had a profound influence on the development of social policy, particularly the institutional approach. Titmuss argued that government actions to provide for social welfare have desirable moral consequences such as institutionalizing altruism, increasing solidarity, and promoting reciprocity and social responsibility. Titmuss further maintained that social goods such as public education and streets should not be bought and sold.

A Critique Current evidence does not provide a great deal of support for any one of these hypotheses as the overall explanation for the development of the social welfare system. Instead, different hypotheses might cast light on the development of specific welfare policies and programs. For example, concern for quelling social unrest certainly influenced the passage of the Social Security Act of 1935. Religious leaders have often spoken out in support of programs for the poor, motivated by and seeking to appeal to others' social conscience. Debates over work requirements and marriage incentives for TANF recipients reflect a societal impulse to control women's lives. Many people believe that benefits such as unemployment insurance and health and safety standards in the workplace would not have developed without pressure from the labor movement. We cannot expect that all the players involved in passing policy will be motivated by the same forces, even if they agree on the same aim. For example, people who favor a residual approach to income-support programs generally champion free-market strategies and want to downsize the public sector, and people who favor an institutional approach to social welfare may support public investment to prepare a well-educated workforce, which contributes to a healthy marketplace economy. If we can recognize these diverse influences and their potential common ground, this understanding can help us craft and enact strengths-based policy that benefits our clients.

Examining the development of welfare states in different countries can help us to better understand our own. Esping-Andersen (2002) argues that welfare systems vary substantially depending on the roles the three pillars of welfare—the market, the family, and government—play in providing for basic needs and managing risks such as unemployment and disability. Although changing demographics and political shifts are pressuring some retreat from institutional approaches, Scandinavian countries have traditionally been examples of countries where citizens rely on the state to provide for basic needs as a right of citizenship. Other countries may rely on a combination of market and family resources, while some use an insurance model, whereby private and government agencies pool contributions to guard against risks. Countries adopt welfare models that grow from particular class relationships and ideological identities. Thus, different countries ascribe different importance to the moral obligation of the government versus that of individuals to provide an adequate standard of living. Countries also vary in the extent to which they integrate their welfare systems into their economies, such that public benefits provide adequate protection in times of market failure and promote work when markets expand. Variations in welfare programs reflect the type of society those in power wish to create, how they respond to internal and external pressures, and how they implement and sustain that vision as economic, political, and social contexts change.

In the United States, the concept of "welfare" initially meant well-being. The U.S. Constitution refers to the promotion of the general welfare, which was understood to mean the advancement of population well-being (Katz, 2008). However, the understanding of the term "welfare" has gradually shifted. In the United States, many people now equate welfare with means-tested public assistance programs. The U.S. welfare system combines private and public components, with most Americans benefitting from these investments in substantial ways (Abramovitz, 2001), even if relatively few people can identify the roles that social welfare programs play in their own lives (Mettler, 2010). Public components of our multifaceted welfare system include public assistance, social insurance, public social services, and tax policies. Private components include employee benefits, philanthropy, and private social services (Katz, 2008). Because of this complexity and fragmentation, total welfare spending and programs' effectiveness can be difficult to measure.

The Enabling State and the Capacity-Building State

The emphasis on social rights and citizen entitlements that influenced the development of welfare states is being replaced by increased emphasis on the responsibility of individuals to meet their own needs. Increasingly, programs are moving from universal to selective criteria and making eligibility criteria more restrictive to limit the number of individuals receiving benefits. The U.S. is not alone in these shifts. Particularly as new arrivals to Europe strain the existing social contract, some nations such as Germany and the United Kingdom have explicitly denied migrants access to social benefits, justifying this action with claims that extending benefits to newcomers provides an incentive for migration and strains program sustainability (Costamagna, 2016). In some cases, countries have even restricted the movement of those receiving benefits, in a redefinition of citizenship that evidences further retrenchment (Lafleur & Mescoli, 2018).

As popular support has decreased for the idea that eligibility for welfare benefits should be a fundamental right, we have seen the rise of the **enabling state**, whereby public benefits are provided to help people be more productive workers (Gilbert, 2002). From this perspective, governments provide benefits to children to help them become productive adults, while older adults receive benefits primarily based on their prior workforce contributions. Those able to work but unemployed receive only time-limited benefits, while only those deemed unable to work receive benefits without work requirements. Even then, they are regularly reevaluated for potential to work. This approach has been criticized for quantifying the value of a person in terms of their capacity as a worker rather than recognizing their inherent human rights. By this equation, people who are unable to work or for whom no jobs are available may be devalued.

This does not mean that encouraging employment and supporting individuals' basic needs are necessarily competing aims. Research has identified multiple ways work can contribute to individuals' well-being, even apart from its contributions to their financial security (McKee-Ryan et al., 2005; Turner & Turner, 2004). Advanced welfare states have long emphasized the connection between public benefits that enable people to be healthy and well-educated and citizens' obligations to contribute to society. However, these systems also subsidize education and training more heavily than in the United States, particularly at the early childhood and post-secondary levels. Combined with policies such as paid family leave, which balance personal and corporate needs, investments in education and training equip individuals to fulfill labor market obligations in the rapidly changing economy. With this more comprehensive approach, social welfare programs can serve the needs of capitalism as well as of individuals. These kinds of initiatives align with a **capacity-building state**, which focuses on strengthening the skills and competencies of people and on helping them secure the resources they need for full economic and social inclusion. In addition to prioritizing investment in human capital and social connection, capacity-building states include income support to assist people who face significant structural barriers that trap them in poverty. Social workers need to work alongside affected populations to mobilize resources for investments that will increase opportunities and improve outcomes for groups that have been oppressed.

Economic and Political Schools of Thought

The United States has a long history of pluralism. In our policymaking process, no one group holds all the power. Instead, many groups are actively involved in creating and implementing public and private policies at the federal, state, and local levels, informed by a variety of philosophies. These strands all contribute to our social welfare system. We begin our exploration of this topic by discussing three fundamental economic philosophies: Keynesian economics, supply-side economics, and democratic socialism. We will then shift our focus to the political arena and examine how different political philosophies and the three branches of government affect social welfare.

Keynesian Economics The economic school of thought known as **Keynesian economics**, also referred to as demand-side economics, is based on the writings of John Maynard Keynes, an English economist. Keynes rejected the traditional *laissez-faire* philosophy that free-market competition would automatically facilitate full employment and make government intervention both unnecessary and undesirable. Instead, he posited that modern economies are not self-correcting; instead, government stabilization efforts are necessary to keep a capitalist economy running smoothly. Specifically, Keynes argued that the government should stabilize the economy through use of **fiscal policy**—that is, by increasing or decreasing spending and taxes in response to economic conditions. When individuals or private businesses do not consume or invest enough, the government must intervene so that the economy continues to grow even during times of elevated unemployment and stagnant wages. For example, when older adults or poor families spend their cash assistance, grocery stores, clothing stores, and other businesses also benefit. Demand-side economics also emphasize the importance of public investment in **human capital**—that is, programs such as education, health care, and job training that make people more productive—to increase national wealth.

Keynes' theory guided some U.S. social policy during the Great Depression and influenced the Obama Administration's approach to the Great Recession as well. New Deal programs that sought to increase demand for goods and services by providing income opportunities to people in need bear the distinct stamp of Keynesian ideas. Overall, Keynesian principles are integral to modern liberalism and its efforts to develop a comprehensive public welfare state. **Liberalism**, which stresses both liberty and equality, is a political philosophy that endorses individual freedom while advocating government intervention to ensure an adequate minimum living condition for all. Today, elected officials in the Democratic Party typically support the type of government intervention Keynes proposed.

Supply-Side Economics In contrast to liberals, classic or traditional conservatives advocate a *laissez-faire* economy and a minimal welfare state. The work of conservative economist Milton Friedman and his theories of **monetarism** inform some conservative initiatives. Friedman argued that Keynesian strategies of using fiscal policy to smooth out business cycles harm the economy. According to Friedman, government policy should be restricted to promoting steady growth in the total amount of money circulating in the economy.

Friedman's economics aligned with Ronald Reagan's policy preferences and gained considerable momentum in the 1980s. However, supply-side economists have largely rejected Friedman's emphasis on increasing the money supply by manipulating interest rates and instead have focused on tax cuts as engines of economic growth. The term "supply-side" stems from the concept that allowing people to retain a larger portion of their income after taxes will encourage them to work more hours and thereby increase the supply of goods and services available to consumers (Roberts, 1988). Supply-side proponents argue that tax cuts, particularly for high earners, lead to increases in investment, spending, and savings, which in turn expand the economy and create jobs. Ultimately, some of these benefits should "trickle down" and improve economic conditions for low-income groups, as wealthy people reinvest tax cut windfalls in consumption and business creation. Supply-side economics provided much of the rationale for the large tax cuts enacted during the administrations of Ronald Reagan, George W. Bush, and Donald Trump, as well as in some states.

Democratic Socialism A third economic philosophy, **democratic socialism**, argues that, because capitalism is predicated on the pursuit of individual self-interest and profit, it inevitably increases social inequality and cannot therefore be relied upon to advance the public good. Democratic socialists further posit that expansion of government investments in social welfare comes through the struggle of the working class and its allies. As their name suggests, democratic socialists work through the democratic process to pursue change in the economic system and expansion of social welfare. However, many democratic socialists maintain that welfare programs function as a flawed substitute for the fundamental social changes that are needed to achieve social justice.

While many Americans are suspicious of anything associated with socialism, growing dissatisfaction with economic and political power arrangements is drawing more Americans—particularly Millennials—to democratic socialism (Anapol, 2018). Membership in the Democratic Socialists of America grew from 7,000 members to 50,000 in the two years following President Trump's election, young people hold more positive views of socialism than capitalism (Newport, 2018a), and a growing number of democratic socialists won Democratic primaries in 2018. However, many Americans still hold misconceptions about socialism and how it operates, and these beliefs are further complicated by misrepresentation of the term. Fundamentally and historically, socialism requires the means of production to be owned by the government; however, today, even in countries often described as "socialist," only a small number of firms are government-owned (Boaz, 2018). Instead, what distinguishes these welfare states from an economic system like in the United States is greater government exertion of regulatory authority and the construction of a far more robust social safety net.

The Political Continuum

Political philosophies fall along a continuum from very conservative to very liberal. Among other distinctions, these political philosophies encompass different beliefs about how to organize an economy (since controlling economic resources is a critical tool for advancing political power) and different perspectives on the role of government in individuals' lives. Issue stances and labels have shifted over time. Further, a growing proportion of Americans reject traditional political party labels. In 2017, 42 percent of Americans identified as political independents (Jones, 2018). Although most of these independents still "lean" toward one party's platform, they are more likely than partisan affiliates to reject ideological labels (Pew Research Center, 2019a). As you will see in our discussion of neoliberalism, the words "liberal" and "conservative" have been applied to a wide variety of beliefs. Here, we delineate the major differences between the political agendas of conservatives and liberals that influence current policy debates. We also discuss the rise of economic nationalism in the United States and around the world, manifest in policies such as trade protectionism, the political fortunes of figures such as President Trump and Brazil's Jair Bolsonaro, and movements, including the United Kingdom's withdrawal from the European Union, known as "Brexit."

Conservatives and Liberals Although most conservatives are fiscally conservative and advocate for a minimal welfare state, their social and political priorities diverge. **Social conservatives** oppose the expansion of personal liberty in areas such as reproductive health care and LGBTQ+ rights. They assert traditional beliefs about the family, religion, and the role of women. They oppose government spending on activities they deem incompatible with those beliefs and often support government action to promote their social agenda. Strict constitutionalists, **classical conservatives** advocate preservation of personal wealth, private ownership, and a *laissez-faire* approach to economics. They traditionally focus their attention on the economy, defense spending, and foreign affairs and are often more socially liberal than social conservatives. **Fiscal conservatives** prioritize reducing government spending and the federal debt. They favor relying on the market to distribute the resources people need and typically seek to limit the government's role in promoting social welfare. Believing that public social programs often harm the social order, they advocate for the transfer of responsibility for welfare from the government to the private sector. At a minimum, they insist that social welfare programs be compatible with values of self-reliance and personal responsibility, as well as with a market economy. Social conservatives' capacity to rally voters around issues such as abortion has made them a potent force in the Republican Party, although some have felt conflicted since the rise of Donald Trump as the party's standard-bearer. To learn more about the policies that conservatives support, go to the websites of the Hoover Institute (**www.hoover.org**) and the Heritage Foundation (**www.heritage.org**), two conservative think-tanks.

Despite the term's root, neoliberals espouse many of the same beliefs as conservatives, with some differences in emphasis and approach. For example, neoliberals do not necessarily support *laissez-faire* economics; rather, they press for government to operate more in line with market principles and direct public resources to facilitating economic growth. Thus, neoliberals often support policy initiatives to privatize welfare programs, allow unfettered trade across national borders, and provide job training and work incentives. David Harvey (2005) describes neoliberalism as deregulation, privatization, withdrawal of government, and exaltation of market rights, rather than a collective responsibility for well-being. According to this definition, neoliberalism's imprint on U.S. policymaking today is evident. Additionally, the social work profession has been profoundly affected by neoliberal influence. In post-secondary institutions, pressures to trim budgets and emphasize revenue production have altered the educational experience, while neoliberal thinking has permeated many social service organizations, threatening retreat from advocacy engagement and commodifying the delivery of social work services (Eikenberry & Kluver, 2004).

Liberals believe in an active government role in achieving a just society. They have traditionally supported the goals of full employment, expanded access to health care, and advancement of civil rights. Some who advocate these policies refer to themselves as "progressives" rather than liberals, while some may claim the mantle of Democratic Socialists.

At the beginning of the 1980s, with the defeat of Jimmy Carter and the ascendance of Ronald Reagan, some politicians historically allied with liberals began working to develop a more moderate approach, in the hopes of retaking power from conservatives. These more moderate "liberals" still supported an active government role in achieving economic growth and social justice, and they remained mostly united around social issues such as civil rights, including women's rights, gay rights, and racial equality. Nevertheless, they differed from traditional liberals in their emphasis on institutions other than the government as agents of change and in agreeing with conservatives on the need to reduce the federal deficit. Individuals and organizations operating from these viewpoints tend to support free trade in the belief that open markets promote economic development and greater prosperity. They advocate investment in human capital, believe that welfare policy should align with labor policy, and do not see pursuit of corporate profits as necessarily in conflict with the social good.

Today's highly polarized political climate can obscure differences among these factions by emphasizing the divides between liberals and conservatives and squeezing out those who seek to occupy centrist positions. A typical Republican is more conservative than 94% of Democrats and the typical Democrat is more liberal than 92% of Republicans (Dimock et al., 2014). Nonetheless, those identifying as conservatives have diverging positions on many issues, and there are major differences among liberals as well, including regarding free trade, government spending, and the extent to which corporate power should be curtailed. The 2016 primary contest between socialist Bernie Sanders and centrist Hillary Clinton, high-profile primary contests in 2018, and debates over Democratic Party leadership in Congress illustrate these divides. To learn more about the work of liberal think-tanks espousing various iterations of liberal ideologies, go to the websites of the Center on Budget and Policy Priorities (**www.cbpp.org**) and the Brookings Institution (**www.brookings.edu**).

Other Political Influences Communitarians, libertarians, populists, and economic nationalists are also part of our political landscape. Emphasizing the need to rebuild communities and encourage two-parent families, **communitarians** represent a mix of liberal and conservative traditions. Communitarians advocate for individual rights and equality; however, they also believe that institutions need to build character, and they favor greater local government and community involvement in promoting social welfare. **Libertarians** believe that government grows at the expense of individual freedom. Therefore, they are critical of taxation, reject the argument that government should be involved in social or economic activities, and seek to restrict or eliminate the public welfare system. The platform of the Libertarian Party can be found at **www.lp.org**. The Tea Party, a grassroots political movement that helped elect conservative Republicans in 2012 and claims many members of Congress among its adherents, has its roots in both the libertarian and the social conservative camps.

While the term means different things to different adherents and in different contexts, in political science, populism is the idea that society is separated into two groups at odds with one another: "the pure people" and "the corrupt elite" (Mudde & Kaltwasser, 2017). **Populists**, then, claim to represent the unified "will of the people," in opposition to an enemy. Populism's historical roots include the French and Mexican Revolutions and, in the United States, a nineteenth-century farmers' movement for land reform, direct election of U.S. senators, government ownership of railroads, and a graduated income tax. Today, leaders assuming the label of populism may identify as liberals who seek to overturn an unjust status quo or may identify with the political right, advancing policies of trade protectionism and often expressing authoritarian and nativist views.

Many populists champion policies and rhetoric of **economic nationalism**, the practice of using policy to bolster and protect national economies in the context of world economic markets (Pryke, 2012). From a strengths perspective, economic nationalism can be seen as a way to invest in domestic infrastructure, increase economic growth to facilitate greater prosperity, and employ careful planning in order to better anticipate and manage economic threats. However, as deployed today, economic nationalism is often accompanied by a narrow characterization of whose interests economic policy should advance. As political scientist Francis Fukuyama describes, nationalists "play by democratic rules but harbor potentially illiberal tendencies due to their longing for identity and unity" (2018, p. 69). This means that economic nationalism can veer into xenophobic policies. Additionally, by exalting domestic economic interests above all other concerns, nationalism can also disrupt global cooperation toward shared priorities, including combating climate change and advancing human rights. This was tragically evident as fires raged in the Amazon rainforest in 2019, as the Brazilian president resisted international efforts to help combat the fire, claiming they insulted Brazilian national sovereignty. People, including social work clients, have undeniably experienced substantial economic upheaval due to globalization. At the same time, international arrangements and cross-border economic activity have contributed to an improvement in standards of living around the world (Samimi & Jenatabadi, 2014). Strength-based policy practitioners should work to ensure that the fruits of globalization are broadly and fairly distributed, while recognizing that all nations can benefit from global partnership.

Implications for Understanding Policy

How can we use this knowledge about the political and economic schools of thought that influence our policy landscape to understand the development of a particular policy at a given time? Think back to the historical context of the New Deal policies of the 1930s when the economic instability of the Great Depression fueled initiatives informed by Keynesian economics. On the other hand, sluggish economic growth and high inflation in the 1970s ushered in the conservative supply-side economics and political realignments of the 1980s. The interplay of the economic and political contexts of these periods brought very different approaches.

The concept of "political capital" describes political power in terms analogous to currency—something that can be accumulated and, then, spent to pursue desired aims. In 2008, during a severe economic crisis, the country elected Barack Obama, who promised to reform financial markets, the health care and immigration systems, and U.S. environmental policy. Because a public eager for decisive change had elected Obama with a sizable proportion of the vote and given Democrats a majority in Congress, Obama was seen as having the political capital to press for major reforms. Similarly, when President George W. Bush was reelected in 2004, he believed he had the political capital to increase funding for the wars in Iraq and Afghanistan. Political capital can have a dramatic effect on whether proposed changes are implemented. However, as President Obama experienced when his priorities on immigration and the environment faltered after his hard-fought win on health care reform, political capital can be quickly depleted, particularly if external conditions change.

Today, government itself is often under suspicion. Americans have little confidence in policymakers' ability or willingness to address the problems of people's daily lives. Only 17 percent report having faith that the federal government will do what is right even most of the time—lower even than during periods of recession (Pew Research Center, 2019b). In the current, hyper-partisan political environment, those operating from different political philosophies have few common goals. There are few shared understandings of the social problems we face. We seem unable to even see each other as members of the same nation. Increasing insecurity and inequality intensify polarization (McCarty, Poole, & Rosenthal, 2016) and can lead to marginalization and scapegoating of those perceived as "other." Politicians interested in retreating from the social contract can exploit this lack of consensus to abandon commitments, including to universal social investments with substantial benefits across the entire population. The two major political parties spend a great deal of money and time vying for media attention, control of issue framing, and, ultimately, votes. Each party wants to control the legislative, executive, and judicial branches of government to push policies that reflect their ideological approaches. We turn now to the influence of these three branches on our social welfare system.

The Three Branches of Government

There are three branches of government at both the federal and the state levels: legislative, executive, and judicial. In theory, each branch performs separate and distinct functions. Simply put, the legislative branch makes laws; the executive branch promulgates rules and regulations, enforces the laws, and develops budgets; and the judicial branch interprets the laws. All three influence our social welfare system in complex and interrelated ways. Social workers who are aware that all three branches make policy can craft strategies to more effectively influence social policy in each arena.

At the federal level, the **executive branch** includes the president, the vice-president, the cabinet, the president's advisers, and all the offices and agencies that serve the president. At the state level, the governor, the cabinet, and all the offices and agencies charged with executing state policy belong to the executive branch. When they develop budgets, champion legislation, and create the rules and regulations necessary to implement laws, these entities are making social policy. Focusing on changing regulations via executive agencies may yield quicker results than legislative processes. Indeed, some advocates believe many issues can be resolved more easily through this venue, alleviating the need for legislative action. However, Congress and/or state legislatures may object to this approach, considering it executive overreach; in some cases, these disputes may become constitutional questions for the judicial branch to decide.

Further, as has been evident in the past few years, it can be difficult to ensure that policy made through this channel will survive an executive transition. Nonetheless, social workers regularly influence policy by becoming involved in developing and amending executive actions and regulation.

Congress, the major component of the federal **legislative branch**, is bicameral, consisting of two chambers of elected officials, the House of Representatives and the Senate. Both chambers are charged with passing legislation. They are independent of each other but must agree on proposed legislation for it to become law. Most states also have bicameral legislatures.

Laws begin in the form of a bill, which is a proposal for legislation. Although anyone can have ideas about what laws are needed, only a Senator or Representative can introduce a bill in Congress, either individually, in collaboration with colleagues, or through the auspices of a congressional committee. This person is termed a sponsor. Other members who want to support the bill can become co-sponsors. A bill that originates in the House of Representatives begins with the letters H.R.; one that originates in the Senate begins with S. The bill is then assigned to a committee, which studies the bill. This is the stage where individuals representing diverse viewpoints can testify at public hearings. After a committee report is issued, if the committee decides to recommend the bill for passage, it moves to the floor of the House or Senate. There, members debate the bill, may amend it, and ultimately decide whether to pass it.

After a bill passes out of the chamber where it was introduced (House or Senate), it must also be voted on and passed by the majority of the members in the other chamber. If the two chambers do not agree on language for the bill, a conference committee of members from both chambers meet to resolve the differences. Both chambers must then pass the new conference version before it goes to the executive—the president or the governor. At the federal level, the president can either sign or veto the bill or allow the bill to become law without a signature. If the president vetoes the bill, both chambers must approve it with a two-thirds vote to override the veto. While the House and Senate work together to pass legislation, their duties are not identical. Appropriations bills, which actually authorize spending the money required to conduct government functions, can only originate in the House of Representatives. Only the U.S. Senate has the power to confirm certain presidential nominees, the federal judiciary, and some executive branch positions, as well as the power to approve treaties. Exhibit 4.1 illustrates the legislative process.

The **judicial branch** comprises the court system. Both federal and state judiciaries include a supreme court, intermediate appellate courts, and courts of original jurisdiction. Intermediate appellate courts hear and review appeals from cases already heard in lower courts, while courts of original jurisdiction are those in which a case is first heard. Courts will only try cases where they have jurisdiction. This requires identification of the appropriate geography and level of judiciary. There must be a justiciable case, which means that courts do not hear questions that involve only theoretical concerns rather than actual disputes. If, for example, advocates wanted to challenge state laws that restrict the rights of college students to vote by deeming student IDs unacceptable identification, they would have to determine whether to challenge the law based on a violation of the U.S. Constitution or relevant state statutory or constitutional principles.

EXHIBIT 4.1

The Legislative Process

LEGISLATIVE PROCESS

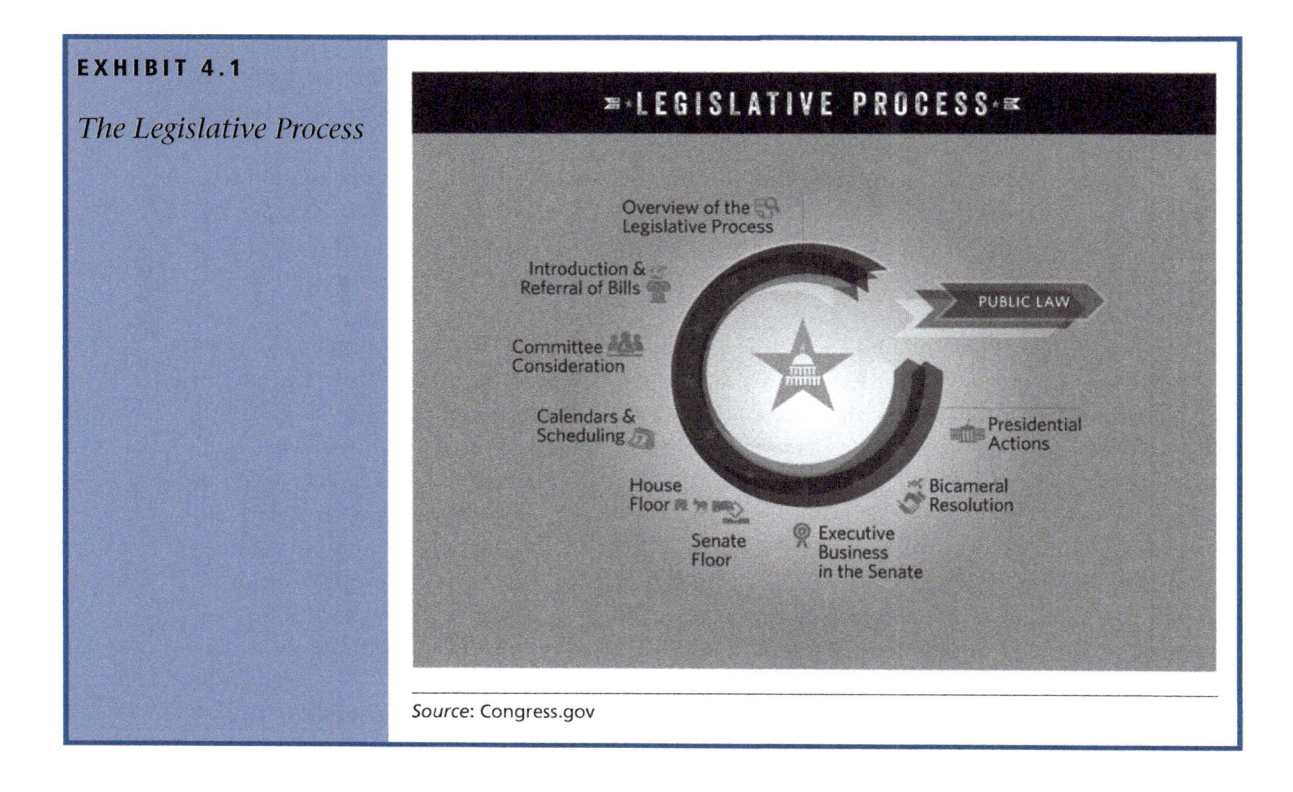

- Overview of the Legislative Process
- Introduction & Referral of Bills
- Committee Consideration
- Calendars & Scheduling
- House Floor
- Senate Floor
- Executive Business in the Senate
- Bicameral Resolution
- Presidential Actions
- PUBLIC LAW

Source: Congress.gov

They would also need to identify a student impacted by this law who would be a willing plaintiff in the case.

The U.S. Supreme Court of nine justices with lifetime appointments heads the judicial branch. The president nominates justices for confirmation by the Senate. While either side in a case may petition the U.S. Supreme Court if not satisfied with the decision of a lower court, the Supreme Court accepts only a fraction of the cases it is asked to hear. All the other courts in the country must adhere to the Supreme Court's rulings.

When the judicial branch interprets legislation, rules on legislative intent, or determines whether legislation violates the Constitution, it exerts great influence over social policy. For example, in 2010, the Supreme Court conservative majority overturned well-established precedents with substantial bipartisan backing that supported campaign finance limits. Justices invoked protection of free speech to justify the ruling (*Citizens United v. Federal Elections Commission*), which has significantly increased the capacity of corporations and other entities to influence candidates and debates, in ways that ultimately help to determine what policies are enacted. History offers other examples of the judiciary's influence in areas such as civil rights, income support, mental health, and the due process afforded within the social welfare system. Often, social work advocates turn to the courts to seek redress of grievances when legislative and executive channels do not yield desired changes. The resulting decisions can reshape social policy for generations.

THE IMPACT OF FUNDING POLICIES

Public policies influence public revenues by increasing or decreasing taxes and by promoting growth or contraction of the economy. Social policies also determine who gets how much of the economic "pie." You only have to observe one year's state legislative session or nonprofit organization's budget process to learn that dollars are finite. Although social workers should support efforts to expand resources through progressive taxation and sustainable growth strategies, they must never lose sight of this reality. The amount of funding allocated determines the extent to which programs can meet clients' needs. As you examine federal and state budgets, you can determine how funding approaches shape outcomes for your clients.

The Federal Budget and Spending Policies

The federal budget is a policy document that exerts a powerful influence on all our lives. It represents the priorities of lawmakers, which may or may not align with what citizens would prefer if they fully understood the available options and trade-offs. Each year, the White House prepares a budget for the new federal fiscal year, from October 1 through September 30, through the Office of Management and Budget (OMB). It then submits the budget to Congress for authorization and appropriation. In fiscal year (FY) 2018, the federal government spent $4.1 trillion, or approximately 20.3 percent of the nation's gross domestic product (Congressional Budget Office, 2019b). **Gross domestic product (GDP)** is the total monetary value of all goods and services produced in a country annually. While critics point out that GDP fails to account for the environmental and human consequences of economic activity (Ivkovic, 2016), instead assigning all value to economic transactions (Cass, 2018), it is the measure used to compare economic growth or contraction over time, as well as to compare economic conditions internationally.

Mandatory versus Discretionary Spending   The majority of the federal budget is earmarked for **mandatory spending**, which is government spending directed toward **entitlement programs**—those programs for which all people who meet the eligibility requirements legally qualify—as well as for interest payments on the national debt. The most prominent examples of entitlement programs are Social Security and Medicare. Mandatory spending is essentially outside of appropriators' control during a given budget year. New policies that change budget *obligations* can influence mandatory spending, but *appropriations* decisions—about the amount of money to be spent—cannot. In theory, Congress possesses the power to limit mandatory spending by modifying entitlement programs. For example, recall that Aid to Families with Dependent Children (AFDC) was once an entitlement program, until the legislation that replaced AFDC with TANF abolished this entitlement. Similarly, members of Congress have proposed replacing Medicaid's entitlement with a block grant. In an example of how politics influence spending, however, Congress is not quick to tamper with major entitlement programs. Particularly in the case of universal entitlements such as Social Security and Medicare, these investments benefit most Americans and therefore tend to be very popular with voters.

Congressional decision-making, then, focuses on that portion of the federal budget (approximately one-third) that is termed **discretionary spending**. At the federal level, discretionary spending refers to all the spending authorized by the 13 appropriation bills that are passed each year by Congress and signed by the president. It includes funding for national defense, transportation, housing supports, educational and social programs such as Head Start, and agriculture, as well as spending on the basic operations of government. Each year, Congress and the White House struggle to establish priorities concerning which programs to fund and how much money to allocate to them. Underscoring the extent to which budgets are as much about ideology as they are about financing, these debates center not just on the allocation of dollars, but also on the relative value of government activity in those spheres. One difference between discretionary and mandatory spending is that the government imposes a ceiling on discretionary spending. If that money is completely used, the government has no obligation to allocate an additional amount. These ceilings are subject to separate congressional approval and have been hotly contested in recent years by those who want to reduce spending.

General tax revenues fund all discretionary spending, some mandatory spending, and interest payments on the national debt. These are not the only revenue streams. Payroll taxes and tax expenditures also figure into the accounting of social welfare spending and influence the development of adequate health and welfare services. Nonetheless, the collection and distribution of general tax revenues, including the adequacy and equity of these processes, have important implications for social workers and clients. Look at Exhibit 4.2 to see how federal dollars were spent in FY2018. Three major categories—health care, including Medicare, Medicaid, and marketplace subsidies; Social Security; and defense spending—each made up approximately one-fifth of the budget. Many of these dollars are mandatory. Safety net programs other than

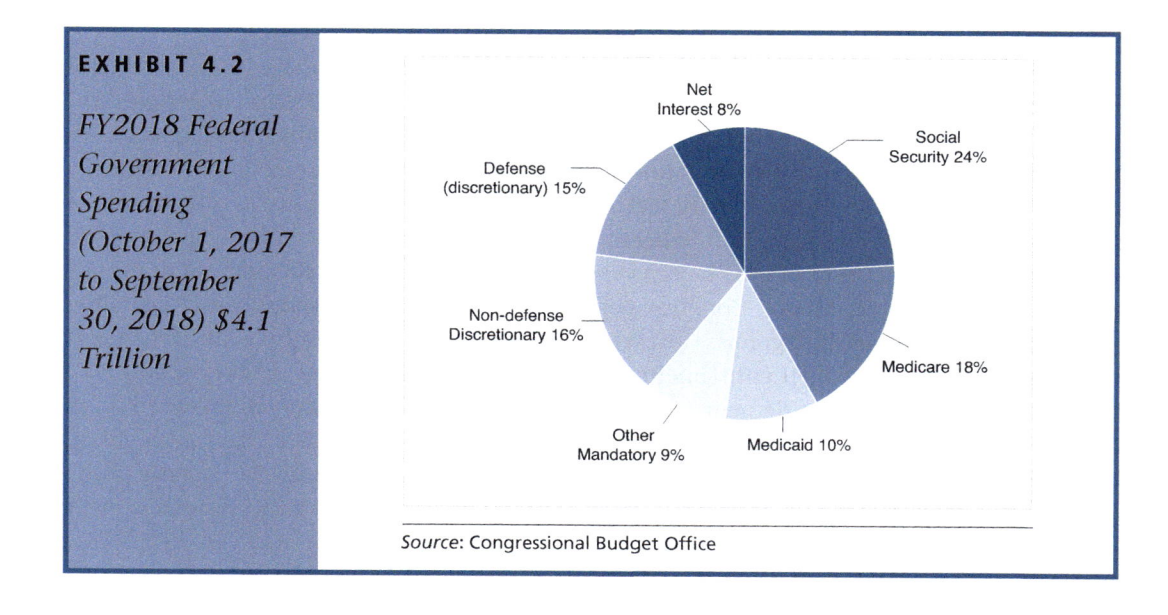

EXHIBIT 4.2

FY2018 Federal Government Spending (October 1, 2017 to September 30, 2018) $4.1 Trillion

- Net Interest 8%
- Social Security 24%
- Defense (discretionary) 15%
- Non-defense Discretionary 16%
- Other Mandatory 9%
- Medicaid 10%
- Medicare 18%

Source: Congressional Budget Office

these income support and health investments made up approximately one-tenth of the budget. These include unemployment insurance, Supplemental Nutrition Assistance Program (SNAP), the Earned Income Tax Credit, TANF, free- and reduced-price lunch and breakfast programs in schools, Supplemental Security Income (SSI), utility and childcare assistance, programs providing aid to abused and neglected children, and various other programs that provide aid to people facing hardship. Again, many of these expenditures are mandatory and, therefore, outside of the appropriation process. The United States is also obligated to pay interest on our previous debt obligations, which amounted to approximately 8 percent of the budget. The 16 percent of spending in the "non-defense discretionary" category includes veterans' health care, medical and scientific research, disaster relief, transportation, housing assistance, and education. As these funds support many valuable services social workers provide, it is imperative that social workers interested in shaping federal and state programs track **appropriations**, or the actual allocation of money to be spent, in addition to monitoring and influencing budget proposals.

The Federal Deficit and Federal Debt The federal government runs a surplus when the amount of all tax revenue exceeds spending in a given year. Conversely, it runs a deficit when spending exceeds tax revenues. In FY2018, the federal deficit totaled $779 billion; for FY2019, it was projected to be $896 billion (Congressional Budget Office, 2019a). The federal deficit is calculated on a yearly basis. See Exhibit 4.3 for information on total deficits or surpluses, from 1969 projected through 2029.

The national debt is the total amount of federal debt, which includes the sum of all previously incurred annual federal deficits. Different measures are used to account for national debt, some of which consider debt held by government accounts, such as Social Security trust funds, and some of which look only at net debt, which is debt minus financial assets held by the

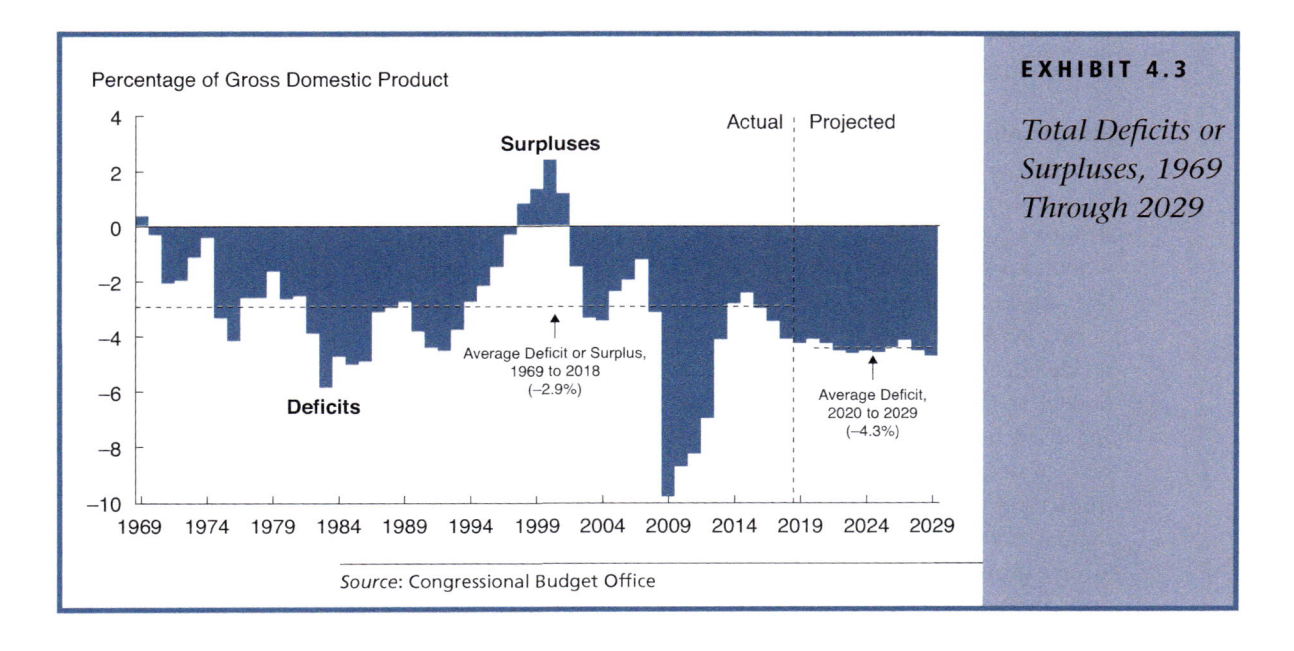

EXHIBIT 4.3

Total Deficits or Surpluses, 1969 Through 2029

Source: Congressional Budget Office

federal government, such as student loans. Using the most common public debt measure, in FY2018, the national debt approached $16 trillion, or almost 78 percent of GDP (Congressional Budget Office, 2019a). To find the current size of the national debt, visit the U.S. Department of the Treasury website (**www.treasurydirect.gov**), and search for "Debt to the Penny." Federal spending on the wars in Iraq and Afghanistan and to stimulate economic recovery contributed to the increase in the national debt, as did reductions in revenues that resulted from the recession and from tax cuts in 2001 and 2003. Although it is too early to determine the ultimate impact, the nonpartisan Joint Committee on Taxation predicts that the 2017 Tax Cuts and Jobs Act will increase federal deficits by $1.46 trillion over the next decade, an effect that will add to debt pressures. Although programs for low-income Americans are often the target of public criticism, outside of health care, future expenditures on programs that serve low-income Americans are projected to fall below the average for the last 40 years, as a percentage of GDP (Greenstein, Kogan, & Horton, 2018). Social workers should be prepared to explain the ways that increased health care spending and insufficient revenues contribute to the nation's long-term fiscal challenges and to frame programs that help those disadvantaged as investments in our collective well-being and capacity.

Social Security and Medicare do not affect the public debt. Although these entitlement programs are included in the overall budget, because they are designed on an insurance model, they are funded through payroll taxes that flow into the Social Security Trust Fund and the Medicare Hospital Insurance Trust Fund. Although many critics complain about the percentage of the federal budget devoted to these programs, current rates of payroll taxes, which can also be thought of as insurance premiums, are sufficient to fund Social Security retirement until 2034 and Social Security Disability Insurance until 2052 (Social Security Administration, 2019b). Even after that date, current policies will fund more than three-quarters of the Social Security Trust Fund's obligations without further reform until 2093, suggesting that relatively modest changes enacted soon could ensure long-term sustainability. The Medicare Hospital Trust Fund faces greater fiscal pressures but is solvent through 2026 (Centers for Medicaid and Medicare Services, 2019a).

Budget Allocation Issues Political differences over central funding issues—who should pay, who should benefit, and which programs should grow or shrink—must be resolved, at least temporarily, before the budget can be approved (Schick, 2000). Government spending is a redistributive process, meaning that it results in gains for some and losses for others. For example, when expenditures for defense escalate, fewer dollars are available for social programs unless lawmakers are willing to let the federal deficit increase dramatically. The deficit did just that during 2009 and 2010, as the United States simultaneously combated global security threats and tackled deep recession. Exhibit 4.4 shows the change in government spending as a proportion of GDP in the 60-year period from 1968 to projections through 2028. As illustrated, mandatory spending has increased dramatically and is projected to continue to grow, to an estimated 15 percent of GDP in 2028, compared to an average of less than 10 percent for the 50-year period from 1968 to 2017 (Congressional Budget Office, 2018a). Particularly sharp increases in mandatory spending are noted in the period surrounding the Great Recession, when programs that always grow during economic downturns (called **countercyclical programs**, including SNAP and unemployment insurance) increased in response to greater need.

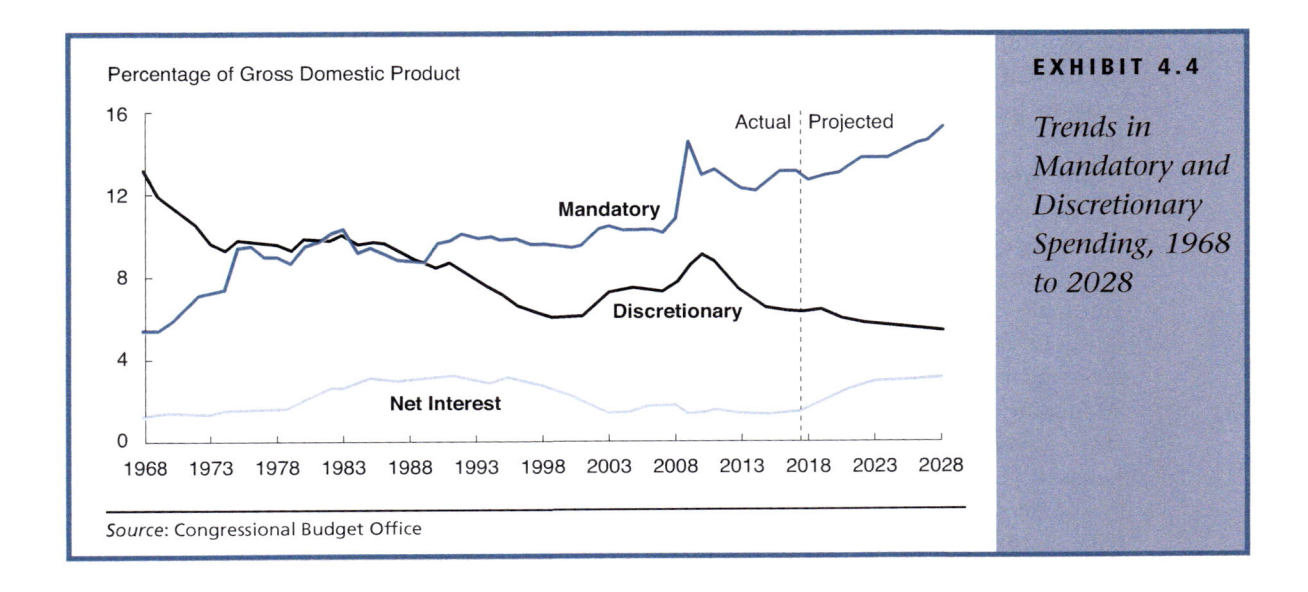

EXHIBIT 4.4

Trends in Mandatory and Discretionary Spending, 1968 to 2028

Percentage of Gross Domestic Product

Source: Congressional Budget Office

In contrast to trends in mandatory spending, the percentage of GDP consumed by discretionary spending has fallen steadily throughout this period. Decreases in discretionary spending are projected to continue for at least the next decade. Indeed, the Trump Administration's budget proposals would reduce non-defense discretionary spending to less than 50 percent of its FY2010 level. Further, these cuts are not equitably distributed but instead would fall disproportionately on low-income individuals and families who depend on safety-net programs (Reich, 2018). While many of the president's proposed cuts have been ignored by Congress, powerful political actors are clearly advancing a budget vision that deemphasizes investment in and support for working families and communities struggling with poverty.

Beyond direct spending on services, the government promotes social welfare through other policies such as tax incentives, infrastructure investment, and antidiscrimination laws. The federal government can also influence policy by withholding federal dollars. For example, the federal government can pass laws requiring states to implement policies such as restrictions on teenage drivers or standards for the issuance of identification cards as a condition for receiving federal funds. If a state fails to implement these policies, the federal government can withhold funds from that state.

State Budgets and Spending Policies

State budgets also have important ramifications for social welfare. In FY2018, state and local government expenditures contributed $2.9 trillion to national economic activity, including in critical areas of social investment (Nunn, Parsons, & Shambaugh, 2019a). As discussed in Chapter 3, beginning with the Reagan Administration, the federal government increasingly shifted responsibilities for social welfare to the states. Federal and state budgets are linked in multiple ways, although the difference in power between the federal government and states means that this relationship is primarily one-directional. States receive financial support and incentives for programs such as Medicaid, for which they are required to provide matching funds; states that fail to provide these funds lose federal monies. Additionally, changes in the federal tax code impact state budgets, because most states link their tax policies to federal law. Further, when the federal government retreats from some areas of responsibility, states often must step in to fill the resulting gaps.

For some programs, such as TANF, federal support takes the form of block grants. This mechanism allows states discretion over how to spend federal allocations. However, block grants are capped, so that if the need for services increases, the federal government will not automatically provide additional funding. Some states now are following the federal government's lead and using a variety of funding strategies to cut back on spending. This can leave local governments and community-based organizations to bear additional burdens for addressing pressing concerns such as homelessness and food insecurity. Because lower levels of government have less capacity to respond to economic crises and other extraordinary needs, this devolution of responsibility for social welfare puts client groups at great risk.

Moreover, unlike the federal government, most state governments are required by law to balance their budgets. When the economy is not growing, states must increase taxes, reduce spending, and/or identify new sources of revenue. In some cases, struggling states attempt some combination of these strategies. Unfortunately, spending cuts often target social welfare programs, regardless of their effectiveness or demonstrated need. Even among populations reliant on social welfare spending, not all populations are equally affected by state budget cuts. In particular, because public funding for child development mainly comes out of state budgets, children often bear the brunt of state cuts. However, when states are severely squeezed, the pain is relatively widespread. In cycles of economic crisis, state budget cuts can deepen a recession, as laid-off public workers and individuals whose benefits have been cut are less able to participate in economic activity. As evidence of the disparities in state and federal experiences of recession, more than five years after the official end of the Great Recession, tax collections in 29 states had not rebounded (Pew Charitable Trusts, 2015a), and a similar share had not restored K-12 education funding to its 2008 level (Leachman, Masterson, & Figueroa, 2017).

In general, a state's economic resources and political climate determine which programs will be cut and how drastically. Powerful business interests in some states have successfully pressed for tax cuts based on the supply-side claim that lower taxes will spur economic growth. Corporate power is often amplified at the state level, as state governments react to business threats to relocate if the state raises taxes. As is true at the federal level, women, people of color, and people with low incomes are generally underrepresented in state government. As a result, their interests are seldom prioritized, and the education and social programs designed to assist them are especially vulnerable to pressures to reduce spending.

For all these reasons, states' ability to help people meet their needs is more limited than the federal government's. The federal government has often assumed the responsibility to protect people's interests when states are unwilling or unable to do so adequately (Gordon, 1998). Because the federal government can run a deficit, it is able to keep borrowing and spending even when tax revenues are insufficient. However, the increasing federal deficit and national debt can create economic instability, generational strain, and political tensions—realities that underscore the need to pursue revenue generation as part of overall economic policy.

Tax Strategies

Tax policy can be a powerful instrument for ensuring that people's basic needs are adequately met. However, it is often used as a tool for redistributing resources from lower and middle socioeconomic groups to the wealthy. Indeed, tax policy can even destroy the revenue foundation on which an effective public safety net can be built. Therefore, it is important for social workers to understand some fundamentals of the tax system.

We pay taxes to fund local, state, and federal services and benefits. While all taxes can be used to finance social welfare investments, they are not equal in terms of their effects. **Regressive taxes** require people with lower incomes to pay higher rates or proportions of their income, compared to higher-income taxpayers. For example, sales taxes on food and clothing are regressive because low-income people spend a higher percentage of their incomes on these necessities. Sales taxes are typically used to fund services at the local level, although some states rely heavily on sales taxes as well, particularly where states have reduced income taxes because of ideological preferences or to compete for corporate investment. In contrast, **progressive taxes** require people with higher incomes to pay a greater percentage of their income, compared to lower-income taxpayers. Federal and state income taxes are usually examples of progressive taxes. However, tax deductions and other mechanisms can reduce the progressivity of income tax structures.

A type of tax that you began to pay when you started your first job is commonly called a **payroll tax**, which your employer deducts from your pay and sends to the government. Some payroll deductions, while called "taxes," are not intended to be a source of general revenue for the government and so are not true taxes. Instead, the amounts deducted for the Federal Insurance Contribution Act (FICA) and for Medicare are premiums you are paying to public insurance programs from which you are entitled to draw benefits if you become disabled or when you retire. Employees pay only half of these payroll taxes; employers pay the other half. Referring to payments made for OASDI and Medicare as insurance premiums rather than payroll taxes highlights that these monies fund public insurance programs. Nonetheless, these deductions are a substantial part of the "tax" obligation of many Americans; many people pay more in payroll taxes than in income taxes. Further, because these insurance premiums/payroll taxes are not assessed on some of the incomes of very high earners or on non-wage income (such as interest earned on investments), they are regressive.

An additional area of tax policy that exerts a powerful influence on social welfare is that which governs tax expenditures. Economists apply the term **tax expenditures** to tax incentives (exemptions, deductions, and credits) that the government extends to particular groups to assist them in obtaining services such as housing and health care, or to reward them for taking actions such as saving for retirement or for their children's college educations. Tax expenditures are one way that Americans receive financial support from the government. Although tax credits, deductions, and exemptions typically do not draw the attention that proposals to increase appropriations or cut taxes do, tax expenditures represent lost revenue the government is not able to use for other purposes, such as paying down the debt, providing more military funding, or increasing social welfare expenditures. The government determines that this money will remain with the person filing taxes instead of being collected for other purposes.

These tax breaks operate in much the same way as direct expenditures. Recall that mandatory spending does not go through a direct appropriation process each year, and neither do most tax expenditures. Rather, they continue and may even expand without any congressional action. Further, many tax expenditures and social programs target the same goals. For example, when corporations are given tax breaks to encourage employer-provided pensions and individuals' tax obligations are reduced based on their contributions to retirement accounts, tax expenditure policy addresses the goal of retirement security, as does Social Security.

As direct benefits to individuals that are merely less visible than TANF or Social Security payments, tax expenditures are an important part of the social policy "toolbox" that policymakers use to advance various social agendas. For example, Pell Grants, subsidized student loans, and tax breaks for college tuition all aim to offset the costs of pursuing higher education. All represent considerable federal government expense; analysts estimate that higher education-related tax credits, deductions, and exclusions will cost the federal government $132.4 billion between 2018 and 2022 (Joint Committee on Taxation, 2018), while spending on Pell Grants was more than $28 billion in FY2018 (U.S. Department of Education, 2017). However, size is not the only metric by which investments should be evaluated. There is evidence that, compared to direct investments such as need-based financial aid, education tax expenditures are distributed less equitably and operate less efficiently. Tax credits are provided only after students have come up with the money for tuition, deductions can be complicated to claim, and many needy students do not receive any benefit from these complex and poorly targeted provisions (York, 2019). Such evaluations raise concerns about needed reforms to make tax expenditures more potent investments in social welfare.

Looking beyond higher education, in FY2017, more than 200 tax expenditures totaling almost $1.7 trillion were paid to individuals and corporations. That amount equated to almost 9 percent of GDP, more than half of all federal revenues received in that year (Congressional Budget Office [CBO], 2018a). The importance of tax expenditures is well recognized; in fact, the president is required to submit a tax expenditure budget to Congress. Exhibit 4.5 documents

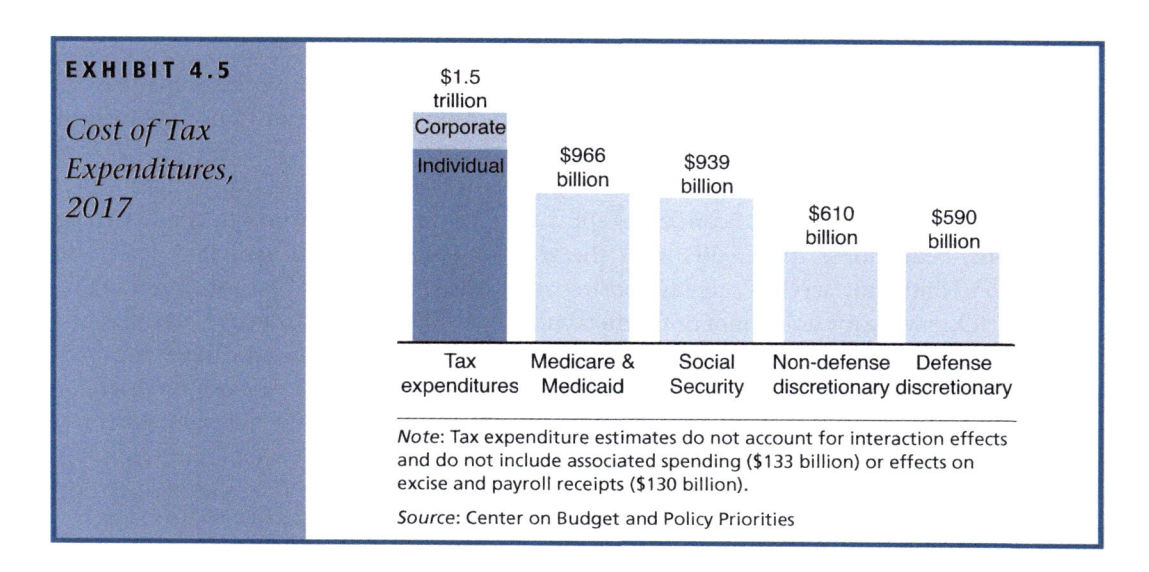

EXHIBIT 4.5

Cost of Tax Expenditures, 2017

Tax expenditures (Corporate + Individual)	$1.5 trillion
Medicare & Medicaid	$966 billion
Social Security	$939 billion
Non-defense discretionary	$610 billion
Defense discretionary	$590 billion

Note: Tax expenditure estimates do not account for interaction effects and do not include associated spending ($133 billion) or effects on excise and payroll receipts ($130 billion).

Source: Center on Budget and Policy Priorities

the use of tax expenditures at the federal level. As you can see, tax expenditures dwarf spending on other social programs often considered "too expensive."

While similar in intent and comparable in size, the distributive effects of direct and tax expenditures are dramatically different. Specifically, more than half of the combined benefits of tax expenditures accrue to households in the highest one-fifth of the population, with 24 percent going to households in the top 1 percent and only 4 percent to households in the lowest income quintile (CBPP, 2019). Exhibit 4.6 illustrates the distribution of tax entitlements by income. After changes in the Tax Credit and Jobs Act (TCJA) take full effect, analysts anticipate that this distribution will swing even more decisively in the direction of those most advantaged. As the TCJA increased the standard deduction and capped state and local income tax deductions, fewer Americans are expected to itemize their tax returns. As a result, while middle-income households received 6.4 percent of the mortgage interest deduction in 2017, they will receive only 4.3 percent in 2018, while those with incomes in the 95th to 99th percentiles will receive almost 30 percent (Gleckman, 2018). Additionally, the TCJA capped the refundable Child Tax Credit, while extending its benefits to wealthy families. In an echo of supply-side economics, some justify these policies and the inequities they fuel by arguing that expenditures targeted to upper-income households will improve the economy. However, this argument is rooted in ideological debate more than economic fact. Expenditures for low-income people also provide an economic stimulus because those with low incomes must spend most of their money immediately on necessities.

Although this is seldom the case, tax expenditures can be used to promote social justice. For example, the Earned Income Tax Credit (EITC), which is refundable, redistributes financial resources to low-income working families. Importantly, because it is administered through the tax code, the EITC lifts households out of poverty without the stigma and administrative costs of some means-tested programs.

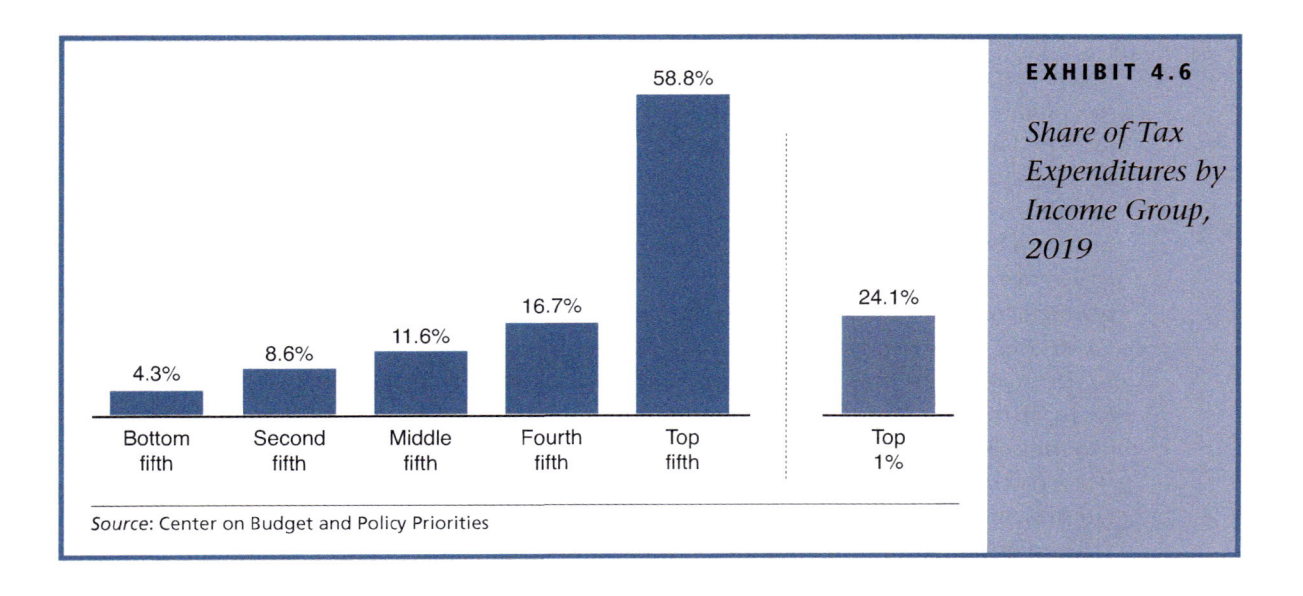

EXHIBIT 4.6

Share of Tax Expenditures by Income Group, 2019

Income Group	Share
Bottom fifth	4.3%
Second fifth	8.6%
Middle fifth	11.6%
Fourth fifth	16.7%
Top fifth	58.8%
Top 1%	24.1%

Source: Center on Budget and Policy Priorities

Tax expenditures and direct appropriations are not the only ways the government uses tax policy to influence behavior and outcomes. For example, higher taxes on tobacco and alcohol are used to discourage smoking and drinking. Some states are experimenting with taxes on certain beverages and foods to encourage healthier nutrition. Of course, when the targeted behavior is dramatically discouraged, revenues are reduced, making these taxes an effective policy lever but a poor long-term revenue source. Additionally, strengths-based social workers recognize the need to consider such tax policies through a lens of equity, in addition to efficiency. When policies fail to consider the social determinants of behavior, tax incentives and penalties can unfairly reward privileged individuals and punish those disadvantaged.

EVALUATING CURRENT U.S. SOCIAL WELFARE EXPENDITURES

To evaluate social policy, we must carefully consider social welfare expenditures. Typically, the term **social welfare expenditures** refers to all spending necessary to sustain core social welfare programs. Core federal programs include TANF, Social Security, Medicaid, Medicare, SSI, SNAP, Head Start, various housing and job training programs, educational grants, veterans' benefits, and unemployment benefits. State and local programs include education (early childhood, K–12, and post-secondary), programs for people with mental illness, health and social services, corrections, and workers' compensation. Although administered on state or local levels, these programs are often subsidized in part by the federal government.

In the United States, the largest component of social welfare spending is social insurance, particularly Old Age, Survivor, and Disability Insurance (OASDI, commonly called "Social Security") and Medicare. Significantly, most of the recipients of social insurance benefits are not poor, although many would fall into poverty were it not for these programs.

The Nature of U.S. Social Welfare Spending

Recall that, beginning in the 1980s, there was growing pressure to curtail welfare benefits, reconfigure universal programs, and institute strict means testing. A sluggish economy, increased mistrust of government, and the growing pressures of globalization all fueled support for these cutbacks. Some scholars also link increasing diversity to reduced public support for welfare spending (Alesina & La Ferrara, 2005, among others), which suggests that the growing inclusion of people of color in welfare programs, due to civil rights gains, also contributed to preference for retrenchment. The conservative political philosophy that emerged during this period favored privatization of social welfare activities and the devolution of many fundamental services to state and local levels. Today, state and local governments have a more prominent role in many aspects of policy decision-making than the federal government, particularly in terms of the key investments in infrastructure, education, and other components that help determine long-term productive capacity (Nunn et al., 2019a).

As social workers often observe in practice, this approach increased fragmentation in a welfare system already notorious for its lack of cohesion. However, although some programs have suffered drastic cuts and few are able to keep up with increasing demand, aggregate funding for social welfare programs has mostly increased on an annual basis. These increases reflect the difficulty of enacting sweeping policy changes. Organized constituencies often resist loss of benefits, elected officials face political risks in withdrawing needed investments, and demographic pressures compel spending, particularly in entitlement programs.

When social welfare is defined broadly, most social welfare expenditures are not targeted toward low-income people. However, the popular definition of "social welfare" is often limited to assistance for people categorized as needy. This not only contributes to people's resistance to invest in public social welfare programs they do not perceive as benefiting "people like them," it also obscures the substantial role public policy plays in facilitating the well-being and success of those already advantaged. For example, when people identify social welfare expenditures, they are more likely to think of means-tested financial aid than tax incentives for families' college savings, even though, as described above, both policies serve to place higher education more readily within reach. Crucially, while they serve similar ends, programs directed primarily at people with higher incomes are often more strengths-based than those aimed at low-income people; the former, for example, encourage asset-building and place people in control of their own decisions, while the latter carry some stigma and are more tightly controlled (Elliott & Lewis, 2018). Using a more comprehensive definition of social welfare helps draw attention to what has been termed "the upside-down welfare state" (Abramovitz, 2001, p. 298), where more substantial and valuable assistance is provided to those with the least need, by objective measures.

Adequacy of Current Expenditures for Social Programs

In addition to the principles of economic efficiency and equity, social workers should consider the adequacy of social welfare programs, including those provided by the tax system. **Adequacy** refers to the ability of social welfare programs to sufficiently meet public needs. Determining whether public social welfare expenditures are adequate is a complex and value-laden task that can only be considered accurately in comparison to policy goals and some conception of an "ideal" state of social welfare. Accounting for the adequacy of social welfare programs requires looking at the extent to which they address people's daily needs. This, in turn, means looking at actual costs of living. However, this is a complicated process. Different families have different spending needs, depending on whether members have disabilities or whether there are young children who need childcare. Households eligible for more generous assistance programs may find a given income "adequate," while those earning higher incomes but lacking those supports may struggle to make ends meet. And the cost of living in New York, for example, is very different from Missouri. One way to assess social welfare programs in the United States is to look at equity and adequacy in the context of income distribution.

Income Distribution   Income distribution in the United States is highly unequal. In 2017, median household income was $60,336. However, average income of households in the top 5 percent was $385,289, while households in the lowest quintile had an average income of $13,258 (Fontenot, Semega, & Kollar, 2018). Even when the wages of households in the lower tiers of the U.S. economy increase—2018 saw the biggest wage gains in a decade—inflation often means that their purchasing power barely budges (Desilver, 2018).

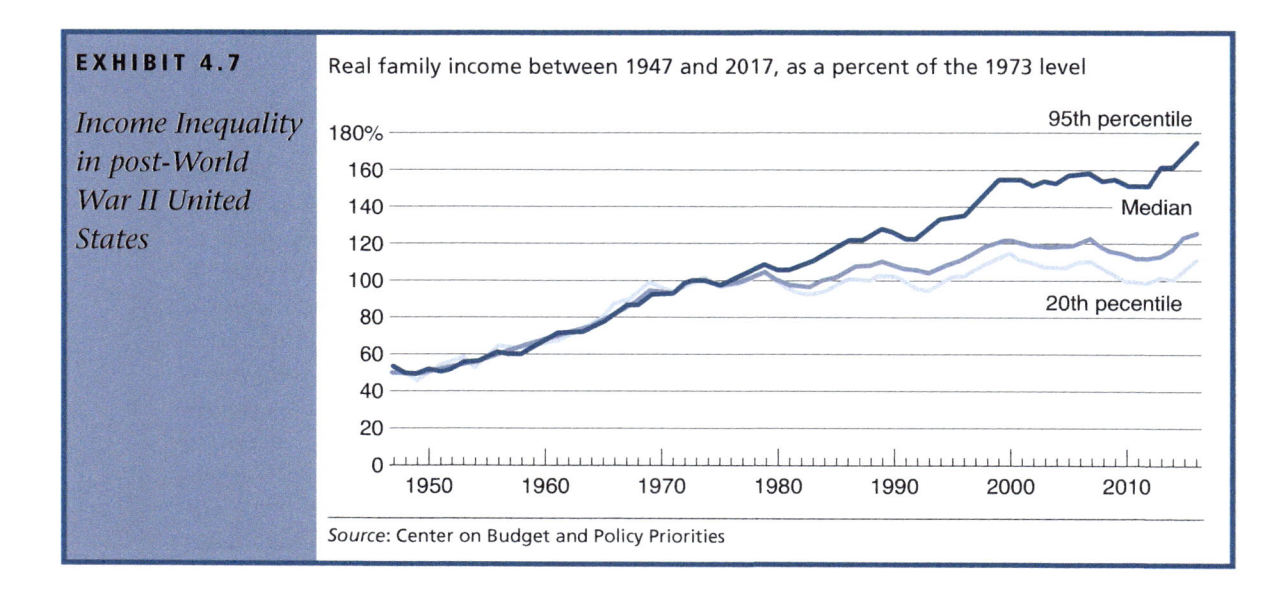

EXHIBIT 4.7

Income Inequality in post-World War II United States

Real family income between 1947 and 2017, as a percent of the 1973 level

Source: Center on Budget and Policy Priorities

Social welfare programs and tax strategies can be used to more equitably distribute income. However, as Exhibit 4.7 illustrates, since 1980 the gap between income classes has increased dramatically. Note that those with the highest income have experienced substantially greater income growth than have those in the other groups. Despite the myth that the United States is a classless society where individuals can rise from poverty to prosperity (Reisch, 2017b), economic mobility rates are low. Indeed, analysis has found that the chance of surpassing one's parents' economic standing is only about 50 percent for those born in 1980 or later, compared to more than 90 percent for those in prior generations (Chetty et al., 2016). Importantly, there is evidence that income inequality plays a major role in making it harder for Americans to improve their economic position; if inequality had not risen dramatically starting in the 1970s, upward mobility rates today would be more like 80 percent (Chetty et al., 2016).

Further, mobility has not vanished; instead, like so much else in the economy, it is inequitably distributed. For Americans born in 1984, those at the top of the income ladder have a 70 percent chance of surpassing their parents' earnings, while those near the bottom are half as likely to achieve that feat. Disadvantaged Americans do not just *feel* "stuck"; in many cases, they are, and that contributes to intensifying anxiety and growing hopelessness. That these effects contribute to alarming trends of suicide and overdose—what economists Case and Deaton (2015) have called "deaths of despair"—illustrates how economic conditions directly impact well-being. Further, economic fortunes are not only relatively fixed but also inequitably distributed, with people of color, those with disabilities, and older women disproportionately clustered in the lowest income quintiles. Indicative of the extent to which race determines Americans' economic outcomes, children of color, especially Black boys, are more likely to experience downward mobility than to improve their standing in adulthood (Chetty et al., 2018). If our policies adequately and equitably distributed economic opportunities, these children would have a fairer chance to succeed.

As Thomas Piketty, a prominent French economist, has pointed out, the rise in the top-percentile income share is correlated with declines in top marginal tax rates (Piketty, 2014). This adds to the evidence that suggests that escalating inequality is at least partially fueled by U.S. policy decisions. Further, contrary to the claims of supply-side economists, tax cuts for the very rich have not resulted in greater per capita economic growth (Piketty, 2014). Nor has economic growth brought widespread prosperity. Instead, inequality intensified in the recovery from the Great Recession; during the expansion of recent years, the stock market has climbed to historic highs, but many Americans struggle to make ends meet and feel largely left out of the "recovery" altogether. In 43 states, incomes of the top 1 percent grew more quickly than incomes of the bottom 99 percent, such that, nationally, the top 1 percent of families made more than 26 times as much as the bottom 99 percent in 2015 (Sommeiller & Price, 2018). Ensuring that lower-income households will benefit from economic expansion will clearly require intentional policy measures to redistribute opportunities.

Inequality in Wealth Wealth inequality is even starker than income gaps. Here, the divide reflects not only the compounding effects of income inequality, but also the ways that policy facilitates asset-building for wealthy households—including tax laws favorable to corporations, lower marginal tax rates on the highest incomes, tax incentives to encourage saving and investing, and reduced estate taxes on people with great wealth—while constraining wealth accumulation among those economically disadvantaged. The share of wealth held by the richest 400 Americans tripled between the early 1980s and 2016, such that they own more than the 150 million adults in the bottom 60 percent of the wealth distribution (Zucman, 2019). The growing concentration of wealth illustrated in Exhibit 4.8 has reached levels last seen in the United States in the 1920s—the period immediately preceding the economic collapse of the Great Depression.

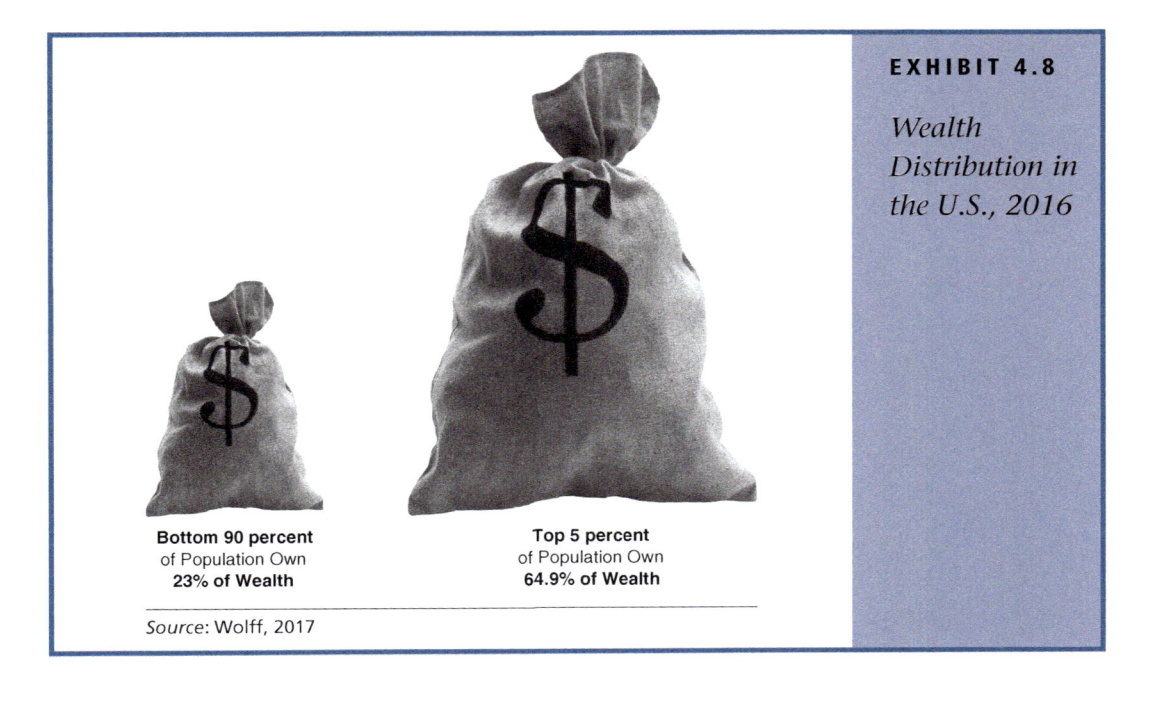

EXHIBIT 4.8

Wealth Distribution in the U.S., 2016

Bottom 90 percent of Population Own **23% of Wealth**

Top 5 percent of Population Own **64.9% of Wealth**

Source: Wolff, 2017

Wealth is not just about money, but also about power. Wealth inequality in the United States today resembles China and Russia, nations not known for advancement of the democratic values on which ours is supposed to rest (Zucman, 2019). Increasing concentration of wealth and the growing gap between the rich and poor have allowed the economic elite to consolidate power, use that power to influence the political process, and pursue policies that prevent workers' wages from rising with productivity (Bartels, 2002). Inequality, then, becomes not only the result of social policies unfair to those in and near poverty, but also a contributor to those same policies. After the 2016 election of Donald Trump, when many voters attributed their support to his stated intention to address their economic anxieties and avenge their perceived loss of economic dignity, former Labor Secretary Robert Reich's 2015 assertion sounded like an accurate prediction:

> The most important political competition over the next decades will not be between the right and left, or between Republicans and Democrats. It will be between a majority of Americans who have been losing ground, and an economic elite that refuses to recognize or respond to its growing distress.
>
> (Reich, 2015)

Inequality pulls Americans apart, as the "haves" and "have-nots" live very different realities, even within the same country. This is perhaps nowhere demonstrated more dramatically than in the nation's astronomically high racial wealth gap, depicted in Exhibit 4.9. The result of a legacy of institutionalized racism and ongoing disparities, the racial wealth gap both contributes

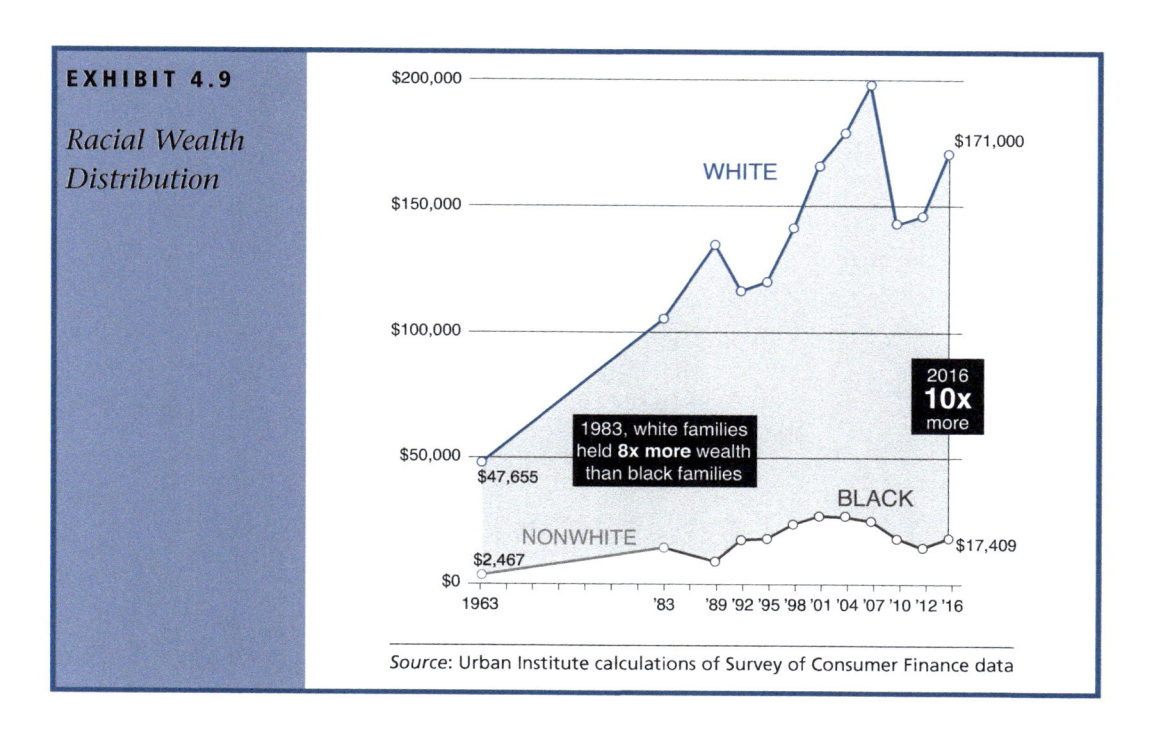

EXHIBIT 4.9

Racial Wealth Distribution

- WHITE: $171,000 (2016)
- NONWHITE: $2,467 (1963)
- BLACK: $17,409 (2016)
- 1983, white families held **8x more** wealth than black families ($47,655)
- 2016: **10x** more

Source: Urban Institute calculations of Survey of Consumer Finance data

to and results from divergent outcomes for White Americans and people of color. Between 1934 and 1962, the Federal Housing Administration and Veterans Administration financed more than $120 billion worth of new housing; because of racial restrictions on mortgage lending and property ownership, less than 2 percent was available to households of color (Lipsitz, 2006). Tracing this inequity forward, in 2016, the median White household wealth was $171,000, compared to $17,409 for African Americans (Urban Institute, 2017). Using average measures, White family wealth was seven times greater than Black family wealth and five times greater than Latinx family wealth in 2016. And, rhetoric about our "post-racial" nation notwithstanding, this divide seems likely to grow. Homeownership, which represents the greatest asset of most Americans, has fallen in Black households almost every year since 2004, as pervasive racism, rollbacks in government protections, and the lingering effects of the Great Recession saw African-American homeownership fall to 43 percent in 2017, virtually erasing the gains made since the passage of the Fair Housing Act in 1968 (Joint Center for Housing Studies, 2018).

U.S. Social Welfare Expenditures Compared to Those of Other Countries In the United States, direct public welfare expenditures as a percentage of GDP have historically been lower than those of other industrialized countries. Further, spending is often fragmented. Cities and counties may invest separately from federal and state initiatives aimed at the same needs, often with little coordination. Some local areas have more resources of their own from which to finance additional investments; this contributes not only to complexity, but also to inequity among different groups and parts of the country. On the global stage, the United States is exceptional in that corporate and voluntary sectors have long been integral to our social welfare system. Those expenditures often go uncounted in international comparisons (Hacker, 2002). In fact, it has been argued that if tax expenditures and private social benefits are considered, U.S. social welfare spending is relatively high per capita. Of course, private benefits can often be withdrawn, as observed in the decline in corporate-sponsored pension plans. Tying benefits to employment also means that losing a job may mean losing benefits, and those who lack connection to the labor market are often locked out of these benefits entirely. Thus, risk is shifted onto the individual when the private rather than the public sector provides benefits.

The Organisation for Economic Co-operation and Development (OECD), an international organization devoted to promoting economic growth and world trade, collects data on the spending of various countries. The social expenditures primarily fall into three broad categories:

1. pension payments such as old-age cash benefits, including survivors' benefits;
2. income-based support for working-age people experiencing need due to illness, disability, or loss of earnings; and
3. health and other expenditures for children, older adults, and people with disabilities, as well as programs that train people to return to work.

These data do not include similar benefits provided by private sources, or in the many levels of government such as towns and counties. As described above, because U.S. social welfare services rely more heavily on city-, county-, and state-level spending, as well as on the participation of private entities, these comparisons underestimate social welfare spending in the United States.

EXHIBIT 4.10

Public Social Expenditure as a Percent of GDP, 1960, 1990, and 2018

Source: OECD Social Expenditure database

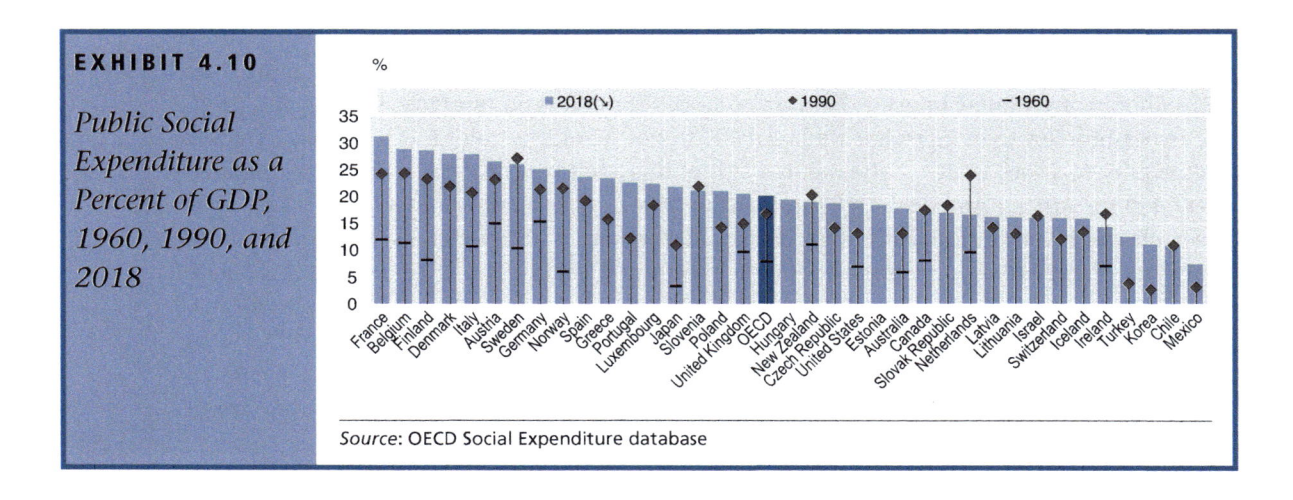

Exhibit 4.10 compares social expenditures in the United States to other countries. As shown, public social expenditures for items like health insurance, pensions, and income support to working-age populations consumed a larger share of GDP in most nations in 2018 than in 1990. Further, global public social spending is concentrated on pensions and health, while family support constitutes only 2.1 percent of GDP, on average, and is seldom targeted to those with the lowest incomes (OECD, 2019a). Finally, the percentage of the U.S. GDP dedicated to public social spending (18.7 percent in 2018) is less than the average among these developed nations and far below the countries with the most generous supports.

In recent decades, most Western governments have either reduced spending on social programs or arrested their growth, often in response to changing demographics, sluggish economic growth, and/or increasing pressure to reduce taxation. For example, as a condition for debt bailout, the European Union imposed austerity measures on Greece that included substantial cuts to public workers' pay, public pensions, and public education. Other countries adopted their own cuts in response to pressure from international lenders and/or domestic debt strains. Italy increased health care fees and cut pensions and family tax benefits, Ireland cut public workers' pay and social welfare benefits including the child allowance, and the United Kingdom increased the retirement age and cut public jobs.

Due to the government's hesitance to fund more social welfare provisions, Wilensky and Lebeaux (1965) defined the United States as a "reluctant welfare state." However, **welfare pluralists** reject the notion that the United States is a laggard in the social welfare arena. They do not believe that needs should be met primarily by the government but instead argue that people can and do enhance their well-being with the help of neighbors or families, by purchasing services on the market, or by obtaining help from voluntary organizations.

The question thus arises: How do we assess whether the approaches used in the United States address people's needs as effectively as the largely publicly financed programs in other countries? What insights are revealed when we look at countries' approaches to social welfare through the lens of the strengths perspective? One strategy is to examine health and welfare indicators, including infant mortality, childhood poverty, mental and physical health, and elder welfare. In the United States, the infant mortality rate is higher than most European countries as well as many other countries, including Canada, Australia, South Korea, Croatia, New Zealand, Singapore, Japan, and Cuba (World Bank, 2018a). Infant mortality is half as common in Scandinavia and extremely rare in Japan, with only two deaths per 1,000 live births, compared to almost six per 1,000 in the United States (Central Intelligence Agency, 2017). This outcome undoubtedly reflects the lack of universal health care in the United States, as well as inequities that make some populations especially vulnerable to poor health outcomes. Specifically, the mortality of African-American infants is more than twice that of non-Latinx White infants (Kochanek, Murphy, Xu, & Arias, 2017). The United States also has a high rate of childhood poverty compared to other developed countries. Of course, countries differ on these indicators for a variety of reasons. Nevertheless, the adequacy of the social welfare system and the persistence of racial inequality are certainly among them.

Investing in the workforce by providing effective public education, health care, and other supports can improve health and economic outcomes. Although some in the United States contend that instituting higher taxes to pay for these investments will damage the nation's position in the global economy, many developed countries with more comprehensive social welfare systems and higher taxes than the United States are very competitive. It appears, then, that political forces, more than economic ones, explain the U.S. reluctance to finance and administer a more robust public social welfare system. Before consenting to the higher taxes needed for the kind of universal public programs likely required to improve outcomes, Americans must accept shared responsibility for our collective well-being.

The Role of the Private Sector

Of course, governments do not fund or administer all social welfare programs. Many operate through the private sector, which is composed of for-profit and nonprofit organizations such as hospitals, long-term care facilities, addiction treatment centers, community groups, religious institutions, foundations, and social service agencies. An increasingly prominent type of private organization is a social enterprise. **Social enterprises** address unmet needs or solve social or environmental problems through market-driven approaches, including by providing employment opportunities to those with significant barriers, selling transformative products or services, or producing revenue that is then funneled to nonprofits. In some cases, existing nonprofits may incorporate social enterprise models into their operations to generate revenue; in other cases, for-profit companies may integrate social impact goals alongside traditional profit motives. Social enterprises illustrate a principal characteristic of private sector entities: they employ a variety of funding strategies and so can be very flexible. They often have a mix of clients, some of whom pay privately for services, some of whom rely on third-party private resources such as philanthropic grants, and some of whom rely on public funding. For example, in a for-profit long-term care facility, it is not uncommon for taxpayer money in the form of Medicaid to pay the bills for more than half of the residents, while others pay with their own resources. Such facilities are often able to hold costs down for private-pay clients and still make a profit because public funding largely finances infrastructure and fixed costs.

Although privatization is an increasingly significant trend in social welfare, private organizations have limitations that make them imperfect substitutions for public commitment to the social contract. Private entities are not well-suited to meet needs during economic crises, when demand increases as private contributions decrease. Privately funded organizations are also vulnerable to changes in public policy, political pressures, and economic contexts. For example, the TCJA has reduced the number of Americans who itemize their taxes, which is expected to make it harder for private nonprofits to solicit charitable contributions. Even in the best conditions, government sources provide a substantial portion of funding for many private agencies; further, the capacity of even the largest private nonprofit organizations is a fraction of the government's size and scope. For example, while the leading anti-hunger charity, Feeding America, distributes an impressive $5 billion in food every year, the federal government spends more than $105 billion each year to combat hunger, including approximately $80 billion on SNAP (Lubrano, 2013). Although significant as part of the overall social welfare system and as a demonstration of Americans' commitment to collective well-being, the private sector clearly lacks the capability to fund a welfare system that can adequately meet people's needs.

Benefits and Drawbacks of Different Combinations of Funding Strategies

The United States has a long history as a pluralistic system in which both public and private funding contribute to the provision of social welfare services. Still today, each has a role to play. Innovative or controversial services, such as abortion counseling or experiments with Universal Basic Income, may be unable to secure public funding, at least initially. In these cases, private funding may be particularly important. Philanthropy and voluntary donations have provided valuable "seed capital" to important social policy innovations and can also ensure that communities with relatively low populations and limited political power receive at least some funding. At the same time, private supporters are not subject to the same scrutiny or oversight as public programs and so can exclude people they consider "unworthy" and attach inequitable conditions to their support. For these reasons, public funding may be preferable when the service is especially vital, unprofitable, or focused on a particularly vulnerable population. Investments in public health and infrastructure are examples of such services, as is protection against child and elder abuse.

Public and private funds can also be combined. For example, if you are attending a public university, it is likely that private contributors financed many of the buildings on your campus and funded many scholarships. If you are attending a private college, it is likely that public funds are being used to provide student loans and Pell Grants to low-income students; some of your professors may be conducting research using public funds. In considering the benefits and drawbacks of different funding combinations, many analysts emphasize that taxation can generate large amounts of public funds, thereby ensuring more year-to-year stability, while private funding is generally much more limited but may be nimbler in response to emergent needs. Private and public funding both have their advantages and trade-offs, so social workers need to consider both when attempting to develop funding strategies.

THE ECONOMY OF THE AGENCY

Social work agencies have an economic context that is shaped by local, state, and federal government pressures. They must also attend to the political context, including the ways demographic changes create opportunities and challenges, as well as the types of responses various stakeholders demand. To provide programs and services, an agency must have enough resources to pay staff salaries and benefits and to cover such costs as office space and supplies. These costs are beyond tangible benefits that go to clients like housing subsidies or foster care payments. Every social service agency employs administrators who are responsible for ensuring that the agency can meet its obligations. In most agencies, these administrators also have authority to make decisions about service delivery. For example, administrators of primarily privately funded agencies realize that they can serve clients who cannot afford to pay only if they attract sufficient private donations and/or clients who do not require financial assistance. This can serve as an incentive to develop services that appeal to potential donors or to prospective self-pay clients. Similarly, in agencies that are reimbursed based on client diagnoses, administrators know that, if they want to raise the rate of reimbursement, they will need to serve people with more severe diagnoses and/or change their treatment modalities. This has led to the phenomenon of "charting for dollars," in which providers make diagnoses with an eye to those that will bring in sufficient funds. For example, a young person who may need family counseling could also be diagnosed as having a mental illness such as depression, because of the greater reimbursement that accompanies that diagnosis.

The financial implications of how an agency is funded can critically influence agency programs and policies. Therefore, when you are having a difficult time grasping the logic of a policy, useful advice is to "follow the money." Does the agency receive public or private funding or a combination of both? How does the way each agency is funded create incentives or disincentives for clients and workers? In the spirit of student inquiry, ask to see agency budgets. When you are in a position to make critical decisions about resource allocation, encourage approaches that involve clients to the greatest extent possible. Social work agencies should be laboratories for the kind of policy development we want to see in larger systems. This begins with identifying ways to include those who are most affected by budget decisions. Considering the economic context and asking these questions can help you better understand and anticipate changes in your agency. Further, understanding state and federal budgets and how changes in either can influence your agency will help you advocate for your clients.

The Ramifications of Globalization

From the vantage point of an individual social welfare agency integrating multiple funding sources to ensure effective services for clients, the workings of the global economy can feel very distant. However, the forces of globalization have important implications for social workers, agencies, and clients. **Globalization** refers to the economic, political, and social integration of nations and markets. Globalization has increased our access to ideas, cultures, and products from around the world. Today, Americans work, learn, and interact globally. The increased ease of shipping, traveling, and communication allows for quicker movement of goods, services, information, and currency. These changes are political as well as economic, particularly as companies' mobility allows economic gains to be distributed as profit rather than shared with workers and governments. In response to fears of corporate abandonment, governments have shifted the tax burden for basic services onto the backs of individuals. This is a fundamental realignment of the social contract.

For much of the modern era, there has been hope that greater global communication and economic interdependence would motivate increased cooperation. Americans still broadly support globalization and cross-border trade in principle, with nearly three-quarters believing trade is a good thing and twice as many Americans supporting globalization as opposing it (Stokes, 2018). There is also evidence that global movement of people has tangible economic benefits for American communities. Immigration is offsetting population loss and providing valuable infusions of working-age adults in regions with aging populations; in the future, these changing demographics will provide crucial inputs for economic growth and stability (Frey, 2019a). However, those who believe our economy is doing poorly are less likely to trust globalization to improve standards of living and other economic outcomes; only 29 percent of those who see the economy in this light believe that global trade increases wages, for example (Stokes, 2018). And, as more begin to question whether the technological advances, greater availability of low-cost products, and ease of global communications are worth the apparent trade-offs in employment instability and financial insecurity, economic and political nationalism have challenged optimism about globalization.

Today, there are real concerns that international arrangements may be collapsing. The future of the European Union is imperiled after the United Kingdom's 2016 vote to leave. President Trump has upended longstanding alliances, instead signaling a greater willingness to partner with autocratic leaders also ambivalent about global cooperation. Motivated both by the quantifiable trade deficit between the United States and other countries, as well as by the more diffuse sense that U.S. industrial might is waning, the Trump Administration has initiated trade disputes with Canada, the European Union, Mexico, and China. The government has used tariffs and other protective measures to advance U.S. interests, actions that have prompted retaliatory provisions. While the resulting trade war has had particularly significant economic impact on U.S. agriculture, many diplomatic experts and other global observers worry more about the long-term effects on global cooperation than about immediate financial fallout. President Trump is not alone in championing nationalism, nor in using trade policy as a tool to protect domestic economic interests, rather than pursue international exchanges. Across Europe and elsewhere, nationalist parties have made significant gains in elections many see as referenda on the idea of globalization as a threat to people's ways of life.

Globalization and other major changes in our economy, like the loss of manufacturing jobs and increasing prevalence of automation, have changed work environments. People are now more likely to hold a variety of jobs for short periods rather than have a long-term career with one employer. These changes reduce the ability of many workers to depend on employer-provided health and income security benefits and alter people's understanding of the "deal" they receive in exchange for their labor. Globalization also links the relative health of the U.S. economy with that of other nations, introducing an unprecedented level of mutual vulnerability. For example, as the United States struggled to emerge from the Great Recession, financial crises in Greece and elsewhere threatened our precarious recovery and demonstrated the degree of interconnection between global markets.

Undeniably, some of the backlash against globalization is xenophobic in nature, reflecting a mistrust of those perceived as "foreign." At the same time, many people have legitimate concerns about the ways that global economic arrangements affect their lives, and about the relative inability of elected officials to constrain powerful corporate actors. Large transnational corporations have successfully influenced multilateral trade agreements so that they explicitly grant corporations the right to appeal government decisions that could usurp their profits, eroding the power of the nation-state to use policy to protect environmental or labor interests.

Globalization and Social Development As global economic change dislocates workers and alters economic arrangements, the need for social services grows. When governments reduce spending on social programs in an attempt to make their economies globally competitive, people in need suffer. As a politically viable pathway to improving people's well-being in today's political and economic contexts, social welfare can be framed as social investment, designed to strengthen people's skills and capacities so that they can more productively participate in the economy and provide for their own social needs (Midgley, 2012).

The social development approach is such a strategy. Initiated by social workers, the **social development approach** seeks to harmonize economic development with social welfare policy by redistributing resources in ways that promote economic growth (Midgley & Sherraden, 2009). Social development pursues new ways of removing barriers to economic participation to develop human capital to its fullest potential. This approach involves government intervention, but primarily in the form of social investment with positive rates of return. Among other things, government funds can be used to train people for meaningful and well-compensated jobs, enhance community-held assets such as social infrastructure, and encourage saving and productive investment.

Perhaps because social workers shaped the social development approach, it is not surprising that this strategy reflects the strengths principles of starting from common human needs, helping people remove barriers to their goals, and providing opportunities for people to build on their strengths. If social investment enables people currently in poverty to train for rewarding jobs, own a share of community assets, and become productive in their own businesses, they will become part of the economy. Further, their full participation will strengthen the economy in ways that benefit everyone. Social development is transforming lives and communities around the globe, from Children's Savings Accounts in low-income communities as different as Oakland, California, and rural Wabash County, Indiana, to support for entrepreneurs in developing countries in Asia and Africa, to universal asset development policies in Israel, Singapore, and Canada. To learn more about this approach, go to the website for the Center for Social Development (**http://csd.wustl.edu**).

Consistent with social work's increasing emphasis on environmental justice as a core value of the profession and a central aim of social policy, many social development approaches have an explicit focus on environmental sustainability. Efforts to support people in developing local approaches to providing adequate food, secure housing, and productive transportation options can meet not only current needs but also future concerns for the natural environment. Particularly as climate change and destruction of resources threaten both economic prosperity and human health, policies that facilitate sustainable economic development and equitably distribute these opportunities will be a global imperative. They must also be U.S. priorities.

CONCLUSION

Social workers, policymakers, and others committed to social justice are faced with the task of restructuring the U.S. welfare state so it can respond more effectively to changing political, economic, environmental, and social forces. The values of reciprocity, social integration, cohesion, and choice can be reflected in public social policy, but only if advocates of social justice make successful claims for basing policy on these values. Social workers must clearly articulate how social programs contribute to overall well-being.

As you have learned in this chapter, political and economic contexts are intertwined. Together, they exert great influence over which policies gain support. You can influence the economic context by doing research and advocacy that highlights the positive economic effects of capacity-building and frames clients' strengths as valuable assets. You can shape the political context by voting for candidates who share social work values and are likely to support policies that prioritize clients' goals. In a pluralistic society such as ours, where many groups vie to influence social policy, we must find ways to amplify clients' voices. Together, we must press for policies that improve clients' opportunities for political and economic gains.

MAIN POINTS

- To understand the social policies that determine how they will practice and what benefits their clients will receive, social workers must examine the economic and political contexts in which policies are developed.

- Economic contexts include the production, distribution, and consumption of income, wealth, and resources. Political contexts include power-seeking in public affairs. They are intertwined, and both exert powerful influences on social welfare policy.

- The United States has a mixed economic system in which markets are regulated and some major industries and utilities may be government-owned.

- Explanations of how economic and political contexts have influenced the development of social welfare include hypotheses that focus on the use of welfare policy to even out economic cycles, control workers, and maintain our capitalist system.

- In the United States, both the public and private sectors (for-profit and nonprofit) are actively involved in providing social welfare benefits and services.

- The legislative, executive, and judicial branches of government all create social policy. All are important arenas for policy development and evaluation.

- The size of the federal budget and national debt, mandatory spending for entitlement programs, and interest on the federal debt all limit discretionary spending, the area of budget policy that reflects the priorities of the current president and Congress.

- U.S. social welfare and tax policies contribute to widening income and wealth inequality.

- Globalization influences social policy and must be taken into account in developing a new consensus to support a more effective, pluralistic welfare system.

EXERCISES

1. Consider the many forms of public social welfare benefits you receive. Have you or anyone in your family received unemployment insurance, TANF, EITC, Medicaid, subsidized housing, or student financial aid? How about fiscal welfare such as mortgage interest deductions, childcare tax credits, or tax incentives for saving? Using what you learned in this chapter about the indirect and direct ways public benefits are distributed, compile your own list.
    a. What was the impact of those benefits on your life or on the lives of those who received them? How might your outcomes have been different without these benefits?
    b. Did or do you experience any stigma associated with your receipt of these benefits? Why do you think people who receive some forms of benefits are stigmatized, while those who receive others are not?
    c. What can you do to change negative attitudes toward people receiving benefits that are commonly stigmatized?
2. What are the benefits and drawbacks of our marketplace economy? Is poverty an inevitable consequence of a marketplace economy? Why or why not?
3. Go to the websites of the Republican National Committee, Democratic National Committee, Libertarian Party, and Democratic Socialists of America.
    a. What are the major policies and issues highlighted? What factors do you think explain the differences? What do differences suggest about the areas each party prioritizes?
    b. How might the populations you serve fare under the policy approaches advocated by each party? What does this analysis suggest about the significance of the political context in shaping the policy landscape?
    c. How are parties reaching out to women, people of color, people with disabilities, and LGBTQ+ voters?
4. Find out how your community has used tax exemptions or tax credits to attract or keep businesses in your town in the last five years.
    a. How large were the tax exemptions? What were the outcomes and who benefited?
    b. Did the community attract businesses that created jobs providing a livable wage? Did the businesses stay?
5. Identify a U.S. Supreme Court decision that has affected the lives of client groups. Here are some examples you might consider: *Loving v. Virginia*, 1967; *Roe v. Wade*, 1973; *Citizens

United v. Federal Election Commission, 2010; *Obergefell v. Hodges*, 2015; *King v. Burwell*, 2015. After you have identified a ruling that interests you, explain the case to a colleague/classmate. Discuss how it influences social work. What were the key issues considered by the Court? How would social work practice be different if the justices had reached a different decision?

6. Go to the Sanchez case at **www.routledgesw.com/cases**. Identify one federal policy and one state social policy that influence the services or benefits for which members of the Sanchez family may be eligible. Specifically, how does an approach to social welfare that bases eligibility on citizenship impact the Sanchez family?

7. Go to the RAINN case at **www.routledgesw.com/cases**. Review the funding section.
   a. How do you think sources of funding impact the capacity of this private nonprofit organization to provide its services?
   b. What opportunities and concerns might arise when providing these services through a private organization rather than a public one?
   c. How might a client experience this organization differently based on race/ethnicity or sexual orientation?

8. What federal and state policies have direct impacts on RAINN and its services? What public agencies are responsible for developing and enforcing regulations governing RAINN's services? How might the political context, particularly attitudes about the rights of women, potentially shape support for RAINN and its objectives?

9. Go to the Carla Washburn case at **www.routledgesw.com/cases**. What entitlement benefits does Mrs. Washburn receive? How would changes in entitlements, such as raising the retirement age for Social Security or requiring higher co-pays for Medicare, impact her?

10. One of the important insights from the 2016 presidential election was how often political polls turn out to be inaccurate. However, polls are still tools for understanding political opinion. Find polling about an issue that interests you. What can you find out about how the poll was conducted? Who was asked for opinions, how were the questions phrased, and how were people contacted? What do you believe might compromise this poll's accuracy? Who would likely be interested in the poll's findings? Who would be surprised? Who might try to question the legitimacy of the poll?

CHAPTER 5

Basic Tools for Researching Need and Analyzing Social Policy

The significant problems we have cannot be solved at the same level of thinking with which we created them.

Albert Einstein

YOU CAN BUILD YOUR POLICY PRACTICE SKILLS BY APPLYING what you have learned about the historical, political, and economic contexts that shape social policy to this chapter's information about the policy analysis process. We begin by exploring needs determination as the foundation on which effective social policy is built. We then examine traditional problem analysis methods and explore how examining strengths and goals and linking them to needs determination can contribute to more effective policy and programs. To help students more easily identify promising avenues for change, this chapter considers opportunities for policy analysis within the social work agency, where social workers can work to center discussion of need and articulation of goals on the experiences of clients, to influence the organizational context of their work and the outcomes it can produce for those served.

POLICY ANALYSIS FUNDAMENTALS

Although social policy may address individual needs, it also typically benefits society. This can be a selling point, but these dual aims may sometimes work at cross-purposes. Efforts to make social welfare policies meet societal goals may render those policies less effective for meeting clients' goals. For example, cities may be willing to fund homeless shelters not just to provide refuge for homeless populations but also to clear homeless people from around businesses. This can catalyze provision of resources to meet clients' shelter needs but may lead to the establishment of shelters away from business hubs where the people the shelters serve might be most likely to locate work.

You can identify which societal needs a social welfare policy prioritizes by examining how policymakers define the need. Consider the example described above. If we define the problem as homeless people needing shelter *and* discouraging shoppers, then establishing a policy to fund a shelter away from businesses is an obvious solution. In contrast, if we view individuals experiencing homelessness as people with strengths who face barriers to resources, we may prioritize helping them quickly find a permanent home in proximity to essential supports, to create a base where they can recover from the crises that have contributed to their homelessness. We may further attend to structural inequities—including those that fall along lines of race and gender—that make some groups more vulnerable to homelessness.

Social Conditions and Social Problems

Articulation of need shapes more than just the types of programs developed. It also influences the likelihood of any policy response at all. For example, for years our society accepted gender and racial discrimination in employment as a social condition, simply "the way things are." When a woman or a person of color could not get a job that paid a living wage, it was their personal problem, not an issue demanding societal action. This distinction is critical for determining the policy response. Whereas a personal problem negatively affects an individual in a way perceived as unique, a social problem systematically harms a group of people, meriting a public intervention. Therefore, a social problem generally requires a structural solution—addressing the root causes of the problem—rather than a personal one. Policies that prohibit discrimination in employment are examples of solutions that aim to bring about systemic change in addition to improving conditions for individuals. In contrast, a response focused on the personal nature of these problems would center on interventions designed to increase a given individual's chance of securing and keeping a job.

Before social policies can be developed, it is usually necessary to convince at least a sizable segment of the public that a problem exists that warrants intervention. It is important to recognize that the scope and seriousness of a problem are not the sole criteria for determining whether public concern rises to the point of action. Rather, the critical elements are the power, influence, and capacity of the group to tell a story that helps people "see" the problem (Mildred, 2003) and envision collective action. Very often, the people affected by a problem play an active role in achieving this public recognition. For example, as you read in Chapter 3, groups experiencing prejudice have struggled long and hard to focus public attention and outrage on the problem of discrimination.

Social norms, demographic shifts, and political changes can "tip" an issue from consideration as a social condition to definition as a social problem. Social work students can see evidence of these dynamics playing out today. For example, while the unaffordability and unavailability of quality childcare was long considered a personal problem, belonging uniquely to mothers who worked outside the home, the concentration of working mothers with young children, growing media and public attention to childcare costs, and mounting research on the importance of nurturing early learning environments are reshaping the facts surrounding childcare into social problems that demand some policy response.

As this example illustrates, to increase public recognition of social problems, advocates use a variety of strategies. These include:

- conducting research and collecting data to identify the barriers that the problem creates;

- building alliances with other groups, particularly those with greater access to power;
- attracting public attention;
- communicating with government officials and thought leaders;
- using litigation to establish a legal basis for the claim;
- mobilizing through direct action (rallies, marches, picketing, sit-ins); and
- employing economic tactics such as sanctions and boycotts.

Once advocates achieve public recognition of a problem, they can garner support for policies and programs to alleviate it. Social workers play important roles in all phases of problem definition and response. Indeed, many of the agencies that employ social workers are designed to allocate and ration resources for the alleviation of a condition that society (or, at least, some powerful elements within it) has labeled a social problem.

Alternative Views

To advance more accurate assessment of the causes of social problems, social workers must understand how others view them. When analyzing existing policy, it is vital to examine how policymakers and the public understood the social problem at the time the policy was developed. At the same time, you should consider whether there are alternative ways of understanding those needs that might lead to more effective policy, particularly where social problems are still largely neglected. Additionally, you should consider how policies may be failing to keep pace with evolving understanding of social problems or, conversely, how achieving policy advances may help the public to reconsider a social problem and its origins. In all these efforts, we must help policymakers see social problems from a perspective compatible with the real experiences of affected populations. When you are thinking about alternative understandings of need, carefully consider the questions you need to ask, rather than quickly moving to seek answers. For example, many policies are designed to address the problem of poverty. Before asking, "How can we best end poverty?" we must first ask, "Why are people poor?"

There are a variety of explanations for the causes of poverty. Some argue that people are poor because they lack a work ethic or have impaired intellectual capacity. These arguments ignore the structural causes of poverty, such as inequity in educational systems, insufficient supply of well-paid jobs, and discrimination. Because beliefs about the causes of poverty lead to policy approaches, these narrow views often emphasize individual remediation and even sanctions, rather than social changes. While social workers know that individuals' unique challenges must be addressed, they also know that current policies do not adequately address many of poverty's structural causes. Furthermore, policy-informed social workers recognize that these structural causes also contribute to personal problems, resulting in a vicious cycle.

Next, we consider the conceptual underpinnings of the strengths perspective and how to apply this perspective to reframe questions and find alternatives to existing approaches.

Defining Needs and Problems: The Social Constructionist Approach

To integrate the strengths perspective into the process of social problem definition, you need some background on its conceptual underpinnings. The strengths perspective reflects a **social constructionist approach**, which posits that our explanations of all human interactions—including social problems—are based on socially and personally constructed views of reality (Geertz, 1973; Gergen, 1999). This suggests that personal beliefs and group consensus shape what people consider to be "real" at a given time.

To comprehend the social construction of reality, consider historical periods when many people were convinced that witchcraft and personal sin caused natural disasters and personal suffering. Over time, objective observations dispelled many of these beliefs. Even when we attempt to be objective, however, our preconceptions shape our observations. Leading scholars in the natural and social sciences acknowledge that the observer shapes all observations and the meanings attached to those observations. Meaning is socially constructed and interpreted through the lens of individuals' own lived experiences. This does not mean that facts do not exist, cannot be rigorously examined, or have no influence on social policy analysis. Indeed, in today's contested environment, which has thrust the phrase "alternative facts" into our political lexicon, social work's willingness to acknowledge the ways our own backgrounds influence our understandings of events may serve as a model for using evidence to probe our own biases in pursuit of greater knowledge. For the purpose of integrating the strengths perspective into social policy, it is unnecessary to enter into a lengthy debate about the existence of objective reality. However, it is important to understand how reality has been constructed in relation to core social policy issues. Further, we must recognize this is a dynamic process—and one we can influence. The following discussion illustrates how people can interpret the same realities from very different perspectives based on their values, ideologies, and past experiences.

The Social Construction of Teenage Pregnancy Different people identify different causes for problems such as teenage pregnancy and define problems in ways that reflect these perceived causes. For example, some blame teenage pregnancy on moral failure. Based on this construction of the problem, they are likely to argue that abstinence is the only viable solution. Others blame schools for failing to provide adequate sex education; their proposed solution would be to provide teenagers with information about contraceptives. Still others point to the structural disadvantages facing some teenagers and advocate for improved pathways to opportunity. For the teenage mother herself, the pregnancy may not be seen as a problem. Instead, it may represent a rite of passage or a chance to claim her autonomy.

Lacking a consensus on the causes of teenage pregnancy, we have developed often-conflicting policies related to sex education, contraception, adoption, child support, and welfare. Based on our differing views of why teenagers become pregnant, policies may evolve rapidly, diverge dramatically among places that evidence different orientations to the problem, and/or coexist in contradiction, as legacies of opposing views. Ultimately, the inability to understand that there is more than one "correct" way to view this issue limits our capacity to work effectively on behalf of the mother, the child, and our communities.

The Social Construction of Family Violence Although there are always differing beliefs within a society, there can also be widespread agreement about some social issues. While such consensus shapes society's responses, consensus can also change over time. Changing definitions of and views about workplace sexual harassment provide evidence of this evolution, as do different understandings of racial justice today compared to historically. Consider, too, an issue of vital concern to social work: family violence. In the United States, until relatively recently, violence against family members was widely perceived as a man's prerogative. Indeed, many people believed that it was the father's duty to keep order in the home, and violence was an acceptable tool with which to accomplish that duty. This was evident in legislated definitions of unlawful family violence, judicial rulings in criminal and civil courts, and media coverage of the issue. Over time, however, that consensus changed. Today, a husband who beats his wife is guilty of committing a criminal act, and family violence is characterized as unacceptable in political debates and national conversations.

In many states, however, parents are still allowed to administer physical discipline to a child. In fact, there are undoubtedly many people whose views support physical punishment as compatible with or even essential to successful child rearing. Even beyond the home, some schools and religious institutions assert their right to physically punish children, even as few would seriously make similar claims regarding adult women. Thus, the consensus regarding the physical punishment of children in the United States has not changed as dramatically as the consensus regarding violence against a partner.

Understanding Different Views of Reality If you understand that views of reality differ over time as well as among people at any given time, you can begin to see definitions of needs and problems in a new light. People have different perspectives depending on their place in society, their personal experiences, and their held identities. They may, therefore, interpret the same problem in fundamentally different ways. Differences in problem definition, in turn, may be at the heart of many disputes over policy responses. Further, not all definitions of social problems are given equal weight. Although there is growing pushback against the influence of elites, our society privileges some problem definitions. Elected officials, religious leaders, media personalities, foundations, think-tanks, and university researchers are all in positions that empower them to define social problems in the policy arena. Their opinions are widely circulated, and frequently large segments of the population, including members of the target population themselves, accept those opinions as fact. Conversely, people in need generally are not privileged, and their opinions are seldom considered when the problem is defined. Armed with these insights, you can ask what motivates groups to define problems in a certain way. You can also consider how that definition may ultimately shape social policy and contribute to positive or negative outcomes for clients.

Understanding how social problems have been constructed will also help identify the prevailing causal theories underpinning those definitions. Policies are supposed to result in intervention either to eliminate the causes or lessen the consequences of a social problem. However, many times, little or no research has been conducted to support the supposed causal relationship. These gaps in problem understanding have important implications for policy development and subsequent social work practice. Where there are significant gaps in our understanding about the causes of a problem, any intervention designed to respond will almost inevitably be flawed.

USING STRENGTHS PERSPECTIVE PRINCIPLES TO CONSIDER NEEDS DETERMINATION

As a reminder, in strengths-based policymaking, client strengths and goals are legitimate starting places for developing social policy. Social workers emphasize the structural barriers that impair clients' abilities to meet their needs and then build on individual and community strengths to remove these barriers. You can revisit Quick Guide 1 from Chapter 1 for a review of strengths principles for policy. We begin this section with a discussion of how to apply the first two principles.

Needs Definition Shapes Policy

Strengths perspective principles 1 and 2 assert that (a) social policies should be developed based primarily on analysis of client strengths and goals rather than problems and deficits; and (b) the definition of need should incorporate clients' perspectives. You can apply these principles when you analyze the way in which a policy defines need. Moreover, after you explore a particular definition of need, these principles can help you consider alternative definitions that may better serve clients' interests.

Policies that created high-rise public housing projects are excellent examples of how policymakers addressed a social problem—inadequate housing for low-income people—without considering the way members of the target population understood their needs. If anyone had bothered to ask low-income families, very few would have responded that they want to live on the ninth floor of a building surrounded by concrete and thousands of other low-income people. However, because policymakers focused only on the problem as they saw it—creating affordable housing in an available location—they crafted ineffective solutions. Public social policies are not the only places social workers find examples of responses that do not adequately incorporate clients' perspectives. Social work agencies are also subject to pressures that can lead to privileging considerations other than clients' goals in the process of need definition and policy development. For example, a family service agency that has funding to provide parent education classes may define clients' needs in terms of insufficient parenting knowledge and skills, even if clients' own priorities are utility assistance and affordable health care. However, even when the policies we analyze do not reflect a strengths approach, we can still use a strengths lens to evaluate them.

Social workers who use a strengths perspective view the intended beneficiaries of social policy as interdependent components of the general population (Rapp et al., 2006). As a result, rather than placing initial focus on the social problem, they focus on how members of the larger society influence and are influenced by the target group. They believe that we should consider the strengths and goals of the target population as well as potential community resources that could be leveraged to help address needs.

When you consider strengths principles as part of policy analysis, you begin to recognize when the experiences of people in need have been distorted by an emphasis on alleged deficits or pathology. For example, you can use strengths perspective principles to reframe questions about the causes of poverty. You might ask, "What resources or opportunities are necessary for people in our society to succeed in jobs that will support a family above the poverty level? Who does not have these opportunities? Why does this happen?" Further, a strengths-based, solutions-focused approach is goal-oriented. Client groups are asked about their vision of appropriate goals early in the process.

In the case of poverty, client groups have already provided some answers to these questions. As individuals and as part of social movements including the Moral Monday and Fight for $15 campaigns, people experiencing poverty have articulated goals including educational equity, a higher minimum wage, and training to enable people to succeed in jobs that facilitate upward mobility. Centering your work on clients' goals does not mean ignoring urgent needs and complex, intertwined social problems. However, a strengths approach does not dwell on individual deficits. Instead, policy practitioners steeped in the strengths perspective focus on solutions and examine which pathways to power and resources are available as they work collaboratively toward different policy options.

Social workers and students of social policy can find numerous examples of how a focus on deficits has failed to produce effective solutions. Indeed, this is often one of the first lessons students encounter in practice as they come face-to-face with policies that are failing those they seek to help. Therefore, it is time to experiment with a different approach. However, lest we fall into the same mistakes that characterize the deficit-focused approach, it is important to remember that seeking a single cause to explain complex needs is too simplistic.

ANALYZING SOCIAL PROBLEMS FROM AN EXPANDED VIEWPOINT

Strengths principles can be integrated into social problem analysis. The approach discussed here builds on the work of several policy analysts (Chambers, 2000; Dolgoff and Feldstein, 2013; Gilbert & Terrell, 2013; McInnis-Dittrich, 1994). To understand the definition of social problems that shaped a social policy, you need to:

- examine how the problem or need is defined and documented;
- consider how values and self-interest shape this definition and documentation; and
- determine which causal theories have been developed and what consequences are ascribed to the problem (what is believed about why the problem exists and why it is, in essence, "problematic").

Defining and Documenting Problems or Needs

To illustrate how a social problem is defined and documented within a policy, we will use the example of the Stewart B. McKinney Homeless Assistance Act (Public Law 100-77). This policy, now commonly referred to as McKinney–Vento, was originally passed in 1987 and is administered by the Department of Housing and Urban Development (see Exhibit 5.1). On May 20,

> **EXHIBIT 5.1**
>
> *The McKinney–Vento Act: A Bi-Partisan Initiative*
>
> (R) Stewart B. McKinney   (D) Bruce F. Vento
>
> Republican Stewart B. McKinney and Democrat Bruce F. Vento both served in the U.S. House of Representatives. Although from different political parties, they worked together to champion the rights of those experiencing homelessness. President Ronald Reagan signed the Stewart B. McKinney Homeless Assistance Act into law soon after McKinney's death in 1987. In 2001, President George W. Bush reauthorized homeless assistance as the McKinney–Vento Homeless Education Assistance Improvements Act. The McKinney-Vento Act is a prime example of the kind of sweeping reform bipartisan cooperation can make possible.
>
> *Source*: images: Library of Congress

2009, President Obama signed into law the Homeless Emergency Assistance and Rapid Transition to Housing (HEARTH) Act to expand upon McKinney–Vento. You can review the text of this legislation online. Search for the Helping Families Save Their Home Act (Public Law 111-22); the HEARTH Act is part of that larger policy.

The McKinney–Vento Homeless Assistance Act, passed in 1987, was the first major piece of federal legislation designed to respond to homelessness. In the decades leading up to passage, some towns and cities experiencing difficulties coping with growing homeless populations were exerting pressure to have homelessness defined as a national problem. The original Act contained findings that homelessness is a national crisis and that states and localities need federal assistance to deal effectively with this crisis. Because homelessness had previously been considered largely a local problem, the redefinition was critical to garnering federal resources. In the 2009 amendment, the findings section states:

The Congress finds that—

A lack of affordable housing and limited scale of housing assistance programs are the primary causes of homelessness; and
Homelessness affects all types of communities in the U.S., including rural, urban, and suburban areas.

(Public Law 111-22, Division B, Section 1002)

The findings in the 2009 amendments further assert that the primary causes of homelessness are lack of affordable housing and inadequate housing assistance programs. Policies and programs to increase affordable housing and provide housing assistance to those experiencing or at risk of homelessness can result in structural change to address these causes. The foreclosure crisis of 2009 affected many Americans, and many policymakers cast homelessness as part of this wider problem. Indeed, making the HEARTH Act of 2009 part of the Helping Families Save Their Home Act connects the housing insecurity many families face with the need to help people who are homeless. Conversely, had this legislation defined the cause of homelessness as primarily individual in nature—stemming from addictions or mental illness, for example—then the programs and policies emanating from it would have likely been far different. The main thrust of the HEARTH Act is to highlight and incentivize proven strategies for preventing and ending homelessness, such as getting people rehoused as quickly as possible after they lose their homes and intervening with emergency aid prior to individuals becoming homeless. These kinds of strategies recognize that an economic crisis is the primary immediate cause of homelessness. Focusing on strategies such as rapid rehousing, which emphasizes permanent housing, allows those assisting individuals who are homeless to quickly work toward solutions.

When examining legislation, it is important to look at the definitions. The definitions will provide insight into how policymakers conceptualize the need the legislation is designed to address. Continuing with the example of the McKinney–Vento Act, the original 1987 legislation defines a homeless person as:

An individual who lacks a fixed, regular, and adequate nighttime residence; and an individual who has a primary nighttime residence that is a private or public place not designed for, or ordinarily used as, sleeping accommodation for human beings; an institution that provides a temporary residence for individuals intended to be institutionalized; or a supervised publicly or privately operated shelter designed to provide temporary living accommodations (including welfare hotels, congregate shelters, and transitional housing for the mentally ill).

(McKinney–Vento Homeless Assistance Act, 1987)

Those working with people at risk of homelessness criticized this definition as too limited to help those who need assistance to *prevent* their fall into homelessness. In response, the HEARTH Act of 2009 expands the definition to include people at imminent risk of losing housing so that preventive work can be done with these groups.

To identify the official definition of homelessness in the HEARTH Act of 2009, look first at the legislation itself. Sometimes, legislation contains a section called "general provisions," "legislative intent," or "findings" that provides this information. In the HEARTH Act, there is a section called "definitions of homelessness." The HEARTH Act expands the statutory definition of homelessness to include the following situations:

- People who lived in a shelter or a place not meant for human habitation prior to temporarily residing in an institutional care setting would be considered homeless upon their exit.

- People who will imminently lose their housing and lack the resources to find other housing, including those who are being evicted within 14 days, people living in a hotel or motel and who lack the resources to stay for more than 14 days, people who are doubled-up and must leave within 14 days.

- Unaccompanied youths and homeless families who have not lived independently for a long time, have experienced persistent instability, and will continue to experience instability because of disability, health problems, domestic violence, addiction, abuse, or multiple barriers to employment.

- People who are fleeing or attempting to flee domestic violence.

(National Alliance to End Homelessness, 2009)

The new definition of homelessness also puts increased emphasis on homeless families. Additionally, in 2015 the HEARTH Act was updated to establish the definition of those "chronically homeless," important because many programs are targeted to this subgroup. You can review the definition at **www.hudexchange.info/homelessness-assistance/hearth-act**.

While this definition is lengthy and detailed, in other legislation, need is vaguely defined. This leaves definitions open to a variety of interpretations at the point of implementation. Policymakers working on the HEARTH Act wanted to ensure that those developing programs would target funding to a specific population, so they developed the chronically homeless definition carefully.

Of course, as with the other social problems we have discussed, there are alternative definitions of homelessness. Even within the federal government, definitions vary. For example, the U.S. Department of Education uses different criteria to assess eligibility for homeless services for students. Professional literature as well as sources such as homeless shelters and advocacy organizations might define homelessness in different ways. These definitions, in turn, influence understanding of what homelessness looks like, who experiences it, and which policy approaches will be most successful in ending homelessness. For example, if only individuals who are living "on the streets" or in designated homeless shelters are considered homeless, the size and characteristics of the homeless population will be considerably different than if individuals and families living "doubled up" with other family members or temporarily institutionalized in corrections or health care systems are also counted.

Once we have defined homelessness, we can count cases to document need. However, because different researchers define the problem differently, studies sometimes provide wildly divergent estimates of the size of the homeless population. For example, should a person who has been sleeping on her relative's couch for the last month after her home was destroyed by fire be classified as "homeless"? In such a case, would it matter if the person were an unaccompanied youth instead of a working-age adult, or if she had received emergency assistance to recoup her losses from the fire or not? Agreeing on a definition and then counting the number of homeless people in a given area is not an easy task, even though it is a critical step in determining the extent and nature of the need to which policy must respond. Despite disagreements surrounding definitions of homelessness, HUD issues an assessment of homelessness to Congress annually. You can access the Annual Homeless Assessment Report (AHAR) by going to **www.hudexchange.info** and searching for AHAR.

This analysis of the definitions of homelessness highlights the central point that all social policies—whether their overriding objective is social assistance, social control, or both—are based on socially constructed beliefs concerning people and social conditions (Loeske, 1995). A social condition sometimes goes largely unnoticed by the larger society until it is identified as a problem. For example, emergency-room staff can log the number of women injured by their spouses and police can record the number of domestic violence calls to which they respond, but these numbers will not even be collected and analyzed if the social condition of intimate partner violence is not identified as an indication of deviant behavior. In the case of homelessness, until the homeless population began to infringe on economic activity and population quality of life, city officials seldom documented numbers of homeless people. It was only then that officials became more interested in gathering information to control the homeless population, thus initiating the process whereby homelessness was defined as a national problem worthy of federal intervention.

Defining the problem helps quantify the number of people who have a need. This can help convince policymakers to act. Advocates can use data that support a particular definition of a social problem to attract media attention, which can then help to secure and sustain a spotlight on the existence of the problem and a specific definition of it. Focusing on negative outcomes for particular groups, such as higher rates of homelessness for veterans and former foster children, can highlight injustice. Often, you can access information on differential outcomes from statistical reports compiled by the U.S. Census Bureau, U.S. Justice Department, Centers for Disease Control and Prevention, and other government agencies; from professional literature; from organizations dedicated to serving marginalized communities; and from your own practice. It is important to have an understanding of the problem that includes divergent views, so that you learn to see the issue from others' perspectives and, where possible, can consider how they might be part of your efforts.

It is also important to question whether the problem has been identified in ways that make it possible to evaluate how policy affects outcomes for the target group. In the HEARTH Act, the defined problem is homelessness. Using a strengths perspective, we can evaluate the effectiveness of the subsequent policy in terms of clients' accomplishments in reaching goals. For example, how many formerly homeless people have now acquired adequate permanent housing? How quickly are those experiencing homelessness rehoused? How are people supported in maintaining and thriving in permanent housing? Is the policy serving some subpopulations more successfully than others? Whose needs are not being met as well, and what policy reforms might improve their outcomes?

Values, Ideologies, and Problem Definition

Examining the values that define a condition as a social problem provides insight into the "should statement" that underlies the perception of that problem. *Should statements* are implicit in most descriptions of social problems and in the resulting policies. The statement that people *should* work and meet their own needs is reflected in many public assistance programs and rooted in our belief in self-reliance. Policies that direct assistance to families with children are rooted in the belief that children *should* have adequate food, clothing, and shelter. Many people—particularly those supporting abstinence-based pregnancy prevention—believe teenagers *should* abstain from sex. Many of our policy debates today center on the idea that governments *should* decrease spending. Look for *should* statements in the information you read depicting social problems and policies. For example, the purpose statement of the original Homeless Assistance Act places special emphasis on homeless programs that serve families with children, elderly people, and veterans. These groups historically have been considered the "worthy" poor who *should* receive help.

Social movements can do a great deal to shape the definition of a problem and to document the problem in ways that reflect their values and ideologies. By examining who wins or loses when a problem is defined in a specific way and the size of the victory or loss, you can often gain insight into which group was able to dominate the problem-definition process. For example, people with disabilities who are living in the community need both social and medical services. However, physicians' groups are generally more influential than social services providers. This power imbalance helps explain why medical needs often receive greater attention and funding than social needs. Of course, if people with disabilities were driving the agenda, there might be a different emphasis entirely; indeed, gains in civil rights protections for people with disabilities largely reflect instances where these individuals have succeeded in the task of problem definition and have been able to shape policy according to their goals.

Professional groups, corporations, and myriad advocacy groups all work to promote the definition of a need or problem that serves their own interests. In the case of the original Homeless Assistance Act, it was in the interest of states and localities to define homelessness as a federal issue, and they lobbied for that outcome. Similarly, social workers themselves often define needs for a target population in terms of what services their agency can provide. For example, social workers have helped point out the special needs of homeless people who have mental illness and have pressed for policies that provide outreach and case management services for homeless people who are mentally ill.

Causal Theories

It is necessary to understand what causes and consequences policymakers attribute to a social problem because related policy is supposed to eliminate those causes and/or lessen those consequences. The findings section of the HEARTH Act asserts that a lack of affordable housing and the limited scale of housing assistance programs are the primary causes of homelessness. Given that definition, the HEARTH Act focuses on more widely implementing programs that have proven effective in targeting the immediate causes of homelessness and helping families avoid recurring episodes of homelessness. This emphasis stems from successful advocacy on the part of people experiencing homelessness and their allies and from a growing recognition that preventing homelessness is the most cost-effective and successful approach.

Teenage pregnancy provides another example of the complex nature of causes and consequences associated with a social problem. Lack of self-control on the part of adolescents, absence of parental supervision, media and societal attitudes about sex, availability of birth control, and the women's movement have all been identified as causes of teenage pregnancy. The consequences attributed to this problem include unwanted pregnancies, abortions, and longer-term outcomes such as child maltreatment and welfare dependency. Research has connected some of these consequences, sometimes in a circular fashion. For example, children who were unplanned are more likely to become teenage parents themselves (Hoffman, 2008). This illustrates how consequences sometimes become a cause.

However, consider that, historically, many women became mothers in their teens; in fact, this was often the community expectation. Reflect on how and why attitudes about teen sexuality have changed. You can see that the business of determining cause and consequences can lead to redefining the social problem. Further, social policies based on some formulations of cause may create or exacerbate social problems rather than alleviate them. For example, policies stemming from a belief that exposure to information about sex leads to teenage pregnancy may force schools to exclude information on birth control from curricula, which may lead to increases in teenage pregnancy (Stanger-Hall & Hall, 2011).

Social workers who are attuned to political dynamics and other constraints that influence program and policy development will likely be unsurprised to learn that policy analysis and development are not always systematic. Realities of available funding and pressures to align with dominant views may inhibit adequate research to support the supposed causal chain and interventions. Even in social work agencies, ineffective programs based on incomplete, outdated, or inaccurate understanding of a social problem and its causes may be allowed to continue, as inertia and human bias interfere with needed change. Acknowledging this deficiency, strengths-based practitioners and researchers work to investigate connections between problem, intervention, and outcome. Increasingly, these evidence-based practitioners are involving the groups they are studying in the research. For example, researchers are asking people who have successfully overcome a problem such as substance use disorder how they did so and what lessons from their experience might help others. Other researchers are asking people who are still addicted to help identify the barriers to recovery. Involving the target population in this research is consistent with the strengths principle that people are experts on their own needs and goals.

Some of the policies you will analyze may reflect strengths-based thinking more than others. When a policy ignores the goals of the target group and instead emphasizes meeting societal goals, that policy is not strengths-based. When a policy or program fails to adequately interrogate assumptions about clients, their priorities, and the roots of their challenges, social problems are unlikely to be resolved. The voices of people in need can lead to policy change. In Chapter 6, you will learn how to encourage this process.

Claims-Making

We now shift our focus from analysis of problems and needs to the claims-making process. Claims-making connects the social problem and the resulting social policy. Even if policymakers agree that a need exists, they may not agree that the need merits attention. Even when advocates succeed in identifying champions with enough prominence to ensure that the social problem stays at the forefront, these leaders often will disagree about how to address the need. Those pursuing policy change must make a compelling claim for resources that clearly asserts not only the need for action but specifically what needs to be done. Recall from Chapter 1 that claims-making is the process that promotes recognition of a social condition as warranting policymaker action. Values undergird claims. The claim that mothers receiving cash assistance should face more stringent work requirements is linked to the value of personal responsibility. The claim that parents should have paid leave during the first weeks of their child's life is linked to the value of family bonds and of a child's right to a strong start in life. Claims often contain underlying appeals to our sense of morality in the form of calls for compassion, social responsibility, and fairness. Holding a demonstration to demand equal rights for Latinx families or lobbying Congress to provide affordable prescription coverage for older adults are both examples of claims-making. Of course, not all claims-making attempts are equally likely to succeed. Both the strategies pursued and alignment with broader political and economic contexts influence outcomes. Crucially, engaging the client group in envisioning potential solutions often makes it possible to center on an effective way forward.

The Various Bases of Claims-Making Claims can be made on a variety of bases. In some cases, claims are based on rights. For example, women could make a claim for a policy response to domestic violence only after they won the right to be considered more than the property of their husbands. In many situations, power is the basis for claims-making. If individuals or groups wield enough power, they can make a successful claim. For example, Congress often passes policies that give large tax breaks to corporations because executives have sufficient power to advance their claims for preferential treatment. People and groups with power can also help press for claims based on rights or other criteria. This is why advocates pressing a claim typically attempt to mobilize a wide and powerful foundation of support. For example, advocates working for health care reform attempted to get the powerful pharmaceutical industry to back their efforts. Advocates pushing for more welcoming immigration policies have found common cause with some labor unions that want immigrant workers to have legal status as a protection on the job, as well as with some employers who want avenues to legally hire needed workers.

Other bases for claims include comparative disadvantage and, more broadly, an appeal for social justice. The claim may be made that public schools should provide free breakfast for children from low-income families because these children are at a disadvantage when they try to learn on empty stomachs. Recent advances in criminal justice reform have largely centered on appeals to justice and illumination of the racial and economic disparities that pervade our current system. Further, consider how advocates make claims on behalf of elders and children in general. Reflecting a belief in social justice, advocates claim that we should help elders and children because we are responsible for their well-being. Advocates make a further claim for children based on utility. Specifically, they argue that, if we do not invest in children, they will not be prepared to take on important roles in our society, and we will all suffer. For elders, advocates can make a claim based on reciprocity. This population worked hard, fought our wars, and raised children; now they deserve our care. Here, it is not only the need or problem that propels action. It is the claim that policymakers have a responsibility to meet the need based on values held in common or, more typically, based on claims of utility in combination with appeals based on values. Some needs will go unmet because claims sufficient to induce action have not been advanced.

When analyzing how advocates have made claims that policies need to change, it can be helpful to examine the historical basis of claims for the original policies. For example, recall how general agreement that society has a moral obligation to care for impoverished women and children underpinned programs such as Aid to Families with Dependent Children (AFDC). In the 1990s, proponents of stricter work requirements claimed that mothers needed to take more personal responsibility and work outside of the home. As the basis of the claim shifted, so did the language. When making claims for stricter work requirements, proponents often used the term "welfare mothers" rather than "women and children" to refer to people receiving assistance. This language pivoted from claims based on the moral imperative to protect vulnerable people and support families, to the prevention of the immorality of perceived irresponsibility. Analysis and careful media consumption can also reveal ways in which different information arenas actively shape—rather than passively transmit—construction of social problems, including through the selection of images, phrasing, and representative voices (Kellner, 2004). Social workers must consider this interplay of values, morality, and language when they craft claims or refute the claims of those who seek to undermine or co-opt reform.

Returning to the original McKinney–Vento Act, it is clear from the findings section that successful claims for federal involvement on behalf of homeless children, elders, and other groups were made to get the law passed. By 2009, when the HEARTH Act passed, the need for federal involvement had already been established. The claim emphasized in the HEARTH Act was that more evidence-based housing assistance should be provided to an expanded class of eligible recipients to effectively combat homelessness. Generally, information concerning the bases for claims-making often can be found in the initial sections of a law.

Assumptions Embedded in Claims-Making When you are considering claims-making, it is important to be aware of the assumptions embedded in the claim. For example, a claim for spending on older adults based on the belief that they deserve care in return for their past contributions will likely promote policies that increase funding for long-term care facilities rather than encourage employment and social engagement, even though growing numbers of older adults may want and need to work. In contrast, a need for policies that support older workers and lessen age discrimination may prompt advocates to craft a claim that emphasizes the importance of removing structural barriers confronting older workers and facilitating overall productivity. These claims will rest on somewhat different value bases, emphasizing equality of opportunity and the significant contributions elders can and do make. This is another example of the importance of involving client groups in crafting and advancing claims, including preferred solutions.

Successful claims-making can also result in the establishment of rights that can then be the foundation of future claims. For example, eligible older adults now have the right to health care through Medicare and can take legal action if Medicare refuses to pay for covered care. Indeed, today's battles over civil rights are waged primarily on the foundation of legal claims established in policies passed more than 50 years ago. Examining how such successful claims were structured, limited, and promoted helps us understand current policy and enact future policies.

When a claim is made, it must compete for resources with other claims that may be more compelling. For example, after the terrorist attacks of September 11, 2001, claims for increased defense spending were more successful than claims for greater social spending, and even more successful than claims for defense spending had been in previous contexts. Additionally, policies that had long been championed unsuccessfully, including for stricter rules on state-issued photo identification and reorganization of federal immigration enforcement offices, passed after their proponents recast their claims in terms of national security against the terrorist threat.

In earlier chapters, we examined key factors that influence whether claims-making succeeds. For example, the economy influences the identification of social problems and the resources available to address them. History sets the stage for policies to emerge, and politics influence who has power. Recall how economic conditions during the Great Depression increased public acceptance of an expanded federal role in promoting social welfare. Values and ideology fuel social movements that press claims for certain policies. Members of the Townsend Movement pressed the claim that people who had worked all their lives should not become paupers in their old age. Government-funded pensions for veterans provided historical precedent for intervention, and some European countries had already established public pension systems, providing international precedent, too. The interplay among all these factors propelled passage of the landmark Social Security Act.

After you explore the claims-making process for a policy, evaluate the extent to which claims are strengths-focused. Do claims emphasize the structural barriers that prevent clients from meeting their needs? Do they reflect social work values of self-determination and social justice? Do they provide a foundation on which to base future claims, in furtherance of clients' goals for their lives? If you determine that a claim does not meet these criteria, consider alternative claims-making approaches that incorporate a strengths perspective.

A FRAMEWORK FOR POLICY ANALYSIS

When you are analyzing a policy or program, it is easy to become overwhelmed by the vast quantity of information available. Scholars have developed a variety of frameworks for policy analysis (Chambers & Bonk, 2013; Dolgoff & Feldstein, 2013; Gilbert & Terrell, 2013; McPhail, 2003; Popple & Leighninger, 2012). These frameworks vary. Some focus primarily on the historical context, on understanding the problem, or on examining social policy through a gendered lens, while others focus on key policy elements, separately and in terms of how they interact. The framework presented below is a thorough and relatively simple way to begin analyzing policy. We will use this framework in Chapters 7 through 11 to help you quickly grasp the major components of social policies. Framework elements include:

- policy goals;
- benefits and services;
- eligibility rules;
- service delivery systems; and
- financing.

While frameworks vary in their emphasis on strengths, you can approach your analysis from a strengths perspective. You can use strengths perspective principles to evaluate the extent to which policy goals, benefits and services, eligibility rules, service delivery systems, and financing reflect attention to client and community strengths. These principles affirm that social policies should (a) help remove barriers that limit clients' full participation in their community; (b) emphasize access, choice, and opportunities for clients that can lead to empowerment; and (c) be evaluated in terms of client outcomes.

Policy Goals and Objectives

A **policy goal** is a statement of the desired human condition or social environment the implementation of a policy is expected to accomplish. For example, a goal of the legislation that established the Special Supplemental Nutrition Program for Women, Infants, and Children (WIC) is to safeguard the health of low-income women, infants, and children up to age five who are at risk of poor nutrition (Food and Nutrition Service, 2009). Measures of the health of these populations, then, can be used as benchmarks by which to evaluate the efficacy of WIC.

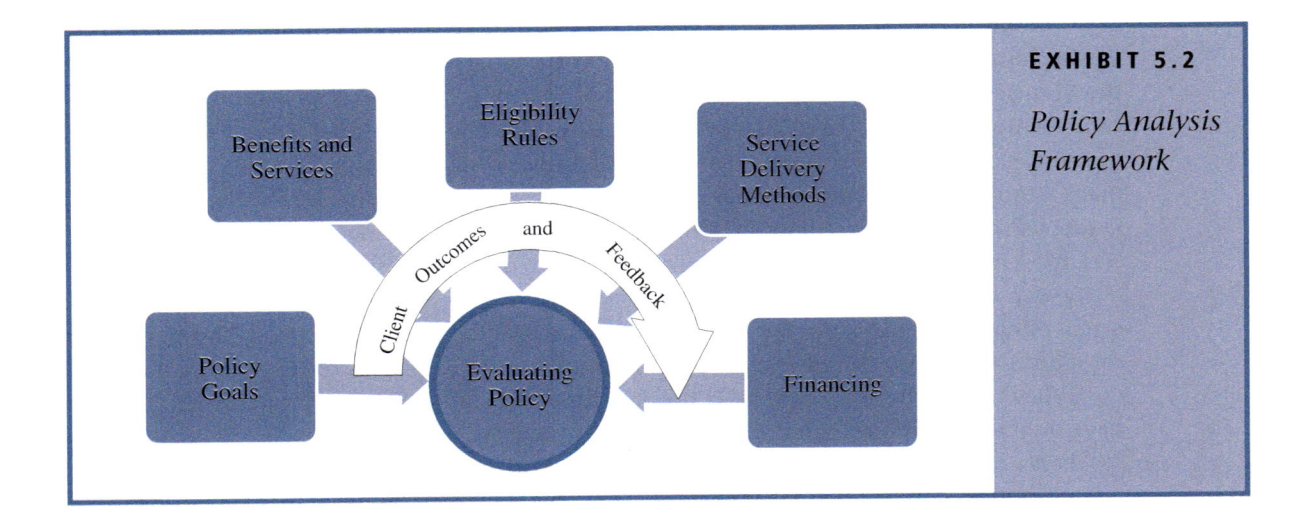

EXHIBIT 5.2

Policy Analysis Framework

While goals may be stated in general or abstract terms, **policy objectives** spell out in detail what a policy should accomplish. Objectives are specific statements that operationalize desired results. They provide detail about services and outcomes on which programs are evaluated. Several different objectives may be developed for the same goal. For example, one objective for WIC is to increase the birthweight of infants in low-income families. Another objective is to increase breastfeeding. In the latter case, if the objective specifies a desired percentage of increase, it provides a specific statement of expected outcome by which to evaluate effectiveness.

Locating Goals and Objectives As with claims and the definition of needs, policy goals and objectives are often found in the preamble or general provisions of the enabling legislation. You can also investigate the legislative history that contains the background material legislative committees use in framing the legislation. Program descriptions, available from agencies that administer the programs created by the policy, also provide information on policy goals. In the HEARTH Act, a section establishes a federal goal of ensuring that individuals and families who become homeless return to permanent housing within 30 days.

Manifest and Latent Goals Goals can be both manifest and latent. **Manifest goals** typically are publicly stated, whereas latent goals are not. **Latent goals** may reflect some policymakers' intentions, but they are often goals on which it would be difficult to achieve consensus or that would not be considered socially acceptable. For example, a manifest goal of homeless assistance legislation is to fund services for homeless people; a latent goal may be social control so that homeless people do not interfere with business. As this example illustrates, it is possible for the manifest goal of a policy or program to be consistent with social work values and the strengths perspective while latent goals are not. This is another reason it is important to critically analyze the intents and effects of social policies.

When you examine a policy's goals and objectives, you need to determine whether goals are clear and measurable. Goals should also primarily attend to ends rather than means. When the stated goal is instead concerned with the means of reaching that goal, people can lose sight of the desired result. For example, the goal of increased coordination in the original McKinney–Vento Homeless Assistance Act was concerned with the means required to meet the needs of the homeless population rather than the end of reducing homelessness. Although increased coordination may lead to a reduction of homelessness, framing the goal this way could lead to measuring efficacy based on how many coordinating meetings were held rather than on how many people are no longer homeless. However, in this case, the "purpose" section of the legislation also contains the stated goal of meeting the needs of the homeless. In social work agencies, too, emphasis on the activities staff are expected to conduct can obscure needed attention to the outcomes these activities are expected to produce. For example, a policy may articulate a goal of having clients complete family budgets or attend financial education classes without explaining how these activities connect to clients' goals of exiting poverty. This could lead to the policy being judged a "success" if the activities are completed, even though clients' needs have not truly been met. Families may remain in poverty.

Policy analysis should also include evaluation of whether the activities the policy prescribes can actually accomplish the stated goals. For example, one possible manifest goal of a program that promotes adequate nutrition for pregnant mothers is to improve the health status of their babies. Activities designed to achieve that goal, which the policy could specify, include distributing food and information that would help safeguard the health of mothers and their children. We could measure how successfully the program accomplishes this goal by comparing the percentages of low-birthweight babies born before and after the policy was implemented in a specified area.

In contrast, if the specified goals and activities had been simply to distribute surplus food to pregnant women and children, evaluation of the program would focus on how much food was distributed rather than the health of the mothers and their children. Any adjustments made may focus on increasing distribution, without necessarily positively affecting health. Indeed, if the food distributed was not sufficiently nutritious, or if mothers lacked information and resources to use the food to improve their families' health, accomplishment of the activity may not achieve the goal. Therefore, from a strengths perspective, it is important to focus on client outcomes. Your evaluation should use data from reliable sources that are as objective as possible. When you rely on a given source, always assess the ideological perspective(s) it represents, so that you have a better sense of any biases, as well as the extent to which data may be unrepresentative of the diversity of the target population and/or too dated to accurately reflect the current landscape.

Incorporating Clients' Perspectives   Typically, the goal of the policy and the type of intervention prescribed are determined by policymakers who may not possess expertise in the underlying issue. In such cases, the policymakers turn to "experts." However, these are frequently members of privileged or higher-status groups who may have little knowledge of clients' realities. Critically, failure to incorporate the clients' perspective often leads to the adoption of inappropriate and ineffective goals (Rapp et al., 2006). For example, people with developmental disabilities who want a rewarding job may instead receive a lifetime of "vocational training" because the prescribed policy goal is to just keep them safe during the day. Not coincidentally, this goal often reflects the priorities of experts who run centers serving those with developmental disabilities. In contrast, a policy developed using the strengths perspective would reflect clients' goals of securing and maintaining a satisfying, paying job. Social workers have been instrumental in reforming policies in many arenas to incorporate clients' perspectives. State policies that facilitate immigrant students' access to higher education, ease the process of transitioning from public assistance to paid employment, and support kinship caregivers in child welfare systems are all examples of policies that are improving outcomes by making clients' goals the policies' intended aims.

Benefits or Services Provided

When analyzing a policy or program, it is important to examine the benefits or services it provides. Benefits and services may include food assistance, counseling, job coaching, a Social Security check, or the opportunity to vote, among others. Protection from discrimination, air pollution, or harmful financial products can also be a benefit. In certain cases, program benefits may be stigmatizing. For example, school systems sometimes provide vouchers that families can present at specific local stores to purchase back-to-school clothing. Medical clinics may require families to line up in the heat to receive free dental care. If the clothing voucher clearly marks the shopper as indigent, the child may feel ashamed. If a family is recognized from news coverage of the dental clinic, they may feel "outed" as people in need. In these ways, some benefits and services may discourage usage. There is evidence that some youth who are eligible for free and reduced lunches do not receive this nutrition assistance because they are ashamed to apply. Recognition of this deterrent effect has increased use of community eligibility processes, which allow schools to provide free meals to all students without requiring household-level application (Food Research and Action Center, 2017).

Analyzing benefits and services from a strengths perspective leads to a number of questions: Is the benefit or service designed to remove societal barriers that prevent people from meeting their needs, or does it focus primarily on correcting what is perceived as problematic behavior of the target population? How much consumer choice is allowed? Cash benefits usually provide the most choice; however, if a service is unavailable, cash may not help. For example, if children with disabilities need therapeutic preschools and none are available, then the service must be developed to address the need.

The strengths perspective also raises the question of whether benefits or services incorporate the strengths and resources of the community. For example, policies may prescribe that nutrition programs for seniors serve a uniform menu across the city or, alternatively, may permit local groups to develop different menus, consistent with nutrition guidelines. In the latter case, program coordinators could hire local cooks to develop culturally appropriate, healthy menus. The original McKinney–Vento Homeless Assistance Act provided funds to a wide variety of programs that assist homeless people. Such an approach makes it possible to build on existing community resources and tailor programs to the community. There are trade-offs here, however. The quality of the programs funded by the Act varies widely, and such customization may be more expensive, resulting in greater service gaps.

Finally, it is crucial to evaluate whether the benefit or service will result in positive outcomes for clients. For example, when the goal is to reduce substance use among teenagers, a policy that provides a rack of pamphlets in each high school warning against drug use will probably be ineffective. Research and practice wisdom both confirm that combating substance use requires not just provision of information but also attending to contributing risk factors.

Eligibility Rules

Some eligibility rules allow people to receive benefits only if they have made prior contributions recognized by the entity providing the benefit. For example, Social Security retirement benefits are available only to workers who have paid into the system for the required amount of time, although spouses and children of qualified workers are also eligible for certain benefits. Other benefits are available based on attachment to the workforce but do not require employee contribution. For example, employers fund workers' compensation, although workers in some industries and in the informal economy do not have these protections. As a social worker, you should always consider social justice and equity when you examine eligibility rules. For example, historically, women have been disadvantaged whenever eligibility for benefits was based on attachment to the workforce. Because they often performed unpaid care work, women were eligible only if they were legally married and their husband had the required work record. Similarly, people of color were historically less likely to have worked in jobs that provide Social Security benefits.

Eligibility for many of the services and benefits clients receive is based on a means test and awarded only to people whose income and assets fall below a certain level. Some policies require that recipients demonstrate functional as well as financial need. For instance, older adults can receive Medicaid funding for nursing facility care only if they have exhausted their financial resources *and* are functionally impaired. Since they hinge on an assessment of impoverishment, means tests can be stigmatizing and may discourage people in need from applying for services. Asset tests, in particular, force individuals to deplete even a small financial cushion, which can result in greater economic insecurity. Processing eligibility determinations based on means tests can be expensive, too. As described in Chapter 4, programs available only to select populations usually have higher administrative costs than those more universally available. At the same time, benefits with less stringent eligibility rules may lead to overwhelming cost, as a larger number of prospective beneficiaries qualify for assistance.

In addition to administrative determinations, eligibility rules may be based on judicial decisions. For example, a judge may rule that a family should receive services designed to prevent further child maltreatment. A teenager may be assigned to probation and receive the assistance of a probation officer. Beyond the level of an individual client, significant eligibility-related public policy has been enacted through the judicial system, as in *Goldberg v. Kelly* (1970), which established that clients have due process rights in benefit determinations, and in recent state cases (*Eneliko v. Dreyfuss, Hendrick v. Department of Health & Human Services,* and *V.R. v Ohl*) that found that a child's receipt of Supplemental Security Income does not make a family ineligible for other means-tested financial support (Drought & Heintz, 2017).

In addition, many physical and mental health benefits require that licensed professionals certify the need for services. In these cases, eligibility is based on professional judgment. Although rules and guidelines typically direct their judgment, professionals have some discretion in deciding who will receive services. Scholar Michael Lipsky (1980) termed this power "street-level bureaucracy," a characterization that resonates with many social workers as they reflect on the extent to which their decisions determine clients' access to and experiences with social policies.

When considering eligibility rules from a strengths perspective, determine whether they create incentives for people to develop their capacity to meet their needs or whether such positive steps could result in lost benefits. For example, do low-income parents automatically become ineligible for a childcare subsidy if they manage to land higher-paying jobs? Does this prevent their permanent exit from poverty by subjecting them to the "benefit cliff"? Or are policies constructed to encourage and facilitate people's growth toward their goals?

Service Delivery Systems

A critical dimension of policy analysis is examination of the system by which services are delivered to those who want and need them. This delivery system may take many forms, all of which have implications for policy efficacy. Public or private agencies can deliver services, and private institutions can provide publicly funded services under public supervision. For example, the publicly funded Medicaid program pays for long-term care services that are often provided by private facilities. Similarly, Medicare-funded health care is often provided by private hospitals that are regulated by public agencies.

If a policy is not meeting its goals, one thing to consider is whether the services are being delivered as intended. Often called process evaluation, this analysis is carried out to determine whether the agency is implementing the policy as prescribed—an essential first step before one can assess whether the policy is "working." If a social worker finds that staff charged with implementing the policy are taking shortcuts or money has not been expended for necessary outreach, for example, it will be hard to determine whether these implementation failures are responsible for the policy falling short of its goals or whether other changes are needed.

Services can be delivered in a variety of ways, and these approaches can influence outcomes. Community institutions that do not typically provide social services can become important parts of the delivery system. For example, some communities have hired social workers in public libraries to work with homeless people who use these facilities. Social workers play critical roles in schools, public health agencies, and some police departments. Many community mental health systems train clients to support their peers. Employee assistance programs provide social work services to workers in large corporations or through health insurance plans. Taking advantage of technology, social workers are experimenting with delivering services such as case management, support groups, and family therapy online. In addition, certain benefits, such as Social Security payments, are routinely delivered through direct deposit.

Returning to analysis of McKinney–Vento, rapid rehousing is one intervention shown to combat homelessness. However, the delivery of services associated with rapid rehousing can vary among communities. A social worker may be assigned to recruit landlords willing to take tenants with rental subsidies. Staff at homeless shelters or community outreach programs may be charged with identifying people in need of housing assistance and placing them into appropriate housing. Exhibit 5.3 illustrates a logic model for the Rapid Rehousing Service Delivery System. Logic models

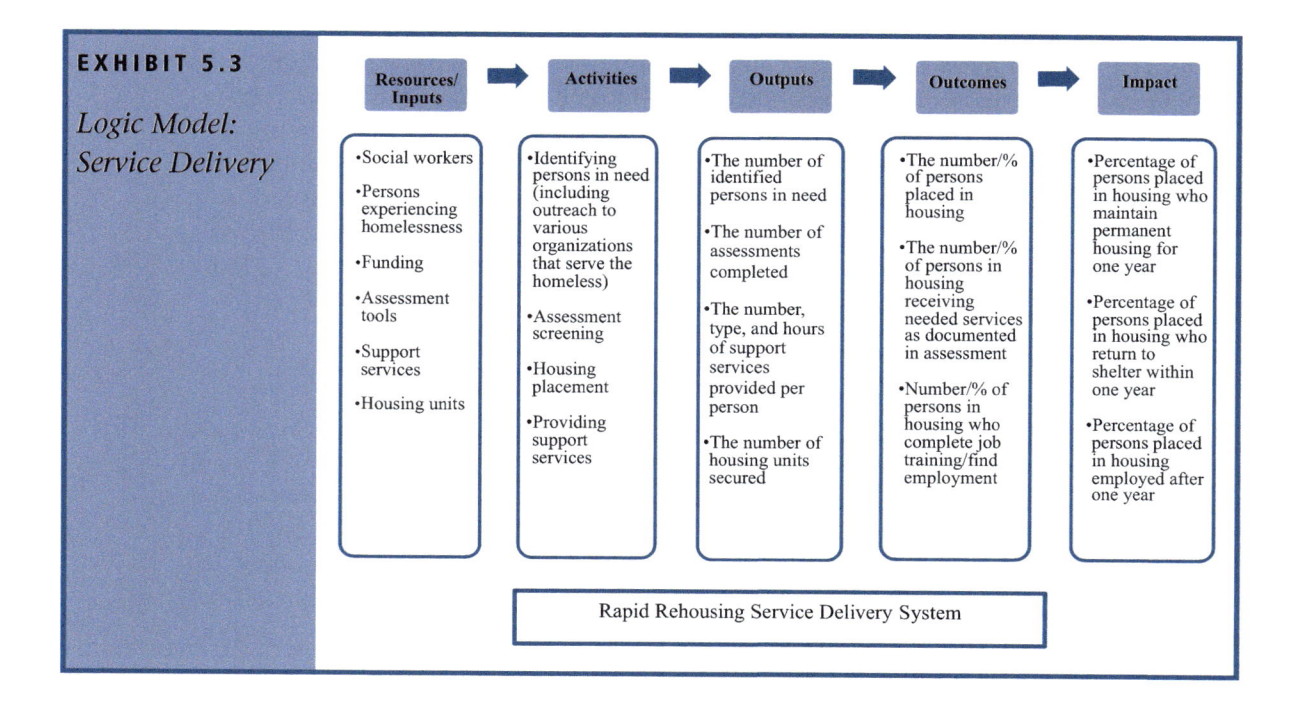

EXHIBIT 5.3

Logic Model: Service Delivery

Resources/Inputs → **Activities** → **Outputs** → **Outcomes** → **Impact**

Resources/Inputs	Activities	Outputs	Outcomes	Impact
• Social workers • Persons experiencing homelessness • Funding • Assessment tools • Support services • Housing units	• Identifying persons in need (including outreach to various organizations that serve the homeless) • Assessment screening • Housing placement • Providing support services	• The number of identified persons in need • The number of assessments completed • The number, type, and hours of support services provided per person • The number of housing units secured	• The number/% of persons placed in housing • The number/% of persons in housing receiving needed services as documented in assessment • Number/% of persons in housing who complete job training/find employment	• Percentage of persons placed in housing who maintain permanent housing for one year • Percentage of persons placed in housing who return to shelter within one year • Percentage of persons placed in housing employed after one year

Rapid Rehousing Service Delivery System

illustrate the resources/inputs delivered by the policy, activities conducted using these resources, the outputs produced as a result of the activities, and the outcomes and ultimate impact the policy is expected to produce. Logic models can help social workers organize policy analysis by outlining the components to be assessed. Here, a social worker could check whether the inputs/resources necessary for rapid rehousing were available and utilized. Process evaluation could determine whether the activities were conducted as designed and whether these activities delivered the desired outputs. That way, if the outcomes were not achieved or the ultimate impact not realized, the policy analyst has valuable insights as to where the policy may have gotten off track.

To examine a service delivery system from a strengths perspective, consider whether it builds on assets that already exist or instead creates separate structures. For example, separate schools and recreation facilities can be set up for people with disabilities, or existing facilities can be modified so that people with disabilities can use them. History has repeatedly illustrated that separate structures are inherently unequal. Further, consider whether a service delivery system offers clients choice, thereby maximizing the social work value of self-determination and preserving human dignity. For example, SNAP benefits allow people to shop in a variety of grocery stores and even farmers' markets, while historically people had to go to surplus-food distribution sites with few options to receive subsidized food.

Service delivery systems should be staffed by workers who reflect the diversity of the target population. Services should be physically accessible and culturally responsive to people of all backgrounds. For example, locating a program in a primarily White neighborhood limits access for people of color. If the delivery system does not consider availability of public transportation, gaps in that infrastructure may impede clients' access. Providing services in only one language can also restrict access. Policy can require providers to construct service delivery systems to be accessible to certain groups, perhaps compelling them to offer extended hours, provide in-home visits, or hire multilingual staff. However, most policies focus on the types of benefits provided rather than on problems in service delivery systems. In part, this is because policymakers are not service delivery experts. Unfamiliar with how service delivery is supposed to work, policymakers may nonetheless be receptive to social workers' ideas about options for improving delivery systems. Indeed, social workers may find that the arena of service delivery is a particularly fruitful place for their policy practice. For example, social workers have successfully advocated for integration of physical and mental health care and have secured changes in social service agencies that have resulted in greater representation of diverse staff, better utilization of technology to bridge divides, and more service provision in underserved rural and urban communities.

Financing

When you analyze a social policy or program, consider how it is funded. Funding that is not assured from year to year can result in chaos for providers and clients. Because private funding depends on voluntary giving, its stability and adequacy fluctuate. Entitlements have the most year-to-year stability; however, even publicly funded entitlements can meet the fate of the AFDC program, which was eliminated in 1996 and replaced with a less secure and largely inadequate block grant. Although public funding is generally more stable and adequate than funding from other sources, federal government shutdowns over budget disputes and budget shortfalls in many states illustrate its potential volatility.

Recall that certain publicly funded programs, such as Social Security retirement, are based on the insurance principle and require prior contributions. Other public programs, such as Temporary Assistance to Needy Families (TANF), are funded through general revenue appropriations that specify how tax dollars are to be spent. Federal taxes, state revenues, or some combination of the two may provide the funding for public programs. Many federal funding streams require that programs match federal funds from other sources. For example, the McKinney–Vento Homeless Assistance Act provides federal funds to augment state, local, and private funds. In the climate of devolution, local governments provide increasingly significant funding for social services, including public health, school-based supports, mental health, and housing initiatives.

In some programs, those who receive the service pay for it out-of-pocket. For example, a church or a for-profit company might institute a childcare program that requires parents to pay with their own money. Clients also may pay privately for counseling or for some rehabilitation services or addiction treatment. Strengths-based social workers carefully consider whether policies that require clients' contributions pose barriers to clients' pursuit of their goals.

When analyzing financing, it is also important to consider how service providers are reimbursed or paid. If service providers are paid the same amount regardless of clients' outcomes, they have less incentive to attain policy goals. The HEARTH Act of 2009 provides an example of how reimbursement policy can promote desired outcomes. Because the purpose of the HEARTH Act is to reduce homelessness, the legislation stipulates that HUD will provide financial incentives to community agencies that implement strategies proven to reduce homelessness. These strategies include programs to rapidly rehouse homeless families as well as permanent supportive housing programs for people who experience chronic homelessness.

Cost-Effectiveness and Outcomes

Analysis of the effectiveness of policy goals, benefits and services, eligibility rules, service delivery systems, and financing must be centered on outcomes for clients. However, policymakers may discontinue a program if it is not cost-effective. Of course, a program abandoned due to costs cannot have any impact. Particularly when budget crises loom, if social workers cannot document both the cost-effectiveness of a program and its positive outcomes, their initiatives will be in great danger. On the other hand, social workers who document program effectiveness can use that information to maintain and even increase funding. Additionally, social workers should be careful to include the cost of inaction in the cost–benefit analysis, since social problems seldom resolve themselves. Although it can be difficult to precisely quantify future costs and harms of failure to act, policymakers should evaluate cost-effectiveness of a given policy in a way that incorporates the cost of later intervention. When possible, call on someone skilled at doing fiscal analysis to help with cost calculations. You can bring a focus on positive outcomes for your clients, while also incorporating discussion of the benefits to the broader society of efficiently implementing effective programming.

CONCLUSION

Each element of the policy analysis framework explained above needs to be examined to determine how it contributes to outcomes for clients. Such evaluation is crucial to establishing the merit of a policy or program and convincing policymakers that it should continue, be modified, or be discontinued in favor of a more effective alternative.

You can utilize this framework to evaluate any social policy. Your analysis may identify ways policies can be improved. You may also demonstrate that certain policies result in negative outcomes for clients. For example, eligibility rules that limit TANF payments to five years or less create hardships, including hunger and homelessness, for children whose parents have not been able to find adequate employment. As a professional social worker, you will be expected to be capable of judging the merits of existing policies, using research to identify promising alternatives, and advocating for more effective policies.

MAIN POINTS

- There are many ways to view social problems or needs. The way in which the problem or need is constructed will greatly influence the policy solutions developed.
- Careful policy analysis is the foundation for effective policy practice. Policy analysis begins with understanding how a problem is defined, focusing on how values influence policy, and researching the causal theories developed.
- Research that either supports or refutes causal theories about problems and their origins should be carefully evaluated. Social workers may need to conduct their own evaluation to determine the full scope of the policy's impact on clients' needs and goals.
- Strengths-based policy analysis seeks to identify the needs of people as well as their strengths, goals, and resources, to guide policy and program development.
- Early in the problem definition process, social workers who take a strengths-based, solutions-focused approach to policy analysis should ask client groups about their vision for appropriate solutions and engage them in imagining a better future.
- Claims-making is the process of persuading policymakers of the need to act to improve a social condition. A successful claim must be made before social policy will be enacted.
- Claims can be based on rights, comparative disadvantage, utility, and/or appeals for social justice.
- A strengths-based analysis framework focusing on the following areas can help determine policy effectiveness: goals, benefits or services provided, eligibility rules, service delivery system, and financing.
- Using reliable sources, each element of the policy and program analysis framework should be examined in terms of its relationship to positive outcomes for clients.

EXERCISES

1. Social work is a values-based profession.
    a. How does this statement apply to policy analysis?
    b. What specific values does a strengths-based policy analysis emphasize?

2. Immigration policy influences the Sanchez family in multiple ways. Examine how people interested in immigration reform are engaging in claims-making.
    a. On what basis do immigration reform advocates assert that policies need to change—human rights, comparative disadvantage, utility, or social justice? Do different advocates rely on different primary claims?
    b. Are members of target populations actively involved in this process? Give examples.
3. In Riverton, as well as in your community, people who are homeless differ in many ways. People experiencing homelessness include former foster children, people with mental illness and other disabilities, veterans, two-parent families, single parents with children, and people with histories of substance use.
    a. How do you think public attitudes about providing resources to each of these groups may differ? What information on these groups might you present to help increase public support for assisting people who are homeless?
    b. How could Riverton construct a service delivery system capable of meeting the diverse needs of these different groups?
4. Consider the Carla Washburn case. Even though it is common to see grandparents raising grandchildren, social policies seldom reflect this reality.
    a. Research groups trying to get increased support for these grandparents. Note what actions they are taking, whether they focus on strengths as well as needs, and how they construct their claims for benefits and recognition.
    b. Advocates for children and for elders sometimes rely on claims that are perceived to advantage their target population over another. How do such tactics fail when confronting complex situations involving interrelated populations, as when grandparents are raising their grandchildren?
    c. Review the information you have on Carla Washburn. How do you think you might engage her in claims-making regarding the needs of grandparents raising grandchildren? Construct a short news story about these needs and illustrate how you and Mrs. Washburn could use her story in claims-making for these grandparents.
5. Go to the RAINN interactive case that focuses on an online service delivery system. Given the information provided in the interactive case, evaluate the program in terms of whether it delivers services in a cost-effective manner. How might this delivery system—and the calculation of its cost-effectiveness—change as technologies evolve?
6. Look at editorials and letters to the editor in news media. Starting with your local area, try to find instances where authors use different terms for the same people or events to evoke different values in debating an issue.
    a. Are there references to "children at risk" or "juvenile delinquents"? Is there focus on "addicts" or "unemployed mothers and fathers"?
    b. Do some issues and populations receive little attention? Why do you think this is so?
    c. Whose voices are represented in the coverage? What images are used to illustrate the issues, and how might those images shape public opinion?
    d. Identify the values the authors aim to evoke. As a social worker, what words could you use to evoke the values you believe should undergird the discussion?

CHAPTER 6

Social Policy Development

POLICY DEVELOPMENT IS THE PROCESS BY WHICH POLICIES are created and implemented to meet identified needs. While policy development might seem like a mysterious process, as the immigrant students whose advocacy is described in Exhibit 6.1 experienced, it is one you can come to understand and even influence. Policies can be designed to build on strengths and reflect the goals of the client group. Your research can help you better understand your clients and their needs, as well as the effects of different policies on their outcomes. Your communication and relationship skills can help you convey these critical truths to policymakers and make the case for change. In fact, the NASW Code of Ethics and our social work values impel you to take on these challenges, in pursuit of a more equitable policy landscape.

In this chapter, we first explore the steps in the policy development process. We then focus on ways social workers can use strengths principles to intervene in that process. If you think a policy is serving your clients poorly, you can help change it, and you can pursue this policy development in a way that engages your clients as co-creators of that change.

Effective social work involves a variety of skills and unfolds in various domains, including individual therapy, coalition building, program development, and policy practice. Social workers must guard against focusing on only the psychological aspects of clients' pain while ignoring political, economic, and social factors that contribute to their problems. This is not an "either/or" proposition. Social workers have traditionally recognized that helping clients involves a toolkit of skills appropriate both to work with individuals and to policy advocacy (Middleman & Goldberg-Wood, 1990). In fact, it is often work with individual clients that makes social workers aware of the need for policy change and fuels their passion for policy practice. Because social workers have close connections to clients and can cultivate strong relationships with policymakers, our profession is ideally positioned for **policy entrepreneurship**, defined as actions to take advantage of opportunities to influence policy outcomes (Kingdon, 2003). When you do a dual assessment of your clients, you will see patterns that point to the need for policy reform. You will recognize the connections between "presenting problems" and their root causes in ineffective policy, systemic discrimination, and/or policymakers' neglect of vulnerable populations. These connections undergird social workers' involvement in policy development, what scholar Michael Reisch refers to as the process of converting "private troubles" to "public issues" (2017b, p. 31). In addition, when fair and effective policies undergird social work practice, practice activities are more likely to be successful.

EXHIBIT 6.1

Immigrant Students Wage Long Campaign for Equitable Educational Opportunities

Credit: Rob Sagastume

In 2015, Missouri lawmakers wrote a provision into the budget that would penalize public universities if they did not charge immigrant students the higher international tuition rate, even when they were longtime state residents and graduates of Missouri high schools. This policy effectively locked these talented young people out of public post-secondary institutions. In response, immigrant students advocated to change the policy. They formed coalitions with immigrant-serving organizations around the state, used social media to stay connected with advocates in every legislative district, quantified the lost tuition and other economic impacts when students left the state, mobilized hundreds of supporters for lobby days and protests, and secured support from university leaders.

Their most potent tool was their own stories. Immigrant students like social worker Rob Sagastume (BSW 2017, MSW 2018), shared their journeys in visits with legislators and in media interviews, and these stories touched policymakers' hearts and changed many minds. Sagastume, who came to the United States from Honduras as a child and graduated at the top of his high school class, became undocumented when he aged out of his family's residency petition. While searching for a way to continue his own education, Rob encountered leaders from the Kansas/Missouri DREAM Alliance (KSMODA). He became

> **EXHIBIT 6.1**
>
> *Continued*
>
> KSMODA co-director and started a peer mentoring program to encourage other immigrant students to continue their educations—and to share their stories as advocates. He studied social work to improve his skills in organizing grassroots leaders, assembling persuasive arguments, assessing prospective opponents, and evaluating strategies. He completed a practicum in the state capitol to build deeper relationships with policymakers.
>
> And, true to his social work values, Sagastume also helped other students build their capacities. Their personal witnesses were powerful testimonies that based claims on universal values of opportunity, belonging, and hard work. They became increasingly skilled at navigating the political environment and conveying complicated information about immigration law and budget processes to stakeholders. They proved they could activate large constituencies and demonstrated their tenacity, especially after succeeding in having the punitive language stripped two years in a row, only to see it reinserted. And they made compromises; after recognizing they lacked the votes to make undocumented immigrant students eligible for instate tuition statewide, they instead pushed to return control of tuition pricing to individual educational institutions. When success on that front was reversed three times, they demonstrated their tenacity, vowing #CantStopWontStop and strategizing ways forward. To sustain their advocacy, these young people rely on many of the same strengths that helped them succeed in a new country, against great odds. They take comfort in community, hold fast to their vision, and take the high ground, arguing that the state should live up to its own ideals of opportunity and fairness. And, as when Rob thought his own dreams might be out of reach, they refuse to give up.

To illustrate how social workers can engage in policy advocacy from their practice roles, consider how, as a school social worker, you may see increasing numbers of children who are homeless and have problems in school. You will likely be working with families around behavioral issues and providing referrals to help with rehousing. At the same time, to provide the most effective social work interventions and help your clients reach their goals, it is also important to address policies contributing to the problem of homelessness. You can make sure that what you see in your work comes to the attention of policymakers. These may include city council members with jurisdiction over zoning laws, school administrators who allocate funds for in-school interventions, and members of Congress considering reauthorization of programs under the Department of Housing and Urban Development. Policymakers need to know how the numbers of homeless children are increasing, and they must recognize the impact homelessness has on school performance. You could also make sure they have information on the best models used to respond to homelessness in other communities. Most social problems have been addressed in some fashion, and social work advocates who scan the landscape to look for promising interventions and valuable lessons will develop a reputation for being conduits of good ideas. School policies may need to change so that children who are homeless can shower and change clothes before starting their school day. Teachers may need additional training to equip them to meet the academic needs of homeless students. Your community may need to develop policies to prioritize families for rapid rehousing. State and federal policies beyond homelessness may also need to improve, such as those that tackle issues like job creation, minimum wage, family income supports, and housing affordability.

You are not expected to take on all these issues. There is no mandate—from the NASW Code of Ethics, your future employer, or your policy instructor—to tackle policy development on all these fronts. You are, however, expected to consider how these issues influence your clients and to then act, alongside your clients, where you can. It is important to recognize your clients' strengths and how they might contribute to efforts to bring about more just policies and programs. All clients can be invited to collaborate in ways that align with their own goals. Indeed, participating in advocacy can be an integral part of the helping process. You can use advocacy skills to push for policies within your employing organization that support your involvement in policy practice to promote social justice.

STEPS IN POLICY DEVELOPMENT

Policy development ideally emanates from the process of policy analysis. However, although policy analysis involves analyzing each element of an existing policy, not all policy development aims to change policies. Sometimes policy analysis leads social workers to oppose any significant policy changes; in these cases, social workers use policy development skills to preserve the status quo. Especially in periods of retrenchment, this kind of policy practice is crucial to retain programs upon which we all rely.

Quick Guide 3 summarizes what you have learned thus far about policy analysis and policy development. The list below provides a more detailed overview of the policy development process. Each bullet integrates the strengths perspective into an element of the process:

- **Define needs or social problems and strengths in partnership with clients.** The strengths perspective views definitions as negotiated, not fixed or imposed. When defining goals and strengths and identifying needs and structural barriers, include the perspectives of the target group.

- **Document needs, strengths, and goals in partnership with clients.** Measure the amount of need, the dimensions of structural barriers, and clients' strengths and preferred goals.

- **Identify initial policy goals in partnership with clients.** Seek out information on clients' goals and carefully consider those goals as important priorities.

- **Engage in claims-making to carve out the space for clients to self-determine a path to their identified goals.** Strengths-based policy practice uses claims to advance a vision of social justice.

- **Negotiate the definition of policy goals.** Work with policymakers to ensure that they include client perspectives when developing policy goals.

QUICK GUIDE 3 Policy Analysis and Development Overview

BACKGROUND/CONTEXT
- How do historical policy approaches to this social problem/need shape current policy?
- What was the cultural milieu at the time these historical approaches were taken? In what ways are the current political and economic contexts the same or different?
- Who were the key players involved in developing historical policies? Whose interests were the policies intended to serve?
- Is there reason to think that historical policy approaches would work better or worse today?
- Did these historical policy approaches build on the strengths of the target population? How?
- Alternatively, were these policy approaches predicated on a pathology or deficit view of people in need?
- How have definitions of this problem/need and policy approaches to address it changed over time?

UNDERSTANDING THE SOCIAL PROBLEM/NEED
- What causal theories have been developed based on this definition of the social problem? What evidence supports these causal theories?
- What consequences are ascribed to the problem?
- What are the direct and indirect effects of the policy? How are they distributed in society?

POLICY ANALYSIS
- What are the goals of the policy or program? What is the logical link between the goals and positive outcomes for clients?
- What benefits or services does the policy provide?
- What are the eligibility rules? In other words, who gets the benefits or services?
- How are services/benefits delivered?
- How are services/benefits financed?
- What evidence is there that each element of the policy leads to positive outcomes for the client population, is cost-effective, and is sustainable?
- Is the policy politically, socially, and economically feasible?
- Does the policy incorporate key social work values such as self-determination and social justice?
- How is the target/client population involved in evaluating the policy/program?

POLICY DEVELOPMENT
- Who is the target/client population? What specific needs are you trying to meet?
- What policy options have been identified to address these needs? Has the target population been involved in defining the need and policy options?
- What specific policy changes are being advocated? How can a claim be made for the need for these policy changes?
- What actions will be necessary to get this policy enacted? How can the target population be involved?
- Once implemented, how can you ensure that the policy will be evaluated and improved based on client outcomes?

- **Legitimize policy goals with the public.** Publicize information on the opportunities and resources people need to meet their goals. Frame policy goals to align with key social values and work to find common ground with important constituencies.

- **In partnership with clients, formulate policy alternatives that meet established goals.** Identify ways clients currently overcome barriers to reach their goals. These are important strengths and should be heralded as such. Identify programs that help clients overcome those barriers; these are best practices. When formulating policy in collaboration with clients, it is crucial to assess workability and evaluate the various elements of proposed policy alternatives. Strengths-based social workers facilitate client empowerment when they position clients as experts on their own needs and experiences and relevant policy actors capable of advancing promising solutions.

- **Develop, enact, and implement the policy or program in partnership with clients.** Client involvement does not stop at the point of policy formulation. Instead, clients' needs, goals, and perspectives should inform design and implementation at all stages.

- **Evaluate outcomes in partnership with clients.** To improve policy, evaluation and ongoing assessment should emphasize client outcomes and client feedback.

An example of a social policy developed without incorporating the elements of this process illuminates their importance. A group of state legislators developed a policy proposal to require that all Temporary Assistance to Needy Families (TANF) recipients undergo drug testing to receive their benefits. However, they did not discuss their proposed policy with TANF recipients or advocacy groups. They did not even research who was receiving TANF in their state. They did not realize that many TANF recipients were grandparents raising grandchildren. Advocates contacted the media to publicize this proposal and its effects on this group of TANF recipients. Advocates asserted that grandparents who needed financial help while caring for their grandchildren should not have to "pee in a cup" to get that help. These claims were successful, and the proposal was defeated. The policymakers who proposed mandatory drug testing had little idea of the strengths or needs of TANF recipients like these grandparents. They did not consider engaging them in policy development. The time, effort, and taxpayer money spent on this failed legislation did nothing to improve the effectiveness of TANF or to meet the needs of these families.

Determining Need and Making Claims

In Chapter 5, we described how people have defined needs and made claims for existing policies. This chapter highlights how the strengths perspective can inform the development of new or reformed social policy. People typically identify initial policy goals early in the problem definition and claims-making processes because they have some preconceived idea of the policies they expect to champion. For example, if civic leaders have noted a need for supervised out-of-school-time activities, they may propose a policy with the goal of establishing after-school programs through the Parks and Recreation Department. However, it is important to scrutinize policy goals from the beginning to ensure they include the goals of the client group. In this case, asking the young people in the community directly about their needs, barriers to getting those needs met, and preferred after-school intervention will make it much more likely that they will benefit from any program that is implemented. If young people have negative perceptions of the Parks and Recreation Department, want to spend their after-school time receiving academic assistance, or prefer internships or employment to recreation, involving them in the policy development process from the beginning will facilitate policymaking that meets their needs, rather than the needs policymakers perceived.

Groups Involved in Needs Determination and Claims-Making Major policies are rarely crafted quickly. Typically, a variety of provider, client, and advocacy groups identify needs, engage in claims-making, and try to direct policy development. Legislators typically have a plethora of interest groups vying for their attention. Because all these constituencies may operate independently and even in opposition to one another, policy development often unfolds slowly. Groups may have identified specific policymakers to champion their causes or to target for persuasion. For example, an advocacy group for people with developmental disabilities may work closely with a senator who has a son who has a disability. Similarly, a service provider group that owns independent living facilities may have the ear of a legislator who formerly owned such facilities. An immigrant rights organization may focus its energies on a conservative Catholic senator whose faith may make her sympathetic to their cause. Although social work policy practitioners should be prepared to encounter opposition, if it is possible to get several groups or stakeholders to agree on a message and a policy goal, advocacy efforts may be more effective. While powerful interests can advance their claims even in the face of considerable opposition, policymakers are more likely to address an issue when constituencies are unified in support of a particular position. The student whose advocacy is described in Exhibit 6.2 amplified his impact by recruiting others to participate in his claims-making efforts.

Legislators bring varying amounts of expertise on different subjects to policymaking. For example, a legislator may be very familiar with transportation needs because of his career in trucking but might know little about social services. Another policymaker may have little background in curriculum and instruction but considerable experience with budgets and financial management. In such cases, legislators turn to people who possess expertise on the subject. Legislators are pressed to enact agricultural policy, taxation, water standards, educational reform, and many other initiatives. Federal policymakers must attend to foreign concerns as well as

---

EXHIBIT 6.2

Social Work Students Engage in Claims-Making on Behalf of Their Clients

A student at a university in the Southwest worked to increase public awareness of homelessness in his state. He helped to organize a demonstration on the grounds of the state capitol, where more than 200 people camped overnight in tents or cardboard boxes. He also helped to arrange a photo exhibit and presented information on homelessness at legislative committee meetings in support of a bill that would provide $20 million for housing resources.

domestic issues. They must weigh competing claims to determine who to trust and whose appeals to prioritize. Social workers can educate legislators, influence their understanding of needs, and help to ensure that claims are made successfully.

The Legislative Agenda Fundamentally, claims-makers who want to enact legislation must compete to get their issue on the legislative agenda. The term **agenda**, as used here, means "the list of subjects or problems to which government officials, and people outside of government closely associated with those officials, are paying some serious attention at any given time" (Kingdon, 2003, p. 3). Claims for attention must compete with many other claims that policymakers may find more compelling. This phase of policy development may include conversations that bring the issue to policymakers' attention. However, for the issue to progress to the point that legislators introduce and act upon a bill, it will somehow need to move to what is termed the "decision agenda" (Kingdon, 2003).

A problem or need only moves to the decision agenda when it presses on policymakers in some way. For example, if the media are covering a problem or need, there may be pressure for change. This was the case when high-profile cases of sexual abuse occurring within institutions such as churches and universities led to legislation to change the statute of limitations for bringing criminal charges against perpetrators. Media coverage of problems in the child welfare system also brings those issues to the decision agenda, particularly when a child is abused in foster care or dies after an allegation of maltreatment at home. Crises focus the public's attention on an issue. For example, media reports of an older nursing home resident wandering away and dying of exposure due to inadequate supervision can give rise to public clamor for more stringent regulation of facility staffing levels. If specialists have accumulated research about the need and best practices, these moments may open **windows of opportunity** for conveying this information to policymakers. By striking while policymakers' attention has been captured, advocates may find a more receptive audience for their proposals. Other, more predictable openings occur when policies or programs are up for renewal, routine evaluation reports are made, or budgets are negotiated.

Elections also influence which issues move to the decision agenda. In Kansas, after several years of drastic budget cuts prompted by the governor's tax "experiment," several new legislators were elected after promising to overturn the tax policies and restore funding for public education and social services. Shortly after taking office, these legislators advanced tax changes to increase revenues, even overriding the governor's veto (Ehrenfreund, 2017). Policymakers who were elected after promising to reduce immigration or restrict abortion will similarly prioritize advancing those issues. In addition to taking tangible policy action, they will likely seek to keep those concerns on the broader agenda.

The process by which an issue moves to the decision agenda influences the resulting policy. For example, public outrage may prompt rapid action. In some cases, this action may be undertaken so quickly and with so little research that resulting policies may fail to resolve underlying problems or result in significant unintended consequences. Many argued that this was the case immediately following the terrorist attacks of September 11, 2001, when legislation such as the USA PATRIOT Act advanced quickly through Congress to address perceived security breaches while significantly eroding privacy and due process protections.

It should be clear by now that policy development is not a technical, step-by-step process. Rather, it tends to be messy and inexact. Policy development is very much influenced by economic, political, and social contexts, which is why this text began with a consideration of how these forces have shaped policy throughout history. Many people participate in policy development. When input from different groups coalesces at a time when policymakers are open to considering initiatives in that area—or can be convinced to be so—policy can be developed or changed. Although this can sound like a magical "aligning of the stars," that does not mean that social workers are just to sit and wait for the right time to pounce. Instead, policy practitioners can actively help to shape this process—what some have called the converging of the multiple streams of policy development: problem definition, proposal/policy recommendation, and politics (Kingdon, 2003). Regardless of the stream on which social workers focus their efforts, those who will be most successful in influencing social policy over the long term are those who learn to "read" the landscape and to adjust their policy practice accordingly.

Crafting Policy Goals

Once social work policy practitioners and target groups determine which goals to pursue, they can formulate and evaluate policy alternatives to meet those goals. Key actors' ideas about potential ways to meet needs and reach goals typically emerge in the need-identification and claims-making processes. Remember, key actors are those who hold significant power to influence policymaking by their position, political influence, or expertise. They include elected officials, agency staff, advocacy groups, and researchers.

Of course, client groups have expertise from their lived experience. However, because this expertise is seldom fully acknowledged, they may not be viewed as key actors unless other stakeholders intentionally position them as such. Efforts to develop policy goals that promote social justice should include work to ensure that client voices are heard, as in Exhibit 6.3.

EXHIBIT 6.3

An Unexpected Policy Proposal from a Client

A social worker employed as a case manager in a transitional housing program for homeless teens invited policymakers to come to a graduation ceremony where adolescents would be recognized for completing the program. Afterward, the social worker connected one of the teens to a county commissioner she knew was interested in youth development. In their conversation, the commissioner asked the teen if there was one thing she could think of that would have been helpful to her when she was trying to get through high school as a homeless youth. To the case manager's surprise, the teen responded that she struggled to get food assistance because her parents still listed her as a dependent (even though she did not receive any support from them) and because the U.S. Department of Agriculture (USDA) did not conduct Supplemental Nutrition Assistance Program outreach at high schools. The county commissioner promised to follow up. By the end of the week, the USDA had committed to community office hours at high schools with homeless teens and to at least exploring ways for youth to apply as households separate from their parents.

Achieving Consensus While, to observers, policymaking can appear like a "winner-take-all" exercise, most policy change includes at least some compromise. The process is too long and twisting for a single policy entrepreneur to easily ram through a solitary idea. Instead, enacting new policies requires melding together the diverse goals of key actors to reach consensus. This can be difficult. Often, stakeholders may agree about some of the elements of a problem, but this consensus might fall apart at the point of formulation of policy alternatives. For example, groups may agree on the need for more public support for people with developmental disabilities; however, some factions might advocate for more funds for group homes, whereas others might favor family-directed in-home care.

Even in today's polarized policy context, there are some needs on which we can readily find consensus. Most policymakers would agree that it is important to have healthy babies. Conflict comes at the points of determining the causes that contribute to the need and the best ways to achieve our shared goals. For example, details such as the type and amount of assistance mothers should receive are more contentious. At times when obtaining consensus might be impossible or unrealistic, amassing enough public support may be critical to getting policies approved or enacted. Groups attempting to stop health reform in 2009 worked very hard to stir up opposition, but advocacy groups involved in claims-making helped to legitimize the policy goal of increasing access to care. Later, when congressional Republicans attempted to repeal the Affordable Care Act (ACA) in 2017, broad public support for the goals of the ACA—particularly regarding equitable coverage for people with preexisting health conditions—prevented their success, even though many in the public remain skeptical of or even resistant to some of the mechanisms included in health reform.

To find avenues for moving forward, ask clients, policymakers, and other stakeholders how they would like things to be better, what they see as options for reaching this new state, and what examples they see where these improved outcomes have been accomplished. These conversations should consider the costs of not moving forward, as well. While any policy change includes some risks and inevitable trade-offs, evaluation should also incorporate the potential harm of inaction, as people try to continue coping with the problem without sufficient resources. The policy proposals that get implemented usually incorporate a variety of ideas that one person would not have developed alone. It is easier to craft policy goals and options around which consensus may develop when advocates understand stakeholders' goals.

Utilizing the Strengths Perspective The strengths perspective mandates that efforts to develop policy goals include assertive outreach to client groups, whose priorities should be central to the process. Social workers engaged in policy development have many options regarding the best ways to engage client groups. Public hearings often elicit feedback on proposed policies and lend legitimacy to the policies that are ultimately passed. Social workers can remove barriers to participation in these venues by considering transportation, childcare, financial assistance, and client preparation. Social workers can also connect client groups to media outlets open to presenting clients' perspectives and use social media to elevate clients' voices.

Examining the Feasibility of Policy Alternatives

To ensure that resulting policies address stated policy goals and the targeted social problem, the policy development process must consider the feasibility of proposed solutions within the social, economic, and political contexts. People attempting to develop policies try to craft a workable solution and then convince policymakers to support it. "Workability," however, is not an entirely objective determination. Social work values guide our evaluation of workability. To determine whether a solution is workable, consider the following elements:

- *Expected outcomes*. First, can the proposed solution realistically be expected to help the target population reach their goals? Some proposed "solutions" could make things worse for the target group.
- *Unintended outcomes*. Consider whether the proposal could have unintended negative outcomes, such as harming the environment.
- *Value base*. Are the values this proposal supports consistent with social work values and the strengths perspective?
- *Level of risk*. Is the proposed solution low-risk? Is it likely to succeed?
- *Ease of implementation*. How much would the existing service delivery system have to change to accommodate this policy change?
- *Cost*. Can the policy be funded with existing resources? If a tax increase would be needed to fund the proposal, what is the likelihood that increase would be passed? Take **opportunity cost** into account, as pursuing any given approach will inevitably reduce the resources available for alternative solutions.
- *Flexibility*. Is the policy flexible enough to withstand environmental stressors like economic downturns or demographic shifts, to provide some choice to the varied members of the target group, and to address additional societal goals?
- *Communicability*. Is the policy easy to communicate to policymakers, the public, and the target population? Is there likely to be considerable buy-in regarding the viability of this approach?
- *Likelihood of passage*. Are there enough policymakers and allies who support or could be persuaded to support its passage? How strong is the opposition?

Here is an example of how to use these criteria to consider a policy designed to improve the performance of low-income children in school and, ultimately, to increase their graduation rate. Parents and the larger community are united in supporting this goal. Social justice, equal opportunity, and concern for future prosperity are values that motivate the goal. Community activists therefore proposed a policy to provide full-day preschool programs. Research indicates that if these programs are accessible, carefully designed, and well implemented, they lead to higher graduation rates (Stegelin, 2004). Research further reveals that such programs are cost-effective and that state and federal funding as well as philanthropic money may be available; they may also have corollary benefits in facilitating parents' work participation and improving children's physical and mental health (Hahn et al., 2016). The proposal is low-risk in that many communities have already successfully implemented such programs. In addition, the preschool classes will be conducted at existing schools. Allowing each school the flexibility to design outreach to best reach parents and respond to unique needs will increase the likelihood of sustained success. Such an approach will address criteria concerned with *expected outcomes*, *value base*, *level of risk*, *costs*, and *ease of implementation*.

The concept of all-day preschool is easily communicated to parents and the media. Widespread parental support for the proposal makes its passage more likely. However, some taxpayers may oppose any program that will increase property taxes. Others argue that the problem of low graduation rates needs a more immediate solution than this long-term intervention will provide. Since school board members are concerned with their electability on much shorter timelines than the 14 years it will take to see results from this investment, securing federal, state, or philanthropic support for the program will be crucial to obtaining school board approval. Such a funding mix could also help to minimize opportunity costs, since school district funds would not need to be diverted from summer school or enrichment programming. This proposal meets the criteria of *communicability* and *likelihood of passage*, provided the always-difficult issue of funding can be successfully negotiated. In total, then, this proposal appears to be workable.

In contrast, increasing a high school's graduation rates by making discipline policies more restrictive and placing struggling students in separate, remedial schools would not fit the *values* and *strengths perspective* criteria. The assumptions behind such a policy—that student behavior is the sole cause of low graduation rates and that students cannot be supported toward successful graduation—clearly conflicts with a strengths-based approach. However, layering onto the preschool program efforts to identify high school students at risk of dropout and to provide them with targeted assistance may increase the perceived workability of the approach to the social problem. By working on both prevention and early intervention, the program would provide students and families with resources and opportunities that may have previously been unavailable.

If a policy proposal does not fit the criteria outlined above, it may be eliminated from consideration. In some cases, however, a generally distasteful proposal is presented to motivate decision-makers to compromise and pass the preferred policy before the alternative policy gains momentum. For example, groups might put forward a proposal to abolish free after-school programs for all middle school students in a district to save tax dollars, when the policy they actually favor is to require higher-income families to pay a fee for participation. They propose abolishing the program in the hope that those who oppose any change will compromise if they believe the program's existence is threatened. It should be emphasized, however, that these tactics can reduce client participation in policy development, as clients might be uncomfortable advocating an approach they do not support. They also contain a significant level of risk, particularly if the political environment is such that these seemingly "extreme" proposals may gain momentum.

Finally, when examining the workability of policy alternatives, an approach should not be automatically rejected because there is not yet evidence it will work. Proposals may be feasible and promising but untested. While it is more difficult to work out the details of piloting an untested approach, that may be an effective strategy, particularly if it arises from people familiar with the nuances of client needs, strengths, and goals. Some of our most cherished social policies—Social Security, universal public education, Medicare—began as policy innovations that, over time, demonstrated significant potential for positive outcomes.

Enacting and Implementing Policy

The next phase of policy development focuses on how policies are enacted and subsequently implemented. We often think of state and federal legislators enacting policy, but increasingly city and county governments make social policy decisions regarding education, health and mental health, housing, and civil rights. Additionally, as discussed in earlier chapters, the executive and judicial branches also make policy. The organizations where social workers are employed also make policies that govern their work and the ways in which clients interact with the agency. The specific processes of determining need, making claims, and enacting policy will vary somewhat depending on the setting, but the concepts are essentially the same. Need must be recognized and defined, claims-making must take place, and the issue must gain enough attention from policymakers to warrant action.

Generally, once a policy is approved, policymakers must appropriate money to implement it. Many times, a poorly negotiated appropriation process results in inadequate funding, which can blunt the policy's impact. Sometimes, a policy cannot even be implemented, despite winning passage, because appropriations never follow.

After a policy is enacted and funded, agency staff will work out, often in consultation with outside experts and key stakeholders, the details of who will be eligible and how the benefit or service will be delivered. Legislation is seldom so specific that administrators know exactly what is to be done. For example, legislation may give a state agency the authority to license and regulate childcare providers. However, it might not specify the number of infants one provider can care for, the type of space that is appropriate, an inspection schedule, or consequences for providers not meeting regulations. The legislation may not even define "infant" or stipulate the training care providers must receive. In such a case, the state agency might hold a series of meetings with legislators, providers, and parents to develop rules and regulations. Many times, federal, state, and even local agencies may be required to engage in a rule-making process that includes public input. In other instances, one or more staff members may develop written or unwritten implementation guidelines. Some local and private agencies also codify their implementation plans in this way, but many agencies have few, if any, written guidelines for implementing policies and programs. While this may allow social workers more flexibility and professional discretion, it can also create ambiguity that makes it difficult for clients to understand and exert their rights.

Client groups can and should be part of the implementation process. Their participation in rule development promotes service delivery that is sensitive to their backgrounds and responsive to their needs. Often, clients can become service providers. Providing services through community agencies with which clients are already comfortable may be more effective and cost-efficient than constructing a delivery system from scratch.

Evaluating Policy Outcomes

As described in Chapter 5, evaluation involves determining whether a program accomplishes the goals of the policy and whether it meets or at least reduces the identified need. The evaluation should examine outcomes for clients and highlight clients' perspectives on effectiveness. Ideally, evaluation of the extent to which policies meet clients' needs should be both the starting point and culmination of policy development, as advocates, administrators, and clients consider together what the effects are, how they compare to the goals, and how modifications might improve outcomes. Seen through this lens, evaluation is ongoing, circular, iterative, and client-centered.

Given their knowledge of promising practices and practice wisdom regarding clients' needs and strengths, social work policy entrepreneurs can also play crucial roles in policymaking in social work agencies. Indeed, when evaluation points to needed reforms, work to change policy and practice at the agency level can be highly effective and often more expeditious than advocacy at the state and federal levels. However, even more than engagement in legislative policy development, these efforts may affect your position in the agency. Before engaging in this work or any policy practice, think through the potential impact of your activism and seek consultation from trusted colleagues.

Although policymakers may try to anticipate outcomes, policies frequently generate **unanticipated consequences**—unexpected events that result from the implementation of a policy. A policy can make things better for the general population but worse for the target group, or better or worse for some other groups (Ellis, 2003). For example, building a housing project for older adults with low incomes may involve tearing down existing housing that serves low-income families. In this case, the unanticipated consequence might be an increase in the number of homeless families. Of course, "unanticipated" does not necessarily mean unpredictable. Policymakers could have foreseen these consequences if they had developed outcome scenarios to try to determine displacement effects. Other unanticipated consequences may include higher than expected costs. Additionally, one policy or program could have an unintended effect on the eligibility or effectiveness of other policies. For example, when a family receives a lump sum refund from the Earned Income Tax Credit, they might have to spend it immediately or risk losing eligibility for programs such as Medicaid, which have very low asset limits. To deal with this negative program interaction, some policymakers eliminated asset tests or developed policies that shield some assets from eligibility determinations. When thinking through policy options, it is important to carefully consider potential interactions. However, no matter how careful you are to anticipate results, every policy is likely to have unexpected consequences. By monitoring implementation, you can discover unanticipated outcomes as early as possible and plan for dealing with them.

SOCIAL WORK POLICY PRACTICE AND THE ECOLOGICAL PERSPECTIVE

The NASW Code of Ethics directs us to engage in policy practice to put our values into action. Analysis is necessary, but it is not enough. Effective social workers act to bring about policy changes that benefit their clients. Some social workers have full-time policy practice jobs such as lobbying, serving as legislative aides, conducting analysis for advocacy organizations, or developing rules in public agencies. Others may engage in policy practice as part of their larger responsibilities. This policy practice may include monitoring legislation, testifying at legislative committee hearings, or mobilizing supporters in support of, or in opposition to, policy changes. Many social service agencies realize too late that they need to keep track of policy changes. Although some social workers believe that if they do good work, that is enough, people who want to cut funding for social services or take other actions contrary to our clients' interests are often willing and able to invest time and money to change policies. As a result, social workers must be similarly committed if clients' needs are to prevail. In preparing for and engaging in this work, social workers can learn a great deal from the successful strategies proponents from different political and professional perspectives have used to shape policy. However, this book focuses specifically on *social work policy practice*—that is, work to change social policy that influences your clients and our profession and that is informed by the NASW Code of Ethics (Jansson, 2013).

Like most social workers, you will likely be busy providing direct service. As one person, what can you do to promote policies that will benefit your clients? The next part of this chapter equips you with beginning tools to influence social policy. When you see foster children shunted through multiple placements or elders with inadequate care, you need not feel powerless. Social workers' value base, theoretical knowledge, assessment and communication skills, and relational competencies provide a foundation for effective policy practice. When you carve out time to hone your policy practice skills, you can turn your passion into strategies with which to realize positive outcomes for your clients. You'll have the ability to make a difference and concrete ideas about how to integrate policy practice into your work in any practice arena.

The **ecological perspective** in social work focuses on the ways in which people and their environments influence, change, and shape each other (Germain, 1991). Certainly, there is ample evidence that individuals are deeply affected by such forces as the economy, social structures, and the political context. Further, the ecological perspective directs attention to the risks and protective factors in the environment—built and natural—that either help or impede people's efforts to reach their goals. Social policies and programs are part of our environment. They can help clients by providing needed benefits and services, or they can create barriers when, for example, they foster discrimination. To shape effective policy, social workers can use an ecological perspective to understand the multiple interactions and feedback mechanisms that connect clients and policies.

The ecological perspective can help us discern the difficulties people face meeting their needs and how we may engage in policy practice to remove these barriers. Jim Taylor, a social work theorist, built on the ecological perspective to explore the concept of "social niches."

Social niches are "the environmental habitat of people, including the resources they utilize and the people with which they associate" (Taylor, 1997). A housing development, school, or community center, and the people and resources associated with each, can all be social niches.

Taylor further distinguished between entrapping niches and enabling niches. People in **entrapping niches** face barriers that prevent them from fulfilling their needs. They frequently have restricted access to people or resources outside their niche. Entrapping niches are stigmatizing and often serve as obstacles that people struggle to overcome. Taylor proposed that many social workers' clients are isolated in niches where very few empowering resources are available to them. They have little contact with people, ideas, institutions, and information that might help them more readily achieve their goals.

In contrast, **enabling niches** provide resources, rewards, and incentives instead of barriers. For example, Kretzmann and McKnight (1993) have identified community assets such as excellent schools, interested adults, and vocational training programs as crucial supports, especially for young people; these assets are hallmarks of enabling niches.

Transporting niches are places where people can get the help they need to move out of entrapping niches. Settlement houses are examples of efforts to create transporting niches. On a micro level, supportive relationships with social work professionals can serve as transporting niches for individual clients. Social policies can also create transporting niches.

The strengths perspective builds on the ecological approach. Reality is co-constructed; that is, people influence one another's views. Along with questions about needs and problems, questions like "What are your strengths and community resources, and how can they be developed?" are important in formulating effective policy strategies.

POLICY RESEARCH AND PRACTICE

To help create a reality for clients that provides opportunities for self-determination and increased access to necessary resources, social workers need to develop a well-honed set of policy practice skills. Research skills will be vital so that you can provide information to policymakers on social problems and promising approaches. Of course, research facts alone seldom carry the day; policy practitioners also need compelling messaging and positive relationships with at least some of the relevant policymakers. Indeed, the use of relationship is as integral to policy practice as to all social work. As you become engaged in policy practice, you will learn that the people you are pressing for policy changes are often facing budget constraints and political pressures. If you can use your relationship skills to find common ground and to identify and build on existing strengths and resources rather than create an "us versus them" mentality, you will develop the networks necessary for effective policy practice.

This does not mean that social workers should expect that good intentions or even good information will win over all opponents. Instead, while our professional values and ethical dictates place some tactics used by others in the political "game" off-limits, we must acknowledge these realities to operate effectively. We can seldom afford to ignore opposition, but skillful deployment of policy practice skills can often neutralize it. Further, as the students in Exhibit 6.1 found, social work advocates should be prepared to defend hard-fought gains, engage on multiple "fronts," and work with a variety of allies. Additionally, since social workers care about so many issues and may work with different groups as political allegiances and contexts evolve, policy practitioners should avoid burning any bridges unnecessarily, instead calling on our relationship skills to find common cause when and where we can.

Beyond analytic and research skills, then, social workers skilled at policy practice have political, values-clarifying, and organizing skills (Jansson, 2013). Political skills enable social workers to understand and use power effectively. Values-clarifying skills help them determine whether the policy options under consideration are consistent with social work values and, then, to frame policy alternatives in value terms that policymakers may be more likely to accept. Finally, organizing skills assist social workers in negotiating consensus and mobilizing constituencies. In deploying these skills, social workers assume the role of a collaborator and resource to help attract attention to clients' perspectives and to complement clients' efforts to advocate on their own behalf.

While this chapter presents policy practice tasks in a linear order, you may be working on several tasks simultaneously. Your policy practice will build on the proud traditions of the profession, which has long played a role in policy development and reform, while reflecting the opportunities and demands of the current context. This chapter is just the beginning of your maturation as a social worker in policy practice.

Identifying and Defining the Target Client Population

To consider policy change, it is important to clearly identify, define, and describe the characteristics of the target group (Ellis, 2003). How many members of the target population live in your town, state, and nation? What are their ages, gender identities, and ethnicities? What is their socioeconomic status? How many have a disability? What are their strengths? What do you know about their histories, including how they have coped with their needs to this point? To illustrate the process of identification of the target population, if you were interested in addressing the needs of children in foster care, you would need to be aware of the legal definitions in your state specifying who is considered a foster child. If you were particularly concerned with the number of placements foster children experience, it would be important to examine how the gender, age, race, ethnicity, and disability levels of children entering the foster care system influence the number of placements and how these identities may intersect. The state agency in charge of foster care may be able to provide this information, or you may need to conduct your own investigations using other methods. To take an informed approach to policy change, you need to know the size and variation of the client population as a starting point to receiving input from its members. You would want to pay particular attention to individuals who may be disadvantaged and to ways policy may compound these challenges.

Identifying strengths can help you construct solutions to otherwise seemingly unsolvable problems. Social workers, then, should document individual and community strengths and assets as well as the barriers client groups confront. Often, members of the target group are already involved in political action. For example, in some states, former foster children actively engage in reform initiatives. Similar client groups have formed in policy arenas such as mental health, child sexual abuse, and domestic violence. You can connect with these organizations by asking your professors or field instructors, attending legislative hearings, and performing online research.

However, sometimes no official organization is already active on behalf of a target group. There may be fragmented organizations that have difficulty accessing policymakers or advocacy organizations engaging in policy practice without authentic collaboration with affected populations. In these cases, you can use your social work skills to help a client group develop a shared vision. You can identify common ground between clients and policymakers and help clients consider which policy initiatives have the best chance of passing. Sometimes, sweeping changes may not be the place to start. Instead, focusing on tangible interim solutions may help the group find a promising point of entry. If you have developed policy research skills, you can also share information about what kinds of programs have helped others in similar circumstances. Clients' perspectives can help you draw valuable lessons from other initiatives and identify ways other models may fail to fully meet the needs of these clients and their communities. Exhibit 6.4 provides a list of initial tasks for the stage of the policy development process that centers on defining, connecting to, and learning about the target group. The time you spend becoming familiar with and documenting the needs, strengths, and goals of the client population will be invaluable in helping to craft a compelling message that gets their needs on the agenda. These insights will also help you develop effective policy options.

Examining Your Perspective

As discussed in earlier chapters, the way in which a situation is viewed is significantly influenced by the viewer. This observation also applies to you as a social worker. It is important, therefore, to examine your views and their effect on your policy practice. Ask yourself, "How does my family background shape my views? What education and experiences influence my perspective?" While your perspective and passion motivate your policy practice, they may also contribute to bias. Pursuing policy practice from a strengths perspective, which situates clients' needs and interests at the center of policy development, can guard against this.

Understanding your own perspective will also help you identify potential allies. For example, your perspectives may have been influenced by membership in a church, and faith-based groups

---

EXHIBIT 6.4

Initial Tasks in Defining Target Group

- Contact advocacy groups with client membership to get their perspectives.
- Conduct a literature review that includes popular media, organizational reports, other professional publications, and academic literature.
- Note how various groups portray the affected client group and characterize their problems.
- Ask social workers practicing with the affected client population to provide input on the population's strengths, needs, and goals. Analyze demographics, identify location, and estimate the size of the target group.
- Help formulate an analysis of the client group's strengths, needs, and goals that incorporates the group's vision of preferred reality.

may be potential allies. At the same time, think about what is likely motivating those who have opposing perspectives. Consider ideological and philosophical differences as well as the desire to play to a certain constituency. Do you know who supports your opposition, financially or otherwise? Time spent investigating these issues will help you craft more effective strategies for your policy practice moving forward. As you move toward refining and then advancing your potential policy solutions, you may forge coalitions with at least some people or groups who hold perspectives that you have opposed. While all your alliances must uphold your social work values, your coalitions will be strengthened by your efforts to understand different stakeholders' perspectives, reach out to less likely partners, and institute practices that ensure that client groups have meaningful representation.

Getting on the Agenda

Remember that many policies and needs are simultaneously vying for policymakers' attention. Typically, interest in policy change develops gradually as need is recognized and claims are successfully made. Recall, however, that policymakers' overall agenda is separate from their decision agenda, which includes those issues on which they may effect policy change (Kingdon, 2003).

Exhibit 6.5 describes a social worker's labor through the incremental process typical of efforts to get onto the decision agenda. This example illustrates how social workers can carve

---

EXHIBIT 6.5

Getting on the Agenda: A Real-Life Scenario

A social worker employed in a State Department of Human Services was asked to write up an idea she had read about for parents of children with developmental disabilities to be eligible for special state-backed loans to buy homes. This would allow their children to remain in the community through adulthood. This approach is strengths-based in that it reflects the goal of many people with developmental disabilities to remain in their communities; meets needs in non-segregated, normative ways; and builds on families' strengths. Having worked with local advocacy groups for people with developmental disabilities, she knew that these groups supported these general policy goals. In the cafeteria before work, she brought the idea to the attention of the department head. She then wrote up the idea as a concept paper, hoping it would be the subject of legislation during the coming term. Later that fall, the young social worker was congratulated because the concept paper was to be incorporated into the agency's "C" budget proposal. However, as the "C" budget was the agency's wish-list, it would probably be years before this initiative would be incorporated into a decision agenda. In this agency, a proposal moved from the "C" budget only if there was sufficient money, political pressure, and time. Family advocates pressed the agency to make the proposal a high priority. The legislature finally enacted policies to develop homeownership loans some years later. This was primarily because of the work of clients' families, but the social work policy entrepreneur also played a part in making it happen.

out a little time for policy practice and use relationships, research, and writing skills to place an issue on the agenda. It also illustrates the importance of exercising patience, being committed to an issue for the long haul, helping clients develop the power to move issues, presenting not only the need but also a possible policy response, and leveraging connections to build alliances.

Strategies for Utilizing the Strengths Approach The strengths perspective emphasizes clients' perspectives at all points in the policy development process. How can you help ensure that policymakers understand clients' needs, strengths, and goals?

You can begin by collecting stories that illustrate capacity rather than incapacity. Create "story banks" of clients' struggles and successes that you can draw upon when you have a chance to talk to policymakers or influence public opinion. Although effective policy practice requires logic and research skills, personal stories can illustrate the need for policy change, capture policymakers' attention, and spark emotional connection. Of course, to protect client privacy, you must never make names or identifying information public without clients' express written permission. Even when using stories anonymously, you must have clients' permission to share them.

You can also find out if researchers are doing **participatory action research** in your area. In participatory action research, practitioners, researchers, and people in target populations collaborate to conduct research to contribute to social action. Community meetings, surveys, interviews, and focus groups involving members of the target population can also help you gather information on needs, strengths, and goals.

You will need to use your assessment skills to evaluate your work environment and determine what is allowable policy practice as part of your duties. Many agencies now understand the need for policy practice and would welcome your well-conceived efforts. You will likely not do all the things discussed thus far to help get your clients' issues on the policy agenda, but you can choose to do something.

Working with Others When you are engaged in claims-making to get an issue on policymakers' agendas, it is critical to locate and work with like-minded people. If you go to an advocacy meeting or sign up for electronic alerts and have some time and energy to give, you will most likely be very welcome. And if you join forces with people whose policy interests at least somewhat overlap with yours, your efforts at claims-making will likely be more successful than if you labor in isolation. Coalitions' amplification of claims is one of their most valuable contributions to the policy development process. Where one individual's or agency's claim that a need demands attention or that a proposal is worthwhile could be easily ignored—and often is—by policymakers, advocates' ability to command attention is often greatly increased when different organizations join forces. Examine how claims have been made in the past and what approaches have been effective. Where possible, adapt them to emphasize the strengths and contributions, as well as the needs, of the target population. Identify key actors who must be convinced of the merit of the claim and consider how it might need to be framed to garner their support. Then, in collaboration with members of the target group, develop a clear statement that explains why policymakers should provide benefits or services to your target population.

Identifying Policy Options That Include Client Perspectives

To identify policy alternatives that build on clients' strengths to meet needs, list proposed policy options that clients and other experts have identified during the claims-making process. Determine whether any of these options are widely supported. Brainstorm with potential allies about how ideas might be combined and new options crafted. Conduct a literature review and contact stakeholders to determine whether other entities have tried similar initiatives and, if so, what lessons might be learned from those experiences. Include legislation that has been successfully enacted and consider where policies that have been implemented with one population may be relevant for another. For example, a community effort to end youth homelessness applied the concept of seamless service delivery to break down silos between agencies that can make it hard to navigate systems (Williamson, 2018). When the effort dramatically reduced youth homelessness, it was then modified to work with homeless families. Also take note of failed attempts and what went wrong. Successful policy practitioners learn from mistakes—including their own.

Negotiating Policy Goals

You can help draw attention to clients' perspectives and goals by facilitating client–policymaker interaction. For example, social workers involved with older adults routinely invite legislators to speak at senior centers and provide transportation so that older adults can visit their legislators. Preparation for such meetings could emphasize how to focus the interaction on specific policy goals. These approaches can be effective with executive policymakers as well as elected officials. One organization that works with families involved in the child welfare system set up a meeting with parents whose children were in state custody and the administrators in charge of reunification to discuss each side's concerns and help policymakers see parents' perspectives.

You and your clients deserve access to policymakers whose decisions affect your lives. You can request time from elected leaders, appointed decision-makers, and their staff to talk about policy strategies that will meet your clients' needs. Armed with first-hand knowledge acquired from talking with clients and analyzing your own practice, you will be ready to engage in a discussion that will help you identify which strengths-based policy goals are most likely to receive support. When you use your policy analysis and presentation skills to prepare a concise written summary of the need and your proposed policy solution, including its feasibility and likely positive outcomes, this policy brief can enhance the effectiveness of your communication. If you follow-up with a "thank you" and additional information that may be helpful, you will establish a contact that allows you to give and receive feedback. Many social workers have been surprised by their ability to open lines of communication even with policymakers they would not have expected to be receptive. However, having access is not the same as having power. Contributions from key players and coalitions of voters can exert considerable power over policy decisions. Nonetheless, information and transformative interactions can help change people's minds.

Helping to Get Policy Enacted

Although it is important to dream on a grand scale, you should carefully consider the feasibility of your ideas before suggesting them to policymakers. Otherwise, your proposal may fail even if there is widespread agreement that the need deserves attention. This may subsequently make it more difficult for you to advocate successfully for another policy change.

Considering Whether a New Law Is Needed Many times, when social workers see a problem, a policy intended to address it exists but is ineffective. The policy may be underfunded or poorly implemented. In such cases, the appropriate policy change may not be new legislation but, rather, increased funding or more enforceable regulations. Social workers can use a policy analysis framework similar to the one presented in Chapter 5 to examine the components of the existing policy and consider which should be adjusted to improve client outcomes. Could minor enhancements bolster parts that are mostly working? Has the evidence base shifted, such that the policy needs updating, but not wholesale reform?

Although it may seem more glamorous to advocate an entirely new approach, when infrastructure and experience administering a policy already exist, working for adequate funding or minor adjustments can be the most effective approach. For example, advocates committed to improving educational services for students with disabilities have labored for years to convince Congress to fully fund the Individuals with Disabilities Education Act (IDEA), arguing that the efficacy of this legislation cannot be assessed until the policy is fully funded and appropriately implemented. In other cases, an effective policy response may just need to be scaled up so that the intervention can reach more members of the affected group. This is often the case where social work agencies have piloted a promising approach; when it demonstrates substantial improvement in client outcomes, policy can be developed to replicate the model in other contexts. Collecting information to document how such scaling could be beneficial and then conveying that information to policymakers can be a rewarding way for social workers to engage in policy development.

In addition, policymakers may create sanctions for ineffective implementation or may build in external evaluation to better monitor operations. For example, the Trump Administration's plans for countering the opioid epidemic include tying Medicaid and Medicare payments to improved practices in opioid prescribing, as well as the establishment of a national prescription drug monitoring program to track prescriptions and enforce limits. When a program is sanctioned for ineffectiveness, funds can be withheld or fines can be levied. Conversely, policymakers may offer incentives in the form of greater funding or other rewards for meeting or exceeding specified outcomes. This has long been the case in child support enforcement, where states can earn additional federal appropriations by improving their collection rates and implementing cost-effective systems.

Without passing new legislation, agencies can often change the rules that stipulate how to administer a program, including to ensure proper training and balanced workloads for staff charged with implementation. If agency regulations do not require training and funds are not available to provide it, little training may be provided. When program staff are not adequately trained, programs seldom work well.

Analyzing Costs Social work values and ethics emphasize that some "goods" are impossible to quantify precisely. The value of a healthy child or an older adult's quality of life should not be reduced to a dollars-and-cents calculation. However, although policymakers certainly base decisions on more than cost, cost-effectiveness is important. You can most easily include a cost–benefit analysis in your consideration of feasibility by working with an expert who can help perform the analysis, or by using already completed analyses as a starting point. If a legislator has already introduced a bill dealing with the policy in which you have an interest, the agency involved has likely been asked to generate a **fiscal impact statement**. This is an estimate prepared by a government agency that predicts how legislation would affect public finances. You may be able to use this information either to bolster or to refute the cost–benefit claims of other groups. Keep in mind, however, that the official fiscal "note" may be based on a particular perspective on the proposed legislation, depending on the preferences of those charged with developing it.

Your analysis should also draw attention to the costs to clients and to society of *not* implementing policies. Returning to the preschool example, advocates interested in increasing access to quality, affordable, early childhood education have pointed to research that indicates that at-risk children who attend high-quality preschool programs are less likely to be incarcerated as teens and adults (Reynolds et al., 2011). If the relatively small cost per child of preschool education is compared to the yearly cost of incarcerating a juvenile offender, the potential for significant return on investment is clear. Such calculations attempt to quantify the "cost of failure," when not acting makes it much more likely that negative and very expensive consequences will occur (Bruner, 2002). Including the cost of failure in the cost–benefit analysis requires synthesizing research evidence connecting current needs and future social problems (Bruner, 2002). Another good example of this calculation is contrasting the huge costs associated with premature births with the cost of making prenatal care more widely available. However, when calculating the cost of failure, guard against promoting the idea that, if not for a social program, all potential recipients will inevitably experience negative outcomes. This is neither accurate nor consistent with the strengths perspective. Nonetheless, it is often possible to calculate the percentage who are likely to experience negative outcomes if nothing is done and to compare those aggregate costs to the aggregate costs of prevention or early intervention. It is often the case that return on investment in clients' capacities outweighs initial expenditures. At the least, this approach underscores that inaction is not free, an analysis that places program costs in a more complete context.

Evaluating Policy Based on Client Outcomes

If policymakers agree on desired outcomes, evaluation can focus on whether these outcomes are achieved. This means that convincing policymakers to specify in the enabling legislation that evaluation will be based on client outcomes ensures that (1) resulting reporting will also focus on clients' perspectives and (2) efforts to improve the policy will center on effectiveness at meeting clients' needs. For example, a social work student who had been in foster care worked with an advocacy group to develop a policy proposal with the goal of increasing educational attainment for children who have been in foster care. They proposed legislation to provide free tuition at state post-secondary institutions for children aging out of care. Because policymakers were concerned with the number of former foster children who were experiencing homelessness and other adverse outcomes, they were interested in initiatives that might increase these youths' ability to thrive and prosper. Significantly, the specified goal—increased educational attainment for youth who had been in foster care—was quantifiable and therefore could be tracked by the agency responsible for foster care. Wisely, the student urged that the legislation mandate this tracking. It is important to think about outcome measures that include clients' goals early in the process so that they can be evaluated alongside policymakers' goals. In this case, policymakers were interested in decreasing youths' reliance on emergency assistance as they age out of foster care. These outcomes could all be monitored.

Failure to evaluate policies can contribute to their ineffectiveness. If problems are not detected, policies cannot be adjusted accordingly. This can harm clients, who need policies to not only exist but to truly meet their needs. Additionally, over time, this breach can make policymakers lose faith in an approach. For example, a policy may specify that juvenile offenders receive services in a group home. However, if no one tracks residents' rates of repeat offenses, policymakers cannot determine whether the program is effective, would work well with only minor changes, or needs major revamping. Further, the social workers who staff the group home will have no evidence with which to defend the efficacy and cost-effectiveness of their work. To ensure that programs are achieving desired outcomes, savvy and client-centered social workers monitor client outcomes even if not required. Consider finding out how the agencies where you may want to work evaluate their policies and programs. You can contribute your analytical skills to this aspect of the policy development process.

When evaluating policies, it is also important to analyze the different effects they have on different groups. Intersectional analyses reveal the ways in which individuals' different identities affect their experiences with policies (Crenshaw, 1989). Social workers can use policy impact analyses to understand these differences (Johnson, 2005). This type of analysis attempts to determine the consequences of policy interventions—before, during, and after their implementation—on the well-being of different groups. A policy impact analysis examines the distributional effect of policies across social groups, in terms of benefits or services received as well as harm done, and identifies differences in impact based on gender, race, ethnicity, age, socioeconomic status, and geographic location.

For example, a policy that specifies that applicants for service must apply online may speed up eligibility determination for people who are computer literate but could greatly disadvantage those without Internet access or older adults who might not use computers. Policies that have increased admissions requirements at colleges and universities may make it more difficult for students who attend underfunded, underperforming high schools to gain access to higher education, while contributing to inequality by increasing the prestige of the degrees earned. Because of entrenched inequities, even policies that are race or gender "neutral" on their face may have disproportionate intersectional impacts. Further, policymakers or even social workers may consider policies evidence-based before they have been tested with different groups. This is problematic; so-called evidence-based initiatives should not be implemented wholesale without considering their efficacy with all groups with which they will be implemented. Many social work policy practitioners are providing important leadership in efforts to disaggregate data by race, gender, and other salient identities, in pursuit of deeper understanding about the roots of structural inequities and how they manifest in different policies.

To analyze outcomes once a policy is enacted, we need to know the condition of the target group prior to the intervention. This information is called **baseline data**. Ideally, information gathered in the need determination stage will provide baseline data. Of course, even if you know that the outcome improved after implementation of a policy change, it will take more research to establish that the change actually *caused* the improved outcome. Be careful not to overstate the policy's impact. Nonetheless, if more members of the client groups had positive outcomes after receiving services or benefits compared to members of the same groups in the baseline year, then the policy might have improved conditions. Remember that there will likely be repeated attempts to reform a specific policy. Earlier information gathered on outcomes will be useful in incrementally improving the policy.

A PLACE TO START

Now it is time for you to put together the content provided in this chapter and consider how you can use it. Think critically about the social work agencies where you work, volunteer, or do fieldwork. What policies govern their programs? How does funding drive their work? How are the programs evaluated? Are outcomes for clients central in evaluations? Is evaluation used to improve programs? What "brick walls" do social workers at these agencies encounter in trying to help clients, and how could policy practice forge a way around these obstacles? What promising programs might be scaled up, so that a promising practice becomes part of how larger systems operate, and how might such scaling improve clients' outcomes? What challenges might you face in seeking to convince the agency to support your involvement in policy practice? How could you use your skills to make a successful claim that policy practice should be part of your work—and of the organization's mission?

Like the students depicted in Exhibit 6.6, the social policy landscape today provides many examples of students and practitioners engaged in policy practice. You can learn from others' experiences in the policy process by connecting to your state/local NASW chapter, participating in webinars and Twitter chats sponsored by macro-engaged social workers (**macrosw.com**), and reading about past student contest winners at Influencing Social Policy (**influencingsocialpolicy.org**). Take time to envision how you may get involved in policy practice as a social worker.

If you have not already done so, registering to vote and getting others to vote—including your clients—is a very good place to start. Working on voter registration can get more people involved in the policy process. Obtain contact information for those who represent you at the city, county, state, and federal levels. They cannot effectively represent you and your clients if they do not have information on what is working and what needs improvement.

EXHIBIT 6.6

Social Work Students Mobilize for Policy Change

Source: Influencing Social Policy

Seeking Support

If you are in field placement, ask your field instructor for guidance about where to start in policy practice. Your agency may already designate staff to follow legislation and talk to policymakers about needed changes. If so, see if you can work with these colleagues. If you are not yet in a field placement but have volunteered with an agency, agency staff may be willing to talk with you about the policy changes they would like to see. The skills you practice when setting agendas, building relationships, and making claims will help you in any policy practice venue.

During your social work career, your policy practice may include forming coalitions with clients and constituent groups, analyzing and developing proposals, preparing issue briefs to share with policymakers, and advocating for policy enactment. You may even become engaged in efforts to take an issue to court. Many NASW chapters sponsor training to increase the political effectiveness of social workers. Nationally, the NASW seeks to educate and mobilize social workers to press for a more just society; joining your chapter of the NASW is a good place to begin establishing yourself as a policy-informed and policy-engaged social worker. The NASW publishes *Social Work Speaks*, a collection of policy statements on a variety of issues, designed to guide social work policy advocacy (National Association of Social Workers [NASW], 2018a). The NASW also has a political action arm called Political Action for Candidate Election (PACE). PACE endorses and contributes financially to candidates who support the NASW's policy agenda.

> **EXHIBIT 6.7**
>
> *Policy Practice Inspires Student to Run for Office*
>
> Social work students in a Midwestern state were concerned about growing numbers of teen pregnancies in the high school where they were placed for their practicum. For a social policy class project, they developed and executed an action plan to offer more comprehensive sex education courses in high schools across the state. They met with students to learn about their experiences with sex education and what changes they thought should be made. They developed informational programs, including skits designed to increase public support for comprehensive sex education. They met with their local school board representatives and state legislators to advocate for comprehensive sex education. After working on this advocacy and observing the intersection between social work interests and education policy, one of the students decided to run for and was elected to the school board.

We know that people are most familiar with policy issues that have a direct impact on them and their communities. If legislative bodies reflected the makeup of the public more closely, they would include many more women, people of color, and low-income individuals. Such legislators might be more likely to support the policies that social workers champion. Large numbers of eligible voters who could help elect such candidates are not registered or seldom vote, however, contributing to the chasm between the electorate and their representatives. Compared to those who are more privileged, marginalized populations often face many more hurdles to voter participation, including restrictive registration laws, lack of transportation, and inflexible work schedules. Many lack confidence that their voices can really make a difference in political outcomes. There is a great need for **political activism**—actions taken to influence the outcome of elections or government decisions—to increase involvement among marginalized populations. Some students become so involved in political activism that they decide to run for political office. Exhibit 6.7 provides an example of one social work student's successful political campaign.

Taking Action

An **action plan** is an important tool that details steps you will take in planning and implementing your action strategy. A thoughtful plan can alert you to the potential influence of your actions and those of your allies. When the work involved in making an impact seems overwhelming, break it down into small, manageable tasks. Your skills will improve with practice, and others will take notice. Exhibit 6.8 describes one group of students' careful planning and successful implementation of policy change strategies. To learn more about developing an action plan, explore the Sample Action Plan provided in Quick Guide 4 at the end of this chapter.

Two principles should guide development of action plans:

- First, keep it simple. Remember, the goal is to involve people from a variety of backgrounds, many of whom may not, at least initially, be as invested in your issue or proposed strategy as you are.

- Second, if your group expends most of its energy in planning, there will not be any left to put the plan into action. Think realistically about how much time and effort group members have and then contain the planning so that it does not use up the momentum.

> **EXHIBIT 6.8**
>
> *Social Work Students Successfully Advocate for Legislation*
>
> College students concerned about the overrepresentation of youth of color in their state's juvenile justice system tracked a legislative bill that addressed this problem. Recognizing that the issue was not well understood, they devised a strategy that involved first developing relationships with key actors—including legislators, state agency staff, law enforcement, and religious leaders—and then making sure these stakeholders had current information on the problem and possible solutions. The students successfully advocated for the bill, which was designed to reduce biases in the juvenile justice system. Their fellow students joined them in celebrating a legislative victory when the governor signed the bill into law.

Integrating Other People into Action Plans A written action plan helps clarify strategies (Ellis, 2003). Also, if the action plan is developed as a group endeavor, it can help create consensus about what needs to be done and divide responsibility among stakeholders. People who are involved in drafting the action plan will be more likely to work to implement it. A concise action plan can serve as a relatively easy way for different stakeholders to begin strategizing together. If possible, contemplate potential future developments, including unexpected opportunities and crises, so that you can plan for how you might respond. After developing the action plan, review it with people who have experience in your chosen area. They often can identify misinformation and offer constructive feedback. They may join your effort or know other people who will.

Focusing Your Efforts Working from a strengths perspective, you could focus your policy practice on increasing public awareness of a policy alternative that builds on the strengths and goals of clients. One approach would be to help local media develop a series of stories about innovative strengths-based policies, such as those that address the need for affordable high-quality childcare for single working mothers or the need for affordable home and community services for low-income elders. Grassroots efforts might use Twitter to collect petition signatures for a city council ordinance preventing discrimination against the LGBTQ+ community or start a blog profiling experiences of homelessness. A concerned mother used Facebook to start the organization One Million Moms for Gun Control to press for stricter gun control legislation following several deadly mass shootings. In just over a month, more than 40,000 grassroots advocates "liked" the page. Similarly, after a mass shooting at their high school, students in Parkland, Florida, used direct action, social media, and the power of personal narrative to put gun safety on the national agenda, mobilize thousands of activists, and make #neveragain a viral hashtag that has reshaped how a generation of young people sees their political power (Wright, Molloy, & Lockhart, 2018). Similarly, Exhibit 6.9 describes students' use of technology to successfully oppose anti-immigrant policy in their state. In today's media environment, your ability to communicate directly with your policy targets and potential allies does not depend on outlets' willingness to cover you. You and your clients can create your own coverage and tell your own story.

Interacting with Your Opposition Expect to encounter opposition. Remember, some conflict is inevitable when resources and power are at stake. There may be groups whose goal is simply to block all initiatives. They may feel they benefit most from maintaining the status quo, or

> **EXHIBIT 6.9**
>
> *Social Work Students Can Use Social Media to Influence Policy*
>
> A group of students was concerned about efforts to repeal their state's policy extending in-state tuition rates to undocumented immigrant students. The students particularly objected to claims, advanced by those pushing the repeal, that the existing policy was unfair to U.S. citizen students paying out-of-state tuition. Seeking a way to frame this issue as one about access to opportunity, not tuition prices, the students conceived a communications strategy they titled "You Don't Speak for Me." Primarily using Facebook, they identified U.S. citizen students paying out-of-state tuition at colleges around the state. They invited these students to submit short videos of themselves—mostly recorded via smartphones—giving their names, schools, home states, and fields of study. All the videos concluded with personal statements affirming support for immigrant students and telling anti-immigrant policymakers: "You don't speak for me." The resulting videos were widely shared on social media. Immigrant rights advocates forwarded copies directly to legislators prior to the vote and credited the students with helping to defeat the repeal attempt.

they may have an interest in denying the "other side" a victory. You will need to learn how to work with those who share your concerns and deal with those who do not. There may even be other social workers who have different priorities. Policymakers and opponents may try to pit your constituencies against each other, but you can use your shared vision and common value base as the foundation from which to resolve disputes and find workable solutions.

It is helpful to become savvy about vested interests with a stake in your issue who espouse ideologies different from your own. Consider how much power they have and the methods they use to acquire and keep power. Realistically assessing the barriers to policy change is important. As discussed above, you will find key policymakers who will be your allies, and you may find common cause with people who you initially identified as your opposition. Your social work skills can help you craft compromises that stay true to social work principles and honor clients' priorities. And your skills, relationships, and values will keep you from giving up in the face of opposition or sacrificing so much that clients lose something essential.

Supporting Client Groups Members of client groups may already possess well-developed policy practice skills. If they do not, you can connect them to opportunities to build capacity. Temper efforts to encourage their involvement with a careful assessment of the level of risk such involvement represents for them. This assessment is particularly important when you are considering confrontational strategies such as public protests or boycotts. While these tactics sometimes may be necessary, they may also involve more risk. Remember social workers have an ethical obligation to gain informed consent before involving clients in any change effort, including policy practice. While social workers must proceed cautiously to avoid paternalism and ensure that clients' preferences are paramount, carefully consider the possible consequences before championing a high-risk policy initiative.

Interacting with Policymakers Before communicating with key stakeholders such as policymakers, investigate their backgrounds and philosophies. Try to identify legislators with past professional or personal involvement with the issue. Package your ideas so that they are attractive to policymakers. You know the importance of "starting where the client is" in practice. Similarly, "starting where policymakers are" and framing proposals to fit their interests, where possible, will likely secure more support. For example, a legislator who lost a family member to cancer or diabetes might be willing to champion increased spending for community outreach initiatives to reduce risk of these diseases. At the very least, a little research will help you avoid alienating a policymaker needlessly. Policymakers who believe people should rely on themselves may be cautious about increasing spending on public welfare programs and put off by an advocate who decries "a bootstrap mentality," but they might be convinced to support efforts that provide target populations with opportunities to improve their conditions if they are framed as giving clients a chance to help themselves. When possible, your policy brief and other policy communications should employ framing that presents issues and proposed solutions in terms that appeal to policymakers. However, policymakers will sometimes reject social workers' accurate presentation of issues that do not align with policymakers' own worldviews. A social work advocate who testified about the racial wealth gap was challenged by a state representative who was convinced it could not be true that Black college graduates see less return on their degree than White graduates. However, her footnoted evidence (Emmons & Noeth, 2015) and careful appeal to policymakers' values of equal opportunity and fair reward for hard work were convincing to many others on the panel. While this example illustrates the unlikelihood of persuading every policymaker, a goal-focused, consensus-oriented approach may help some dissenting legislators actively engage in developing effective policies, even in today's polarized political landscape.

When you work as a change agent, staying focused on finding solutions may foster consensus about desired outcomes. The solution-focused approach, much like the strengths approach, emphasizes goals, strengths, and resources rather than problems. Individuals who take a solution-focused approach begin by asking people to envision their preferred future and then encourage them to begin to take steps, even in small increments, toward creating this preferred future. Many times, people want the same positive outcomes but have different views about how to achieve them. In these situations, policy practice begins with reaching consensus on goals and, then, considering different strategies that could pursue them. Reflecting the extent to which policy practice builds on other social work techniques and competencies, this solution-focused approach to policy practice applies many of the same skills used in practice with individuals.

Facing Limits on Political Activism Sometimes, social workers do not get involved in policy practice, especially political activism, because they fear it would violate the terms of their employment. In fact, this self-censorship often results from social workers' misunderstanding of relevant limits. In some cases, social work agencies may indicate that political activism is prohibited under the Hatch Act, a federal law that restricts the political activity of federal employees, District of Columbia government employees, some state and local employees working with federally funded programs, and others whose activities are wholly financed by federal loans or grants. These restrictions are absolutely constraints on the policy engagement of social workers employed in these settings. Further, many states have adopted provisions similar to the Hatch Act. However, social workers in these organizations may be able to engage in advocacy using other funding. Further, although private nonprofit organizations that qualify for 501(c)(3) tax-exempt status must follow certain rules regarding political activism, the limits on lobbying are so generous they pose little obstacle. There are, then, many ways in which a social worker can be politically active without violating these rules. The website Bolder Advocacy (**www.boldereradvocacy.org**) offers further information on these regulations. In an extension of their policy practice obligations, social workers whose employers unduly proscribe their policy activities can advocate for their professional right and ethical responsibility to engage in such practice.

CONCLUSION

This chapter provided an overview of the policy development process and of policy practice, examined your professional responsibility and opportunities to become involved, and suggested some initial strategies. Your social work practice and research classes will help you further develop skills you can use to influence policy. Using books that detail specific strategies and tactics to use in policy practice, including those from an explicitly social work perspective (e.g., Hoefer, 2019) and those aimed at more general activist audiences (e.g. Rowe-Finkbeiner, 2018), you can study how to build coalitions, leverage evolving technologies, or use sophisticated frameworks for cost-effectiveness modeling. Simply by practicing social work, you will develop knowledge and hone skills that make you a valuable part of the policy development process. Start now with one contact or one action to influence social policy. As your career unfolds, chances to get involved in policy practice will abound if you are attuned to the opportunities and to your obligation to influence policy.

MAIN POINTS

- Policy development is the process by which policies are created and implemented to meet identified needs. Policies should build on strengths and reflect the goals of client groups.

- Tasks in the policy development process include defining and documenting needs, problems, and strengths; identifying policy goals; engaging in claims-making; formulating policy alternatives that meet goals; developing, enacting, and implementing policy; and evaluating outcomes.

- Social, cultural, and economic factors influence social policies and help to determine the feasibility of proposed reforms.

- The NASW Code of Ethics states that social workers have a responsibility to engage in social work policy practice. This involvement requires many skills. Some are particular to policy practice, including policy analysis and political, value-clarifying, and organizing skills, while some are core to social work, including assessment and relationship building.

- Strengths-based policy practitioners actively incorporate clients' perspectives and priorities. Strengths-based and solution-focused strategies can help chart a path forward when stakeholders disagree on policy direction.

- Policy impact analysis, intersectional policy analysis, and cost-effectiveness analysis are important tools for examining social policies.

- In addition to influencing legislation, effective policy practice can also influence rules created by the executive branch and private organizations, as well as judicial opinions that may limit or expand services and opportunities for clients.

- While a written action plan can help guide policy practice, think realistically about how much effort your group can give and avoid using all the group's energy on planning.

- You can use the ideas presented in this chapter to engage in policy practice that will advance your clients' interests and fulfill your professional obligations.

QUICK GUIDE 4 Sample Action Plan—Narrative

The Action Plan template on the following pages will help you determine necessary steps, assign and monitor duties, and evaluate outcomes when you engage in policy practice.

Jamal is a 17-year-old boy who ran away from home. His mother was verbally and physically abusive, and he never knew his father. Jamal has been able to stay with his aunt for the last six months, but she has told Jamal that he must find other living arrangements by the time he is 18. Jamal does not have any future living situation arranged and currently lacks employment. He has been struggling in school, and his grades are just average. Jamal wants to go to college but does not know how to make that happen. He does not understand the college or financial aid application processes, and he lacks direction for what to study. Most urgently, Jamal does not have a safe place to live once he has to leave his aunt's house. Told not to trust anyone outside of the family, he is scared to tell anyone his situation. Hard-working, resourceful, and smart, Jamal will soon be homeless.

You learn about Jamal's needs, strengths, and goals. You highlight his resilience and intellect and affirm his right to set ambitious goals for his future. As you begin to work with him to explore housing options and support for financial aid and college admissions, you also conduct a dual assessment. You examine the policies that are contributing to Jamal's needs and assess the barriers that present obstacles to reaching his goals. As you often do, you start by reaching out to social work colleagues who are experts in these areas. While, as a school social worker, you know the college admissions and financial aid processes well, you have relatively limited experience navigating the systems that support homeless youth.

You take your long-time friend, Heather, out for coffee and, without disclosing anything about Jamal or his situation, ask for her help figuring out where to begin and what options might exist for an aspiring college student without a secure place to live. Heather tells you that many young people in your community are facing these kinds of challenges. Full-time students are not eligible to live in properties funded with Low-Income Housing Tax Credits (LIHTC), which closes off some options. A few years ago, Congress authorized a program that provides 36 months of housing vouchers for transition-age youths, but housing authorities must find private landlords to make these vouchers work for full-time students because of the LIHTC exclusion. If Jamal is not a full-time student, he could live in a project-based rental; however, you have some concerns about that option because of what you know about lower college completion rates for part-time students. You find groups in the community proposing different solutions. One possible avenue seems to be convincing the college Jamal decides to attend to keep dormitories open year-round for students who need permanent housing. You know that institutions often provide year-round housing for international students, so you think you could at least push for that with the schools Jamal is considering. You also know from your school social worker conferences that there are conversations in Congress about making federal Pell Grants, which pay for college costs for low-income students, year-round. That would help a student like Jamal, too. You are still not sure where to begin, but you are compelled to act.

In addition to your work to help Jamal access informal and formal supports that will build on his strengths and help him meet his needs, consider how you would go about researching youth homelessness in your area, so that you are better informed and better positioned to be a resource to young people in this situation. What organizations would you contact? How would you find out how many young people in your community are in similar situations and what policies and programs address this issue?

After gathering information about the population of homeless youth, you examine the community resources available. You discover that programs are constrained by policies that narrowly define who should be helped and create gaps that people like Jamal—currently not defined as homeless and just about to reach the age of adulthood—often fall through. As a youth "doubled-up" in someone else's home, Jamal has never even been assessed by the systems that serve as gatekeepers to homeless assistance.

When you do a literature search, you will find that a federal bill introduced in 2015, entitled the Homeless Children and Youth Act, was reintroduced in 2019. This proposed legislation looks like it may be designed to help young people like Jamal. Use resources such as **helphomelesskidsnow.org** to learn more about this proposal. Then, learn about some of the opposition to this bill. Why does the National Alliance to End Homelessness, a well-known advocacy group, oppose it? To read more about their stance go to **www.endhomelessness.org/library/entry/opposition-statement-to-homeless-children-and-youth-act**. These conflicting opinions illustrate the complexity of policy development, the battles over scarce resources, and the challenges inherent in trying to get different groups to agree on a policy direction. After reviewing these and other sources, decide if the Homeless Children and Youth Act is a bill you support. Use the following Action Plan template to think through steps involved in (a) working for the bill's passage or (b) looking for alternative routes to policy change.

In addition to working for more effective national policies, you also know that change can happen at the state level. In your research you learn about "host homes," and you know that some states and communities have used this as a model for helping homeless youth. Some states have proposed legislation to support this approach, including by exempting these homes from some licensing regulations. To learn more about host homes for homeless youth, see what some organizations in Seattle, which has particularly high housing costs and a large homeless youth population, has done to explore this option (**raikesfoundation.org/blog/posts/host-homes-could-provide-housing-every-homeless-young-adult-king-county**). Learn about the state of Washington's legislation to support host homes. Research whether your state is proposing similar policies. If state-level change is already happening, track that bill. If no bill is currently being proposed in your state, consider what avenues you might pursue for change at the state level.

Finally, consider what agencies in your community would be invested in helping the homeless youth population. What agency-level policy changes are needed to ensure that homeless youth secure the housing and support services they need? If you were a worker in one of those agencies, how might you help to change their policies? What policy practice strategies might you use to influence the university Jamal decides to attend? How could community organizations catalyze advocacy to make the university more accessible and supportive of students experiencing homelessness?

Once you have chosen the policy you want to champion, create an action plan. The following pages provide an action plan template. Although you should consider all the items on the Action Plan, you can tailor it to fit your objectives and approach.

ACTION PLAN		
ACTION PLAN TASKS TO ADDRESS IDENTIFIED PROBLEM	WHO WILL DO IT?	DATE DONE

Months 1–2: Identify the Target Population and Examine Your Perspective

1. Identify target population affected by recognized problem.
   - Define the specific issue/problem.
   - Contact advocacy groups and conduct research to determine who is affected; document the number affected and the demographics of this population.
   - Consider what you know from your own practice experience about the strengths of the target group.
2. Do a literature search and policy scan to research possible policy solutions.
   - Investigate other areas' efforts to identify any relevant lessons.
   - Identify advocacy groups at the local, state, and national levels with similar interests. Review their materials to look for evidence of effective approaches. Consider what might influence the extent to which their experiences translate to your challenge.
3. Examine your perspectives.
   - Why are you interested in this issue? What outcome would you like to see?
   - What motivates you to advocate for change? Identify your beliefs and values and consider how they may influence your policy practice.
   - Do you belong to civic, church, or professional groups that might share your interests?
     - If so, develop a strategy to engage with these organizations. What appeals could you use to gain their support?

Months 2–3: Getting on the Agenda
1. Talk to key actors about the issue.
   Speak to advocacy groups about whether they are already working on the issue or are interested in focusing on the issue. If not, ask if they are aware of others interested in the issue, and the best way to connect with these groups. As you conduct this outreach, think about how forging coalitions with these partners might affect your policy development process.
Legislative Advocacy:
   - Visit your legislators' websites and/or social media profiles to look for connections to your issue. Review media coverage that features your legislators to investigate their positions.

ACTION PLAN		
ACTION PLAN TASKS TO ADDRESS IDENTIFIED PROBLEM	WHO WILL DO IT?	DATE DONE

- Contact your elected officials. Introduce yourself, share your position, and assess their interests in the topic. Remember to protect the confidentiality of clients when explaining the need for change. Be sure to thank your legislators for the visit.

Agency Advocacy:

- Seek support from colleagues by adding the issue to team meetings.
- Organize a worker-level group to assess the implications of the issue for the organization's operations (financial, service delivery, community relationships). This could be an informal group that meets over lunch or an official working group. Your choice will depend on the strategy you have outlined and the agency leadership's position on your issue.
- Elicit support for the proposed change by presenting positive implications for your work. Discuss how to present it to agency administration.
- Based on discussion with staff and supervisors, determine the most effective ways to gain support of administration and/or Board leadership.

2. Locate and engage with people who want to help address the identified issue.
    - Examples could include other students, service providers, client groups, social work colleagues, or a policymaker willing to sponsor a bill.
3. Try to get media coverage.
    - Write a letter to the editor of your local newspaper.
    - Call a local radio station to see if they will air a story. They are likely to be more interested if there is a personal "hook," so see if you can identify clients or service providers eager to tell their stories. Again, remember that informed consent and confidentiality are essential social work ethical requirements.
    - Use social media to engage stakeholders, frame the issue in a way that supports your claim, and capture policymakers' attention. You may also be able to find influencers with an active social media presence who can help amplify your messages.

Months 3–4: Identifying Policy Options and Negotiating Consensus on Policy Goals

1. Clarify the issue and discuss policy goals and solutions.
    - Work with like-minded advocates to develop a clear statement that articulates reasons decision-makers should:
        - support your recommendations;

ACTION PLAN		
ACTION PLAN TASKS TO ADDRESS IDENTIFIED PROBLEM	**WHO WILL DO IT?**	**DATE DONE**

- persuade their colleagues to support your policy goals; and
- provide additional funding and regulatory authority if necessary.
- Create a written policy brief that outlines the need, provides evidence from your research, and makes a claim for your proposed change(s). When possible, incorporate what you have learned about policymakers' priorities. Ideally, this will be a one-page information sheet you and your allies can use to deliver a consistent, compelling, and concise message.
- Identify alternative solutions. Consider your likely or actual opposition. Are there ways you might reach a compromise? What do you need to understand about their perspectives?

2. Negotiate consensus.
   - Meet with client groups to determine a mutually acceptable goal and solutions to addressing the issue.

Months 5–6: During Legislative Session—if applicable

1. Track the legislative process.
   - Look for a legislator or committee to introduce and/or support the bill(s) you have outlined. Don't be surprised if a bill is not introduced or fails to have a hearing or otherwise gain traction, during the first year.
   - Maintain contact with key actors or agency administrators. Attend the meetings of other advocacy group(s) working on similar issues.
   - Continue to increase awareness of the issue through media and community organizing.

Months 7–8: Evaluating Your Efforts

1. Evaluate the campaign.
   - Even if the policy you supported was not advanced or your plan was not implemented, evaluate whether public awareness and/or support for the issue have increased. Did any policymakers express interest in pursuing the policy later? Have attitudes changed in ways that might make passage of your proposal more likely in the future?
   - If your policy change was implemented, try to determine how many people, from what client groups, benefited. In addition to serving as the principal measures by which to evaluate impact, you can use these data to increase community interest and awareness around the issue.
   - Regardless of whether your intended outcome was achieved, review the steps you took to determine which were the most and least effective and why.

ACTION PLAN		
ACTION PLAN TASKS TO ADDRESS IDENTIFIED PROBLEM	WHO WILL DO IT?	DATE DONE

2. Use evaluation to think about strategies for the next attempt.
    - Strategies may include:
        - periodically meeting with interested policymakers to encourage continued work on the issue;
        - organizing a letter-writing or social media campaign encouraging people to contact policymakers to increase awareness of the need; and
        - staying in contact with advocacy groups to strategize about how to accomplish your goals.
3. Keep records of all your research and contacts.
    - Issues have a way of coming up repeatedly. Particularly if an incident opens a window of opportunity, you will want to be ready to provide information on possible ways to address the problem.
4. If policymakers worked to get changes made, be sure to thank them.

EXERCISES

1. Go to the Riverton case at **www.routledgesw.com/cases**. What perceived needs face the Riverton community? What do you see as some of the strengths of the community?
    a. Based on your review of the Riverton case, which key actors would you talk to about homelessness and the underlying factors that contribute to these concerns?
    b. Imagine that you are working as a case manager in Riverton with individuals experiencing homelessness. You want to convince the city council to allocate more money toward permanent housing rather than temporary shelter. Using the Action Plan, how might you begin? With whom would you want to work? What strategies might be most effective?
2. To make an effective case for changes in immigration policy, it can be helpful to involve families impacted by current policies.
    a. How might the Sanchez family become involved in advocacy? What do the NASW Code of Ethics and the strengths perspective, respectively, suggest about possible roles for members of the Sanchez family in this policy practice arena?
    b. If they do become involved, how could you reduce the risk that the Sanchez family would experience negative consequences for their activism? What positive consequences might family members who engage in activism experience?
    c. How would a social worker coming from a different cultural background than the Sanchez family need to approach this difference in planning for effective policy practice?
3. Go to the Carla Washburn case at **www.routledgesw.com/cases**. In doing a dual assessment, you identify public home and community-based services as critical programs that

help older adults stay in the community. However, you are concerned these programs will be cut during times of economic downturn. Contact an advocacy group for older adults in your state, such as the state chapter of AARP, and find out what kind of advocacy they are doing to protect these home- and community-based programs.

4. Go to **www.socialworkersspeak.org**. This website is part of NASW's effort to influence how the media portrays social work issues. What issues are people discussing on this website? Do you think this discussion is helping to change policies on behalf of clients? What improvements can you suggest?
5. Think about an area of policy practice where you have passion. What issues do you think are the most pressing? How might you get your social work colleagues involved in helping to improve policies in your area of interest? Suggest at least three specific strategies.
6. Given the policy practice interest you identified, should you focus your involvement on the agency, state, or federal levels? What are the benefits and drawbacks of each level?

CHAPTER 7

Civil Rights

SOCIAL WORK IS COMMITTED TO THE PROTECTION, preservation, and advancement of civil rights. Key to our work for social justice, **civil rights** are legally enforceable protections that prevent the government, other entities, or individuals from arbitrarily abusing others. The rights that dominant populations take for granted—for example, the right to vote, the right to fair treatment in employment, the right to live where desired, and the right to be treated justly by law enforcement—are often denied to oppressed populations. This unfair reality has driven oppressed groups and their allies to advocate for the enactment, enforcement, and expansion of civil rights protections. In this chapter, we will examine policy advances that have promoted more equitable civil rights and some of the challenges that remain. The first section builds on the historical base from Chapters 2 and 3, while the second section highlights key policies directed toward securing and expanding the rights of marginalized individuals and groups.

One of the many benefits of being a social worker is getting to work with people from diverse backgrounds. The NASW Code of Ethics specifically requires that social workers "act to expand choice and opportunity for all people, with special regard for vulnerable, disadvantaged, oppressed, and exploited people and groups" (National Association of Social Workers [NASW], 2017a). Social workers embrace diversity. Characteristics such as race, ethnicity, age, gender, sexual orientation, gender identity, or disability are not valid bases for withholding societal benefits such as adequate education, housing, health care, employment, social services, or protection from mistreatment. Yet, African Americans, Native Americans, Latinx, Asian Americans, immigrants, women, people with disabilities, older adults and people who are lesbian, gay, bisexual, transgender, or queer (LGBTQ+) face threats to their civil rights that contribute to the problems that bring them into contact with social workers. The quality of the civil rights policies that protect these groups heavily influences their outcomes and can either impede or bolster the social worker's capacity to help them reach their goals. Your charge is to use what you learn about where and how people are still denied crucial rights to pursue social justice throughout your social work career.

BACKGROUND AND HISTORY

Taking an ecological approach helps us focus on the environmental barriers groups face in meeting their needs and achieving their goals. Perhaps the most obvious barrier disadvantaged groups face is their underrepresentation in positions of power. People of color, women, people

EXHIBIT 7.1

U.S. Marshals Escort Ruby Bridges, the First Black Child to Attend a Previously All-White Elementary School in the South, to and from School in 1960

Credit: Department of Justice

with disabilities, and other marginalized groups are less likely to serve in the U.S. Congress, on our nation's courts, in most state legislatures, in executive positions in corporate America, and even in leadership positions in many social service agencies. When people make policy for target groups whom they perceive to be different—that is, the "other"—those policies are unlikely to adequately reflect the goals, strengths, and needs of these target groups. In fact, many historical and current policies have erected barriers that entrench racism, sexism, heterosexism, and other unjust biases. The existence of such systemic oppression means that disparities can reproduce themselves without requiring deliberate action on the part of any individual. Importantly, systematic oppression also advances the status of privileged groups, who are artificially aided by not needing to compete fairly with those unjustly denied their rights.

Although race is an arbitrary classification with little basis in biology, racism clearly continues to influence interactions in our society. **Racism** is prejudice or discrimination directed against someone of a different race based on the belief that one's own race is superior. Social workers can see the imprint of racism not only in individual encounters, but also in policies that have disparate effects and, sometimes, even intentions regarding people of color (Neubeck & Cazenave, 2001).

A key component of racist ideologies is that they connect physical characteristics with traits such as intelligence, work ethic, or criminal behavior. Consequently, they tend to divide people into "superior" and "inferior" groups—a classification that manifests along other lines as well. **Sexism** is discrimination based on gender. **Heterosexism** is discrimination against people who are LGBTQ+, on the basis of sexual orientation or gender identity. **Ageism** is discrimination based on age, usually directed toward older adults, but often toward children as well.

Members of oppressed groups receive inequitable treatment and experience inequitable outcomes in many areas—in inferior educational opportunities, poorer medical care, and unjust police protection, for example. These injustices stem both from institutional structures and, sometimes, from the more individualistic discrimination of people within those systems. Systemic oppression often compounds. For example, individuals in some groups lack equitable access to quality education and job opportunities, disparities that amplify economic gaps between populations and reinforce disadvantage in a destructive cycle. Further, many individuals belong to multiple groups with overlapping disadvantages, a phenomenon known as *intersectionality*. For example, older African-American women experience sexism, ageism, and racism, and it can be difficult to disentangle how these oppressions interrelate.

Because of the ways that biases have pervaded society, portrayals of the strengths and capacities of oppressed groups are often hard to find. Dominant groups frequently overlook, ignore, gloss over, or simply accept discrimination. Instead of the unacceptable injustices it reflects, inequity is seen as part of "the way things are" or the expected result of groups' supposed inferiority. While some argue that the United States has made progress against the most overt forms of discrimination and that unjust policies are relics of the past, social workers see otherwise. We witness how inequitable policies continue to disadvantage our clients. Exhibit 7.2 quantifies continued injustice. While some of these indicators encompass policy arenas other than civil rights, vigorous enforcement of existing protections and more expansive application of civil rights principles would help to move the needle on many of these disparities. Indeed, civil rights campaigns in U.S. history have often taken on policy battles—in education, poverty, and housing—that have civil rights dimensions, and, in the process, have secured significant progress toward a vision of greater justice.

Although some attribute poorer outcomes to individual deficits, evidence implicates societal barriers as the primary drivers of these disparities. As policy analysts, you need to ask how social policies contribute to the systemic barriers that produce inequities. Further, as policy practitioners, you need to work with oppressed groups to craft policies that more effectively meet their needs.

EXHIBIT 7.2

Indicators of Continued Injustice

- **High rates of children of color living in concentrated-poverty communities.** Thirty percent of African-American and Native American children live in communities where at least 30 percent of the population is poor, compared to 7 percent of Asian/Pacific Islanders and 5 percent of non-Latinx White children (Annie E. Casey Foundation, 2018). Growing up in low-income communities—even if one is not personally poor—can influence later life chances (Sharkey, 2013).
- **High rates of sexual violence against women.** Every two minutes, someone is sexually assaulted in the United States, including one in six women and one in 33 men. Every year approximately 207,754 people are victims of sexual assault. About 44 percent of rape victims are under age 18. More than half of sexual assaults go unreported (Rape Abuse and Incest National Network [RAINN], 2016).

EXHIBIT 7.2

Continued

- **Large differences in educational attainment**. The percentage of Americans with a college degree varies greatly, with 69.6 percent of Asian Americans and 47.6 percent of non-Latinx Whites having a post-secondary degree, compared to 28.7 percent of Blacks and 18.6 percent of Latinx (U.S. Census Bureau, 2017). Students of color also attend institutions that are, for the most part, less selective and that convey less social and occupational status (Kolodner, 2015; Ryan & Bauman, 2016). They are also more likely to accumulate student debt in the pursuit of their degrees (Huelsman, 2015).
- **Rising incidence of hate crimes**. Hate crimes increased 17 percent between 2016 and 2017. Of the 7,106 single-bias hate crimes reported in 2017, almost 60 percent of victims were targeted based on race/ethnicity/ancestry bias, and 17.6 percent based on sexual orientation. Of the 1,679 religious bias crimes reported in 2017, 58 percent were anti-Jewish, and 18.6 percent were anti-Muslim (Federal Bureau of Investigation, 2018). High-profile hate crimes such as the mass murder at a Pittsburgh synagogue also contributed to some groups' greater sense of insecurity.
- **Police violence**. In 2017, African Americans were 25 percent of those killed by police, despite being only 13 percent of the population. Additionally, most of the unarmed people killed by police were people of color, and officers were charged with crimes in only 1 percent of all cases (Mapping Police Violence, 2018).
- **Older adults and younger people with disabilities are often institutionalized rather than having the choice of receiving services in the community**. Especially for older adults, more public funds for long-term care continue to go to nursing facilities rather than to home- and community-based services. This funding distribution runs contrary to people's preferences, thereby undermining their strengths.
- **Unfair and unequal pay for women**. In 2017 in the United States, women employed full-time earned 80.5 percent of what men employed full-time earned (Institute for Women's Policy Research, 2018). This means that women are paid less to do comparable jobs, a divide that contributes to poverty in female-headed households (DeNavas-Walt & Proctor, 2015).
- **High poverty rates for people with disabilities**. Among people aged 16 and older who have a disability, 19.9 percent are living below the poverty level, compared to less than 11 percent of those without disabilities (U.S. Census Bureau, 2018a).
- **Very high poverty rates for elderly women of color**. In 2017, women made up nearly two-thirds of all poor people age 65 and older. More than one in five Black women aged 65+ lived in poverty, as did 19 percent of Latina elders and Native American older women (National Women's Law Center, 2018).
- **High rates of suicide for LGBTQ+ youth**. LGBTQ+ youth are almost five times more likely to attempt suicide than heterosexual youth (Centers for Disease Control and Prevention, 2016a).

EXHIBIT 7.3

Equality versus Equity

EQUALITY VERSUS EQUITY

In the first image, it is assumed that everyone will benefit from the same supports. They are being treated equally.

In the second image, individuals are given different supports to make it possible for them to have equal access to the game. They are being treated equitably.

In the third image, all three can see the game without any supports or accommodations because the cause of the inequity was addressed. The systemic barrier has been removed.

Source: Interaction Institute for Social Change

To counter the effects of prolonged injustice, it is critical to consider not only equal rights but also policies that can help oppressed groups that have suffered structural discrimination for years. In other words, when populations begin from very unequal starting points, policies that afford "equal opportunities" to each group can still result in highly inequitable outcomes. Look at Exhibit 7.3 for a graphic illustration of inequitable outcomes and how they can be changed. The last panel illustrates what happens when the systemic barriers that create structural discrimination are removed. **Structural discrimination** refers to entrenched societal practices that favor one group over another. Structural discrimination reflects the power of the dominant group to enforce its prejudices throughout society and to discriminate against groups based on characteristics fixed at birth such as gender, race, and ethnicity. It includes institutional oppression whereby policies, customs, and practices reinforce systematic mistreatment of certain groups and produce inequities. The effects of these policies and practices accumulate and block life opportunities, just as the societal privilege dominant groups enjoy opens doors.

In examining policy options and strategies for decreasing discrimination, the strengths and resources of oppressed groups are often central to successful efforts. For example, the mobilization of African-American religious leaders played a crucial role in securing voting rights for people of color. Cesar Chavez, Dolores Huerta, and other Latinx activists organized farm laborers to press for an end to discriminatory practices and for access to opportunities. As depicted in Exhibit 7.4, these efforts elicited solidarity from others committed to

EXHIBIT 7.4

Coretta Scott King and Cesar Chavez Unite to Fight for Farm Workers' Rights, 1973

Source: Bob Parent

expanding civil rights and advancing a more inclusive vision of justice. LGBTQ+ advocates have won tangible policy victories and contributed to dramatic shifts in public attitudes about equity for their communities. Women have won critical gains in the effort to protect their own rights and have also played crucial roles in other movements for justice. And movements for people with disabilities have centered on the voices and aspirations of those most affected by policies regarding access and full inclusion. Historically and still today, civil rights efforts draw on the strengths of oppressed communities.

Social work students, like their clients, come from varied backgrounds. Perhaps you grew up hearing about your Native American heritage and the proud traditions of your ancestors. You may be familiar with historical images of "Whites Only" drinking fountains and lunch counters, and you are likely familiar with some of Dr. Martin Luther King, Jr.'s speeches. You may be active in efforts to ensure that transgender students' identities are recognized in school policies and that LGBTQ+ people are protected from discrimination at work. Conversely, you may have limited familiarity with the struggles of disadvantaged groups. As a social worker, you cannot understand current civil rights debates if you do not know this history. You should consider how your own identities shape the advantages and disadvantages you experience. Your instructor can provide you with a list of films, readings, and online resources to familiarize yourself with movements that have shaped our nation's understanding of civil rights, from autobiographies of central figures to ethnographies that examine oppressed communities' efforts to define their own futures. You may also want to talk with friends, family members, or community leaders whose life experiences can add to your understanding of our nation's struggles for civil rights and social justice. Social work students should examine their schools' curricula for full inclusion of diverse perspectives, intentionally read authors of color and those representing LGBTQ+ experiences, and challenge unjust policies within their educational institutions and field placements.

CIVIL RIGHTS IN THE UNITED STATES: PROMISING FOUNDATION FOR ONGOING STRUGGLES

The Constitution, particularly the Bill of Rights, serves as the foundation of civil rights protections in the United States. The Bill of Rights refers to the first ten amendments to the Constitution, which were ratified in 1791. Importantly, most core civil rights in the U.S. Constitution are not confined to citizens but, instead, apply equally to non-citizens who fall under U.S. jurisdiction. Rights reserved for citizens, such as the right to vote or to hold elective office, are spelled out; in other cases, people can assert their rights regardless of citizenship status. For example, the 14th Amendment to the U.S. Constitution states (emphasis added):

> No state shall make or enforce any law which shall abridge the privileges or immunities of citizens of the U. S.; nor shall any state deprive *any person* of life, liberty, or property, without due process of law; nor deny to *any person* within its jurisdiction the equal protection of the laws.

Protections under the Bill of Rights include:

- freedom of religion, freedom of speech, freedom of the press, and the right to assemble (First Amendment);
- freedom from "unreasonable searches and seizures" (Fourth Amendment);
- protection against self-incrimination (Fifth Amendment);
- the right to "a speedy and public trial, by an impartial jury" (Sixth Amendment); and
- protection against excessive bail and "cruel and unusual punishments" (Eighth Amendment).

Subsequent amendments to the Constitution have expanded civil rights. For example, recall from Chapter 2 the amendments approved during Reconstruction that officially abolished slavery and extended voting rights and due process to former slaves.

Disenfranchised Groups: Civil Rights and Social Justice

In this section, we focus on the successes and shortcomings of efforts to enhance civil rights and promote social justice for groups that have historically faced discrimination. To do this, we must also examine the effects of social policies directed toward these groups.

African Americans Chapters 2 and 3 trace the historical struggle for African-American civil rights, from slavery to Jim Crow through the Civil Rights Movement and the implementation of affirmative action. The Supreme Court decision in *Brown v. Board of Education*, which declared school segregation to be unconstitutional, is one of the Civil Rights Movement's landmark achievements. African-American leaders also successfully advanced policy victories through the legislative process, winning the Civil Rights Act of 1964, which outlawed racial discrimination in employment and mandated equal access to public accommodations, and the Voting Rights Act of 1965.

Although these victories required decades of struggle, winning their passage proved easier than ensuring their effective enforcement or, certainly, than achieving real racial equity. To be sure, the struggle continues. The number of schools where less than 40 percent of students were White approximately doubled between 1996 and 2016, while the concentration of Black students attending such "segregated schools" rose to 71 percent (Stancil, 2018). Overt "door slamming" has declined, but discrimination against renters and aspiring homebuyers of color persists, resulting in tangible costs and lost chances; African Americans are particularly disadvantaged in these transactions (Turner et al., 2013). While the Black unemployment rate fell in 2017, it is still nearly double the rate for Whites (U.S. Bureau of Labor Statistics, 2018a). Indeed, contemporary protests such as those in the National Football League aim to emphasize the extent to which realities of racial inequity fall short of constitutional ideals and our national image as a land of opportunity and freedom.

Inequities in the criminal justice system provide a particularly vivid illustration of the way race shapes life outcomes. While recent bipartisan policy shifts to decriminalize some non-violent offenses and to facilitate successful offender reentry may alter this future, research indicates that if high incarceration rates continue, one in three Black men will go to prison at some point in their life (Sentencing Project, 2013). Here, as in so many policy domains, social workers must consider not only the responsibility individuals bear for their own outcomes but also the contributions of policy. For example, although Blacks and Whites use drugs at similar rates, the imprisonment rate of African Americans for drug charges is almost six times that of Whites (Pettit & Sykes, 2017). Many of the defendants who end up incarcerated, whatever their race or ethnicity, are poor. They often rely on indigent defense services from systems that are short-staffed and inadequately funded. Even the fact of poverty can result in incarceration; people who cannot afford locally levied fines or costs associated with their own court proceedings, or who violate ordinances against public sleeping, for example, can end up in jail (Edelman, 2017).

Because people of color are more likely to be poor, these policies are examples of those that may be racially neutral on their face but yet have dramatically different racial implications. **Smart decarceration**, or the pursuit of policies to substantially reduce the incarcerated population and redress social disparities among the incarcerated while maximizing safety and societal well-being (Epperson & Pettus-Davis, 2015), is an urgent civil rights imperative. The NASW supported the First Step Act, signed into law in December 2018, as a worthwhile step in the direction of more equitable criminal justice policy. Social workers welcomed this legislation's provisions to expand job training and other programming to reduce recidivism, as well as sentencing modifications, including reductions of mandatory minimum sentences and expansion of "safety valve" alternatives to harsh detention consequences. There is hope that this bipartisan federal action reflects shifts that may ripple into state policy and pave the way for more substantial pivots from the racially unjust, expensive, and often inhumane status quo.

In 2015, a gunman murdered nine people at a prayer service at Emanuel African Methodist Episcopal Church in Charleston, South Carolina. The gunman later indicated that he was hoping to start a race war. The Charleston shooting is a horrific example of the extent to which racism continues to motivate extremism. Perhaps even more alarming, when an anti-racist counter-protestor was killed at a "Unite the Right" rally in Charlottesville, Virginia, President Trump's official statement was one that many saw as seeming to condone at least the beliefs—if not the actions—of racists. First condemning the "egregious display of hatred, bigotry and violence on many sides," Trump later added that he saw "people that were very fine people, on both sides," including the White supremacists responsible for the violence. This apparent equivocation adds to the sense many African Americans have that they are less safe and their lives less valued because of the color of their skin. The killings of Trayvon Martin, an unarmed 17-year-old Black student, by a neighborhood watch coordinator in Sanford, Florida, and of Michael Brown, an unarmed 18-year-old African American, by a police officer in Ferguson, Missouri, sparked widespread demonstrations and catalyzed a growing outcry against institutional violence. As part of their work for freedom and justice for people of color, the Black Lives Matter movement has raised national awareness of police brutality directed toward Black people, among other dimensions of racial injustice. For more information about their work, go to **www.blacklivesmatter.com**.

Although the elections of Barack Obama marked a victory in the work to achieve equality for African Americans, many believe that we have moved backward today. Indeed, writer and social commentator Ta-Nehisi Coates is among those who see Donald Trump's election as at least partially an intentional backlash to the temporary triumph of a person of color to the nation's highest office (Coates, 2017). Certainly, the struggle is far from over. The corrosive legacy of slavery and other official public policies of racial brutality is not yet fully understood and acknowledged, let alone accounted for. We may even be moving in the wrong direction. The Trump Administration has reportedly considered rolling back decades-old rules used to determine discrimination in areas such as housing, education, and law enforcement. According to the proposed new standards, the rules would consider only policies' racial *intent*, not their disparate *impact*—a shift that would make it harder to reckon with the policy roots of inequity (Meckler & Barrett, 2019). In June 2019, the U.S. Supreme Court agreed to hear a case (*Byron Allen v. Comcast*) that could undermine civil rights protections dating to Reconstruction. If the defendant prevails, people alleging racial discrimination would be required to prove that bias was the sole reason for adverse action, thus essentially allowing institutions to justify discrimination with any racially neutral rationale. The NAACP warns that the Supreme Court could make the "oldest civil rights statute virtually impotent" (Jan, 2019), further eroding the foundations on which marginalized groups attempt to defend their rights. Although high-ranking public officials today are increasingly called to account for statements and actions of overt racism, the effects of persistently discriminatory policies are often overlooked. The United States must grapple with these realities if we are to build a more just society.

Undeniably, however, African Americans instrumental in advancing the Civil Rights Movement achieved dramatic gains that changed the experiences of people of color in the United States. This activism also blazed a trail that inspired other social movements focused on rights for women, people with disabilities, and other oppressed groups. Leadership for civil rights causes most often comes from members of the group experiencing discrimination. Exhibit 7.5 highlights one Black social work leader's significant contributions to these efforts. However, other groups may be motivated to join the struggle in response to appeals to shared values, particularly when movement tactics underscore the harm discrimination causes. Still, change does not happen without conflict, particularly not when individuals' own interests are involved. This conflict can help people build their strengths and force dominant groups to address their concerns. Many African Americans continue to provide leadership in struggles for social justice. For more information on this history, visit the website of the NAACP (**www.naacp.org**) and click on the "History" link.

Native Americans The U.S. government has denied Native Americans civil and human rights throughout most of the nation's history. Non-Native representations often focus on this brutal treatment and its consequences, reducing Native Americans' experiences to what Ojibwe author David Treuer describes as "a list of the tragedies we had somehow outlived" (2019, p. 11). Strengths-based social workers acknowledge the horrors inflicted on Native communities but see Native Americans as a strong, resilient, and diverse population, made up of many tribes with different traditions and beliefs, who nonetheless share some common civil rights priorities. Of central concern for many Native Americans is **tribal sovereignty**, the right of Native peoples to self-govern, determine tribal membership, regulate tribal business and domestic relations, and manage tribal property. Sovereignty implies a government-to-government relationship between the federal government and the tribes. However, as noted in Chapter 2, as far back as 1831, the U.S. Supreme Court ruled in *Cherokee Nation v. Georgia* that tribes are "domestic dependent nations" (Commager, 1958, p. 256). Subsequent government actions such as the Dawes Act of 1887 further undermined tribal sovereignty. In 1934, the Indian Reorganization Act gave tribes more autonomy in handling their own affairs. However, termination policies instituted in the 1950s further eroded both tribal sovereignty and traditional cultural practices. To challenge these policies, groups like the American Indian Movement (AIM) employed direct action, while others used the courts to press for the restoration of land, water, and fishing rights. The Indian Self-Determination and Education Assistance Act of 1975 affirmed Native Americans' rights to be self-governing and to have greater authority over federal programs for their communities.

Advancing claims often based on treaties and sovereignty rather than the U.S. Constitution, Native Americans' struggles for civil, economic, and human rights continue today. It was not until 2009 that a settlement was reached in one case regarding Native Americans' rights to full accounting of the money held in "trust" for them by the Department of Interior, as outlined pursuant to the Dawes Act (DiNitto & Johnson, 2016). The settlement requires the U.S. government to provide funds for land consolidation and post-secondary scholarships for Native students. Policies that influence the ability to practice and pass on traditional religious beliefs, languages, and social practices are particularly important to many Native Americans.

EXHIBIT 7.5

Whitney M. Young

Whitney M. Young was born in Kentucky in 1921. His father was the president of an all-Black boarding school and his mother was the first African-American postmistress in Kentucky. Young earned an undergraduate degree in science, and as a soldier in World War II, he was trained in electrical engineering at MIT. After the war, Young earned his master's degree in social work and began volunteering at a local branch of the National Urban League. He became president of the League in 1961. While at the National Urban League, Young significantly increased its size and budget. He successfully urged major corporations to hire Black workers for jobs that previously had been held only by Whites. Because of his close relationships with influential business leaders, many African Americans felt that Young had "sold out" to the establishment. Young himself denied these accusations, insisting that it was critical to work *within* the system to bring about change. At the same time, Young did take a strong stance on civil rights. In 1963, he assisted in organizing the March on Washington. Besides his position at the National Urban League, Young served as president of the National Association of Social Workers (NASW) from 1969 to 1971. While at the NASW, he ensured that the organization focused on major social justice issues, such as poverty, racial justice, and ending the Vietnam War. After his death in 1971, Young was remembered as an influential civil rights leader who was able to break down many of the barriers facing African Americans.

> Every man is our brother, and every man's burden is our own. Where poverty exists, all are poorer. Where hate flourishes, all are corrupted. Where injustice reigns, all are unequal.
>
> Whitney M. Young

Source (image): Library of Congress

The U.S. government has often compromised Native peoples' religious freedom by denying them access to religious sites. For example, the Supreme Court refused to prevent the federal government from building roads through lands that tribes consider sacred, even though one justice acknowledged that this construction "could have devastating effects on traditional Indian religious practices" (Postrel, 1988). During the past decade, Native American advocates developed the Tribal Supreme Court Project, which seeks to develop new litigation strategies and coordinate tribal legal resources to strengthen Native Americans' position in this important arena. For more information on civil rights issues affecting Native Americans, visit the Native Americans Rights Fund (**www.narf.org**) and the Center for Native American Youth (**www.cnay.org**).

Another area of policymaking significant to many Native Americans is environmental protection. Here, claims of sovereignty often align with concerns about long-term sustainability. In an especially high-profile example, members of the Standing Rock Sioux tribe and thousands of supporters maintained a months-long standoff over the construction of the Dakota Access pipeline on land the Sioux claimed was awarded to them in a treaty years ago. Then-President Obama halted construction of the pipeline, citing concerns about environmental risks and infringement on Native rights, but President Trump overturned the decision.

An additional implication of Native American sovereignty centers on economic development. Native Americans' long-term experiences with bias and structural discrimination have resulted in disproportionately low educational attainment and high rates of poverty, infant mortality, unemployment, and substance use. To catalyze economic development and control their own economic outcomes, many tribes have opted to open casinos on their lands. However, because gaming is regulated by the U.S. government, tribes first must obtain permission from the state. This requirement has resulted in many legal disputes concerning sovereignty.

Not all the challenges facing Native American communities are unique to their arrangement as sovereign nations. Native Americans, already disadvantaged in electoral participation by obstacles such as long distances to polling places and persistent poverty that often depresses turnout, found themselves facing another obstacle in the 2018 midterm election: voter identification rules that required a street address, which few Native people living on reservations have. Yet again, tribes resisted attacks on their rights. Native American leaders, including many of the Standing Rock Sioux who were active in the Dakota Access pipeline struggle, went door-to-door to educate people about the law, provided free voter identification cards to tribal members, and gave people free rides to the polls. Because of these efforts, North Dakota's 2018 Native American high voter turnout was unprecedented.

Latinx Communities The Latinx community is very diverse, comprised of individuals with distinctly different social backgrounds and current needs. For example, Mexican immigrants living in Texas may have very different histories and opportunities than Cuban Americans in Florida or Puerto Ricans in New York, or even Mexican Americans whose families settled in Chicago or Los Angeles generations ago. Although the number of powerful Latinx government leaders and businesspeople is increasing, Latinx continue to be overrepresented among families with low incomes and underrepresented in positions of power. As is the case for African Americans and Native Americans, Latinx individuals and entire communities live with the legacy of past discrimination, including school segregation and denial of employment opportunities. Even when discriminatory practices were less overt, failure to provide services to meet students' needs—as English-language learners, sometimes, or as first-generation students in the United States—resulted in unequal outcomes, as did lack of investment in infrastructure and services in Latinx neighborhoods. Further, although more than 60 percent of Latinx individuals and more than 50 percent of Latinx adults were born in the United States (Flores, 2017), immigration policy inequitably affects Latinx lives. More than half of Latinx worry that someone they know could be deported (Lopez, Gonzalez-Barrera, & Krogstad, 2018), and they are more likely than other Americans to rank immigration as a top policy priority (Pew Research Center, 2017).

In recent decades, the Latinx population in the United States has grown significantly, due to both a relatively high birth rate and continued immigration. Today, Latinx are 17 percent of the nation's total population (Flores, 2017) and 25 percent of U.S. children under age 18 (Child Trends, 2018). According to U.S. Census Bureau projections, Latinx will constitute almost 30 percent of the nation's population by 2060 (U.S. Census Bureau, 2015). Further, historic undercounting of Latinx communities means that the population's actual size may be even greater than official statistics suggest. Although a growing share of Latinx worry about their place in the United States and feel targeted by anti-immigrant rhetoric and increasingly harsh policies (Lopez, Gonzalez-Barrera, & Krogstad, 2018), as numbers of Latinx voters and elected officials grow, there is reason to hope that growing political power will lead to policies to reduce discrimination and expand equitable opportunities. For more information on work to improve opportunities for Latinx Americans, access the website of Unidos US (**www.unidosus.org**).

Today, immigration policy is a source of sharp debate in the U.S. political system. President Trump campaigned on a promise to build a wall along the U.S.–Mexico border and frequently characterizes Latinx communities as threats. In 2018, he deployed the U.S. military to the border, where they used tear gas to prevent Central American asylum-seekers from entering the country. In 2019, the United States endured the longest federal government shutdown in history, largely over the president's dispute with Congress regarding funding for construction of the border wall. When Congress' spending bill appropriated less than the almost $6 billion Trump had demanded for the wall, the president declared a national emergency so that he could unilaterally authorize construction to stem what he called an "invasion" of migrants—an action subsequently rebuked by Congress, but without the votes necessary to override a presidential veto. States, border communities, Native tribes, and other interests are using lobbying pressure, litigation, and other strategies to oppose the border wall as a policy and the use of executive authority to impose it. However, in July 2019, the U.S. Supreme Court allowed President Trump to divert more than $2 billion in Pentagon funds to begin construction. Meanwhile, the flow of families seeking refuge from poverty and violence in Central America reached a 15-year high in 2019. As a result, pressures on detention capacity and security resources have mounted, along with the stakes in the immigration policy debate. Detained migrants, including thousands of children, experience increasingly harsh conditions, as the U.S. Department of Homeland Security withholds hygiene supplies and basic humanitarian relief in an attempt to deter those seeking asylum. In September 2019, the Trump Administration reached a deal to divert asylum seekers to El Salvador, thereby signaling a willingness to send people fleeing poverty, violence, and corruption to a country known to be dangerous, in an effort to discourage the journey to the United States. Combined with highly publicized border deaths, including those that took place in U.S. custody, these conditions and actions attract condemnation from some members of Congress and of the American public. However, in the current landscape, concern has not translated into policy intervention to address the roots of these problems.

While the president's voice is particularly prominent, other groups are also demanding that the government limit immigration and strengthen border patrols. Arrayed on the other side of this issue are immigrant rights organizations and immigrants themselves, who push for policies that would recognize immigrants' economic and social contributions and afford fair access to opportunities. Many Americans embrace the ideals of fairness and welcoming that pro-immigrant movements advance. Even at the height of controversies over refugee admissions and border security, polls found record-high numbers of Americans who view immigration as a "good thing" for the nation (Brenan, 2018).

Nonetheless, policy trends continue to move in a decidedly unwelcoming direction. For example, some states have changed their calculation for SNAP eligibility to make it more difficult for U.S. citizen children with immigrant parents to receive food aid. Federally, the Trump Administration included SNAP in the expanded list of services that count against a family in a determination of "public charge," which can prevent adjustment of immigration status or even entry to the United States. Under these new rules, which took effect in October 2019, aspiring immigrants must prove they have health insurance and submit extensive documentation to demonstrate that they will be "self-sufficient". These restrictions threaten to separate more immigrant families and further disadvantage low-income individuals and communities in immigration determinations. Strict public charge rules, misinformation about which benefits are included, and extensive publicity about harsh consequences intensify social workers' concerns about the reluctance of families with mixed immigration status to seek services. For example, a child born in the United States to a low-income family is likely entitled to health care coverage. However, when families include older siblings not born in the United States or immigrant parents not eligible for public benefits, confusion about eligibility may keep them from getting health services for their child.

President Trump's stated desire to end birthright citizenship, such that children born in the United States would not be U.S. citizens unless their parents were also citizens, has ratcheted up these anxieties. Families are routinely thrown into crisis when parents are deported and must choose whether to leave behind a U.S. citizen child or attempt to rebuild their lives in their country of origin, even though their child may never have lived there. The trauma of family separation was amplified on the global stage in 2018, when a new policy of "zero tolerance" for people crossing the border illegally led to separation of thousands of families, including those with very young children. While the Trump Administration prefers rules that would undermine the emphasis on family reunification and admit only highly skilled workers, today's pathways for people to bring their family members to the United States as immigrants date to the Immigration and Nationality Act, passed in 1965 as part of the legislated expansion of civil rights. Social workers are among those concerned about the implications of abandoning this policy principle.

Given the lengthy and sometimes sparsely populated Mexican border, deep connections between people in the United States and family members in other countries, the sometimes-impassable system of navigating to lawful immigration status as a would-be American, and the economic significance of immigrants to businesses and local governments, immigration policy is undeniably complex. It is also clear, perhaps more than ever in today's context, that immigrant rights are civil rights. Seen through this lens, U.S. immigration policy says more about our nation than about those seeking to join it.

Asian Americans Over 21.4 million U.S. residents are of Asian descent (U.S. Census Bureau, 2018b). Because Asia comprises myriad countries and regions, there are more than 20 Asian-American subgroups in the United States, and the Asian-American population is very diverse. Although small in comparison to other racial and ethnic groups, its numbers and economic and political influence are growing. Between 2000 and 2015, the Asian-American population increased by nearly 72 percent, the most of any group. Immigration was the major factor driving this rapid increase. Asians have accounted for one-quarter of all immigrants who have arrived in the United States since 1965. This rapid population growth suggests that Asians will become the nation's largest immigrant group by 2055 (Lopez, Ruiz, & Patten, 2017). After Spanish, Chinese is the most widely spoken non-English language in the United States (U.S. Census Bureau, 2015).

Exhibit 7.6 presents projections from the Pew Research Center (2015) concerning changes in racial and ethnic composition in the United States by 2065. This exhibit graphically illustrates expected increases in the Asian-American population, which currently comprises approximately 6 percent of the U.S. population. Three of the largest Asian-American groups are Chinese, Asian Indian, and Filipino, followed by Vietnamese, Korean, and Japanese. While their individual and collective stories are testament to their resilience and the strength of their

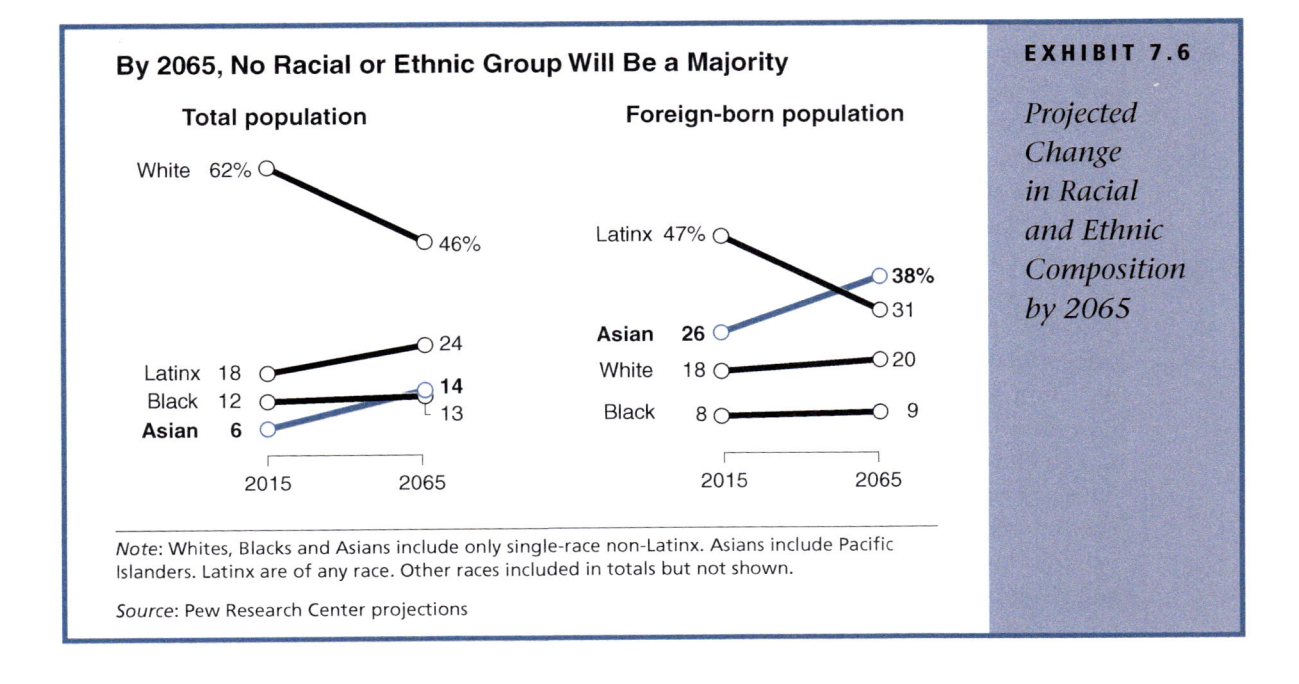

EXHIBIT 7.6

Projected Change in Racial and Ethnic Composition by 2065

By 2065, No Racial or Ethnic Group Will Be a Majority

Total population
- White: 62% → 46%
- Latinx: 18 → 24
- Black: 12 → 14
- Asian: 6 → 13

(2015 → 2065)

Foreign-born population
- Latinx: 47% → 31
- Asian: 26 → 38%
- White: 18 → 20
- Black: 8 → 9

(2015 → 2065)

Note: Whites, Blacks and Asians include only single-race non-Latinx. Asians include Pacific Islanders. Latinx are of any race. Other races included in totals but not shown.

Source: Pew Research Center projections

family and community ties, like many other ethnic and racial groups, Asian Americans experience discrimination. For example, Chinese immigrants have experienced exploitation in the workplace, from the mid-1800s, when they performed very dangerous work building the nation's railways, to the present time, when newly arrived immigrants have been discovered toiling in urban garment industry sweatshops and working long hours as domestics. These ongoing abuses illustrate the need for stronger enforcement of labor and civil rights laws.

Because many Asian Americans have been able to complete higher education and secure good jobs, people sometimes assume that all Asian Americans are doing well. This stereotype has led to a portrayal as the "model minority," an image that ignores discrimination and obscures the high rates of poverty that some Asian Americans experience. Asian-American advocacy groups are working to dispel stereotypes and develop the political influence needed to remove remaining barriers to full participation in society.

When their policy interests align, Asian Americans have found common cause with other oppressed groups. Asian Americans and Latinx have developed coalitions to push for immigration reform and humane treatment in immigration detention facilities. Some Asian Americans have also joined forces with African Americans and others concerned about overreaches of government authority and the erosion of civil liberties. Asian Americans have found common cause with other communities of color who experience barriers to equitable educational opportunities, particularly in post-secondary institutions. For more information about Asian Americans' advocacy priorities and alliances, go to the websites for the Asian Pacific American Advocates (formerly known as the Organization of Chinese Americans, at **www.ocanational.org**), the Japanese American Citizens League (**www.jacl.org**), and the Southeast Asia Resource Action Center (**www.searac.org**).

Sexual Orientation and Gender Identity The struggle for equal rights for people who are lesbian, gay, bisexual, transgender, or queer (LGBTQ+) has been a central part of the civil rights struggle in the twentieth and twenty-first centuries, often intersecting with, drawing from, and inspiring other movements for civil rights. Historically, millions of Americans regularly suffered discrimination based on sexual orientation, defined by "a person's emotional, sexual, and/or relational attraction to others. This can include attraction to people of the opposite sex/gender (heterosexual), the same sex/gender (gay/lesbian), or multiple sexes/genders (e.g., bisexual)" (Poirier et al., 2014).

Today, discrimination based on sexual orientation and gender identity continues to pose barriers to full social inclusion. **Gender identity** is a person's internal sense of belonging to the categories of "male," "female," "both," or "neither." **Transgender** is an umbrella term for people whose gender, gender identity, or expression of gender is in some way different from social norms for their assigned birth sex (NASW, 2015a). Propelled by activism such as that depicted in Exhibit 7.7, transgender individuals' struggles for civil rights, recognition, and opportunity have moved center stage at the local, state, and federal government levels in recent years. However, efforts to end discrimination against these groups are not new. Although the 1950s were a period of social isolation for gays and lesbians, the development of early activist organizations laid the groundwork for the gay rights movement. The Stonewall Riot of 1969 was a turning point for LGBQT+ civil rights and sparked new activism across the country.

EXHIBIT 7.7

Youth at Equality Rally Advocating for Transgender Rights

Credit: Shutterstock

   As gay and lesbian activists convinced organizations to alter policies regarding sexual orientation and pressured institutions to equitably meet their needs, professionals' interactions with LGBTQ+ individuals have changed dramatically. For example, in 1974, the American Psychological Association removed homosexuality from its official list of mental disorders and put forth a new definition of homosexuality as an alternative form of biopsychosocial development (Oltmanns & Emery, 1995). This signaled a greater professional willingness to acknowledge the validity of previously stigmatized expressions of sexuality. In 1977, the delegate assembly of the NASW passed a public policy statement that called on social workers to help eradicate homophobia. It further proposed that the NASW establish a National Task Force on Gay Rights to begin implementing this policy (Tice & Perkins, 2002). The National Committee on Lesbian, Gay, Bisexual, and Transgender Issues (NCLGBTI) is now mandated by NASW bylaws. The Committee reports on a regular basis to the NASW Board of Directors on matters of policy and coordinates with the Program Committee on related activities. The 2008 revision to the NASW Code of Ethics incorporated sexual orientation and gender identity into existing non-discrimination standards. People who are transgender have made some similar progress; where a diagnosis of "gender dysphoria" was formerly required to access transition-related medical care, such services are now considered "medically necessary" (White Hughto et al., 2017).

Notwithstanding these advances, heterosexual privilege is built into many facets of our society. Still today, privileges that dominant groups take for granted, such as the right to use the public restroom in which one feels most comfortable and to be protected from unjust firing, are battlegrounds for LGBTQ+ communities. Further, as has been the case for other groups, in recent years, some of the hard-won progress of the LGBTQ+ movement for civil rights has been eroded by federal executive order, local and state government infringement, and public backlash. In these fraught times, advocacy groups are particularly concerned about LGBTQ+ youths. These young people often face discrimination in their schools and alienation from their families. Largely due to ostracization, they have higher than average rates of homelessness and suicide. Repeated experiences of discrimination and bullying place LGBTQ+ youths at increased risk of involvement with court and child welfare systems and negatively influence their outcomes in those systems. For more information on advocacy work for LGBTQ+ youth, visit **www.thetrevorproject.org**.

Paralleling the civil rights journey of African Americans, some of the LGBTQ+ communities' greatest victories were won in U.S. courts. In 1996, the Supreme Court, in *Romer v. Evans*, struck down an amendment to Colorado's constitution that barred cities and localities from enacting laws protecting gays and lesbians against discrimination. Among the court's arguments was that the amendment violated the "equal protection of the laws" provision of the 14th Amendment (Dripps, 1996). Despite this ruling, many municipalities and states fail to include sexual orientation and/or gender identity in their lists of "classes" deserving civil rights protections. Discrimination remains widespread, and federal policy provides little protection. In 2019, the U.S. Supreme Court ruled that the Civil Rights Act's prohibition on sex discrimination does not include those discriminated against based on sexual orientation or gender identity, even though the federal Equal Employment Opportunity Commission and several lower courts have ruled in favor of workers on these bases.

In 2003, the Supreme Court struck down sodomy laws, ruling that intimate consensual sexual conduct was part of the liberty protected by substantive due process under the 14th Amendment. Then, on June 26, 2015, the U.S. Supreme Court ruled 5–4 in *Obergefell v. Hodges* that the due process and equal protection clauses of the 14th Amendment to the U.S. Constitution guarantee people in same-sex relationships the fundamental right to marry. This historic decision, like civil rights rulings that preceded it, including *Brown v. Board of Education*, was a consolidation of cases that had been heard in lower district courts. With the 2015 ruling, the U.S. Supreme Court compelled states to honor same-sex marriages conducted in other jurisdictions, grant marriage licenses to same-sex couples, and confer the rights of marriage—including to make medical decisions for each other, inherit property, file joint tax returns, and share custody of children—to same-sex couples equally as to opposite-sex couples. *Obergefell v. Hodges* was decided two years after the U.S. Supreme Court's ruling in *United States v. Windsor*, which overturned Section 3 of the 1996 Defense of Marriage Act (DOMA), effectively requiring the federal government to recognize same-sex marriages.

While a major civil rights victory and the product of years of strategic organizing by LGBTQ+ activists, the *Obergefell* ruling has not completely silenced debate over marriage equality. In the months following, some jurisdictions stopped issuing marriage licenses altogether to avoid having to issue them to same-sex couples, while many states considered or even passed "conscience" laws that protect professionals who refuse to provide services on an equal basis to same-sex couples. In 2018, the U.S. Supreme Court sided with a Colorado baker who cited religious freedom as his rationale for refusing to make a wedding cake for a same-sex couple. Although the 7–2 ruling was narrowly decided, hinging on a finding that the Colorado Civil Rights Commission showed hostility to the baker over his religious beliefs, it has added to uncertainty about the security of civil rights protections for LGBTQ+ Americans and the extent to which others' religious objections can limit them.

While civil rights policies are crucial "backstops" against individual and institutional discrimination, social movements set their sights on changes in norms, attitudes, and political will, in addition to tangible policy victories. Today, popular support for marriage equality is growing worldwide. At the time of the *Obergefell v. Hodges* ruling, same-sex marriage was already legal in more than 20 other countries, including Argentina, Brazil, Canada, England, France, Norway, Spain, South Africa, and Uruguay; by 2018, the number had risen to 27, including Australia, Colombia, and Germany. Americans express more support for LGBTQ+ rights today than at any point in history (McCarthy, 2018). Openly LGBTQ+ policymakers, celebrities, and corporate leaders are contributing to the changing landscape for LGBTQ+ civil rights, and a new generation of LGBTQ+ leaders continue to drive toward social justice for this population. The NASW is committed to full legal and social acceptance and recognition of lesbian, gay, bisexual, transgender, and queer people (NASW, 2015b).

Marriage equality has not been the only battle in the campaign for greater civil rights for LGBTQ+ individuals. In 2011, President Obama signed a bill repealing the controversial "Don't Ask, Don't Tell" policy that required LGBTQ+ military service members to conceal their sexual orientation. In preparing to implement the inclusive new policy, military experts cited the laudable service of LGBTQ+ soldiers, as well as U.S. interests in attracting all qualified candidates to the armed services. In 2016, then-Secretary of Defense Ash Carter announced that transgender individuals could openly serve in the military; later that year, gender-transition medical care was officially provided as a benefit for service members. The Trump Administration has moved to reverse at least some of these policy advances, however. A 2018 directive prohibits military service by transgender persons "who require or have undergone gender transition" (Mattis, 2018, p. 2). In 2019, the U.S. Supreme Court lifted injunctions that had kept this policy from being implemented. Instead, the conservative majority on the Court allowed the restrictions on transgender people serving in the military to go into effect while the legal battle continues in lower courts (Barnes & Lamothe, 2019).

Many of the LGBTQ+ community's struggles for civil rights are contested at the state and local levels. At least seven states allow discrimination against prospective parents in adoption and foster care decisions, based on sexual orientation, and a few states have even broader "exemptions" from general anti-discrimination laws—provisions that essentially license discrimination. Only 19 states offer explicit protection for LGBTQ+ individuals in housing, employment, and public accommodations; other states prohibit discrimination based on sexual orientation but not gender identity (Human Rights Watch, 2018b). Transgender Americans are particularly vulnerable; the Movement Advancement Project (2017) identifies only 16 states' policies as fully protective of transgender rights.

In 2016, several states took up so-called "bathroom bills" that sought to restrict use of public restrooms to those matching the gender on a person's birth certificate, effectively denying the legitimacy of their transgender identity. After the passage of such a bill in North Carolina, companies, municipalities, and others rushed to condemn the discrimination and announce boycotts, but state legislators in more than 20 other states considered anti-LGBTQ+ legislation, including eight other states that similarly sought to restrict bathroom usage. In the Obama Administration, the U.S. Department of Education issued guidelines cautioning that public schools receiving federal funds may not discriminate based on gender identity. After challenge by 13 states, a federal judge blocked enforcement of a directive that public schools allow transgender students to use bathrooms and locker rooms corresponding to their gender identity. In 2017, the rule was overturned by the Trump Administration, which has also reversed Obama-era rules that recognize gender identity protections in health and human services.

Potentially even more sweeping and, ultimately, damaging to the cause of LGBTQ+ rights, the Trump Administration has considered narrowly defining gender as a biological, immutable condition determined by genitalia at birth (Green, Benner, & Pear, 2018). Spearheaded by the U.S. Department of Health and Human Services, this policy change would establish a legal definition of sex under Title IX, the federal civil rights law that bans gender discrimination. When the memo announcing the potential policy was revealed, protestors took to the streets and to social media, using the hashtag #wewontbeerased. To learn more about the campaign for equal rights for LGBTQ+ Americans, visit the Human Rights Campaign (**www.hrc.org**).

People with Disabilities Advocacy by people with disabilities and their families has changed the face of social policy. The Education for All Handicapped Children Act of 1975[1] mandates free public education for all children with disabilities. Amendments passed in 1986 extend services to children with disabilities from birth through age five (Pollard, 1995). Other legislation, such as the Mental Health Bill of Rights Act (2011) and the Developmentally Disabled Assistance and Bill of Rights (2000), expand protection and care for people with mental illness and developmental disabilities. However, these laws offer protection only in public activities and programs.

As discussed in Chapter 3, the Americans with Disabilities Act (ADA) of 1990 helped remove barriers to full inclusion for people with disabilities (Pollard, 1995). The ADA requires businesses and employers to make "reasonable accommodations" to allow people with disabilities to perform job functions. This law has significantly increased opportunities and access to needed resources for people with disabilities. We explore the ADA in depth in the section on major policies and programs. In 1999, the Supreme Court held in the landmark decision *Olmstead v. L. C.* that Title II of the ADA requires that states, whenever possible, place individuals with disabilities in community settings rather than in institutions. The Supreme Court called on the states to develop "comprehensive, effectively working plans" to provide services to people with disabilities in the most integrated settings possible. Subsequently, George W. Bush signed Executive Order No. 13217, Community-Based Alternatives for Individuals with Disabilities. This initiative went beyond the *Olmstead* decision in calling on federal agencies to assist states and to examine whether their own policies present barriers to community-based services. The order empowered the Attorney General and the Secretary of the Department of Health and Human Services to enforce *Olmstead*. President Obama committed to more rigorously enforcing *Olmstead* and to providing additional funding to aid in compliance. As depicted in Exhibit 7.8, Lois Curtis, one of the original plaintiffs whose battle for community services rather than institutionalization catalyzed the *Olmstead* ruling, met President Obama in 2009, on the anniversary of the decision.

EXHIBIT 7.8

President Obama and Lois Curtis Commemorate the Olmstead Ruling

Credit: Official White House Photo by Pete Souza

The civil rights campaigns waged by individuals with disabilities place a strengths-based and capacity-building perspective at the center. Policies are advanced that help people meet their needs and pursue their own goals, and target groups take the lead in articulating objectives and determining strategies. The struggle to fully implement *Olmstead* continues. These efforts support the core social work value of self-determination and inspire other campaigns for social justice. They have led to important reforms throughout the social policy landscape and may lead to greater community integration for people with disabilities. To learn more about the *Olmstead* decision and its enforcement, go to **www.ada.gov/olmstead**.

The number of people with disabilities will grow much larger as (1) the Baby Boomer generation ages and (2) new medical advances make it possible to save the lives of people with serious injuries and congenital disorders. Disability rights groups can be expected to continue to press their case legislatively as well as through the courts and through direct action. The combination of growth in the population with disabilities and the loudly voiced goal of people with disabilities to remain in the community creates fiscal and adaptive challenges. Meeting these challenges will require strategic planning to best use and most equitably distribute public resources. Like other groups facing discrimination, people with disabilities experience higher rates of poverty—both a consequence and a cause of some of the inequities they experience. Supportive services and vigorous enforcement of civil rights protections will be necessary to improve their quality of life.

People with Mental Illness People with mental illness have experienced both gains and setbacks in their pursuit of civil rights. Although people with mental illness have the right to refuse treatment, they may be committed involuntarily for treatment in a psychiatric hospital if they exhibit dangerous behavior or are deemed incapable of self-care. Once committed, they have the right to treatment; however, a client's right to treatment in the least restrictive environment has been less well established (Marty & Chapin, 2000). Further, many people have the theoretical *right* to care, but not necessarily the resources with which to secure the services they need.

Courts often have been unwilling to protect the right to community-based treatment when states cut options because of funding shortfalls, since that might lead to creation of a guaranteed right to services that do not exist—at least not in sufficient supply. Although *Olmstead* was a victory for social justice and a crucial advance in civil rights, unless the government provides treatment once people have reentered the community, they are in danger of struggling without needed support. This danger has become more acute as states have cut funding for home- and community-based services and for mental health centers. A 2015 report found that states were still recovering from a collective $4.35 billion cut from the overall mental health system after the recession (National Alliance on Mental Illness [NAMI], 2015a). Further, individuals may struggle to access the services that would help to stabilize them in moments of crisis and, then, prevent the development of more critical needs, since there is no established right to prevention or early intervention approaches.

The consequences of inadequate treatment are becoming ever-more evident with the growth in numbers of people with untreated mental illness in prisons and homeless shelters. According to analysis by the National Alliance on Mental Illness (2015b), almost 30 percent of women and 15 percent of men who are booked into jails have a serious mental health condition. It is conservatively estimated that 25 percent of the total homeless population have serious mental illness (Treatment Advocacy Center, 2018). Racial inequities manifest in these figures, as people of color are less likely to receive appropriate care for mental illness (Agency for Healthcare Research and Quality, 2016) and more likely to experience punitive approaches. In recognition of the intersection of race in these other civil rights domains, in 2018, the NAACP, a leading civil rights organization championing issues of concern to African Americans, passed a resolution condemning the over-prescription of psychiatric medication for children of color, particularly in the child welfare system. Strengths-based social workers recognize that protecting the civil rights of individuals with disabilities and mental illness centers the goals and priorities of client groups, including their desire to receive the types and amount of services required to meet their needs—no more and no less.

One strategy to improve mental health treatment is to push for access to and reimbursement for mental health services comparable to physical health benefits. Passed in 1996, the Mental Health Parity Act required employers with more than 50 employees who offer health insurance to include comparable mental and physical health benefits. Of course, mental health parity policies do not address barriers to services for those without any insurance coverage. Until there are sufficient high-quality, affordable mental health care services, many people with mental illness will continue to go without adequate treatment. The Bazelon Center for Mental Health and the Law provides in-depth coverage of current civil rights issues for people with mental illness (**www.bazelon.org**).

Older Adults   The U.S. population of older adults is quite diverse and will become increasingly so. For example, the proportion of the population aged 60+ who are people of color is expected to increase to 21.1 million—28.5 percent of the older adult population—by 2030. More than 2.4 million older adults identify as LGBTQ+. Further, there are wide gaps in the economic well-being of older adults, largely reflecting inequities throughout the lifespan. Social policies must reflect this diversity.

Changes in the economy—particularly the decrease in the provision of private pensions—and in society—including the increasing number of older adults and new social expectations about active roles in later life—have increased the number of older adults engaged in the workforce. However, workplace discrimination is part of many older adults' experiences. The 1964 Civil Rights Act did not prohibit discrimination on the basis of age. Three years later, however, the Age Discrimination in Employment Act (ADEA) prohibited employment discrimination against people between the ages of 40 and 70, while allowing employers to continue to enforce mandatory retirement and to pursue other discriminatory practices for those older than 70. In 1986, the ADEA was amended to eliminate the age cap. This revision abolished mandatory retirement for most employees and made age discrimination illegal for all employees 40 years and older (Equal Employment Opportunity Commission, 1999). In 1990, the Older Workers Benefit Protection Act (OWBPA) further amended the ADEA to specifically prohibit employers from denying benefits to older employees.

Despite laws enacted to protect older workers and the increasing political and economic power of older Americans, most workers over age 45 report having either experienced or witnessed age-based discrimination in the workforce (Perron, 2018). Expanding older adult worker populations, pervasive ageism, and policies that have eroded some protections contribute to this discrimination. In the 2009 case *Gross v. FBL Financial, Inc.*, the Supreme Court held that in an ADEA discrimination claim, the plaintiff/employee must prove by a "preponderance of the evidence" that age was the "but for" cause of the employer's actions; in other words, the worker must demonstrate that the adverse action (e.g., firing or demotion) would not have happened, but for discrimination based on age. Some courts have interpreted this as a higher standard for proving age-related discrimination, compared to other cases, where the identity in a protected class (e.g., gender, race) need be only a "motivating factor." By putting the burden of proof on the employee claiming discrimination rather than on the employer, this ruling makes it more difficult for a worker to win an age discrimination case. As a result, older workers often pursue age discrimination claims in state court, where 43 states include age within their omnibus antidiscrimination laws, subject to the same standards as in other cases (Lipnic, 2018).

Inadequate access to mental health care for older adults has long been an area of concern. Their need for mental health treatment is well-documented, and research indicates that mental health treatment for older adults is effective. However, many mental health providers serve relatively few older clients. Providers' ageism and older adults' reluctance to seek help undoubtedly contribute to this problem, as do more universal barriers such as lack of access to transportation and concern about out-of-pocket costs. In long-term care facilities, the issue is often overreliance on psychotropic medication to control behaviors among residents with dementia or mental illness. In November 2017, the Centers for Medicare and Medicaid Services (CMS) implemented a new rule limiting the duration of use of psychiatric medications for long-term care facility residents and requiring physician examination for these medications to be continued. However, media investigations continue to reveal inconsistent enforcement and ongoing abuses of residents' rights and preferences regarding treatment.

Older adults suffer discrimination when their right to self-determination in end-of-life decisions is infringed. The Patient's Self-Determination Act of 1990 requires all hospitals participating in Medicare and Medicaid to inquire whether adult inpatients have advanced health care directives and to provide information on pertinent state laws and hospital policies. An **advance directive** is a document or statement produced by the patient specifying their choices for medical treatment—including no treatment. An advance directive can also be used to designate a person who will make those choices should the patient be unable to do so. Although the 1990 law is intended to protect patients at the end of life, the lack of trained hospital staff has limited its effectiveness. Further, as a society, we have yet to effectively address the unacceptably high levels of untreated pain many older adults experience at the end of life. Recent state and federal efforts to restrict access to pain medication in the wake of a growing epidemic of abuse of opioid painkillers have exacerbated the problem. New safety precautions have had the unintended consequence of making it more difficult for individuals who rely on these sophisticated pharmaceuticals to adequately address their pain. Conflict surrounding assisted suicide continues to compromise the rights of patients, including older adults, to self-determination. For more information on policy issues that impact older adults' rights, investigate the advocacy of the AARP (**www.aarp.org/research/ppi/health-care**).

In many spheres, compassionate ageism—the stereotypical belief that all older adults are frail and incapacitated—has led to the development of public and corporate policies that hinder older adults from fully participating in society. Strengths-based social workers recognize that many older adults can and do contribute to their communities in varied and important ways, and that more older adults would be so engaged if policies and support structures facilitated this participation. The development of such systems is a primary goal of older adults and of the social workers who help advance their claims for civil rights.

Women and Civil Rights Although women have made great gains in education—even surpassing men in college completion rates—and although they can enter many professions that were previously closed to them, the struggle for gender equity is ongoing. The Equal Pay Act of 1963 prohibited wage discrimination on the basis of sex, but there were many loopholes in this legislation, and the gender pay gap continues. While some gender divides are narrowing, if change continues at this slow pace, women will not reach pay parity until 2059 (Institute for Women's Policy Research, 2018).

When gender equity in the United States is compared to that of other countries, we clearly have much work to do. The Global Gender Gap Index developed by the World Economic Forum is a tool for comparing gender-based inequalities on economic, political, education, and health-based criteria. In 2017, the United States ranked 49th out of 144 countries. This is a drop from our 2015 ranking, largely due to the progress made by other countries to more dramatically close gender gaps. Discrimination against women manifests in all facets of U.S. society, including at the highest levels of government, as illustrated by the United States' low 96th-place global ranking on the dimension of political empowerment. As described in Chapter 3, the 2016 and 2018 national elections in the United States saw strong voter participation by women and record numbers of women elected to local, state, and congressional seats. However, given that one of the metrics used to calculate global gender parity is "years with a female head of state," the United States is clearly a laggard on the world stage.

Although majorities of Americans support equal pay legislation, the Pay Check Fairness Act has yet to pass in Congress. Designed to close some of the loopholes in the Equal Pay Act, this legislation would require that employers demonstrate that wage differentials between men and women with the same position who do the same work stem from factors other than sex. It would also prohibit retaliation against people who ask about their employers' wage practices. The case of Lilly Ledbetter, described in Exhibit 7.9, eventually led to passage of the Lilly Ledbetter Fair Pay Act of 2009, described in more detail later in the chapter. Affirmative action policies and litigation, discussed in the following section, have also helped women achieve gains

EXHIBIT 7.9

Lilly Ledbetter

Lilly Ledbetter was born Lilly McDaniel in 1938 and was raised in a small town in Alabama in a home that had no electricity or running water. Lilly and her husband Charles had two young children at home when Lilly applied for a job at a Goodyear tire factory in 1979. One of the few women hired as management, Lilly endured continuous sexual harassment and discrimination during her 19 years with the company. Lilly was near retirement when she received an anonymous note telling her that she was making much less than her male counterparts. Lilly had signed an agreement not to talk with co-workers about her pay, so she was unaware that she was paid less than men in the same position. Once she became aware of the disparity, she filed a sex discrimination lawsuit against Goodyear. Lilly's case went all the way to the U.S. Supreme Court, which ultimately decided against her, ruling that she had waited too long since the incident of discrimination to file her lawsuit. After the Supreme Court's ruling, Lilly lobbied members of Congress about the need for change. Lilly's efforts culminated on January 29, 2009, when President Obama signed into law, as his first official piece of legislation, the Lilly Ledbetter Fair Pay Act of 2009.

Image Credit: Lilly Ledbetter

in the workplace. However, retreat from affirmative action could imperil some of the advances women have made, especially in terms of access to employment opportunities.

Because women are often the primary caregivers for children and elders, the lack of policies to adequately support people who care for dependents places women workers at a disadvantage. This contributes to the **feminization of poverty**—that is, the disproportionately high number of women who live in poverty. Additionally, low wages for women are a major cause of childhood poverty. Women are also more adversely affected financially by divorce than are men (Smock, Manning, & Gupta, 1999). Moreover, women who have been poor all their lives face old age with inadequate retirement savings and pensions. For men, the poverty rate decreases after age 65, but women face a greater risk of poverty in later life (Issa & Zedlewski, 2011). For more information on the struggle for gender equity, go to the website of the National Organization for Women (**www.now.org**).

Women also continue to fight for the right to control their own bodies. Although abortion has been legal in the United States since *Roe v. Wade* in 1973 and more than two-thirds of Americans want that decision to stand (Kaiser Family Foundation [KFF], 2018a), policy changes—especially in recent years—have imposed many restrictions on women's exercise of this right. George W. Bush signed two controversial bills relating to abortion rights. The first, passed in 2003, banned late-term, so-called "partial birth" abortions. The second, passed the following year, defined a violent federal crime against a pregnant woman as two crimes—one against the woman and one against the fetus. Critics charged that by affirming that a fetus has separate rights, Congress was contradicting the underlying philosophy of *Roe v. Wade*. More recently, 21 states sued the Trump Administration over rules, temporarily blocked by the courts, that would cut federal funding from clinics that provide or discuss abortions unless they physically separate their provision of cancer screenings and other preventative health care from any abortion-related services or information.

Primarily, however, the abortion rights debate has been waged in the courts and in state legislatures. Between 1973 and 2016, states passed 1,193 state laws restricting abortion rights, including requirements for parental notification and/or counseling, restrictions on institutions' provision of abortions, and other mechanisms; more than 25 percent of these bills were passed after 2010 (Guttmacher Institute, 2016). While many of these proposals have been implemented, advocates have been successful in challenging some measures. The Supreme Court ruled in the *Whole Woman's Health v. Hellerstedt* case that a Texas law that required abortion providers to have admitting privileges at local hospitals and maintain facilities similar to surgical outpatient centers created an undue burden for women seeking abortions. The law was overturned, and the ruling was hailed as a victory for supporters of women's right to a safe, legal abortion. Louisiana's restrictive legislation met the same fate in 2019, a particularly notable ruling since it came after President Trump's two Supreme Court picks shifted the Court's overall composition to a more conservative alignment.

As state lawmakers and advocates contemplate a potential overturning of *Roe v. Wade* by this Supreme Court, state activity on abortion policy has intensified. Abortion opponents have pressed for sharp restrictions, often with an objective of creating test cases for the Supreme Court. Georgia, Kentucky, Mississippi, and Ohio passed, and several other states introduced, legislation that would ban abortion at six weeks—often before a woman would even know she was pregnant. Alabama and Missouri made abortion illegal even in cases of rape or when necessary to save a woman's life; Alabama's policy made abortion a felony, punishable by up to 99 years in prison. At the same time, more than 100 state bills expanding reproductive rights have been enacted in recent years, many related to access to contraception and equitable coverage for prenatal and maternity benefits. Officials in Vermont, Colorado, and elsewhere have sought state policies and practices to protect access to abortion, largely propelled by activism from women alarmed by the mounting threats. However, the battle over contraceptive coverage in the Affordable Care Act illustrates that even access to birth control remains a contentious policy issue. After the Trump Administration's rulings to allow employers to deny insurance coverage of contraceptives on religious or moral grounds were struck down by federal courts in early 2019, those opposed to contraception vowed to continue their efforts.

Women are much more likely than men to report severe intimate partner violence in which they are beaten, shot, threatened with a gun, or choked, with one in five women reporting such violence. In addition to the psychological toll and physical threat such violence imposes, women often face economic disadvantages that make it difficult for them to leave abusive relationships. Congressional action to provide a federal response to gender-related violence resulted in passage of the original Violence Against Women Act in 1994. We provide an overview of this legislation and its reauthorizations in 2005 and 2013 later in this chapter. For more information on violence against women and enforcement of the Violence Against Women Act, see the Office on Violence Against Women at the U.S. Department of Justice (**www.justice.gov**).

Sometimes changing societal attitudes can lead to a policy change, and sometimes new laws can create the conditions that ultimately reshape societal views. Both types of change have led to improvements in women's access to equitable opportunities. In 2013, the U.S. military announced that it would lift the ban on women serving in active combat roles. In January 2016, all military positions and occupations were opened to women. However, full inclusion does not mean fair treatment. In 2018, a military report found that sexual assault in the military had increased 38 percent since 2016; further, paralleling sexual violence in other institutions, most perpetrators were known to victims, but reporting is relatively rare (U.S. Department of Defense, 2019).

In the military and in all workplace settings, the right to be free of harassment and evaluated fairly is a civil rights issue. Sexual harassment creates a hostile working environment and can limit tenure and promotion. Many people who encounter harassment on the job either suffer through it or leave, both actions with significant potential psychological and economic consequences. For years, women endured gender-based harassment—including innuendo, unwanted sexual contact, and unfair assignment of work duties—privately, while trying individually to resist and change work cultures. Then, in 2017, after a series of high-profile exposés of sexual harassment and workplace assaults were leveled at men in politics, business, and entertainment, women used the hashtag #metoo to display their solidarity. Adopting the mantra coined in 2006 by a sexual assault survivor to empower girls and women of color who had been abused, this movement has shifted social norms and brought down powerful men whose abusive behavior was previously tolerated. It has also contributed to tangible policy change, including new anti-sexual harassment policies in many companies and in several states and localities. However, the confirmation fight over Supreme Court justice Brett Kavanaugh, after emotional testimony from a woman who alleged he had sexually assaulted her as a teenager, underscored the extent to which treatment of women remains a polarizing battleground in American society. You can find more information on protection in the workplace at the U.S. Equal Employment Opportunity Commission website (**www.eeoc.gov**).

Sexual violence on campus is a civil rights issue. Title IX of the Education Amendments of 1972 requires schools to address sex discrimination, sexual harassment, and sexual violence on campus or risk losing their federal funding. Although Title IX protects all students, women are much more likely to be victims of sexual violence, and fear of violence is more likely to limit women's access to education. Demands from advocates on and off campus pressured university administrators to address this issue, and changes enacted in the Obama Administration increased accountability and victim protection. However, policy changes in the Trump Administration have swung the pendulum back. After Education Secretary Betsy DeVos proposed new rules she said would balance the rights of those accused with those of assault survivors, the Department of Education received more than 100,000 comments (Meckler & Svrluga, 2019). Universities were concerned about new requirements to guarantee those accused a live hearing with the right to cross-examine their accusers. In many cases, institutions were also reluctant to retreat from recent efforts to change school climate, increase training, and emphasize prevention (Melnick, 2019). Survivors and their advocates were upset about the limited definition of sexual harassment and narrowing of the scope of cases requiring investigation and the university officials responsible for responding. On the other hand, parents of those accused welcomed what they saw as a correction to overreach in the previous, nonbinding, guidance, and free speech advocates celebrated loosening of prohibitions. At this crossroads on campus sexual violence policy, examine your school's record and consider how well its policies protect the civil rights of students, particularly women. For additional general information, visit **www.aclu.org/know-your-rights/title-ix-and-sexual-assault**.

The number of women in prison in the United States has increased dramatically in the past few decades—at twice the pace of men's incarceration. Most women are imprisoned for nonviolent crimes, often drug-related offenses. The effects of gender inequality, sexual violence, and motherhood must be considered if policies and programs are to be implemented to stem increasing rates of female incarceration and to improve outcomes for incarcerated women. Lack of equity for women continues to result in negative outcomes for families and children. In later chapters, when we examine issues of poverty, housing, health care, and child welfare, you will see these relationships illustrated often. If we are to effectively address social problems, civil rights issues at the intersection of age, disability and immigration statuses, race, and gender will need focused attention.

MAJOR POLICIES AND PROGRAMS

Examination of history provides ample illustration of social policies that serve to deny rather than protect the civil rights of African Americans, Native Americans, Latinx, Asian Americans, women, older adults, people with disabilities, and LGBTQ+ people, as well as some of the ways these groups have successfully exerted their rights. Now, our focus shifts to analyzing major policies and programs implemented to protect civil rights, eliminate discrimination, and help repair the damage wrought by discriminatory policies. Civil rights policies are often powerful examples of strengths-based approaches to creating the conditions in which people can overcome barriers and pursue their goals. At the same time, examining specific laws provides us with insight into what additional policies are needed to achieve further progress in civil rights.

The Civil Rights Act of 1964

The Civil Rights Act of 1964 was an omnibus bill directed against the various forms of segregation and discrimination that characterized U.S. society—particularly in the Southern states—in the 1960s. This landmark law attempted to decrease discrimination by:

- barring the unequal application of voter registration requirements;
- outlawing segregation in hotels, restaurants, theaters, and other public accommodations;
- encouraging school desegregation and authorizing the U.S. attorney general to file lawsuits against schools that resisted integration;
- empowering federal agencies to withhold funds from programs that practiced segregation; and
- creating the Equal Employment Opportunity Commission (EEOC) to oversee antidiscrimination efforts in employment.

Exhibit 7.10 summarizes the central features of the 1964 Civil Rights Act. We will use exhibits like this to (1) help you quickly grasp the major components of social policies and programs and (2) give you practice using the policy analysis framework when you are trying to understand a policy. These exhibits typically summarize original laws, and we discuss later amendments in the narrative. We do this because the original laws illustrate intent and typically are good examples of the principles that undergird policy changes. Further, if you understand the fundamentals of the initial law, it is much easier to understand the reforms reflected in amendments and reauthorization.

The Civil Rights Restoration Act of 1987, which became law despite President Reagan's veto, amended the Civil Rights Act of 1964 by strengthening enforcement of nondiscrimination laws in private institutions that receive federal funds. The Civil Rights Act of 1991 further amended the 1964 law. Designed to address a series of Supreme Court decisions that rolled back support for employees who sued over discrimination, this law is an example of how the branches of government interact in policy development. The Act strengthened federal civil rights enforcement by mandating monetary damages in cases of intentional employment discrimination and by extending protection against employment discrimination to employees of

EXHIBIT 7.10 *Civil Rights Act of 1965*	Policy goals	To remove barriers to voter registration, end discrimination in public accommodations and programs receiving federal assistance, encourage school desegregation, and establish the Equal Employment Opportunity Commission to oversee anti-discrimination efforts in the workplace.
	Benefits or services provided	Enforcement of the right to register to vote; the right to use public accommodations such as hotels, restaurants, and theaters; desegregation of schools; and the right to obtain employment.
	Eligibility rules	All people are eligible regardless of race, color, religion, or national origin. Employment protection also covers discrimination based on sex.
	Service delivery system	Mandated that places of public accommodation remove barriers by desegregating. The U.S. attorney general is authorized to file suits to enforce rights.
	Financing	Federal general revenue is used to fund enforcement.

Congress and some high-level political appointees. In addition, it extended civil rights requirements to include U.S. and U.S.-controlled employers operating abroad. Although the legislation broadened many aspects of civil rights law, it also included provisions prohibiting the use of quotas to increase representation of minority groups and placed a cap on the damages paid in cases of intentional employment discrimination and unlawful harassment.

The Voting Rights Act of 1965

By 1965, televised accounts of the murder of voting rights activists and of violent resistance from state troopers on the protest march from Selma to Montgomery, Alabama, made it clear that stronger federal intervention was necessary to overcome practices that disenfranchised African Americans. Responding to activists' demands for strong voting rights legislation, President Lyndon Johnson pressed Congress to act. This pressure—from the grassroots Civil Rights Movement and the powerful allies who leaders enlisted—led to the passage of the Voting Rights Act (Exhibit 7.11). This legislation temporarily suspended literacy tests and provided for the appointment of federal examiners with power to (1) approve or block election practices before they were implemented and (2) register qualified citizens to vote (U.S. Department of Justice, 2000). In 1964, the 24th Amendment to the Constitution had outlawed the use of poll taxes. In 1975, amendments to the Voting Rights Act added protections from voting discrimination for groups whose native language is not English.

It did not take long for the Voting Rights Act to begin to reshape the American electorate. From 1964 to 1968, the percentage of eligible Black voters who were registered rose from 23 percent to 59 percent in the Deep South states of Alabama, Georgia, Louisiana, Mississippi, and South Carolina. As the number of registered Black voters increased, so did the number of Black elected officials. Prior to 1965, fewer than 100 Black elected officials held office in those five

EXHIBIT 7.11

Voting Rights Act of 1965

Policy goals	To enforce the 15th Amendment to the Constitution, granting all citizens an equal opportunity to vote.
Benefits or services provided	Protection against the use of literacy tests or other requirements that deny or reduce voting rights.
Eligibility rules	All citizens are eligible to vote regardless of race.
Service delivery system	Federal examiners register voters and approve election practices prior to their use. The U.S. attorney general is directed to enforce the law and challenge discriminatory practices.
Financing	Federal general revenue funds enforcement.

states plus Virginia and North Carolina. By 1975, that number had risen to more than 1,000, primarily in county and municipal offices, with one Black man serving in Congress and 68 African Americans as state legislators (Hudson, 1998). In 2008 and 2012, the United States elected a Black president; 2012 was the first U.S. election in which African Americans voted at a higher rate than Whites. In 2018, women of color increased their ranks as candidates at the federal and state levels more dramatically than any other group (Reflective Democracy, 2018). Still, while people of color were 39 percent of the population in 2017, they were only 10 percent of elected officials (Reflective Democracy, 2017).

Strengths-based policy practitioners understand that voting rights are an issue themselves *and* the precondition to progress in other realms, since people who cannot exercise their right to select their own political representation have little chance to ensure that policies will reflect their priorities. Far from a relic of history, voting rights controversies still very much shape policy debates. While social workers have ample cause for overall concern about voting rights, there are some bright spots. To expand electoral opportunities, some states have expanded early voting, extended voting hours, and increased the number of polling sites. In 2018, 25 states had either introduced or implemented automatic voter registration (Anderson, 2018). However, more states have moved in the opposite direction, as depicted in Exhibit 7.12. The 2016 and 2018 elections saw record numbers of U.S. citizens whose rights to vote were suppressed by various policies and procedures. Recounts were stopped in Michigan and Pennsylvania in 2016, and the 2018 midterm election included a North Carolina congressional race that was subsequently voided when it turned out a political operative had stolen absentee ballots and employed other illegal tactics to influence the outcome. Since both election cycles featured contests decided by very small margins, it is quite possible that the retreat from robust voting rights protection altered at least some of the outcomes.

Even though there were only 31 confirmed instances of voter fraud in the United States between 2000 and 2014, out of more than a billion votes cast (Anderson, 2018), many state and federal policymakers framed "voter fraud" as a greater threat to democracy than voter suppression. President Trump claimed non-citizen voters explained his loss of the popular vote and then briefly set up a national voter fraud commission to pursue greater restrictions. Fueled by the specter of unauthorized voting, 25 states put new voting restrictions in place between 2010

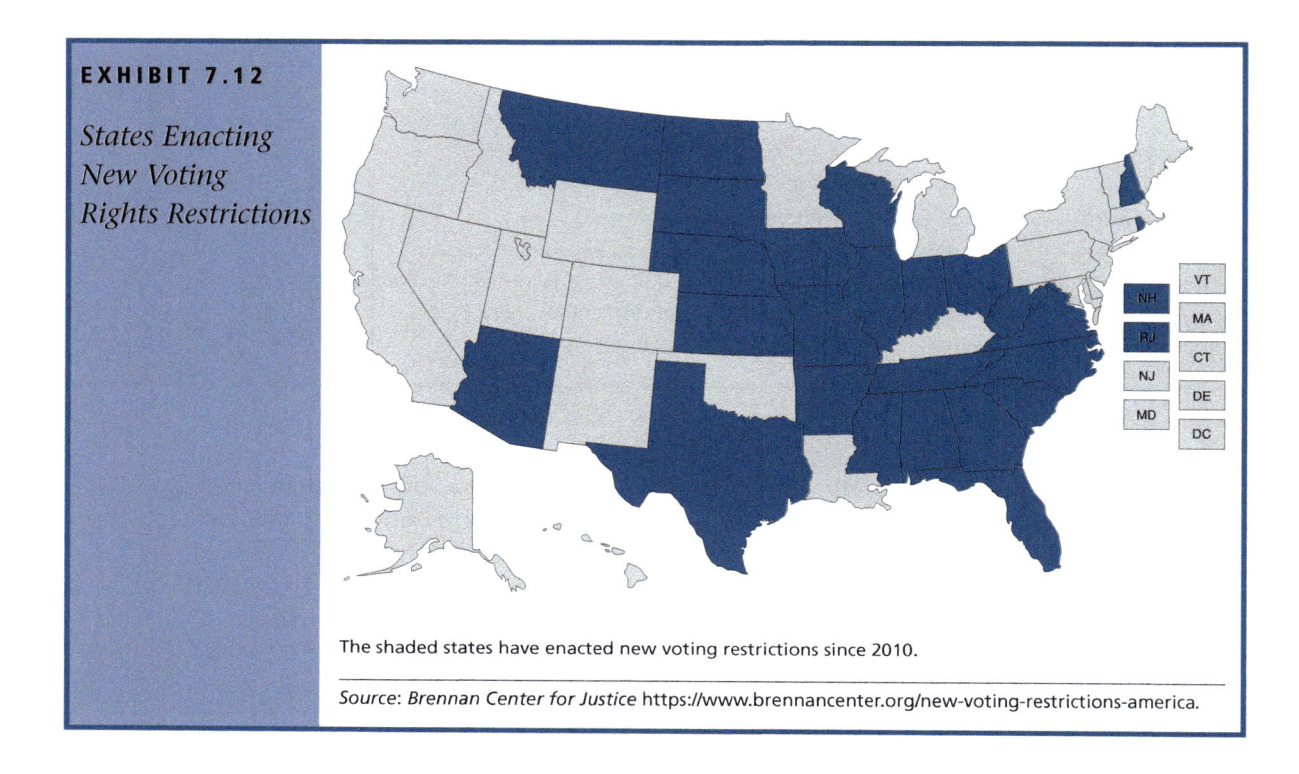

EXHIBIT 7.12

States Enacting New Voting Rights Restrictions

The shaded states have enacted new voting restrictions since 2010.

Source: Brennan Center for Justice https://www.brennancenter.org/new-voting-restrictions-america.

and 2019 (Brennan Center for Justice, 2019). Fourteen states enacted more restrictive voter identification laws, including six with strict photo ID requirements; 13 made it harder for citizens to register to vote; eight reduced early voting opportunities; and three made it harder for ex-offenders to restore their right to vote. These laws have prompted legal challenges, some of which have succeeded. The net effect, however, has been to make it significantly more difficult for citizens to exercise their constitutional right to vote, particularly when they also face barriers such as language, transportation, or inflexible work schedules. States have purged voters whose signatures are deemed not to match, who have not voted frequently, or who do not respond to mailed notice; reduced voter outreach; eliminated paper ballots that are more familiar to older voters and those less comfortable with technology; and changed polling places, often without adequate notice. In recent elections, more than one million Florida voters were removed from the rolls solely because they voted infrequently, Ohio tossed absentee ballots for spelling errors, and Michigan purged 450,000 voters mismatched in the controversial and error-prone Cross-Check system (Anderson, 2018). In the 2018 midterm election, voters in states such as Georgia and Florida alleged that mail-in ballots never arrived, voting machines malfunctioned, lines were prohibitively long, and provisional ballots were unfairly discarded. Of course, few of these injustices are novel. States have long sought to suppress the votes of certain groups. These are the practices the Voting Rights Act sought to prohibit and the injustice it sought to remedy.

In 2013, the Supreme Court struck down Arizona's Voter ID law, one of the first to require that prospective voters submit proof of citizenship when registering to vote. The ruling relied on the federal Motor Voter Act, however, not the Voting Rights Act. The court ruled that Arizona could not reject the federal voter registration form in favor of its own requirements but did not rule that requiring proof of citizenship is necessarily an undue infringement on voting rights. Immediately following the ruling, the architects of the Arizona law announced plans to push the Federal Elections Commission to require proof of citizenship on the universal federal form. In the meantime, challenges to other states' proof of citizenship and photo identification requirements continue to wind through the courts, with arguments largely centering on the extent of the hardship presented to prospective voters and states' purported interests in such measures as counters to potential voter fraud.

Also in 2013, the court handed down an even more consequential ruling for voting rights advocates in the *Shelby County v. Holder* case. At stake was whether people of color continue to face barriers to voting in states with a history of discrimination and, further, whether electoral rules in these states should continue to face additional scrutiny. The justices, in a 5–4 decision, ruled that Section 4 of the Voting Rights Act was unconstitutional. Section 4 specified a "coverage formula" to determine which states and local governments need to get approval before changing their voting laws. The court decided that nine states, mostly in the South, should no longer be required to receive advance federal approval to change their election laws. In some ways, the Voting Rights Act was a victim of its own success; because Black voter registration rates approached those of Whites, the Supreme Court ruled that the Voting Rights Act is no longer needed. Based on this decision, state voting restrictions are now subject only to "after the fact" litigation. This puts the burden of proof on those alleging discrimination instead of requiring states to affirmatively demonstrate that their proposed changes will not deprive voters of their rights. While the court left open the possibility that Congress could craft new standards by which to identify jurisdictions that still warrant additional regulation, without the substitution of new standards, this core of the Voting Rights Act is effectively void.

The consequences are already apparent. In 2016, there were 868 fewer polling places in counties previously subject to Voting Rights Act preclearance (Lopez, 2016); when polling places disappear, the change reduces turnout (Haspel & Knotts, 2005). The federal government's involvement in states' electoral processes has shifted dramatically. For example, in 2017, the Department of Justice sent letters asking states how they keep their voter rolls updated but not about efforts to expand and protect voting rights. While the 2016 election exposed vulnerabilities in the electoral process, political will has focused primarily on external threats—including foreign influence—rather than the entrenched interests that undermine the sanctity of our political process. As a result, in 2018, the Economist Intelligence Unit index classified the United States as a "flawed democracy," and 40 percent of American voters—and more than half of voters of color—doubt that U.S. elections are fair (NPR/Marist, 2018). Historically, voting rights have been at the center of our civil rights battles. It appears that this will be true in the future, as well.

Affirmative Action

A collection of agency-level policies, institutional practices, and available avenues of redress of discrimination, affirmative action evolved in the 1970s as advocates of equal opportunity became convinced that simply banning discrimination was insufficient to help marginalized groups overcome the effects of past discrimination. Often misunderstood and misrepresented, **affirmative action** is best understood as a tool for reducing discrimination in a broad spectrum of domains including, but not limited to, employment, education, and housing (NASW, 2015c). Core affirmative action strategies—proportional representation, numerical quotas, and set-asides for disadvantaged groups—have been relatively successful in securing access to opportunities previously restricted largely to White males. Nevertheless, affirmative action has always been controversial. Critics question its fairness and effectiveness and frequently refer to affirmative action as "reverse discrimination," to suggest discrimination against the dominant group arising from policies designed to overcome discrimination against oppressed groups. These reactions may be partly explained by some Whites' view of racism as "zero-sum," such that decreasing bias against Black Americans inevitably results in bias against Whites (Norton & Sommers, 2011). Resistance to affirmative action is also motivated in part by a vision of this country as one that is basically fair. From this perspective, what needs fixing are the people in marginalized groups who are not doing well, rather than the systems that influence their outcomes.

Critics have challenged affirmative action policies in the courts. In 1978, *The Regents of the University of California v. Bakke* came before the Supreme Court. Allan Bakke, a White male, had been denied admission to the medical school, even though he had a higher grade point average than some candidates of color who were admitted. The court struck down the use of strict racial quotas in school admissions, while leaving open the door to different ways of considering race in admissions criteria. When Bakke was subsequently admitted to the medical school, the decision fueled the reverse discrimination controversy.

In 2003, two major Supreme Court decisions essentially upheld the *Bakke* ruling. Both cases involved the University of Michigan. The university's College of Literature, Science, and the Arts had instituted an admissions system in which all candidates who received a rating of 100 points on a scale of 150 were accepted. In 1998, the college instituted an affirmative action program that automatically awarded 20 points to all Native American, African-American, and Latinx applicants. Two White students challenged this system as reverse discrimination. In *Gratz v. Bollinger*, the court declared the program unconstitutional. However, in *Grutter v. Bollinger*, it ruled in favor of the law school's affirmative action approach, which considers race a factor in admissions but does not employ a strict numerical system (NASW, 2009).

Significantly, the court confirmed the argument of affirmative action proponents, that promoting racial and ethnic diversity on college campuses is a legitimate strategy for achieving social justice, even while it limited some of the mechanisms institutions might employ to pursue this aim. In 2013 in *Fisher v. University of Texas*, the Supreme Court reasserted that consideration of race in admission policy must be "narrowly tailored." The justices sent the case back to the lower court, with the mandate to provide stricter scrutiny of the University of Texas's affirmative action plan. In 2016, the Supreme Court again ruled on *Fisher v. University of Texas*, sustaining the university's narrow use of racial preferences in undergraduate admissions when used to ensure a diverse student body.

The Supreme Court has also placed greater restrictions on affirmative action policies concerning employment. In the 1995 case *Adarand Constructors v. Peña*, the court invalidated a set-aside program established by the federal government that awarded special consideration to minority-owned construction firms. While affirmative action aims to create a more level playing field by remedying widespread patterns of past discrimination, the ruling specified that such an arrangement is legitimate only when people can demonstrate that they have *personally* been the victim of clearly identified acts of discrimination in the past. It further mandated that all federal affirmative action programs be subjected to "strict scrutiny," which means that there must be a demonstrated compelling government interest for the policy (Weiss, 1997).

Increasing diversity has led many people to believe that U.S. society has reached a point where we no longer need affirmative action. However, some see persistent racial and ethnic gaps in outcomes such as educational attainment and economic security as evidence that we still have a long way to go before we achieve equity; many of these individuals believe affirmative action remains essential. In this context, social workers' efforts to reveal the structural nature of disadvantage, rather than to perpetuate a view that gaps are caused exclusively by individual failings, may increase the likelihood that some institutional responses will emerge, even if their specific form changes. Some colleges and universities are promoting diversity while circumventing court-imposed restrictions by providing support based on socioeconomic status rather than on race or ethnicity, approaches that will likely assist some students of color while potentially reducing attention to racial disparities. Other institutions are taking steps to acknowledge how they historically benefited from slavery and other oppressive practices and are modifying admission, financial aid, and other policies as partial restitution for this injustice.

The federal government can influence state and local policymakers, academic institutions, corporations, and other entities by requiring them to adhere to specific stipulations as a condition for receiving federal funds. In the past, the federal government has used this power to require affirmative action to advance civil rights, particularly in the 1960s, when widespread discrimination under state rule spurred federal involvement in civil rights protection. However, the trend of return to more state control could lead to diminished support for civil rights in some parts of the country, which raises concerns about equity. Additionally, there are signs that the Trump Administration intends to focus resources of the Department of Justice's civil rights division not on equalizing the chances of groups oppressed throughout our history, but on investigating university affirmative action admissions policies deemed to discriminate against White applicants (Savage, 2017). This aligns with the goals of affirmative action opponents and signals that disputes will continue, particularly centered on access to higher education as a critical gateway to economic and political opportunity.

The Education for All Handicapped Children Act of 1975

The Education for All Handicapped Children Act of 1975 mandated that a free and appropriate public education must be made available to all children with disabilities. The law specified that education and related services should be designed to meet the unique needs of these children. The Act also required that students with disabilities be "mainstreamed"—that is, educated with their peers without disabilities to the maximum extent "appropriate," a caveat that leaves some implementation of the Act up to interpretation. The federal government was to assist states and localities so they could provide for the education of all children with disabilities. The law also mandates federal oversight to ensure the

EXHIBIT 7.13	Policy goals	To provide free and appropriate public education to all children.
Education for All Handicapped Children Act of 1975	Benefits or services provided	Special education and related services. Creation and use of an Individualized Education Plan (IEP) for each eligible child. Education in the least restrictive environment.
	Eligibility rules	Children aged 3–21 with disabilities.
	Service delivery system	Public schools provide appropriate education. Multidisciplinary teams within the public schools prepare IEPs, incorporating family and student input.
	Financing	Federal funding is provided to states to encourage public education of children with disabilities.

effectiveness of efforts to educate children with disabilities. You can examine the details of this law in Exhibit 7.13.

In 1990, this statute was amended, and its title was changed to the Individuals with Disabilities Education Act (IDEA). When the legislation was reauthorized in 2004, it became The Individuals with Disabilities Education Improvement Act. Some parts of IDEA were permanently authorized in 2004, while funding for Part C (Infants and Toddlers with Disabilities) and Part D (National Activities) was authorized through FY2011 and authorized since on a continuing basis through annual appropriations. IDEA secures the right of children to a "free and appropriate public education" by making federal funding for special education contingent upon compliance with IDEA rules and requirements. IDEA is strengths-based, in that it requires **inclusion**—that is, the education of children with disabilities in the classroom with their peers without disabilities—to the maximum extent possible. This approach reduces the stigma children with disabilities may otherwise feel and builds their capacity to succeed.

Although school districts continue to struggle to meet the mandates of this legislation, especially because IDEA has never been fully funded, its enactment significantly increased the chance that children with disabilities receive an adequate public education. IDEA has also led to new standards for teacher training and curriculum development that increase schools' ability to provide instruction that works for students' different learning styles. This is another example of how ensuring the civil rights of a disadvantaged population also has profound benefits for those outside the target population. IDEA has become a powerful tool for parents' advocacy on behalf of their children. There are ongoing bipartisan efforts to fully fund IDEA and ensure that all children receive adequate educational services. For more information, visit the Individuals with Disabilities Education Act page at the U.S. Department of Education website (**www.ed.gov**).

The Americans with Disabilities Act of 1990

The Americans with Disabilities Act (ADA) was designed to ensure full access to services and benefits for people with disabilities. The purposes of this Act are:

- To provide a clear and comprehensive national mandate for the elimination of discrimination against individuals with disabilities;

- To provide clear, strong, consistent, enforceable standards addressing discrimination against individuals with disabilities;

- To ensure that the federal government plays a central role in enforcing the standards established in this Act on behalf of individuals with disabilities; and

- To invoke the sweep of Congressional authority, including the power to enforce the 14th Amendment and to regulate commerce, to address the major areas of day-to-day discrimination faced by people with disabilities.

(Americans with Disabilities Act of 1990)

Outlined in Exhibit 7.14, the ADA embodies strengths-based policy development. There is a guiding principle in the disability community: "Nothing about us without us." In keeping with that principle, groups made up of people with disabilities worked to craft this legislation based on their goals. Those who crafted the ADA understood that because disability is a social construct, it is open to interpretation and modification (NASW, 2003). They were tireless in their efforts to secure passage of the ADA.

People with disabilities and their allies worked hard to change the discussion of disability from a focus on individual deficiencies to one that insisted that strengths, needs, and goals of

EXHIBIT 7.14

The Americans with Disabilities Act of 1990

Policy goals	To eradicate discrimination directed toward people with disabilities, increase employment opportunities, and ensure equality of opportunity and access.
Benefits or services provided	Protects the right to equal opportunity in public accommodations, employment, transportation, state and local government services, and telecommunications.
Eligibility rules	People with a physical or mental impairment that limits one or more major life activities.
Service delivery system	Businesses and employers make and pay for reasonable accommodations. Department of Justice negotiates, mediates, and files suit in cases of discrimination unless they are employment-related, in which case the Equal Employment Opportunity Commission handles the complaint.
Financing	Federal general revenue funds enforcement.

people with disabilities be center stage. Claims-making was based on appeals to social justice, equity, and the right to self-determination, all core social work values that reflect the strengths perspective. While the ADA has not ended discrimination against people with disabilities, and while enforcement remains problematic, this legislation provides a powerful example of how policy change can contribute to shifts in social norms. Because Americans now have more opportunities to experience people with disabilities as full participants in society, views are evolving to more positively and accurately recognize these individuals' strengths.

Some businesses and employers have challenged the need to comply with the ADA. Their reasons for resistance include cost and concern that people with disabilities create heightened liability risks. In these battles, courts have often sided with defendants rather than people with disabilities. However, efforts to promote voluntary compliance, coupled with a willingness to pursue mandatory compliance through the courts, have resulted in increased access to facilities and opportunities previously inaccessible for people with disabilities. The 2008 Amendments to the Americans with Disabilities Act (AADA), which broadened the definition of disability and the scope of coverage under the ADA, mitigated the effect of a series of Supreme Court decisions that more narrowly interpreted the ADA of 1990. In 2010, the federal government published final regulations for the ADA, including standards for accessible design. To learn more about work to ensure rights for people with disabilities, visit the National Disability Rights Network (**www.ndrn.org**).

The Reauthorization of the Violence Against Women Act, 2005 and 2013

Then-Senator Joe Biden, author of the Violence Against Women Act (VAWA), explained that the Act specifically names women because women are far more likely to experience intimate partner/domestic violence than men; however, "nothing in VAWA denies services, programs, funding, or assistance to male victims of violence" (cited in Brown, 2005). Enacted in 1994, the original VAWA provided funding to increase investigation and prosecution of violent crimes against women, supported education and prevention programming, increased pre-trial detention of people accused of these crimes, imposed automatic and mandatory restitution requirements on those convicted, and allowed civil redress if prosecutors leave cases unprosecuted. VAWA also created special provisions in U.S. immigration law to protect battered non-citizens, including allowing them to petition for permanent immigration status independent of abusive spouses. As such, this legislation began to address the intersections of ethnicity, class, gender, and immigration status that increase risk of violence.

The Battered Immigrant Women's Protection Act of 2000 updated the provisions of VAWA. Legislation in 2005 reauthorized VAWA funding for fiscal years 2007–2011, amended and strengthened federal criminal law pertaining to these cases, strengthened protections for immigrant victims, and created new protections for victims living in public housing. Exhibit 7.15 provides an overview of this legislation. VAWA was reauthorized in 2013 for another five years. Congress did not act on VAWA before the federal government shut down for five weeks at the end of 2018. In the resulting chaos, programs that serve domestic violence survivors feared for their clients' safety. Organizations had to cut back on services, including home visits, emergency financial assistance, and counseling. Some turned survivors away from shelters after having to

> **EXHIBIT 7.15**
>
> *The 2005 Reauthorization of the Violence Against Women Act*
>
> | | |
> |---|---|
> | Policy goals | To fund services for sexual assault victims and screening for exposure to domestic and sexual violence and to increase enforcement of protections for immigrant victims of violence. To create a health care initiative that trains professionals and medical students to recognize domestic violence. |
> | Benefits or services provided | Provides services to people who have been victims of violent crimes. |
> | Eligibility rules | Person must be a victim of a violent crime. |
> | Service delivery system | The U.S. Department of Justice oversees implementation. State and local agencies are responsible for granting services. |
> | Financing | Funded by federal grants. |

furlough staff. Hours before a deadline that would have ceased federal funding, the Department of Justice issued a temporary extension. However, although VAWA has considerable bipartisan support, its funding lapsed in February 2019 when Republicans and Democrats could not agree about whether to reauthorize the existing legislation or make changes, including increasing resources for Native American women, expanding youth prevention programming, enacting stricter gun laws for perpetrators of violence, and addressing the risks faced by transgender individuals. Advocates continue to push for long-term reauthorization, without which they face a continually uncertain future. In April 2019, the U.S. House of Representatives passed a five-year reauthorization, but, as of publication, a bipartisan push in the Senate had not yet succeeded.

The Lilly Ledbetter Fair Pay Act 2009

As described earlier, Congress passed the Lilly Ledbetter Fair Pay Act in 2009. The Act's provisions, outlined in Exhibit 7.16, clarify that pay discrimination claims "accrue" whenever an employee receives a discriminatory paycheck, when a discriminatory pay decision or practice is adopted, or when an employee becomes subject to or is otherwise affected by the decision or practice. The legislation affects pay discrimination claims made based on sex, race, national origin, age, religion, and disability.

The Matthew Shepard and James Byrd, Jr. Hate Crimes Prevention Act 2009

Matthew Shepherd and James Byrd, Jr. were both victims of hate crimes. Both were brutally murdered, and law enforcement investigators concluded that their murderers were motivated by homophobia and racism, respectively. However, the murders were not considered hate crimes under the definition at the time. The Matthew Shepard and James Byrd, Jr. Hate Crimes Prevention Act of 2009 expanded the scope of the 1968 hate crimes legislation that applied to

EXHIBIT 7.16

The Lilly Ledbetter Fair Pay Act of 2009

Policy goals	To ensure that victims of pay discrimination have an opportunity to file a claim for legal recourse.
Benefits or services provided	Guarantees and enforces the right to equal pay. No statute of limitations applies, since each paycheck restarts the option for individuals to file a lawsuit.
Eligibility rules	A person must demonstrate discrimination based on Title VII in regard to being paid less than other employees.
Service delivery system	Mandates the requirement for equal pay in the workforce. The U.S. attorney general is authorized to file lawsuits to enforce rights.
Financing	Federal general revenue funds enforcement.

EXHIBIT 7.17

The Matthew Shepard and James Byrd, Jr. Hate Crimes Prevention Act of 2009

Policy goals	To classify attacks based on sexual orientation, gender, gender identity, or disability a federal hate crime; to give federal authorities greater authority to investigate hate crimes; to broaden the scope of crimes falling under hate crimes protection.
Benefits or services provided	Provides federal assistance for the investigation and prosecution of hate crimes committed against persons because of their gender, sexual orientation, gender identity, or disability. Grants are available to law enforcement agencies that have incurred extraordinary expenses associated with the investigation and prosecution of hate crimes.
Eligibility rules	Must be a victim of a hate crime, as defined in federal statute.
Service delivery system	State and local agencies investigate and prosecute hate crimes with federal assistance; federal agencies can investigate when other agencies do not do so.
Financing	Funded federally through the Department of Justice.

people attacked because of their race, religion, or national origin to include crimes committed because of a person's gender, sexual orientation, gender identity, or disability. It also removed the prerequisite that victims be engaged in a protected activity, such as going to vote, at the time of the attack and gave federal authorities greater authority to investigate hate crimes that local authorities choose not to pursue. Exhibit 7.17 provides an overview of this legislation.

ONGOING CHALLENGES IN CIVIL RIGHTS

There is no question that the United States has made significant progress toward protecting and enhancing civil rights. Perhaps some of the most important changes have been an increased recognition of discrimination and a willingness to use a variety of strategies to end discriminatory practices. Groups that have experienced discrimination, including people of color, women, people with disabilities, and people discriminated against based on sexual orientation or gender identity, have demanded policy changes and an end to unfair treatment. They have organized and, increasingly, they are finding common cause in each other's struggles, as in the alliances between LGBTQ+ and immigrant populations and the broad-based coalitions that participated in the women's marches following the inauguration of President Trump. The successes of disadvantaged groups in changing policy and in electing individuals to represent them have reshaped the country's political and social landscapes.

However, there is much more work to do. Indeed, many of these groups feel that they have lost ground, as they face threats they had thought were vanquished forever. People actively opposed to civil rights occupy crucial positions in government and wield considerable influence in many arenas. People of color still experience discrimination, which results in disproportionately negative educational, health, and employment outcomes. These outcomes are the legacy of unjust laws in the past and of **de facto segregation**—segregation caused by social practices, political acts, or economic circumstances, not by explicit laws. The result is that disproportionate numbers of people of color continue to live in disadvantaged neighborhoods with under-resourced schools, fewer essential services, and severely limited job opportunities. Nor are people of color the only Americans to feel that civil rights are increasingly precarious. The Anti-Defamation League reported a 57 percent increase in anti-Semitic incidents in 2017—the largest increase on record and an alarming indicator of continued threat to people's fundamental civil rights (Anti-Defamation League, 2017). The number of transgender Americans killed in 2017 was the most ever recorded, and many communities report experiencing increasing levels of animosity and threat (Human Rights Watch, 2018a).

To advance civil rights and social justice, social workers must do more than oppose overt acts of repression and discrimination. We must also analyze unjust systems and construct more equitable institutions. For example, a major reason why women and people of color earn lower wages than White males is that they are still disproportionately represented in the lowest-paying jobs, sometimes termed the **secondary labor market**. These jobs, including those in childcare, housekeeping, and temporary positions, generally do not provide health insurance, and some are hazardous to workers' health, with high rates of work-related injuries. Although it is important to open more job categories to women and people of color, adequately compensating people who perform labor in any part of the economy is a crucial civil rights issue. To accomplish this goal, we need to develop methods of determining the comparable worth of jobs and strategies for enforcing comparable pay scales, and we need to help workers build the power they need to demand fair reward for their labors.

Although affirmative action has increased access for groups previously excluded from many employment and educational opportunities, it has not leveled the playing field. The recession's disproportionate impact on people of color illustrates how entrenched inequality ensures that Americans do not experience even our worst economic pains equally. Not only did people of color enter the recession behind, compared to White households, their losses were steeper and their recovery slower (McKernan et al., 2014). These disparate experiences compound generations of inequity. Further, because so many opportunities in our country—such as education, access to health care, and retirement security—hinge on one's ability to finance them, the racial wealth gap translates to patterns of deep disadvantage.

Women of color suffer from the realities of intersectionality. Women experience racism differently than men of color do, and they experience sexism differently than White women do. They are often subject to more negative outcomes than other members of either group. For example, despite being one of the most educated and civically engaged groups in the country, African-American women earn less than either African-American men or White women. If these women have a disability or are not heterosexual, they may experience discrimination in different ways. To craft effective social policy to deal with multiple sources of oppression, we must construct movements that cross divides to counter injustice however it manifests.

Enacted in the wake of the September 11, 2001 terrorist attacks, the PATRIOT Act made it possible to authorize the detention of immigrants on mere suspicion and to use secret evidence in immigration proceedings that the immigrant can neither confront nor rebut. At the same time, requirements for increased cooperation between federal, state, and local law enforcement agencies led to increased racial profiling and strained relationships between immigrants and law enforcement. While years of advocacy by organizations concerned about infringement of civil liberties led to changes in some parts of the PATRIOT Act in 2015, tensions between security, liberty, and human rights continue. The Trump Administration has threatened to withhold federal funding from any jurisdiction that does not force local law enforcement to assume immigration enforcement duties, an action so far constrained by the courts. Meanwhile, concern about the reported human rights abuses by Immigration and Customs Enforcement, Customs and Border Protection, and private contractors administering immigration detention facilities (ACLU, 2018) has led some to call for fundamental reform in the nation's immigration enforcement (Hinkle & Levinson-Waldman, 2018).

Efforts to restrict immigration have been a recurring theme in our history. However, this moment feels different to many advocates, with anti-immigrant policies and attitudes championed at the highest levels of government. Human rights violations and economic crises in other parts of the world contribute to the flow of refugees, but refugee admissions are at the lowest level in modern history. President Trump has proposed new asylum rules that impose stricter scrutiny and lengthen detention times for those fleeing violence and devastation; he has even threatened to close the U.S.–Mexico ports of entry entirely. The United States has traditionally been a pluralistic nation that benefits from new arrivals. However, instead of putting energy into integrating newcomers, crafting a workable process of naturalization, and prioritizing targeted and humane enforcement, federal might is currently deployed to keep would-be immigrants out. Strengths-based social workers recognize a need for immigration and refugee policies that (1) reaffirm the contributions immigrants have made and continue to make to this country; (2) permit the United States to respond humanely to refugees while protecting our national security; (3) celebrate linguistic and cultural diversity; and (4) support human rights (NASW, 2012a). Strengths-based immigration reform would make unification of immigrant families and protection of immigrants' rights cornerstones of national policy.

While some states and localities have made strides as places of welcoming, federal policy is mostly aimed in the opposite direction. Today, advances in immigration policy, such as the Obama Administration's Deferred Action for Childhood Arrivals (DACA) and Deferred Action for Parental Accountability (DAPA), seem to have been temporary promises, cruelly withdrawn. DACA was an executive action that provided employment authorization and protection from deportation for immigrant youth who came to the United States before they turned 16 and are either students or graduates of U.S. high schools. Nearly 690,000 students received DACA between its announcement in June 2012 and September 2017, when President Trump announced it would phase out the administrative relief. These students—commonly known as "Dreamers"—are strong advocates for further immigration reforms and possess many talents valuable to the United States. Most DACA recipients are in the labor force, and 62 percent of those not working are enrolled in school (Zong et al., 2017). Further, despite significant obstacles to educational attainment, DACA recipients are almost as likely as all U.S. adults in the same age group to be enrolled in college (Zong et al., 2017). Employment data suggest that DACA can be a means to occupational mobility and fuel for overall economic growth. Like the immigrant students for whom it was intended, DACA's fate is currently in limbo, with the U.S. Supreme Court scheduled to decide its fate in the 2019-2020 term. For now, while a federal court order has forced the U.S. Citizenship and Immigration Service to resume accepting DACA renewals, the Trump Administration's refusal to extend DACA protection to new applicants is a blow to the aspirations of a generation of promising young immigrants.

Similarly, DAPA would have prevented family separation by providing work authorization and some protection from deportation for immigrant parents with U.S. citizen or Lawful Permanent Resident children. Several states quickly challenged this executive order, and federal courts issued an injunction blocking it from going into effect. In 2016, the Supreme Court deadlocked over the legality of DAPA. In June 2017, the Department of Homeland Security rescinded DAPA entirely, leaving millions of adult immigrants as they have been stuck for years: working in the United States, hoping to realize the promises of this land of opportunity, but largely locked out.

Social workers can encounter immigrants in many settings. They need to understand these individuals' needs and have basic knowledge of immigration policy, including the protections afforded to professionals working with clients who might be undocumented. The NASW opposes "mandatory reporting of immigration status by health, mental health, social service, education, police, and other public service providers" (NASW, 2015d, p. 179). However, some policymakers have threatened to hold providers criminally liable for "harboring" unauthorized immigrants if they fail to comply with reporting obligations. Enabling everyone in the United States to meet basic needs is imperative to maintain a healthy and civil society. Toward this end, the NASW continues to work to educate policymakers about the need for comprehensive immigration reform (NASW, 2015d).

NEXT STEPS

Given the history of civil rights struggles in the United States and the challenges we face today, how can we secure and protect civil rights? The NASW Code of Ethics calls on social workers to advocate for equal rights and champion social justice for all people. Some incorrectly believe that the strengths perspective is incompatible with conflict strategies to help oppressed groups. In fact, there is a close relationship between the strengths perspective and empowerment theory, which is rooted in conflict theory. Conflict theory focuses on how individuals and groups struggle to increase their power and maximize benefits, which in turn leads to political and social change. Strengths-based and empowerment-oriented interventions both focus on client and environmental strengths and strategies, including education (transfer of knowledge and skills, often among individuals in similar circumstances), self-help, social networking, advocacy, and social action. Both approaches strongly support client participation in all aspects of decision-making that affect their lives and seek egalitarian working relationships between social workers and their clients (Chapin & Cox, 2001).

Social work's commitment to social justice encompasses work to protect civil and human rights. Human rights are broader than civil rights and include the universal right to an adequate standard of living that supports health and well-being. These rights are premised on a belief in the inherent dignity and inalienable rights of all members of the human family (NASW, 2015e). Our commitment to human rights can help guide policy practice with diverse groups. Using a human rights framework can help social workers explore how the deprivation that many groups experience demands both remedies to address underlying injustice as well as supports to help people cope. To learn more about how social workers around the world collaborate to secure human rights, go to the website of the International Federation of Social Workers (**ifsw.org**).

Work that identifies and bolsters the strengths of oppressed groups and helps them remove barriers to reaching their goals is at the heart of the strengths perspective. Indeed, the strengths perspective can be used to rethink civil rights initiatives. Rather than being viewed as a struggle where one group loses when another group gains, these efforts can be framed as capacity building, because increased opportunities enhance groups' ability to be productive, engaged participants. Decades of research have demonstrated that when groups are socially diverse, they are more innovative than homogeneous groups (Phillips, 2014). Diversity is key to success in our challenging future. In recognition of this truth, many policymakers, philanthropists, and social change champions are promoting equity agendas to inform policy development and advocacy efforts. Diversity, equity, and inclusion (DEI) initiatives in government, universities, and the corporate sector are promoted to help systems plan and establish coordinated action to foster more equitable representation and power-sharing throughout organizations. These strengths-focused initiatives offer a template for pursuing social justice in a range of settings.

Reconsidering "Neutral" Policies

Advancing civil and human rights often starts with looking at problems through a lens of critical inquiry that probes for the root causes of observed injustices. Social workers must analyze policies that, in theory, apply equally to all Americans, to determine whether, in practice, they adversely affect people from different backgrounds or identities. Policies apply to large categories of people, and individualizing policies to fit diverse needs is a complicated process. Failing to do so, however, can inflict disparate harm on some groups or leave populations out of services to which they are entitled. As an example, low-income elders with disabilities are eligible to have their long-term care paid for through Medicaid. Theoretically, Native Americans should have equal access to that benefit because Medicaid prohibits discrimination based on race or ethnicity. However, facility policies often have requirements that make them inaccessible to

Native American elders, including certain types of beds and dietary regimens. An elder raised in a traditional Native American culture may be more at ease in a bed at a lower level, surrounded by sacred objects from home, eating familiar foods. When viewed from this perspective, policies that appear to be neutral on the surface in fact create barriers that limit access or reduce service effectiveness for particular populations. Exploring this issue from a strengths perspective suggests alternative approaches that center on the experiences and needs of all affected populations. For example, nursing home regulations could incorporate traditional values of tribal caring, or tribes could receive resources to design community-based long-term care alternatives that meet their needs.

Another example of a seemingly neutral policy that disparately affects some groups is the requirement to produce proof of citizenship, such as a birth certificate, to get benefits ranging from a driver's license to Medicaid. People of color, Latinx, people living in poverty, and the very old are all less likely than more privileged groups to have a U.S. birth certificate readily available. For example, a social worker worked with a 91-year-old veteran who had been told that documentation of his 20-year history of military service was insufficient to allow him to renew the driver's license he had held for 40 years. New laws required that he submit a birth certificate to renew his license, but, because he was born at home, he never had one. Finally, his 94-year-old brother attested that he was present at the client's birth in Texas. While the requirement to produce a birth certificate appears neutral because it applies to everyone, many observers, including the Supreme Court, have acknowledged that these policies may impact some groups differently. These policies could be modified to accomplish stated policy aims with less imposition on specific groups. For example, alternative forms of documentation that prove identity might be accepted, fees to request birth certificates could be lifted when the documents are required, and practices such as presumed eligibility could provide continuous service while verification is completed.

If you look carefully at the effects of policies, you undoubtedly will find many more examples of purportedly "neutral" policies that disparately affect some groups. When policymakers are primarily White and/or male, their lived experience of **White privilege** and/or **male privilege**—societal privileges that benefit people identified as part of dominant groups—may make it more difficult for them to recognize how policies can have differentially negative effects on people who do not belong to those groups. This is not always accidental; people in powerful groups may preserve their privilege by packaging policies so that they appear neutral. It is important to educate policymakers about cultural differences and the effects of years of accumulated oppression and to help them craft more responsive and progressive policies. However, until people of color and other disadvantaged groups are much better represented among the ranks of policymakers, policymakers are unlikely to prioritize using policy to dismantle obstacles.

The Role of Social Workers

The NASW is committed to affirmative action and is working to increase diversity in the profession (NASW, 2015c). Schools of social work actively recruit students from diverse backgrounds. Many have instituted curricular approaches to help sensitize students to groups who have experienced discrimination and increased the resources provided to help students from oppressed groups overcome barriers to professional education.

Social workers must scrutinize each new piece of proposed policy for differential effects on people of different backgrounds. Further, discriminatory rules and regulations can often be changed without creating new legislation. Social workers on the front lines who are aware that certain policies perpetuate discrimination can help craft more effective and equitable rules. Typically, the more flexible the regulations, the greater the opportunity for professionals to respond to individuals' unique needs. Although greater flexibility may also lead to abuse, it is impossible to legislate for all eventualities. Rather, allowing professionals latitude and then closely monitoring for outcomes can reap more satisfactory results for client groups.

Our civil rights laws defend people who are members of **protected classes**, that is, people who are members of specified groups, including women; any group that shares a common race, religion, color, or national origin; people over 40; and people with physical or mental disabilities. However, our laws do not protect people from discrimination because they are poor or homeless or, in some cases, if they are LGBTQ+. Heterosexism and, especially, classism, have yet to be challenged sufficiently to develop a body of law that adequately protects these groups. Further, many of our age discrimination policies protect older adults but not children. For example, although older adults cannot be stripped of their basic right to self-determination without court action, we presume children are incapable of self-determination even when it is evident that they understand what is in their best interest. Finally, it is necessary to more carefully examine how the intersection of identities affects people who are members of two or more protected classes and to develop policy initiatives that address multiple and dynamic forms of discrimination. Social work advocacy for all experiencing oppression is needed if we are to develop a robust framework of civil and human rights.

It is also helpful for social workers to publicize information concerning progress toward equal opportunity in a form the public can understand. For example, the National Urban League has developed equality indices that measure disparities in financial well-being, education, health, housing, civic engagement, and social justice. Whites are used as the benchmark because, as the 2018 Equality Index explains, "the history of race in America has created advantages for Whites that continue to persist in many of the outcomes being measured" (National Urban League, 2018). The index summarizes how well African Americans and Latinx are doing compared to Whites—essentially, measuring the share of the "pie" that people of color get. The 2018 Equality Index showed essentially no change in the relative standing of African Americans to Whites on economic measures, compared to 2005, some progress in health, and a sharp drop in social justice. Latinx communities made some progress relative to Whites in all areas except civic engagement; Latinx measures of health continue to exceed those of Whites (National Urban League, 2018).

Because both public and private monitoring of outcomes are necessary for laws to achieve stated goals, social workers can advocate for more effective, comprehensive monitoring by federal and state agencies charged with enforcing civil rights legislation. These efforts should include demands for adequate funding for these agencies and the effective use of technology to foster greater transparency so that individuals with civil rights concerns can monitor enforcement. This is a particularly urgent need today, as the Department of Justice, under the Trump Administration, has instructed attorneys to back away from consent decrees in civil rights cases, instead defaulting to settlements without court oversight unless there is an unavoidable reason to require it (Huseman & Waldman, 2017). Consent decrees, which spell out the specific steps that must be taken to remedy the harm and allow further intervention if the terms are not met, have been used to ensure enforcement following settlement of a civil rights case. This shift, then, made without accompanying written policy guidance, threatens to remove a crucial tool for civil rights advocacy.

Social workers must recognize our responsibility to be involved in policy practice and to call attention to policies that lead to unequal access; otherwise, such policies and practices will continue to put disadvantaged groups at risk. Quick Guide 5 lists some questions you can use to discover inequities in settings where you practice. If you conclude that access to service is unequal, you can utilize the information in Chapter 6 to generate ideas about how you might resolve the problem. Using a solution-focused approach, what would need to change in terms of specific policies, programs, and environment for the agency to be more inclusive? Start by personally challenging and rejecting racist, classist, ageist, sexist, or heterosexist attitudes and behavior in your own life. Who you are as a person largely determines who you will be as a social worker, which in turn informs your professional stance against oppression.

QUICK GUIDE 5   Agency Analysis

Social workers need to continually monitor agency policies and practices to reduce discrimination. You can do this by taking a close look at an agency with which you are familiar. The following questions will give you a starting point for examining practices and identifying the appropriate outcomes to monitor:

- Does the agency serve a larger proportion of people from one racial or ethnic group or gender than is representative of the service area? If so, what is the rationale for this disparity?
- Where is the agency physically located? Location can create access problems for certain groups.
- Is the agency accessible to people with physical disabilities and inclusive of transgender individuals' needs?
- Do agency practices advance gender equity? For example, do employee family leave policies equitably support parents, or are women's careers hindered by birth and childcare? Are parents equitably involved in issues pertaining to their children, or are mothers presumed to carry this caregiving responsibility?
- Who works in the agency? Do the gender and ethnic compositions of workers resemble those of the population served?
- Do the gender and ethnic compositions of agency administrators and managers resemble the population served?
- Do clients whose first language is not English have access to staff who speak their preferred language?
- Does the agency attempt to build on clients' ethnic and cultural identities, or does it typically impose the identities of staff members?
- Does the agency acknowledge and effectively serve the LGBTQ+ community, including same-sex couples and families?
- Does the agency advocate to dismantle structural discrimination? What strategies are used to pursue these aims?

CONCLUSION

People of diverse backgrounds bring energy, new perspectives, and productive contributions to all areas of life. Social workers can help celebrate these differences and not allow them to be the basis for denying access to education, employment, health, or social services. The struggle for civil rights and social justice is intense and urgent. As the demographic profile of the United States becomes more diverse, barriers to equitable opportunity will make our society less capable of thriving economically and socially. We need to join with others to resist oppression and develop more effective policies to ensure that our society realizes goals consistent with social work values. The strengths perspective serves as a reminder that protecting the civil rights of disadvantaged individuals is not only a moral imperative but also a matter of national well-being. The full participation and contribution of people who represent our country's great diversity enriches us all.

MAIN POINTS

- Civil rights are legally enforceable protections afforded to individuals to prevent arbitrary abuse by the state or others. Societal barriers to accessing equal rights for oppressed groups affect outcomes such as poverty, unemployment, and educational attainment.

- The Constitution, including the Bill of Rights, is the foundation of civil rights protection in the United States. Subsequent constitutional amendments and civil rights movements of the 1950s and 1960s helped secure additional rights for oppressed groups.

- Core civil rights protections in the Constitution extend to non-citizens in the United States, except in cases where the U.S. Constitution reserves particular rights for citizens.

- Structural discrimination refers to entrenched societal practices that favor one group over another based on group characteristics such as skin color. It includes institutional oppression, whereby policies, customs, and practices produce inequities.

- Intersectionality refers to the ways in which different types of discrimination interact when, for example, a person belongs to two or more marginalized groups, as is the case for African-American women or LGBTQ+ immigrants.

- Groups such as Black Lives Matter have pressed for policy reform, including changes to police and corrections systems that have treated people of color unjustly.

- Besides having to struggle to secure citizenship and individual civil rights, Native Americans have fought for tribal sovereignty. Today, Native Americans' lives and voices give testament to their resilience, diversity, and strength.

- Both Latinx who are native-born U.S. citizens and those who are newly arrived immigrants experience structural discrimination. For a variety of reasons related to language barriers, cultural differences, xenophobia, and entrenched disadvantage, immigrant groups are especially vulnerable to civil rights violations.

- Efforts to reduce discrimination based on sexual orientation have focused on employment, housing, education, and family rights, as well as on the prevention and prosecution of hate crimes.

- In June 2015, the U.S. Supreme Court ruled that due process and equal protection afforded marriage rights to same-sex couples. This was a significant advance in civil rights.

- Rights for people who are transgender, including the right to use bathrooms that correspond to their gender identity and to serve openly in the U.S. military, are currently contested.

- People with disabilities have fought for access to services, educational and employment opportunities, and non-institutionalized care. Advances in the civil rights of those with disabilities increase these individuals' integration into society and, in turn, build the collective capacity of the nation.

- Employment discrimination and end-of-life decisions are critical arenas where older adults are seeking more protection.

- Women's rights initiatives have focused on suffrage, education, employment and pay equity, sexual and domestic violence, and reproductive freedom. While women have made substantial strides in advancing their rights and the rights of other oppressed groups, women in the United States have yet to achieve gender equity to the extent found in many other countries.

- Women who have experienced sexual assault and harassment, including in the workplace, have catalyzed a social movement to change norms regarding treatment of women.

- Affirmative action is based on the idea that steps are warranted to repair the damage wrought by past and present discrimination. It has been used as an effective tool to reduce discrimination. However, it remains controversial, and recent court rulings have limited the tools available to institutions seeking to enact affirmative relief.

- Major legislation influencing the rights of people, regardless of their race, color, religion, or national origin, includes the Civil Rights Act of 1964 as amended in 1987 and 1991 and the Voting Rights Act of 1965.

- The Education for All Handicapped Children Act of 1975 provides for free and appropriate public education for all children with disabilities. This policy and subsequent legislation requiring inclusion of students with disabilities to the greatest extent possible have increased students' opportunity for adequate public education.

- The Americans with Disabilities Act of 1990 (ADA) mandates equal opportunity, regardless of disability status, in applying for and securing access to jobs. The ADA also removed barriers to services and facilitated full integration into society.

- The Matthew Shepard and James Byrd, Jr. Hate Crimes Prevention Act of 2009 expanded the scope of 1968 hate crimes legislation to include crimes committed because of a person's gender, sexual orientation, gender identity, or disability. It also removed the prerequisite that victims be engaged in a protected activity, such as going to vote, at the time of the attack, and gave federal authorities greater authority to investigate hate crimes that local authorities choose not to pursue.

- Immigration policy is a flashpoint today. Human rights abuses on the U.S.–Mexico border and in detention facilities, proposals to further restrict asylum and immigrants' access to public benefits, and the withdrawal of executive orders that protected some immigrants from deportation have contributed to harsher political and legal contexts for immigrant communities.

- Social workers must carefully examine social policies that may appear to be neutral to ensure they do not, in fact, disadvantage some groups.

- By identifying the strengths of oppressed groups and removing barriers to goal attainment, social workers can increase social justice.

EXERCISES

1. The Sanchez family is a mixed-status family; some family members are citizens, and some are not. Visit the website for the National Immigration Law Center for information about immigrants' eligibility for federal benefits.
    a. What difficulties might the family encounter in navigating the eligibility requirements for federal safety net programs?
    b. How might the Sanchez family fare differently in different states? What agencies might you contact in your state to learn about non-citizens' eligibility for state-funded benefits and services?
    c. What barriers not related to eligibility may discourage the family from making use of benefits? Think about language differences, cultural distance, and other factors.
    d. If the Sanchez family lived in your state, what climate might they encounter? How has this climate changed in recent years? If possible, connect to a social worker or organization working with immigrants in your state to understand their perspectives on the current context.
    e. Can you suggest ways that a social worker might help the family navigate immigration laws and receive services? How would connecting the Sanchez family to services benefit their larger community?
2. Policies often violate the civil rights of people who are homeless, whether by infringing their right to vote, denying homeless children an equal right to education, or criminalizing behaviors common among those who are homeless, such as sleeping on sidewalks. Visit the websites of advocacy groups to get ideas for how to help protect the rights of people who are homeless. Learn about communities' efforts to enact homeless "Bills of Rights" to frame the needs of people experiencing homelessness as core civil rights concerns. As the social worker in the Riverton interactive case:

a. Identify three strategies you could use to help protect people in Riverton who are homeless if their civil rights are violated.
   b. Articulate the kinds of civil rights provisions on which you would rely, including specific court cases, if applicable.
   c. Discuss in small groups how communities can reconcile the civil rights of the homeless with the concerns of the community, as articulated in the Riverton case.
3. Carla Washburn receives a small pension from Social Security (OASDI). Although OASDI is available regardless of race and gender, it results in very different outcomes for different older adults.
   a. How do you think Mrs. Washburn's identities as an African American and a woman have influenced her financial security in old age? How does the intersection of these identities affect the benefits she might receive from OASDI?
   b. What can social workers do, through practice and policy advocacy, to help level the playing field for older adults like Carla Washburn?
4. As you learned earlier in the chapter, Native American tribes have pressed for recognition of their sovereign relationship with the federal government. Explain what it means to have a sovereign relationship and identify at least two implications for social policy based on your understanding of this relationship.
5. Equal rights for those who are transgender is one of the crucial frontiers in civil rights.
   a. What is the status of laws in your state regarding transgender rights, including those related to modifying the gender listed on one's birth certificate and to using a public bathroom that corresponds with one's gender identity?
   b. Consider a social work agency with which you are familiar. What are its policies regarding equitable treatment of those who are transgender? If the organization does not have any specific policies for this client group, how might you influence the policy development process?
   c. Consider the downloadable case "Willow's Transition," which your instructor can provide. What are the policy issues a social worker engaged with Willow's family should consider? How does policymaking at different levels and in different sectors—federal, state, local, and school—affect someone like Willow and the resources and tools available to a social worker supporting her?
6. Is the Black Lives Matter movement active on your campus? If so, what policy changes do they want to see? How does this agenda compare to the policy priorities of the social work profession?
   a. Identify a policy on your campus that would need to change to improve conditions for students of color. Consider the effects of "neutral" policies, including degree requirements, financial aid, and housing.
   c. Consider what steps would be needed to change the policy. Review the Action Plan template provided in Chapter 6 if you need ideas about a place to start.
7. Many colleges and universities are reviewing and reforming their policies and practices for addressing sexual harassment and assault. Find out what administrators on your campus are doing to protect students. Have these policies been changed recently? If so, what considerations guided administrators' decisions? How were students—including those who

have experienced sexual harassment or assault—included in this policymaking? Are future changes planned, including in response to prospective changes at the federal level?
   a. In your opinion, are adequate steps being taken?
   b. If not, what would you suggest?
8. Schools across the country are increasingly recognizing the damaging effects of bullying and implementing policies and programs to address this problem. LGBTQ+ youth are at increased risk of being bullied, as are students with disabilities. Find out what sorts of policies and programs your local schools have implemented to curb bullying.
   a. Are there any policies or programs aimed specifically at protecting the civil rights of LGBTQ+ youth in these schools? Has the school system assessed its culture, particularly regarding inclusion of LGBTQ+ students and faculty?
   b. In your opinion, are these policies adequate and enforceable? If not, what could you do to improve them?
9. The RAINN interactive case describes the organization's work with survivors of sexual violence. How do you think the #metoo movement has affected the work of organizations like RAINN? If possible, reach out to an organization that provides resources and support to those who have experienced sexual violence. What policies is the organization championing? What do leaders see as the effects of shifting social norms on their work with survivors of sexual violence? How has the organization navigated the effects of coverage of high-profile incidents of sexual violence on survivors, staff, and on the policy debates of which they are part?
10. The website **mappingpoliceviolence.org** maps incidents of fatalities involving police. Review some of the cases profiled, particularly those close to where you live or go to school. How would you approach the issue of police violence in communities of color from a strengths perspective? How would you assess and articulate the goals of affected groups, and what approaches would you use to advance claims that center on civil rights? How can research such as the data presented on this site play a role in this policy practice?
11. Find out what social workers and other advocates for social justice are doing in your community to protect and advance voting rights. You can start by researching the activities of the ACLU, NAACP, and/or the Mexican-American Legal Defense and Education Fund (MALDEF) in your area. How are they using litigation, legislative advocacy, and direct action to promote voting rights? Identify at least two actions you and other social work students could take to be part of these efforts.
12. Ta-Nehisi Coates' article "The Case for Reparations" includes interactive maps that illustrate how African Americans were locked out of the accumulation of property wealth. Coates asks readers to consider how policy could begin to account for the horrific costs slavery and racial terror have imposed on communities of color. Read the article and write a reflection that analyzes why you believe the United States has not reckoned with the need for reparations, what you think it would take to close racial wealth gaps, and strategies that might be used to make this case (**www.theatlantic.com/magazine/archive/2014/06/the-case-for-reparations/361631/**). You might also review online coverage of Coates' testimony in the U.S. Congress about the need for reparations, as well as policymaker and media response to these debates.

13. Investigate whether your state has made policy changes to support employment of individuals with disabilities. Conduct an online search for legislative changes, talk with policy advocates working in this arena, and/or talk with individuals with disabilities about tangible changes they have observed in (a) their access to benefits while seeking employment or (b) the availability and appropriateness of employment supports. How well do you think these efforts have balanced individuals' needs for services with their goals regarding employment and independence? What policy changes do you think would further build on the strengths of people with disabilities, and what systems would need to be involved for these changes to be realized?

NOTE

1. While this language was considered acceptable at the time, except where it refers to specific bill titles, person-first language (e.g. "people with disabilities") will be used in this text, rather than pejorative terms.

CHAPTER 8

Income- and Asset-Based Social Policies and Programs

The test of our progress is not whether we add more to the abundance of those who have much; it is whether we provide enough for those who have little.

Franklin D. Roosevelt

Economic growth without social progress lets the great majority of people remain in poverty, while a privileged few reap the benefits of rising abundance.

John F. Kennedy

SOCIAL WORKERS AROUND THE WORLD HAVE LONG concerned themselves with supporting those living in poverty and with efforts to reduce financial deprivation. In the U.S. context, too, the profession has often emphasized the needs of those in poverty and sought to raise the national consciousness of poverty and its ill effects. Today, social work students see the effects of poverty on people in communities that have always struggled to keep their families housed and fed, as well as on those who were once solidly middle class but have been buffeted more recently by the corrosive effects of rising inequality and the collapsing safety net. The specter of poverty distresses even many Americans who are not officially poor, as they fear that their own economic insecurity could send them into the ranks of the impoverished. Today, fewer Americans believe that economic well-being is within their reach (Jones, Cox, & Navarro-Rivera, 2014), and statistics on mobility bear these fears out (Chetty et al., 2016). While the chances in the United States of moving from poverty to prosperity are very limited—70 percent of those born in the bottom income quintile never even make it to the middle (Pew Charitable Trusts, 2013)—falling from the middle class is often as simple as losing a job. For too many people, "economic mobility" primarily means moving downward. Further, some families remain disadvantaged for generations. While the Great Recession exposed the fragility of many households' economic positions, poor Americans faced considerable threats to their health and security long before that crisis. They continue to face those threats today, even years after economists declared the nation's economy officially "recovered."

As the discussion of needs determination in Chapter 5 pointed out, there are many competing social constructions of the problem of poverty, only some of which are supported by

INCOME- AND ASSET-BASED POLICIES   259

research, practice wisdom, or people's lived experiences. Some assert that individuals who are poor have a distinct "culture" and that their beliefs and behaviors perpetuate their poverty. However, research has found a relationship that is largely the opposite; poverty may influence how people think and act, but these differences do not explain or cause poverty (Rauscher, 2014). Others define poverty as lack of human capital. However, while limited education makes it harder for people to leave poverty (Pew Charitable Trusts, 2012), even earning a college degree is not guaranteed protection in today's economy (DeNavas-Walt & Proctor, 2015). In keeping with our profession's commitment to social justice, many social workers point to structural explanations for poverty, including discrimination by race and gender, the capitalist arrangements that compensate people poorly for many essential jobs, and failings in the safety net that trap many people with disabilities, children, and older adults. While individual circumstances can clearly contribute to experiences of poverty, it is important to recognize the ways in which underlying forces shape these outcomes. Although differing beliefs about what causes poverty point to many strategies for overcoming the barriers people in poverty face, the most immediate concern is access to financial resources to meet their needs.

This chapter examines major government policies and programs designed to reduce poverty, as well as approaches that could help end poverty entirely. We provide tools to help you evaluate anti-poverty policies and programs using strengths-perspective principles and an intersectional lens. You are encouraged to consider policies' effects on reducing overall poverty, as well as the extent to which approaches are equitable for all groups.

DEFINITIONS OF POVERTY

It is not just beliefs about the causes of poverty that are contested; even the definition of poverty varies. A basic needs perspective views poverty as the lack of sufficient resources to fulfill basic human needs, including food, shelter, health care, and education. A capabilities perspective defines poverty as the absence of opportunities to achieve capabilities required to be sheltered, well-nourished, adequately clothed, healthy, and active (Sen, 1999). An asset view focuses on the importance of wealth, even distinct from income, for securing positive outcomes. While these perspectives each capture valuable dimensions of the experience of poverty, income is the criterion many health and social service programs use to determine eligibility. It is also the way most people think about what it means to be poor.

An income perspective on poverty deems people poor if their income falls below a specific threshold. Experts who define poverty based on income frequently distinguish between absolute and relative poverty. **Absolute poverty** refers to a system whereby the government determines an objective income threshold or **poverty line**, which is then used as a measure of who is poor. In the United States, this threshold is based on an original calculation of minimal income required to purchase food and other necessities, updated annually for inflation. If an individual's or a family's income falls below the poverty line, then that individual or family is defined as poor. If, conversely, an individual has income even one dollar above that threshold, they would not be defined as officially "poor," even though their actual well-being may be practically indistinguishable from someone who falls below the line. Policymakers typically use absolute measures of poverty as the reference point when crafting eligibility for means-tested programs.

Poverty can also be defined in relative terms. Societal standards that determine how much income is required to afford what is generally considered an adequate standard of living at a given time and place heavily influence definitions of relative poverty. This approach considers context, then, to a much greater degree than absolute poverty measures. What is considered a necessary material possession and how much income is needed to secure it varies from country to country and even among communities within a country. For example, many Americans might not consider a television to be a necessity, but perhaps all Americans would define a refrigerator as essential. In some communities, having enough money to pay for funeral services may be a cultural necessity, such that lacking these resources makes one definably "poor."

The differences in public benefit programs such as health care and housing subsidies impact whether income is sufficient to cover basic needs and further complicate comparisons of poverty rates. A given household needs to have a higher income to afford all its basic needs in a country that does not have universal health care or childcare, for example, than in one where the government provides both services as basic rights. Within a nation, individuals whose immigration status, criminal history, or other characteristics make them ineligible for public assistance might experience deprivation even with higher income than someone receiving such supports. Housing that is considered adequate by U.S. standards is different from housing considered adequate elsewhere. Within the United States, obtaining adequate housing costs far more in some urban areas—especially on the coasts—than in rural areas in the Midwest; however, as will be discussed below, the absolute threshold of poverty is the same in these different communities. One common measure of relative poverty is income less than 50 percent of the median—the point at which half of all households have a higher income and half have a lower income—in a country or political subdivision. This can result in relative poverty thresholds that vary considerably, in dollar amount, in different areas.

The Poverty Line/Poverty Threshold

The federal government uses an absolute income threshold, or poverty line, to determine who is poor. The poverty line has also been described as the *poverty index*, *poverty threshold*, or *poverty level*. Mollie Orshansky, an analyst at the Social Security Administration, initially developed the official U.S. poverty threshold in 1964. In search of a better way to measure poverty, Orshansky based this measure on a survey of American households conducted in 1955. This survey indicated that families with three or more members spent approximately one-third of their post-tax monthly income on food. Orshansky, who grew up in poverty, wanted to use one of the more generous food plans developed by the Department of Agriculture as the foundation for the threshold (Payne, 2017). However, the government selected the cheapest of four economy food plans developed as the basis and then multiplied the cost of that plan by three. Significantly, this food plan—referred to as the "Thrifty Food Plan"—outlined a diet that, while nutritionally adequate temporarily, might not be conducive to long-term nutrition and health (Fischer, 1992). Also, there is abundant evidence that families' finances are considerably different now than they were in 1955, making the poverty threshold an inaccurate barometer of economic need. For example, in 2016, the Pew Charitable Trusts found that households in the lower third of the income distribution spent more than 40 percent of their income on housing. Given increased costs for health care and transportation, these expenses have squeezed households' food budgets significantly. For today's poverty threshold to be roughly equivalent to the original, households' food budgets would need to be multiplied by a factor of eight (Payne, 2017).

The U.S. Census Bureau is responsible for measuring poverty. In 2018, the poverty threshold for a family of four with two children under the age of 18 was $25,465 (U.S. Census Bureau, 2018c). If a family's income was lower than this amount, the Bureau considered that family poor. An individual younger than age 65 with an income of $13,064 qualified as poor, whereas a person who was 65 or older and had an annual income of $12,043 was poor (U.S. Census Bureau, 2018c). In 2017, 39.7 million people in the United States—approximately 12.3 percent of the overall population—were living below the federal poverty threshold (Fontenot et al., 2018). Calculations to determine who is poor are based on pre-tax income, including financial assistance from the government, such as Social Security and Supplemental Security Income (SSI). However, the poverty line does not consider non-cash benefits such as housing subsidies and Supplemental Nutrition Assistance Program (SNAP) benefits, nor does it include a family's assets, debts, or adjustments for extraordinary expenses. Unlike earlier federal calculations of poverty levels that considered such factors as farm and non-farm residence and the gender of the head of the household, the current poverty line is adjusted only for family size and, in the case of older adults, age. Although cost of living and availability of supports varies greatly by state and local contexts, the poverty line does not take geographic location into consideration. For these and other reasons, most analysts agree that official poverty measures have many flaws. Later, we discuss initiatives to improve these measures, as well as a change proposed by the Office of Management and Budget (OMB) under the Trump Administration, which could serve to make poverty measures even less accurate reflections of people's financial realities.

Poverty Guidelines

The federal government uses the poverty threshold primarily to measure poverty for statistical purposes. The stability of the measure allows comparisons across years and can reveal patterns in poverty. In contrast, the government uses *poverty guidelines* to determine financial eligibility for many federal programs. The U.S. Department of Health and Human Services (USDHHS) publishes poverty guidelines in the *Federal Register*. Even though many social workers consider the poverty threshold much lower than the actual income needed to secure a decent standard of living, some public means-tested programs such as Medicaid and Temporary Assistance for Needy Families (TANF) require clients to fall far below this line to qualify for assistance. In 2019, the poverty guideline for a family of four was $25,750 for the 48 contiguous states and the District of Columbia, $29,620 for Hawaii, and $32,190 for Alaska (USDHHS, 2019). The poverty guideline is adjusted using the annual average Consumer Price Index (CPI). SNAP, Head Start, Special Supplemental Nutrition Program for Women, Infants, and Children (WIC), and Children's Health Insurance Programs (CHIP) are among the programs that use USDHHS poverty guidelines to determine eligibility. However, many of these programs, in recognition of the inadequacy of the measure, allow individuals to qualify with incomes that exceed the line by a specified percentage.

Alternative Poverty Measures

It is difficult to gauge the effectiveness of safety-net programs when poverty measures exclude non-cash benefits such as SNAP and refundable tax credits such as the Earned Income Tax Credit (EITC). In effect, any successes these programs have in lifting families out of poverty are ignored in the official poverty measure, even though research has revealed their substantial effects on the well-being of American families (Huang, 2015). To account for these investments and adjust for the dramatic changes in household accounting that make the current line an inaccurate representation of economic hardship, the U.S. Census Bureau now issues an alternative poverty measure along with the "official" measure (Short, 2012). While not intended to replace the official measure as the criterion for benefit eligibility, the Supplemental Poverty Measure (SPM), released for the first time in 2011, attempts to determine the extent to which incorporating expenses such as taxes, child care, and health insurance, as well as benefits such as subsidized housing and nutrition supports, alters poverty statistics. In 2017, the overall SPM rate was 13.9 percent (Fox, 2018). The SPM also provides different thresholds based on whether households rent or own their homes, given often-dramatic differences in housing cost burdens based on ownership status. Although it uses a different formula, the Supplemental Poverty Measure still defines poverty in absolute terms; those whose incomes fall below this line are "poor," while those who earn above the line are not.

While alternative measures of poverty have distinct advantages, the prospect of shifting to an entirely new poverty measure raises both political and practical concerns. A change would complicate comparison of poverty statistics from different time periods. Furthermore, many policymakers fear that using a more realistic poverty threshold could produce significant increases in poverty rates. Regulatory changes sought by the Trump Administration threaten to make official poverty guidelines less accurate measures of Americans' economic positions. In 2019, OMB proposed using the chained Consumer Price Index—rather than the overall CPI—for annual inflation adjustment, a change the administration acknowledged would lower the poverty guidelines and, then, may result in many Americans losing their eligibility for programs such as Medicaid, SNAP, and Head Start. This effort—and the alarm it provoked among social workers and others who work with people in poverty—illustrates the extent to which defining and measuring poverty is itself contested. To find out more about poverty and how it is studied, explore the website of the Institute for Research on Poverty (**www.irp.wisc.edu**).

INCOME-SUPPORT POLICIES AND PROGRAMS

Unlike many other developed countries, the United States does not have policies that guarantee a minimum income for each child, a basic income for childless adults, or paid family leave for caregivers. Instead, we have enacted policies to provide a patchwork of income supports. Some U.S. antipoverty programs require prior attachment to the workforce as a condition of eligibility. Others are available only to low-income citizens, or certain qualified resident immigrants, who meet some additional criteria such as disability or having children in the family. Most are designed to provide only short-term assistance and to relieve only the most severe deprivation, rather than to provide long-term financial support adequate to meet a household's needs.

INCOME- AND ASSET-BASED POLICIES   263

Income-support programs are categorized as either universal or selective. Although all have eligibility requirements, the government provides universal programs to eligible individuals regardless of income, whereas selective programs are typically means-tested and designed for people in poverty (Blau & Abramovitz, 2007). Some programs are entitlements, meaning that the government has a legal obligation to provide benefits to all who meet eligibility requirements. Some entitlement programs, such as unemployment insurance and Old-Age, Survivors, and Disability Insurance (OASDI), are universal and provide benefits to a broad category of people. To be eligible, individuals must prove sufficient qualifying periods of attachment to the workforce, but eligibility is not tied to demonstrated financial need. Veterans' benefits, for example, are an entitlement based on prior military service. Other entitlement programs, including SNAP, SSI, and the EITC, are selective and means-tested. Individuals can become ineligible for these benefits if their financial situations change so that they are no longer poor enough to qualify.

Many of the programs that serve people in poverty are not entitlements. These programs include TANF, WIC, the Elder Nutrition Program under the Older Americans Act, and public housing. People who apply and are eligible might not receive the benefits and services they need from these programs, depending on federal and state budgetary constraints. In some cases, there are additional requirements people must meet to receive or maintain these selective benefits, such as working a certain number of hours or keeping their apartment clean. These rules are used to influence individuals' behavior and to ration scarce resources.

UNIVERSAL PROGRAMS

In this section, we consider universal programs designed to provide income in the face of predictable events, such as old age, and unpredictable events, including disability that interferes with ability to work. In addition to providing crucial, direct assistance to those in need, these programs help stabilize the economy, because beneficiaries typically spend income provided right away on necessities such as food, clothing, shelter, and health care.

Old-Age, Survivors, and Disability Insurance: How It Benefits Both the Young and Old

As described in Chapter 3, the Social Security Act established several major income-support programs, including unemployment compensation and financial assistance for aged and blind individuals and dependent children. Nevertheless, as popularly used, the term *Social Security* generally refers to Old-Age, Survivors, and Disability Insurance (OASDI). Congress established OASDI to provide pensions to covered workers and their families when income is lost due to retirement, old age, or disability. Workers do not automatically qualify for OASDI. To receive a retirement benefit, they must work in jobs covered by OASDI and pay into the program for a requisite period during their working lives.

OASDI is more than a retirement program. It is also an insurance program that benefits young people. More than one in four of today's 20-year-olds will become disabled before reaching age 67, the current age at which they can begin to receive full retirement benefits. For most young people, OASDI provides the only long-term disability insurance they will ever have. Disabled workers and their dependents account for about 20 percent of total benefits OASDI pays (Social Security Administration [SSA], 2018a). Additionally, many children receive survivor benefits due to the death of a parent.

Currently, 88 percent of U.S. workers aged 20 or older are fully insured through the Social Security system. Almost 62 million people—almost 19 percent of the U.S. population—received OASDI benefits in 2017. OASDI has two parts: one for workers who have retired and one for those who become disabled prior to retirement. Exhibit 8.1 illustrates the increases in awards to retired and disabled workers. You can see that as the oldest of the Baby Boomers—people born between 1946 and 1964—began to reach retirement age, awards to retired workers rose. Other economic, demographic, and social factors, including medical advances that have allowed people to survive conditions that previously could have resulted in premature death, increases in obesity and opioid addiction, and structural shifts that have altered regional economies, have also contributed to disability rates. The spike in disability benefits during the Great Recession was partly due to the relatively weak economy. As jobs disappeared in many communities, workers with disabilities struggled to adjust and applied for disability insurance when they found themselves unable to work at any available job. This trend helps to explain the decline in growth in the past few years, as the economy has largely stabilized. Notably, the 2019 OASDI trustees report extended the date when the disability insurance trust fund is expected to run out by 20 years—to 2052 (SSA, 2019a). Officials attributed the improving finances to a variety of forces, including the strengthening economy; broader access to health care, particularly due to the Affordable Care Act; and a 2015 congressional action to reallocate a small percent of taxes from Social Security's OASI fund to its disability insurance fund. This reversal in fortunes

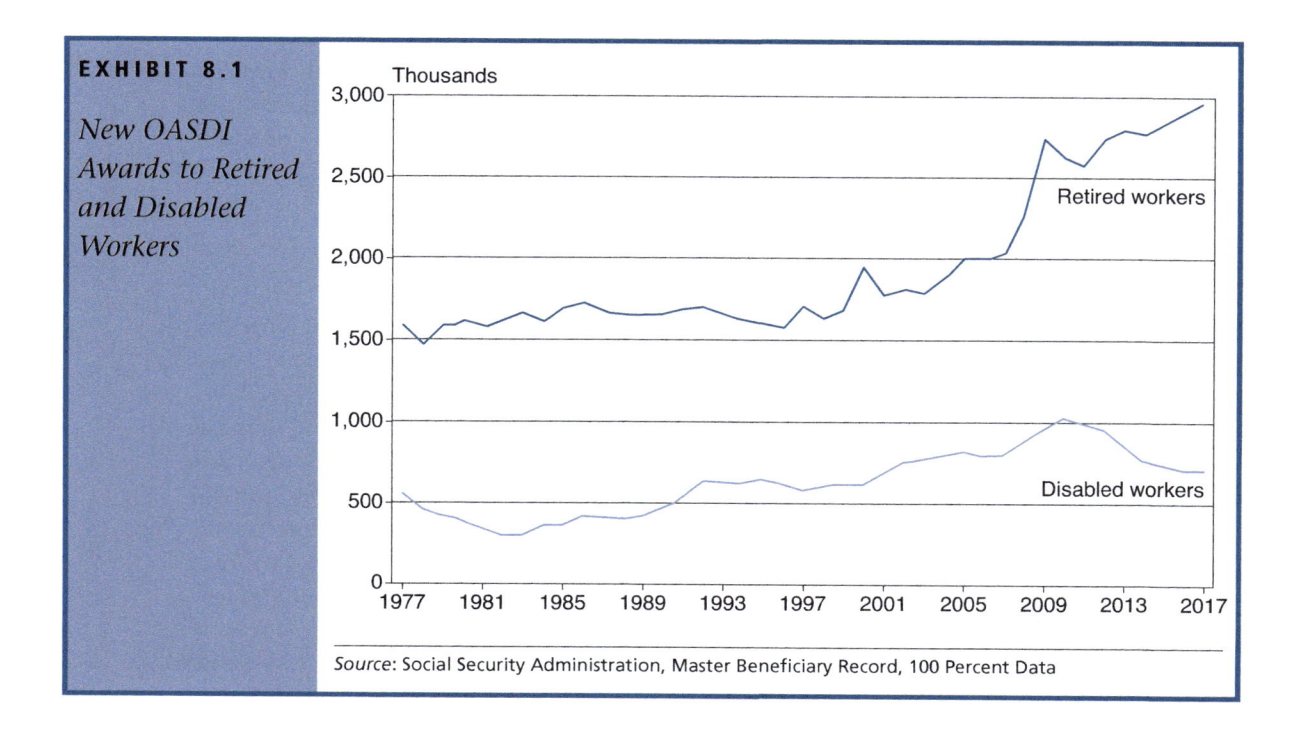

EXHIBIT 8.1

New OASDI Awards to Retired and Disabled Workers

Source: Social Security Administration, Master Beneficiary Record, 100 Percent Data

underscores interactions in different policy arenas and illustrates how policy changes can alter trends—sometimes in dramatic ways.

Eligibility for OASDI benefits is dependent on age or disability and earned work credits. For example, to be eligible for old-age retirement pensions, in general, a person must complete 40 credits of work. A covered worker can earn four credits each year by working for at least a threshold amount of wages (SSA, 2013). In 2018, a worker earned one credit for every $1,320 in earnings, up to a maximum of four credits per year (requiring $5,280 in earnings). Once people earn the requisite number of credits, they become eligible for early retirement benefits at age 62. Early retirees receive a lower monthly pension—for some, up to 30 percent lower than if they waited to their full retirement age. People born before 1938 are eligible for full Social Security benefits at the age of 65. However, beginning in 2003, the age at which full benefits are payable increased in gradual steps from 65 to 67 (SSA, 2018b). People born after 1959 are not eligible to receive full benefits until age 67. Some experts advocate moving the age of eligibility even higher as life expectancy increases; however, such changes would disproportionately disadvantage some people of color and others whose life expectancies are shorter than the national average. Currently, if a person voluntarily elects to delay retirement until age 70, their benefits increase for each month OASDI payments are postponed. Eligibility for survivor and disability benefits requires fewer credits when death or disability occurs at a younger age.

Beneficiaries receive payments via direct deposit into a checking or savings account or through a debit card. In 2017, the average monthly Social Security benefit for a retired worker was about $1,404 (SSA, 2018a). The actual benefit amount varies widely based on length and amount of employee contribution. As a result, there are substantial differences in average benefits by gender; retired women received an average of $1,244 per month in OASDI retirement, compared to $1,545 for men (SSA, 2018a). Beneficiaries with disabilities received average monthly payments of $1,197; those with a spouse and one child who is under the age of 16 or disabled received $1,898. While each additional child of a disabled or deceased worker receives an average of $366 or $858 per month, respectively, there is no minimum amount that all eligible workers or their families must receive.

Payments are processed through the U.S. Treasury Department, and the administrative costs associated with providing OASDI are low. While people are in the labor force, their earnings are taxed to pay for Social Security benefits for those who have already retired. Both employers and employees pay the FICA tax up to a certain maximum income. In 2018, employers and employees each paid 6.2 percent of an employee's gross income in FICA taxes, for a total of 12.4 percent. Social Security payroll taxes are collected under the authority of the Federal Insurance Contributions Act (FICA) and listed on pay receipts as FICA. When the government collects more taxes than it needs to pay benefits in a given year, the surplus is invested in U.S. Treasury Bonds. Decades ago, when the ratio of workers to retirees grew with the entrance of the Baby Boom generation and unprecedented numbers of women, the Social Security surplus swelled. Today, that accumulated surplus is crucial to keeping the system solvent. However, in recent years, cash flow into the fund has been less than expenditures for a variety of reasons, including the growth in the older adult population. Large numbers of older workers lost jobs and took early retirement during the Great Recession. Other workers contributed less during the recession as their wages declined or they spent periods out of work. In 2017, there were about 2.8 workers for every Social

EXHIBIT 8.2 *Old Age, Survivors, and Disability Insurance (OASDI), 1935*	Policy goals	To protect workers and their families from loss of income due to retirement, disability, or death.
	Benefits or services provided	Monthly payments.
	Eligibility rules	Determined by age, disability, or death; payment of payroll taxes; and satisfaction of work credit requirements.
	Service delivery system	Social Security Administration offices determine eligibility and send funds by check via U.S. mail or by electronic bank transfer.
	Financing	Payroll taxes (insurance premiums) paid by employees and their employers.

Security beneficiary; this ratio is expected to decline gradually to 2.2 by 2033. Other variables could intervene to shift this equation, including changes in immigration policy or birthrates, economic cycles, OASDI policy changes (in retirement age, benefit amounts, or eligibility criteria), and long-term trends in lifespan and health. Crucially, however, this accounting does not mean the system is insolvent. Indeed, OASDI still has large surpluses.

OASDI's fiscal and political success depends in part on its structure as a social insurance program, where the government provides the institution through which people share the risks and rewards associated with participation in a capitalist economy. As proposals to reform OASDI are debated, then, social workers should be wary of changes that would undermine this insurance principle. As history has illustrated, universal programs that are designed on the insurance principle and cover a wide constituency across income levels are much less likely to be cut than means-tested programs designed for people in poverty. Exhibit 8.2 above summarizes OASDI using the analysis framework. The date shown in the exhibit is the year when the original legislation was passed. For more detailed information on Social Security, go to Social Security Online (**www.ssa.gov**).

Unemployment Insurance

Unemployment insurance serves two primary functions: (1) it ensures that unemployed workers receive minimal cash assistance, allowing them to meet basic needs such as housing, food, and clothing; and (2) it helps shore up the economy during periods of high unemployment. As such, unemployment insurance is both a stabilizing force in the economy and a protection for workers whose well-being is largely dependent on labor market outcomes over which they have little control. Approximately 97 percent of all permanent wage and salary workers are covered by unemployment insurance. When economic cycles push more people out of work, demands on unemployment insurance and other counter cyclical programs rise. In March 2019, more than 1.7 million unemployed workers received unemployment insurance benefits (U.S. Department of Labor, 2019), but a record 20 million Americans received unemployment insurance in 2009, as the unemployment rate rose to 10 percent and the nation grappled with deep and lasting recession.

Eligibility for unemployment insurance benefits is based on attachment to the labor force, which is determined by examining wages earned and weeks worked. Benefits are intended for people who are unemployed due to external circumstances—rather than those who were fired for cause—and who will continue to actively seek work. Beneficiaries also must be able and willing to work if an appropriate job becomes available. These latter requirements become particularly significant during recessions or labor restructurings, when many Americans become frustrated with their long job searches and then stop seeking work. As the economy changes, including with the proliferation of low-wage jobs and advances in automation, a growing number of people—particularly men—in their prime working years are dropping out of the labor market entirely. In 2016, more than seven million American men aged 25 to 54 were not working but not defined as unemployed (Tuzeman, 2018). Analysts believe that polarization in the labor market may keep many of these men out of work indefinitely, a prospect that raises important questions about future economic growth and the adequacy of the current unemployment insurance system.

Unemployment insurance is unique in that it is the only universal program created by individual states with federal oversight. Individual states design the program's benefit and tax structures, within parameters allowed by the U.S. Department of Labor. This arrangement causes variations in eligibility and benefits, across states. In 2018, maximum weekly unemployment benefits ranged from a high of $795 per week in Massachusetts to a low of only $235 per week in Mississippi. However, the actual benefit received depends on the worker's previous earnings. In all but three states, unemployment insurance is funded entirely by taxes on employers. The remaining three states tax employees as well. Both the states and the federal government collect these taxes, and companies that comply with state requirements are eligible for substantial tax credits (U.S. Department of Labor, 2012). During periods of economic growth, taxes are collected and saved for times when larger numbers of workers become unemployed. Most states pay benefits for up to 26 weeks, although four states provide less and two states—Montana and Massachusetts—provide more. Five states adjust the duration of unemployment insurance as the state unemployment rate changes. You can find information on unemployment insurance at your state government website. In times of economic crisis, the federal government has stepped in to provide additional funding to protect and extend benefits in states with high unemployment. For example, the American Recovery and Reinvestment Act, passed in 2009, allowed some people in states with high unemployment rates to receive up to 99 weeks of benefits.

Even if they are trying to find a job, many Americans who are out of work do not qualify for unemployment insurance. They include part-time, temporary, and self-employed workers, as well as those who work in the informal economy, such as many domestic workers and independent contractors. Additionally, many people become ineligible for unemployment insurance before they find a job. Even as the unemployment rate hits a 50-year low, unemployed Americans have more trouble finding a job than in previous economic cycles, and their chances deteriorate the longer they stay out of work (Nunn, Parsons, & Shambaugh, 2019b). Only a fraction of the 6.2 million Americans counted as unemployed in January 2019 received unemployment insurance. Advocates have analyzed the current structure of the labor market and

> **EXHIBIT 8.3**
>
> *Unemployment Insurance, 1935*
>
> | | |
> |---|---|
> | Policy goals | To provide income to meet basic needs for workers who have lost jobs and to stabilize the economy by encouraging spending. |
> | Benefits or services provided | In most states, cash assistance for up to 26 weeks. |
> | Eligibility rules | Workers must be unemployed due to no fault of their own and must meet requirements of wages earned and weeks worked in the past year. They also must actively seek work. |
> | Service delivery system | State agencies determine eligibility. Claims are filed weekly or biweekly. |
> | Financing | Funded primarily by taxes on employers. |

how it exposes workers to the insecurities that systems such as unemployment insurance were designed to counter; many have called for substantial changes to better meet the needs of workers in the non-traditional arrangements that increasingly typify "employment" in the modern "gig economy" (McKay, Pollack, & Fitzpayne, 2018). Exhibit 8.3 above summarizes the features of the unemployment insurance program as it exists today.

Workers' Compensation

Workers' compensation was the first social insurance program in the United States. In 1908, Congress enacted a workers' compensation program for federal employees, and states soon began enacting their own programs. The federal program—which, like unemployment insurance, is funded by employers—provides some protection for workers injured on the job and survivors of those killed at work. In addition to paying for medical care to treat the injury, workers' compensation provides cash to ensure that people are not without income due to work-related injuries. Benefit levels vary by state; however, most states pay recipients two-thirds of weekly earnings at the time of injury. The duration of payments depends on whether the resulting disability is temporary or permanent. Surviving spouses of deceased workers receive burial expenses and payments until they remarry, and children receive benefits until an age set by the state. The workers' compensation program can be very difficult for an injured worker to navigate. Social workers, attorneys specializing in workers' compensation, and other professionals might need to become involved to successfully press a claim. Exhibit 8.4 provides an overview of the workers' compensation system, through the lens of the analysis framework.

Workers' compensation covers most of the nation's wage and salary workers. In general, people are eligible for benefits regardless of fault for the accident. The major exceptions to this rule are their gross negligence, willful misconduct, or intoxication while working. Private employers purchase policies through insurance companies, which distribute benefits following an injury. State and federal statutes govern these insurance companies. In most cases, the state organizes the

> **EXHIBIT 8.4**
>
> *Workers' Compensation, 1908*
>
> | | |
> |---|---|
> | Policy goals | To protect workers against the effects of occupational injuries and to compensate families of those injured or killed at work. |
> | Benefits or services provided | Cash and medical assistance. |
> | Eligibility rules | Workers must be injured or killed on the job in accidents unrelated to their own intoxication, gross negligence, or willful misconduct. |
> | Service delivery system | States organize programs under federal legislation. Insurance companies receive claims and award benefits. |
> | Financing | Employers purchase policies from insurance companies. |

delivery system. Businesses pay premiums based on company size, level of risk to employees, and experience rating. The way claims are handled varies greatly by state. Workers who are encouraged to settle for lump-sum payments often find that these funds do not equal their lost wages. Further, many workers experience long delays between the time of injury and the time benefits begin. To find out more about workers' compensation in your state, go to the U.S. Department of Labor website and search for Workers' Compensation. You will find a link to your state's workers' compensation board.

Veterans' Benefits

Veterans' benefits include pensions and disability compensation. Disability compensation provides income for those with disabilities that resulted from or were exacerbated by military service, while veterans' pensions are for low-income veterans and their surviving spouses. Veterans can receive the greater of these two benefits, but not both. These benefits are intended to restore veterans' capabilities to the greatest extent possible and to improve the quality of their lives and the lives of their families. In 2018, 4.7 million veterans received disability compensation, with an average annual award of $14,862; an additional 273,000 received an average of $12,006 in pension benefits (Congressional Budget Office [CBO], 2018b). These recipients represent approximately a quarter of the U.S. veteran population (U.S. Census Bureau, 2018a). The number of veterans receiving disability and pension payments has risen substantially in recent years, particularly following U.S. engagement in military conflicts in Afghanistan and Iraq. The need for social workers to serve veterans and assist them in navigating available resources is increasing.

To be eligible for veterans' benefits, an individual must meet minimum service requirements and have received an honorable or general discharge from active military service. The level of disability compensation a veteran receives depends on the degree of disability, ranging from monthly payments of $140 to $3,057 for a sole veteran. The payments can be even greater depending on the veteran's marital status and number of children (U.S. Department of Veterans' Affairs, 2018a). While disability compensation depends primarily on the extent of disability, veterans' pensions are means-tested benefits paid to low-income veterans with a permanent and total disability unconnected to their service or to low-income veterans age 65 or older regardless of physical condition (U.S. Department of Veterans' Affairs, 2013). Veterans' benefits are financed primarily through federal general revenues, with some military personnel making co-payments, and are administered through the Compensation and Pension Service, a division of the Department of Veterans' Affairs (VA). While the benefits and eligibility qualifications are complex and too varied to present in a summary table, you can go to the website for the Department of Veterans' Affairs for more information.

SELECTIVE PROGRAMS

In 2017, 12.8 million children (persons under 18) were growing up in poverty. That's a child poverty rate of 17.5 percent. Children living in female-headed single-parent households had a poverty rate of 40.8 percent, almost five times the rate of children in married-couple families (8.4 percent) (Fontenot et al., 2018). Driven by economic conditions, demographics, and other social forces, child poverty rates vary greatly from state to state. In Louisiana, the state with the highest proportion of children in poverty in 2017, 28 percent of children were poor. In New Mexico and Mississippi, the rate of childhood poverty was approximately 27 percent, and in West Virginia it was 26 percent. New Hampshire, Utah, and North Dakota had the lowest childhood poverty rates in 2017—still unacceptable at between 10 and 11 percent (Children's Defense Fund, 2018).

Being a child is not the only characteristic that increases one's risk of experiencing poverty. Poverty rates are also much higher in communities of color than in communities largely comprised of non-Latinx Whites. In 2017, the poverty rate for all African Americans was 21.2 percent. The poverty rate for Latinx was 18.3 percent. In contrast, the poverty rate for non-Latinx White people was 10.7 percent. Not only are some groups far more likely to be poor, the experiences of those officially in poverty can be quite different. Although the poverty line defines poverty absolutely, social workers understand that life close to or far below the poverty line may feel very differently to those positioned there. In 2017, 5.7 percent of all Americans, including 3.2 percent of those aged 65 and older, lived in deep poverty, defined as having an income less than half the poverty threshold (U.S. Census Bureau, 2018d).

While patterns of poverty, particularly by race and gender, are entrenched in social and economic structures of inequality, for many people, poverty is a temporary experience—and far more prevalent than many Americans believe. Social worker and scholar Mark Rank and his colleagues have studied lifetime risk of poverty to expose the predictable risks to which most people are vulnerable and highlight disparities in chances of experiencing poverty. This research found that by age 60, more than 60 percent of the American population will have experienced at least a year of poverty in adulthood (Rank & Hirschl, 2015). When childhood poverty is considered as well, it becomes increasingly difficult for most Americans to avoid poverty entirely. You can calculate your own poverty risk using the Poverty Risk Calculator, which accounts for factors that influence the experience of poverty, such as age, race, gender, education, and marital status (**https://confrontingpoverty.org/poverty-risk-calculator/**).

Informed by the ecological perspective, social workers understand that poverty risk depends on context as much as individuals' intrinsic characteristics. In particular, educational deficits, mismatch between where jobs are located and where people live, lack of public transportation, persistent discrimination, and global economic shifts present structural barriers that prevent many in disadvantaged populations from experiencing economic mobility. New analysis by the U.S. Census Bureau and academic researchers maps earnings based on the neighborhood where someone grows up, to identify characteristics of places that either facilitate or hinder prosperity. You can explore outcomes for those who grew up where you did or where you live now using the Opportunity Atlas (**www.opportunityatlas.org**). Overall, data reveal that while poverty is more pervasive than many realize, some populations are at far greater risk than others.

Women of every demographic and in every geography are overrepresented among the poor. Although more than 58 percent of working-age women are in the labor force, they are disproportionately represented in low-paying jobs with few benefits. They are often expected to balance the demands of unpaid caregiving with paid employment, a tension that disadvantages them as workers and results in higher levels of stress. These strains are particularly great for single mothers in poverty, for whom there is now very little public assistance. While the public generally supports a mother's decision to stay at home to care for children when the family can provide the necessary income, single mothers in poverty have very little safety net to meet their needs for income or childcare—let alone both.

As social norms surrounding women's "proper" roles in the workforce have changed significantly over time, public policy aimed at improving the economic situations of women and their children increasingly emphasizes work as the ladder to upward mobility. Nonetheless, analysis indicates that mothers transitioning from public assistance work predominantly in low-paying jobs that seldom allow them to move out of poverty. As they attempt to exit means-tested aid, these mothers face many of the same barriers that necessitated their reliance on income support in the first place. For these families and millions of poor people in the United States, work—at the jobs available to them in today's economy—is insufficient to meet essential needs.

Temporary Assistance for Needy Families

The Social Security Act established the federal cash public assistance program Aid to Families with Dependent Children (AFDC, originally Aid to Dependent Children) as an entitlement. However, the 1996 TANF legislation eliminated the individual entitlement to cash assistance. Formerly, under AFDC, states were required to aid all families that met eligibility requirements. The federal government funded at least half of AFDC benefit costs, so federal welfare spending increased as AFDC caseloads rose. In contrast, TANF is a block grant that allows each state to determine under what circumstances it will provide cash assistance to poor families. In exchange for assuming responsibility for "welfare," states are no longer required to assist any individual or family (Committee on Ways and Means, 2000). States get a lump-sum payment that represents roughly what they received for AFDC and related services in 1994 and have a "maintenance of effort" (MOE) requirement to continue to spend each year at a level equal to at least 75 to 80 percent of what they spent on AFDC and related services in 1994 (Committee on Ways and Means, 2000).

States do not have absolute control over TANF regulations. They must meet some federal stipulations, including work requirements and a cumulative five-year limit on cash assistance using federal funds. States can enact rules stricter than the federal government's recommendations. For example, Kansas, Arkansas, and Connecticut all have two-year lifetime TANF limits, and Arizona limits recipients to only 12 months of aid. Time limits in 21 states are four years or less (Council on State Governments, 2016). Further, the TANF block grant is now an attractive revenue source for filling funding gaps for a variety of state programs. States have reduced TANF spending to divert funds to other purposes, including child welfare investigations, state Earned Income Tax Credits, early childhood education, and even state expenditures far afield of poor children's interests. In Michigan, for example, TANF funds have been used to provide scholarships to expensive private colleges for upper middle-class students, with the rationale that higher education helps to prevent and reduce the incidence of out-of-wedlock pregnancies, one of the four purposes of TANF (Clark, Esch, & Delvac, 2016).

History and Development of TANF The debates leading up to the passage of TANF illustrate the role that historical, economic, social, and political contexts play in shaping policy. Few of the themes that emerged during the welfare reform debate of the 1990s were new. Ideological conflict about the morality of single motherhood, "deserving" versus "undeserving" poor people, and race have historical roots. Even the elements of TANF policy that were presented as novel were not. Low benefit levels in AFDC meant that many recipients already engaged in paid labor to provide more adequately for their families, a fact obscured by the debate over work versus "dependence" (Abramovitz, 1996).

As the number of families receiving AFDC benefits rose in the 1970s, policymakers' focus increasingly shifted to moving recipients into paid work. Growing political support for strict work requirements, even for mothers with very young children, coincided with societal shifts toward greater participation of middle- and upper-income women in the workforce. Working outside the home and being the only parent handling childcare and household tasks—as is the case for TANF recipients, who are disproportionately single mothers—is a monumental undertaking. These challenges are particularly acute if the parent lacks advanced education and cannot compete for highly compensated employment with which to purchase additional support. Children of working mothers can thrive if they have high-quality childcare and plenty of parental involvement, but these inputs are not within reach of most TANF recipients. Further complicating the precarious existence of low-income families, some states have passed policies that seek to prevent those struggling with addiction from receiving TANF, while, in other cases, rules that require frequent reverification of eligibility and/or invoke complicated sanctions may make it difficult for families in crisis to comply with program regulations. State laws prohibit use of TANF benefits in certain businesses or for certain goods or services; in many cases, the penalty for violating these rules may include permanent sanction for the entire family.

TANF Goals Section 401(a) of the Social Security Act states that the purpose of TANF is to give states more flexibility in operating a program that is intended to serve the following purposes:

- Provide assistance to needy families so that children may be cared for in their own homes or in the homes of relatives.

- End dependence on government benefits by promoting job preparation, work, and marriage for needy parents.

- Prevent and reduce the incidence of out-of-wedlock pregnancies.
- Encourage the formation and maintenance of two-parent families.

(Committee on Ways and Means, 2000)

Family Formation Goals As we have seen, one stated goal of TANF is to reduce the number of out-of-wedlock pregnancies by promoting marriage. In 2005, Congress reauthorized TANF with a renewed focus on strengthening families through the promotion of responsible fatherhood and healthy marriages. TANF reauthorization gave states more flexibility to assist two-parent families. While this priority emerged in a period of conservative Congressional control, such family formation initiatives have some bipartisan appeal. President Obama took special interest in programs to promote responsible fatherhood. During his tenure, programs designed to strengthen fatherhood, including in families where parents are or have been incarcerated, were implemented. A rigorous evaluation of one such program (Hsueh et al., 2012) provides insight into the costs and benefits of attempting to promote marriage through policy intervention. Supporting Healthy Marriage (SHM) is a skills-based program designed to help low-income married couples strengthen their relationships and achieve more positive outcomes for their children. From February 2007 to December 2009, the program recruited 6,298 couples and randomly assigned them into one of two groups, only one of which was offered SHM. The remaining couples were a control group not provided SHM services. The SHM program spent an average of $9,100 per treatment couple each year. Although the program produced a consistent pattern of small positive effects on multiple aspects of couples' relationships, such as marital happiness and decreased physical and psychological abuse, the program did not significantly affect whether couples stayed married at the 12-month follow-up (Lundquist et al., 2014). It is important that social workers ask critical questions about the efficacy of programs that states are funding through TANF, particularly since many of these initiatives come at the expense of cash benefits to poor families.

TANF Work Requirements and Sanctions Pressure to push more aid recipients into the paid workforce was a major impetus for the creation of TANF. An emphasis on work, with increasing requirements for work and penalties for not working enough, is now pervasive throughout safety-net programs—part of the historic fixation on work as the answer to poverty. The Personal Responsibility and Work Opportunity Reconciliation Act of 1996 (PRWORA) mandates that a specific percentage of families receiving TANF be involved in work activities and that this percentage rise over time. In 1997, the requirement was 25 percent; in 2002, it increased to 50 percent. The Deficit Reduction Act of 2005 (DRA), which reauthorized TANF, also increased work requirements (Administration for Children and Families, 2012). Federal TANF legislation requires all recipients to be involved in work activities, which may include limited training and education activities directly related to work, within two years after they begin to receive assistance. However, many states impose immediate work requirements, and few allow higher education to count as a work activity. There is some allowance made for families that face extraordinary barriers to work, but 90 percent of two-parent families must be engaged in work, typically for at least 35 hours per week (Huang, 2015). States may choose to exempt parents with a child under the age of one year, although in recent years many states have pushed mothers to return to work quickly after giving birth. Even as states have cut essential work supports, including childcare and transportation assistance, they have made work requirements less flexible; in 20 states, applicants are required to demonstrate that they are searching for work even before they receive any cash assistance.

The PRWORA further requires states to reduce TANF cash benefits for adults who do not meet work requirements. In all states except New York and California, families can immediately or eventually lose their entire cash grant due to work requirements, a fate experienced by more than two million families (Pavetti, 2018). Most states impose "full-family sanctions," which terminate benefits for the whole family if a parent does not meet work requirements. Additionally, some states have chosen to eliminate other benefits as well if the family head does not meet work requirements. The federal government will also reduce the amount of the block grant to any state in which the specified percentage of TANF recipients is not participating in work activities. To avoid these penalties, many states have opted to reduce the number of TANF recipients who can enroll in the first place. States have the option of exempting up to 20 percent of families receiving TANF from the five-year time limit and may use their own funds to assist families who have exceeded the limit. However, many states have taken TANF policy in the opposite direction. They have continued to utilize punitive tactics to prioritize work over assistance, despite evidence that such an approach increases families' hardship without increasing employment (Pavetti, 2018). Indeed, research has found low employment rates among families who leave TANF because of sanctions; these families often spiral into crisis and extreme deprivation following the loss of benefits. Exhibit 8.5 summarizes the major features of TANF.

A third of states raised TANF benefits in 2018 or 2019; for five of these, it was the first benefit increase in more than a decade. Even with these increases, benefits are at or below 60 percent of the federal poverty line in every state; many states' benefits are below 30 percent of the federal poverty line. In 2018, TANF benefits in the median state were just $447 per month for a family of three; in 14 states, such a family received less than $300 per month. Additionally, as an illustration of how state-level variations increase inequality and can produce dramatically different

EXHIBIT 8.5 *Temporary Assistance for Needy Families (TANF), 1996*		
	Policy goals	To promote families by helping parents care for children in their own home, supporting two-parent families, and discouraging out-of-wedlock pregnancies. To reduce poor families' dependence on government aid by focusing on work and marriage.
	Benefits or services provided	Monthly cash assistance. Services to promote work and reduce dependency.
	Eligibility rules	Means-tested. Families must meet work requirements and not exceed the state's time limits.
	Service delivery system	State welfare agencies determine eligibility and administer payments to eligible families.
	Financing	Federal block grant to each state. States are required to contribute additional funding.

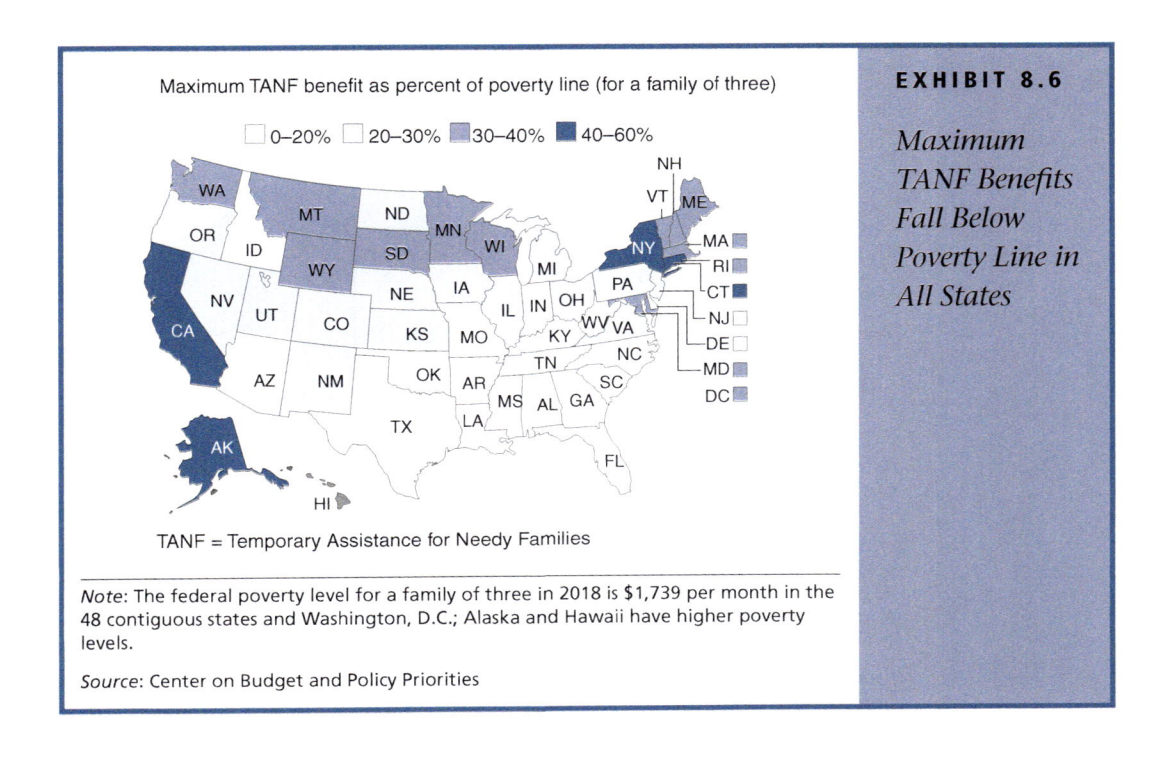

> **EXHIBIT 8.6**
>
> *Maximum TANF Benefits Fall Below Poverty Line in All States*

Maximum TANF benefit as percent of poverty line (for a family of three)

☐ 0–20% ☐ 20–30% ▨ 30–40% ■ 40–60%

TANF = Temporary Assistance for Needy Families

Note: The federal poverty level for a family of three in 2018 is $1,739 per month in the 48 contiguous states and Washington, D.C.; Alaska and Hawaii have higher poverty levels.

Source: Center on Budget and Policy Priorities

outcomes for those differently positioned, TANF recipients of color are disproportionately likely to be in states with particularly low benefit levels (Burnside & Floyd, 2019). These low benefit levels are not entirely due to pressures of the devolved TANF model; two-thirds of states reduced cash assistance for poor families with children by over 40 percent in real terms between 1970 and 1996, even prior to the shift to TANF. Then, because TANF legislation does not adjust the block grant, TANF benefits have fallen by 20 percent or more in inflation-adjusted terms in 36 states (Burnside & Floyd, 2019). Exhibit 8.6 shows how profoundly TANF fails to reduce child poverty.

In Fiscal Year (FY) 2017, total federal and state spending for TANF was $28.7 billion, about $14 billion of which was in the form of federal block grants (U.S. Department of Health and Human Services, 2018a). The cash assistance portion of TANF was just over $7 billion in 2017 (U.S. Department of Health and Human Services, 2018a), less than half than in 1996. Exhibit 8.7 depicts states' allocation of TANF dollars in 2017, only about a quarter of which went to direct cash assistance. In contrast, when TANF was first instituted, states spent 70 percent of allocated funding on basic assistance. Further, even the meager benefits provided today are largely unavailable to many—even most—low-income families and children in many states. On average, only 23 percent of low-income families received TANF in 2016 (Center on Budget and Policy Priorities [CBPP], 2018a). In 13 states, fewer than 10 percent of low-income families receive TANF, and in no state does TANF cover more than 65 percent of poor families. This has resulted in a dramatic retreat from AFDC's entitlement, as illustrated in Exhibit 8.8. About 4.4 million families received direct financial assistance in 1996, the year the TANF block grant was created; now, even as the number of poor children has grown, only 1.3 million families receive such assistance (Pavetti, 2018).

EXHIBIT 8.7

How States Spend TANF Dollars

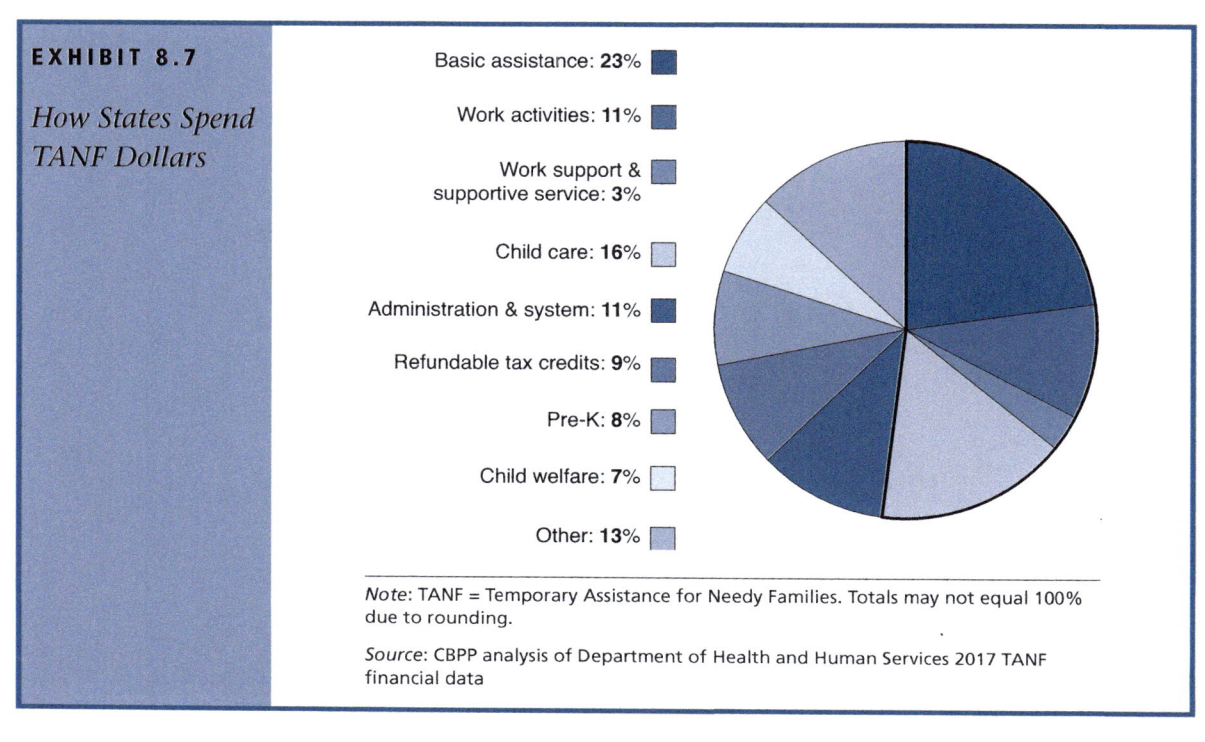

- Basic assistance: **23%**
- Work activities: **11%**
- Work support & supportive service: **3%**
- Child care: **16%**
- Administration & system: **11%**
- Refundable tax credits: **9%**
- Pre-K: **8%**
- Child welfare: **7%**
- Other: **13%**

Note: TANF = Temporary Assistance for Needy Families. Totals may not equal 100% due to rounding.

Source: CBPP analysis of Department of Health and Human Services 2017 TANF financial data

EXHIBIT 8.8

TANF Declines as a Safety Net for Poor Families

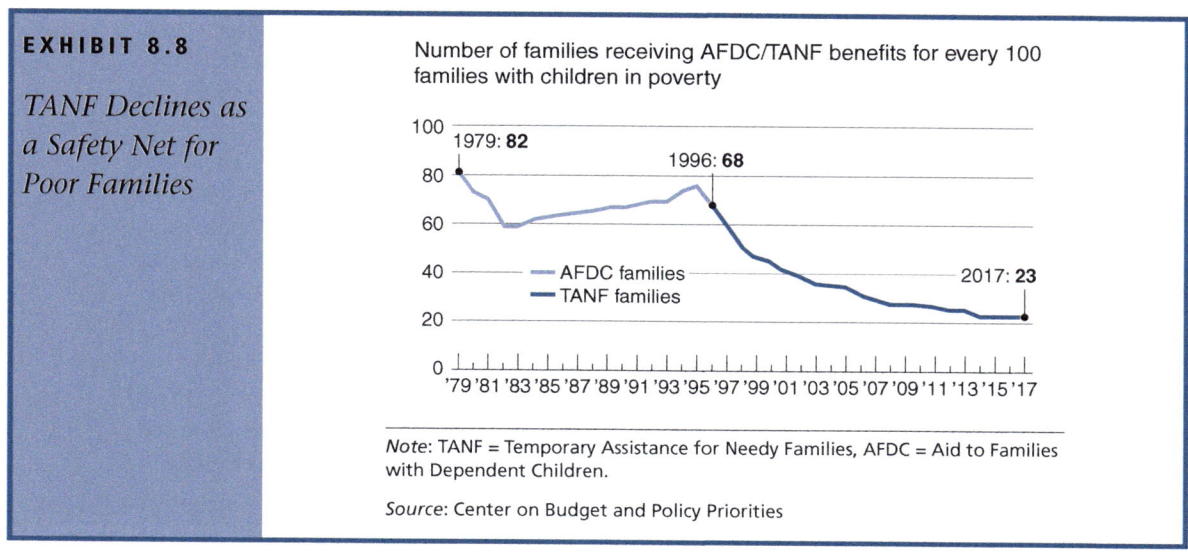

Number of families receiving AFDC/TANF benefits for every 100 families with children in poverty

- 1979: **82**
- 1996: **68**
- 2017: **23**

Note: TANF = Temporary Assistance for Needy Families, AFDC = Aid to Families with Dependent Children.

Source: Center on Budget and Policy Priorities

With inadequate benefit levels, eroding purchasing power, insufficient reach, and wide variation in eligibility rules, sanctions, and supports by state, TANF fails to lift most families out of even deep poverty. Crucially, these bleak outcomes are consistent with the goals articulated in the TANF legislation, which include reducing welfare dependence and promoting marriage, but *not* reducing child poverty. We know that poverty is a powerful predictor of all sorts of negative outcomes for children, from dropping out of school to poor physical and mental health to teenage pregnancy to juvenile crime. TANF could and should be an important tool in preventing these outcomes; however, realizing that potential will require substantial policy change. To compare eligibility requirements for TANF in your state with those in other states, visit the National Center for Children in Poverty (**www.nccp.org**) and go to State Profiles. Find out what choices your state is making. Is your state one that has unspent federal TANF reserves that it could be investing in low-income children? As a social worker, how would you prioritize allocating such funds to poor families in your state? In addition to recent benefit increases, some states have added funding for transportation, childcare, and other services designed to help parents succeed in employment. However, many others have enacted increasingly strict sanctions and limits, which have the effect of further weakening TANF as a resource for poor families (Wiltz, 2015).

Work Instead of Welfare The 1996 PRWORA legislation combined welfare and existing employment policy, such that a large portion of employment policy is now focused on welfare recipients or those who might otherwise use TANF. The 1997 Balanced Budget Act established welfare-to-work (WTW) grants as a component of the TANF Funding Work Incentive Program. The following year, the Workforce Investment Act required that a wide range of state programs for job seekers, including WTW, unemployment insurance, vocational rehabilitation, adult education, and post-secondary vocational education, be brought together into a one-stop system.

Of course, when unemployment is high, work opportunities are more difficult to find, especially for those disadvantaged. Even in a context of relatively low unemployment, many Americans face barriers to successful employment. These include families where parents and/or children experience disabilities, addictions, low literacy, and/or domestic violence. With so much income-support policy now carrying work requirements, sanctions for not meeting work goals make it increasingly difficult to meet basic needs. Authors Kathryn Edin and Luke Shaefer (2016) document the stories of several of the 1.5 million American households with cash incomes of less than two dollars a day—a number used to measure poverty in the developing world. In many states, millions of families have no resources other than food assistance, in the form of SNAP, with which to meet their needs. The result is persistent hunger, homelessness, ill health, stunted child development, and family instability. Research has even found that living with this financial stress lowers IQ and makes it harder to complete even basic functions, let alone to find a route out of poverty (Mani et al., 2013). Almost without exception, these are families that want to work. However, they desperately need a safety net to hold their lives together.

Non-Cash Programs That Assist Low-Income Families

Other programs help low-income families meet basic survival needs without providing cash assistance. These programs include SNAP, WIC, public housing, and the Tenant-Based Housing Assistance Program (Section 8). Due to space constraints, we discuss these programs relatively briefly. However, you will likely encounter these programs in your practice. For many of the individuals and families that receive them, these supports are essential investments in their survival.

The Supplemental Nutrition Assistance Program   The Supplemental Nutrition Assistance Program (SNAP, formerly the Food Stamp Program) was established to address hunger in the United States by helping low-income people purchase nutritionally adequate food. It also serves to increase demand for U.S. food production, an effect that makes SNAP important to U.S. agricultural interests as well as those concerned with poverty. In FY2018, SNAP assisted over 40 million Americans in more than 20 million households (U.S. Department of Agriculture [USDA], 2018a). To be eligible for benefits, individuals or families must have monthly gross incomes that are less than 130 percent of the federal poverty guidelines—$2,720 per month for a family of four in 2018 (USDA, 2018b). In some states, people applying for SNAP must also have countable assets under $2,250, or $3,500 if at least one person is age 60 or older or is disabled. Under federal rules that allowed states to raise or eliminate asset limits for SNAP, 34 states allowed low-income households to receive food assistance without having to liquidate their assets (Prosperity Now, 2018). However, new rules proposed by the Trump Administration would end automatic SNAP eligibility for those already receiving other federal and state assistance, instead requiring these individuals to undergo asset tests. The proposal, touted as a way to standardize rules nationwide and ensure that SNAP is only a "temporary safety net," are expected to cut food assistance to approximately three million people. Current federal law requires SNAP recipients aged 18 to 59 to work part-time or agree to accept a job if offered one. Those who do not meet requirements of 80 hours of work per month are limited to only three months of SNAP benefits in three years. However, states can seek waivers from the U.S. Department of Agriculture to temporarily suspend this limit in areas with insufficient jobs. While every state except Delaware has sought such a waiver at some point since 1996, several states have instituted additional work participation requirements for SNAP eligibility. Seventeen states have extended disqualification periods, six disqualify the whole family if the household head does not comply with work requirements, and four do both (National Conference of State Legislatures, 2018a). As more than 70 percent of SNAP recipients are in households with children, these sanctions have potentially serious consequences for child well-being.

In late 2018, Congress rejected a provision that would have inserted a stricter work requirement in the portion of the federal Farm Bill that includes SNAP. However, just before he signed the legislation, President Trump announced a proposed rule that would administratively narrow the conditions in which states can waive SNAP work requirements. Instead of allowing states to waive such requirements whenever their unemployment rates are at least 20 percent higher than the national average, the new rule would only allow states to seek waivers of work requirements when their unemployment rate exceeds 7 percent. Analysts estimate this rule could push as many as 755,000 people off federal food assistance. It also illustrates the extent to which rulemaking can modify or even subvert legislative action and, then, the importance of social work advocacy in regulatory arenas. If unchanged, this policy will tie the hands of states that have sought to maintain more generous allowances for those who are out of work. Further, it could impair SNAP's ability to respond quickly and adequately to economic downturns (Bauer, Parsons, & Shambaugh, 2019). Already, several

EXHIBIT 8.9

Supplemental Nutrition Assistance Program (SNAP)

Policy goals	To supplement households' food budgets. To support U.S. agricultural production through the subsidy of food consumption.
Benefits or services provided	Electronic Benefit Transfer (EBT).
Eligibility rules	Adjusted monthly income less than 130 percent of federal poverty guidelines. Participation in required work activities unless exempt or waived. Ownership of less than $2,250 in assets unless state has eliminated asset test.
Service delivery system	Benefits transferred to card that can be used to purchase allowable food items at approved retailers, including most grocery stores, as well as many convenience stores and farmers' markets.
Financing	General tax revenues.

states have passed or considered legislation to eliminate waivers or increase enforcement of SNAP work requirements. Exhibit 8.9 provides a summary of the existing provisions of the federal SNAP policy.

For people who are eligible, SNAP is an entitlement. Indeed, this explains why SNAP participation rose significantly during the Great Recession; unlike TANF, SNAP is designed to grow with increases in need. Further, the program is, for the most part, uniform across states, and because most low-income people are eligible regardless of where they live, it is easier to swiftly deliver benefits to low-income families. Nonetheless, some elements of SNAP create unnecessary barriers. Many immigrants are ineligible for the program for their first five years as lawful permanent residents, although children are eligible no matter how long they have been in the United States (USDA, 2016). Also, since states normally pay half of the administrative costs, cuts in state budgets for staff needed to process applications and/or conduct outreach may depress participation. Importantly, SNAP participation rates are especially low among working-poor families, indicating that these households may face barriers to learning about, applying for, and using these critical food resources. These limitations notwithstanding, Exhibit 8.10 compares the responsiveness of TANF and SNAP to the increased economic need of the recession, using one of the most "generous" states—New York—to illustrate the inadequacy of TANF's block grant approach and the extent to which people turn to SNAP in times of increasing need.

SNAP provides monthly allotments in the form of Electronic Benefit Transfer (EBT) cards to eligible beneficiaries. Recipients use these cards to purchase specified food items in retail stores or, in some cases, farmers' markets or other outlets. As with the poverty threshold, the benefit formula assumes that families will spend 30 percent of their net income on food. The average three-person SNAP household received about $378 per month in benefits in FY2019; the maximum monthly benefit was $505. The average recipient received about $126 per month

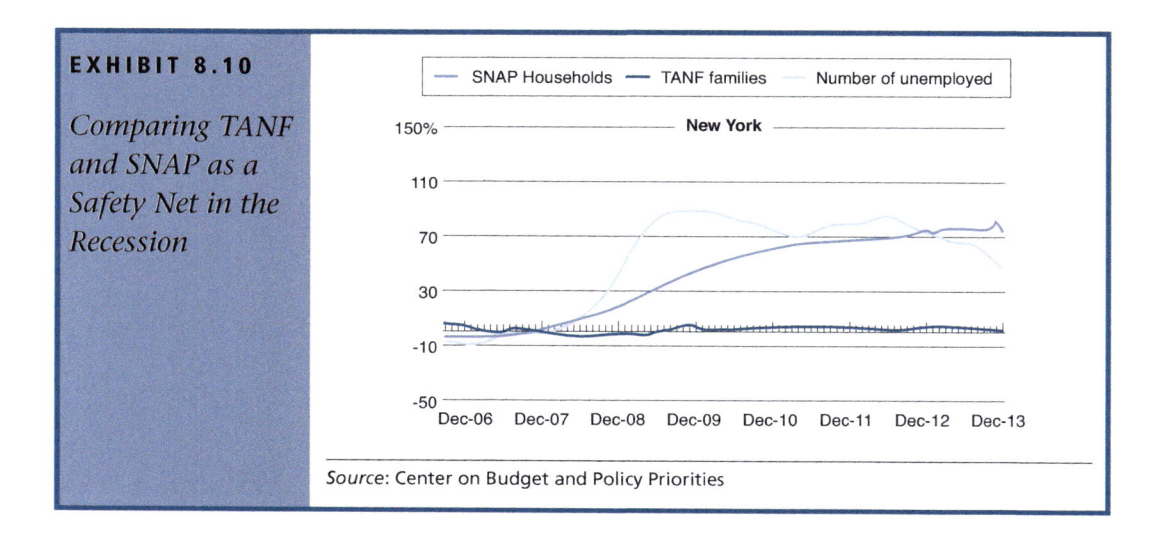

EXHIBIT 8.10

Comparing TANF and SNAP as a Safety Net in the Recession

[Chart: New York — SNAP Households, TANF families, Number of unemployed, Dec-06 through Dec-13, y-axis from -50% to 150%]

Source: Center on Budget and Policy Priorities

(or about $1.40 per meal) (CBPP, 2018b). SNAP pays larger benefits to very poor households than to households closer to the poverty line because those families need more help affording an adequate diet. To promote healthy food choices and exert some control over purchases, the federal government and many states put restrictions on the types of products that can be purchased using SNAP benefits. A problem for many families is that SNAP benefits cannot be used to purchase personal care items, including diapers.

SNAP is funded through general tax revenues. At the federal level, the Department of Agriculture administers the program through the Food and Nutrition Service, which has established eligibility, allotment, and benefit distribution guidelines. State- and local-level programs distribute benefits within the parameters of these federal regulations. For more information on SNAP and other programs to reduce hunger, go to the Food Assistance Programs website at the U.S. Department of Agriculture (**www.usda.gov**).

The Women, Infants, and Children Nutrition Program In 1972, the Special Supplemental Nutrition Program for Women, Infants, and Children (WIC) was established to help improve the health of low-income women, infants, and children up to age five who are nutritionally at-risk. Although selective, 62 percent of all infants born in the United States are eligible for WIC, 80 percent of whom participate in the program (USDA, 2018c). During FY2017, the number of women, infants, and children receiving WIC benefits averaged more than seven million per month. Of these, 3.76 million were children, 1.79 million were infants, and 1.74 million were women (USDA, 2018d).

To be eligible for WIC, applicants must meet the following criteria:

- All recipients must have incomes at or below 185 percent of the poverty line.

- All recipients must be determined to be nutritionally at-risk by a health professional.

- Women are eligible while they are pregnant. After the baby is born, the mother receives benefits for one year if she breastfeeds and for six months if she does not, a rule that both encourages breastfeeding and attempts to meet mothers' nutritional needs while breastfeeding. A woman need not be a single mother to be eligible.

- Until their first birthday, infants are eligible for benefits specifically designed to address the needs of very young children.

- Children are eligible for WIC benefits—specifically, food items associated with sound child nutrition—until their fifth birthday.

WIC benefits include nutritious food, nutrition counseling and education, and referrals to health care and other social services. In most states, WIC participants receive checks or vouchers to purchase food in local retail stores. Some states issue an electronic benefit card to participants; all states are required to implement WIC EBT statewide by October 1, 2020.

WIC is not an entitlement. Instead, WIC is funded by a federal grant appropriated by Congress. This grant may not be sufficient to cover all eligible women, infants, and children. However, while estimates suggest that WIC serves fewer individuals than are eligible, WIC participation tracks the number of low-income infants and children much more closely than TANF, reaching an estimated 73 percent of low-income children under age five (Carlson, Neuberger, & Rosenbaum, 2017). Some states' success in reaching more WIC-eligible families suggests that enrollment growth requires increasing awareness, reducing the stigma associated with public assistance, and helping families navigate application during the stressful period surrounding pregnancy and birth. In 2014, California, Minnesota, Maryland, and Vermont had the highest overall WIC coverage rates, while several states approached participation close to 100 percent of eligible infants (USDA, 2017). At the federal level, WIC, like SNAP, is administered by the Food and Nutrition Service. At the state and local levels, various agencies administer WIC programs through state and county health departments, hospitals, community centers, schools, Indian health facilities, and similar entities. Go to the WIC website at the U.S. Department of Agriculture (**www.usda.gov**) for more information.

Public Housing With the supply of rental housing reduced during and following the recession, wages that fail to keep pace with other costs, and cultural and economic changes leading more Americans to rent rather than buy, communities across the nation face affordable housing crises (Colburn & Allen, 2016). In many markets, even moderate-income households struggle to afford housing. For low-income families, paying rent can often mean sacrificing other essentials. In 2016, 83 percent of renter households with incomes below $15,000 and 77 percent of those with incomes between $15,000 and $30,000 were cost-burdened, defined as paying more than 30 percent of their income for housing (Joint Center for Housing Studies at Harvard University, 2017). As are other economic outcomes, housing cost burdens are inequitably distributed by race; in 2015, 46 percent of Black and 33 percent of White renter families were cost-burdened (Pew Charitable Trusts, 2018). Unaffordable housing has a variety of negative effects on families, including contributing to overcrowding, lengthy commutes, and residence in substandard conditions. Research has found that housing cost burden compromises child well-being, largely by forcing families to divert investment from critical needs in nutrition, childcare, and health care (Harkness & Newman, 2005). To see what someone needs to earn to afford housing in your community, visit the National Low-Income Housing Coalition's calculator (**nlihc.org/oor**).

Through the U.S. Department of Housing and Urban Development (HUD), the federal government provides housing assistance to low-income Americans who cannot afford rent in the private market. However, in many communities, insufficient funding means that people encounter long waiting lists that give them little chance of receiving assistance to securely and affordably house their families. There were almost two million people living in public housing in 2018 (U.S. Department of Housing and Urban Development [HUD], 2018), with millions more who could qualify if resources were available. In large part because affordable housing is so scarce, turnover among public housing residents is low. A person can continue to live in public housing until their income is high enough to afford rent in the private market. In many communities and for many families, this may never happen.

Eligibility for public housing is based on income. Specifically, families and individuals are eligible if they earn less than 80 percent of the median income in the geographic area. Those whose incomes are below 50 percent of the area median income receive preference for scarce public housing spots. Housing policies are therefore unique in that they define need in terms of poverty relative to a person's location, rather than against an absolute line. Because median income varies by region, an individual may be eligible in one community but not another. To further ration this limited resource, public housing is denied to people who have not exhibited good habits at other rental properties. Individuals with drug-related convictions can also lose their eligibility for public housing, even long after they have served their sentences. Many states institute more stringent bans than required by federal law and exercise considerable discretion in enforcement (Curtis, Garlington, & Schottenfeld, 2013). These rules disproportionately impact people of color, who have frequent and more unjust encounters with law enforcement and suffer discriminatory implementation by local housing authorities (Weiss, 2016).

At the federal level, general revenues finance the public housing program. HUD provides federal funds to local housing agencies, which manage the housing. These agencies oversee collecting rent from tenants, enforcing leases, and maintaining the housing so that it continues to meet acceptable standards. For more information on public housing, go to the website of the U.S. Department of Housing and Urban Development (**www.hud.gov**).

Tenant-Based Rental Assistance Program   This program serves the same purpose as the public housing program: to provide low-income people with decent, safe, and affordable places to live. However, its benefit structure and delivery system are different. Instead of providing an actual apartment or home, the Housing Choice program uses a voucher system that permits eligible families to choose privately owned houses or apartments that meet program requirements and have reasonable rent that will be subsidized.

People who apply for these vouchers must meet the same income eligibility standards as public housing recipients. Nearly 90 percent of households that receive rental assistance are elderly, disabled, working (or worked recently), or have access to work programs through TANF. Only a small share of non-elderly, non-disabled adults receiving housing assistance are persistently unemployed (Mazzara & Sard, 2018). Housing Choice is financed through general federal revenues, and funding is limited. HUD provides funds to local housing offices, which

INCOME- AND ASSET-BASED POLICIES   283

issue vouchers to families when their names reach the top of the waiting list. However, a study by a national low-income housing organization found that 53 percent of waiting lists for Housing Choice were closed to new applicants and another 4 percent were open only to certain target populations (National Low-Income Housing Coalition, 2016). The median waiting time for those who make it onto the lists is 1.5 years, but 25 percent of local communities have waits of at least three years.

The cost of housing as a percentage of the median incomes is increasing, a problem that strains families' finances and can force people into homelessness. In 2018, an average of 553,000 people in the United States experienced homelessness on a given night; 65 percent of these individuals found shelter, but the rest were on the street or in a place not fit for habitation (Henry et al., 2018). Recent trends in homelessness reflect both the continuing challenges that many Americans face in meeting their housing needs, as well as the progress some targeted housing investments have made. African Americans are particularly overrepresented among those experiencing homelessness; 40 percent of the homeless population but only 13 percent of the total population is Black (Henry et al., 2018). Young people who are homeless—an estimated 36,000 unaccompanied youth in 2018—are particularly likely to be unsheltered, demonstrating the extent to which existing services fail to meet their needs. Particularly in cities with very expensive housing markets (Los Angeles, New York, San Francisco, Seattle), homelessness is an urgent crisis, prompting threats from President Trump and other politicians to demolish tent cities and use police power to make sleeping on the streets intolerable. However, policies have demonstrated promise in preventing and responding to homelessness in several demographics. Family homelessness (23 percent since 2007), chronic homelessness (26 percent since 2007), and veteran homelessness (48 percent since 2009) have all declined, as investments in rapid rehousing and care coordination have improved outcomes for these populations.

While homelessness is the most vivid indicator of the nation's housing crisis, there is evidence that inadequate supply of affordable housing and insufficient public investment in housing support have long-term implications for families' economic mobility, as well as immediate effects on economic well-being—even when they manage to remain housed. Unaffordable housing in areas of strong job growth can crowd out those who could find promising opportunities there, and families may be particularly reluctant to move in search of better employment and educational opportunities if they are not certain they can afford to live in the upwardly mobile communities. Analysis of a federal demonstration that provided housing vouchers to families for the explicit purpose of encouraging them to move to lower-poverty neighborhoods—Moving to Opportunity—found that it significantly improved college attendance rates and earnings for children who were younger than 13 when their families moved (Chetty, Hendren, & Katz, 2016). Children also lived in better neighborhoods as adults and were less likely to become single parents.

These effects are substantial and lasting; however, insufficient funding and difficulty recruiting enough participating landlords meant that HUD only enrolled 4,608 families in Moving to Opportunity, which stopped accepting applicants in 1999. As Exhibit 8.11 shows, household mover rates have fallen considerably compared to periods of greater economic mobility in the 1950s and 1960s. To counter this trend and encourage families to locate in communities that offer the greatest opportunities, federal, state, and local policymakers are considering various reforms. For example, land

EXHIBIT 8.11

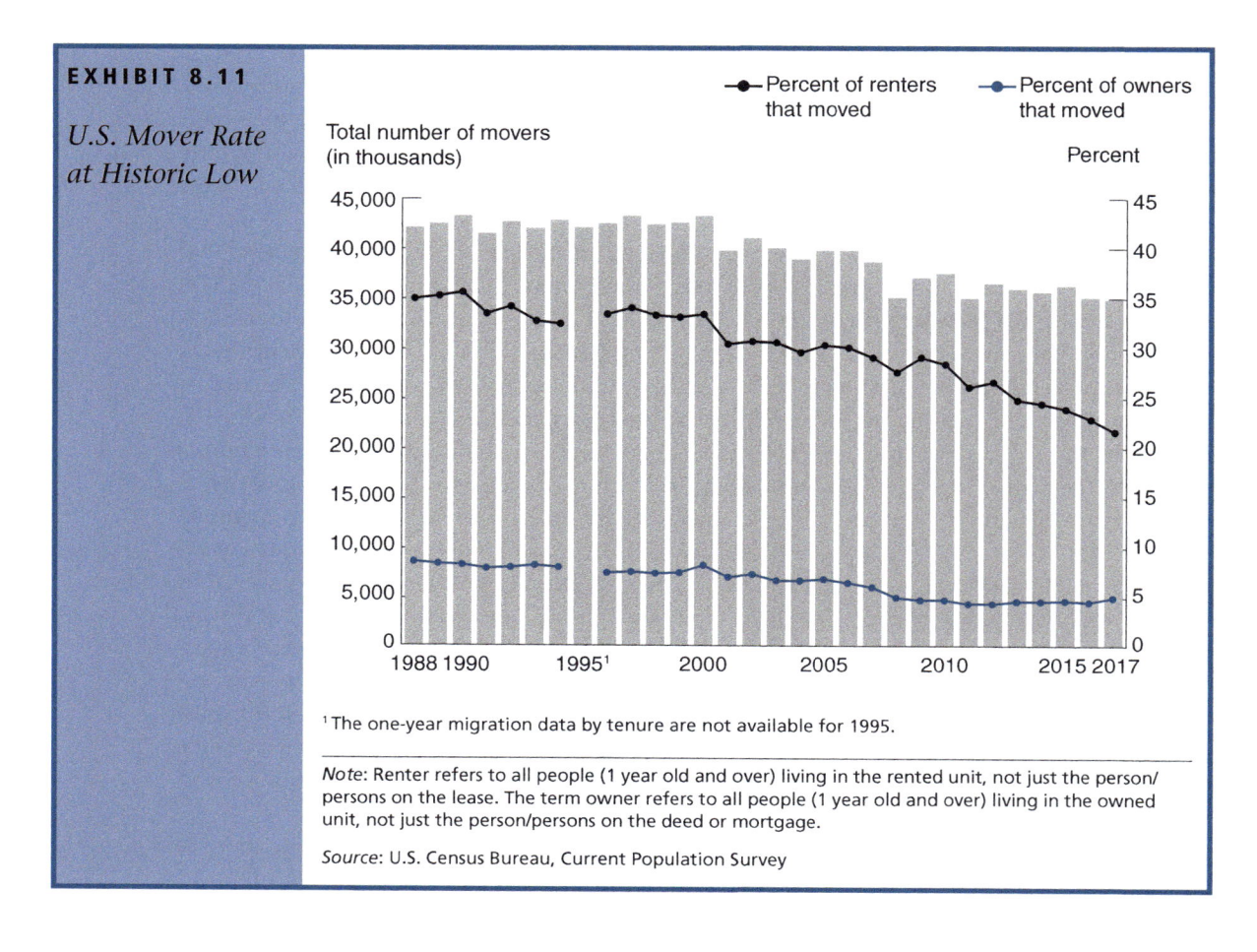

U.S. Mover Rate at Historic Low

[Chart: Total number of movers (in thousands) shown as bars, with percent of renters that moved and percent of owners that moved shown as lines, from 1988 to 2017. Total movers hover around 40,000–43,000 thousand through the 1990s and early 2000s, declining to around 35,000 thousand by 2017. Percent of renters that moved declines from about 35% in 1988 to about 22% in 2017. Percent of owners that moved declines from about 9% to about 5%.]

[1] The one-year migration data by tenure are not available for 1995.

Note: Renter refers to all people (1 year old and over) living in the rented unit, not just the person/persons on the lease. The term owner refers to all people (1 year old and over) living in the owned unit, not just the person/persons on the deed or mortgage.

Source: U.S. Census Bureau, Current Population Survey

use changes such as inclusionary zoning increase housing density and could increase the supply of affordable housing (Shoag, 2019). Other proposals include tax credits for renters to help close the gap in tax incentives provided to those who own rather than rent.

HOME Investment Partnership Programs This initiative, typically referred to as HOME, is the largest federal block grant exclusively designed to create affordable housing. HUD funds this initiative, and states and localities can apply the funds in a wide variety of ways, including rehabilitating properties, providing rental assistance, and subsidizing homeownership by low-income households. All 50 states have HOME programs.

The Low-Income Housing Tax Credit program also gives states and localities the equivalent of nearly $8 billion in annual budget authority to issue tax credits for the acquisition, rehabilitation, or construction of rental housing targeted to low-income households. States may also use Community Development Block Grant funds for affordable housing production, and some states use their own funds to meet residents' housing needs. Overall, public funding for low-income housing is inadequate. Today, rapidly growing need far outstrips availability.

Supplemental Security Income

Before Congress created the Supplemental Security Income (SSI) program in 1974, states had a patchwork of programs that assisted people with limited or no income who were elderly, blind, or had other disabilities. The federal legislation replaced this arrangement with a means-tested entitlement that is uniform across the nation. In October 2018, almost 8.2 million Americans, approximately 2.5 percent of the population, received monthly SSI cash benefits (Social Security Administration [SSA], 2018c). To receive SSI benefits, individuals must have very low incomes, including both cash and non-cash assistance. Additionally, assets must be below $2,000 for individuals and $3,000 for a couple, excluding certain items such as a home, a car, and life insurance policies under $1,500 (SSA, 2018d). Congress last updated the asset limits in 1989.

Other eligibility requirements include age (65 or older for age-based benefits), physical or mental disability that prevents work for at least one year, or blindness. Approximately 1.2 million U.S children receive SSI benefits, making up 14.2 percent of SSI recipients (SSA, 2018c). As depicted in Exhibit 8.12, the numbers of children receiving SSI increased substantially in the 1990s, in part through expansion of the mental health conditions with which children could qualify. Although rates of children receiving SSI for mental disabilities grew less than the incidence of childhood mental illness overall, this growth nonetheless contributed to an increase in the share of the SSI beneficiary population under age 18 (Perrin et al., 2016). SSI benefits provide crucial income supports to low-income families of children with disabilities, who face considerable barriers to work, additional costs for treatment, and extraordinary housing needs. In 2010, research found that SSI benefits raised the family income of 46 percent of child SSI recipients above the federal poverty line (Bailey & Hemmeter, 2010); in some cases, the child's SSI benefits provided most of the family's income.

In 2019, the maximum monthly SSI benefit was $771 for individuals and $1,157 for a married couple when both are eligible (SSA, 2018e). The SSA administers the SSI program through

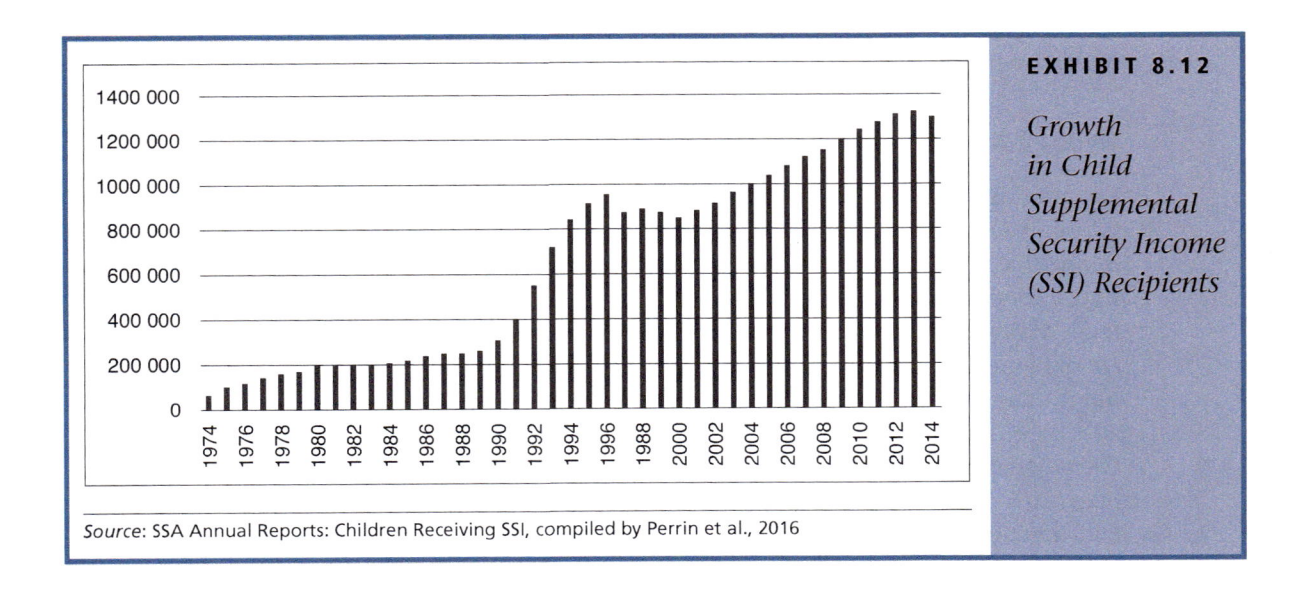

EXHIBIT 8.12

Growth in Child Supplemental Security Income (SSI) Recipients

Source: SSA Annual Reports: Children Receiving SSI, compiled by Perrin et al., 2016

EXHIBIT 8.13 *Supplemental Security Income (SSI), 1974*	Program goals	To provide income assistance to the aged, blind, and people with disabilities who have limited income and assets.
	Benefits or services provided	Monthly cash benefit.
	Eligibility rules	Means-tested. Must be 65 or older, blind, or disabled.
	Service delivery system	Social Security Administration offices administer SSI. Funds are sent by check via U.S. mail or Electronic Bank Transfer.
	Financing	General federal tax revenue.

regional and district offices. Some states also provide a state supplement to SSI. Although the SSA oversees both OASDI and SSI, the two are very different programs. OASDI is an insurance program. Under the Federal Insurance Contributions Act and the Self Employment Contributions Act (SECA), workers and employers pay Social Security insurance premiums/taxes that fund OASDI. SSI is not insurance and is not tied to work history. Rather, it is financed by general U.S. Treasury funds (SSA, 2018f). Exhibit 8.13 summarizes the features of the federal SSI program.

Before the passage of the PRWORA in 1996, legal immigrants were eligible to receive SSI under the same eligibility rules as citizens; today, most immigrants are ineligible for most means-tested programs including SSI, TANF, and Medicaid until they obtain citizenship or reside in the United States as lawful permanent residents for five years. Further, use of any federal or state funds for income support for undocumented immigrants is prohibited. To find out more about eligibility for SSI, research Supplemental Security Income on the SSA website (www.ssa.gov). To find out how to help clients more effectively access SSI, do an online search for your state's SSI/SSDI Outreach, Access, and Recovery (SOAR) program. This program is designed to increase access to SSI/SSDI for eligible adults and children who are experiencing or at risk of homelessness and have a serious mental illness, medical impairment, and/or a co-occurring substance use disorder. These efforts have greatly increased application approval rates.

General Assistance

General Assistance (GA) is provided to help poor individuals and families who do not qualify for or are awaiting approval for federal programs such as SSI and TANF. GA programs provide minimal assistance and are generally a last resort for people in need. GA is administered by states, counties, and localities, which determine benefits, eligibility criteria, and delivery systems. Many of these programs are called General Assistance, but some are referred to by a variety of names such as General Relief, Poor Relief, or City Welfare. The federal government does not fund or regulate GA. Budget constraints and public attitudes increasingly hostile to those who depend on public assistance have led many states to eliminate GA. In 1989, 38 states had GA programs; by 2015, that figure was only 26, although Pennsylvania reinstituted its GA program in 2018. In the states that do provide GA, programs vary dramatically in the amounts and duration of benefits as well as eligibility rules. Only 11 states provide any benefits to childless adults who do not have a disability (Schott & Hill, 2015). Typically, payments are

EXHIBIT 8.14

General Assistance (GA), 1935

Program goals	To help low-income people who are ineligible or awaiting approval for federal assistance programs meet their survival needs.
Benefits or services provided	Temporary or long-term cash and/or in-kind assistance.
Eligibility rules	Means-tested. Eligibility varies but usually is reserved for people with very little or no income. Some states specifically restrict GA to "unemployable" people with disabilities.
Service delivery system	States, counties, and localities determine eligibility and provide cash, in-kind assistance, or both.
Financing	Funded entirely by the states, counties, and localities that administer the programs, although these entities may apply some federal funding to this purpose.

low; in addition to cash, they may take the form of in-kind benefits such as food or clothing. Due to differences in reporting and in the types of GA programs localities offer, it is difficult to determine the total number of GA recipients. Because cities and states finance GA, capacity to fund GA is drastically reduced at times of greatest need. Nevertheless, because GA can often be made available quickly to people who do not qualify or are waiting to qualify for other benefits, it can be a lifesaver for very poor Americans. Exhibit 8.14 describes GA.

The Earned Income Tax Credit

Congress enacted the Earned Income Tax Credit (EITC) in 1975 to mitigate the impact of Medicare and Social Security taxes deducted from the wages of low- and moderate-income families with children. The goal of EITC is to encourage people to work and to assist them in paying for the expenses they incur because of work.

In 2017, more than 26 million working families and individuals received EITC refunds for the 2016 tax year (CBPP, 2018c). The EITC lifts millions of people, many of them children, out of poverty each year. As such, EITC has been described as the largest anti-poverty program in the United States. However, not all workers are eligible for the EITC—only citizens or lawful permanent residents who meet all other eligibility requirements. Benefits vary depending on income level and number of children. During the 2016 tax year, the average EITC was $3,176 for a family with children, compared with just $295 for a family without children (CBPP, 2018c). Military and disability status are also considered in determining eligibility, as combat pay and some disability benefits may be counted as earned income. For tax year 2018, to qualify for EITC, recipients with one child had to earn an income from work that was less than $40,320 ($46,010 for married, filing jointly). Recipients with three or more qualifying children had to earn work income below $49,194 ($54,884 for married, filing jointly) (Internal Revenue Service [IRS], 2018).

The EITC reduces recipients' federal tax liability and provides a refundable credit to tax filers who have already paid more than the amount owed. To apply for the EITC, individuals must file a federal tax return with the IRS. The IRS administers the program and issues refunds to eligible taxpayers. This mechanism minimizes administrative costs and reduces the stigma often attached to anti-poverty benefits. In 2018, the maximum credit was $6,431 for a family with three or more qualifying children, while the maximum credit for families with no qualifying children was $519 (IRS, 2018). This difference reflects the extent to which the EITC is designed to be an income support for working *families*. Indeed, EITC benefits for childless adults are insufficient to offset federal tax obligations, making this group the only demographic consistently taxed into poverty (Marr & Huang, 2019). People who receive the EITC may opt to receive one lump sum at the end of the year or smaller allotments added to their paychecks throughout the year. Depending on state rules, receiving a refund can negatively affect an individual's eligibility for Medicaid, SSI, SNAP, TANF, or low-income housing; if recipients do not spend their refunds within a certain timeframe, the balance could be considered against asset limits. This serves as a disincentive to saving, even though policy demonstrations have underscored the potential for receipt of the EITC to encourage asset-building among low-income savers (Roll et al., 2018).

EITC benefits reduce general revenue funds, since fewer taxes are collected from individual tax returns. Importantly, EITC has been found to have a positive impact on children's health, academic achievement, and well-being. Among other positive effects, EITC receipt increases children's test scores (Dahl & Lochner, 2010; Maxfield, 2013), reduces family stress, improves nutrition, reduces incidence of low birthweight (Hoynes, Miller, & Simon, 2015), and improves health behavior (Baughman, 2012). As low-income children become adults, prior EITC receipt leads to greater work participation and higher incomes (Bastian & Michelmore, 2018). In total, this evidence suggests that future public cost avoidance could offset the costs of the EITC (Chetty, Friedman, & Rockoff, 2011).

Another tax credit aimed at helping working families is the Child Tax Credit (CTC). The tax law Congress passed in 2017 increased the CTC and made it partially refundable, a change that may increase its potency in combating poverty. Already, in 2016, the EITC and the CTC together lifted an estimated 8.9 million people out of poverty and reduced the severity of poverty for approximately 19.3 million more (CBPP, 2018c). Exhibit 8.15 illustrates this impact.

Twenty-nine states have implemented their own EITC, usually calculated as a percentage of the federal credit (National Conference of State Legislatures, 2018b). Overall take-up rates of EITC are greater than for other means-tested programs; an estimated 78 percent of those eligible claim the EITC. Still, increased outreach, additional taxpayer assistance to navigate the complicated benefit, monthly refund disbursement, and improved efforts to reduce IRS miscalculations could make the already-efficient and effective EITC a more powerful tool in the government's anti-poverty policy repertoire and a more valuable assistance to low-income working families (Fichtner & Dutta-Gupta, 2017). Social workers are among those working to connect eligible workers to valuable EITC benefits. Exhibit 8.16 summarizes this anti-poverty program that is delivered through the tax code.

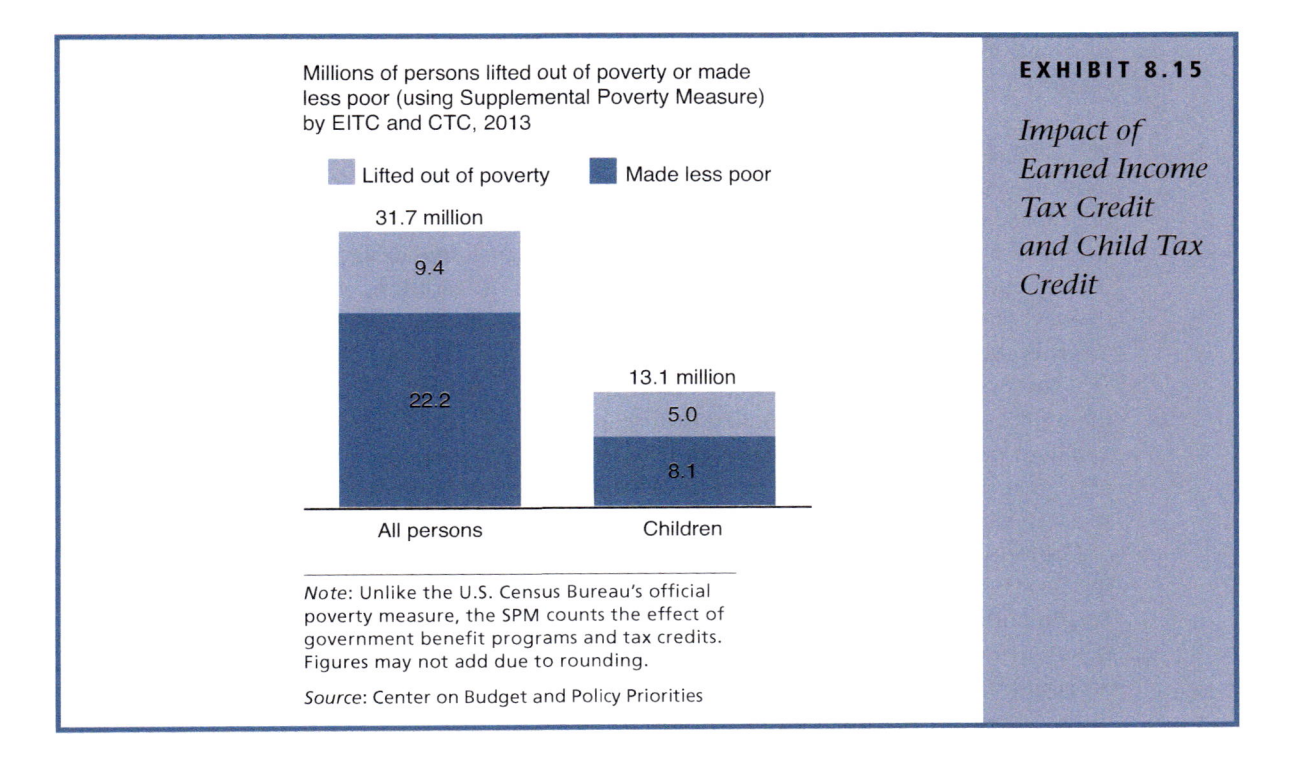

EXHIBIT 8.15

Impact of Earned Income Tax Credit and Child Tax Credit

Millions of persons lifted out of poverty or made less poor (using Supplemental Poverty Measure) by EITC and CTC, 2013

- Lifted out of poverty
- Made less poor

All persons: 31.7 million (9.4 lifted out of poverty; 22.2 made less poor)

Children: 13.1 million (5.0 lifted out of poverty; 8.1 made less poor)

Note: Unlike the U.S. Census Bureau's official poverty measure, the SPM counts the effect of government benefit programs and tax credits. Figures may not add due to rounding.

Source: Center on Budget and Policy Priorities

EXHIBIT 8.16

Earned Income Tax Credit (EITC), 1975

Program goals	To decrease the impact of payroll taxes on low-income families with children, encourage people to enter the workforce, and increase work effort.
Benefits or services provided	Tax credit of up to $6,431 in 2018. Beneficiaries may use the credit to reduce federal taxes owed or opt to receive a cash refund.
Eligibility rules	In 2018, recipients with three or more qualifying children had to earn income below $49,194 ($54,884 for married, filing jointly); income limits for families with fewer children are lower, and tax filers with no child had to earn less than $15,270 ($20,950 for married, filing jointly). Note that unemployment insurance does not count as earned income but may impact the amount of EITC.
Service delivery system	Recipients must file tax returns with the Internal Revenue Service, which administers the program.
Financing	Decreases the amount of tax revenue the federal government collects.

EVALUATION OF INCOME-SUPPORT POLICIES AND PROGRAMS

We have examined several income-support policies and programs. This section provides a more in-depth evaluation of two of the major programs, TANF and OASDI, guided by strengths principles. Recall that removing structural barriers to necessary resources is a key tenet of the strengths perspective. Therefore, policy and program goals and designs should focus on access, choice, and opportunities that lead to empowerment. In addition, we should judge the effectiveness of these programs according not only to whether they achieve societal goals, but also whether they help clients achieve their own goals.

The strengths perspective asserts that clients are the experts on their own needs and should therefore be consulted when policy is developed and evaluated. As conduits for clients' perspectives on TANF policy, welfare rights groups provide valuable insights. To view advocacy that gives voice to welfare recipients and other low-income Americans, access the websites or social media profiles of organizations that work with families in poverty, such as the Coalition of California Welfare Rights Organizations and Community Voices Heard. You may also see if the Poor People's Campaign, a grassroots movement that takes on many of the same issues Dr. Martin Luther King, Jr., was working on when he was killed—racism, poverty, and inequality—is active in your community. Many low-income individuals are using social media to weigh in on policy debates that affect the programs on which they rely and to inform policymakers and others about the realities of a life in poverty in the United States today. Some welfare rights groups are also part of the global struggle for human rights. You can learn more about global campaigns for human dignity by studying the United Nations' Universal Declaration of Human Rights (**www.un.org/en/universal-declaration-human-rights/index.html**).

Crucially, examining the outcomes of anti-poverty programs in the United States is impossible to do accurately or justly without attending to the influence of race. Structural barriers, including educational and workplace inequities, prevent some people of color from succeeding in the labor market. These forces also separate them from some components of the income support system, such as OASDI and unemployment insurance. This analysis underscores the need for evaluation of anti-poverty programs and the outcomes they produce to take into account the extent to which U.S. social policy—historically and currently—has contributed to the challenges against which different groups now struggle. In debates around welfare rights, wealth inequity, reparation for past harms, and investments in shared prosperity, social workers' voices are sorely needed.

Positive Impact of Safety Net Programs

While anti-poverty policies are imperfect and the "War on Poverty" that President Johnson declared in 1964 is certainly unfinished, the U.S. poverty rate has fallen considerably in the past 50 years, particularly when measured by a Supplemental Poverty Measure that accounts for in-kind benefits. Further, the effectiveness of anti-poverty programs has increased over this period; in 1967, government assistance lifted above the poverty line just 5 percent of those who would otherwise be poor; by 2016, that figure had jumped to 44 percent (CBPP, 2018b).

EXHIBIT 8.17

The Effect of Safety-Net Programs

Safety Net Cut Poverty Rate Nearly in Half in 2014

- Counting no government assistance (before taxes)
- Counting all government assistance (after taxes)

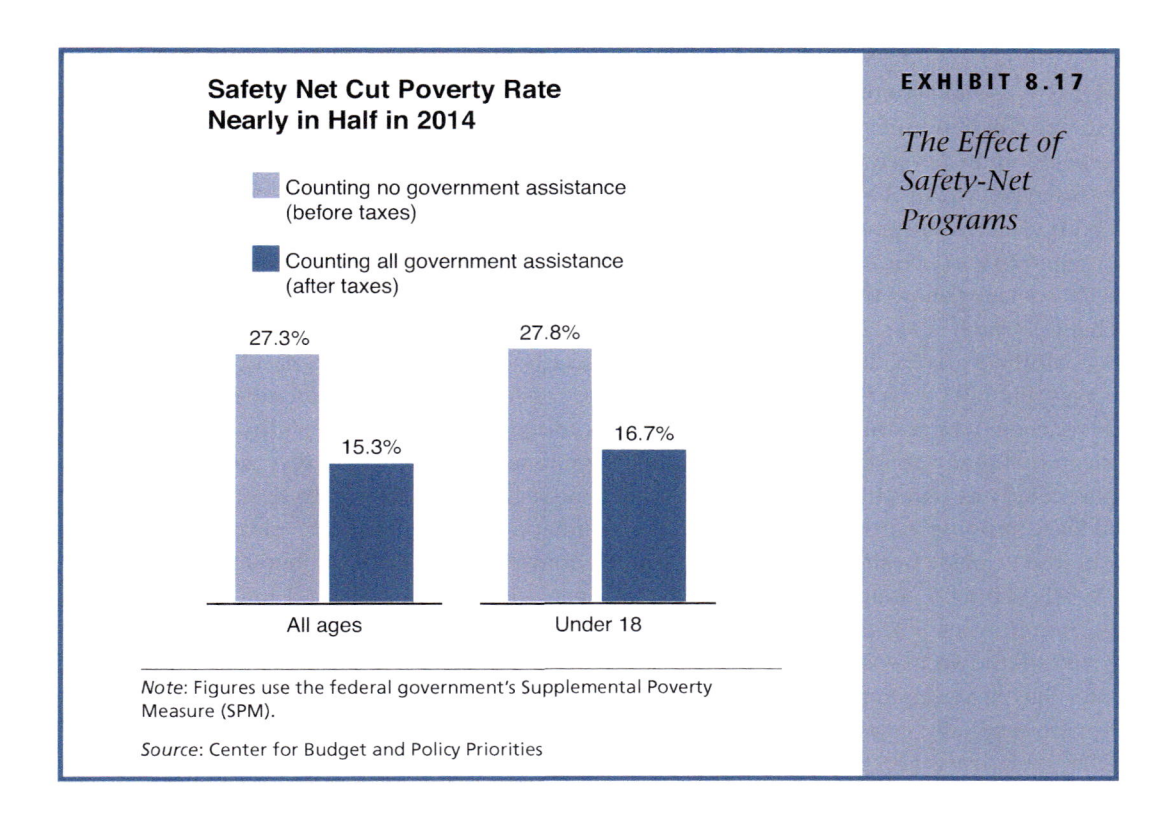

All ages: 27.3% / 15.3%
Under 18: 27.8% / 16.7%

Note: Figures use the federal government's Supplemental Poverty Measure (SPM).

Source: Center for Budget and Policy Priorities

As Exhibit 8.17 indicates, if these safety nets had not existed, almost twice the percentage of Americans would have been living in poverty in 2017. Understanding outcomes of programs like these is essential to improving our efforts to help people living in poverty.

TANF from the Strengths Perspective

A central, broadly shared goal of TANF clients is to move their families out of poverty. However, TANF is designed not to end poverty but rather to lessen dependence on public assistance. This has been the benchmark by which TANF "success" is measured. Indeed, evaluations indicate that TANF reduced welfare caseloads (69 percent over the past two decades) and increased employment, although these effects were due in part to the strong economy in the latter half of the 1990s and, in other cases, to changes in eligibility requirements, which reduced TANF caseloads without necessarily improving well-being. This evaluation largely ignores questions about whether employment enables people to emerge from poverty or how well children do after their families exit TANF. In contrast, from a strengths perspective, analysis of TANF should center on criteria other than declining caseloads. Further, evaluation should include examination of outcomes by race and ethnicity to consider the intersectional effects that may disproportionately disadvantage people of color.

Although child poverty rates for some groups dropped precipitously in the late 1990s, they began to rise and continued to rise in the second decade of the twenty-first century. The poverty rate for children under 18 is higher than for adults. For children under age six, 20 percent are growing up in poverty, as are about 31 percent of children living in single-parent homes. Thirty-three percent of Black children, 33 percent of Native American children, and 26 percent of Latinx children are poor. In comparison, 11 percent of Asian children and of White, non-Latinx children live in poor families (Kids Count, 2018). These figures are particularly alarming given what we know about the deep and lasting effects of poverty on children's development and later chances (Barch et al., 2015; Luby et al., 2013; Tucker-Drob & Bates, 2015).

Mothers leaving TANF—or unable to access cash assistance at all—typically find jobs with wages that fall below the poverty level and in sectors/occupations that provide few benefits or advancement opportunities. Further, difficulties completing complex eligibility determinations mean that many do not receive other public income supports for which they would be eligible, particularly as states have "decoupled" those benefits (Cawley, Schroeder, & Simon, 2016) and reduced funding for outreach and case management. The "benefit cliff" means that workers can lose valuable health care, childcare, and/or housing benefits if their incomes increase only slightly (Romich, Simmelink, & Holt, 2007). Even when people can find full-time work, the minimum wage is seldom enough to support a family. In 2019, the extended federal government shutdown exposed the precarious accounting of the nearly 80 percent of U.S. workers who live paycheck-to-paycheck, never earning enough to really get ahead. Low-income families are especially vulnerable to financial shocks and persistent economic instability. The Pew Charitable Trusts (2015b) found that the typical household earning less than $25,000 only has enough savings to replace six days of household income; families of color are particularly vulnerable on these financial margins.

Many welfare rights groups and other advocates for economic justice endorse the living wage as a strategy for alleviating the problems associated with poverty-level wages. A **living wage** is the income level necessary to live adequately within a given community. Living wage campaigns seek to pass local ordinances requiring businesses that benefit from public money—such as government contracts, loans, or tax incentives—to pay their workers a living wage. In many cases, advocacy for living wage policies has included highlighting the public cost of means-tested assistance for low-wage workers who would not need benefits such as SNAP and Medicaid if they were paid fairly. The precise wage that is considered "livable" varies by community, but the goal is to ensure that no worker earns below the poverty line. You can use the Living Wage Calculator developed by faculty at MIT to calculate the living wage in your community (livingwage.mit.edu).

Other advocates have focused on specific industries, as in the successful Fight for $15 movement, which began in and still concentrates on fast-food workers. Currently, 29 states have minimum wages higher than the federal minimum wage of $7.25 per hour, although many of these are still not truly livable wages. To create a living wage, policymakers in Arizona, California, Maine, Massachusetts, New York, and Washington have increased their state minimum wages substantially, often including a provision that automatically increases the minimum wage as inflation pushes prices up. In most of these states, the minimum wage will soon be $15 per hour, although this is not necessarily a wage that will enable households to meet all their financial needs, given the high cost of living in some areas. Further, ballot measures increasing the minimum wage have won voter support in recent years in places such as Alaska, Arkansas, Missouri, Nebraska, Ohio, and South Dakota. The University of California-Berkeley Labor Center has catalogued dozens of counties and municipalities that have passed living wage ordinances through a combination of legislative action and public referendum. You can see if there has been action on this issue in your community and view the evidence that many people see today's minimum wage as insufficient at **laborcenter.berkeley.edu/minimum-wage-living-wage-resources/inventory-of-us-city-and-county-minimum-wage-ordinances/**.

Family economic security increasingly requires more than just an adequate cash income for one worker. To account for the other crucial advantages that accrue to those who have "good jobs," living wage campaigners and their allies also advocate for benefits such as health coverage, paid vacation, and family leave. While living wage movements and successful labor organizing efforts have won some recognizable victories on behalf of working people in the United States, declining real wages and the shift toward more highly skilled information-based industries have meant that only the massive entry of women into the workforce has made it possible for families to continue consumption levels similar to those in the 1970s. To support families in reaching their goals of economic security, family well-being, and a chance at upward mobility, we must reconsider the "deal" workers get in the labor market, as well as the policy investments that complement employment arrangements.

Strengths-Based Priorities for TANF Reform   Within the context of the current economic and social policy landscapes, what changes in TANF policy would more effectively meet the needs and support the goals of low-income families? First, states need to focus their use of TANF funds on core functions such as more adequate cash benefits and more effective employment supports, rather than diverting those funds to other purposes. Further, parents in the paid workforce should have affordable access to high-quality childcare, transportation, and training for jobs that pay a living wage. The strengths perspective also encourages us to carefully analyze the barriers that prevent families from reaching their goals, including inadequate education, addiction, domestic violence, physical or mental illness, or geographic isolation. Families who have difficulty succeeding in the labor market often face many of these barriers simultaneously. Focusing on overcoming these barriers rather than on enforcing work requirements would better serve their needs and long-term U.S. policy interests. Other needed reforms grounded in the strengths perspective include policies to protect women's family formation and marital choices. Additionally, policies to encourage parents' involvement in their children's lives, such as the option of working only part-time or receiving work credits for involvement in school activities, may help mitigate the heightened risks of school failure, teen pregnancy, and delinquency that poor children face.

Restoring the concept of cash assistance as a federal entitlement might help ensure that at least the basic survival needs of children in poor families are met. Social work values and our collective interests in future productivity and societal well-being demand that our nation's children be provided with a safety net when other systems fail them. Analysis suggests that child poverty costs the country more than $500 billion per year (Coley & Baker, 2013), in addition to the negative effects on psychological well-being and intellectual development that are difficult to quantify. To improve the adequacy of anti-poverty policy, the NASW supports integrating welfare, housing, economic, education, child welfare, and mental health policies to create a comprehensive and holistic approach to confronting poverty (NASW, 2015f).

Another strengths-based strategy to reform TANF is to reconsider the five-year time limit on receipt of federal funds. This time limit fails to consider circumstances that can force some individuals to rely on public assistance for a longer period (Edin & Shaefer, 2016). Even individuals who work may not earn enough to survive without public income support, resulting in economic crises if families abruptly lose benefits. If the five-year limit is not abolished, it needs to be modified to stipulate that the clock may be stopped in some instances. For example, policies could specify that periods when a parent must care full-time for a family member with disabilities will not be counted against the limit. Individuals could have extended periods of eligibility if they demonstrate consistent work effort, even when jobs are unavailable. The NASW supports eliminating time limits as well as family caps. Enacted in 22 states after TANF allowed the rule and still in place in 14 states, family caps prohibit benefits for babies born after a household enrolls in TANF (Thomhave, 2018). Family caps unduly restrict family formation decisions and compromise health and well-being by placing additional strains on the family's budget. Instead, policies should be developed that support families' efforts to move out of poverty.

States have authority over key policies that govern basic safety net programs, including not only TANF but also SNAP and Medicaid, and could take steps to align these programs with strengths-based principles. For example, states can raise and, in some cases, eliminate asset limits for these programs. However, federal rule changes are reducing states' latitude to make sure strengths-based investments in low-income households' capacity. Disturbingly, when programs send people in poverty the message that if they ever accumulate assets beyond a bare minimum, the safety net they rely on will not be available, they may be discouraged from taking steps that could move their family permanently out of poverty (Ratcliffe et al., 2016). When states eliminate asset limits, they may facilitate upward mobility among those trying to leave poverty. This move can also reduce administrative costs by streamlining eligibility determinations.

OASDI from the Strengths Perspective

Just as with TANF, any strengths-based evaluation of OASDI should start by examining the perspectives of the target group. Consumer groups such as the Gray Panthers and advocacy organizations such as AARP provide insights into how OASDI has benefited generations of Americans and how the program may need to change. They speak to the importance of OASDI in protecting workers and their families from loss of income due to retirement, disability, or death. The monthly OASDI check gives consumers a choice of how best to meet their needs, and the program's structure keeps administrative costs low. Because eligibility is determined by age, payment of payroll taxes, and disability, beneficiaries do not have to submit to humiliating means tests or navigate complicated application processes.

Women and OASDI   If not for OASDI, more than half of women over 65 would be living in poverty. However, even with Social Security, older women are nearly twice as likely as older men to be poor. Because older women have experienced gender inequity in educational and employment opportunities over a lifetime, they often enter old age with shorter, less consistent, and lower-paid employment histories than men. While a minimum benefit that considers part-time as well as full-time work would be particularly beneficial for women, OASDI does not provide such a policy. Although providing coverage for a spouse in the amount of half of the worker's earnings does partially recognize the spouse's role in supporting the worker, this amount varies not by the spouse's contribution but by the worker's earnings. This effectively penalizes spouses of low-income workers, who are likely to be economically disadvantaged themselves. In addition, couples who divorce before their tenth anniversaries are not eligible for survivors' insurance. Also disadvantaged are women who have worked alongside a low-income spouse. When both spouses work outside the home, the couple may pay more taxes and receive lower yearly Social Security benefits at retirement than a one-earner couple with the same income.

Individuals do not earn Social Security credits for unpaid labor they perform caring for children and older adults. Therefore, women, who have traditionally been expected to assume these duties, are disadvantaged first when they are not paid for this work and again at retirement when their contributions are not recognized. Many women will be unable to secure adequate retirement income unless policymakers reform Social Security so that caregivers receive credits for their caregiving. It is therefore important to preserve OASDI features particularly important to women. These features include a progressive benefit formula that aids lower-income earners; benefits for children and their parent caregiver when a working parent is disabled or dies; spousal and survivor benefits for married women, divorced women, and widows; and a full cost-of-living adjustment.

Protecting benefits from inflation is essential for women who, on average, live longer than men. Conversely, proposals to use a chained Consumer Price Index (CPI) to reduce OASDI's cost-of-living adjustment would exacerbate the disproportionately high risk of poverty that very old women currently face. Chained CPI calculations assume people can substitute lower-cost products when prices of goods (e.g., types of meat and fresh vegetables) and services (e.g., transportation) rise. However, many older adults are already living close to the margins and would have difficulty absorbing rising prices and falling benefits. Having seen policymakers use chained CPI to calculate increases in tax brackets and the standard deduction in the 2017 tax reform and as the cornerstone of proposed changes to poverty guidelines, advocates for low-income older adults are concerned that this approach could be used to cut Social Security.

People of Color and OASDI A system that bases eligibility on salary earned and time spent in covered jobs disadvantages people who have experienced racial discrimination during their working lives. Because earnings determine benefits, White males who earn higher wages receive higher benefits. At the same time, workers of color and those in lower-paying sectors are less likely to have significant retirement benefits outside of OASDI, making inadequacies particularly detrimental to their financial well-being. OASDI provides 90 percent or more of income for 31 percent of Latinx and 33 percent of Black older adults (Dushi, Iams, & Trenkamp, 2017). Without Social Security, the poverty rate among elderly Latinx would approach 50 percent, and the poverty rate among elderly African Americans would exceed 50 percent (Romig, 2018). Raising the retirement age, as some policymakers have proposed, would further disadvantage older workers of color. While life expectancy has increased overall, workers with higher incomes often live longer than those with low incomes, who are disproportionately people of color. However, arguments that OASDI is unfair to people of color because they are less likely to receive the retirement benefits for which they have contributed overlook the fact that these workers may receive disability and survivors' benefits. Because people of color face significant health disparities, these elements of OASDI are especially important for them.

Is OASDI Regressive or Progressive? The Social Security tax is regressive because both high- and low-income employees contribute at the same rate—an obligation that is more burdensome for those with lower incomes. Amplifying this inequity is the income cap on the FICA tax. In 2018, employees did not pay the tax on income above $128,400. This means that an individual earning below this annual income pays FICA taxes on a larger percentage of their total income than an individual earning far above it. However, distribution of benefits is progressive in that low-wage earners receive a proportionally higher rate of return on their contributions. In this way, OASDI has a redistributive function.

OASDI: Solvency and Reform Proposals for reforming Social Security retirement to extend solvency beyond the current anticipated date of 2034 include the following:

- raising the retirement age, although workers in physically demanding jobs, as well as those with disabilities, may find it difficult to work longer;
- increasing the tax that workers and employers pay into the system;
- requiring that high earners pay FICA taxes on their entire incomes;
- dedicating taxes on estates worth more than $3.5 million to Social Security reserves; and
- mandating that all federal and state workers take part in the national retirement program.

Young people, concerned about the solvency of OASDI, have questioned whether Social Security benefits will be there for them. While many young people already benefit from OASDI in the form of disability and survivors' benefits, this insurance element is often overlooked. Further, anxieties about the future of OASDI retirement benefits add to the context of economic insecurity that has characterized the lives of many young Americans in recent years. Buffeted by student debt, job instability, and the slow recovery of balance sheets following the Great Recession, workers in the Millennial generation have less retirement wealth than older generations did at their age (Gale, 2019). While demographic, economic, and social forces contribute to changing attitudes about the viability of "retirement" as currently understood, young adults are correct to conclude that the sustainability of Social Security is of particular significance for their own future financial well-being.

One highly controversial proposal for reforming Social Security is to privatize the system, although the recession and subsequent stock market volatility cooled enthusiasm for privatization. While privatization plans vary, they would use Social Security funds to create private investment accounts, toward which younger workers could redirect a portion of their FICA taxes. However, setting up and administering such a system would involve substantial costs.

In addition, private accounts would divert funds from the current program, thus hastening the arrival of an OASDI solvency "crisis." Finally, since most workers' employment-based retirement is already heavily invested in private systems that carry risk of financial loss, the political prospects of shifting entirely to such private models are dubious.

Although strategies to help people save and accumulate assets are in keeping with the strengths perspective, pursuing these approaches by reducing income support could intensify economic inequity and deprivation. Such a change would also undermine the social insurance principle of OASDI, which pools risk and softens the exposure inherent in a capitalistic system. Today, relatively minor adjustments to payroll taxes, benefits, and eligibility rules can ensure OASDI solvency far into the future, without abandoning this crucial intergenerational contract.

From the strengths perspective, OASDI provides consumer choice by transferring cash benefits that can be spent as people desire. Non-stigmatizing and universal, OASDI enjoys public support despite calculated efforts to undermine it. Advocacy to protect and improve OASDI is sorely needed. You can contribute to these efforts by getting your facts straight and speaking up when OASDI is discussed. As policymakers seek to reform OASDI, social work advocates can arm themselves with knowledge of the program's successes.

PROMISING DIRECTIONS IN ANTI-POVERTY POLICY

As described here, several of our current policy efforts make significant contributions to preventing, reducing, and ameliorating poverty. OASDI has transformed the economic realities of millions of older Americans, SNAP ensures that hunger does not necessarily accompany financial hardship, and the EITC uses the tax code to efficiently and effectively augment the wages of low-income families. These successes notwithstanding, however, too many Americans contend with poverty in a time of relative prosperity. Millions more live in economic insecurity, feeling "poor" even if their incomes are somewhat above the official threshold. There are promising avenues the nation could pursue to better distribute available resources to these households. Seen through the strengths perspective, these policy directions could amplify people's capacities, build on the incomplete foundation of existing policy, and equip the nation to meet the evolving challenges of an unknown financial future. In this final section, we describe a recent national effort to systematically examine and then collectively confront child poverty, as well as two promising areas of policy innovation: asset development and universal income support. These are not the only approaches worth pursuing, certainly. The next generation of social workers and allies will make their own contributions and leave their own marks on the nation's journey to end poverty.

A Roadmap to Ending Child Poverty

In 2015, Congress commissioned the National Academies of Sciences, Engineering, and Medicine to conduct a comprehensive study of child poverty in the United States. The Academies were directed to identify evidence-based programs and policies that could achieve the goal of cutting child poverty in half within ten years—a timeframe that necessitated an emphasis on interventions that could quickly increase parents' resources and result in tangible improvements in families' well-being. Among the findings was substantial evidence that policy has made significant strides in reducing poverty, improving children's health, and stabilizing families. The report cited evidence included in this chapter, including the relationship between the EITC and children's outcomes and the positive impact of helping low-income families relocate to low-poverty neighborhoods when children are young. Had U.S. anti-poverty programs not been operating, child poverty would have been considerably higher; eliminating SNAP alone, for example, would raise the child poverty rate to 18.2 percent (National Academies of Sciences, Engineering, and Medicine, 2019).

This analysis helps to make the case that policy change can place even ambitious goals within reach. Child poverty in the United States fell by 50 percent between 1967 and 2016, in large part due to changes in a variety of policy domains. This history suggests that effectively tackling child poverty is a question of *political will* more than technical challenge. The National Academies analyzed the costs and projected effects of different policy options and "packages." While no single option considered could meet the goal of reducing child poverty by half, combinations of changes to tax, housing, and work support policies could make substantial progress. As was the intention, this analysis lays out a roadmap that policymakers can follow to reduce child poverty, calibrating selection of options to satisfy aims such as increasing work participation, limiting public expenditure, and fueling economic growth, while committing to approaches with demonstrated potential to make child poverty a relic of our past, rather than a tragic part of children's futures. The Academies' specific recommendations to reduce child poverty are outlined in Exhibit 8.18. You can read the National Academies' Roadmap to Reducing Child Poverty, see simulations of projected effects of different approaches, and evaluate the policy options for yourself at **www.nap.edu/catalog/25246/a-roadmap-to-reducing-child-poverty**.

EXHIBIT 8.18

Roadmap to Reducing Child Poverty

PROGRAM AND POLICY OPTIONS TIED TO WORK:
- expanding the Earned Income Tax Credit (EITC);
- expanding child care subsidies;
- raising the federal minimum wage; and
- implementing a promising training and employment program called WorkAdvance nationwide.

MODIFICATIONS TO EXISTING SAFETY NET PROGRAMS:
- expanding the Supplemental Nutrition Assistance Program (SNAP);
- expanding the housing choice voucher program; and
- expanding the Supplemental Security Income (SSI) program.

OPTIONS USED IN OTHER COUNTRIES:
- introducing a universal child allowance (which can also be thought of as an extension of the federal child tax credit, delivered monthly instead of once a year); and
- introducing a child support assurance program that sets guaranteed minimum child support amounts per child per month.

MODIFICATIONS TO EXISTING PROVISIONS RELATING TO IMMIGRANTS:
- Increasing immigrants' access to safety net programs.

Asset-Based Approaches

A strengths-based approach to ending poverty must include attention not only to income but also to assets, as the foundation on which people can build toward their goals. The term "assets" can even be synonymous with strengths, although the financial context is more specific, defined as equity in a home or other property, deposit accounts, and investments such as stocks. Assets are more than a storehouse for future consumption. They provide a hedge that facilitates productive risk-taking, a buffer against life crises such as unemployment and health emergencies, a vehicle for transferring wealth across generations, and a platform for upward mobility. Indeed, evidence suggests that asset accumulation may have profound psychological and behavioral effects (Yadama & Sherraden, 1996). Critically, as described in Chapter 4, inequality in asset distribution in the United States is vastly greater than income inequality (Wolff, 2017). This stark divide and growing understanding of its implications have prompted proposals to facilitate asset accumulation among people with low incomes and other disadvantages. While asset-based anti-poverty policy is sometimes considered a "new" approach, the concept of using government intervention to help Americans build a solid financial foundation is certainly not novel. U.S. tax policy invests hundreds of millions of dollars in wealth promotion (Levin, 2014). Historically, public policies have helped many Americans accumulate life-changing assets, albeit with inequitable effects.

Social worker Michael Sherraden has been one of the primary advocates for an asset-based approach to combating poverty. In his book, *Assets and the Poor: A New American Welfare Policy* (1991), Sherraden proposed that the U.S. shift from a welfare paradigm focused on income maintenance to one that strives to narrow inequality in asset ownership. As it stands today, even when families receive assistance fulfilling their basic consumption needs, they remain in poverty and, therefore, are denied the advantages conferred by asset accumulation, including the ability to plan for the future they want. The injustice of asset inequality is particularly acute given assets' effects on children's educational outcomes (Elliott, 2013). By failing to assist low-income households in accumulating assets, U.S. anti-poverty policy is not only hindering households' economic security today, it is crippling their children's upward mobility tomorrow (Elliott & Lewis, 2018).

Asset poverty is measured by examining the extent to which people have sufficient assets to continue to meet their basic needs during temporary hard times. In 2014, more than 25 percent of the U.S. population was *asset poor*, defined as lacking enough in assets to cover three months' expenses without income. More than 40 percent were *liquid asset poor*, meaning they could not survive three months without selling off property they own (Prosperity Now, 2018). Trends in asset poverty parallel income poverty data in many respects; for example, asset and liquid asset poverty rates are higher for households of color, with nearly 60 percent of African-American households in some states living in asset poverty (Prosperity Now, 2019). Importantly, in every state, asset poverty rates were greater than income poverty rates.

Attending to asset poverty as a dimension of financial deprivation does not mean that income is irrelevant. Indeed, Sherraden emphasized that asset development should complement income assistance, not replace it. However, asset-based policy may also help prevent poverty, both in the short term by helping to smooth over income losses and in the longer-term by enabling households to build greater economic security.

A number of policies and programs exist to help middle- and upper-class Americans accumulate assets. Indeed, some argue that public expenditures on these programs create an "upside-down" welfare state where wealth is redistributed to people at the top of the income ladder. Asset-policy advocates are working to devise strategies that can help low-income families equitably benefit from policies that aid in asset accumulation. With some modifications, structures such as 529 state college savings plans and tax-advantaged Individual Retirement Accounts (IRAs) could fuel wealth-building in low-income as well as high-income households. However, given the inequities in current wealth distribution and the inadequacy of current structures for meeting the needs of those in poverty, there is a need to create new, more explicitly redistributive structures.

In his book, Sherraden suggested establishing savings accounts for people living in or near poverty that would match individuals' deposits with public or private funds. He called them Individual Development Accounts (IDAs) and proposed that they be universal, with increased matched amounts and greater incentives for people in poverty (Sherraden, 2000). Inspired by Sherraden's vision of helping people save their way out of poverty, federal, state, and local entities passed IDA legislation and established projects designed to position people for opportunities associated with upward mobility, including higher education, job training, homeownership, and/or entrepreneurship. The federal government determined that IDAs cannot be considered assets when determining TANF eligibility (Edwards & Mason, 2003), and some states followed suit, paving the way for asset complements to anti-poverty policy.

Large-scale evaluations of IDA programs indicate that low-income people, including even the very poor, can save; further, people use their IDAs to make asset-building purchases (Delgadillo, 2015; Grinstead et al., 2011; Schreiner, Clancy, & Sherraden, 2002; Zhan, 2003). Account-holders reported increased feelings of short-term and long-term security, more hope for the future, and greater self-confidence (Corporation for Enterprise Development [CFED], 2009). Crucially, asset-based anti-poverty policy has significant appeal across ideological divides. Liberals tout progressive benefits while conservatives appreciate that low-income individuals are expected to contribute and to use the money for development. These policies build on a strengths-based view of people as competent and able to set and reach goals when public policies facilitate growth.

In the global economy of the future, workers will be less likely than in previous generations to have steady employment over a lifetime. In this environment, access to assets can enable a person to fund training, weather downturns in the job market, or start a business that can provide a path out of poverty. Children in low-income households that save are less likely to be poor as adults (Cramer et al., 2009), and low-income children who have savings accounts dedicated for higher education are more likely to graduate from college (Elliott, 2013)—still the clearest route to long-term financial security (Daly & Bengali, 2014).

Bolstered by evidence that low-income individuals will save with the right support and that the experience of accumulating assets may have substantial positive effects on individual well-being, U.S. researchers and policymakers continue to develop asset-based initiatives to help low-income families. One such initiative, building on the IDA foundation, is Children's Savings Accounts (CSAs). Sometimes called Child Development Accounts (CDAs), they establish savings accounts early, ideally at or near birth, seed them with public and/or private dollars, and provide progressive matching and other support to help families save for their children's futures. The hope is that these approaches can cultivate early identification with higher education, improve children's outcomes throughout the educational system, and move financial aid away from debt dependence. To date, research has affirmed these aspirations; on many fronts, it seems that investing in children's assets can realize more equitable outcomes, even for those who remain in income poverty.

Although not yet nationwide, policy innovations are testing CSAs and delivering transformative assets to young people in places as diverse as Indiana, Maine, New Mexico, California, Pennsylvania, and Missouri. As is usually the case with devolved approaches, policy and program design vary. Some CSAs incentivize behaviors associated with upward mobility, such as academic preparation, parental engagement in children's education, and/or financial planning. Some states have used their 529 college savings plans to provide universal accounts for all babies, financed with $100 to $1,000 in initial investment. An evaluation of a universal CSA in Oklahoma found that the early assets substantially increased children's social and emotional development, particularly among low-income families (Huang et al., 2014). Further, even though the assets were dedicated to higher education and could not be used to supplement family income, the existence of the CSA mitigated about half of the negative effects of poverty on child development; essentially, assets' effects on families' expectations of future chances were strong enough to counteract much of the weight of poverty (Huang, Kim, & Sherraden, 2017).

Some CSAs are administered through school districts, where administrators' attention has been captured by findings that early assets can close achievement gaps between high- and low-income students (Elliott, Jung, & Friedline, 2011; Elliott et al., 2016). And, encouraged by evidence that helping students avoid debt may increase the return on a college degree, some organizations that provide college scholarships are looking for ways to fuel children's asset-building, too. Key scholars and experts on racial equity have suggested that the federal government establish universal accounts at birth. Seeded with a lump sum inversely correlated to parental wealth—all children would get an account, with larger federal deposits for poor children—such policy could serve as a hedge against widening inequality (Hamilton & Darity, 2010). Strengths-based social workers see that policies that put people in charge of their own decisions and equip them with tools with which to confront their challenges are superior to many of our current programs, which often require families to submit to invasive questioning and go along with others' ideas for their lives, to get what they need to survive.

While asset-based initiatives can be critical complements to public income-support programs, social workers must continue to eliminate the structural barriers that keep people in poverty, such as discrimination in employment, inferior educational institutions, and inequitable wages. Further, policymakers should design asset strategies carefully. Diverting crucial funds from programs that help low-income families meet basic needs would erode an already badly frayed safety net. Developing, implementing, and evaluating additional ways to extend support for asset accumulation to moderate- and low-income families, in pursuit of an integrated economic mobility system, may help families build a more financially secure future. For more information on strategies to place asset building within reach of all households, particularly for the benefit of children living in and near poverty, go to the website of the Center on Assets, Education, and Inclusion at **aedi.ssw.umich.edu/**.

Universal Basic Income: Fundamental Reform to End Poverty

In addition to proposing adjustments to existing anti-poverty programs, critics of policies designed to help people in need have recommended fundamental reforms to the way support is provided. Expansion of asset-based policy is one such proposal. Another, which is gaining traction around the world and across the U.S. political spectrum, is Universal Basic Income (UBI). Under a Universal Basic Income policy (sometimes called Basic Income Grant, or BIG), every individual, regardless of income, would receive a uniform benefit. Unlike other policies outlined in this chapter, UBI would be explicitly designed to end poverty—by simply providing enough income, every month, to ensure that no one falls below the poverty line. The precise calibration of UBI policy would have to be determined; some proposals call for $1,000 for everyone, each month, while others set different amounts for families with children, seniors, or those with disabilities (Lowrey, 2018). Some UBI proposals would tax the benefits heavily for high-income households, while payments to low-income families would go largely untaxed.

However, the "universal" in UBI is absolute; in all policy designs and in pilots implemented in Germany, the Netherlands, Finland, Canada, Kenya, and Stockton, California, every person enrolled receives the monthly payment regardless of age, income, or employment status. Universality would make UBI an immediate entitlement and could provide considerable political protection, since everyone would have a stake. Indeed, interest in UBI is growing among conservatives who see writing a check (or transferring money electronically) as more efficient than our current patchwork of anti-poverty policies, as well as among those alarmed by TANF's shrinking reach and the rise of extreme poverty in households that essentially have no income at all (Smith & Chandy, 2014).

UBI also resonates with many in the public who are anxious about increasing automation, economic insecurity, and a growing sense that work alone is insufficient to provide a solid financial future (Lowrey, 2018). At the same time, UBI would be a departure from our current approaches to income support, and the analysis to support it is still evolving. Some UBI critics interpreted the early results of Finland's UBI trial as evidence that Universal Basic Income cannot deliver on its promises, since the first two years of the randomized pilot found no significant effects on unemployed adults' work participation and little reduction in other benefit receipt. However, positioned within the context of Finland's reforms to its social insurance system, observers see reason for some optimism. Those receiving the UBI reported greater confidence in their future, improved health, and better overall well-being—even when they had not yet found work (Kangas et al., 2019). As technological change, growing inequality, and many measures of individual and population distress proliferate around the globe, social workers see real promise in a policy that appears to help people weather these storms.

Globally, UBI is not without precedent. Most developed countries already provide some sort of universal children's allowance, viewing it as an investment not only in the child's future, but also in the nation's long-term prosperity. However, in the United States, benefits are primarily provided through the tax structure, which mutes their redistributive potency. Despite the "buzz" it is generating in some circles, UBI is not on the immediate policy agenda. Like earlier proposals to create a minimum family income, concerns about cost and work disincentives challenge UBI's enactment. The precise cost would depend largely on whether UBI would replace or complement existing welfare policies, and it is difficult to determine how UBI would influence work effort—particularly in the uncertain labor market of the future. Some have proposed wage subsidies—delivered within a worker's paycheck, rather than after the fact, as in the EITC—as an alternative to UBI that would preserve the role of "work" in defining Americans' lives and identities (Cass, 2018). What is undeniable is the need for policies designed to help lift families out of poverty and strengthen the social contract. UBI is one such attempt. It could reduce inequality and provide a crucial safety net for

Americans whose jobs are lost to robots or to other countries (Lowrey, 2018). To learn more about UBI/BIG, go to the website of the U.S. Basic Income Guarantee Network (**www.usbig.net**).

CONCLUSION

Inclusive economic growth and intentional measures to create equity are essential aims of a capacity-building state. Income programs provide a safety net so that people who lose or can't find jobs can survive hard times and find stability, while policies that help them build assets open the door to opportunities. Our nation pays directly and indirectly for people who do not have the means to participate fully in the economy. To align our policies with social work values, meet people's needs, and provide for our collective welfare, we must find effective strategies to change unfair and unproductive outcomes.

Additionally, in today's increasingly globalized context, our consideration of anti-poverty policy reforms should look beyond our borders. As has already been described, other countries have promising ideas that could make valuable contributions to our policy landscape. Further, poverty in other parts of the world affect Americans, including in ways that may alter our policy options, today and in the future; poverty rates contribute to migration, affect global labor markets, and drive utilization of natural resources. Strengths-based social workers recognize our interdependence, see global poverty as part of the ecology that shapes U.S. social and economic policies, and commit to solidarity with people in poverty—in all nations.

Poverty in the Global Context

To measure the incidence and extent of global poverty, the United Nations uses a Multidimensional Poverty Index (MPI), which reflects acute deprivation in health, education, and standard of living. This expands on money-based measures by considering factors that influence experiences of deprivation, including years of schooling, access to clean water, asset ownership, and infant mortality. In the 105 countries included in the MPI Report, roughly 1.3 billion people—about 23 percent of the population of these countries—live in multidimensional poverty (Oxford Poverty and Human Development Initiative, 2018). By some indicators, global poverty resembles poverty in the U.S. context. For example, half of the multidimensionally poor are children under age 18, and those living in rural areas are overrepresented (Oxford Poverty and Human Development Initiative, 2018). Also like the United States, the world has made considerable progress in reducing global poverty and yet has much more to do. Social justice demands and an increasing commitment to cultural humility and cross-border solidarity are propelling some social workers into careers focused on lessening global poverty. As with all aspects of social work, a strengths approach to this effort centers the voices of people experiencing poverty in these countries when developing interventions. To learn more about United Nations initiatives to address global poverty, read UN Human Development Reports (**http://hdr.undp.org**).

Anti-Poverty Social Work Practice

Helping people meet their basic needs is often the first step in effective social work practice. To help you align your practice and policy study, Quick Guide 6 provides a brief description of the major programs discussed in this chapter and information on how to help your clients apply for benefits.

As a social worker, you will likely meet families who struggle to get by with few resources. They may need help filling out complicated application forms and navigating benefit processes. Unfortunately, benefits frequently are inadequate and in short supply. Policy practice to expand benefits and improve access is sorely needed. In addition to making sure clients know about available benefits, social workers should seek to inform public debate about the causes and consequences of poverty, the struggles facing people living with low incomes, the inadequacy of our poverty line for measuring the true scope of need, and the consequences of the wealth divide. Further, social workers and policymakers should develop and test more strategies

QUICK GUIDE 6 Income- and Asset-Based Programs

Old-Age, Survivors, and Disability Insurance (OASDI)	Insurance program for workers who pay payroll taxes/insurance premiums, based on earned income, into the Social Security Trust Fund. The program pays monthly benefits to those who are eligible, including retired workers, survivors (spouses and children) of deceased workers, and disabled workers (when their work history qualifies). Benefit amounts depend on earnings and years of contribution. For more information and details on the application process, see **www.ssa.gov**.
Temporary Assistance for Needy Families (TANF)	Monthly cash assistance for low-income families with children under 18 who qualify. Must be engaged in employment or work-related activities within two years of enrollment. Requirements and benefits vary by state. For more information about application, go to **www.acf.hhs.gov/ofa/help** and select your state.
Supplemental Security Income (SSI)	Cash assistance for low-income adults and children with disabilities; must meet functional and income requirements. Low-income people age 65 and older without disabilities are also eligible. For more information on the application process, see **www.ssa.gov/pgm/ssi.htm**.
Supplemental Nutrition Assistance Program (SNAP)	Nutrition assistance program for qualifying low-income individuals and families; provides resources via electronic transfer. For more information about application, see **www.fns.usda.gov/snap**.
Women, Infants, and Children (WIC)	Nutrition assistance program intended to enhance health and wellness for qualifying low-income pregnant women, mothers, and young children. For details on the application process, see **www.fns.usda.gov/wic**.
General Assistance (GA)	Short-term cash assistance provided by some states/cities to low-income adults who do not qualify for other assistance.
Earned Income Tax Credit (EITC)	Tax credit issued for qualified income; the amount of credit depends on the number of qualifying children claimed on the tax return along with factors such as military service, disability, and adjusted gross income. For information, visit **www.irs.gov** and search for Earned Income Tax Credit.
Individual Development Account (IDA) and Children's Savings Account (CSA)	Investments intended to help low-income savers attain financial stability or pursue upward mobility. Find where programs are available and how policies are changing by reviewing resources at Prosperity Now: **http://prosperitynow.org**.

INCOME- AND ASSET-BASED POLICIES   **305**

to help low-income families escape poverty. We need effective safety-net programs, equitable asset-building strategies, and sufficient job creation. Failure to provide this vital infrastructure imperils economic growth and places our children at risk. Our future depends on having an educated, healthy, and engaged population that has opportunities to succeed. More attention to capacity-building approaches can help close widening gaps so that more Americans can look toward their futures with a foundation of financial security and a meaningful chance of upward mobility.

MAIN POINTS

- The U.S. Census Bureau primarily uses the poverty threshold or *poverty line*, which was $25,465 for a family of two adults and two children in 2018, to determine who is poor for statistical purposes. The USDHHS issues poverty guidelines, adjusted for Alaska and Hawaii, and uses them to determine eligibility for federal programs.

- Poverty can also be defined in relative terms, whereby people are judged to be poor if they do not have sufficient resources to maintain a standard of living considered adequate in a given society at a particular time.

- The capabilities perspective defines poverty as the absence of opportunities to achieve capabilities to be sheltered, well-nourished, adequately clothed, healthy, and active in the community.

- Recognition of the inadequacy of the current poverty threshold as a measure of what people need to afford a decent standard of living has led to calls for alternative measures. Ideally, such measures should consider the value of in-kind benefits, the true cost of necessities like housing and health care, and the tremendous variations in costs across different communities.

- Asset poverty measures should complement income-based assessments to provide a clearer picture of financial vulnerability.

- Income-support programs may be either universal or selective. Entitlement programs, which can also be universal or selective, require that benefits be distributed to all people who meet program criteria, regardless of total cost.

- Old-Age, Survivors, and Disability Insurance (OASDI), Unemployment Insurance, workers' compensation, and veterans' benefits are examples of universal income-support programs provided to eligible people regardless of income.

- The fiscal and political success of OASDI depend on its structure as a social insurance program, where the government provides the institution through which individuals share the risks and rewards associated with participation in a capitalist economy. As debate about OASDI reform continues, social workers should be wary of efforts that could undermine this insurance principle.

- Selective income-support programs are means-tested and include Temporary Assistance to Needy Families (TANF), Supplemental Nutrition Assistance Program (SNAP), Supplemental Nutrition for Women, Infants, and Children (WIC), public housing, Supplemental Security Income (SSI), General Assistance (GA), and the Earned Income Tax Credit (EITC).

- TANF reflects changing attitudes about the role of women in society and our obligation to those experiencing financial challenges. Where parents in poverty used to receive a guaranteed cash grant to support their children, TANF is a block grant that serves a declining percentage of poor families. Many states provide only enough support to bring recipients to about half the official poverty line and use strict sanctions and time limits to try to control participants' lives.

- Although badly frayed, our public safety-net programs keep many people out of poverty and still others from falling even further into poverty.

- When evaluating the effectiveness of safety-net policies, strengths perspective principles emphasize examination of client goals and outcomes as the measure of success. Policy and program goals and design should focus on removing structural barriers and increasing opportunities.

- Children's Savings Accounts (CSAs) have gained traction as platforms for asset accumulation, particularly given the potential for improved outcomes for children who grow up with the economic security an asset base can provide.

- Such asset-based programs may complement, but should not replace, income-support programs, to construct an integrated economic mobility system for low-income Americans.

- The Multidimensional Poverty Index (MPI), which goes beyond money-based measures to consider factors such as years of schooling, access to clean water, assets, and infant mortality, can be used to compare poverty globally.

EXERCISES

1. Go to the Sanchez family case at **www.routledgesw.com/cases**. What benefits discussed in this chapter do you think Joey and Vicki might be eligible to receive?
   a. What further information would you need to determine their eligibility?
   b. How might the stigma attached to some means-tested programs impact this immigrant family, given their values and life experiences?
   c. How might recent changes regarding immigrants' inadmissibility on grounds of public charge affect the willingness of the Sanchez family and others in their community to seek assistance from programs such as SNAP, subsidized housing, and Medicaid? How would you, as a social worker, help immigrants navigate their options according to the current regulations?

d. Since the Sanchez family lives in a mostly immigrant community, how might policy changes in 1996 have affected the neighborhood's well-being? What policy reforms would positively impact families like them?
3. Go to the Carla Washburn case at **www.routledgesw.com/cases**. Financial struggles are among the challenges many grandparents raising grandchildren, like Mrs. Washburn, face. Find out what benefits grandparents raising grandchildren may receive in your state. Do eligibility rules differ for grandparents applying for different means-tested benefits, such as TANF, SNAP, WIC, and subsidized housing?
    a. Must grandparents in your state return to work in order to receive TANF benefits? What barriers do you think Mrs. Washburn would face if she applied for these benefits?
    b. Identify three policy or program changes you believe are needed to help grandparents provide an adequate standard of living for their grandchildren and for themselves.
4. Go to the Riverton case at **www.routledgesw.com/cases**. It is often difficult to get benefits such as SSI or veterans' pensions without a home address. If you were a social worker in Riverton, how could you address this problem for an individual client? What policy changes would you explore to aid similar clients?
5. The wealth gap manifests in many ways, including disparities in Internet access. Typically, people without their own computers must access online services in public spaces. What problems can you see with the RAINN model of service delivery for people without private Internet access? Who in your community might lack equitable access to RAINN's services, given this digital divide? As service delivery models evolve, what strategies could organizations use to make sure people in poverty are not further disadvantaged by lack of access to online services?
6. Is there an active living wage campaign in your community today? Investigate organizations like Fight for $15 and similar efforts to learn more about these movements and their demands. How could you become part of the effort in your area to promote a living wage? List the steps you could take.
7. How has government policy influenced your family's asset holdings? For example, has your family received mortgage interest deductions that subsidize homeownership? Do you (or did you) live in a neighborhood that had racial restrictions on property ownership? If so, how did your racial identity interact with these policies to influence your access to wealth? Did your parents receive tax benefits associated with 529 state college savings accounts? Have you received any tax benefits for retirement saving? Conversely, did you have to complete asset tests when you filled out the Free Application for Federal Student Aid (FAFSA)? What about asset tests associated with receipt of public assistance? How have these policies affected your economic security and your prospects for upward mobility?
8. Ask a member of your family, a neighbor, or a friend who is age 65 or over what Social Security means for them. How would their lives be different without that income support?
9. For millions of Americans living in and near poverty, especially those cost-burdened by housing, eviction is a near-constant threat and frequent occurrence. Several municipalities are reviewing eviction practices and patterns to highlight the ways eviction destabilizes households and can trap families in even more dire financial straits. Visit the Eviction Lab

website (**evictionlab.org**) to see maps of evictions and explore eviction rates and stories from your community.
10. While income support policies are increasingly important in the uncertain labor market of today and the projected future, in-kind (non-monetary) supports are also crucial supports on which many poor families rely. People in your community are likely already advocating in the local and state policy arena for quality affordable childcare, mass transit, and food assistance. Find out how you can join with social workers and others to advocate for needed anti-poverty reform by going to the website of your state chapter of the NASW.
11. Anti-poverty groups operate SNAP challenges that ask people to commit to stay within the SNAP budget of approximately $1.40 per person, per meal. Public officials, business leaders, and others have taken the SNAP challenge to help them understand what those who receive SNAP face in trying to eat healthy foods on a tight budget. You can find resources for low-cost meals and grocery discount tips online to try to keep yourself to a SNAP budget for a week or even a month. What was hard about surviving within these constraints? How did the SNAP budget affect your nutrition, meal preparation, and overall well-being?
12. TANF and OASDI are framed and discussed very differently in U.S. media coverage and public conversation. Review and analyze media covering welfare and retirement issues. How do we talk differently about these populations? What do these differences say about our values and beliefs, and what do they mean for shaping policy in these respective areas?
13. Use the Poverty Risk Calculator (**https://confrontingpoverty.org/poverty-risk-calculator**) to investigate your own risk of poverty. Then, experiment with how changing key aspects of your circumstances—your race, educational level, marital status, and age—influence your poverty risk. What do these changes tell you about how these factors contribute to your risk of experiencing poverty? What kinds of changes might decouple these factors from the risk of poverty?
14. The United Way's ALICE (Asset Limited, Income Constrained, Employed) Project is designed to improve data collection, programming, and policy regarding households that are not officially defined as "poor" but nonetheless struggle to meet basic needs. Explore the state- and county-level data for the communities where you live, practice, and/or attend school (**www.unitedforalice.org/home**). How do ALICE calculations differ from the official poverty statistics? How might anti-poverty policy be changed to better meet the needs of these households?
    a. Examine the news coverage generated by the ALICE project (**www.unitedforalice.org/in-the-news**). How does including low-income families in the discussion of poverty change the conversation?
    b. How might your own policy practice raise awareness of the challenges faced by individuals and families living near poverty?

CHAPTER 9

Policies and Programs for Children and Families

Let us put our minds together and see what kind of life we can make for our children.
Sitting Bull

WHEN WE SEARCH FOR STRENGTHS IN THE FAMILY AND community, our attention turns naturally to children. Many adults devote their lives to helping children build on their strengths. This commitment to children's well-being enhances both the present and the future. However, by many measures, American children face considerable odds. In 2017, more than 17 percent of children under age 18 lived in poverty (Fontenot et al., 2018). Children who grow up in economic disadvantage are more frequently exposed to violence, substance use, and environmental threats. Systemic barriers, including discrimination and inequities in school funding, create obstacles to learning and compromise well-being. We are learning more about how early exposure to the toxic stress associated with adverse childhood experiences influences lifelong outcomes, including later behaviors and even genetic predisposition to certain health conditions (Shonkoff et al., 2012). These risk factors can interact to produce negative outcomes for children, particularly the very young. Even their lives are threatened, as poverty contributes to the high rate of infant and child mortality in the United States compared to peer nations (Thakrar et al., 2018). Nor do these disadvantages disappear when poor children arrive at adulthood. Children who grow up in poverty are increasingly stuck there, as economic mobility rates decline (Chetty et al., 2016), particularly in some parts of the country (Chetty et al., 2014). Without sufficient investment, opportunities that could help them exit poverty, such as higher education, are often closed to those without financial resources (Ratcliffe & Kalish, 2017). Outcomes for children who spend at least half of their childhoods in poverty—the "persistently poor"—are particularly compromised, with only 16 percent consistently connected to work or school in their late 20s (Ratcliffe & Kalish, 2017). Children raised in poverty and children of color suffer significant health disparities, which may translate into increased disability and earlier deaths.

Of course, it is not only children growing up in poverty who face adverse conditions. American young people are buffeted by threats on many fronts. Suicide is the second leading cause of death among young people 10 to 24 years of age (Centers for Disease Control and Prevention [CDCP], 2017a). The growing ubiquity of social and other digital media has effects on the anxiety, depression, and social interactions of children and youth, including in ways we still do not entirely understand (Hoge, Bickham, & Canton, 2017). More than 20 percent of youth ages 12 to 19 are obese (CDCP, 2016b). More than 1,000 young Americans die of gun violence each year (Fowler et al., 2017). High-profile incidents of child maltreatment, including sexual abuse in churches and other institutions, have exposed the risks children face throughout society. Social workers work closely with the more than 442,000 children currently in foster care (Children's Bureau, 2018), where instability in placements and the trauma of family disruption can create lasting challenges to children's development.

In 2016, Child Protective Service (CPS) agencies received almost 4.1 million reports of suspected child abuse nationwide, involving 7.4 million children (U.S. Department of Health and Human Services [USDHHS], 2018b). Almost 60 percent of these referrals were screened in, with more than 3.5 million children receiving either an investigation or an alternative response (USDHHS, 2018b). An estimated 676,000 children were victims of child abuse and neglect, a rate of 9.1 per 1,000 children. Younger children were the most endangered. Infants under one year of age had the highest victimization rate—24.8 per 1,000. Seventy percent of child fatalities were among children under the age of three. Improved reporting systems and increased detection efforts, such as screening newborn infants for drug exposure, have helped to identify families that need services. At the same time, poverty and unemployment are major contributors to the family stressors that increase child abuse (Briar-Lawson et al., 2009). As some research suggests that these may be relatively permanent features of the U.S. economy for many families (Coibion, Gorodnichenko, & Koustas, 2013), there are concerns about the child welfare system's ability to respond to growing need, particularly as traditional support systems provided by extended families and community institutions are less available and/or less adequate than they once were. Further research is needed to examine risk factors for abuse and unravel the relationships among them, as are investments in the functioning of our nation's families.

Although children represent our future, current policies and programs fail to meet the needs of many of our youngest and most vulnerable Americans. Fiscal pressures and short-sighted policy decisions may further constrain investments in children's well-being. According to the Urban Institute, in 2017, only 9 percent of the federal budget was spent on children younger than 19 (Isaacs et al., 2018). Looking forward, children's programs are projected to receive just one cent of every dollar of the projected $1.6 trillion increase in federal spending over the next decade. The federal government will soon spend more on interest payments on the debt than on children (Isaacs et al., 2018). Additionally, because much of current public spending on children is delivered through state budgets, such as in early childhood education and K-12 public schools, there is significant inequity in funding arrangements.

All children need investments and support as they grow. However, most children's policies in the United States have been designed as residual interventions rather than as universal resources. This means that many American families only receive services once problems have already arisen, even though all families could benefit from additional help with the daunting task of raising a child to successful adulthood. In particular, child welfare policies have developed primarily when the family and other systems that serve children have failed. This emphasis on the child in danger, separate from the family unit, contrasts with the universal family allowances that many other developed countries provide. For example, in 2016, Canada launched the Canada Child Benefit, which provides a non-taxable monthly payment to families with children under 18. While the amount of the child benefit varies depending on family income and the number and ages of children, all Canadian families with children are eligible for benefits, which may be as much as $6,496 per year per child (Canada Revenue Agency, 2018). Due largely to these investments in children, Canada met its goal of reducing poverty by 20 percent three years ahead of schedule, bringing its poverty rate to the lowest in history (Statistics Canada, 2019). Such public investments are designed to keep families and children from becoming vulnerable. In contrast, U.S. interventions are targeted to crises. The United States, then, can be understood to have not a "child welfare" policy that supports the universal well-being of children, but instead a "child risk response system." Children inevitably fall through the resulting cracks.

Without universal policies to support all our nation's children, the programs we have leave grave risk factors for children and major stressors for families. Increasing child hunger provides particularly vivid evidence of the negative effects of our inadequate support. It is especially severe on weekends and in the summer, when many children do not have access to school-supplied meals, and in geographic communities characterized as "food deserts" for their lack of accessible, affordable food. Similarly, even though most children need at least some care not provided by a parent at some point during their development, the United States has no universal childcare system. Research has underscored the importance of early educational investments in catalyzing children's later success in school and in life, but our preschool programs are inadequate, often inaccessible, and seldom affordable. These gaps and challenges have significant implications for child well-being. Synthesizing the correlates between insufficient policies and adverse child outcomes will help you think critically about the kinds of reforms needed.

In this chapter, we focus on policies and programs dealing with child protection and care, family preservation, adoption and foster care, and juvenile justice. As you will observe in practice, these systems frequently intersect. Inadequacies in one domain may ripple into another, as when the high cost of childcare forces parents to leave their children with insufficient supervision, which may trigger child welfare involvement. Similarly, children and families who are caught up in the juvenile justice system are often involved with other service providers. For example, the accused child may be in foster care, or the family may be receiving family preservation services.

Although social workers recognize the challenges all families face, we will also examine programs for subgroups of children whose unique situations demand policy response, including those with special developmental needs and those who have child support enforcement orders. Of course, we have already covered some policies relating to children's well-being, including anti-discrimination regulations and anti-poverty programs. We will cover a good deal more in the coming chapters, including the health and mental health care systems. In the chapter on aging, you will learn how healthy aging has its roots in healthy, economically secure childhoods. The challenges children face and the policies that attempt to respond, then, overlap issue areas and cross jurisdictions. As a social worker, your efforts to help an individual child or a large group of children will require you to interface with many sectors. In all these domains, using a strengths approach to craft effective child and family policy allows us to develop programs that enhance the ability of families to care for their children and that reduce the incidence of the family struggles that put children at risk.

HISTORY AND BACKGROUND OF PROGRAMS PROTECTING CHILDREN AND FAMILIES

Social workers have long been leaders in the fields of child welfare and juvenile justice. In contrast to fields of practice where other professions dominate, such as health care and education, the child welfare system has been primarily a social work domain since the beginning of the twentieth century. Jane Addams and her colleagues from Hull House lobbied the Illinois legislature to create a separate juvenile court. As a result of their efforts, the first juvenile court opened in Cook County, Illinois, in 1899 (Allard & Young, 2002). This approach spread across the country, and by 1925, all but two states had juvenile courts.

Most states did not pass laws to protect children from physical abuse by their parents until the mid- to late 1800s. Because children were viewed as their parents' property, it took the determined efforts of women's groups and other concerned citizens to convince legislators to pass such laws. Widely publicized cases of severe abuse helped build public support for laws that allowed the courts to place children in need of protection in institutions or with other families. However, the laws did not specify who was responsible for investigating child abuse and enforcing child protection statutes.

Activists and philanthropists founded the first Society for the Prevention of Cruelty to Children in New York in 1875. Subsequently, similar private societies were established across the country. These societies investigated cases of alleged child abuse and neglect, presented the cases in court, and advocated for legislation to safeguard children's welfare (Downs, Costin, & McFadden, 1996). Because private societies dedicated to the protection of animals were much more organized during this period, child protection agencies modeled their programs and strategies on those efforts.

As far back as 1935, Title IV-B, the Child Welfare Services Program of the Social Security Act, established the protection of children as a focus of public social service. Nevertheless, it was not until the powerful medical profession "rediscovered" child abuse in the 1960s that child maltreatment appeared on the national policy agenda (Brissett-Chapman, 1995). The 1963 publication of a medical survey on "battered child syndrome" ignited public action. By presenting child abuse as a syndrome recognized by the medical profession, this report enhanced the validity of claims for intervention. By the mid-1960s, every state had passed legislation for the reporting of child abuse and intervention to protect children (Petr, 2004).

Currently, the federal government provides funds to states and counties to help support child welfare services. Specifically, Title XX of the Social Security Act provides block grants for social services to states. In addition, Title IV-E provides reimbursement for a portion of states' costs for foster care and adoption. Finally, Title IV-B provides grants to states for child welfare case management and child cruelty prevention. The U.S. Children's Bureau, established in 1912, oversees policies and funding affecting child welfare systems.

CHILDREN AND FAMILIES TODAY

The face of childhood in the United States is changing, and the environments in which children are growing up differ from those of past generations. Family composition and economic status, educational contexts, and the influence of technology have all changed—sometimes quite dramatically—in ways that alter children's experiences of childhood and their likelihood of emerging prepared for a smooth transition to a successful adulthood. Examining these differences provides insight into the types of policy reforms needed to better protect children's rights and interests.

Children today grow up in much smaller families than were typical during the Baby Boom of 1946 to 1964. In 2017, almost 24 million (32 percent) of U.S. children were living in single-parent homes (Livingston, 2018). Having two parents does not ensure that children will receive the support they need, as adults who grew up with abuse in two-parent homes can attest. However, current construction of family patterns does mean that children have access to fewer traditional sources of support. Rates of childhood poverty are higher in single-parent families (Sawhill & Thomas, 2005), and many single parents face difficulties in the labor force, particularly given the high cost and relative unavailability of childcare (Madowitz, Rowell, & Hamm, 2016). Families have also become much more mobile, and distance can prevent members from supporting younger relatives as they might have in previous generations.

In 2017, the U.S. fertility rate fell to a 30-year low, contributing to shifting demographics that make children a smaller proportion of our population. In 2018, only 23 percent of the population was under the age of 18, compared with 36 percent in 1960. This percentage is projected to decrease to approximately 19.8 percent by 2060. However, this does not mean there are fewer children in the United States today. In fact, the population aged 18 and under is larger than ever, and the number is expected to continue to grow (U.S. Census Bureau, 2018e). Exhibit 9.1 illustrates demographic trends and projections from 1950 to 2060.

American children today, then, are more likely to grow up in relatively small, increasingly single-parent families, geographically distant from other relatives. The racial and ethnic

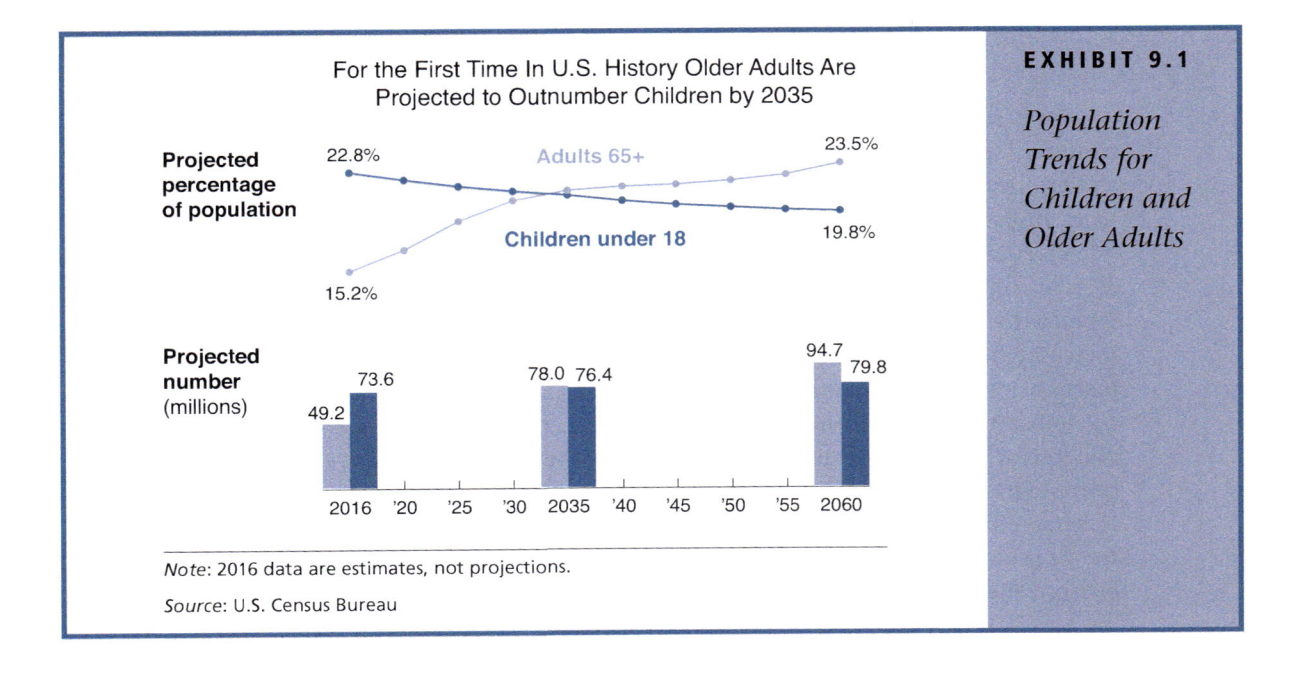

EXHIBIT 9.1

Population Trends for Children and Older Adults

For the First Time In U.S. History Older Adults Are Projected to Outnumber Children by 2035

Projected percentage of population:
- Adults 65+: 15.2% → 23.5%
- Children under 18: 22.8% → 19.8%

Projected number (millions):
- 2016: 49.2, 73.6
- 2035: 78.0, 76.4
- 2060: 94.7, 79.8

Note: 2016 data are estimates, not projections.

Source: U.S. Census Bureau

EXHIBIT 9.2

These Are Our Children

Credit: Shutterstock and Rosemary Chapin

composition of U.S. children is also evolving. Exhibit 9.2 represents children from diverse racial and ethnic backgrounds in approximate proportion to the percentage of children 18 and under with similar backgrounds living in the United States today.

In 2018, 49.9 percent of American children were non-Latinx White, 13.7 percent were African American, 25.8 percent were Latinx, 1 percent were Native American, and just over 5 percent were Asian/Pacific Islander (Frey, 2019b). Reflecting both growing diversity and the increasing fluidity of racial and ethnic designations, 4 percent of children were officially identified as belonging to two or more racial groups. Experts project that Latinx children will increase to almost 35 percent of the child population by 2050. The number of U.S. children who are children of immigrants is also increasing. In 2050, it is estimated that 34 percent of children will be immigrants or children of immigrants (Murphey, Guzman, & Torres, 2014). Because children in some ethnic and racial groups have different needs and face particular risks, demographic trends portend a need to reexamine the adequacy and equity of current policies. Additionally, because these trends foreshadow demographic shifts within the overall U.S. population, the

EXHIBIT 9.3

Child Poverty by Race and Ethnicity, 2017

Group	Percentage
American Indian	33%
Asian and Pacific Islander	11%
Black or African American	33%
Latinx or Latino	26%
Two or More Races	18%
Non-Latinx White	11%
Total	19%

Source: National Kids Count, a Project of the Annie E. Casey Foundation

---

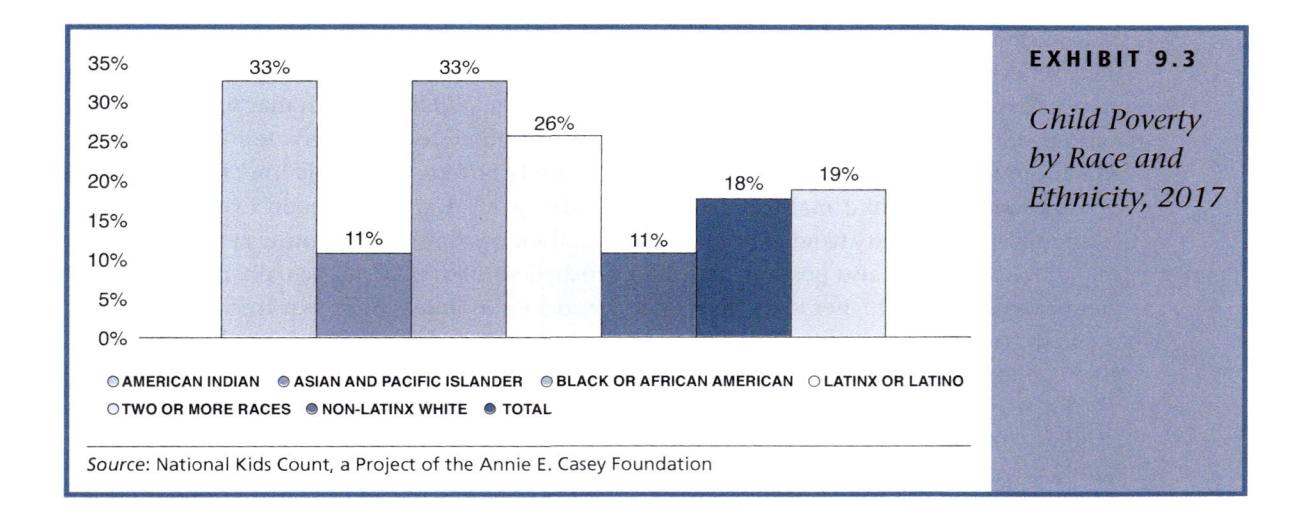

extent to which child policy meets the needs of increasingly diverse generations is an important signal of our policy readiness for a diversifying nation.

Along with recognition of the need for universal investment in children's health and safety, social workers must consider how intersecting identities, particularly around race and class, contribute to children's experiences of risk. Many statistics are bleaker for children of color. The infant mortality rate for Black children is about 2.2 times that of non-Latinx White children (Kaiser Family Foundation, 2016a). As illustrated in Exhibit 9.3, poverty rates for infants and children of color and those in some ethnic groups are considerably higher than for White children. Among children aged two and under, 32.7 percent of African Americans and 27.3 percent of Latinx live in poverty, compared to less than 12 percent of non-Latinx White toddlers (Fontenot et al., 2018). In large part because of interlocking disadvantages and their cascading effects in families, the percentage of children of color in foster care is disproportionately high. Even though African Americans represent only 14 percent of all U.S. children under the age of 18, they are 23 percent of children in foster care (USDHHS, 2018c).

Impact of High Poverty Rates on Child Welfare

In addition to the long-term consequences of poverty on children's development and later achievement (Hair et al., 2015), research has found a strong relationship between poverty and child maltreatment. The relationship between poverty and child maltreatment is a complex one that must be interpreted with care (Drake & Pandey, 1996). Federal law defines **child maltreatment** as "serious harm (neglect, physical abuse, sexual abuse, and emotional abuse or neglect) caused to children by parents or primary caregivers, such as extended family members or babysitters" (Child Abuse Prevention and Treatment Act, 1974). Child maltreatment occurs across all socioeconomic groups. Most parents living in poverty do not abuse or neglect their children. Further, although there is a correlation between poverty and maltreatment, this does not mean that poverty *causes* maltreatment. In the United States, the absence of universal support—such as childcare and medical care—often requires parents to use their personal resources to secure these services. Of course, because parents living in poverty are less able to navigate these marketplaces, they may be unable to provide adequately for their children, which may lead to neglect. Further, the strains associated with poverty may contribute to or exacerbate mental distress, which can result in other types of mistreatment. Family poverty may sometimes be understood as a *consequence* of child maltreatment, as parents' own adverse childhood experiences may compromise their ability to adequately provide for their own children (Bunting et al., 2018; Metzler et al., 2017). It is also possible that impoverished families may not actually have maltreatment rates markedly higher than those of other socioeconomic groups, but that maltreatment in impoverished families is more likely to be reported to Child Protective Services (CPS). Further, after coming into contact with CPS, these families may be more vulnerable to adverse findings.

There is some evidence to support all these explanations for the link between poverty and child welfare outcomes. Researchers connected reductions in Kansas' safety net for low-income families—particularly Temporary Assistance for Needy Families' (TANF) harsh sanctions and strict time limits—to increases in child welfare referrals and foster care placements, as families struggled to contend with an increasingly difficult economic context (Ginther & Johnson-Motoyama, 2017). Advocates for Native American children have emphasized that authorities seldom account for culturally specific safety nets and tribal resources in assessing Native families for neglect (Akee, 2019). These individual oversights and systemic biases can overestimate Native children's experiences of neglect and place them at greater risk of removal from their homes. Other research has found that interactions between poverty and other risk factors, such as substance use, depression, and social isolation, increase the risk of maltreatment. Further, parental stress has been found to be a risk, and families dealing with economic hardship experience significant stress in their daily lives. It is vital that we address the forces that can destabilize families and that the strengths of all families are equitably and amply uplifted.

The Child Welfare System

Child welfare policy has created a child welfare system. The U.S. Department of Health and Human Services (USDHHS) defines the child welfare system as "a group of services designed to promote the well-being of children by ensuring safety, achieving permanency, and strengthening families to care for their children successfully" (Child Welfare Information Gateway, 2012). Although the child welfare system is sometimes defined broadly to include services designed to be preventive, such as Head Start, the core child welfare services are investigation, foster care, adoption, and preservation services for families in which child maltreatment, including abuse and neglect, is reported or suspected.

The largest category of child maltreatment, **neglect**, is the failure of caregivers to provide for basic needs such as nutrition, shelter, emotional care, and supervision. Almost 75 percent of maltreated children experienced neglect, while 18 percent were physically abused and 8.5 percent were sexually abused[1] (USDHHS, 2018b). State CPS agencies report data on child maltreatment. Importantly, these figures do not include all instances in which children are harmed. If an acquaintance or stranger harms a child, child welfare agencies generally do not intervene, as law-enforcement agencies have exclusive responsibility for those cases. Additionally, because child abuse and neglect tend to be underreported, particularly within some populations and for certain types of offenses, it is likely that child maltreatment is an even larger problem than official statistics suggest.

The United States does not have a cohesive child welfare system. Federal, state, county, and tribal laws and practices overlap, and a mix of public and private organizations provide services. Systems vary from state to state, as does the assistance that families receive. In some states, public agencies such as departments of social services or child and family services contract with private, community-based organizations to provide services to families. These services may include adoption, foster care, family preservation, residential treatment, addiction treatment, parenting education, mental health care, employment assistance, and financial or housing assistance. While those who urge more federal financing and oversight of child welfare are largely aiming to give children an equal chance no matter their residence, part of the rationale for state jurisdiction is to keep control of such vital programs at a level of government closer to families, in the hope that programs will be better able to respond to unique needs in their communities. This may also mean that policymakers are more accessible and social work advocates have more opportunity to influence child welfare policy.

History offers tragic evidence of the need for vigilance in ensuring that children's interests are paramount in the development and operation of child welfare policies. Racism, classism, and anti-immigrant bias have undeniably affected child welfare practices. Even more horrifying are scandals such as the child trafficking of Georgia Tann and the Tennessee Children's Home Society. Lax state regulation of adoption and powerful accomplices, including politicians, judges, and social workers, made it possible for Tann to engage in publicly sanctioned child trafficking for years, stealing poor children from their homes and essentially selling them to influential families (Austin, 1993). Public horror led to state reforms of adoption laws in the 1950s, and these initiatives continue today, as families work to ensure that child welfare policies balance individuals' rights and the government's interests in protection. Some states' moves toward greater privatization of child welfare again threaten to allow profit interests to influence child welfare practices. These changes can also complicate advocacy, as private entities may not respond to advocates in the same way that publicly accountable governments might.

In addition to their obligations to investigate reports of suspected maltreatment, child welfare agencies often provide services to youths in the juvenile justice system as well as to families who seek out services on their own or who are referred by schools or community organizations. Although juvenile justice typically is not considered part of the child welfare system, families in these two systems often face similar problems and contend with similarly high stakes. Critically, both systems have social control functions and wield the power to remove children from their homes. You will need to understand the policies and programs that structure each of these systems if you are to work effectively with children and families.

The Juvenile Justice System

Children and youths who are charged with crimes receive services through the juvenile justice system, which includes law enforcement, juvenile courts, and corrections. In marked contrast to the approach employed within the rest of the American criminal justice system, the juvenile justice system's emphasis on rehabilitation reflects the concept that young people are developmentally different from adults and, therefore, more amenable to treatment. Children and youths under 18 who come into the juvenile justice system may be experiencing mental illness, substance use disorder, and/or learning disabilities. They might have a history of child maltreatment or other trauma. Their backgrounds, then, may be very similar to those of children involved in the child welfare system. The juvenile justice system's limited ability to address these underlying issues contributes to what observers often critique as its failure to successfully rehabilitate those who enter its jurisdiction.

Although media coverage, particularly of high-profile cases, may contribute to the public perception that young people have become more crime-prone and dangerous, studies indicate that this is not the case. Juvenile arrests grew in the late 1980s, peaking in 1996. From 1996 to 2017, however, juvenile crime fell more than 72 percent. Juvenile violent crime followed a similar trajectory, falling dramatically between 1993 and 2012 (Office of Juvenile Justice and Delinquency Prevention [OJJDP], 2018). Particularly after juvenile arrests fell 59 percent between 2008 and 2017, juveniles account for a small percentage of the overall arrest rate. Still, more than 800,000 juveniles were arrested in 2017 (OJJDP, 2018). While many states' policies were made harsher for juvenile offenders following the increase in juvenile crime in the 1990s, trends in recent years have moved in the other direction. As of 2017, only five states automatically send 17-year-old offenders to the adult criminal justice system (Campaign for Youth Justice, 2018). Since 2005, 17 states and the District of Columbia have taken steps to remove youth from adult jails, including by restoring judicial discretion over sentencing and raising the age "floor" when youth can be transferred to adult facilities (Campaign for Youth Justice, 2018). Other states have proposed including young people in the juvenile justice system until age 21 or 22, in recognition of their still-developing mental and emotional capacities.

As a result of these policy changes, there has been a 64 percent decrease in the number of juveniles held in adult prisons. Bolstered by federal policy and court decisions that have advanced juvenile offenders' rights to humane rehabilitation and by trends toward less severe sentencing for some adults, reformers are working on additional changes that will ensure age-appropriate responses to juvenile offenders. Such policies are important steps toward better outcomes for adolescents who have become involved in the criminal justice system. Juveniles in adult prisons are more than 36 times more likely than the overall juvenile offender population to commit suicide and are at greater risk for sexual assault than any other population of inmates (National Juvenile Justice Network, 2016). Moreover, after these youths are released, they are re-arrested sooner, more often, and for more serious offenses than their counterparts who went through the juvenile system. In keeping with the profession's commitment to child well-being, the National Association of Social Workers (NASW) recognizes that children and youths are developmentally different from adults and works to advance policies that treat juvenile offenders in ways that reflect these differences (NASW, 2015g). Importantly, this approach is not only more appealing as a strengths-based approach that aligns with social work values, there is also evidence that it is more effective. Juveniles who are given effective intervention are less likely to reoffend as juveniles or to commit crimes as adults (Thompson, 2016; Weaver & Campbell, 2015).

Even with recent improvements in policy and practices, many youths continue to experience inadequate and inappropriate justice system responses. A pervasive and alarming problem is the inequitable processing of youth of color, such that they are overrepresented in adult prisons, juvenile correction facilities, and overall interactions with law enforcement (Shook & Goodkind, 2009). Even as juvenile detention decreased by 47 percent between 2003 and 2013, racial disparities in juvenile incarceration increased 15 percent (Rovner, 2016). Due to these diverging trends, Black youths are more than four times more likely and Latinx youths twice as likely as non-Latinx White youths to be detained in a juvenile correctional facility (Rovner, 2016). As movements demanding that all elements of law enforcement treat people of color more equitably have highlighted, Black youths are more than twice as likely as White youths to be arrested. In 2015, Black youths accounted for about 14 percent of the total youth population but 43 percent of incarcerated male juveniles (Sawyer, 2018). Exhibit 9.4 illustrates racial disparity in adjudication of juvenile offenders by state. As depicted, there is a disparity gap in the incarceration of Black juveniles compared to non-Latinx White juveniles in almost all states. Further, in many states, these disparities have increased in recent years; where states have made progress in diverting White juveniles from incarceration, youth of color have often been disproportionally underserved by these reforms.

Inequity in the juvenile justice system also manifests along lines other than race. A large percentage of incarcerated youth have learning disabilities, emotional disturbances, or other special needs (Burrell & Warboys, 2000). These issues can contribute to involvement with the juvenile justice system, particularly as gaps in mental health care make it difficult for young people to access needed treatment. Additionally, the unique psychosocial needs of LGBTQ+

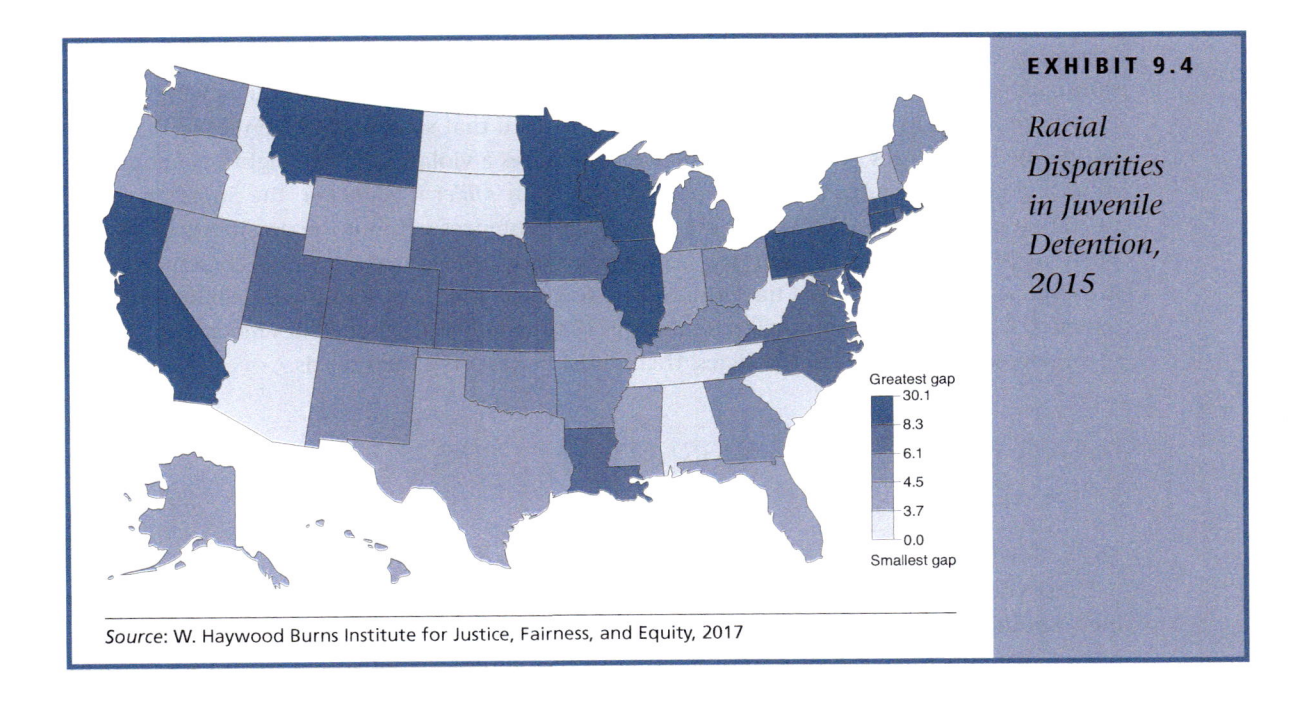

EXHIBIT 9.4

Racial Disparities in Juvenile Detention, 2015

Greatest gap
30.1
8.3
6.1
4.5
3.7
0.0
Smallest gap

Source: W. Haywood Burns Institute for Justice, Fairness, and Equity, 2017

EXHIBIT 9.5

Adolescent Boys in a Juvenile Detention Facility

Credit: Steve Liss

adolescents in both the juvenile justice and child welfare systems are often overlooked. The experiences of these populations underscore the dire need for effective reform.

The March 2005 U.S. Supreme Court ruling in *Roper v. Simmons* abolished the death penalty for juveniles. Other Supreme Court decisions have aligned with the reasoning in *Roper v. Simmons*, relying on scientific evidence regarding the ways in which youths' brains and decision-making differ from those of adults (National Juvenile Justice and Delinquency Prevention Coalition, 2013). In 2010, *Graham v. Florida* determined that sentencing juveniles to life without parole for offenses other than homicide constitutes a violation of the Eighth Amendment regarding cruel and unusual punishment. In 2012, in *Miller v. Alabama*, the Supreme Court ruled that children cannot be given mandatory life sentences without the possibility of parole. Then, in 2016, the Supreme Court applied retroactively its decision that teenagers sentenced to life in prison for murder must have the chance to appeal their case and the possibility of being released (Rovner, 2018). Exhibit 9.5 reminds us that juvenile justice statistics reflect the lives of young people. Juvenile justice policies, then, must better serve their needs.

MAJOR POLICIES AND PROGRAMS AFFECTING CHILD WELFARE AND JUVENILE JUSTICE

The following section examines major child welfare and juvenile justice policies. In child welfare, you will observe tension, at times, between protecting children and preserving families. Similarly, ideological and societal shifts strongly influence the extent to which juvenile justice policies emphasize rehabilitation or retribution. Finally, the quality and types of services available for children and families vary greatly from state to state. Some states that made recession-era cuts to public services such as child welfare have not restored those appropriations. In other states, political influences rather than fiscal constraints are the primary determinant of investments in child well-being. Because of these forces, child welfare social workers seldom have all the tools they need to adequately perform their jobs. High rates of worker turnover also continue to negatively impact child welfare services. Given their firsthand knowledge of these challenges, social workers are uniquely positioned to advocate for changes that will enhance outcomes.

The Child Abuse Prevention and Treatment Act

In 1974, the federal government became involved in child abuse prevention with the passage of the Child Abuse Prevention and Treatment Act (CAPTA) (Public Law 93-247). CAPTA established "minimum definitions that serve as a baseline for intervention" (NASW, 2012b). The law also provided states with federal funds with which to develop reporting systems for the investigation of child abuse and neglect. For state-by-state information on child abuse and neglect and information on a variety of child welfare policies, visit the Child Welfare Information Gateway website at **www.childwelfare.gov**. This site, maintained by the Children's Bureau of the USDHHS, is an excellent source of information on child maltreatment and the policy response.

Congress has amended CAPTA numerous times to reauthorize its provisions, strengthen and expand programs centered on prevention and reporting, and address emergent concerns affecting child welfare. A 1978 amendment included provisions for comprehensive state adoption programs, and the Keeping Children and Families Safe Act of 2003 (Public Law 108-36) provided community-based grants for the prevention of child abuse and neglect. In 2009, the NASW submitted testimony to the House of Representatives calling for the reauthorization and full funding of CAPTA to allow for the implementation of effective prevention strategies, as well as more culturally appropriate services and initiatives to recruit and retain professional child welfare workers. The following year, President Obama signed the CAPTA Reauthorization Act of 2010. This reauthorization increased grant funding, promoted coordination of services between CPS entities and domestic violence agencies, and refined the focus of community-based child abuse prevention grants. CAPTA was further amended by the Justice for Victims of Trafficking Act of 2015 and the Comprehensive Addiction and Recovery Act (CARA) of 2016, both of which focused on special populations—child victims of trafficking and children in families with substance use challenges. These amendments illustrate how CAPTA has evolved to help child welfare systems address emerging needs. However, sometimes, as in the case of CARA, statutes have failed to define or operationalize important concepts. This leaves implementation largely up to states and can result in considerable differences in the approaches' effectiveness. Many child welfare advocates expected CAPTA to be reauthorized in 2018. There is some momentum in this direction. In Fiscal Year (FY) 2019, Congress added $60 million to the state grants in CAPTA—the largest increase in the policy's history—and legislation to reauthorize CAPTA passed the House of Representatives in May 2019. However, as of publication, CAPTA was still operating on continuing resolutions.

EXHIBIT 9.6 *Child Abuse Prevention and Treatment Act (CAPTA), 1974*	Policy goals	To strengthen the identification, reporting, and investigation of child maltreatment. To monitor research and publish information about child abuse and neglect.
	Benefits or services provided	Programs for reporting, investigating, treating, and preventing child abuse and/or neglect. National Center on Child Abuse and Neglect established as an information clearinghouse.
	Eligibility rules	Children under age 18 at risk of or victims of abuse or neglect.
	Service delivery system	At the federal level, the Office on Child Abuse and Neglect in the Children's Bureau of the USDHHS administers the Act. State and local agencies are responsible for investigating and responding to child maltreatment.
	Financing	Federal grant to states based on the population under age 18.

In line with NASW recommendations, CAPTA reporting requirements now include data on the number of CPS personnel, average caseloads, education and training requirements, demographic information, and the number of children referred for early intervention services under the Individuals with Disabilities Education Act (IDEA) Part C (NASW, 2015h). In this way, CAPTA has contributed to our understanding of child welfare needs, a crucial first step in charting an agenda for further policy changes. Exhibit 9.6 applies the policy analysis framework to CAPTA.

The Juvenile Justice and Delinquency Prevention Act

Also in 1974, Congress passed the Juvenile Justice and Delinquency Prevention Act (JJDPA) (Public Law 93-415). Reauthorized in 2002, programs operated without an authorization after 2007. As knowledge about youth development increased and juvenile crime decreased, social workers and other advocates eager to see sweeping change in juvenile justice policy struggled for years to secure JJDPA reauthorization. Then, in 2018, Congress passed a five-year JJDPA reauthorization. Advocates heralded the action, citing increased funding for juvenile justice programs, establishment of core safety standards that will improve treatment during and following detention, and financial incentives for states to end racial and ethnic disparities in juvenile justice. Today, all states but Wyoming, Connecticut, and Nebraska participate in the JJDPA and receive a formula grant for their compliance. Specific requirements of the reauthorized JJDPA include segregating youth from adults in detention; improving screening for sex trafficking, mental illness, and substance use disorder; and phasing out shackling of pregnant young women (Johnson, 2018). These enhancements align with the goals of the original Act: to aid state and local governments in preventing and controlling juvenile delinquency, improve the juvenile justice system, and emphasize community-based treatment for juvenile offenders.

The Office of Juvenile Justice and Delinquency Prevention (OJJDP) in the U.S. Department of Justice works to achieve the goals of the JJDPA. Historically, although the Act focused on

> | | | |
> |---|---|---|
> | Policy goals | To prevent and control juvenile delinquency and improve the juvenile justice system. | **EXHIBIT 9.7** |
> | Benefits or services provided | Community-based treatment when appropriate to protect juveniles from unnecessary detention and from harmful exposure to adult inmates. | *Juvenile Justice and Delinquency Prevention Act (JJDPA), 1974* |
> | Eligibility rules | Juveniles determined to be offenders and other at-risk youths. | |
> | Service delivery system | Office of Juvenile Justice and Delinquency Prevention in the U.S. Department of Justice has oversight over state and local government actions taken to reach goals. | |
> | Financing | Federal funds provided to state and local governments. | |

rehabilitating youthful offenders, it has not provided sufficient resources to build an effective system. The omnibus spending bill that included JJDPA reauthorization provided a $5 million funding increase to support innovative state efforts to reduce risk of harm to court-involved youth, ensure fair treatment of youth of color, and improve system response to delinquency. The bill also included an increase in funding for delinquency prevention, including new obligations for initiatives such as opioid prevention (Campaign for Youth Justice, 2018). Given the erosion of funding prior to reauthorization, however, state and local governments will likely need much more funding if they are to develop juvenile justice systems that can achieve the goals of the Act. Even with declining rates of juvenile crime, the system lacks capacity to prioritize prevention, early intervention, and diversion, while ensuring the safety of court-involved youth and supporting youth reentry (NJJDPC, 2015). Exhibit 9.7 summarizes the features of the JJDPA. For more information on juvenile justice legislation, visit the website of the OJJDP at **www.ojjdp.gov**.

The Indian Child Welfare Act

Earlier, we discussed the Indian Child Welfare Act (ICWA) as an excellent example of strengths-based policy development, where problem definition and policy change are guided by the client group. Here, we briefly review the conditions that propelled the passage of this unique piece of child welfare legislation. Recall that federal policy for Native Americans historically facilitated marginalization, forced acculturation, and even attempted annihilation. White authorities forced religious conversion, placed children in boarding schools, and systematically stripped them of their Native cultures. These practices continued for decades. Between 1969 and 1974, approximately 35 percent of Native American children were in foster homes or institutions (Matheson, 1996). Eighty-five percent of these placements were in non-Native homes (American Academy of Child and Adolescent Psychiatry, 1975).

Native American leaders were determined to halt this cultural genocide. After hundreds of hours of testimony by leaders and affected families from several tribes, Congress passed the ICWA (Public Law 95-608) of 1978, declaring, "The wholesale separation of Indian children

EXHIBIT 9.8	Policy goals	To protect the best interests of Native American children and families. To set minimum standards for removal and placement of Native children and for termination of parental rights. To recognize and strengthen the role of tribal government in child welfare decision-making.
Indian Child Welfare Act (ICWA), 1978	Benefits or services provided	Endorses keeping Native American children with their families or facilitating placement in homes that reflect their culture. Tribes are actively involved in decision-making.
	Eligibility rules	All children who are members of federally recognized tribes, with membership determined by individual tribes.
	Service delivery system	Tribal and urban Native American agencies have authority over state and federal courts to protect the best interests of their communities' children.
	Financing	Federal funds provided to Native American agencies.

from their families is perhaps the most tragic and destructive aspect of American Indian life today." The ICWA mandates that "active efforts" (compared to the "reasonable efforts" required in other child welfare policies) be made to ensure that Native American children remain with their families. It further empowers tribes and their courts to oversee decisions regarding Native children. The phrase "active efforts" mandates that social workers involve the child's extended family and tribe, including tribal service providers, and that they tailor their work to the tribe's cultural values. It may also mean providing transportation or otherwise facilitating connection to resources, rather than just providing referrals. Exhibit 9.8 applies the policy analysis framework to the ICWA.

Implementation of the ICWA has often been compromised by differences in states' capacity to support Native families and in their commitment to partnering with tribes. Tribes, too, vary in their capacity to implement the ICWA, and federal funding has been insufficient for tribes with few resources of their own. To more fully implement the ICWA, the federal government must provide adequate funding to establish, staff, and monitor Native child and family services. In addition, greater cooperation between states and tribes and increased employment and retention of Native American staff are essential if the ICWA is to achieve its goals. While some states have developed special courts where Native practices are prominent, Native parents in other parts of the country find few culturally appropriate and readily accessible tools to help them raise their children and comply with state expectations. Further, Native children and youths are still disproportionately likely to be removed from their homes for maltreatment, and there are not enough Native placements to serve these children (Casey Family Programs, 2015).

Many child welfare advocates believe that inconsistent implementation of ICWA has not only compromised its outcomes but also endangered its existence. In 2013, a Native father's parental rights were relinquished without his ICWA-required appearance before a judge, and a misspelling of his name delayed tribal notification of the case. When the U.S. Supreme Court subsequently ruled in *Adoptive Couple v. Baby Girl* that the ICWA's requirements to pursue additional efforts to preserve the Native American family before terminating parental rights may be waived when the child has never lived with the Native father, Native child welfare advocates roundly denounced the decision as a subversion of the policy's intent and a violation of the rights of the father and his tribe.

Other legal challenges to the ICWA have sought to invalidate it even more explicitly and completely. In a 2015 case regarding a Native child adopted by a non-Native family, a federal judge in Texas sided with a conservative group's challenge to the ICWA and ruled that the policy is racially discriminatory. Subsequently, an appeals court found that children are not harmed by the ICWA's requirement that states involve tribes in child welfare decisions affecting Native families; in June 2019, the U.S. Supreme Court declined to hear the issue. While the Indian Child Welfare Act makes tribes' unique legal status, not the child's race, the basis for the higher standard to which states are held in removal proceedings, subsequent challenges and ongoing disputes are likely. Exhibit 9.9 underscores that, in all these policy questions and legal decisions, Native children's lives are at stake.

The Fostering Connections to Success and Increasing Adoptions Act of 2008 attempted to address implementation challenges related to the ICWA. This legislation provides more federal financial support for tribal foster and kinship care, recruitment and training of caregivers, and foster care and adoption services. In the past, tribes could not access Title IV-E funds to administer their own foster care and adoption assistance programs unless they had an agreement with the state to access these funds. The Fostering Connections to Success and Increasing Adoptions Act now gives tribes the option of directly accessing and administering Title IV-E funds. The Act also allows tribes to access a share of their state's Chafee Foster Care Independence Program (CFCIP) funds to provide independent living services to tribal youths in the state (Children's Defense Fund, 2010). To learn more about current initiatives to protect American Indian children, go to the website of the National Indian Child Welfare Association at **www.nicwa.org**.

EXHIBIT 9.9

Child in Traditional Native Dress

Credit: Shutterstock

Adoption Assistance and Child Welfare Act

The Adoption Assistance and Child Welfare Act (AACWA) of 1980 (Public Law 96-272) established family preservation as a major goal of the child welfare system. This was a marked departure from the system's prior emphasis. In the 1960s and 1970s, the philosophies, financial incentives, and professional attitudes in state foster care systems emphasized "child saving" rather than "family saving" (Petr, 2004). Because the system did not emphasize permanent relationships in biological and/or adoptive families, children in the child welfare system often grew up without the family bonds research suggests are important to healthy development (Fox & Hane, 2008; Sroufe et al., 2005). Fueled by growing dissatisfaction with the impermanence of foster care placement and concerns about the long-term implications for children whose home environments were extensively disrupted, the AACWA aimed to prevent out-of-home care.

The AACWA established financial incentives for states to emphasize permanency planning. To receive certain federal funding for their child welfare services, states are required to make a judicial determination that they have used "reasonable efforts" to prevent unnecessary out-of-home placement (Petr, 2004). If such placements are found necessary, states subsequently must make "reasonable efforts" to reunite separated families. Unfortunately, the legislation does not define what constitutes "reasonable efforts." Therefore, state child welfare agencies vary widely in their efforts to increase permanency, and children continue to languish in foster care. In 2017, although permanency (either reunification with the biological family or adoption) was the case plan goal for 83 percent of children in foster care, the median number of months a child had been in foster care was almost 13; the average was more than 20 months (Children's Bureau, 2018). Exhibit 9.10 summarizes the features of the AACWA.

EXHIBIT 9.10

Adoption Assistance and Child Welfare Act (AACWA), 1980

Policy goals	To reduce the number of children in foster care for extended lengths of time through development of written permanency plans that emphasize family preservation, reunification, or adoption.
Benefits or services provided	Promotes "reasonable efforts" to preserve the family. Establishment of a permanency plan for each child in foster care.
Eligibility rules	Children and families being investigated and/or treated for abuse and neglect.
Service delivery system	The U.S. Department of Health and Human Services is responsible for federal oversight. State and local agencies are responsible for investigating and responding to abuse and neglect and implementing program changes. Courts periodically conduct reviews of each foster care case.
Financing	Federal funds attached to incentives to reach goals.

Family Preservation and Support Services

Particularly as professional understanding of the nature of trauma and its negative effects has evolved, a growing chorus has called for greater emphasis on moving child welfare investments "upstream," to shift efforts toward *prevention* of harm rather than response. As part of this movement, many states and counties have experimented with family preservation initiatives to prevent placement and support timely reunification. **Family Preservation and Support Services** provisions (Public Law 103-66), enacted as part of the Omnibus Budget Reconciliation Act of 1993, reinforce this work.

The Family Preservation and Support Services provisions encourage the development of cohesive, community-based, family-centered supports that involve collaboration between child welfare workers and other service providers. The goals of the provisions are to support the well-being of all family members and to enable parents to create safe, nurturing home environments. Federal funding is provided to states to establish programs and services. Family support services may include parent groups, home visits, and childcare. Family preservation encompasses counseling or respite care and other interventions that help families at risk keep their children in their homes (Ahsan, 1996).

These provisions were reauthorized as the Promoting Safe and Stable Families (PSSF) program in 1997, part of the Child and Family Services Improvement Act in 2006 and the Child and Family Services Improvement and Innovation Act of 2014. PSSF is one of the few programs that provide federal funds to state child welfare services that focus on the prevention of child maltreatment. However, even under this program, families must typically fall into crisis before they become eligible for services. Programs that provide supportive programming for all families, before a crisis develops, are badly needed.

The Multi-Ethnic Placement Act

The Multi-Ethnic Placement Act (MEPA) of 1994 (Public Law 103-82) and its 1996 amendment, the Interethnic Adoption Provisions (MEPA-IEAP), aim to remove barriers to permanency for children in the child protective system. The specific goals of these policies are:

- to eliminate discrimination based on race, color, or national origin of the child or the prospective parent;
- to shorten the time that children wait to be adopted; and
- to facilitate the recruitment and retention of adoptive and foster parents who can meet the needs of children awaiting placement.

(Hollinger, 1998)

The MEPA-IEAP prohibits states and other entities involved in federally funded foster care or adoption services from delaying or denying a child's foster care or adoptive placement because of the child's or prospective parent's race, color, or national origin, or from denying the opportunity to become a foster or adoptive parent for the same reasons. This Act also

EXHIBIT 9.11 *Multi-Ethnic Placement Act (MEPA), 1994*	Policy goals	To remove barriers to permanency by eliminating discrimination based on race, color, or national origin of the child or the prospective parent and by reducing the waiting time before adoption.
	Benefits or services provided	Guidelines established for placement of children with prospective parents and recruitment and retention of adoptive and foster parents.
	Eligibility rules	All children in foster care awaiting adoption except those covered under the Indian Child Welfare Act.
	Service delivery system	State and local child protection agencies follow guidelines that accompany federal funding.
	Financing	Federal funds given to states.

requires that states diligently recruit foster and adoptive parents who reflect the racial and ethnic diversity of the children in the state in need of foster and adoptive homes (Hollinger, 1998). Exhibit 9.11 summarizes the provisions of the MEPA-IEAP.

The MEPA-IEAP does not apply to children covered under the Indian Child Welfare Act because of the unique political relationship between the tribes and the federal government. The special considerations governing child welfare decisions for Native families are rooted in tribes' sovereignty, while in other populations, placement takes precedence. In contrast to the ICWA, the MEPA-IEAP is designed to remove barriers to interracial adoption. However, the MEPA-IEAP does require increased efforts to recruit and retain a pool of prospective parents who reflect the diversity of children in foster care, a demand that supports objectives aligned with those of the ICWA. Although the MEPA is designed to increase recruitment of adoptive parents of color while simultaneously removing barriers to cross-racial adoption, children of color and Latinx children still spend comparatively longer amounts of time in foster care than non-Latinx White children before they are permanently placed (U.S. House Committee on Ways and Means, 2016). Children of color are overrepresented in foster care when compared to their numbers in the general population (Child Welfare Information Gateway, 2017).

Even as policy changes and societal shifts have contributed to increases in transracial adoptions, the impact on children of color of being raised in White homes is still debated. For example, since 1972, the National Association of Black Social Workers (NABSW) has taken a strong stance against transracial adoption, calling for the repeal of the Interethnic Adoption Provisions. They are leading advocates for increased attention to African-American family preservation and kinship care. For more information on the NABSW's position on the MEPA and transracial adoption, visit their website at **www.nabsw.org**.

Some research on transracial adoption indicates that the practice does not negatively affect the child's psychosocial and overall well-being (Hamilton et al., 2015; Juffer & van IJzendoorn, 2007). However, others have suggested that such findings may not definitively make the case for transracial adoption as a child welfare practice. It is likely that different groups of children experience transracial adoption differently, potentially in ways that impact ultimate outcomes. For example, international adoptees may have a different experience in their adoptive American families than African-American children who are adopted by White parents. Research findings that transracial adoptees have relatively high self-esteem and strong racial/ethnic identity are perhaps better understood as testament to the resilience and strength of these young people rather than affirmation of the validity of the practice. Further, some studies have indicated that children of color adopted into White families are prone to identify with the culture of their adopted families instead of their own, which can be problematic because identifying with one's own race and culture is correlated with fewer difficulties in adjusting to the new family (Frasch & Brooks, 2003). Other research points to parenting behaviors and number of placements prior to adoption as important factors related to child well-being in transracial adoptions (Bumpus, 2014). Policy reforms to reduce multiple placements and increase evidence-based training for potential adoptive parents can influence these experiences. Finally, it is important to carefully consider all possible outcomes to make decisions that are not merely better than the available alternatives, but truly in children's best interests. For more detailed information on this legislation, see the Guide to the Multiethnic Placement Act of 1994 and its 1996 amendment, available at the Children's Bureau website at **www.acf.hhs.gov/programs/cb**.

The Adoption and Safe Families Act

The Adoption and Safe Families Act (ASFA) of 1997 (Public Law 105-89) amended the Adoption Assistance and Child Welfare Act (AACWA) of 1980. The AACWA mandated that agencies make reasonable efforts to reunite the child and family and established new timetables for initiating termination of parental rights for children in foster care. Compared to the AACWA, the ASFA placed greater emphasis on child safety and was specifically intended to increase adoptions. The ASFA provides that states are not required to make reasonable efforts to preserve or reunify families once a court has determined that (1) the parent subjected the child to "aggravated circumstances"; (2) the parent committed a felony assault that resulted in serious bodily injury to the child or another of the parent's children; (3) the parent is guilty of murder or voluntary manslaughter of another of their children, or abetted, aided, solicited, or conspired to commit such a crime; or (4) parental rights with another child have been terminated. The Act further requires that permanency hearings be held within 12 months of the child's entry into foster care. If "reasonable efforts" are not required, the timeframe is reduced to 30 days. Additionally, for children who have been out of the home for 15 of the prior 22 months, termination of parental rights must be initiated unless (1) a child is being cared for by a relative; (2) the parent, their representative, or case workers can show a compelling reason why termination would not be in the best interests of the child; or (3) the state has not provided parents with the necessary or timely services that would enable the child to return safely to the home (Wan, 1999).

To expedite the permanency process, the ASFA authorizes the use of concurrent planning when appropriate. **Concurrent planning** provides states with the option of working on an alternative plan for the child, such as adoption, even while they are attempting reunification

(Adler, 2001). The ASFA provides states with incentive payments for any increase in the number of adoptions over the base year. It also provides an additional payment if children with special needs are adopted, makes health insurance available for children with special needs who cannot be adopted without such insurance, and removes geographic barriers to adoption by allowing children to be adopted outside the jurisdiction responsible for them (Adler, 2001).

These changes were intended to reduce the time a child spends in limbo between foster care and permanency (either reunification or adoption). However, current trends underscore the considerable challenges in achieving these aims. More children entered foster care in FY2017 than in 2013 (269,690, compared to 254,622), and there are 20,000 more children awaiting adoption than five years ago (Children's Bureau, 2018). As of September 2017, more than 123,437 children were in foster care awaiting adoption; almost 70,000 had already had parental rights terminated (Children's Bureau, 2018). This is likely due to a combination of factors. Many children come into the child welfare system with complex needs, and it can be hard to find adoptive homes that have the capability and desire to adopt children with special needs. Difficulties finding adoptive homes for older children and a lack of adequate post-adoption services may also contribute to the lengthy stretches many children spend in foster care.

The ASFA asserts that health and safety should be paramount in every decision made about children. If you accept the rationale that earlier and more forceful decisions about whether to reunify or adopt are in the child's best interests, then altering the reasonable effort requirement for permanency planning provides for the "best interests of the child." However, evaluation of the ASFA highlights the difficulty of child welfare decision-making and the reality of unintended consequences, as social workers, judges, and others attempt to reconcile parents' and children's interests when the two appear to conflict. Realizing the potential benefits of concurrent planning requires careful attention to ambiguities (D'Andrade, 2009). Some advocates have expressly urged states to limit concurrent planning to those children deemed unlikely to reunify with their biological families, since the pursuit of alternative placements may divert valuable energies from facilitating successful reunification. Finally, as we discuss later, the strict timelines imposed by the ASFA complicate the reunification prospects of many families, particularly those struggling with multiple challenges.

A diverse group of professionals delivers ASFA services. The court system is involved in deciding the best interests of the child. Social workers and other professionals who provide case management and therapeutic services are responsible for planning and delivering competent treatment and for working with the courts to make recommendations for placing the child. To enhance state capacity and accountability, ASFA provides additional funds to states to develop innovative approaches and makes technical assistance available to states, communities, and courts. Furthermore, it requires states to submit an annual performance report to the USDHHS. In turn, the USDHHS is responsible for reporting performance and developing performance-based incentives (Adler, 2001). The ASFA requires states to implement standards that ensure that children in foster care receive quality services that protect their health and safety (Adler, 2001). Nevertheless, many staff lack adequate preparation, a situation exacerbated by the difficulty of recruiting into the stressful, poorly compensated field. Exhibit 9.12 summarizes the major provisions of the ASFA.

EXHIBIT 9.12

Adoption and Safe Families Act (ASFA), 1997

Policy goals	To emphasize child safety to promote and accelerate permanency for children in foster care.
	To increase the accountability of the child welfare system.
Benefits or services provided	Accelerates permanent placement by promoting adoption and shortening time limits for termination of parental rights.
Eligibility rules	Children are eligible when they are removed from their homes.
Service delivery system	Federal oversight of state and local child welfare agencies that implement mandated changes.
	Court system decides the best interests of the child, with recommendations from social workers and other professionals who provide case management and therapeutic services.
Financing	Federal funding with some state matching funds.
	Federal incentives given to states that increase adoptions.

Family First Prevention Services Act (FFPSA)

The Family First Prevention Services Act (FFPSA) was passed as part of the Bipartisan Budget Act of 2018 (H.R. 1892). The FFPSA reforms child welfare finance streams. Previously, Title IV-E funds of the Social Security Act could be used only to help pay for the costs of foster care maintenance for eligible children, administrative expenses of foster care programs, training for staff and foster parents, adoption assistance, and kinship guardianship assistance. With the passage of the FFPSA, states, territories, and Native American tribes can also utilize these funds for prevention services that would allow at-risk children, deemed "candidates for foster care," to remain with their parents or relatives. After creation of a written, trauma-informed prevention plan that identifies evidence-based services to be provided, states and other eligible entities can be reimbursed for prevention services for up to 12 months. These services could include mental health care, addiction treatment, and/or in-home parenting intervention. The key to securing federal reimbursement is the assessment that the services are necessary to keep children safely at home with their families.

The FFPSA also includes financial incentives to reduce congregate placements and facilitate quicker transition to permanency, as well as additional support for youths transitioning from care. Apart from limited exceptions, the federal government will no longer reimburse states for children placed in group care settings for more than two weeks. Further, approved settings, known as qualified residential treatment programs, must use trauma-informed models, limit their size to six children, employ licensed clinical staff, and formally assess all children within 30 days of placement to determine whether their needs can be met in a family setting. Finally, the FFPSA requires states to compile annual child maltreatment death data and provide information on what they are doing to develop and implement multidisciplinary fatality prevention plans.

Because the legislation offers the potential to expand child welfare services to encompass a more holistic understanding of child well-being, advocates are optimistic that the FFPSA will

EXHIBIT 9.13 *Family First Prevention Services Act (FFPSA), 2018*	Policy goals	To prevent children from entering foster care by allowing federal reimbursement for prevention services such as mental health care, addiction treatment, and in-home parenting intervention. To improve the well-being of children in foster care by incentivizing states to reduce utilization of group care.
	Benefits or services provided	Allows funding previously restricted to foster care to be used for prevention services.
	Eligibility rules	Families are eligible when their children are identified by a state, territory, or tribal entity as "candidates for foster care."
	Service delivery system	States and other entities provide prevention services and/or contract with private agencies to provide them. Regulations restricting operation of group homes accompanied by financial incentives governing reimbursable services.
	Financing	Federal funding, through Title IV-E and Title IV-B of the Social Security Act.

reduce out-of-home placements. However, because most provisions of the FFPSA are discretionary, states will have to be proactive in seizing these opportunities. Pivoting the child welfare system from an emphasis on child-saving to a focus on family-strengthening will likely take considerable time and effort. The National Association of Social Workers sees the FFPSA as a step in the right direction and cheered its passage, citing the law's intention to "provide services to keep children safe with their families and out of foster care" (NASW, 2018b). Many social workers engaged in child welfare agree. However, some state policymakers and child protection administrators worry that the supply of foster families will be inadequate to support children without the ability to rely on group homes. At the same time, some advocates were disappointed that the FFPSA did not eliminate funding for group homes entirely, while others worry that the prevention funding will be inadequate to address families' needs and could then be used to further shift blame to parents whose children still need out-of-home placement (Wexler, 2018). Exhibit 9.13 above summarizes the provisions of the FFPSA, although some aspects of the law remain to be determined in regulations.

Independent Living Transition Services

Many children who are raised in foster care go on to lead full and happy lives. However, youths who grow up in foster care disproportionately experience negative outcomes in adulthood, such as homelessness, unemployment, and incarceration. The abrupt loss of financial and familial support that many youths experience when they age out of the foster care system may leave them ill-prepared for adulthood. As most 18-year-olds continue to depend on their families for a variety of emotional, financial, and developmental support, former foster children often have a hard time making the transition to adulthood without this assistance.

Concern that young people aging out of foster care were not equipped to live on their own led Congress to authorize the Independent Living Program in 1986. It provided funding for states to develop programs to help older foster youth make the transition to independence. The Chafee Foster Care Independent Living Act of 1999 (Public Law 106-109) provided further support for adolescents transitioning to adulthood. Additional assistance for these young people was included in the Fostering Connections to Success and Increasing Adoptions Act of 2008 (Public Law 110-351). Caseworkers are now required to help children complete personal transition plans 90 days before they are set to exit the foster care system. This legislation also created a federally subsidized guardianship program for kinship providers; mandated, expanded, and increased adoption incentives; and provided new funding to promote permanency. An important, optional, provision extended federal funding for youth in foster care to age 21. However, states are not required to apply for this reimbursement, and, as of 2018, only half had done so. More policy reform is needed. There is mounting recognition that supports for young people coming out of foster care may be necessary until age 25 to enhance the chances that they will complete their education and become adequately housed and positively connected to their communities.

The Child Support Enforcement Program

Increasing numbers of children live in single-parent households. In 2016, 22.4 million children—one quarter of all children under age 21 in the United States—lived with only one custodial parent (Grall, 2018). More than one-third of these children lived in poverty. Particularly as TANF cash assistance is reduced, any lack of adequate financial support from the noncustodial parent may mean many of these children grow up without the economic resources needed to thrive. Designed to help remedy this situation, the Child Support Enforcement (CSE) Program was established in 1975 as part of Title IV-D of the Social Security Act. At the federal level, the Office of Child Support Enforcement in the Administration for Children and Families (ACF) within the USDHHS oversees child support enforcement. Each level of government—federal, state, and local—plays a role in the child support enforcement system. Although many custodial and noncustodial parents make informal child support arrangements, CSE only intervenes where legal orders have been made. To guide courts' establishment of child support orders, states adopt child support guidelines and make those available to all judges. States use different methods to calculate child support payments. To learn how child support obligations are calculated in your state, start with your state's CSE agency's website.

    In all states, the first step in child support enforcement is establishment of paternity. The CSE Program also helps locate noncustodial parents and collects child support for families. In 2015, custodial parents were owed $33.7 billion in child support awards, 59.8 percent of which was collected, for an average annual payment of $3,447 to each custodial parent (Grall, 2018). While these payments represent a crucial support to custodial parents and children, leakage throughout the CSE system means that many custodial parents and children receive less child support than they are owed and, importantly, less than they need. There are other dynamics that compromise the efficacy of the CSE system. The requirement that custodial parents cooperate in the establishment of paternity can be a deterrent to some who fear it could damage their child's relationship with the noncustodial parent. When noncustodial parents are unemployed or have challenges that reduce their earning potential, it can be difficult for them to comply with child support obligations. And state and local responsibility in the CSE system can make it difficult to enforce orders across jurisdictions, even though all states are required to follow the Uniform Interstate Family Support Act, which places control of an order under a single state.

Currently, each state administers a CSE Program. In some states, the human services department is responsible for child support enforcement; in others, the department of revenue performs this role. Additionally, many states contract with private agencies to provide certain components of CSE, and Native tribes may administer their own programs. A parent with custody of a child whose other parent lives outside the home may receive services through CSE by applying to the agencies that administer the programs. For families receiving TANF, CSE services are automatic and mandatory. In those cases, CSE uses part of the child support collected to reimburse federal and state governments for TANF payments the family has received. Beginning in 2008, the federal government provided states with incentives to pass through up to $100 per month of child support to TANF families with one child and up to $200 per month of child support to TANF families with two or more children (Wheaton & Sorenson, 2007). As of 2017, half of states had chosen to pass through some child support payments without reducing the family's TANF assistance (National Conference of State Legislatures, 2017). In 2014, states distributed more than $118 million in child support payments to families receiving TANF. Child support payments for families not receiving TANF are sent directly to the families, and these funds are important elements of many families' budgets.

Although not technically a component of CSE, the 1996 legislation that created TANF also improved states' capacity to collect child support. The law established a national new-hire and wage-reporting system and instituted uniform interstate child support forms. It also provided funds to computerize statewide collection systems and authorized tough new penalties, such as revoking driver's licenses, for nonpayment of child support. Following these reforms and other state initiatives, child support collection increased nationally to a record $28.6 billion in FY2015 (Solomon-Fears, 2016). To further aid in these efforts, some states are experimenting with different incentives designed to increase repayment of child support arrears. For example, Kansas forgives some unpaid child support arrears if noncustodial parents save money in an account for their child's college education.

When parents who are in arrears for child support and do not have the means to pay are punished for nonpayment with incarceration, they may lose their jobs, rendering them even less able to support their children. Because poor noncustodial parents are often responsible for child support payments to custodial parents also living in poverty, children's well-being suffers in this inadequate arrangement. In 2015, only 30 percent of custodial parents living in poverty received any child support, and only 17 percent received their full child support order (Grall, 2018). To help noncustodial parents meet their child support obligations, as of 2014, 30 states had programs designed to increase parents' capability to provide financial and emotional support to their children. Some states help noncustodial parents continue their education, and others offer budgeting and financial management assistance. Advocates across the ideological spectrum have urged policy to make child support a more reliable and substantial source of financial support for custodial parents and children. In many European countries, the government guarantees child support to low-income custodial parents even if the noncustodial parent cannot pay or can only make partial payments. As proposed by some advocates, a U.S. child support assurance policy would set a minimum monthly award per child, standardize orders to ensure that low-income noncustodial parents could comply, and use government funding to allow custodial parents to rely on this income each month (Cancian & Meyer, 2018). Because the service delivery system varies significantly from state to state and, in some cases, even among judicial districts, we have not provided a summary analysis of CSE. To find out more about CSE, visit the website of the Office of Child Support Enforcement at **www.acf.hhs.gov/programs/css**.

Legislation for Children with Special Educational Needs

Children who require special services because of a physical or mental disability are considered to have special educational needs. Legislation for children with special needs, such as the Education for All Handicapped Children Act of 1975 and its reauthorization, IDEA of 1990, requires states to provide education and services to meet these children's needs in the "least restrictive environment" (Briar-Lawson et al., 2009). This means that children should be integrated into the educational mainstream to the greatest extent possible. As described in Chapter 7, IDEA was reauthorized in 2004 (Public Laws 108-446), with regulations finalized in 2006. Measures designed to hold education systems more accountable for outcomes for children with disabilities were a major component of the reauthorization. However, federal funding to help schools meet the requirements has been inadequate.

As greater knowledge and improved diagnostic approaches have raised the visibility of children with disabilities, movements on behalf of these children have helped draw attention to the importance of "most appropriate" placements and "least intrusive" interventions. These efforts have been aided by growing realization that the increase in the number of children with recognized special needs makes creation and maintenance of separate facilities and programs financially and administratively infeasible. In 2018, the Centers for Disease Control and Prevention estimated that one in 59 children are on the autism spectrum, almost one in six have some developmental disability, and still others have physical or emotional needs that require special attention. In this context, many advocates promote **normalization**, an approach whereby schools endeavor to create an environment for children with special needs that is similar to that experienced by other children. Parents, educators, social workers, and others have worked to implement policies that allow children with special needs to receive inclusionary services. Some of the most innovative strategies involve wrap-around services and those that modify the classroom environment so that it is more comfortable and successful for children with a wide range of needs. As is true in most strengths-based approaches, these changes may facilitate optimal development of all children, not just those with special needs.

Despite these advances, there are ongoing failures to promote the full strengths of children with special needs. An investigation by the Government Accountability Office uncovered "hundreds of cases of alleged abuse and death" as a result of misuses of restraint and seclusion in schools, and these interventions were disproportionately used on children with disabilities (Miller, 2010). Because these data are mostly self-reported, the incidence may be considerably higher. Further, the Centers for Disease Control and Prevention (2016c) has expressed concern about overreliance on medication for very young children with behavioral issues. Federal legislation has been proposed to prohibit elementary and secondary school personnel from managing any student by using chemical or mechanical restraint, physical restraint or escort that restricts breathing, or aversive behavioral intervention that compromises student health or safety, and to require staff to receive state-approved crisis intervention training. However, this legislation has not yet passed. The 2015 Every Student Succeeds Act, which replaced the No Child Left Behind Act, requires states to develop plans for how they will reduce the use of restraint and seclusion in schools (Every Student Succeeds Act, 2015). However, as of December 2016, only 28 states had adopted policies that limit restraint and seclusion for all students, and only 38 for students with disabilities (Butler, 2019). Nineteen states require an emergency threatening physical injury before restraint or seclusion can be used, but other states leave those decisions to the discretion of school personnel.

Social workers in schools and other agencies regularly serve children with special needs. It is important that you become familiar with policies and programs targeted to these children, including their rights to appeal policies that violate their civil and human rights. Many of the policies that determine how children with special needs are treated are state-specific. For information on your state's programs, contact your State Department of Education.

Quick Guide 7 provides an overview of the policies related to child welfare and juvenile justice analyzed in this chapter. You can use this Quick Guide as a resource in your policy-informed practice with children and families.

QUICK GUIDE 7   Child Welfare and Juvenile Justice Programs

Child Abuse and Prevention Treatment Act (CAPTA)	Federal program that provides funding to states to develop systems for reporting, investigating, treating, and preventing child maltreatment. See **www.childwelfare.gov**.
Juvenile Justice and Delinquency Prevention Act (JJDP)	Federal government provides assistance to states and local governments to address juvenile crime and improve the juvenile justice system. The focus is on community-based treatment to avoid unnecessary institutionalization and protect juveniles from exposure to adult inmates. Oversight is provided by the Office of Juvenile Justice and Delinquency Prevention in the U.S. Department of Justice. For more information, see **www.ojjdp.gov**.
Indian Child Welfare Act (ICWA)	Provides protection to all children who are members of federally recognized tribes through the provision of standards for the removal and placement of Native American children in the child welfare system. Mandates efforts to keep Native children in their homes or place them in homes that reflect their culture. Establishes tribal authority over federal and state courts in the protection of Native American children. For more information, see **www.nicwa.org**.
Adoption Assistance and Child Welfare Act (AACWA)	Federal government provides financial incentives to states to reduce the time children spend in foster care by developing permanency plans that emphasize family preservation, reunification, or adoption. Mandates that reasonable efforts be made to keep children in the home or to reunite them with their families.

The Multi-Ethnic Placement Act (MEPA)	Federal funding provided to states to implement provisions to remove barriers to permanency for children in the child welfare system, except for those covered by ICWA. Aims to shorten the time to adoption by prohibiting child welfare agencies from denying placement based on race, color, or national origin of the child or prospective foster or adoptive parent. Requires that state child welfare agencies actively recruit and maintain foster and adoptive parents reflective of the racial and ethnic diversity of children in foster care. For more information, see www.acf.hhs.gov.
Adoption and Safe Families Act (ASFA)	Amendment to the Adoption Assistance and Child Welfare Act that endeavors to ensure permanency and child safety by promoting adoption and accelerating termination of parental rights. Provides adoption promotion and support services to foster children and adoptive families. Also provides coverage of health insurance for children if necessary to ensure adoption. Federal government provides adoption incentive payments to states if annual adoption numbers increase, and for the adoption of children with special needs.
Family First Prevention Services Act (FFPSA)	Allows federal reimbursement for prevention services, including mental health, addiction, and parenting intervention, designed to help children remain safely in their homes. States will need to create plans in order to utilize federal funds for these prevention services.

EVALUATING POLICIES AND PROGRAMS FOR CHILDREN AND FAMILIES

Evaluating policies for children and families using the strengths perspective focuses attention on enhancing families' capacity to serve as the foundation of support for children. Policy reforms center on reengineering the "front end" of the child welfare system and providing upstream intervention to improve children's outcomes. Policies are assessed based on the extent to which they facilitate families' realization of their dreams for their children's futures. According to strengths-perspective principles, programs must be attuned to the racial, ethnic, social, political, cultural, and economic contexts of families' lives and make structural changes in systems that disadvantage some children. In child welfare, juvenile justice, and other domains, evaluation should track disparate outcomes for children of color and those from low-income families to identify patterns that suggest needed reform. For strengths to be exalted and enhanced, policy must sever the connection between poverty and the risk of child maltreatment, give all children a fair and healthy start, and eliminate disparities in juvenile justice. Many families engaged with the child welfare and juvenile justice systems face co-occurring challenges related to the intersections of their identities of race, class, and gender and the systems' unjust responses to their social positions. Just as surely, these families have strengths that can be amplified. Such an approach will yield benefits for their children and for the larger society.

Evaluating policies and programs using the strengths perspective involves seeking clients' input. Advocacy groups provide parents' perspectives on policy in arenas including child welfare, while other groups position children and youths as experts in foster care and juvenile justice reform. For example, Family Voices, a national grassroots network of families and advocates for children with special needs, promotes the inclusion of all families as decision-makers and supports partnership between families and professionals. Family Voices' publications describe strategies for involving families in developing and evaluating programs. You can learn more about the work of Family Voices at **www.familyvoices.org**. Kansans United for Youth Justice highlighted experiences of juvenile offenders and built a bipartisan campaign that contributed to substantial reforms in state policy. Their publications are available at **www.kansansunited-foryouthjustice.org**.

In many states, child abuse prevention organizations work to strengthen families and help parents reunite with children removed from their homes. Often, these organizations also promote system reform by communicating families' concerns to service providers and judicial decision-makers. The Child Welfare Organizing Project provides support services and training to parents whose children are in the child welfare system, while engaging those parents to educate others about child welfare policy and lobby policymakers for needed changes. You can learn about such efforts at **http://cwop.org**. Teens who are transitioning from foster care are another particularly good source of information about needed change, as illustrated in Exhibit 9.14, which relates a student group's experience mobilizing youths in the foster care system.

Strengths-based policy principles stress involving clients in designing and delivering services. As families define themselves in new ways, strengths-based child welfare policy recognizes the validity of different family forms, including same-sex partnerships and multigenerational extended families. Strengths-based approaches to reforming child welfare services include instituting policies that promote self-help and mutual assistance, as well as investing in approaches that help families overcome the barriers that perpetuate their crises. Policies should ensure that payment systems and accountability measures align with children's understanding of their needs and with families' own goals. Otherwise, reimbursement structures may serve to incentivize continued provision of services without necessarily emphasizing progress toward positive outcomes for children.

Evaluation from a strengths perspective requires attention to basic rights for children in our society. Children today still do not have guaranteed basic rights. Nineteen states still have policies allowing corporal punishment in their schools (Gershoff & Font, 2016); its use with students

---

EXHIBIT 9.14

Student Advocates Target "Aging-Out" Policy (Foster Care)

Students and Foster Care Youth Press for Transition Services

Students at the University of Washington-Tacoma were involved in a community project over two years mapping the system that serves youths who are "aging-out" of the foster care system. They advocated for bills that would extend Medicaid coverage for all children leaving foster care from age 19 to 21. Students organized a group of youth with experience in the foster care system to go to the Capitol for Youth Advocacy Day and empowered the youths to share personal testimony in front of the House and Senate. The successful bill resulted in many youths who were aging out of the system receiving health care until age 21.

with disabilities and disproportionately with youth of color is particularly troubling. On the global stage, the United States is the only member of the United Nations (UN) that has not yet ratified the UN Convention on the Rights of the Child, a human rights instrument that spells out the economic, civil, political, social, and cultural rights of children. While there is some concern that ratification could interfere with states' rights in the arena of child welfare, the NASW continues to advocate for ratification of this critical convention.

In the next section, we evaluate selected components of child welfare and juvenile justice policies. We consider necessary changes that would improve child well-being and increase the effectiveness of social work with these children and families.

Child Protection Policy from the Strengths Perspective

There are two different policy paradigms for child protection. One views child maltreatment as a crime requiring police-style investigation. The second emphasizes social work interventions that focus on assessing the need for a range of services, along with risk and safety. While political pressures, particularly following tragic lapses, have contributed to litigation-oriented rather than social work-operated child protection systems, research indicates that providing parents with needed support can improve child welfare outcomes (Briar-Lawson et al., 2009). Additionally, prevention investment aligns with the state's primary responsibility in child welfare—to ensure the safety of all children in state custody. When necessary efforts are made to ensure that children enter the child welfare system only when necessary, state authorities have a still-daunting but nonetheless more manageable task of safeguarding those children in their care.

Given the multiple agencies often involved in families' lives, there is a need for much greater integration across the physical and mental health, domestic violence, addiction, income support, and child protection systems. Instead, as an example of the fragmented and ineffective system today, although it is estimated that more than half of all families involved with the child welfare system present substance-use problems, few states have enacted policies that allow drug-using pregnant mothers priority access to treatment beds. Long waits and expensive co-pays place quality treatment out of reach for many who need and even want it, and parental addiction is a prominent contributor to the removal of children from their homes—overwhelming state systems and endangering children (Wiltz, 2016).

Social workers' understanding of the complex realities of families' lives points to a need for policies that provide more flexibility in conducting investigations, rather than adhering to a standardized, "one-size-fits-all" approach. These policies should be informed by intersectionality, to account for the ways identities affect individuals' experiences with and outcomes from child protection systems. For example, given the discrimination African-American families often experience within the criminal justice system, the use of a law-enforcement approach in child welfare responses with Black families may be especially problematic. Additionally, for many LGBTQ+ youth, child welfare and juvenile justice systems are oppressive and dehumanizing (Estrada & Marksamer, 2006). Too often, then, these systems reinforce and even amplify societal inequities, instead of intervening to help children and families meet their needs.

Family Rights and Child Safety

As described above, policy changes in the Adoption and Safe Families Act allow courts to terminate parents' rights more easily than under the AACWA. While advocates hoped this approach would facilitate permanency, critics contend that the ASFA works against family reunification. The ASFA's compressed schedule and triggering of termination of parental rights are particularly problematic for parents who face multiple obstacles to reunification that cannot be resolved on ASFA's timeline, including those struggling with addiction and, especially, those incarcerated (Genty, 2003; Lawrence, 2014). Indeed, research has found that incarcerated parents are even more likely than those who have assaulted their children to have their parental rights terminated, particularly when corrections officials refuse to transport parents so that they can be present at required hearings and otherwise exert their desire to stay involved in their children's lives (Hager & Flagg, 2018). Additionally, the majority of substantiated child maltreatment cases are associated with substance use disorder, a condition that can often take far longer than 12 months to successfully address (Young & Gardner, 2003). Further, inadequate financial assistance for low-income families may make it harder for parents to secure housing and other necessities in the time that the ASFA prescribes.

To promote permanency for children in the child welfare system, we need to develop policies and programs that (1) provide support and services for families involved in **kinship care**, which means a child living with relatives without a parent present in the home, and (2) allow parents sufficient time and assistance to regain some control over issues impeding their ability to be effective caregivers. In 2017, only 32 percent of children taken into state custody were placed into kinship care, and only 7 percent of those leaving foster care went to live with relatives other than their parents (Children's Bureau, 2018). Most kinship care placements are arranged privately, without the involvement of a child welfare agency. When children transition directly to kinship care, they have better outcomes than children placed in non-relative foster care, and even better outcomes than children who eventually receive kinship placements after time in the public child welfare system. Specifically, keeping children within their family systems is associated with better health and mental health (Winokur et al., 2015). However, some research suggests that kinship care is associated with relatively less permanency (Zinn, 2009), as some relatives may be reluctant to pursue adoption (Bell & Romano, 2015; Bramlett, Radel, & Chow, 2017). This research underlines a critical fact about child welfare policy: In circumstances this complex and with stakes this high, careful evaluation is needed on a case-by-case basis to determine the best interest of the child.

Family Reunification High caseloads and financial disincentives often work against family reunification. Most federal child welfare funding supports out-of-home rather than in-home services. In addition, the policies and practices of many residential facilities do not support family reintegration. When facilities are located far from families, when family visits and phone calls are considered privileges rather than rights, and when no residential staff are responsible for facilitating discharge and reintegration, family reunification is less likely.

Greater understanding about the effects of trauma on children's development has made the need to intervene to support healthy family functioning prior to any crisis or disruption more urgent. However, the U.S. child welfare system has yet to transition to approaches that would elevate this goal. Laudable policy principles such as reasonable efforts to prevent out-of-home placement, the child's right to the least intrusive intervention and the least restrictive environment, and emphasis on normalization have been difficult to define and operationalize. Nevertheless, by focusing on child development and overall well-being as well as safety, these principles promote a philosophy of child welfare intervention consistent with the strengths perspective. They further make it clear that extremes such as large, impersonal children's institutions and foster care drift, where children spend years moving from one temporary placement to another, are unacceptable. When incorporated into law and enforced with financial incentives, these principles help fortify the efforts of advocates who are petitioning for child welfare reform. For example, rather than employing traditional reimbursement strategies that pay providers a fee for each day children remain in out-of-home care, some states' reimbursement approaches explicitly discourage allowing children to linger too long in foster care.

Teen Pregnancy While, of course, not all teen pregnancies occur among youth who have been in the child welfare system, research has shown that youth in foster care are more likely to engage in risky behavior, including unsafe sexual behavior. Indeed, exposure to harsh and stressful environments early in life can even alter children's sexual development, including by triggering earlier onset of puberty (Belsky et al., 2007), particularly when children lack strong attachments to parents that buffer them from these effects (Sung et al., 2016). As they approach adolescence, then, children who have been involved in the child welfare system face particular risks. In the domain of teen pregnancy, these challenges can be transmitted across generations.

Although the overall number of children born to teen mothers reached a record low in 2016, youths in foster care are much more likely to experience pregnancy than those not involved in the child welfare system. Compared to girls not in foster care, teen girls living in foster care are 2.5 times more likely to become pregnant by age 19; half of young men aging out of foster care report getting someone pregnant, compared to 19 percent of their peers outside the system (National Conference of State Legislatures, 2016). Additionally, although the teen birth rate has fallen more than 50 percent in the past decade, teen pregnancy remains a significant issue for some young women, with one in six teen pregnancies occurring among girls who have already had a pregnancy (USDHHS, 2017).

Further, as the map in Exhibit 9.15 depicts, teen birth rates are more prevalent in some parts of the country than others, ranging from a high of 32.8 births per 1,000 teen girls in Arkansas to eight births per 1,000 teen girls in Massachusetts (Martin et al., 2018). In addition to state policy disparities, these regional differences illustrate the influence of economic, social, and cultural conditions on such outcomes. Teen pregnancy is still higher in the United States than in many other developed nations. This is especially concerning given the consequences for teen parents, their children, and society. Only 38 percent of young women who become pregnant before age 18 get a high school diploma. Daughters born to teen mothers are more likely to become teen mothers themselves, and teen childbearing costs taxpayers over $9 billion annually (National Campaign to Prevent Teen and Unplanned Pregnancy, 2016).

Preventing teen pregnancy among youths in the child welfare system is a critical agenda item. Many agencies are starting to address this issue through strategies such as foster parent and case worker training and pregnancy prevention programming for teens within independent living courses. To learn more about these efforts and federal resources that complement them, visit the Office of Adolescent Health at **hhs.gov/ash/oah**. Although adolescent health initiatives often come under fire from those who promote abstinence-only teen pregnancy prevention, it is through these types of programs that youths are provided with the tools they need

EXHIBIT 9.15

Teen Birth Rate in the United States, 2017

All teen birth rates are per 1,000 youth.

- 8.1–13.8
- 14.2–16.2
- 16.4–21.2
- 21.3–24.6
- 26.6–32.8

Source: Martin et al., 2018

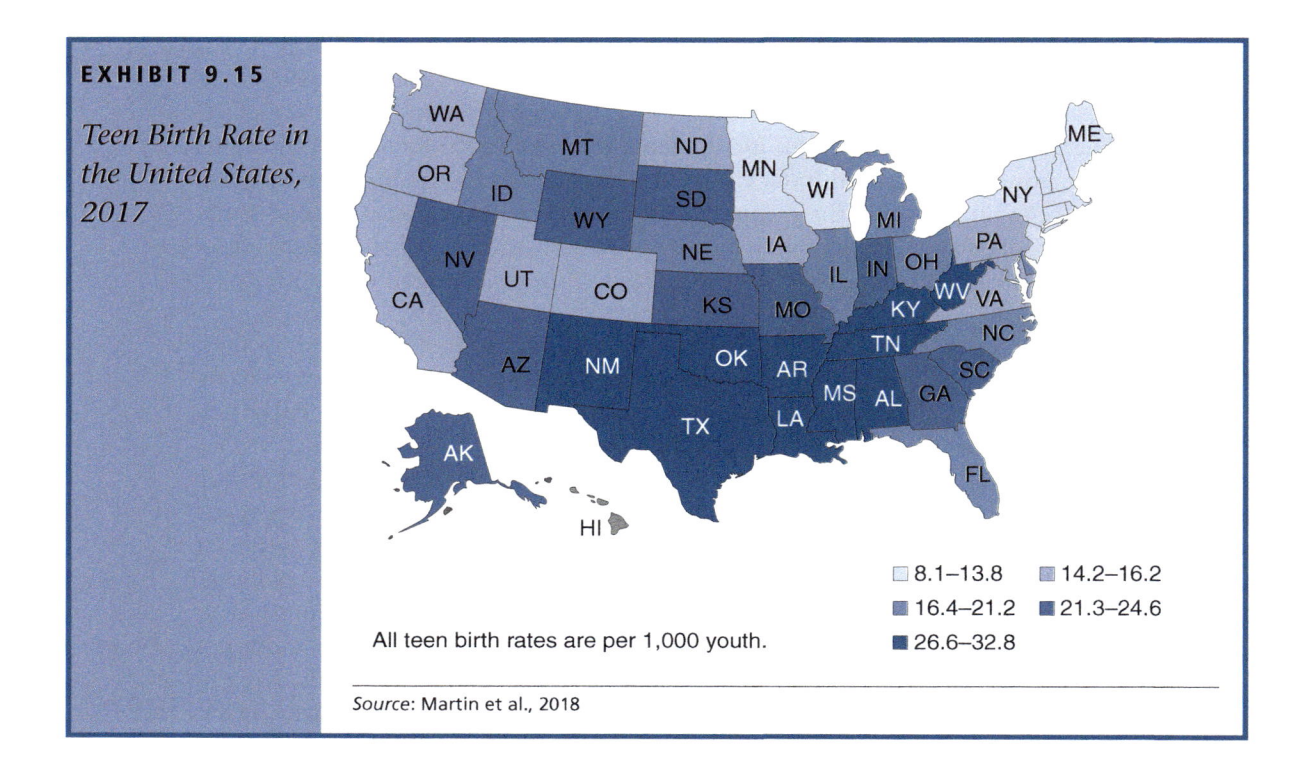

to care for themselves and plan for a productive future within their communities. In addition to pregnancy prevention, child welfare advocates must devise policies that provide the support teen parents need to be successful in reaching their own goals and, if they choose to parent, to be effective in that role.

Privatization Private sector providers have long been important parts of the child welfare system. More recently, private entities have taken on additional functions in many states. One principal privatization strategy is for public entities to buy services for clients through **purchase-of-service (POS) contracting** (Petr, 2004). The state then monitors and oversees the provision of services rather than providing services directly. In one form of privatization, POS vouchers are provided directly to recipients or their families. Some state systems have developed modified managed care models, whereby private entities are paid a set amount per person to provide all needed services. Crucially, if there is no graduation of payment based on severity of need, agencies operating within managed care models have an incentive to "cream"—that is, to provide services to children with fewer needs in order to stretch limited dollars into greater profit. Another concern in some privatization structures is that bids may be evaluated, and contracts awarded, based on the least expensive proposal rather than the strongest track record of success or the most innovative approaches. This can result in serious inadequacies in the child welfare system. Additionally, competition between providers may interfere with efforts to increase cooperation and coordination. Privatization may also jeopardize continuity of care, since each time a private provider loses a contract, families and children experience changes and disruptions on top of those that initially brought them into the system.

Rigorous research is needed to evaluate the efficacy, equity, and efficiency of various privatization approaches. Consistent with the strengths perspective, such research must carefully examine not just cost-effectiveness but also outcomes for clients. Reimbursement policies and privatization contracts should be scrutinized to determine whether they incentivize positive outcomes. Finally, research must examine the impact of privatization on child welfare workers. Because private agencies compete for and may lose contracts, job stability is reduced. When cost is a driving factor, an agency that provides lower pay and fewer benefits for its workforce may be more likely to win the contract. These pressures can take a toll on workers in child welfare systems.

Strategies for Supporting Families More Effectively Parenting is often difficult and stressful even under the best of circumstances. For millions of American families who struggle to ensure that their children's needs are met while balancing obligations at work, economic strains, and challenges such as mental or physical illness, housing unaffordability or instability, and/or community violence, it can appear a nearly impossible task. In many communities, investing in children's welfare and equipping parents to approach parenting from a foundation of strengths must begin with development and subsidy of available, affordable, high-quality childcare. Today, while childcare costs vary dramatically by region and care setting, there are few places in the country where parents can count on having affordable access to the childcare they need. In 35 states, childcare for two children costs more than a mortgage; in 28 states, childcare costs more than tuition at a four-year public university (Childcare Aware, 2017). Average childcare costs can exceed $10,000 per year—high for nearly any household, but completely out of reach for low- and moderate-income families (Whitehurst, 2017). As a result, too many families are forced to compromise their children's well-being by resorting to unsafe or unqualified care arrangements (Herbst & Tekin, 2010), reducing their income by foregoing work, and/or sacrificing other essentials to pay for childcare.

Policies that aim to reduce families' childcare cost burden include subsidies within the Child Care Development Block Grant (CCDBG) and the Child and Dependent Care Tax Credit. However, policymakers, providers, advocates, and parents searching for affordable care largely agree that these investments are inadequately funded and imperfectly conceived, making them insufficient tools for helping families navigate care options for their children. The CCDBG serves approximately 1.4 million children under age 13 from 850,000 low-income working families each month. These families receive subsidies that help pay for the cost of care. However, the gap between the subsidy's reimbursement rate and the cost of care often makes it hard for families to find providers who will accept their subsidies. In 2018, only in three states (Hawaii, Indiana, and South Dakota) did subsidies fully cover the average cost of care (Workman & Jessen-Howard, 2018). Further, only an estimated 15 percent of eligible children receive federal childcare subsidies.

Many states' childcare subsidy programs have long waiting lists and require families to complete time-intensive reviews (Schulte & Durana, 2016). Given the urgency of finding affordable, quality care options, these are delays families literally cannot afford. In light of scarce resources, agencies administering childcare subsidies try to prioritize serving children at risk of adverse childhood experiences, those who are homeless, or those with special developmental needs, although even many of these children do not receive sufficient assistance. Further, even if families qualify for and receive childcare assistance, they may find that relatively modest wage increases dramatically increase their required co-payment. This benefit cliff can shock families' finances, jeopardize children's care, and prevent upward mobility. The Child and Dependent Care Tax Credit is of even less help to low-income families than the means-tested subsidies. The credit is capped at $3,000, even though the annual price for infant care in a childcare center is $4,600 in the most affordable state (Mississippi) and far more in much of the country. It is nonrefundable, meaning low-income families who do not owe taxes do not benefit at all. And, because the credit is awarded only annually, it does not help families afford weekly or monthly childcare bills.

In 2018, Congress increased funding for the CCDBG by $5.8 billion, an infusion of new resources that can support states' efforts to increase access to childcare subsidies to 230,000 children more than the 1.4 million currently served (Adams, 2018). More childcare support is clearly needed, however. Increased CCDBG funding is a policy priority of child welfare advocates such as Prevent Child Abuse America, because these organizations recognize the relationship between insufficient and unaffordable childcare and children's risk of maltreatment. Advocates recommend increasing the rates paid to childcare providers to encourage more to accept subsidies and to improve training and quality, as well as diversifying the types of providers who are approved to deliver subsidized care, to respond to families' preferences and ensure that care is available to meet different work schedules and family demands (Adams, 2018). Creating a more universal childcare subsidy would address the affordability crises experienced by families who earn too much to qualify for the CCDBG or other funds, but too little to pay market rate for their children's care, while ensuring that no child suffers inadequate supervision while their parents attend to work or other obligations (Whitehurst, 2017). Research has demonstrated that availability of affordable childcare options improves parents' labor market outcomes (Schaefer, Kreader, & Collins, 2010), while high-quality childcare supports children's academic and emotional development (Burchinal et al., 2009). If the United States is truly committed to children's welfare, the realities of today's families demand greater attention to and investment in childcare.

Improving the responsiveness of the child welfare system requires funding adequate to provide services immediately when a child has been reported as endangered. One example of an initiative to provide this seamless entry and rapid response, authorized by the Affordable Care Act, is the Maternal, Infant, and Early Childhood Home Visiting Program (MIECHV). The Health Resources and Services Administration (HRSA) and the ACF, both part of the USDHHS, administer this program. Grants are provided to states and jurisdictions for the implementation of innovative evidence-based home visiting programs or for the expansion and improvement of existing programs.

Programs funded through MIECHV provide voluntary home visiting services to pregnant women and women with children up to five years of age who fall within identified priority populations, including low-income families, families where parents have a history of substance use or need addiction treatment, and families with past interaction with the child welfare system. A nurse, social worker, or early childhood educator makes home visits. This program works to improve the identification, provision, and coordination of services for at-risk communities and families by targeting a variety of participant outcomes, including prevention of child injuries or maltreatment and reduction in crime or domestic violence. Research has found that, when delivered by trained workers in adherence to evidence-based models, early home visits can reduce the likelihood of child welfare involvement (McCall, Eckenrode, & Olds, 2009). In February 2018, MIECHV was allocated $400 million per year through FY2022—another victory for child welfare advocates. For more information on this innovative program, see the Maternal and Child Health Bureau page on the USDHHS site at **mchb.hrsa.gov**.

Even if supports such as subsidized, high-quality childcare and early infant intervention are made more universal, families coping with serious challenges will likely need long-term services if their children are to remain safely at home. To truly thrive, these families require even greater investment. High rates of system reentry indicate that some families continue to be vulnerable, and the greater risk of poor outcomes for subsequent generations underscores the importance of transformative interventions. Some advocates have endorsed long-term, low-cost strategies such as mutual aid groups, while others envision more structural changes, including universal health care and universal basic income. As with other policy approaches, these efforts must be evaluated to assess their effectiveness.

As this discussion underscores, true promotion of child welfare requires government, community, and labor policies that support parents in their most crucial role and build on the strengths of family and community networks. Examples of such policies are paid family leave, flexible working hours, and on-site childcare at the workplace. Preventive programs that improve outcomes for children, such as public preschool, should be expanded. Advocates have recommended that when new children enter either the child welfare or the juvenile justice systems, experts should review their cases to determine which preventive services failed to reach them (Briar-Lawson et al., 2009). That information can then be used to close the gaps into which so many children currently fall.

Juvenile Justice from the Strengths Perspective

Adverse events early in life, coupled with insufficient investments in proven interventions, put many young people at risk of involvement in both the child welfare and the juvenile justice systems. Then, when they get in trouble, public sentiment can quickly turn against them, resulting in a policy response that emphasizes punishment rather than rehabilitation. Not surprisingly, programs aimed at prevention and early intervention receive inadequate funding and attention. Although there is still much left to be learned, understanding of trauma and its harmful effects has recently penetrated public consciousness. Scholars have linked community factors to traumatic responses at the family and individual levels and have sought to catalyze collaborations that address root causes of childhood adversity (Ellis & Dietz, 2017). However, policymakers, child welfare professionals, and other stakeholders have often struggled to develop policies in education, child welfare, criminal justice, and health care that prevent exposure to dangerous stress, intervene comprehensively and compassionately to help traumatized children and families, and build community resilience (Ko et al., 2008).

Social workers, who have long recognized that stress affects children's well-being and their likelihood of child welfare and juvenile justice involvement, are involved in initiatives to identify and quantify adverse childhood experiences (ACEs) and permeate policymaking with a trauma-informed perspective. They then work with caregivers and communities to prevent damaging childhood events, treat the consequences, increase supportive resources, and build resilience (Child Welfare Information Gateway, 2016). While focus on trauma may seem incompatible with the strengths perspective, strengths-based policy practitioners see how attention to strengths can generate hope in communities, fuel the call to action, and aid in identifying the kind of policy necessary to support trauma prevention initiatives. Focus on individuals' strengths can even be considered a hallmark of trauma-informed programming; when programs emphasize clients' strengths and "highlight adaptations over symptoms and resilience over pathology," they enhance people's ability to transcend what they have experienced—a primary goal of trauma-informed practice (Elliott et al., 2005, p. 467). Social workers operating from the strengths perspective can emphasize the resilience of individuals, families, and communities and ensure that narratives that elevate discussion of trauma also accurately portray people's tremendous capacity for growth and health. To learn more about trauma-informed approaches to juvenile justice, review the National Child Traumatic Stress Network's principles for reform at **www.nctsn.org/trauma-informed-care/creating-trauma-informed-systems/justice**.

Scholars in a variety of disciplines have found that the prevalence of juvenile crime is reduced when resources are directed toward effective prevention programs. An important element in prevention is facilitation of academic success—important in its own right and a protective factor against adverse outcomes. The education system should include supports that help all children succeed—especially those otherwise at risk. Instead, too many schools punish and exclude some of the very children most in need. Research has found, for example, that zero-tolerance school discipline policies and stiffer criminal penalties are not effective in reducing juvenile delinquency or recidivism rates among youths (Bowditch, 1993; Raffaele-Mendez, 2003). Instead, these discipline practices can create what some advocates have called the "school-to-prison pipeline," catalyzing a cascade of negative interactions.

Further, these policies are inequitably wielded, with particularly harsh consequences for young males of color (Skiba & Rausch, 2006). In the 2014/2015 school year, 17.6 percent of Black male high school students were suspended, compared to only 5 percent of non-Latinx White male students (National Center for Education Statistics, 2019). In 2014, the federal Departments of Education and Justice warned state education commissioners that patterns of disproportionate discipline risk federal civil rights action. As public sentiment in many communities has turned against zero tolerance discipline, more school districts are seeking alternatives. The NASW has also weighed in on this issue, calling on social workers to be proactive in establishing a dialogue among districts and school social workers that focuses on reducing suspensions and providing more effective services for students with disabilities (NASW, 2015i). Removing children who are troubled from school without providing them with treatment does not solve the problem; it leads instead to the creation of more troubled children. There are few employment opportunities for youths who are forced out of school and into the juvenile justice system, and the prevalence of criminal behavior among these youths is higher than for those who remain in school (Ryan, 2013). Juvenile justice reform should include implementing school disciplinary polices that provide more supportive services and help at-risk youths achieve their educational potential (Children's Defense Fund, 2012).

The NASW *Policy Statement on Juvenile Justice and Delinquency Prevention*, issued in 2015, supports changes that would establish interdisciplinary services that reflect social work values and provide developmentally and culturally appropriate services to youths in the juvenile justice system. It also recommends equitable treatment to correct the biases that result in the disproportionate incarceration of low-income youths and youths of color. Further, the NASW recommends cross-system collaboration between the child welfare and juvenile justice systems to address the needs of the significant number of children who cross over. Additionally, the NASW recommends that juvenile justice institutions hire professional social workers with case management, intake, interviewing, cultural competency, and counseling skills to work with youth and families (NASW, 2015g). More recently, a joint publication by the NASW and the Campaign for Youth Justice highlighted policy and practice recommendations to reduce racial disproportionality in juvenile offenders' assignment to adult correctional institutions (Thomas & Wilson, 2018). In this document, the NASW examines racial disproportionality in youth transfer to adult justice systems through the lens of the U.S. Constitution's guarantee of equal protection under the law. When Black youths are 47.3 percent of the youths transferred to adult courts despite being only 14 percent of the total youth population (OJJDP, 2018), there are obvious inequities at work.

Assessment and treatment interventions tailored to the individual youth offender in the community are much more likely to be effective than are generalized treatment programs in large facilities far from home. Effective post-release plans and after-care programs are also important. Policies and funding that make such approaches viable are needed. One initiative currently implemented in a few parts of the country is the Juvenile Mental Health Court. These courts are designed to improve the effectiveness of interventions in cases involving youths with mental illnesses or developmental disabilities who break the law. Youth mental health courts are problem-solving courts that aim to reduce recidivism through treatment. This is an example of developing programs to more effectively integrate the systems that serve youths (National Center for Juvenile Justice and Mental Health, 2006).

A guiding tenet of the OJJDP (2011), "to empower communities and engage youth and families," is based on the understanding that juvenile justice policies and programs need to take into consideration the strengths, experiences, and goals of these young people. Social workers across the nation can advocate for establishment of and investment in prevention, diversion, and early intervention programs that incorporate the recommendations of youths and their families. Some of these programs could be implemented through policy changes at the agency level. Others would require state or federal legislative action. The first step in establishing these programs is to make practitioners and policymakers aware of cost-effective approaches that have successfully reduced juvenile crime. For more information on promising programs in juvenile justice, review the OJJDP's Model Programs Guide at **www.ojjdp.gov/mpg** and examine evidence-based practices at the National Center for Mental Health and Juvenile Justice, at **www.ncmhjj.com**.

The Role of Social Workers in the Child Welfare System

Although social work has traditionally been the lead profession in the child welfare system, high caseloads, low pay, and social work students' increasing interest in more clinically oriented careers have changed this landscape in recent decades. Some states have attempted to save money and reduce case backlogs by reclassifying public child welfare positions so that people without social work degrees can deliver these services. Others have privatized their foster care and adoption systems. As we saw in Chapter 4, these kinds of decisions have a substantial impact on the services that clients receive and, ultimately, on the lives of our most vulnerable families and children.

The NASW has issued a policy statement asserting that (1) the social work profession's core values should guide child welfare services, and (2) an undergraduate or graduate degree in social work should be required for the delivery and administration of public child welfare services (NASW, 2015j). To garner support to secure and sustain these investments in professional service, social workers must educate policymakers about the importance of social work in child welfare.

CONCLUSION

Despite the high correlation of systemic barriers with child maltreatment and involvement with the juvenile justice system, symptom-focused remediation and crisis intervention, rather than efforts to equip all families with needed supports, remain the major focus of work with families and children. Because families are the primary providers for children, policies that support families in that role are basic to promoting child welfare. Policies that provide adequate family income, educational and training opportunities, and affordable, high-quality health care, childcare, and housing help to protect children and empower families. Such policies enhance family functioning and lessen the need for intensive intervention. To learn more about research and advocacy initiatives to ensure equitable opportunities for all children, visit the website of the Children's Defense Fund at **www.childrensdefense.org**. You can also learn about philanthropies promoting child well-being by visiting the websites of the Annie E. Casey Foundation, the Edna McConnell Clark Foundation, and the W. K. Kellogg Foundation. As a social worker, you can investigate promising approaches and commit yourself to strengths-based and client-focused work with children and families. Your practice will be informed by your understanding of the policies shaping the systems with which clients interact, and your practice can also help to change those systems, particularly as you empower clients to tell their stories and advocate for their families.

MAIN POINTS

- Historically, child welfare policies emphasized child saving rather than family strengthening. Policy still displays ongoing tension between the family's right to preservation and the public's desire to protect children.

CHILDREN AND FAMILIES **349**

- In total, the United States can be understood to have not a "child welfare" policy that provides supports for the universal well-being of children, but instead a "child risk response system."

- The demographics of children in the United States have changed in the past 40 years. The proportion of the population under age 18 has been decreasing even as the absolute size of the child population grows. Additionally, the racial composition is shifting, with larger populations of children of color. More children are living in single-parent households.

- Due to the devastating effects poverty can have on vulnerable families, it is imperative that we invest in measures that help parents provide for their families' needs.

- The child welfare system promotes child well-being by providing family preservation, foster care, and adoption services to families and children with reports of suspected child maltreatment.

- Child maltreatment is harm caused by parents or primary caregivers; it includes neglect, physical abuse, sexual abuse, and emotional abuse.

- The first major federal social policy specifically intended to prevent child maltreatment was the Child Abuse Prevention and Treatment Act (CAPTA) of 1974. This Act emphasized the need for increased state efforts in reporting and investigating child abuse and neglect.

- The juvenile justice system was established to promote the rehabilitation of young offenders. The Juvenile Justice and Delinquency Prevention Act (JJDPA) of 1974 was passed to prevent and control juvenile crime and improve the juvenile justice system. The JJDPA was reauthorized in 2002 and again in 2018. The result of years of advocacy, the latest reauthorization increased funding for prevention and early intervention, set core safety standards for youth in detention, and provided incentives to reduce racial disparities.

- Legislation that has influenced the child welfare system includes efforts to ensure that Native American children remain with their families and tribes, prohibition of racial consideration in placement decisions of non-Native children, and emphasis on family preservation and reunification, the latter of which was later tempered by emphasis on safety and permanency.

- Foster children who "age out" of the system face many barriers to successful transition to adulthood because of their experiences with trauma and the lack of supports other young people receive from their families.

- The Fostering Connections to Success and Increasing Adoptions Act of 2008 (Public Law 110-351) extends federal funding for youth in foster care to the age of 21; however, states must apply for this reimbursement, and only half do so. This legislation also creates a federally subsidized guardianship program for kinship providers;

mandates, expands, and increases adoption incentives; and provides additional funding to promote permanency and to support tribal child welfare services.

- Passed as part of the Bipartisan Budget Act of 2018, the Family First Prevention Services Act aims to prevent children from entering foster care by allowing federal funds previously restricted to foster care to be used for prevention services with families determined to be "candidates for foster care."

- Child Support Enforcement (CSE) involves local, state, and federal governments in ensuring that custodial parents and their children receive financial support from noncustodial parents. Participation is mandatory for families receiving TANF; other families can request help in establishing paternity, locating noncustodial parents, establishing a child support order, and collecting payments.

- Legislation for children with special needs emphasizes the importance of normalization and of meeting educational needs in the least restrictive environment. These civil rights protections have reshaped American public education. Many students with an array of special needs are now integrated into mainstream classrooms.

- Although teen pregnancy rates have fallen steadily for more than a decade, youths in foster care still experience considerably higher risk of pregnancy. Programs are needed to provide the support necessary for teens in foster care to reach their goals and, if they choose to parent, to be effective in this role.

- Social workers and others have highlighted the extent to which trauma affects children's outcomes—claims reinforced by recent scientific research documenting trauma's effects on development. The effects of adverse childhood experiences can be addressed by working with caregivers and communities to prevent damaging childhood experiences, treat the consequences, increase resources, and build resilience.

- Educational institutions should provide equitable opportunities for academic achievement, a mandate that requires attention to inequities in discipline policies that can drive children into the justice system. Resources should be funneled to social workers and other providers to focus on positive behavioral interventions.

- While historically, the social work profession has taken the lead in child welfare, the prevalence of social workers in public child welfare is decreasing. The NASW asserts that families have the right to the delivery and administration of public child welfare services by trained social workers. Child welfare policy should prioritize recruitment and retention of a committed, qualified, and competent workforce.

- Despite the high correlation of systemic barriers with child maltreatment and involvement in the juvenile justice system, symptom-focused problem remediation remains the major focus of work with these families. The strengths perspective urges greater focus on family capacity building, including institution of universal supports such as childcare and health care, as well as creation of economic opportunities.

EXERCISES

1. Consider the Sanchez family.
   a. What types of supports do you believe the Sanchez grandparents need to keep their grandson in kinship care?
   b. What policies are needed to make that support possible?
   c. What kinds of services would facilitate Joey's possible reunification with his birth mother?
   d. What considerations should guide child welfare social workers engaged with the Sanchez family as they consider their recommendations regarding the future of Joey's placement? How might Joey's ethnic identity influence social workers' consideration of possible options for his care?
2. Consider the Riverton case.
   a. What policies and programs are in place in your community to help children who are homeless?
   b. Are these services integrated with the child welfare system? What policies facilitate these linkages?
3. Both the Indian Child Welfare Act (ICWA) and the Multi-Ethnic Placement Act (MEPA) were passed to address civil rights issues that influence the out-of-home placement of children, yet they prescribe very different criteria to consider when deciding appropriate out-of-home placements for children. How do you account for those differences?
   a. How do you evaluate each of these policies in terms of the strengths perspective?
   b. What about equity—do you think these diverging policies are fair responses to their respective target communities? How do you evaluate "equity" in this context?
4. Kinship care is an important strategy to help children in foster care remain connected to their families. Investigate the policies that govern kinship care in your state.
   a. Does your state provide payments for kinship care on par with those provided to strangers who serve as foster parents? If not, what is the rationale for the difference? How might this practice affect kinship caregivers and the children in their homes?
   b. Compare services provided to support kinship care under the ICWA to services available to those clients and foster families who are not eligible for the ICWA. What do you find?
   c. What are some initial steps you could take to improve kinship care policy in your state?
5. Consider LGBTQ+ civil rights and adoption.
   a. What are your state's laws regarding adoption rights for LGBTQ+ parents? Are same-sex partners encouraged to adopt together? Does the policy vary depending on whether partners are married or not? What is your state's legislative history around this issue?
   b. Does the state recruit foster parents equitably, or do policies in your state allow private child welfare agencies to discriminate against certain parents?
6. Review media coverage of juvenile justice issues in your community. For example, how are juvenile suspects identified in reporting about their alleged offenses?
   a. How are images and language used to depict and frame the incident and those involved? How does coverage differ from coverage of crimes allegedly committed by adults?
   b. What are the policy implications of this coverage and the reactions it is likely to provoke?

7. Think about the economic, health, and education disparities for children from different groups. How does considering child welfare and juvenile justice policy through an intersectional lens highlight the unique experiences and overlapping injustices of groups such as young women, youth of color, immigrants, and those who are LGBTQ+?
    a. Why do you think these disparities exist?
    b. What do you see as the most important policy reforms needed to address these disparities?
8. Child welfare experts often advocate for better integration of services. What kinds of policy changes do you think would lead to such integration?
    a. Based on your own practice experience, conversations with classmates who have worked in child welfare, and/or investigation of the perspectives of different stakeholders in the system, what barriers can you foresee to implementation of such policies?
    b. How might those barriers be overcome?
    c. How could you draw on a strengths-based foundation to facilitate alliances across disciplines, sectors, and jurisdictional lines?
9. Consider the Brickville case and the plans for redevelopment. Remember, as the social worker in this case, you have already been involved with youths in the community. Create an action plan to help youths in Brickville get their voices heard. Consider appropriate roles for you as the social worker, engaged in strengths-based policy practice with this community.
10. Many policymakers and political candidates are raising the issue of affordable, accessible, high-quality childcare as a public policy imperative. This attention is undoubtedly fueled by the high percentage of American families who report difficulties locating and paying for childcare, as well as employers and other interests concerned about childcare as a workforce and productivity issue. Analyze two proposals regarding childcare being touted in your state or on the federal stage today.
    a. To what extent do these proposals center on the needs of the most vulnerable families?
    b. If the proposals primarily emphasize the concerns of the middle-class, how well would they work for those who are low-income or otherwise at risk? How could they be modified so that they better serve these populations?
11. Select a social work organization of interest to you, maybe where you are doing your practicum, volunteering, or working. Find out whether the organization has any initiatives that utilize trauma-informed principles to work with children and families. Are their practices designed to help clients feel safe? Is the physical space welcoming, including for children and others who may have experienced trauma? How does the agency support workers' need for trauma-informed training? Based on what you learn, think about how you could use your policy practice skills to advocate for trauma-informed approaches at the agency level and how these efforts could improve client outcomes.

NOTE

1. Children may experience multiple forms of maltreatment (e.g., physical abuse and neglect). Each type of maltreatment is counted separately, although multiple instances of the same type of maltreatment are only recorded once.

CHAPTER 10

Health and Mental Health Policies and Programs

POLICIES THAT SUPPORT GOOD HEALTH ARE VITAL TO societal well-being. Helping people maintain or regain their health are essential parts of social work practice. Further, social workers are major providers of mental health services and critical conduits of access to health care. Although the Affordable Care Act (ACA) brought significant expansions in consumer protections and health care resources, the United States is alone among wealthy industrialized nations without universal health care. Indeed, while scientific progress has brought health care advances unimaginable even mere decades ago, lack of equitable access to affordable care continues to plague the system. In the United States, pursuit of good health comes at a high cost. American households collectively spent more than $365.5 billion in out-of-pocket health care expenditures in 2017 (Centers for Medicare and Medicaid Services [CMS], 2018a). Even those fortunate enough to have health insurance coverage through an employer paid an average of more than $5,547 in premiums, plus an average of $1,573 in deductibles (Kaiser Family Foundation [KFF], 2018b). Nationally, health care consumes a growing share of the federal budget and hinders state spending on other priorities (National Conference of State Legislatures, 2018c). Health outcomes, especially for people of color and those with low incomes, lag other nations and our own projections. Further, in the past few years, some important health indicators suggest that the nation may be losing ground. Retreat from the priority of expanded access to care threatens to imperil even modest gains made in improving health outcomes and closing disparities.

While health policy is broader than policies governing access to care, physical and mental health care policies and programs directly and often dramatically influence social work practice. A basic understanding of these policies and of needed reforms will benefit you professionally and personally. This chapter highlights the changes resulting from the passage of comprehensive health reform in 2010, traces ongoing debate over the future of health policy, and takes stock of the status of health care access in the United States today. Commonly known as the Affordable Care Act (ACA), the provisions of the Patient Protection and Affordable Care Act of 2010 (Public Law 111-148), as modified by the Health Care and Education Affordability Reconciliation Act (H.R. 4872) and interpreted by federal regulation, have crucial implications for social workers and those they serve. However, the enduring legacy of this policy is likely more complicated than the image in Exhibit 10.1 would suggest. Devolution of some health care policy to the state level, with its attendant logistical and political complications, has altered the landscape, as have technological advances and evolving demographics. Under the Trump

EXHIBIT 10.1

Health Care Reform Passes in America

Credit: Aislin

Administration, states have more control of health care dollars, particularly through Medicaid, the program that provides health coverage to people in poverty. States have used this latitude to create Medicaid systems where eligibility and benefits differ greatly from state to state. Further, the Trump Administration has pursued regulatory and judicial action to undermine and even undo the ACA, particularly after efforts to overturn the policy in Congress have been unsuccessful. Against this backdrop, social workers and health advocates struggle to confront challenges both persistent and novel: health inequities, growing incidence of chronic disease, escalating needs in an aging population, addiction, treatment-resistant infections, epidemic suicide, and prevalent obesity. In many ways, then, social workers are on the front lines of health policy debates. Our perspectives and our clients' goals and experiences must be positioned at the center to ensure development and preservation of health policies that build on strengths and invest in capacity for healthy functioning.

Because many of the factors that shape physical health care also shape mental health practice, this chapter begins with an overview and evaluation of health care policies and programs. We then examine mental health policy in detail and discuss possible directions for improving overall health.

HEALTH CARE IN THE UNITED STATES

Many factors influence our health, including our genetic makeup, our access to care, and the social and economic factors that affect our opportunities to be healthy. **Social determinants of health** are "the circumstances in which people are born, grow up, live, work, and age, as well as the systems put in place to deal with illness" (Centers for Disease Control and Prevention [CDCP], 2013). As illustrated throughout this text, economics, social position, policies, and politics shape these circumstances. In turn, social determinants have a large impact on health disparities, a fact dramatically illustrated in higher rates of infant mortality and markedly different life expectancies for different racial and ethnic groups. These factors also influence access to health care. Historically, in the United States, health care has been treated as a commodity much like other commodities in the marketplace, with access rationed based on a person's ability to pay. Not surprisingly, then, people with more money traditionally receive better—higher quality, more frequent, more responsive—health care. Indeed, if left unchecked, the market provides health care primarily for those with the means to pay for it and the ability to navigate market structures. However, the complexity of the U.S. health care system means that money alone is insufficient to successfully secure quality care. Further, there are communities, particularly in isolated areas, where health care services are unavailable at any price, due to insufficient supply of providers. Finally, because health care coverage is typically provided through an employer, even those with relatively high incomes may struggle to access health care, if self-employed or not in a job that provides health care benefits.

The premise that health care is something to be bought and sold, rather than a basic human right, is deeply flawed. In important ways, the health care "market" is not really a market at all. It is not realistic to expect buyers (patients) to acquire enough information to determine what tests they need, which hospital has the most reasonable charges and the best quality, and which doctor can oversee care most efficiently and competently. In fact, patients are often powerless buyers, especially when they are gravely ill or struggling with chronic conditions. The commodification of health care imagines that somehow individuals approach health decisions with clear-eyed calculations, ample alternatives, and the ability to negotiate, but this is seldom how health care access plays out.

Most developed countries have chosen to treat health care not as a commodity but as a social utility. In these societies, public funds pay for basic health care, which is available to everyone as a right of citizenship or, in some cases, mere residence in the country. Underpinning this approach is the recognition of two important facts: (1) people need to be healthy if they are to be productive and (2) untreated health problems can be dangerous and corrosive to society. These countries view universal health care as an essential ingredient in building a productive workforce and flourishing society, and then they invest accordingly.

Considering health care as a social utility does not mean it is unlimited. Instead, these countries ration care in a variety of ways, which may include creating waiting lists for elective procedures, developing preferred protocols for dealing with specific conditions, and restricting referrals to specialists. Considerable differences in financing, administrative structure, and technological capability notwithstanding, these systems are characterized by a common commitment to health care access as a core right of the citizenry and a central responsibility of government. Capacity-building, non-stigmatizing, and horizontally equitable, these approaches align far better with a strengths perspective than does the U.S. health care system. While most other developed nations have answered the moral quandary of whether all citizens, at least, should have basic health care, in the affirmative (Reid, 2009), the United States permits profit interests to shape the financing and delivery of health care.

Many Americans *do* receive adequate health care. For people who can afford it, the advanced medical technology available in the United States is excellent, with new advances in pharmaceuticals, diagnostics, and precision treatments achieving unprecedented clinical breakthroughs. However, even for those people who have insurance, decreasing benefits and spiraling costs have compromised the quality of care they can afford. Just because you have health insurance, in other words, you are not guaranteed access to adequate care. While the ACA sought to strengthen regulation of health insurance policies, many of these provisions have been rolled back, such that there is again substantial variation in the protection provided by different insurance plans. Further, even having sufficient, high-quality health insurance coverage does not guarantee adequate care. Access is problematic for many people in a system in which health care providers are in short supply in many geographic areas, medical specialties, and ethnic groups.

In the United States, people who are insured receive their health insurance through either the private or the public (government) sectors. Private health insurance includes employment-based insurance and direct-purchase insurance. The ACA established health insurance exchanges where those without employer-provided insurance can compare plans and purchase coverage that meets government standards. While the exchange is managed by the government, the coverage is purchased from private health insurers. Individuals may be eligible for ACA insurance subsidies, but premium payments are made directly to the insurance company. Government health insurance includes Medicaid, Medicare, the Children's Health Insurance Program (CHIP), and military health coverage. Some families have multiple forms of insurance. For instance, parents may have employer-provided health insurance, while their children receive CHIP, or an older adult may receive Medicaid and Medicare benefits simultaneously.

Some individuals who have health insurance, possibly even from multiple sources, are nonetheless considered **underinsured**, meaning that their coverage is inadequate to provide affordable access to necessary care. Individuals who have "catastrophic" coverage, which only covers care in the event of medical emergencies, as well as those whose insurance has high deductibles they must meet before coverage kicks in, are often considered underinsured. As insurance regulations of the ACA are rolled back, more consumers may find themselves with these types of insurance. In August 2018, the Trump Administration loosened ACA restrictions on "short-term" health insurance plans, which often promise cheaper premiums by limiting coverage, including imposing annual caps on benefits and excluding prescription drugs, maternity care, preventive care, mental health services, and addiction treatment. Previously, such plans could only be sold for 90 days, but the new rule allows 12-month policies, with renewals for up to three years. Many people purchasing such plans may find themselves without coverage for crucial health services (Schwab, 2018).

People who have neither private nor government health insurance fit into the category of "uninsured." About 27.5 million people in the United States, representing about 8.5 percent of the population, had no health insurance in 2018 (Berchick, Barnett, & Upton, 2019). In 2011, before most of the provisions of the ACA had taken effect, that rate was over 15 percent. An estimated 20 million people gained health insurance coverage between 2010 and early 2016. At the end of 2013, just as the health insurance marketplaces created by the ACA came online,

16.2 percent of the nonelderly population and 20.1 percent of nonelderly adults were uninsured; by 2016, these figures had fallen to 10.1 percent and 11.9 percent, respectively (Barnett & Berchick, 2017). However, the uninsured rate increased between 2017 and 2018 across all age demographics, for the first time in a decade. Partial reversals had already been noted among some populations. In 2018, the percentage of working-age adults who were uninsured rose to 15.5 percent, from 12.7 percent in 2016 (Collins et al., 2018). In states that have not expanded Medicaid, more than one-fifth of working-age adults are uninsured today (Collins et al., 2018). Between 2017 and 2018, the percentage of people uninsured decreased in only three states and increased in eight states (Berchick et al., 2019). Disturbingly, more damage to the ACA's gains is expected. Following Congress' repeal of the penalties for not having insurance, in the 2017 tax reform bill, 5 percent of insured adults and 9 percent of those who purchase individual coverage reported that they intend to drop their health insurance (Collins et al., 2018).

In 2018, the uninsured rate even increased among children, one of the subpopulations U.S. health care policy has been most effective at covering (Berchick et al., 2019). However, the U.S. health care system still provides access to coverage for most children, although children living in poverty are more likely than others to be uninsured. In 2017, 7.8 percent of poor children under 19 and 4.9 percent of those who were not poor lacked health insurance (Berchick, Hood, & Barnett, 2018). Coverage also varies substantially by race and ethnicity. In 2018, approximately 5 percent of non-Latinx White Americans were uninsured, compared to 9.7 percent of African Americans, about 7 percent of Asians, and almost 18 percent of Latinx (Berchick et al., 2019). Of immigrants who are non-citizens, over 28 percent were uninsured (Berchick et al., 2018). Some Native Americans receive health care through the federal Indian Health Services (IHS). While this system has increased access to care for this population, the IHS faces problems that limit its effectiveness, including inadequate funding and rapid turnover of providers. Indeed, the U.S. Census Bureau considers someone to be "uninsured" if they have health care coverage only through the IHS, as this coverage is considered insufficient (Berchick et al., 2018).

Employers continue to be the largest source of insurance; of those with insurance, 56 percent are covered by their employers (Berchick et al., 2018). The ACA required employers with 50 or more employees to offer health insurance, helped small businesses provide coverage for their employees, and aimed to increase competition as a mechanism by which to secure better prices. This system is eroding as a safety net, however. In 2018, while 90 percent of workers were employed by a firm that offered health insurance to at least some workers, only 53 percent of workers were actually covered by employer-provided insurance (KFF, 2018b). Further, among those employers offering health insurance, employees' share of costs—in the form of premiums and deductibles—continues to increase. Over the past five years, the average annual deductible among covered workers has increased 53 percent, with 85 percent of covered workers required to meet the annual deductible before services will be paid by the plan (KFF, 2018b). As another signal of employers' desire to avoid responsibility for workers' health care, 16 percent of firms that offer health insurance offer additional compensation or benefits to employees who do not participate in the firm's plan (KFF, 2018b). The changing nature of the labor market, with fewer Americans working as long-term, full-time, "regular" employees, has also disrupted the

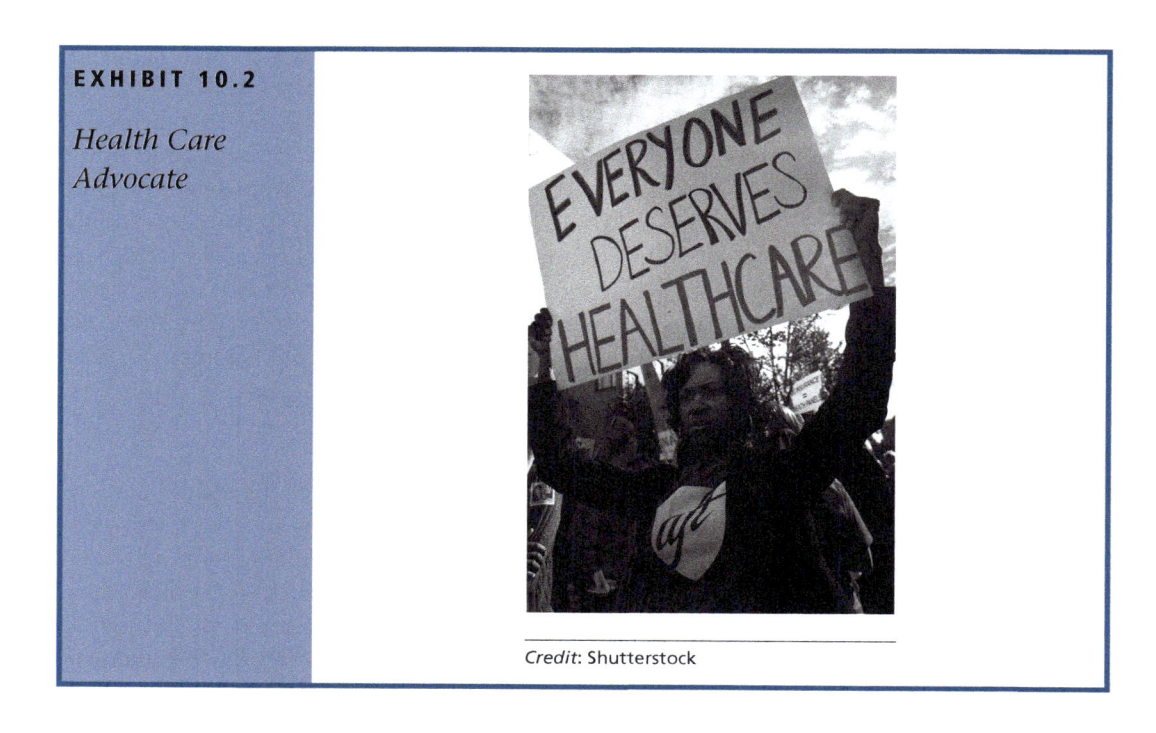

> **EXHIBIT 10.2**
>
> *Health Care Advocate*
>
> Credit: Shutterstock

system of employer-provided health benefits. This means that many middle-class Americans have seen employer-provided health insurance disappear or become more expensive. Although employers are a central component of the U.S. health care system, recent health care debates have underscored the advocate's message in Exhibit 10.2—access to care should not hinge on employment status.

While insurance coverage is a crucial indicator of likely health care access in a health system such as that of the United States, where insurance serves as a gatekeeper to care, it is important not to conflate insurance coverage and health care access. People can and do have the former without guarantee of the latter. Many people in the United States have difficulty accessing health care in part because we have fewer physicians per capita (in 2014, 2.568 per 1,000 people) than most developed countries, and even less than Ukraine, Mongolia, and Kazakhstan (World Health Organization, 2018). These shortages are exacerbated by unequal distribution of health care resources, particularly in some rural and underserved communities. Millions of Americans live in areas designated health care shortages; as many as 25 percent of rural residents report being unable to access care, and more than 10 percent say the situation is worsening, with local hospitals closing in recent years (Harvard T.H. Chan School of Public Health, 2019). Compounding provider shortages, social risk factors such as low incomes and limited English proficiency are associated with decreased access to adequate care and, ultimately, with poorer health outcomes. These outcomes illustrate the power of social determinants. To find the latest information on health status in the United States, visit the National Center for Health Statistics at **www.cdc.gov/nchs**.

The High Cost of Health Care

According to the federal Centers for Medicare and Medicaid Services (CMS), U.S. health care spending grew 3.9 percent in 2017. In 2018, national health expenditures were $3.5 trillion, or $10,739 per person (CMS, 2018a). In 2017, health spending accounted for 17.9 percent of U.S. GDP—by far the highest among the most developed nations in the world. In comparison, health expenditures were 12.3 percent of GDP in Switzerland, 11.5 percent in France, and 10 percent of GDP in Canada (Organisation for Economic Co-operation and Development [OECD], 2019b). Unlike the United States, all three of these countries provide universal primary health care. In 2017, the United States spent over twice as much on health care per capita as the United Kingdom, France, or Canada (OECD, 2019b).

Even though the United States spends the most on health care, some of our health outcomes are not as favorable as those of countries that spend much less. Projected life expectancy at birth in the United States for children born in 2017 was 76 years for males and 81 years for females (World Bank, 2018b). In contrast, children born in Japan in 2017 had a projected life expectancy at birth of 81 years for males and 87 years for females, and babies born in many other developed countries also have a longer life expectancy than in the United States. Further, trends in the United States appear headed in the wrong direction; U.S. life expectancy at birth fell in 2017 for the third consecutive year, the longest sustained decline since World War I and the 1918 influenza pandemic (BMJ, 2018). The principal drivers were drug overdoses and suicides, many among young people in their 20s and 30s. Death rates for Alzheimer's disease, chronic liver disease, and other major causes of death also increased (CDCP, 2018a). Importantly, aggregate indicators in the United States often mask considerable inequities along the lines of race, gender, and class—disparities that underscore failings in our approach to health policy. Life expectancy for women has declined in about 43 percent of the nation's counties, many of which are in rural and low-income areas (Olshansky et al., 2012). Black males also saw a significant increase in their death rate between 2015 and 2016. Life expectancy for a Black baby born in 2016 was 74.8 years, compared to 78.5 years for a White, non-Latinx baby (CDCP, 2017b).

Factors other than health care, including rates of poverty and obesity, community violence, exposure to pollutants, and unsafe workplaces, also influence health outcomes and their racial divides. However, *health care* disparities clearly play a substantial role. For example, recent analysis has found that 60 percent of pregnancy-related deaths are preventable, but health care system failures—including lack of access to care and missed or delayed diagnoses—make pregnancy a more dangerous experience for American women than those in most other industrialized nations; further, Black and Native American women are three times more likely to die from a pregnancy-related cause than non-Latinx White women (CDCP, 2019a). Additionally, access to primary health care can influence other determinants, including by reducing rates of tobacco use and improving nutrition. Although differences in definitions and data collection may account for some of the variation, health outcomes are not as positive for people in the United States as for people in many other countries. As health costs increasingly burden individuals and households, while reducing governments' capacity to invest in other areas, Americans are justified in asking: when it comes to health spending, are we really getting our money's worth?

Health care is one of the largest industries in the United States. In 2017, health care provided 13.1 million jobs (Bureau of Labor Statistics, 2017a). As a component of government budgets, health care costs are very hard to control. Unlike income-maintenance programs, for which the government can calculate the annual cost per person (as in Social Security retirement benefits), federal and state policymakers do not know how much health care an individual will need. They cannot know what costly but promising new medical technologies or medications may be developed. Thus, it is very difficult for policymakers to predict and manage the costs of health care. This is not to suggest that accurate health care budget forecasting is impossible; some countries do a much better job controlling and anticipating health care costs. Like the United States, Japan has a fee-for-service system in which individuals have unrestricted access to specialists, and advanced medical technology is widely available. However, health care spending as a percentage of GDP has increased at a much slower rate in Japan than in the United States, such that government and out-of-pocket spending are markedly lower today. The Japanese have achieved this by combining universal coverage with aggressive regulation of health care prices for virtually all providers and services (Commonwealth Fund, 2017). Other countries deploy different policies to achieve the aim of universal health care. Some countries' municipalities collect the tax that finances universal health care, while other nations take a hybrid approach. Demographics, economics, ideology and values, social movements, and history interact to produce dynamics and outcomes unique to our national context. However, international policy analysis suggests that many approaches to controlling health care costs can produce high-quality care and superior outcomes, at lower cost than the U.S. system.

History and Background of Health Care Programs

Prior to the twentieth century, the federal government's involvement in health care was limited to providing care for military personnel and veterans. By 1909, all states had established a department of public health. Then, with war-related wage controls in force, companies needed to find ways other than salary increases to recruit and retain talent. In 1943, the Internal Revenue Service (IRS) ruled that employees did not have to pay taxes on employers' contributions to group health benefits. This ruling made offering health benefits an attractive tool for employers seeking to attract valuable workers. This approach reflected the American preference for private initiatives and continued reliance on a workforce approach to provide non-stigmatized benefits. These arrangements have implications for health care access and outcomes. Generations later, individuals who experience unemployment, work part-time, or work in marginalized industries are more likely than others to be uninsured.

Growing Federal Involvement in Health Care In 1946, Congress passed the Hill–Burton Act, which provides public funds for hospital construction. In return, hospitals are to provide some free or reduced-charge care for those with low incomes (Division of Facilities Compliance and Recovery, 2016). At the same time, the need for a productive labor force and healthy military recruits, along with humanitarian concerns and fear of epidemics, contributed to growing support for at least limited public entitlement to health care. Moreover, as longevity increased, a political constituency of older adults grew in sufficient numbers and political influence to press successfully for policy change. However, Social Security legislation did not initially include older activists' vision of universal health care for retirees. This exclusion illustrates concerns about federal involvement in health care that persist today. Older adults as well as labor unions and many other advocacy groups later helped press for the addition of Medicare (health insurance coverage primarily for older adults) and Medicaid (a categorical health coverage program for people with very low incomes) to the Social Security Act in 1965.

Medicare, Medicaid, and Civil Rights   President Lyndon B. Johnson signed Medicare into law in 1965. At that time, many U.S. hospitals were racially segregated. While infusing substantial new public investment into health care provision, the new law also specified that hospitals receiving federal Medicare dollars must integrate. While initially there was strong resistance to these regulations, shortly after their implementation, the desegregation of the nation's hospitals was essentially complete (Quadagno, 2000). This action provides a prime example of how financial incentives may be used to expand civil rights. President Obama used a similar approach when he issued a memorandum requiring hospitals to give same-sex couples the right to be with an ill partner. The mandate applied to all hospitals that receive Medicare or Medicaid funding—nearly every hospital in the country. It also affirmed patients' rights to name anyone to be a surrogate decision-maker and instructed hospitals to follow patients' advance directives. This change means that adults' written directives concerning treatment they do and do not want at the end of life are more likely to be honored.

Although Medicaid and Medicare were important steps forward in health care policy, financing of these programs continues to be a major challenge. So that you will more clearly understand options for controlling costs in these and other public health care programs, in the next sections we review some strategies used thus far and how they affect the health care delivery system and the practice of social work.

Background on Approaches to Health Care Finance and Cost Control   Both Medicaid and Medicare were originally structured to be **fee-for-service systems**. In these systems, the government reimburses private health care providers for services provided. This approach is termed **retrospective payment**, because the provider submits a bill after services have been rendered and the insurer then reimburses the provider. This approach creates incentives to provide additional services while offering no incentives to control costs. In fact, it may lead to overservice if providers perform tests or procedures that are unnecessary. Some providers may be tempted to diagnose people with certain conditions and provide services that will facilitate greater reimbursement; in many cases, these assessments and interventions may be influenced by factors other than clients' best interests. Providers may even profit more if their clients do not improve or if they are served in a more restrictive setting than they need, such as a hospital or nursing facility, where services are reimbursed at a higher rate. In addition to intentional efforts to maximize profits, these reimbursement systems serve to shift the "default," such that providers err on the side of utilizing more expensive approaches to health care. Social workers may recognize these pressures in the field of mental health, where it is difficult to secure funding for prevention, and providers may feel incentivized to keep clients coming back for treatment even after their functioning has improved.

Reliance on this system accelerated health care costs without attendant improvement in outcomes, prompting insurers to experiment with a variety of cost-control strategies. Many of these strategies involved **prospective payment**, in which insurers determine ahead of time the average cost for a procedure, such as an appendectomy or uncomplicated childbirth, in a previous year, add an inflation factor, and then set an amount they will pay providers before treatment is provided. For example, insurers reimburse hospitals based on fixed rates for specific diagnoses or *diagnosis-related groups*, regardless of the actual length of a hospital stay or services provided. If a hospital can complete treatment for less than average costs, they profit. Conversely, if the service costs more than what the insurer has agreed to pay, the provider can lose money. This prospect may lead providers to select easier-to-treat patients or even decline to practice in geographic or specialty areas deemed unprofitable (Ellis & McGuire, 1996).

This same prospective approach may be used to determine the average annual costs for 75 percent of healthy people in a certain age range. Public and private insurers can use such an approach to decide how much to pay a **health maintenance organization (HMO)** to care for each such person enrolled in its system. HMOs provide **managed care**, a system wherein the insurer controls the person's health care. Members, their employers, or the government prepay a fixed amount to enroll in the HMO for a specified time, typically one year. Designated providers contract with the HMO to deliver and be reimbursed for health care services. Enrolled patients agree to visit only these providers and to seek approval before receiving health care, and a managing company monitors the cost of treatment.

HMOs assume responsibility for the costs of care for their members. Under such a **capitated approach**, the HMO or managed care provider is expected to provide all elements of health care covered in the enrollee's contract in return for a fixed payment per member. Government insurers can use the same techniques to institute prospective payment systems for high-risk groups that Medicare and Medicaid serve, such as older adults or people with disabilities. As of May 2018, 38 states were contracting with HMOs to cover at least some of their Medicaid populations (KFF, 2018c). In 17 states, more than 90 percent of Medicaid recipients were enrolled in managed care plans (KFF, 2018c).

Unlike fee-for-service retrospective approaches, which may incentivize overservice, prospective payment systems incentivize underservice. If providers can deliver services more cheaply than the prospective payment rate or avoid delivering services altogether, they profit. In these systems, physicians may act as gatekeepers to control access to costly specialists and services. Some managed care systems provide incentives for physicians based on how well they perform this role. Managed care also typically involves administrative oversight to determine whether physician-recommended services are "necessary" and should be approved. Even after their doctors have ordered a test or treatment, patients may have to wait until insurers have determined its appropriateness. Of course, there are limits to the power of health maintenance organizations. Hospitals still must provide adequate care, and patients can appeal premature discharge. However, as is the case in many aspects of social policy, someone's perspective on whether care is "adequate" may depend largely on their position—patient, physician, or insurer. Further, because managed care generally does not cover services outside the network of approved providers, this approach can reduce consumer choice, particularly in areas with relatively fewer health care providers.

Problems in service quality and access, many traced to these incentives and their influences, animated much of the motivation for reform that contributed to the passage of the ACA. Even prior to the ACA, reformers and policymakers had made some progress in this arena. For example, some states passed laws that bar gag clauses in HMO contracts. Gag clauses prohibit physicians from telling patients about expensive or alternative options that their HMOs do not cover. The ACA imposed additional consumer protections, including regulations that prohibit some practices used to control costs, such as denying coverage for many preexisting conditions and charging higher premiums to sicker enrollees. These insurance industry regulations proved among the most popular provisions of the ACA. As is true for many public programs, people come to expect even relatively new provisions as a right. In this way, people can quickly feel entitled to policies, making them resistant to threats. Even after years of legal and political attacks on the ACA, polling in 2018 found that more than 70 percent of Americans prioritize preserving its patient protections (Kirzinger et al., 2018), a political reality that has figured into ACA repeal battles. Some of the executive actions undertaken by the Trump Administration to undermine the ACA, however, have had the effect of loosening restrictions governing insurance. For example, while the ACA required that health insurance plans sold on the marketplaces in every state include sufficient in-network providers, including specialists, in 2018, the Trump Administration relaxed criteria that states use to evaluate their networks. Now, states are no longer required to calculate time and distance standards or make information readily accessible to managed care enrollees (Health Affairs, 2018). Instead, each state has considerable latitude to decide if its network is "adequate" to ensure access to care.

Moving forward, in addition to preserving consumer protections and ensuring navigability of appeals processes for challenging insurers' decisions, advocates should examine financial incentives in managed care to assess how they reward prevention, particularly initiatives that consider the context of disease development, such as rates of smoking, obesity, or exposure to carcinogens. While such measures must be carefully constructed to avoid penalizing disadvantaged individuals for behaviors shaped by their social contexts, properly incentivizing preventive care can help hold down costs and improve health. If this is not done, the short-term nature of many managed care contracts discourages investment in long-term health. In this accounting, less treatment can boost profits.

Yet another approach to restructuring incentives is **payment bundling**, where insurance providers pay providers a lump sum for an episode of care, rather than paying separately for each service. In the case of a knee replacement, for example, the insurance company would pay one entity, such as a hospital. The hospital would have to form a partnership with surgeons and rehabilitation providers and then divide the bundled payment so everyone receives a portion. Ideally, this would create incentives for all partners to provide services that prevent the need for more expensive care. Potentially, this integrated approach, particularly when coupled with the use of evidence-based practice, could help control costs and ensure that patients receive higher-quality, coordinated services.

Health Savings Accounts (HSAs) are another innovation some insurers and policymakers have promoted as a way to hold down costs. Often incorporated into high-deductible health insurance plans, HSAs allow people to place their own pre-tax money in an account that can then be used to pay out of pocket for uncovered routine or long-term care, or to purchase care that counts toward the required deductible. Banks and other financial institutions also offer HSAs, touted by some tax advisors as a way for high earners to set aside pre-tax dollars, particularly since interest earned is not taxable. In 2018, individuals purchasing health insurance through the federal marketplace could contribute up to $3,450 per individual or $6,900 for a family in an HSA that accompanies a high-deductible health plan. HSA funds roll over each year if unspent. Medicare also includes Medical Savings Accounts (MSAs) that similarly help consumers enrolled in high-deductible Medicare Advantage plans finance their out-of-pocket expenses.

Indeed, HSAs could be seen as aligned with a strengths approach, in that they aim to put consumers in charge of their own care. Companies offering HSAs have produced research suggesting that HSA participants are more informed consumers who are better able to compare costs and prepare financially for future health care needs (Alegeus, 2018). However, as discussed earlier, many people lack adequate access to health care information. Further, individuals using HSAs or MSAs to purchase health care typically pay higher prices, absent the special deals insurers strike with providers. Companies' combination of HSAs and high-deductible plans may signal a retreat from more comprehensive employer-provided health care. This shift renders individuals vulnerable if health care costs exceed the balance in their accounts. Indeed, such an approach could lead to a different insurance model for healthy and/or wealthy people, leaving only those more vulnerable in the traditional insurance pool. Because insurance companies base premiums on the expected cost of taking care of those in the insured group, when healthy people leave the pool, average costs per person, and thus premiums, inevitably rise. This is another example of risk shifting from the group to the individual.

Health Reform in the 1990s Although a major initiative of the Clinton Administration to institute national health insurance failed in 1994, some limited health care reforms were enacted during the 1990s. For example, the Health Insurance Portability and Accountability Act (HIPAA) of 1996 (Public Law 104-191) allows workers to continue purchasing their health insurance if they lose or change jobs. In practice, however, the cost of such coverage is often prohibitively expensive, especially for someone who is unemployed. Other HIPAA provisions address the privacy and security of health data. Additionally, Congress passed the Mental Health Parity Act in 1996, which was later strengthened and expanded by the Paul Wellstone and Pete Domenici Mental Health Parity and Addiction Equity Act of 2008. In 1997, the State Children's Health Insurance Program was created as part of the Balanced Budget Act. We discuss these policies in detail later in the chapter.

2010 Patient Protection and Affordable Care Act (amended by the Health Care and Education Reconciliation Act)

President Franklin D. Roosevelt attempted to include a national health insurance program in Social Security in 1935. President Harry S. Truman championed national health insurance. Every Democratic president and some Republican presidents since have wanted to provide affordable health care coverage to more Americans. In 1965, the Medicare and Medicaid programs greatly expanded access to health coverage, but they still did not cover most Americans. When President Obama first signed the ACA, then, he accomplished a task that had eluded all previous administrations. Even though implementation was slow and, at times, thwarted by disputes with states and litigated delays, the ACA has had significant effects on the health care system. However, this law does not provide universal coverage. Despite its characterization as "socialism," it certainly does not institute a **single-payer health care plan**, where the government pays for all health care and thereby is able to control costs. Although actions taken by the Trump Administration have destabilized and weakened the policy, social workers should understand not only the contributions of the ACA to individual and population health, but also ways this policy could provide the foundation on which to continue improving our health care system. As is the case for most innovations woven into our social policy infrastructure, the ACA's greatest asset is its tangible impacts on people's lives.

The 2012 Supreme Court Decision Soon after it was signed into law, some states' attorneys general challenged the ACA's constitutionality. The Supreme Court's subsequent ruling upheld the constitutionality of major parts of the ACA, including the mandate requiring individuals to purchase health insurance. However, the high court struck down the requirement that states expand their Medicaid programs to cover additional populations. This was the first time the Supreme Court had struck down federal funding to states as crossing the line from entitlement to coercion (Gorin & Moniz, 2017). The ruling means that states have the option of whether to expand Medicaid. As of January 2019, 36 states plus the District of Columbia had expanded their Medicaid programs as the ACA encourages (KFF, 2019). In four of these states—Idaho, Maine, Nebraska, and Utah—Medicaid was expanded via public referendum. Other states' refusal to expand Medicaid was largely responsible for the ACA's failure to achieve the health care coverage projected at its passage (Holahan, Buttgens, & Dorn, 2013). Indicative of continued disputes over health care policy is Utah. There, after state policymakers sought to limit the scope of voter-approved Medicaid expansion, the Trump Administration—having since sided with states seeking to overturn the ACA—signaled unwillingness to provide the generous federal funding the ACA promised for a partial expansion. Clearly, health care access is still subject to considerable contest.

Diverging state paths, with some reaping substantial new federal investments for health coverage and others forgoing these monies altogether, also mean that access to care is now very different depending on the state in which someone lives. This inequity is particularly acute for low-income working-age adults, who have few options for affordable health care in states that have not expanded Medicaid (Garfield, Damico, & Orgera, 2018). While this human cost is the most important accounting of the effects of states' decisions about Medicaid expansion, this policy choice has also had ripple effects on state health care systems, including by forfeiting substantial federal revenues. Until 2016, the federal government paid the entirety of Medicaid expansion costs. By 2020, the federal match for the expansion group will have phased down to 90 percent, but expansion will remain largely federally funded (Rudowitz, Hinton, & Antonisse, 2018). As depicted in Exhibit 10.3, the ACA continues to be a potent policy debate for Americans on all sides of the health care reform issue.

EXHIBIT 10.3

Protesters Rally against Proposed Repeal of the ACA

Source: Shutterstock/Rena Schild

Continued Challenges, Regulatory Erosion, and Administrative Undermining While the ACA is still the law, its survival has been uncertain at several key points. Further, many of the legislative, judicial, and regulatory actions against the ACA have left lasting marks and compromised the policy's ability to achieve its objectives. Donald Trump's very first action as president was an Executive Order aimed at thwarting the ACA. In fulfillment of a campaign pledge, Trump issued a directive to the U.S. Department of Health and Human Services (USDHHS) and other agencies involved in administering the ACA to

> exercise all authority and discretion available to them to waive, defer, grant exemptions from, or delay the implementation of any provision or requirement of the [Affordable Care] Act that would impose a fiscal burden on any State or a cost, fee, tax, penalty, or regulatory burden on individuals, families, healthcare providers, health insurers, patients, recipients of healthcare services, purchasers of health insurance, or makers of medical devices, products, or medications; provide greater flexibility to States and cooperate with them in implementing healthcare programs; and encourage the development of a free and open market in interstate commerce for the offering of healthcare services and health insurance, with the goal of achieving and preserving maximum options for patients and consumers.

Even as he sought to secure wholesale repeal of the ACA in Congress and to encourage litigation that would derail it in court, Trump exercised far-reaching executive authority to constrain implementation of the ACA and rewrite the regulations that outline its operation. Several of these actions aimed to prevent people from learning about or navigating the ACA's benefits. For example, the administration canceled advertising for the now-shortened health insurance exchange enrollment period, canceled contracts with private companies that provide enrollment assistance, stopped sending email reminders to those who previously bought insurance on the exchange, and prohibited USDHHS staff from participating in community-based enrollment events. Other changes are largely seen as seeking to destabilize the insurance markets on which the ACA rests. The administration stopped risk adjustment and cost-sharing payments to insurers. These changes have contributed to premium increases, and some fear they may lead insurers to withdraw from some markets altogether (Georgetown University Health Policy Institute, 2018; Kamal et al., 2017). Some of the changes sought have proven to require legislation, while others—particularly the rule allowing virtually all employers to opt out of providing contraception coverage based on their moral objections and a push to make association health insurance plans available that would avoid ACA requirements—have been blocked in federal court. Still, overall, recent years of policymaking regarding the ACA have demonstrated the significance of regulatory authority and the extent to which executive power shapes how policy is experienced by clients.

In addition to these executive actions, President Trump has also sought to work with Republican members of Congress to "repeal and replace" the ACA. However, despite having voted to repeal the ACA more than 50 times, Congress has been unable to agree to a replacement that can garner enough votes. The attempt that came closest was the American Health Care Act (AHCA), which passed the U.S. House of Representatives in May 2017. While the AHCA did not touch six of the ACA's ten titles, it would have given people tax credits to purchase health insurance, allowed differential insurance pricing for older people, turned Medicaid into a block grant, and allowed states to opt out of many ACA protections. After the AHCA passed the House, the Senate crafted its own repeal and replacement, the Better Care Reconciliation Act (BCRA). However, some Republican senators joined Democrats in opposing the BCRA when the Congressional Budget Office (CBO) estimated that it would increase the number of uninsured Americans by at least 15 million (CBO, 2017a).

Having failed in its long-sought aim of undoing the ACA, Congress passed a measure within the 2017 Tax Cut and Jobs Act that many health care advocates believe will do lasting damage to the ACA and, ultimately, the U.S. health care system. Within that tax bill was a repeal of the financial penalty for individuals who do not purchase health insurance—determined in the 2012 Supreme Court decision to be a "tax." As of 2019, then, while the ACA still technically requires people to carry health insurance—either from an employer, from a public program, or purchased through the exchanges—the government does not have any authority to penalize those who do not. This is likely to increase the uninsured population, as some people decide to take the risk of dropping their coverage, while others find themselves priced out of insurance markets that have only less healthy people remaining. The CBO warned that 13 million people will lose health insurance over a decade as a result (CBO, 2017b). It is also possible that the tax bill's limits to deductibility of state and local taxes may squeeze states that use relatively high taxes to finance investments, including health care (Thompson, Gusmano, & Shinohara, 2018).

Seemingly undaunted by previous failures, Republicans in Congress introduced additional measures to repeal the ACA in 2018. However, when midterm elections shifted the U.S. House to Democratic control—in part due to voters' concerns about threats to health coverage—passage of these bills became even less likely. While Republicans mustered significant opposition to the ACA in the months between its passage and full implementation, the politics of health reform have mostly tilted in Democrats' favor since. Recognizing the need for modifications to and protections of the ACA, Democrats have introduced their own legislation to support reinsurance programs, reduce costs for low-income enrollees, and shore up marketplaces. Such changes are necessary; although health insurance marketplace premiums fell in much of the country in 2019, some populations still find them unaffordable. The average cost before subsidies was $612 per month (CMS, 2019b)—a figure many households find daunting. Middle-class older people not yet eligible for Medicare and earning too much for subsidies are most likely to face affordability challenges (Fehr et al., 2019). Without policy changes, the elimination of the penalty for not having coverage will likely lead at least some of these Americans to join the ranks of the uninsured. However, even though relatively minor reforms to the ACA could make it a stronger platform for health policy progress, battles over abortion and Republican resistance have produced an ongoing stalemate. Failed repeal attempts, politically motivated undermining, and thwarted efforts to fix identified inadequacies all come at the expense of Americans' need for reliable access to affordable health care.

All three branches of government have played a role in efforts to overturn the ACA. Twenty states' Attorneys General filed a lawsuit, *Texas v. Azar*, arguing that when Congress reduced the individual mandate penalty to $0 in the 2017 Tax Cut and Jobs Act, it rendered the individual mandate unconstitutional and the entirety of the ACA invalid. In June 2018, the U.S. Department of Justice announced that it agreed with the plaintiffs that, without the tax penalty, the provisions requiring insurance companies to sell to people with preexisting conditions at the same price should be abolished. Seventeen Democratic Attorneys General intervened to defend the law. In December 2018, a federal judge in Texas entered a partial summary judgment invalidating the ACA, and in December 2019, a federal appeals court invalidated the mandate that individuals purchase health insurance, setting up a U.S. Supreme Court decision on the ACA's future. As of publication, the federal government's web portal for individuals to sign up for coverage was accepting 2020 enrollments, but the law's future beyond that is uncertain. This is a critical reminder that people's access to health care—and, indeed, their lives—hinge on the twists and turns of the nation's ongoing debate over health care.

Issues Left Unaddressed The ACA was a giant step forward in the effort to ensure that all Americans have access to quality, affordable health care. As such, organizations like the National Association of Social Workers (NASW) have made opposition to repeal measures prominent policy priorities (NASW, 2017b). However, we must not let our focus on protecting the ACA obscure attention to the many issues that remain to be addressed. For example, the ACA initially contained provisions for long-term care insurance, termed Community Living Assistance Services and Supports (CLASS). The U.S. Department of Health and Human Services determined, however, that the long-term care component was not feasible and would not be implemented. This leaves both young and old vulnerable to the costs of long-term care and exposes the U.S. health care system, particularly Medicaid, to considerable liability. The United States has yet to address the gaping hole that the lack of affordable long-term care insurance leaves in our health care system.

Additional measures to control rising health care costs are needed, as are measures to cover those still uninsured. Even more fundamentally, we need policy that looks at *health*, not just *health care*, to address social determinants and elevate the health status of entire communities.

The ACA did not eliminate many of the factors that contribute to health disparities, such as dangerous working conditions; unhealthy living arrangements; unequal access to health information; lack of diverse, competent providers in underserved areas; and inadequate access to affordable healthy food and safe physical activity. Changes to labor, housing, and educational policies are needed to address these issues. The nation also must contend with the effects of the natural and built environments on people's health, including the threats posed by climate change. As is the case in so many policy arenas, social workers must simultaneously defend previous gains and maintain focus on the essential work that remains.

MAJOR HEALTH CARE POLICIES AND PROGRAMS

The adoption of the ACA, ongoing debates over its future, and shifts in the health care system brought about by changing consumer expectations, evolving demographics, advancing technologies, and emerging health needs have changed all major public health insurance programs. We discuss these changes related to Medicaid, Medicare, and the Children's Health Insurance Program (CHIP). This section ends with consideration of the current health care system and how it is financed.

Medicaid

Title XIX of the Social Security Act established a program with the goal of providing health coverage to families with low incomes and few assets and to certain individuals with disabilities. The program, known as Medicaid, was established in 1965 and is jointly funded by the federal and state governments. Medicaid, which is a means-tested program, is the largest program that provides medical and health-related services to America's poorest families and children. Medicaid accounts for about 17 percent of total U.S. health spending (CMS, 2017). Medicaid is an entitlement program; it is this characteristic that enables it to grow to cover more people during times of rising need. Because states and the federal government share Medicaid costs, state spending also grows as Medicaid ranks swell. However, growth in Medicaid enrollment fueled by the ACA's expansion has less effect on state budgets, since the federal government assumes a larger share of those expenses. Projected average annual growth for Medicaid through 2026 is 5.8 percent (CMS, 2017). In October 2018, more than 66 million low-income Americans received Medicaid, and more than six in ten children received Medicaid or CHIP coverage at some point during the year (CMS, 2018a). Pregnant women who meet income guidelines can also receive Medicaid. Almost half of all U.S. births are now paid for through Medicaid (CMS, 2015). In some states, the percentage of births financed by Medicaid is far higher; in New Mexico, 72 percent of births are paid by Medicaid (KFF, 2016b).

There is evidence that Medicaid's provision of health care access to vulnerable populations has led to significant positive outcomes. Expansions of Medicaid eligibility for low-income children in the late 1980s and early 1990s led to a 5.1 percent reduction in childhood deaths. Expansions of Medicaid coverage for low-income pregnant women led to an 8.5 percent reduction in infant mortality and a 7.8 percent reduction in the incidence of low birthweight (Bhatt &

Beck-Sague, 2018; Center on Budget and Policy Priorities [CBPP], 2016). Research has linked Medicaid expansion to reductions in health disparities (Griffith, Evans, & Bor, 2017), improved diagnosis and care (Loehrer et al., 2018), and higher-quality health services (Charles et al., 2017). Analysis of thousands of health records revealed that racial disparity between non-Latinx White and Black cancer patients' access to timely treatment virtually disappeared in states that expanded Medicaid; this earlier detection and intervention may save lives (Adamson et al., 2019). One of the greatest lessons of the ACA, then, is that affordable health insurance facilitates access to health care, and health care in turn improves overall health, particularly among the most vulnerable populations (Dawson, Kates, & Damico, 2018; Soni, Hendryx, & Simon, 2017).

Exhibit 10.4 depicts Medicaid and CHIP's contributions to reducing the uninsured rate among children. Children are 41 percent of Medicaid enrollees but only 19 percent of the program's expenditures (Truffer, Wolfe, & Rennie, 2017). In contrast, roughly two-thirds of Medicaid spending is attributable to elderly and disabled beneficiaries, even though they make up just a quarter of all Medicaid enrollees. Medicaid is the single largest funding source for nursing homes and facilities for people with developmental disabilities, paying for more than 60 percent of nursing facility residents nationwide (KFF, 2017). Many nursing home residents become impoverished because of the very high costs of nursing home care and thus qualify for Medicaid in old age, even if they did not have low incomes earlier in their lives. Medicaid also helps shore up the gaps in Medicare for low-income older adults and has been the largest single provider of medical care for people with Acquired Immune Deficiency Syndrome (AIDS).

Although Medicaid is supposed to make health care available to those living in poverty, not all people who fall below the federal poverty level are eligible for Medicaid. In the states that have not chosen to expand Medicaid, childless adults over age 21 who are not pregnant, disabled, or elders are generally not eligible for Medicaid, no matter how low their incomes.

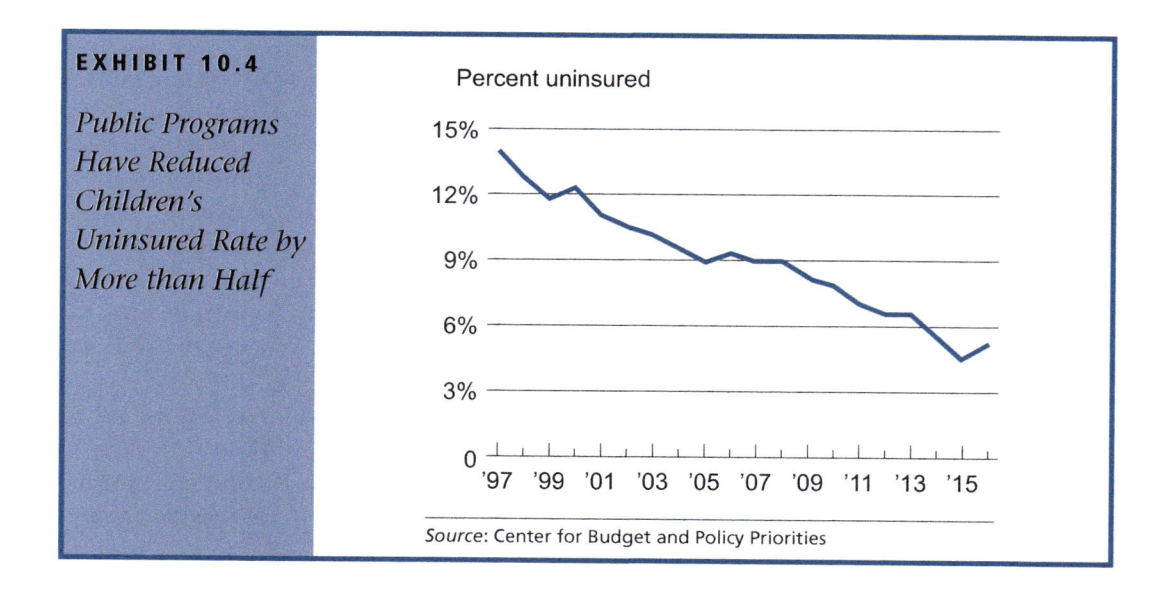

EXHIBIT 10.4

Public Programs Have Reduced Children's Uninsured Rate by More than Half

Percent uninsured

Source: Center for Budget and Policy Priorities

Moreover, many potentially eligible people either are unaware that they might be eligible or feel it would be too stigmatizing to admit they are impoverished. Even when people do apply, they are often met with complex application forms and procedures, requirements to first spend any savings they have accumulated, and long waits for eligibility determination. Despite these limitations, were it not for Medicaid, the number of uninsured people would be much higher.

Mandatory and Optional Coverage To be eligible for federal Medicaid funds, states are required to cover certain groups who meet financial criteria *and* belong to one of Medicaid's categorically eligible groups: children, pregnant women, older adults (65+), adults with dependent children, and people with serious disabilities. States must provide Medicaid coverage for most individuals who receive federally assisted income-maintenance payments. Mandatory populations are:

- children 18 and under in families with incomes below 133 percent of the federal poverty line;

- pregnant women with incomes below 133 percent of the federal poverty line;

- parents and low-income families with children who meet the eligibility criteria for state Aid to Families with Dependent Children (AFDC) benefits that were in effect in 1996;

- most seniors and persons with disabilities who are Supplemental Security Income (SSI) recipients; and

- recipients of adoption assistance and foster care under Title IV-E of the Social Security Act.

(CBPP, 2016)

States are required to cover the mandatory groups and are not allowed to cap enrollment or establish waiting lists for these populations. The ACA eliminated Medicaid asset limits for some adults and all children. However, the ACA did not change asset limits for older adults or those with disabilities; in some states they are still as low as $1,000. Even before the ACA's expansion, states had the option to provide Medicaid coverage for other "categorically needy" groups, such as infants and pregnant women not covered under the mandatory rules whose family incomes are below 185 percent of the federal poverty line, children who meet income and asset requirements for Temporary Assistance for Needy Families (TANF) but are not eligible for TANF, and institutionalized individuals whose income and assets fall below specified limits. States also have the option to implement a "medically needy" program. This empowers states to extend Medicaid eligibility to additional qualified persons whose incomes are too high for inclusion in the mandatory or categorically needy groups. These people are allowed to "spend down" to Medicaid eligibility by incurring medical expenses. Often, older adults and people with disabilities who need long-term care benefit from this option.

Medicaid and PRWORA In 1996, the Personal Responsibility and Work Opportunity Reconciliation Act (PRWORA) allowed states more latitude to expand Medicaid assistance to people in poverty who were not formerly covered. However, PRWORA also separated Medicaid eligibility from eligibility for income-support programs. Families who receive TANF benefits must now also apply for Medicaid, and states have the option of using separate applications, which creates added complications. PRWORA also changed Medicaid eligibility for immigrants. Immigrants who arrived after August 22, 1996, are ineligible for Medicaid until they have resided in the country as lawful permanent residents for five years (CMS, 2010). Although there is an exception for cases deemed true medical emergencies, as the percentage of non-citizens in the United States has grown, these restrictive eligibility rules has contributed to increases in the uninsured population. Some states have elected to use their own funds to provide health care coverage to immigrants who do not meet federal criteria. In June 2019, California became the first state to include undocumented immigrants in the state's Medicaid program; there, children can sign up for Medi-Cal until age 25, and a projected 90,000 young people a year are expected to be covered through this provision, financed entirely with state funds. Other states have extended health coverage only to immigrants with various lawful statuses. However, the growth in the uninsured population in 2018 was particularly substantial among Latinx Americans and non-citizens, who experience particular barriers to health coverage and health care access.

Medicaid Waivers and Variations among States Within broad federal guidelines, each of the states:

- establishes its own eligibility standards;
- determines the type, amount, duration, and scope of services;
- sets the rate of payment for services; and
- administers its own program.

In addition, recent years have seen an increase in states' requests for waivers that allow them to deviate from federal Medicaid rules. While some of these requests have been refused by the federal government, many have been approved. Combined with different decisions on Medicaid expansion, these changes mean that today's Medicaid program, although federal, varies considerably from state to state. Waivers allow states to disregard certain requirements while still drawing down federal Medicaid funds. States have used Medicaid waivers to allow individuals to receive long-term care services in the community rather than in nursing facilities. These waivers are strengths-based, making home- and community-based services available, often allowing individuals to direct their own care options, and improving quality of life (Sonnega, Robinson, & Levy, 2016). These services may also be more cost-efficient than institutional care. Nevertheless, unlike nursing facility care, these services are not an entitlement, and several states have long waiting lists for benefits.

In addition to home- and community-based services, states have sought—and often received—permission to waive Medicaid rules regarding enrollees' financial obligations and service eligibility. In January 2018, the Trump Administration announced that states would be allowed to impose work requirements on Medicaid recipients. In June 2018, a federal judge blocked Kentucky's work requirement, ruling that the state had failed to consider that the proposal would limit access to health coverage—dropping an estimated 95,000 recipients—and, therefore, counter the objectives of the federal Medicaid policy. Undeterred, USDHHS advised states to document that they had followed required procedures, vowed to further articulate the rationale for Medicaid work requirements, and continued approving requests for waivers. However, Arkansas' work requirements were blocked—and Kentucky's were stopped again—in 2019, after the court ruled that states lacked data on the rules' effects on Medicaid recipients. As of March 2019, eight states had been approved to impose Medicaid work requirements, and seven more states had submitted such waivers. Most of these states require Medicaid recipients to work at least 20 hours per week (KFF, 2019). The work requirement itself is not the only potential obstacle Medicaid recipients face. Further, some states require participants to submit proof of employment online, even though many communities lack both employment opportunities and Internet access (Goldstein, 2019).

Other approved state waivers require Medicaid enrollees to pay monthly premiums for their coverage, pay for missed appointments, and/or contribute co-pays above the limits set in federal statutes. In some cases, these requirements only apply to populations covered under Medicaid expansion, while other states impose them on all enrollees. Eleven states have or have requested Medicaid waivers that provide financial incentives for healthy behaviors (KFF, 2019). Indiana takes this a step further, charging a premium surcharge to tobacco users. And several states have behavioral health waivers. Twenty-one states exclude substance use disorder treatment, 14 expanded community-based mental health benefits, and four have waived Medicaid rules to reform their delivery systems. Exhibit 10.5 maps the landscape of Medicaid waivers.

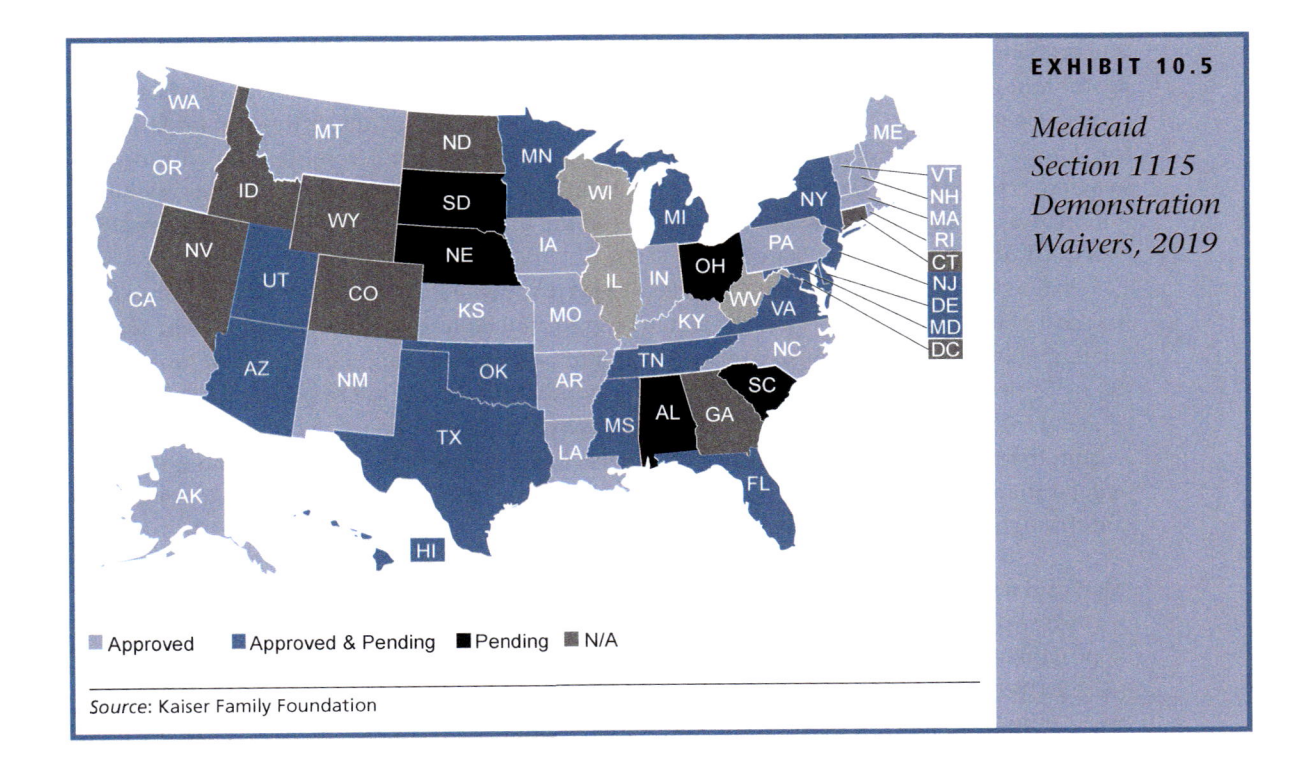

EXHIBIT 10.5

Medicaid Section 1115 Demonstration Waivers, 2019

■ Approved ■ Approved & Pending ■ Pending ■ N/A

Source: Kaiser Family Foundation

While some champion the use of waivers as increasing flexibility, reducing costs, and advancing innovation, others worry that waivers erode Medicaid's core entitlement nature. On this front, particularly notable is the USDHHS' approval, in 2019, of Utah's request to cap enrollment in its Medicaid expansion program if the state runs out of money. While the ultimate fate of this attempt to evade Medicaid's entitlement remains uncertain, this example vividly illustrates the extent to which state policy changes may alter the future of this federal health policy. These concerns are exacerbated by discussion of turning Medicaid into a block grant, a move that would parallel the retreat from entitlement in income support when TANF was implemented. Indeed, Tennessee responded to the Trump Administration's invitation to experiment with Medicaid waivers by proposing such a block grant. While the idea is subject to public debate within the state before formal submission to USDHHS, even in theoretical form, this prospect could have far-reaching effects on the health care system and on health outcomes for low-income Americans. Currently, Medicaid's entitlement status allows it to play a countercyclical role in times of economic downturn, with expenditures rising to cover people who lose their employer-provided insurance coverage. Conversely, if Medicaid is turned into a block grant, enrollment would be limited by predetermined federal grant levels, thus adding to states' economic woes and exacerbating the effects of a recession on vulnerable populations.

Given Medicaid's overall complexity and its increasing state variation, it is crucial that social workers be equipped to help clients navigate this critical health resource and the options it affords. Social workers in hospitals and nursing facilities often assist people applying for Medicaid. Some nonprofit organizations have attempted to connect more eligible individuals to coverage by undertaking Medicaid and CHIP outreach. The ACA explicitly encouraged these health care navigator roles, but the Trump Administration has cut much of the funding for these efforts. Health care navigation is particularly crucial for vulnerable populations, including those in underserved rural areas, those with chronic or complicated health concerns, and communities with diverse religious, cultural, and language needs. You can find out how your state's health care spending for Medicaid compares to that of other states by going to the Kaiser Family Foundation website at **www.kff.org** and looking at State Health Facts.

While Medicaid expansion is financed differently, the federal and state governments share the cost of core Medicaid services via a matching formula that is adjusted annually. The federal matching rate, which is inversely related to a state's average per capita income, can range from 50 to 74 percent. States with relatively poorer populations, then, are responsible for a smaller share of their own Medicaid costs. States can establish their own service reimbursement policies within federal guidelines. In fiscal year (FY) 2017, Medicaid costs totaled $576 billion, with the federal share accounting for 62 percent (KFF, 2018d). See Exhibit 10.6 for a summary of Medicaid through the basic policy analysis framework.

Medicaid and Managed Care   After Congress passed the 1997 Balanced Budget Act, states were no longer required to obtain waivers to enroll Medicaid recipients in managed care plans. Now, approximately 80 percent of all Medicaid beneficiaries receive services through managed care (KFF, 2018d). Managed care allows states greater control over Medicaid spending. Because states pay a pre-set capitated rate, policymakers know in advance what per beneficiary costs will be

Policy goals	To provide health insurance to low-income people (includes those who are elderly, disabled, blind, or in families with dependent children) and to improve access to health care.	**EXHIBIT 10.6** *Medicaid, 1965*
Benefits or services provided	Health insurance for health-related services. Pays for nursing facility care for low-income residents.	
Eligibility rules	Low-income people with minimal assets who fall within the state's "categorically needy" groups.	
Service delivery system	State administration within federal regulations. Federal oversight by the Centers for Medicaid and Medicare Services (CMS). Eligible recipients choose providers who accept Medicaid to deliver health services.	
Financing	Joint federal and state government funding based on the state's average per capita income, with a different cost share—weighted more heavily to federal responsibility—for individuals under expanded eligibility, as called for in the ACA.	

for the year. In addition to improving predictability of costs, states often hope that managed care will help with coordination of services (CBO, 2018c). Unfortunately, managed care plans seldom have much experience with the high-risk clients disproportionately represented among the Medicaid rolls, including frail elders and people with developmental disabilities. Many of these clients may have difficulty accessing and using the information they need to choose plans.

Further, research on the impact of Medicaid managed care on quality, cost, and access has found little evidence that it results in national savings (Sparer, 2012). A few states have seen substantial savings, but they often had relatively high reimbursement rates under fee-for-service, an issue that could have been addressed without moving to managed care. Managed care's record in improving health care access is mixed. There is some indication that emergency visits may have been reduced in states that shifted to managed care, and more people had a usual source of care than under previous systems. However, pregnant women were generally not better off. Many states' managed care organizations report difficulty recruiting enough providers, with enrollee access suffering as a result (Garfield et al., 2018), and quality of care has not been well-studied, even though states require performance measures for managed care plans (Sparer, 2012). Even absent definitive demonstration of benefits, however, more states have shifted to managed care. Many are even placing their most vulnerable long-term care populations into managed care (CBO, 2018c), and some are hiring for-profit managed care organizations to provide Medicaid services. The growth of Medicaid managed care is part of the general trend toward increased privatization. Although responsibility can be partially shifted to managed care providers, states are still ultimately responsible for the care provided to Medicaid beneficiaries. Clearly, the way in which managed care is configured, reimbursed, and monitored influences the outcomes it achieves. Analysis to determine its effectiveness will need to take these differences into account.

Medicaid and Health Care Access   To the extent that it provides some opportunity for oppressed groups to access health care, Medicaid is compatible with values such as social justice. Medicaid's policies that allow individuals to choose their own providers are strengths-based. However, low reimbursement rates make many physicians unwilling to serve Medicaid patients, which limits recipients' access to options and, in some communities, to care altogether. Further, because people are required to "spend down" to poverty before they qualify for Medicaid, eligibility requirements literally undermine people's capacities. While the ACA included structures and incentives to ensure the provision of quality care and to address social determinants of health, Medicaid has relatively few such mechanisms. However, Medicaid has made it possible for millions of men, women, and children to receive desperately needed health services and has lessened the financial strain of seeking health care for many low-income Americans (Finkelstein et al., 2011). Medicaid's imperfections should also be considered within the context of the overall health care system in the United States. As Exhibit 10.7 illustrates, Medicaid compares favorably to private

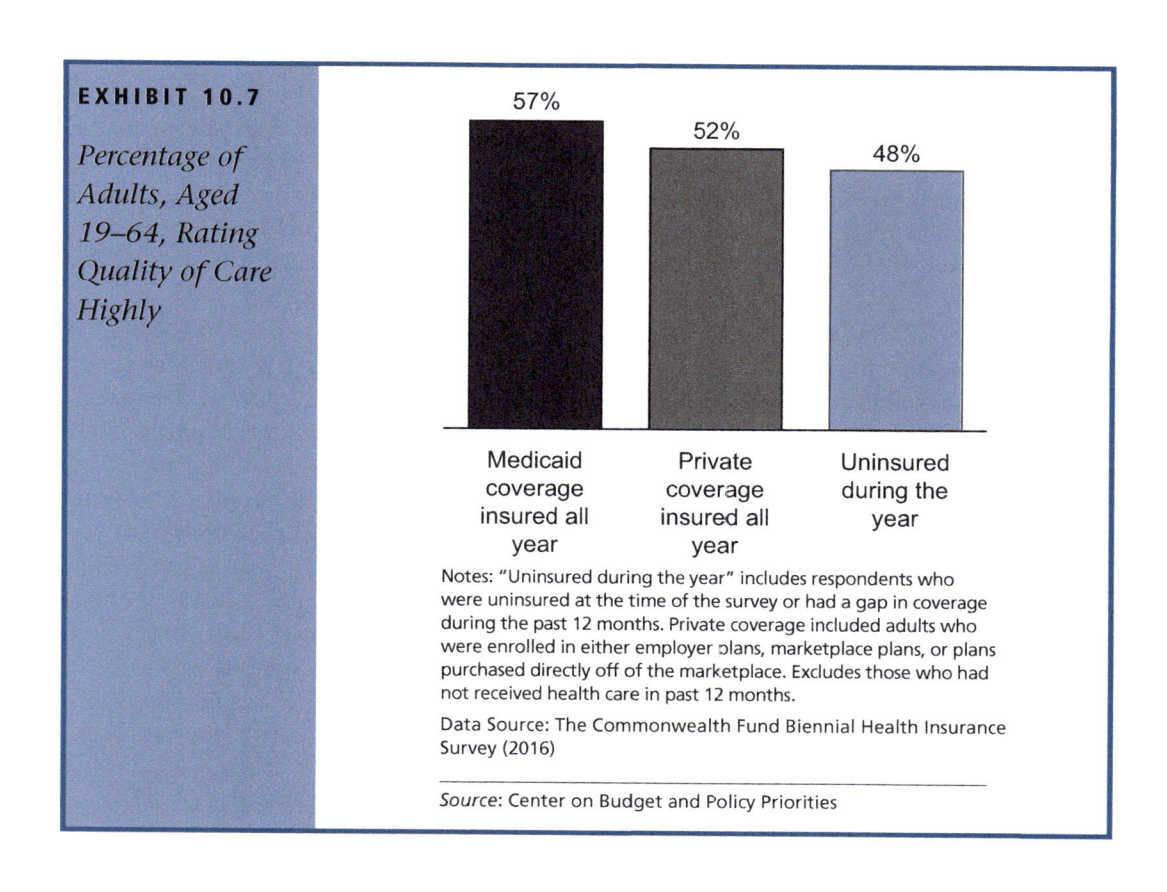

EXHIBIT 10.7

Percentage of Adults, Aged 19–64, Rating Quality of Care Highly

Category	Percentage
Medicaid coverage insured all year	57%
Private coverage insured all year	52%
Uninsured during the year	48%

Notes: "Uninsured during the year" includes respondents who were uninsured at the time of the survey or had a gap in coverage during the past 12 months. Private coverage included adults who were enrolled in either employer plans, marketplace plans, or plans purchased directly off of the marketplace. Excludes those who had not received health care in past 12 months.

Data Source: The Commonwealth Fund Biennial Health Insurance Survey (2016)

Source: Center on Budget and Policy Priorities

health insurance on important indicators, including health care quality. Its importance as a pillar of our health system is clear.

Medicare

Title XVIII of the Social Security Act created Medicare. It is a national health insurance program designed primarily for people aged 65 or older. To be eligible, an individual must be a U.S. citizen or permanent resident. In addition, the person or their spouse must have worked for at least ten years in Medicare-covered employment. Younger people with disabilities who receive Social Security cash benefits for 24 months and persons with end-stage renal disease (permanent kidney failure requiring dialysis or a kidney transplant) are also eligible for Medicare. Fifty-nine million older adults and people with disabilities receive Medicare. In 2015, Medicare benefit payments totaled $702 billion (Cubanski & Neuman, 2018). People can sign up for Medicare through their local Social Security office or online. Exhibit 10.8 summarizes Medicare's features and its component parts.

Medicare Part A, Hospital Insurance (HI) Part A is paid for through payroll taxes. It is compulsory and helps cover the cost of inpatient hospital care, rehabilitation in skilled nursing facilities, some home health care, and hospice care. Each time patients are hospitalized during a new benefit period lasting from one to 60 days, they must pay a $1,340 deductible.

EXHIBIT 10.8

Medicare, 1965

Policy goals	To improve access to medical care by providing health insurance for eligible older adults and people with disabilities.
Benefits or services provided	Health insurance. Part A covers hospital inpatient care. Part B covers doctor visits and outpatient hospital care. Part C allows private companies to contract with Medicare to provide health coverage through managed care or private fee-for-service plans. Part D provides limited prescription drug benefits.
Eligibility rules	Americans age 65+, people with certain disabilities, or people with end-stage renal disease. Part A eligibility is linked to work history or additional payment of premiums.
Service delivery system	Federal administration by the Centers for Medicare and Medicaid Services. Recipients choose physicians or hospitals, and Medicare reimburses providers for services.
Financing	Payroll taxes fund Medicare Part A. The employer and employee each pay half of this premium. Premium payments from older adults and federal general revenue fund Medicare Parts B and D.

They must pay additional charges if their hospitalization lasts more than 60 days (CMS, 2018b).

Medicare Part B This is an optional program that enables people aged 65 and over to purchase medical care. Part B helps pay for outpatient care, doctors' services, laboratory services, some prevention and mental health services, and certain other medical procedures that Part A does not cover, such as occupational and physical therapy. Beneficiaries pay a monthly premium. In 2018, the base premium was $134 per month, while higher-income beneficiaries pay more. Despite evidence that high out-of-pocket costs can influence utilization of needed health care, Medicare beneficiaries must also pay substantial deductibles for most non-preventive services. Unless they have other health insurance coverage such as through employment, if people do not sign up for Part B when they become eligible upon turning 65, they must pay a substantial penalty if they choose to purchase it later. The late penalty, which increases premiums by 10 percent for every 12 months an eligible senior did not enroll, is designed to prevent beneficiaries from waiting to enroll until they urgently need health care.

Medicare Part C, Medicare Advantage The Balanced Budget Act of 1997 created Medicare Part C, named *Medicare Advantage*. Medicare Advantage allows private companies to contract with Medicare to provide health coverage through managed care plans or private fee-for-service plans. People with both Medicare Part A and Part B are eligible to enroll in Medicare Advantage if a plan exists in their area. These plans reduce out-of-pocket expenses and coordinate care. In addition, some plans pay for prescriptions (CMS, 2013). Enrollment in Medicare Advantage has increased substantially, with almost 37 percent of Medicare beneficiaries expected to enroll in 2019 (CMS, 2018c). However, research has found that, far from reducing overall costs, Medicare Advantage generally costs more than traditional Medicare (McGuire, Newhouse, & Sinaiko, 2011).

Medicare Part D Before 2003, Medicare did not pay for prescription drugs administered outside a hospital. Due to ever-increasing costs and growing reliance on pharmaceutical management of health concerns, many older adults could not afford to buy the medications their doctors prescribed. In 2003, Congress passed the Medicare Prescription Drug, Improvement, and Modernization Act, known as Medicare Part D, which went into effect in 2006. Anyone on Medicare can enroll in this optional plan. Consumer savings under Medicare Part D have been modest overall. However, it has had a relatively greater positive impact on low-income beneficiaries with high prescription costs, particularly because they can receive financial assistance with the Part D premium, deductible, and cost-sharing obligations (KFF, 2015). The Trump Administration has announced new proposed rules for Medicare Part D, designed to reduce prescription costs. Some, including encouraging plans to negotiate lower drug prices and increasing transparency of prescription costs, should bring some relief to senior enrollees. Advocates have concerns, however, that some of the cost containment could restrict people's access to essential, albeit expensive, medications. For example, strategies such as closed formularies (limit drugs to certain providers or areas) and step therapy (requires patients to first attempt less expensive prescriptions before more expensive options are authorized) raise concerns for those who have serious and chronic illnesses that require specialized pharmaceutical care (National Kidney Foundation, 2018).

Before Medicare Part D coverage begins, enrollees must pay an annual deductible (no more than $415 in 2019). Then, during the initial coverage period, they must pay a share of the cost of each prescription (either a flat co-pay or a percentage of the cost). Higher-income enrollees also pay an additional surcharge. In 2019, Medicare Part D enrollees nationally paid an average monthly premium of $33.19, although plan costs vary depending on the plan chosen and where they live. In all Part D plans, in 2019, after enrollees paid $5,100 in out-of-pocket costs for covered drugs, they reached "catastrophic coverage." After that point, they pay significantly lower co-pays or coinsurance for covered drugs for the remainder of the year. The "donut hole," which used to leave seniors frequently without coverage, was closed for brand-name drugs in 2019 and for generic drugs in 2020, ahead of the schedule outlined in the ACA. In 2019, beneficiaries who wanted to enroll in Part D had an average of 27 standalone prescription drug plans to choose from, along with many Medicare Advantage plans. This is an increase of 15 percent over the previous year's options (Cubanski, Damico, & Neuman, 2018). Many older adults find it confusing to compare so many plans. However, competition and choice are hallmarks of this program, designed to align with the U.S. health care system's emphasis on health care as a commodity to be purchased in the marketplace.

In addition to the prescription drug benefit, Part D also sought to ensure continued access to basic health services for older adults and individuals with disabilities, especially those living in rural communities, by improving payments to providers. Complex and controversial, Medicare Part D has nonetheless cost significantly less than initial estimates (Park & Broaddus, 2012). Some of the savings can be attributed to the fact that fewer people than expected took advantage of the benefit. Also, although prescription costs continue to burden many Americans, particularly those who require ongoing medication to manage chronic conditions, usage of less expensive generic drugs has increased. Policymakers must implement effective strategies for controlling the growth of health care costs, including prescription drug costs, if we are to have an effective, sustainable health care system. Further, these strategies must ensure that individuals' needs are met. Cost containment should not come at the expense of public health insurance programs' core mandates to increase access to affordable, quality health services.

As discussed in Chapter 8, the number of younger people now receiving Social Security benefits because of disability has grown substantially. If they receive Social Security cash benefits for 24 months, these younger people with disabilities are also eligible for Medicare. Exhibit 10.9 illustrates the percentage of Medicare beneficiaries in different age groups.

EXHIBIT 10.9

Medicare Enrollment

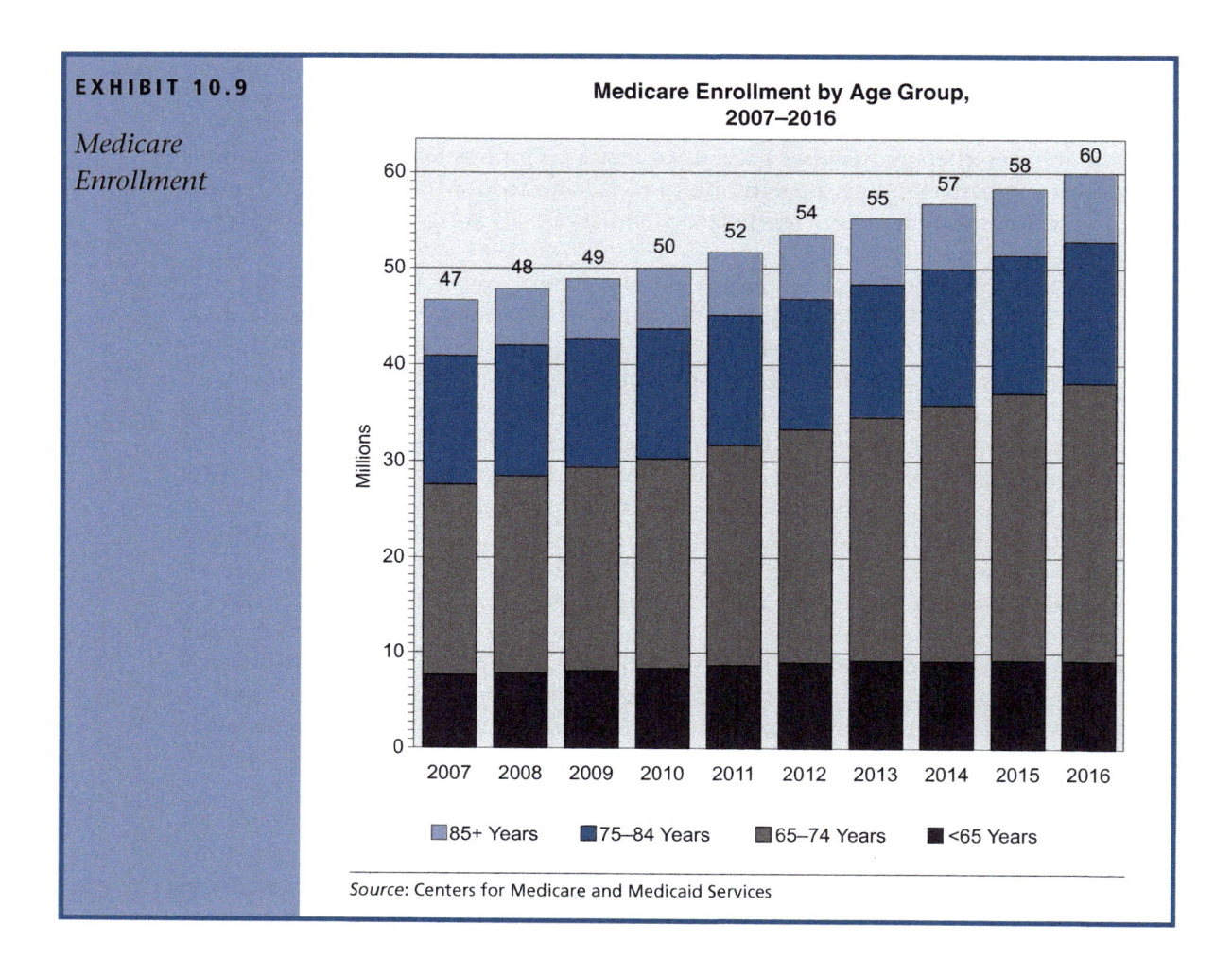

Medicare Enrollment by Age Group, 2007–2016

Year	Total (Millions)
2007	47
2008	48
2009	49
2010	50
2011	52
2012	54
2013	55
2014	57
2015	58
2016	60

Legend: 85+ Years | 75–84 Years | 65–74 Years | <65 Years

Source: Centers for Medicare and Medicaid Services

Medicare Financing

Many people assume that once a person is eligible for Medicare, health care costs are no longer a significant burden. However, premiums, supplemental insurance, co-pays, and costs for non-covered services are major expenses that strain many beneficiaries' budgets. Unlike many health care plans, Medicare does not limit out-of-pocket costs. Medicare beneficiaries' average out-of-pocket health care spending is projected to rise as a share of average per capita Social Security income, from 41 percent in 2013 to 50 percent in 2030 (Cubanski et al., 2018). Out-of-pocket spending increases with age and is highest among women aged 85 and older. Because very low-income older adults are usually eligible for Medicaid, the cost burden on middle-income Medicare households is particularly heavy. In 2016, more than a quarter of all Medicare beneficiaries spent 20 percent or more of their income on health care—an average of $3,024 per year, per beneficiary (Schoen, Davis, & Willink, 2017). Increasingly, consumers rely on managed care options to stem spiraling costs. As in other health care markets, however, mixed outcomes question the efficacy of this approach. When Medicare reimbursement rates do not provide the profit margin anticipated, some HMOs cancel coverage for older adults. Further, some physicians refuse to take Medicare patients because of low reimbursement rates. Despite these limitations and complications, Medicare has helped many older Americans access health care and has contributed to longevity and greater quality of later life.

Medicaid plays a critical role in health care coverage for older adults and those with disabilities. Medicaid may help pay out-of-pocket medical expenses for Medicare beneficiaries who have limited income and assets. For older adults eligible for full Medicaid coverage, Medicaid provides services and supplies. These people are termed **dual eligible**, since they are simultaneously eligible for both major public insurance programs.

When both programs cover a service, Medicare pays first, and Medicaid makes up the difference, up to the state's limit. Compared to other Medicare beneficiaries, those who are dual eligible tend to be sicker and poorer. They are more likely to have activities of daily living (ADL) and instrumental activities of daily living (IADL) limitations and chronic diseases. As people who are dual eligible are among the most expensive for both Medicare and Medicaid, innovations to coordinate care and reduce unnecessary institutionalization for this population could produce cost savings and improve outcomes.

Although changes in the ACA sought to increase Medicare's emphasis on prevention (Chait & Glied, 2018), Medicare still focuses primarily on *acute* care—short-term medical care, especially for serious disease or trauma. While it provides for rehabilitation of up to 100 days in a nursing facility and for hospice care, contrary to what many people believe, Medicare does not pay for long-term care for *chronic* conditions. Some of the services that many older adults require are not covered by Medicare at all. For example, certain health care needs, such as eyeglasses, dentures and dental care, and hearing aids are not covered, nor is transportation for medical appointments. Some people select a Medicare managed care plan specifically to cover these items.

The Centers for Medicare and Medicaid Services (CMS) is the federal agency that administers both Medicare and Medicaid. As in Old Age, Survivors, and Disability Insurance (OASDI), both the employer and employee pay half of the premium that finances Medicare Part A. Beneficiary premiums for Part B are supposed to cover 25 percent of that component's costs, with general tax revenues covering the rest. Significantly, Medicare is administered for a fraction of the cost of many private health insurance programs. This suggests that justifiable concerns about the fiscal sustainability of Medicare reflect overall trends of rising health care costs and the challenges of providing health care for individuals with more expensive health care needs, rather than any features or flaws of Medicare itself.

In 2017, Medicare spending accounted for 15 percent of the federal budget. Between 2010 and 2017, average annual growth in total Medicare spending per capita was 1.5 percent. This marked decrease from the 7.3 percent average annual growth between 2000 and 2010 was largely due to the ACA's reductions in payments to providers and to the influx of younger Baby Boomer beneficiaries, who have lower per capita health care costs than older beneficiaries (Cubanski & Neuman, 2018). Looking to the future, Medicare spending is projected to rise to 18 percent of the federal budget by 2028, as increased use of services, growing enrollment, and rising health care prices push Medicare spending up at an expected annual per capita rate of 4.6 percent.

By analyzing the state of the Medicare Trust Funds, we can assess the program's sustainability. Medicare's Hospital Insurance (HI) Trust Fund currently pays out more than it receives in taxes and other dedicated revenues. The Fund makes up the difference by redeeming trust fund assets, which include Medicare insurance premiums paid in previous years. Slower than expected economic growth during the recession reduced payroll tax contributions to the Funds and strained Medicare's fiscal capacity. In 2018, the Social Security Administration projected that the HI Trust Fund will be exhausted in 2026, three years earlier than estimated in 2017. The Trustees report that lower payroll taxes, due both to lower wages and to legislative changes, as well as increased expenditures for hospitalizations and Medicare Advantage payments, have accelerated the projected date of HI Trust Fund exhaustion (CMS, 2018b).

The imbalance in the HI Trust Fund was part of the impetus for health care reform. The ACA included several proposals to move away from the Medicare fee-for-service system and improve outcomes for beneficiaries. It reduced overpayments to private Medicare Advantage plans and encouraged doctors to provide patient-centered care for the 80 percent of older Americans who have at least one chronic medical condition. It provided new, free annual wellness visits and eliminated out-of-pocket co-payments for preventive benefits, such as health screenings. The ACA also improved Medicare payments for primary care, which protects access and encourages reimbursement based on value, not volume (Bowling et al., 2017). The 2015 Medicare Access and CHIP Reauthorization Act (MACRA) also provides a stable update to the physician fee schedule and links an increasing portion of Medicare payments to patient outcomes and population health (CMS, 2016). However, further reform is needed to ensure that the growing number of older adults and Americans with disabilities have a fiscally sustainable public health insurance system to facilitate their well-being.

The Children's Health Insurance Program (CHIP)

Although Medicaid made strides in covering children from low-income families, large numbers of children remained uninsured until the late 1990s. To help remedy this problem, the Balanced Budget Act of 1997 created the State Children's Health Insurance Program (SCHIP). The Act established SCHIP, now titled the Children's Health Insurance Program (CHIP), under Title XXI of the Social Security Act. This program has made health insurance for children more widely available. This law created a federal block grant to states to offer health insurance for children up to age 19 who are not already insured. Although the program is state-administered, and each state sets its own guidelines regarding eligibility and services, the federal government has established guidelines that each state must meet. Federal and state governments jointly finance CHIP, but the federal government assumes a larger share, with an enhanced federal matching rate that averages 15 percentage points higher than Medicaid's matching rate. However, unlike Medicaid, which provides an individual entitlement such that if a child qualifies, that child will get health coverage, CHIP is a block grant. Federal CHIP funds are capped overall, and each state receives a certain allotment. When that allotment is gone, the federal government is not required to match funds for additional eligible children, and the state has no obligation to serve them via

CHIP. This constrains CHIP's ability to address gaps in coverage, particularly in times of rising need. However, unlike many block grants, CHIP has historically been adequately funded (Guyer, Heberlein, & Alker, 2011).

In 2009, President Obama signed the Children's Health Insurance Program Reauthorization Act (CHIPRA), and SCHIP became CHIP. CHIPRA included a provision allowing children who are lawful permanent residents to participate in CHIP without waiting the requisite five years. However, states are not required to provide this coverage. In recognition of the link between oral health and overall well-being, states are now required to include dental services in CHIP plans. Other covered services include doctors' visits, hospitalizations, emergency room visits, and immunizations. CHIPRA also provided an enhanced match for translation and interpretation services and $100 million in outreach funding. The ACA further boosted the federal match rate for CHIP, a funding arrangement extended in MACRA in 2015. When CHIP authorization ended in September 2017, states were able to use reserve funds to continue children's health care coverage until January 2018, when CHIP funding was again extended through FY2023. This budget deal continued the ACA's enhanced CHIP federal match rate, although it will decline over time. Exhibit 10.10 summarizes the features of CHIP.

Compared to Medicaid, eligibility rules for CHIP are much more generous, enabling working families without insurance to qualify. As depicted in Exhibit 10.11, as of January 2018, 19 states' CHIP programs cover children with incomes at or above 300 percent of the federal poverty level (FPL) (KFF, 2018e). Only two states

EXHIBIT 10.10

Children's Health Insurance Programs Reauthorization Act (CHIPRA), 2009

Purpose	The Children's Health Insurance Program Reauthorization Act (CHIPRA) renews and expands the Children's Health Insurance Program, designed to increase access to health care for low-income children not eligible for Medicaid and not otherwise insured.
Benefits or services	Covered services include doctors' visits, hospitalizations, emergency room visits, immunizations, and dental care. CHIPRA also provides states with outreach funds and some demonstration funding to develop electronic medical records.
Eligibility rules	Uninsured children under the age of 19 whose families have yearly incomes up to 300 percent of poverty, depending on state guidelines. Reauthorization allows states to cover uninsured children and/or low-income pregnant women from immigrant families before they have accrued five years of lawful permanent residence in the United States.
Service delivery system	State administration. Federal oversight by the Centers for Medicare and Medicaid Services (CMS). Recipients choose health care provider.
Financing	Jointly funded by federal and state governments. Federal funds are capped.

EXHIBIT 10.11

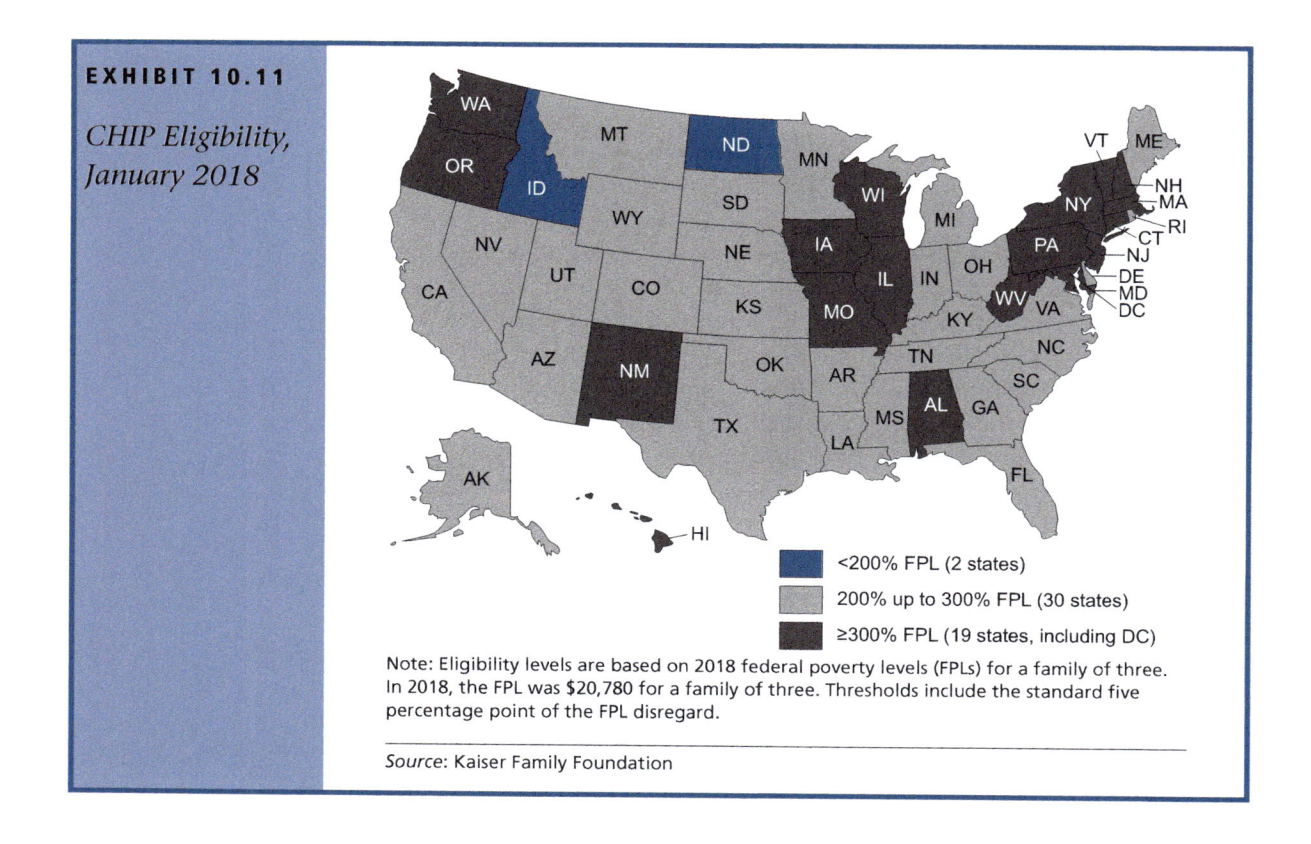

CHIP Eligibility, January 2018

<200% FPL (2 states)
200% up to 300% FPL (30 states)
≥300% FPL (19 states, including DC)

Note: Eligibility levels are based on 2018 federal poverty levels (FPLs) for a family of three. In 2018, the FPL was $20,780 for a family of three. Thresholds include the standard five percentage point of the FPL disregard.

Source: Kaiser Family Foundation

limit eligibility to less than 200 percent of the FPL. In 2017, 9.4 million children were enrolled in CHIP (KFF, 2018f).

The 2010 Patient Protection and Affordable Care Act

The ACA has substantially influenced the provision of physical and mental health care. The American Medical Association, many health care providers, and consumer groups endorsed this health care reform, while most insurance companies and every Republican in Congress opposed it. Several elements of the ACA went into effect in 2010, while others were phased in over several years. Today, while its imprint is felt throughout the health care system, some of the ACA's original provisions have been eroded or altered by administrative action or judicial challenge, while others have been preserved, in some cases gaining popularity as they reshape people's experiences with health care and their prospects for health. While a complete accounting of the provisions of the lengthy legislation and the regulations that implement it is beyond the scope of this text, here we list some of the policy's most significant contributions to social workers' pursuit of dignity, equity, and well-being. These provisions are outlined in the chronological order when they took effect, with notation of any substantial change in subsequent years.

Beginning in 2010:

- Insurance companies were no longer allowed to deny children coverage based on a preexisting condition.
- Insurance companies had to allow children to stay on their parents' insurance until age 26.
- People denied insurance due to a preexisting medical problem were provided with immediate access to insurance plans.
- People on Medicare began receiving help with costs for prescription drugs once their benefits ran out due to the Part D prescription drug "donut hole."
- Insurance companies were prohibited from imposing lifetime dollar limits on essential benefits like hospital stays.
- Funding was provided to expand the number of primary care doctors, nurses, and physician assistants in underserved areas.

Beginning in 2011:

- Medicare began providing free preventive care, including physical exams and screenings, as well as certain vaccinations.
- Insurers must provide a rebate to consumers if they do not spend at least 80 percent of premium dollars on patient care and quality improvements.

Beginning in 2012:

- Incentives were created to encourage physicians to develop integrated health systems to better coordinate and help improve quality of care.
- Changes were implemented to standardize billing and require health plans to provide for the secure and confidential electronic exchange of health information.

Beginning in 2013:

- Medicaid payments for primary care doctors were increased.
- Open enrollment in the Healthcare Marketplace began. Initially plagued by technical problems that complicated sign-up and underscored the complexities of expanding coverage through existing private insurers, the Marketplace offered a choice of health plans that meet specified benefit and cost standards.

Beginning in 2014:

- Uninsured and self-employed individuals could purchase private health insurance plans on government-run insurance exchanges, with subsidies for people with incomes between 133 and 400 percent of the federal poverty line (FPL). The exchanges were designed to guarantee choices of quality, affordable insurance to people who lose or change jobs, move, or get sick. To equalize health care costs, policies had to cover maternity leave and have no gender rating.

- Insurance companies were no longer able to deny coverage to anyone with pre-existing conditions.

- Annual out-of-pocket spending for individuals and families was capped.

- Independent appeals panels were created to contest health insurance decisions.

- Except for those receiving low-income or religious exceptions, U.S. citizens and lawful permanent residents were required to have qualifying health coverage or pay a tax penalty. In 2017, as part of the Tax Cut and Jobs Act, Congress set the penalty at $0, effectively voiding it.

- Tax credits were offered to small businesses to make providing coverage more affordable.

- New plans and existing group plans could no longer impose annual dollar limits on coverage.

- Funds were increased to train primary care providers, including social workers.

- In states that accepted Medicaid expansion, nearly all U.S. citizens under 65 with family incomes up to 138 percent of the FPL qualified for Medicaid. The federal government paid 100 percent of costs for covering newly eligible individuals through 2016.

- Funding was made available for the creation of the Centers for Medicare and Medicaid Innovation (CMI) to experiment with cost-containment approaches, prevention, medical homes, and other practices to improve service integration and patient outcomes.

Beginning in 2015:

- Physician payments were tied to the quality of care they provide.

Beginning in 2016:

- Employers with more than 50 employees were required to provide health insurance or pay a fine per worker each year if any worker receives federal subsidies to purchase health insurance. Fines are applied to the total number of employees minus some allowances.

Enforcement of the patient protections and employer mandates included in the ACA involved both federal and state agencies. Because many states were reluctant to implement the provisions of the ACA, enforcement mechanisms were somewhat slow to develop, making it more difficult for people in those states to reap the benefits and protections the ACA provides.

Further, as described earlier, the extent to which the ACA's impact hinged on regulatory action and financial inducement has made its provisions vulnerable to initiatives by the Trump Administration, which has seen considerable success in its efforts to undermine the ACA using rule-making, strategic appointment of key administrative positions, and selective enforcement.

The Affordable Care Act: Financing and Cost-Control Issues Multiple sources—including new appropriations and taxes, private payments, and repurposing of public health expenditures—fund the ACA. The ACA increased the Medicare Payroll Tax for high-wage earners and expanded it to include unearned income. Families making more than $250,000 per year paid a 3.8 percent tax on investment income. Payments to Medicare Advantage programs were reduced. Industry fees, excise taxes, and other changes in tax law also contributed revenue. Cost-control measures included limits on insurance company profits and a regular review of rate hikes. The Act created health insurance marketplaces based on the belief that competition would drive costs down. The ACA also created an Independent Payment Advisory Board (IPAB) of physicians and health experts to make recommendations to Congress about how to reduce costs. However, the IPAB was controversial from the start, with members of Congress expressing concerns that it would infringe on congressional authority or recommend service rationing. As a result, members were never seated. More successful is the independent Patient-Centered Outcomes Research Institute (PCORI), which develops a research agenda to compare the efficacy of health care interventions. Committed to evidence-based practice, PCORI's intent is to begin a national dialogue about what works and what does not. You can review PCORI's research at **www.pcori.org**.

One of the primary selling points of the ACA was its potential to "bend the cost curve" in health care by introducing innovations that would fundamentally alter financial arrangements and price demands in the health care system. In 2016, the CBO projected Medicare would spend $2 trillion less between 2017 and 2026 than what was forecast in 2009, largely through instituting changes such as bundling services into larger payment groups, reforming Medicare payment models, incentivizing hospitals to avoid costly readmissions and prevent hospital-acquired infections, using value-based purchasing, and improving care coordination. Since 2010, per-enrollee spending growth in private health insurance, Medicare, and Medicaid has been slower than in the previous decade; in 2015, health care spending, which has been tracked since 1960, grew at the slowest rate on record.

However, some worry that the recent—and marked—slowdown in health care spending is attributable at least in part to reversals in coverage growth (Hempstead, 2018). Others point to the projected uptick in total spending over the next decade and express concern that the slower growth depicted in Exhibit 10.12 will not be enough to make health care programs fiscally sustainable, especially because costs per person are still rising. Since social workers cannot accept reduced access as the "price" of lower spending, we must consider other ways to continue constraining health care costs. Without single-payer national health insurance or even a "public option," the government has less leverage over what private providers charge and no way to force the private sector to compete with a government-run choice for health insurance. However, cost control will need to be a high priority in ongoing efforts to improve U.S. health care policy.

Policymakers should ensure that health care financing advances the aim of improving health outcomes. Instead, payment mechanisms have proven a potent leverage point for

EXHIBIT 10.12

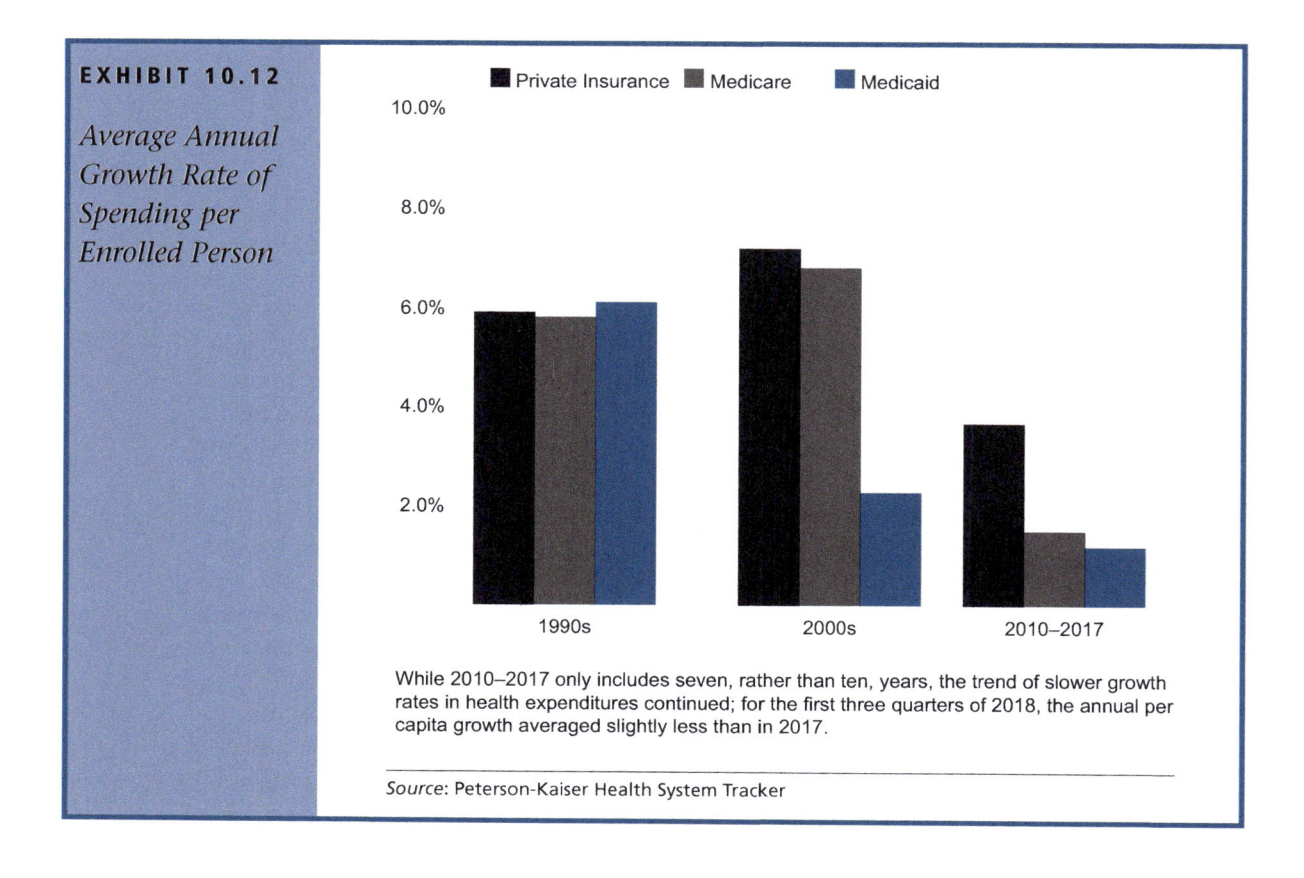

Average Annual Growth Rate of Spending per Enrolled Person

While 2010–2017 only includes seven, rather than ten, years, the trend of slower growth rates in health expenditures continued; for the first three quarters of 2018, the annual per capita growth averaged slightly less than in 2017.

Source: Peterson-Kaiser Health System Tracker

President Trump, whose authority to cut spending on activities that promote the ACA and to stop payments for the private entities that help to operate the health care system has allowed him to subvert some of the ACA's intent, even without repealing the law. In this politicized landscape, the ACA's objectives are often obscured, as is its potential to more fully pivot from an inequitable, costly, and largely inadequate health care system to one that leverages public and private tools to alter incentives, place preventive care within reach, and achieve a healthier population. As strengths-based social workers know, investing in people's capacity to meet their own goals improves outcomes across the board. In this context, when the focus of health care coverage is shifted toward a system that keeps people healthy, this changed emphasis will benefit everyone—and cost far less.

MAJOR MENTAL HEALTH POLICIES AND PROGRAMS

The two principal domains of "health"—mental and physical well-being—are profoundly and inextricably linked. Nonetheless, while events such as high-profile celebrity suicides and tragic incidents of violence sporadically propel mental health concerns into the public consciousness, mental health care seldom receives as much attention as physical health care. Today, however, public attitudes may elevate mental health issues onto policymakers' priorities. In 2017, 72 percent of Americans called mental illness an "extreme" or "very serious" public health problem, a noted increase from past years (Oliphant, 2017). Certainly, mental illness is relatively common; in 2017, more than 46 million American adults experienced mental illness, and more than 36 million received mental health treatment (Substance Abuse and Mental Health Services Administration [SAMHSA], 2018). Even so, many people do not understand that good mental health is essential to overall well-being and, like physical health, requires regular preventive care. Historically, public funding for mental health care was available primarily for people with serious psychiatric problems. Even today, unfair treatment limitations and a fragmented delivery system impede effective intervention. Funding for mental health care is still largely inadequate, and stigma still surrounds mental illness.

In 2017, only 42.6 percent of people with any mental illness, and 66.7 percent of those with serious mental illness, received treatment (SAMHSA, 2018). Further, this treatment is of varying duration, quality, and appropriateness. Although improving mental health care is integral to improving health outcomes in the United States, the current system largely focuses on managing the disabilities associated with mental illness rather than on promoting recovery and building on people's strengths. Social workers provide many of the country's mental health services and play a critical role in improving mental health policies and programs. Improving mental health policy and programs begins with reviewing the historical development of our current mental health system and analyzing the major legislation that shapes the system.

Major mental disorders such as schizophrenia, depression, bipolar disorder, autism, and panic disorder occur worldwide, across racial and ethnic groups. Mental illness affects nearly one in five Americans in any year (SAMHSA, 2018). Fewer adults are diagnosed as having a serious mental illness (SMI), defined as a major mental illness that results in functional impairment and substantially limits their ability to perform ADLs on a long-term basis. This designation is used to determine eligibility for certain public programs. Although people of color are no less likely than White people to suffer from mental illness, they often do not get the help they need. A combination of factors can prevent people from some racial and ethnic groups from even being diagnosed with mental illness, since that often requires at least some access to a mental health provider. Exhibits 10.13 and 10.14 illustrate prevalence of mental illness and receipt of mental health treatment, by age, gender, and race/ethnicity. As depicted, while people who identify as two or more races or Native American are more likely to have a mental illness, non-Latinx White Americans with mental illness are far more likely to receive treatment.

Historical, economic, and cultural factors contribute to these inequities. For example, mental health services for African Americans were not widely available until 1965, when state hospitals were desegregated. There is evidence that an individual's race or ethnicity even affects which diagnoses someone receives (Neighbors et al., 1989; Samaan, 2000). Further, when people of color do get access to treatment, it may be substandard. Barriers to adequate care include stigma, lack of health insurance, treatment that is not culturally competent, lack of inclusive research that specifically investigates needs in communities of color, and insufficient supply of providers and services in isolated areas.

EXHIBIT 10.13

Past Year Prevalence of Any Mental Illness among Adults in the United States (2017)

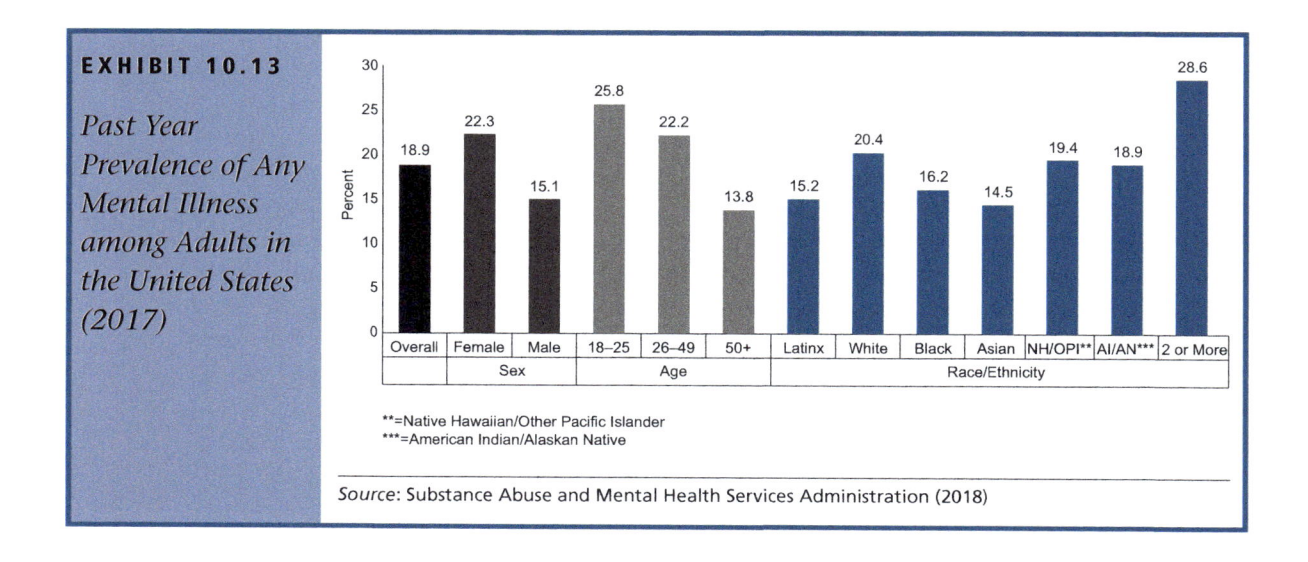

Category	Percent
Overall	18.9
Female	22.3
Male	15.1
18–25	25.8
26–49	22.2
50+	13.8
Latinx	15.2
White	20.4
Black	16.2
Asian	14.5
NH/OPI**	19.4
AI/AN***	18.9
2 or More	28.6

**=Native Hawaiian/Other Pacific Islander
***=American Indian/Alaskan Native

Source: Substance Abuse and Mental Health Services Administration (2018)

EXHIBIT 10.14

Mental Health Treatment Received in Past Year among U.S. Adults with Any Mental Illness (2017)

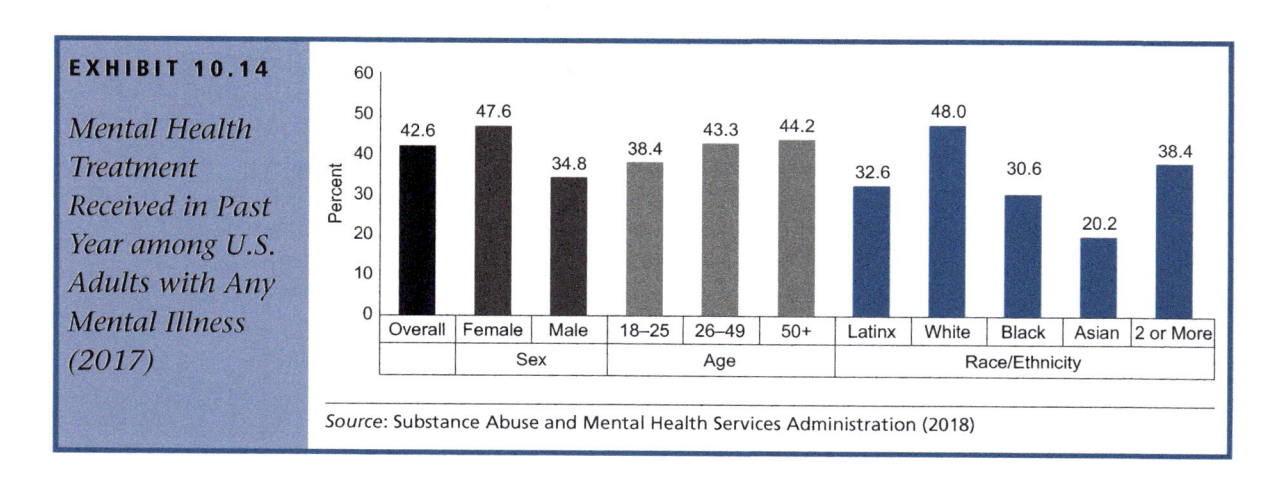

Category	Percent
Overall	42.6
Female	47.6
Male	34.8
18–25	38.4
26–49	43.3
50+	44.2
Latinx	32.6
White	48.0
Black	30.6
Asian	20.2
2 or More	38.4

Source: Substance Abuse and Mental Health Services Administration (2018)

As in the domain of physical health, the consequences of inequity and inadequacy in mental health care are profound. From 2001 to 2017, the U.S. suicide rate increased 31 percent (CDCP, 2019b). Today, suicide is the tenth leading cause of death overall, claiming the lives of nearly 47,000 Americans each year. The suicide rate among males is nearly four times higher than among females, but suicide rates are increasing among all age groups and most demographics and geographies. While less likely to make the evening news, there were more than twice as many suicides as homicides in the United States in 2017. Cuts to mental health services limit access to desperately needed services for people considering suicide, and stigma can keep people from accessing help until it is too late. A deteriorating system leaves many people suffering from mental illness to deal with its effects alone.

History and Background of Mental Health Programs

Prior to the 1800s, people with mental illness were cared for either at home or in almshouses. During the early 1800s, some small, privately funded hospitals were established that emphasized therapeutic rather than custodial care. However, they could serve only a tiny portion of the population with mental illness. As you remember from Chapter 2, Dorothea Dix led a social movement to garner national attention for the plight of people with mental illness. Although she was not successful in securing federal support, her work and that of other advocates spurred the establishment of more than 30 state hospitals by the mid-1800s. This work increased belief in the efficacy of treatment for people with mental illness. However, this care was often largely custodial, and inadequate funding soon led to overcrowding.

In the early 1900s, some states passed laws making it legal to involuntarily sterilize people who were believed to be mentally ill or developmentally disabled. In 1927, the Supreme Court upheld this practice in *Buck v. Bell*. After this ruling, more states passed similar laws; ultimately, more than 65,000 people were involuntarily sterilized in practices that continued, in some states, until the 1970s (National Council on Disability, 2012). These unjust laws underscore that equitable and appropriate treatment for those with mental illness is a civil rights issue.

After World War I, the mental hygiene movement and its emphasis on community care gained momentum, fueled by the recognition of the impact of mental health problems on soldiers returning from war. With the passage of the 1946 Mental Health Act, which established the **National Institute of Mental Health (NIMH)**, the federal government became involved in the delivery of mental health services to the general population. Codifying mental health as a dimension of health, the NIMH is part of the National Institutes of Health (NIH) in the USDHHS. The NIMH is the federal agency primarily responsible for research on mental and behavioral disorders. This agency's research helps shape the nation's mental health policies and programs. You can visit the NIMH website at **www.nimh.nih.gov** to learn about its current research.

Community Mental Health and Deinstitutionalization Although interest in community mental health care grew in the 1950s, state mental institutions continued to provide much of the treatment for people with SMI. The development of medications that helped people with mental illness function outside of institutions, combined with growing awareness of deplorable conditions in some facilities, led to the passage of the Mental Retardation and Community Mental Health Centers Construction Act of 1963 and its 1965 amendments. This landmark legislation gave communities federal funds to construct community mental health centers and provide outpatient services to people with SMI.

Beginning in the 1960s, the deinstitutionalization movement swept through the states, propelled by hopes that community treatment would be more cost-effective and humane than institutional care. **Deinstitutionalization** refers to providing community-based services for people who were formerly served in institutions. Psychoactive drugs made the transition to community living possible for many people. However, although many of the drugs prescribed were found to have serious side-effects, mental health policy and the practices of third-party payers have often discounted the use of other interventions, considering them too expensive.

Federal reimbursement policies, for example, continue to support widespread use of psychoactive medication.

As funding and regulations shifted toward community-based care, thousands of people with mental illness left institutions, new admissions were strictly limited, and many state hospitals closed. Many who were released successfully reintegrated into communities, and this was often an empowering experience for people with mental illness. However, due to inadequate funding, many of those released from institutions received little or no community mental health care. Although the legal rights of people in mental hospitals have been extensively litigated, the right to treatment in the community is less well established. States are largely failing to provide adequate mental health care and treatment in community settings. As a result, some people with mental illness have been re-institutionalized in prisons or nursing homes, while others are living in homeless shelters or on the streets. Initiatives are underway to screen people in these settings for mental illness and, when necessary, refer them for treatment. However, detection and treatment of mental illness are certainly not primary aims of these facilities. Therefore, they are unlikely to meet the treatment needs of people with mental illness who are re-institutionalized there.

Access to affordable, quality mental health care in appropriate community settings is a policy imperative for clients and providers. At the same time, there is an ongoing need for a balanced approach that protects individuals' right to self-determine their treatment—including the choice to refuse it. Strengths-based social workers insist that mental health policy provide equitable and adequate access to care *and* that clients have freedom of choice in pursuing treatment options. In contrast, today's mental health care system often swings between the opposing poles of involuntary commitment and the far more common search for elusive care. In the late 1960s, many states revised their mental health codes to protect consumers' civil rights and standardize criteria for involuntary hospitalization. In most cases, to be involuntarily hospitalized, a person must be found to be a current danger to oneself or others or gravely disabled and incapable of self-care by reason of mental illness. These protections are codified in the Mental Health Systems Act of 1980, which contained a model bill of rights that states were expected to enact and enforce. Court precedents require a factual basis beyond psychiatric danger for civilly committing someone and establish rights to legal representation and due process. Those with mental illness have successfully litigated for freedom from coercive interventions, such as seclusion and brain surgery, and their right to least-restrictive treatment (Bazelon Center, 2018). However, given the insufficient supply of affordable mental health care, the stricter standard for commitment can often mean people must decompensate before they have any legal right to treatment.

Even decades after deinstitutionalization, states still can use civil commitment to compel certain people to accept inpatient commitment (Bazelon Center, 2018). Additionally, nearly all states have measures to compel people to follow *outpatient* treatment regimens—policies that seem particularly cruel in light of cuts to community mental health care options. While most states' laws require some assessment of dangerousness to trigger Involuntary Outpatient Commitments (IOCs), as of 2016, 34 states allowed IOCs based on unwillingness to receive treatment, while in five states, diagnosis of mental illness was itself enough to force outpatient treatment (Temple University, 2018). Balancing the need to protect the civil rights of people who have mental disorders with concerns for their safety and the safety of others is a challenging policy issue, complicated because the question is often not whether someone should be compelled to seek treatment, but rather, how to access treatment that is needed. Mental health centers have never been funded adequately to meet actual need. Although social workers championed deinstitutionalization as a more humane treatment approach, some policymakers viewed it as a way to save money. When institutions were closed without building viable community alternatives, mental health treatment was no longer available for many people. Securing the right to affordable, effective community-based treatment so that people in need receive effective service has thus far proven to be a daunting policy challenge.

Although inadequate funding continues to plague the community mental health movement, the two major federal health insurance programs, Medicaid and Medicare, do provide funding for some mental health services. Medicaid pays for mental health care for people who meet income and disability criteria. Medicare pays for certain kinds of mental health care for eligible people who are elderly and for former workers who have been disabled for at least two years. Additionally, the Social Security Disability Insurance (SSDI) program provides cash assistance for former workers who have mental illness, although the criteria required to qualify for disability assistance with a mental, rather than a primarily physical, disability can make it difficult for people to receive these benefits. Finally, SSI provides cash assistance for people with mental illnesses who have little or no income and meet stringent disability criteria.

As part of Reagan's New Federalism in the 1980s, several categorical programs for substance use disorders and mental health were collapsed into a single Alcohol, Drug Abuse, and Mental Health block grant to states, and funding for these programs was cut by 20 percent (Monitz & Gorin, 2003). Although mental health care is still primarily the states' responsibility, the State Comprehensive Mental Health Services Plan Act of 1986 encouraged a federal–state partnership in this area. This legislation allowed each state to use its block grant to expand community mental health services.

Incarceration of People with Mental Illness   As described in Chapter 7, as states cut budgets for mental health services and people with SMI were frequently left with few resources, many became entangled in the criminal justice system. Although prison is one of the few places everyone is entitled to health care, including mental health care, prisons are ill-equipped to be a de facto major provider of services to people with mental illness. By 2000, the growing number of prisoners with mental illness in state and local correctional facilities helped to motivate the passage of America's Law Enforcement and Mental Health Project Act. This legislation included funds to set up mental health courts, designed to deal with nonviolent offenders in ways that make it more likely they will receive treatment. As with many innovative programs that might be effective if adequately funded, financial support for these special courts has been erratic.

While our prisons and jails continue to hold large numbers of people with mental illness, a new wave of mental health reform is underway to press for changes that will move us away from an approach that has been described as "criminalizing mental illness" (Ollove, 2015). Police are being trained to divert those with mental illness to treatment rather than to jail. Some counties and states are trying to create more housing with supports that will reduce arrests of people with mental illness; others are adding public psychiatric beds. In 2018, the Mentally Ill Offender Treatment and Crime Reduction Act (MIOTCRA) received an $18 million increase in appropriations—its most significant increase ever—to support efforts that promote collaboration between the justice and mental health systems (National Alliance on Mental Illness [NAMI], 2018). Additionally, special Veterans Treatment Courts received a $13 million increase to provide early intervention and treatment for veterans with mental health and substance use disorders (NAMI, 2018). Still, major policy reforms at the local, state, and federal levels are needed to support and sustain a mental health system equipped to meet current challenges and invest in the nation's mental well-being.

Managed Care and Mental Health

States have used managed care approaches to help control costs and coordinate mental health services. As in physical health care, the results have been mixed. Although theoretically, the incentive under managed care is to provide adequate and integrated care to avoid expensive hospitalizations, many times mental health managed care models have resulted in the authorization of only unrealistically limited treatment. For example, short-term psychopharmacology and 15-minute medication sessions with psychiatrists are used to hold down costs, even if other forms of intervention are better suited for that individual's needs. However, given the continued popularity of managed care approaches, social workers need to help investigate ways to use these concepts to create an effective mental health system. Even while working to identify alternatives, social workers should advocate for system reform within managed care to best meet clients' needs.

The Mental Retardation and Community Mental Health Centers Construction Act Development of medication to control symptoms of chronic mental illness, reports of inhumane treatment in some institutions, and the high cost of custodial care in these facilities contributed to the passage of the Mental Retardation and Community Mental Health Centers Construction Act of 1963 (Public Law 88-164) and its 1965 amendments. As described in Chapter 3, the goals of this legislation were to reduce the number of patients in state mental hospitals and to develop a system of community mental health centers that would serve those who had been deinstitutionalized. The federal government provided funds for these purposes to the states through block grants. Although inadequate funding and staffing often created pressure on families to provide care beyond their means, local access to mental health services did increase because of this legislation. The 1975 amendments to the Community Mental Health Act, in combination with Medicare provisions, also increased the availability of mental health services to older adults (Tice & Perkins, 1996). See Exhibit 10.15 for a summary of the Act's provisions.

The State Comprehensive Mental Health Services Plan Act Although the federal government has never played a major role in providing mental health services, Congress encouraged federal–state partnership when it passed the State Comprehensive Mental Health Services Plan Act of 1986 (Public Law 99-660). This legislation authorized states to use federal block grants to expand community mental health services. Although the law permitted states greater flexibility in spending the federal block grants, the money appropriated was inadequate for an effective community mental health system. To compound this problem, states themselves did not dedicate sufficient funds to make comprehensive community-based mental health care a reality. When the FY2018 federal budget increased funding for the Community Mental Health Block

EXHIBIT 10.15

Mental Retardation and Community Mental Health Centers Construction Act 1963, 1965

Policy goals	To reduce the number of patients in state mental hospitals. To develop a system of community mental health centers to provide services in the least restrictive environment.
Benefits or services provided	Community mental health services.
Eligibility rules	People living in the community with mental illness and developmental disabilities.
Service delivery system	Community mental health centers provide local services.
Financing	Federal block grants to the states.

EXHIBIT 10.16

State Comprehensive Mental Health Services Plan Act, 1986

Policy goals	To provide support for community mental health services.
Benefits or services provided	Expanded mental health services.
Eligibility rules	People eligible for mental health services as defined by state policy.
Service delivery system	State agency oversees network of mental health services.
Financing	Federal block grants to the states.

Grants by $160 million, it was the largest increase in the program's history. Exhibit 10.16 summarizes the State Comprehensive Mental Health Services Plan Act's provisions.

Substance Use Disorders

The **Substance Abuse and Mental Health Services Administration (SAMHSA)**, an agency within the USDHHS, was established in 1992. Its purpose is to improve the lives of people with or at risk of mental and substance use disorders. SAMHSA supports the development of policy, programs, and knowledge related to mental health and substance use disorders (SAMHSA, 2010). The estimated 8.5 million adults and more than 330,000 adolescents in the United States who meet the criteria for having co-occurring conditions—that is, both serious mental illness and substance use disorder—are a priority for SAMHSA (SAMHSA, 2018). While many people who have a mental illness do not have substance use disorder—and vice versa—social workers have long been familiar with clients who self-medicate using a variety of substances. Further, the co-occurrence of mental illness and substance use disorders often complicates treatment and, so, necessitates specific policy response.

In 2017, an estimated 19.7 million Americans aged 12 and older had a substance use disorder, including 14.5 million people who had an alcohol use disorder and 7.5 million people who had an illicit drug use disorder (SAMHSA, 2018). These issues have often been regarded as law enforcement priorities, with intervention focusing on punishment of illegal drug use and illegal activities associated with alcohol use (including driving under the influence and underage consumption). However, increased visibility of the pervasiveness of addiction and the liberalization of drug laws in some states are reshaping the context of substance use policy. In 2017, 46 percent of Americans reported having a close friend or family member who has struggled with addiction (Gramlich, 2017). Almost 70 percent of Americans see addiction as a major public problem demanding national attention (Hartig & Doherty, 2018), with a particularly sharp increase in the proportion citing prescription drug abuse as an extremely serious public health priority (Oliphant, 2017).

By early 2018, eight states had declared states of emergency in response to increases in opioid-related deaths and health crises. Governors employed these emergency declarations to reallocate public funds, mandate data sharing, and strengthen collaboration among health and law enforcement agencies (Dedon, 2018). In addition, states have sued pharmaceutical companies for damages associated with the opioid epidemic. This litigation alleges deceptive practices and disregard for public safety, as manufacturers and distributors of prescription opioids sought to increase their profits. Drug company Purdue Pharma settled Oklahoma's lawsuit for $270 million—funds the state intends to use for research and treatment related to its opioid crisis—and then filed for bankruptcy. Three of the biggest drug distributors and a drug manufacturer reached a joint settlement of $260 million with just two Ohio counties. President Trump declared a national emergency after 72,000 Americans died of drug overdoses in 2017—three times higher than the rate a generation ago (CDCP, 2018b). The declaration has been repeatedly extended as federal officials attempt to respond; however, to date, officials have mostly used these expanded powers to commission new studies and expedite state pilot programs (U.S. Government Accountability Office [USGAO], 2018).

In October 2018, even as Congress was largely stymied by intense partisan divides, President Trump signed the Support for Patients and Communities Act. Outlined in Exhibit 10.17, the Act uses regulatory tweaks to make addiction treatment more accessible, prevent illicit synthetic opioids from slipping into the United States, and boost research on non-opioid pain

EXHIBIT 10.17

Support for Patients and Communities Act, 2018

Policy goals	To provide states with additional tools to counter addiction in their communities, with particular attention to opioids; to restrict the supply of illicit opioids and decrease reliance on opioid pain relief; and to invest in addiction research.
Benefits or services provided	Additional funding to remove barriers to addiction treatment; regulatory enforcement to reduce supply of opioids.
Eligibility rules	States determine eligibility and prioritization for the programs they develop.
Service delivery system	Grants to states to increase their capacity to counter addiction, as well as changes within Medicare and Medicaid to attempt to limit over-prescription of opioid painkillers.
Financing	Federal funding, from general revenues; also seeks to provide more flexibility to better leverage existing funds.

treatments. However, while it reauthorizes funding from the 21st Century Cures Act, which put $500 million toward the opioid crisis, the legislation does not pay for the broad and sustained expansion of evidence-based treatment that most social workers see as an urgent imperative. At the same time, physicians and other health care providers have pushed back against new restrictions on prescribing opioid pain medication, fearing the rules will exacerbate the suffering of those who live with chronic pain, particularly older adults. In April 2019, the Centers for Disease Control and Prevention attempted to clarify its opioid prescription guidance, to emphasize that refusing necessary medication for those in severe pain or abruptly ceasing prescriptions without tapering could seriously harm vulnerable patients (Dowell, Haegerich, & Chou, 2019). For more information about mental health and substance use disorder policies and programs, visit the SAMHSA website at **www.samhsa.gov**.

EVALUATING HEALTH AND MENTAL HEALTH POLICIES AND PROGRAMS

As we have seen throughout this chapter, U.S. health care policies have produced mixed results. Medicare, Medicaid, and CHIP provide health care for one in three Americans. Medicare enrollment increased from 19 million beneficiaries in 1966 to more than 59 million in 2018. Medicaid enrollment increased from ten million beneficiaries in 1967 to more than 66 million in 2018. The ACA expanded public health insurance programs and strengthened elements of the employer-provided health insurance system. During the past decade, such efforts reduced the percentage of children without health insurance and extended coverage to a large group of formerly uninsured adults.

However, states' resistance to Medicaid expansion limited policies' reach, and recent regulatory and executive actions threaten progress. Unanticipated and dynamic aspects of the larger economic, political, and social environments create challenges to which policymakers must respond. For example, although most people will continue to be insured through their employers, many people may have a series of employers or be self-employed or unemployed for significant periods. These shifts in the labor market will have ripple effects throughout the health care landscape. In the future, equitable access to affordable, quality health care may require restructuring the link between employment and health care coverage. Enrollment procedures in public insurance programs should be simple, so people who lose their jobs can continue their coverage and those turning to public programs can do so as seamlessly as possible.

Unfortunately, federal policy is moving in the opposite direction. After a decade of decline, the percentage of Americans without health insurance increased in 2018, a trend that suggests growing risk and unmet need. Following months of congressional debate over repealing the ACA, retreat from marketing and outreach, and tax and regulatory changes designed to undermine the ACA, 2019 saw dramatic declines in individuals purchasing health insurance on the federal exchanges, as illustrated in Exhibit 10.18. Enrollment continued to decline slightly between 2018 and 2019 (CMS, 2019b); further, this decline in demand for exchange plans can be only partially attributed to Medicaid expansion and increases in employer-provided coverage. Notably, the 15 states that defied this trend attribute their success to their own advertising, use of state tax incentives, and efforts to attract competitive plans to their exchanges (Burton

EXHIBIT 10.18

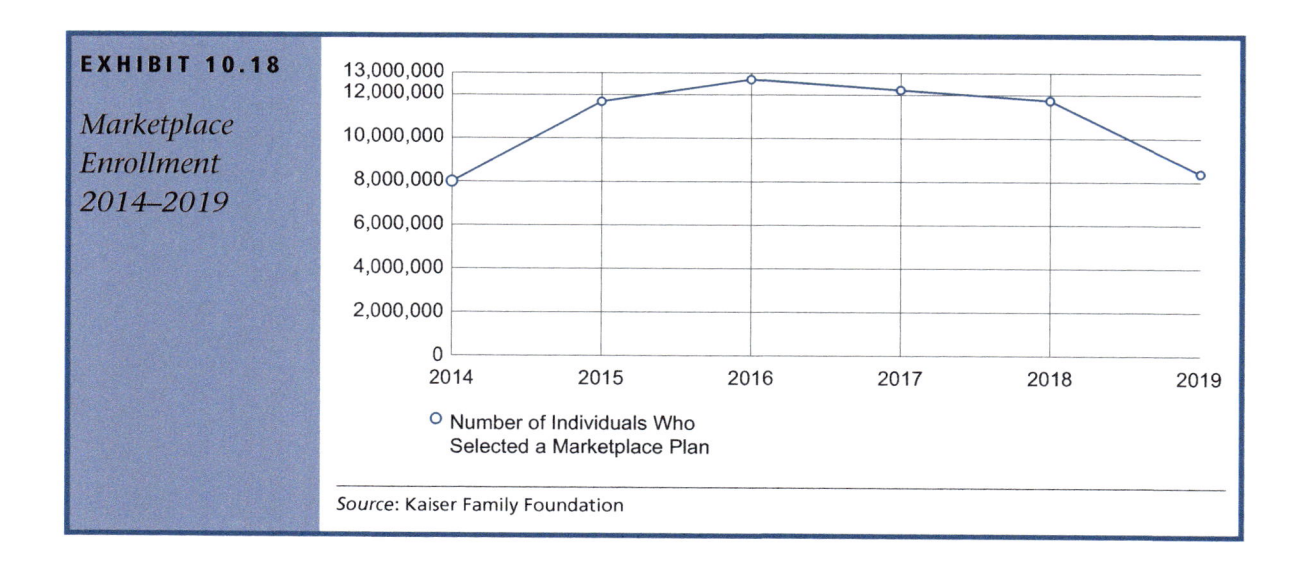

Marketplace Enrollment 2014–2019

[Line chart showing Number of Individuals Who Selected a Marketplace Plan, ranging from about 8,000,000 in 2014, rising to about 12,000,000 in 2015, peaking near 12,700,000 in 2016, declining to about 12,200,000 in 2017, 11,800,000 in 2018, and falling to about 8,000,000 in 2019.]

Source: Kaiser Family Foundation

et al., 2018). These diverging outcomes underscore the significance of state policy in shaping Americans' experiences with health care. Today, states have considerable latitude to determine the scope of services and extent of eligibility for Medicaid as well as the operation of the health insurance exchanges. States expanding Medicaid can choose to provide only a minimal list of benefits to new recipients. They can also cut reimbursement rates, implement cost sharing, and use Medicaid waivers to alter people's outcomes from this ostensibly federal policy. Thus, there is great state variation in implementation of health reform and the costs and outcomes that result.

This devolved model of health care stands in marked contrast to models in many other countries, where public funds pay for health care, and medical centers run by the government are the primary providers. In contrast, the United States chose to expand both public and private health insurance, continue to rely on private-sector provision of services, and empower states with considerable policymaking latitude. Within the continued debate over health care policy, state policymakers continue to experiment with health care reforms. Some of these proposals take the form of retreats from existing benefits, while, in 2018, proposals for single-payer, "Medicare-for-All" health care systems were considered in states such as Colorado, California, Michigan, and New York (Hall & Tolbert, 2018). Beyond reconfiguring state health care programs, voters would likely need to agree to substantial new taxes to implement truly public systems. Supporters would also need to overcome stiff opposition from some providers and the insurance industry. Despite these challenges, state initiatives will undoubtedly shape health reform in the coming years. As noted above, some states used public referenda to expand their Medicaid programs. Seven states have used Medicaid waivers for reinsurance schemes that seek to make coverage more affordable and to stabilize insurance markets (Nicholson & Gruwell, 2018). Of course, states are also active on both sides of court challenges to the ACA. Additionally, states have enacted measures challenging or opting out of aspects of health reform, both by statute and by ballot measure (Cauchi, 2018). Increasingly, then, the U.S. health care system is interpreted, implemented, and often contested by state policymakers, with profound implications for individual and community health and well-being.

Challenges in the Medicare System

Population aging, growth in the number of beneficiaries, and overall continued growth in medical costs ensure that the expenses involved in maintaining the Medicare system will continue to rise. Further limiting reimbursement rates for providers and products could help control costs. In the case of prescription drugs, policymakers may be less reluctant to implement such policies than in the past; however, strong patent protections for medications and limited ability to bargain over prices seem likely to mute the potency of cost-reduction efforts. Further, Medicare provider reimbursement is already so low that, in some areas, it is difficult to find doctors willing to accept new Medicare patients. Absent pressures that would address the root causes of high prices, options for containing the costs of Medicare generally fall into one of three categories: limiting services, raising the age of eligibility, and/or shifting costs to older adults (Quadagno, 1999). These options all raise concerns about effects on beneficiaries, particularly those disadvantaged by gender, race, and/or class. At the same time, efforts to target changes to those older adults who might be comparatively less harmed by them—such as by raising the eligibility age only for higher earners (KFF, 2013)—could undermine public support for the Medicare entitlement. As illustrated in Exhibit 10.19, it is important to consider Medicare's

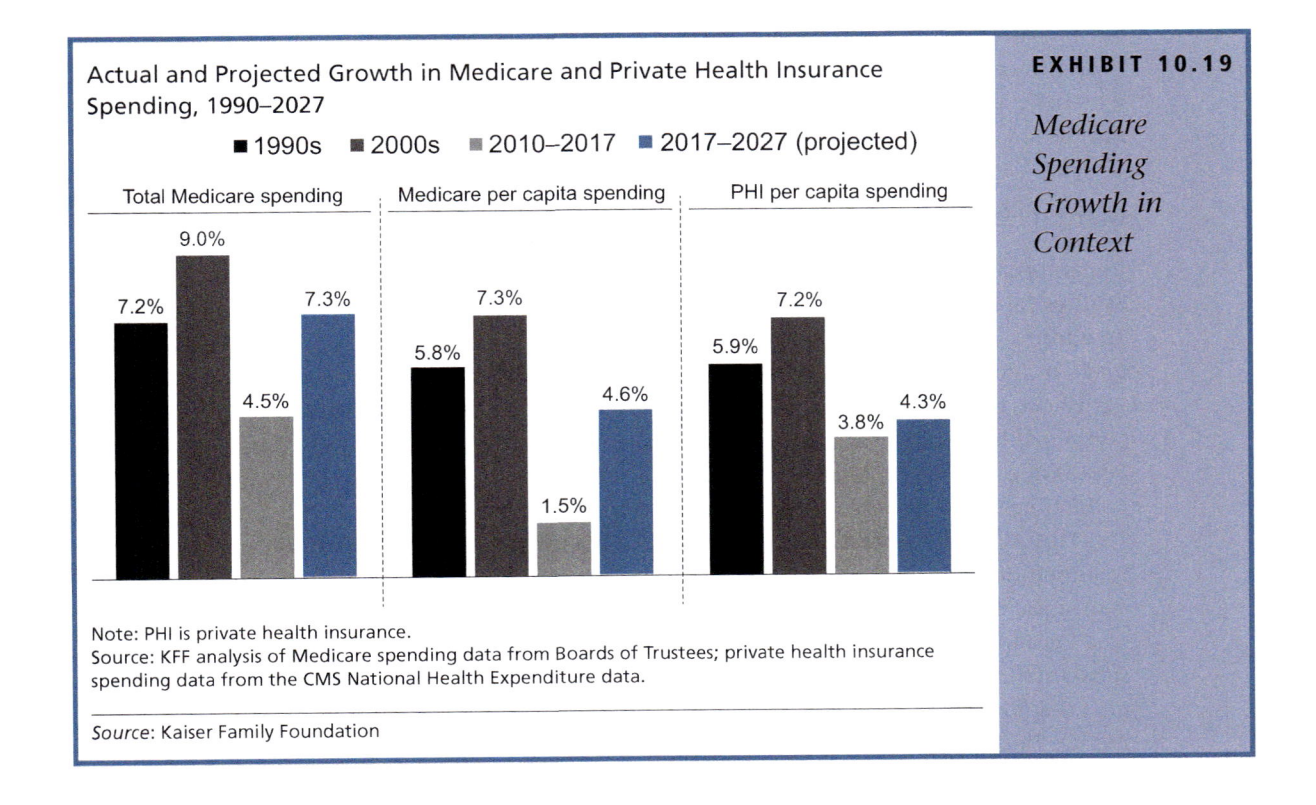

EXHIBIT 10.19

Medicare Spending Growth in Context

Actual and Projected Growth in Medicare and Private Health Insurance Spending, 1990–2027

■ 1990s   ■ 2000s   ■ 2010–2017   ■ 2017–2027 (projected)

Total Medicare spending: 7.2%, 9.0%, 4.5%, 7.3%
Medicare per capita spending: 5.8%, 7.3%, 1.5%, 4.6%
PHI per capita spending: 5.9%, 7.2%, 3.8%, 4.3%

Note: PHI is private health insurance.
Source: KFF analysis of Medicare spending data from Boards of Trustees; private health insurance spending data from the CMS National Health Expenditure data.

Source: Kaiser Family Foundation

fiscal pressures in context. Although Medicare costs have grown rapidly, health care costs in the private sector have grown even more quickly. In fact, Medicare is widely lauded for its cost-effectiveness. To bring the U.S. deficit under control, health care costs in the public and private sectors must be addressed.

Ageism in the Medicare Health Care Cost Debate Particularly in the face of technological advances in health care that are effective but very expensive, attempting to control health care costs is a challenge. As health care is extended to a larger older adult population, these issues will compound. The Social Security and Medicare Board of Trustees projects that Medicare costs will grow from approximately 3.7 percent of GDP in 2017 to 6.2 percent of GDP by 2092 (CMS, 2018a). Methods of controlling health care costs will need serious action so that we can continue to provide Medicare to people who depend on it.

As we evaluate options for controlling health care costs, it is crucial to center debate on our shared obligation to provide a foundation for health for the entire population. Decisions about rationing of limited resources must focus on legitimate bases for making difficult decisions, not on stereotyping or prejudicial assumptions about "worthiness." The goal is not to find a population to blame, whether they be frail elders or extremely premature infants, nor to give credence to the idea that cost should be the sole criterion for determining appropriate health care. We must stop blaming patients in *any* group for increasing health care costs. All patients are deserving of the care they need, and policy levers can be used to reduce the cost of care for any and all populations. While social workers have reason to be discouraged about the erosion of some of the provisions of the ACA and concerned about the long-term trajectories of health care investments, the strong majorities of Americans across the ideological spectrum who believe health care policy should put people over profits suggest there are opportunities to find promising ways forward.

Mental Health Parity and Concerns for Specific Populations

In part because mental health services have never been covered by insurance to the same extent as physical health services, most people with mental illness do not receive the care they need. To address this injustice, advocates have long worked for parity, which means equivalent coverage of both physical and mental health care. In 1996, Congress passed the Mental Health Parity Act, but because of opposition from insurance companies and employers, the legislation contained loopholes that reduced its effectiveness. In 2008, passage of the Paul Wellstone and Pete Domenici Mental Health Parity and Addiction Equity Act required parity in co-payments, deductibles, out-of-pocket expenses, and treatment limits.

The ACA also contained provisions to advance mental health parity. In a March 2016 memorandum, President Obama estimated that the ACA would expand mental health and substance use disorder benefits for 60 million Americans (White House, 2016). All individual and small group private market plans created after 2014 were required to cover mental health and substance use disorder services, which were part of the health care law's Essential Health Benefits categories. Further, insurers could no longer deny anyone coverage because of a preexisting mental health condition. The ACA also required that new health plans cover recommended preventive benefits—including behavioral assessments for children and depression screening for adults and adolescents—without cost-sharing. These are important steps toward achieving parity, but there is still much more work to do.

Veterans' Mental Health Social workers have long worked to establish policies and programs to ensure that veterans receive adequate mental health care. Soldiers returning from Iraq and Afghanistan are exhibiting the same kinds of mental health needs that returning soldiers exhibited in the wake of previous conflicts, requiring the nation to focus increased attention on preparing professionals to provide effective services. The number of soldiers with post-traumatic stress disorder (PTSD) and increased rates of suicide among service members have contributed to recognition of the need for expanded mental health care in the military. However, although President Trump signed a 2018 executive order allowing all veterans to receive mental health care in the first year after service—when they are most vulnerable to suicide risk—veteran health care is otherwise limited to only those veterans whose record of military service is deemed sufficient. The U.S. Department of Veterans' Affairs (VA) estimates that as many as 20 percent of Iraq veterans and 15 percent of Vietnam veterans have PTSD (2018b). Veterans are 1.5 times as likely as civilians to die by suicide. High-profile suicides of veterans on VA hospital property have underscored both the tremendous mental health strains with which these service members contend and the extent to which many perceive the VA's current response as inadequate. Indeed, scandals in the VA health care system and widespread condemnation of lapses in patient care and safety (U.S. Department of Veterans' Affairs, 2018c) have led many to advocate alternative service delivery models to provide veterans' mental health care (Burton et al., 2018). To attempt to address unmet needs, the federal FY2018 budget included substantial increases in mental health appropriations, including a $306 million increase for SAMHSA, $109.8 million more in NIMH research, and $580 million in additional VA funding for services for veterans with mental health concerns (NAMI, 2018). To ensure sufficient supply of professionals equipped to provide these services, the military is recruiting and providing educational stipends for social workers and other mental health professionals to practice on military bases and in veterans' hospitals.

Growing Concerns Related to Children and Mental Health While several states have at least partially restored recession-era budget cuts, funding and research for children's mental health care lag far behind needed levels. Further, fragmentation in funding streams, substantial variation among states, and disproportionate emphasis on pharmaceutical interventions keep many children from accessing necessary services (Cooper, 2008). As in adult mental health, providers often rely on medication to treat children's mental illnesses even in cases where social and behavioral interventions—instead of or in addition to pharmacology—would be more effective. The overuse of medication in the foster care system is of particular concern. A 2012 U.S. Government Accountability Office (USGAO) report reviewed evidence that foster children were prescribed psychotropic drugs at rates over three times higher than other children. Even when comparing babies less than one year old, infants in foster care were nearly twice as likely to be prescribed a psychiatric drug. At the same time, up to 30 percent of children in foster care who may need mental health services did not receive them (USGAO, 2012). After the USDHHS provided additional guidance and oversight, a 2017 follow-up report found an increase in practices to support appropriate use of psychotropic medications for children in foster care, including screening for mental health conditions, developing prescription guidelines, and monitoring a child's response (USGAO, 2017). However, officials said that limited access to mental health services remained a problem, and only four of the seven selected states reduced medication use from 2011 to 2015 (USGAO, 2017). Although medication is useful in treating mental illness, its overuse must be carefully monitored, and alternative treatment options need to be expanded.

Substance Use Disorders, Pandemics, and the Health Care System

While many aspects of health care in this country could use improvement, particularly as evaluated by measures of equity and efficiency, U.S. health care policies have been particularly deficient in two areas: treatment of substance use disorders and response to pandemics.

Substance Use Disorders It is estimated that the yearly economic impact of alcohol misuse in the United States is $249 billion (Sacks et al., 2015); this figure is $193 billion for illicit drug use (National Drug Intelligence Center, 2011). Rates of overdose deaths and hospitalizations contribute to higher child welfare caseloads and more complex child welfare cases (Radel et al., 2018). Treatment options that meet people's needs for flexible, evidence-based, affordable, readily accessible, culturally competent intervention are limited. In their absence, affected individuals, health care providers, and social workers struggle to cobble together a commensurate response. Although the opioid epidemic has catalyzed greater political will to support policies and programs to prevent and treat substance use disorders, the system still lags far behind the need. In 2017, only 12.2 percent of people who needed substance use disorder treatment received it (SAMHSA, 2018). Among adolescents, the percentage receiving needed treatment was even lower—an estimated 8.2 percent (SAMHSA, 2017). Further, despite growing recognition of the economic, social, and health consequences of substance use disorders, spending on mental health and substance use needs is projected to fall as a share of all health spending (SAMHSA, 2014). While some of this decline is attributed to increases in generic prescriptions used to manage symptoms, much is owed to reductions in public treatment facilities, seldom offset by increases in private services (Cummings, Wen, & Ko, 2017).

Even more alarming is new evidence that U.S. health care policies have *contributed* to these disorders through gaps in the mental health system and irresponsible prescribing. In testimony to the U.S. Senate, SAMHSA leadership attributed the opioid epidemic largely to health care providers' overreliance on opioids in the absence of other effective pain relief and to lack of provider capacity to "identify and engage individuals and provide them with high-quality, evidence-based opioid addiction treatment" (McCance-Katz, 2017). Other research found that opioid overdoses were highest in the counties where pharmaceutical companies concentrated their marketing (Hadland et al., 2019). While opioid prescriptions fell in almost 75 percent of counties between 2015 and 2017 (Guy et al., 2019), these substances have permeated much of the country, with devastating effect.

Further, increasing attention to the prevalence and danger of opioid addiction has followed lines of racial inequity manifest throughout the health care system. In the media and by policymakers, people of color who have substance use disorders are often described as "addicts," while other coverage refers to non-Latinx White drug users as "victims" of an epidemic (see Broome, 2018). African Americans are more likely to be denied pain medication at emergency rooms, as providers' biases influence their prescribing (Singhal, Tien, & Hsia, 2016). And, in sharp divergence from the 1990s, when drugs were framed as a law enforcement challenge rather than a public health crisis, the face of substance use disorder today is often "White". Importantly, while in 2015, African Americans were 18 percent of substance use disorder admissions and 12 percent of the population (SAMHSA, 2017), this treatment is often mandated by the criminal justice system and delivered through a law enforcement lens (Cook & Alegría, 2011). In 2015, 48 percent of substance use treatment referrals came through the criminal justice system, making it an important pathway to treatment (SAMHSA, 2017) while raising concerns about access at earlier stages, before the consequences are so dire. Although, as with mental health, people have increased access to substance use disorder treatment when in prison, strengths-based social workers reject this calculus as unacceptable.

Particularly at the federal level, drug policy is still overwhelmingly focused on punishment rather than treatment or prevention. However, largely in response to shifting public attitudes and growing need, several states have moved to address substance use from a public health perspective. In addition to the 33 states that have legalized marijuana for medical use, ten states have decriminalized marijuana for adults aged 21 and older. Many states have sought to give health care providers additional tools with which to counter addictions, including 20 states with prescription drug monitoring programs, 33 with prescription limits, and 12 that increased provider education about substance use disorder (Blackman, 2018). Other states have improved treatment options, often through Medicaid expansion and/or partnerships with community mental health centers. More information about state actions related to substance use treatment is available at the National Conference of State Legislatures. For the latest information on federal drug abuse policy, go to the website of the Office of National Drug Control Policy at **www.whitehousedrugpolicy.gov**.

Pandemics Epidemics that occur across large regions are called **pandemics**. HIV/AIDS is a well-known example of a pandemic. Although HIV/AIDS has presented major challenges to our health care system, the federal government has often been slow to respond. In fact, the Ryan White Comprehensive AIDS Resources Emergency (CARE) Act of 1990, summarized in Exhibit 10.20, is the only major federal policy implemented as a direct response to HIV/AIDS in our country. Because HIV/AIDS patients were initially perceived to be members of marginalized groups, particularly gay men and intravenous drug users, social values that held them responsible for their illness interfered with mounting a timely and effective public health response. Passed after years of work by advocacy groups, the Ryan White CARE Act authorized federal funds for services for people who have AIDS or are HIV-positive.

The crises resulting from the spread of Ebola, Zika, and swine flu viruses illustrate growing global interdependence in the health arena. The U.S. 2018 influenza season killed more than 80,000 Americans and resulted in more than $15.4 billion in lost productivity and more than $10.4 billion in medical expenses. Scientists often struggle to calibrate the influenza vaccine to the strain active in a particular year, while health care providers grapple with shortages of intravenous fluids and personnel during the height of an outbreak. Infectious diseases move rapidly

EXHIBIT 10.20	Policy goals	To improve the quality and availability of care for medically underserved individuals affected by HIV/AIDS.
Ryan White Comprehensive AIDS Resources Emergency (CARE) Act of 1990	Benefits or services provided	Funding for a comprehensive system of care, including testing, primary care, case management, and specialized treatment.
	Eligibility rules	People living with HIV who are uninsured or underinsured.
	Service delivery system	Administered by the USDHHS; services delivered locally, to provide a flexible structure to meet different populations' needs.
	Financing	Grants to cities, states, and community-based organizations.

across borders, and international cooperation is necessary to control their spread. The Centers for Disease Control and Prevention (CDCP) estimates that pandemics are likely to cost more than $60 billion per year over the coming century. However, investing $4.5 billion per year in building global capacity—particularly in surveillance, laboratory networks, workforce training, and emergency management systems—could avert pandemics' catastrophic financial and human costs (CDCP, 2017c). The devastating effects of pandemics make it increasingly clear that U.S. policymakers must pay close attention to the influence of global health conditions. When a disease can reach the United States in less than 36 hours, we must anticipate future needs before they become crises and build capacity to counter them quickly.

The threats posed by outbreaks of infectious disease also underscore the need for ongoing health education, infrastructure development, and community mobilization efforts. Today, while overall rates of childhood immunization remain high (Hill et al., 2018), growth of the unvaccinated preschool population has quadrupled since 2001. Public health officials attribute the rise in unvaccinated children, which in some communities is reaching levels that threaten the overall population's protection against dangerous communicable diseases, to a combination of factors, including cuts to public health systems, particularly in rural areas; barriers that separate low-income and otherwise disadvantaged families from health care providers; and the "anti-vax" movement, which has gained prominence among some vaccine skeptics and those resistant to government intervention in their lives. In 2018 and 2019, these trends contributed to outbreaks of diseases such as measles, thought largely vanquished from the health landscape. In some states, policymakers have sought to head off broader public health crises by increasing enforcement of vaccine requirements in schools, removing exemptions that allow families to avoid immunization, and investing in mobile clinics and co-location of vaccination services.

NEXT STEPS FOR PROMOTING MORE EFFECTIVE HEALTH AND MENTAL HEALTH POLICIES

The U.S. health care system has a foundation of employer-provided health insurance and evidences strong preference for public–private partnerships. While aspects of this approach maximize individual choice, and so are consistent with strengths principles, finding sustainable ways to expand access compels policies to contain rising costs. Ultimately, this means further limiting profits in the powerful health care industry. Under Medicare and Medicaid, most health care is provided privately but reimbursed publicly, with the federal government acting as insurer. It is far too costly for the government to simply pay whatever providers decide to charge. In addition to implementing prospective rate-setting and using the power of the buying group to negotiate lower prices, there is also a need to reduce the administrative overhead incurred when multiple insurance companies—with their own layers of management and often their own profit motivations—oversee health care. Additionally, it is important to design payment systems so that providers have neither incentives to provide nor withhold treatment, but instead base decisions solely on the best interests of the patient (NASW, 2012a).

As Steven Brill (2015) has pointed out, when health care reform is debated in the United States, the focus is primarily on *who will pay?* These debates have largely ignored the arguably most important questions: *what are we getting?* and *are prices too high?* We should expect policymakers to scrutinize all parts of the health care system to identify cost savings. We should insist that policy prioritize sustainable costs for equitable access to essential care and put everything else on the table for negotiation. Otherwise, rising health care costs could further limit investment in education, housing, and other concerns of social workers, as well as result in insufficient attention to and appropriation for investments in health promotion, which can improve quality of life, close disparities, and reduce spending.

Medicare Reform

Entitlements, including Medicaid, Social Security, and Medicare, are under growing pressure, particularly following the passage of the Tax Cuts and Jobs Act in December 2017. Senator Marco Rubio called tax reform the first step before "instituting structural changes to Social Security and Medicare" (*Politico*, 2017), while then-House Speaker Paul Ryan said that "we're going to have to get back next year at entitlement reform, which is how you tackle the debt" (Goodkind, 2018). While political realignments following the 2018 midterm elections made major changes to Medicare somewhat less likely, among the proposals still discussed as possibilities are some that could have dramatic and largely negative effects on older adults' access to affordable health care. Privatizing Medicare would mean older adults get a voucher to purchase health insurance. If they chose a plan that cost more than the average, the beneficiary would have to pay the difference. This would strain the budgets of many elders. Beneficiaries might feel pressured to choose the least expensive plan; however, if those have limited networks, older adults may have inadequate access to providers. Although supporters of vouchers promote them to increase competition and control costs, most Medicare beneficiaries are not able to do extensive comparison shopping. Further, the value of the voucher would likely not keep pace with health care inflation. As a result, more of the costs of care would be shifted to individuals. These threats to Medicare as an entitlement will likely continue to resurface. It is critical that you are familiar with them, so you can speak up when they are proposed.

Mental Health Care

Social workers have long advocated the need to view mental illness and mental health in biopsychosocial terms rather than focusing so heavily on neurobiology. Social workers have also voiced concerns about how insurance systems define mental illness for reimbursement purposes. Official definitions and classifications need to be revised so that providers can seek public reimbursement for treatment of more broadly defined mental health concerns. There should not be a financial incentive, for example, to diagnose a child with a serious mental illness such as bipolar disorder when more generalist family support might be the best approach. Visit the website of the National Alliance on Mental Illness at **www.nami.org** to learn more about mental health advocacy initiatives. As the students in Exhibit 10.21 demonstrated, social workers should be on the "front lines" of policy debates in arenas such as mental health, advancing the profession's values.

Diversity, equity, and inclusion considerations should be paramount in all policy development. To enhance the provision of culturally competent services and leverage health policies as a tool for social justice, we need to support physical and mental health training for people from a variety of backgrounds. Schools of social work should prioritize recruitment and retention of students from historically underrepresented communities. To make the profession an attractive career option, insurers should reimburse social work services at rates comparable to those of other professions. The NASW also advocates for all health settings to employ social workers who are licensed or certified at the appropriate level. The Health Care and Education Affordability Reconciliation Act, which was part of health care reform, included provisions that make it easier for social work students to complete an affordable education. However, the Trump Administration has proposed eliminating the public service loan forgiveness programs that have simultaneously reduced social workers' financial burdens and increased the supply of providers in underserved communities. Clearly, social workers will need to be even stronger advocates if we are to close the gap between the number of future professionals being educated and the needs in the field.

Strategies to Promote Health Social workers can be leaders in the effort to invest in policy approaches that emphasize *health*, not just health care. Such approaches, which urge focus on the multiple influences that affect health, are consistent with the strengths perspective. While emphasizing people's capacity to maintain and improve their own health, health approaches are not about shifting responsibility to individuals but about taking a broader view of what

---

EXHIBIT 10.21

Students Fight for Mental Health Funding

Forty-five social work students created and implemented a social action plan to combat potential state budget cuts to mental health funding. The students testified in front of legislative committees, compiled data on financial burdens facing local mental health facilities, generated alternative options for budget cuts, and worked to increase media coverage of mental health allocations. Together with other advocacy groups, the students helped to restore more than $27 million of mental health funding.

facilitates health. Championed by prominent social work scholar Ann Weick, the health approach encourages practitioners to identify and challenge economic and cultural barriers to health and to advocate for policies and programs that provide clients with essential health-related tools (Saleebey, 2013; Weick, 1986). According to this lens, which increasingly informs the work of philanthropies (Easterling & McDuffee, 2018) and local communities (Quinn, 2016), health policy should begin "upstream" to address the social determinants that shape outcomes. Accordingly, neighborhood safety, workplace conditions, poverty, transportation, community infrastructure, and community connectedness are "health" issues, deserving of policy attention. A health perspective guides us to consider how we can create an environment in which people have the maximum chance for good health—and to make this environmental intervention a policy imperative. Recent research attributing most of the rise in obesity to increases in rural areas (NCD Risk Factor Collaboration, 2019) is evidence of the powerful contribution of environmental context on individuals' health outcomes. Clearly, people's places influence their options—and that landscape has important implications for their health. Social workers need to be alert to the negative health effects of environmental pollution, particularly in areas beset by such injustice, including low-income neighborhoods and tribal communities. Policies that increase access to healthy food and opportunities to safely get exercise in a neighborhood are vital investments in health.

Because it presents the act of seeking out services as a strength, a health approach can reduce the stigma attached to receiving mental health services. Mental health experts working from the strengths perspective advocate for policies that promote recovery and build resilience (Saleebey, 2013). Policies should promote the full community participation of individuals with mental illness. The efforts of people with mental illness to find work should be supported rather than punished with loss of public benefits. Finally, rights to treatment should be strengthened, particularly in the community, and the right to refuse treatment should be protected.

Social Workers and Health Reforms

It is crucial that social workers encourage states to press for the retention of provisions of the ACA that benefit our clients, educate people about the benefits available to them, and insist on enforcement of policies that protect patients' rights to health care. Like the students in Exhibit 10.22, social workers should use our assessment, relationship-building, and community

Social work students organized an online campaign to educate voters about Medicaid expansion. They pointed out the number of uninsured individuals who would be eligible if the state accepted expansion and how expansion would benefit everyone by improving health care, creating jobs, and supporting healthier and more financially stable families. They also collected signatures via an online petition that they sent to the governor, took part in a rally at the state capitol, and recruited other faculty and students to join them. Efforts like these have proven crucial in changing public policy and framing health care as a fundamental right.	**EXHIBIT 10.22** *Students Advocate for Medicaid Expansion*

EXHIBIT 10.23

Many Workers Currently on Medicaid Could Lose Coverage Under Work Requirements

Non-elderly, low-income adults not receiving disability assistance who worked over the course of one year

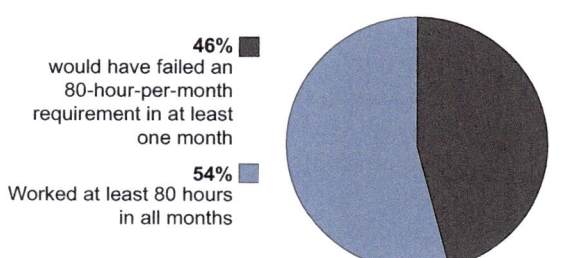

- **46%** would have failed an 80-hour-per-month requirement in at least one month
- **54%** Worked at least 80 hours in all months

Source: CBPP analysis of the Census Bureau's Survey of Income and Program Participation (SIPP) data from June 2012 to May 2013. Sample Includes adults ages 19 to 64 not receiving disability assistance in families with monthly Incomes below 138 percent of the federal poverty line; estimates are weighted by the number of months in which individuals had Incomes below the Medicaid income limit.

Source: Center on Budget and Policy Priorities

---

mobilization skills to help people connect to valuable health resources. Social workers need to understand when and how to sign up clients for public health care programs. We must work to ensure that there are enough providers and that they are delivering accessible, culturally appropriate services. Social workers must oppose efforts to turn Medicaid into a block grant or otherwise undermine its entitlement. Work requirements are a particular threat to Medicaid. Medicaid is designed to ensure that low-income people and those with disabilities have affordable access to health care, not to serve as a work incentive program. Further, while most non-elderly, non-disabled adults who receive Medicaid do work, as Exhibit 10.23 illustrates, nearly half of these working beneficiaries could lose coverage under the strict rules proposed by several states. Social workers should advocate to influence the rules that shape states' Medicaid policies. In states that have not expanded Medicaid or that are considering work requirements, social workers should demand to know why people in their states do not have the same access to Medicaid benefits as people in other states.

Look at the information provided in this chapter and the references cited, think for yourself, and speak up when health policy is discussed. Many people have misconceptions about health reform. You can provide them with information from trusted sources. Mindful of confidentiality, you can also aggregate the experiences of your clients, including those who lack insurance and/or struggle to access needed care. When you do this, you help develop an informed public consensus about health policy. Consider the NASW Code of Ethics, which articulates our mission to "enhance human well-being and help meet the basic needs of all people, with particular attention to the needs and empowerment of people who are vulnerable, oppressed, and living in poverty." What types of health care policies are required to fulfill this vision? The more knowledgeable you become, the more effectively you can help your clients.

It is also important to keep in mind that making health care more widely available will not, by itself, create equality in outcomes. The influential Whitehall Studies conducted in the

United Kingdom found that structural issues related to social class, including occupational hierarchy and perceived locus of control, have profound and enduring effects on health. The studies found a steep inverse association between social class and mortality from a wide variety of diseases. These relationships persist even when access to health care becomes more universal (Marmot & Brunner, 2005). In discussing the implications of their studies, the researchers indicated that those interested in understanding differences in outcomes need to pay more attention to social environments and the consequences of income inequality. Other studies of health care outcomes also draw attention to these factors (Blank & Burau, 2010).

Certainly, these relationships are evident in the United States, where individuals who experience racism, economic oppression, and other marginalization suffer disproportionately on a variety of health indicators, including risk of obesity, chronic disease, and injury leading to early disability. These inequities and their health effects can compound, even across generations, imperiling communities' health. Tragically, low birthweight, preterm labor, and greater infant mortality in African-American babies has been linked to mothers' experiences of racial discrimination (Collins et al., 2004; Mustillo et al., 2004; Smith et al., 2018). Social determinants help to explain why even highly educated and high-income Black women have poorer birth outcomes than their White peers.

At the beginning of the chapter, we highlighted large differences in spending on health care among various countries. As Bradley and Taylor (2013) point out in their book, *The American Health Care Paradox*, there are also large differences in spending on social services. Many other countries spend much more on social investments. These expenditures help to lessen disparities and bolster funding for childcare, paid family leave, mental health care, and other social services. These factors also influence health. One innovation in this direction is the *Accountable Health Communities Model*, an approach to improving health outcomes and reducing costs by systematically identifying and addressing health-related social needs through more effective clinical–community linkages. Other promising initiatives include work to reduce trauma and stress for children in low-income neighborhoods. Increasing recognition of the importance of healthy environments in reducing health disparities places social workers in a key position to lead this critical element of health policy change.

CONCLUSION

Health and mental health policies in our country have created a system in which some people who can afford it get excellent care, but many others do not have even basic health care. While public health programs and policy advances have addressed many barriers to health care access, disparities persist. We have a legacy of neglect of health care for people of color and others from disadvantaged groups. Economic, occupational, social, and environmental policies influence the state of our health, and we must carefully consider the health implications of these policies if we hope to improve quality of life. Faced with an aging population and attendant increases in both acute and chronic health care needs, it is critical that we find ways to control health care costs, promote wellness, and ensure adequate care for people across their lifespans.

MAIN POINTS

- Social determinants of health are "the circumstances in which people are born, grow up, live, work, and age, as well as the systems put in place to deal with illness" (CDCP, 2013). These circumstances also influence access to health care.

- Prior to passage of the Affordable Care Act, more than 15 percent of the American population was uninsured. In 2018, this figure was 8.5 percent. Most people with insurance are insured through their employers.

- Although the United States has the highest per-person expenditure for health care, many health outcomes are not as positive as those in countries that spend far less.

- Medicaid provides health insurance to low-income people who fall within state guidelines for "categorically needy." Federal and state governments jointly fund Medicaid.

- Medicare provides health insurance for eligible people over age 65, people with certain disabilities, and people with end-stage renal disease. Medicare is administered at the federal level and is funded by payroll taxes (Part A), premium payments, and general revenues (Part B). Part C allows private companies to contract with Medicare to provide health coverage through managed care or private fee-for-service plans. Medicare Part D provides coverage for prescription drugs.

- Medicare was used as a vehicle to expand civil rights by requiring hospitals receiving Medicare to be integrated in the 1960s, and again in 2010 to give same-sex couples the right to be with a partner who is sick or dying and to enforce patients' advance directives.

- The State Children's Health Insurance Program, now called CHIP, was established in 1997 to increase the number of insured children.

- Cost-containment efforts have resulted in the introduction of managed care to both public and private insurance systems. The incentive for underservice in managed care necessitates attention to protecting patients' right to adequate treatment.

- While falling short of universal health care, the Patient Protection and Affordable Care Act of 2010, as modified by the Health Care and Education Affordability Reconciliation Act (ACA), has resulted in 20 million more people gaining health insurance.

- Despite years of congressional attempt to repeal the ACA, President Trump and congressional Republicans have failed to advance a workable alternative. However, regulatory changes, executive actions, judicial challenges, and states' refusal to expand Medicaid have all reduced the efficacy of the ACA.

- As gaps widen between states that have expanded Medicaid and made other health investments and those that have used Medicaid waivers and other measures to restrict access, health care depends increasingly on one's place of residence. This creates equity challenges that demand social work advocacy, particularly to protect Medicaid and Medicare as entitlements.

- Health care costs will continue to rise. To build an adequate, sustainable health care system, we must identify and implement effective cost-containment strategies.

- One in five people in the United States experience mental illness. These disorders often go untreated, owing to barriers such as a fragmented delivery system, inadequate funding, stigma attached to service utilization, and lack of cultural competence among providers.

- Deinstitutionalization refers to the policy of providing community-based services for people who were formerly served in institutions. The Mental Retardation and Community Mental Health Centers Construction Act and the State Comprehensive Mental Health Services Plan Act were two major pieces of legislation that contributed to deinstitutionalization.

- Lack of adequate funding to build an effective community mental health service system has resulted in the re-institutionalization of many people with mental illness in our correctional system.

- Overuse of psychotropic medications, particularly with children in foster care, has been repeatedly documented. This approach to mental health treatment is not strengths-based, but alternative approaches are often still inaccessible and/or unaffordable.

- In 2008, Congress passed the Paul Wellstone and Pete Domenici Mental Health Parity and Addiction Equity Act, which closed some of the loopholes that had made the 1996 Mental Health Parity Act ineffective. The 2008 Act required parity in co-payments, deductibles, and out-of-pocket expenses. It also required parity in setting treatment limits.

- More than 72,000 Americans died of a drug overdose in 2017. The growing opioid epidemic these fatalities reflect has spurred new federal and state policies and some increased attention to substance use disorder treatment. However, effective and accessible treatment is still lacking in most communities.

- Suicide rates are climbing at a time when many states have underfunded and even undermined their mental health systems. Suicide claims the lives of nearly 47,000 Americans each year.

- Social workers need to be involved in educating people about publicly funded health care programs, ensuring that rules and regulations developed in their states are equitable, helping people get the health benefits for which they are eligible, and ensuring that patients' rights are protected.

- The United States needs to invest more to anticipate and manage pandemics.

- Promotion of health and wellness, rather than a narrow focus on treatment of illness, is central to the strengths perspective and critical to reducing health disparities.

EXERCISES

1. As discussed in this chapter, research indicates that inequities in health care quality and outcomes persist even when access becomes more universal. Identify four possible reasons these inequities persist and suggest policy changes that would promote equity.
2. Consider how the ACA has impacted you. For example, have you stayed on your parents' insurance longer than would have been possible otherwise? How did the legislation affect you if you had a preexisting condition or disability or if you lost your job? How might you use your own story to help others understand the impact of this legislation? What does this suggest for the importance of stories in advancing policy change?
3. Choose a social work agency where you think you might like to work. Find out whether they provide health insurance to entry-level workers. Is it affordable? Are dependents covered? If you have worked previously, how do these health care benefits compare to what you received with previous jobs? What factors do you think account for the differences?
4. Go to the Sanchez family interactive case at www.routledgesw.com.
   a. How would you determine if Joey, the Sanchez family grandchild, would qualify for CHIP in your state?
   b. Which other members of the family do you think might qualify for the major health care programs discussed in this chapter? What barriers might they face in attempting to qualify for coverage?
   c. How might health insurance make a difference in the lives of the Sanchez family? What barriers to securing health care might they encounter even with insurance coverage?
5. Go to the Carla Washburn case at www.routledgesw.com. Mrs. Washburn receives Medicare. How have the changes in Medicare that were included in the ACA likely affected Mrs. Washburn?
   a. What about the proposals for Medicare reform? How would Mrs. Washburn be affected if Medicare was turned into a private voucher program? What might it have meant if the age of Medicare eligibility was raised to 67? Or if Medicare out-of-pocket costs were increased?
   b. What Medicare reform options would be in the best interest of Medicare beneficiaries like Mrs. Washburn?
6. Go to the Riverton case. How would homeless people in Riverton be affected if the state expanded Medicaid? What if it did not? Contact the staff of your local homeless shelter

or, better yet, volunteer there, and find out how homeless people currently get their health care needs met. Ask if the shelter has been active in advocating for Medicaid expansion.
   a. What do you think are some of the barriers to getting homeless people signed up for health care plans?
   b. What are some strategies for overcoming these barriers?
   c. Some researchers have reported that as many as 80 percent of people who are homeless have a serious mental illness and/or substance use disorder. What policies related to screening, outreach, and treatment do you think organizations would need to implement to get effective treatment for homeless people with these conditions?
7. What types of mental health services will a community like Hudson City need following a disaster?
   a. How could having a strong mental health system in place prior to a disaster position a community to recover more quickly?
   b. Climate change is increasing the frequency and intensity of natural disasters; this, in turn, results in greater economic, social, and health consequences for affected communities. What types of policies could increase Hudson City's capacity to protect residents from natural disasters? How might framing disasters as a threat to community health influence the resources—political and financial—invested in this mitigation?
8. Increasingly, providers are developing online mental health treatment alternatives, such as the one illustrated in the RAINN case. What questions do you think insurers and regulators should consider before funds are made available for online treatment? How can innovations in treatment modalities improve outcomes? How might they help to contain costs? What considerations regarding access to treatment, especially for vulnerable populations, should such service shifts emphasize?
9. The legacy of oppression has produced conditions that have led to health outcomes that are poorer for Native Americans than for other populations. Identify at least three policy changes at the federal, state, or local levels that could result in improved health outcomes for Native American communities.
10. How accessible is treatment for substance use disorders in your state?
    a. How is treatment financed? Is there equitable access for people with low incomes? Are there long waiting lists? Is treatment available in rural parts of your state? Are only certain treatment modalities available?
    b. Are some groups, such as pregnant women, prioritized for treatment? Are people in these groups vulnerable to law enforcement consequences if they seek help? Have interventions been tailored to the special needs of different groups, such as older adults, teens, and members of particular racial/ethnic groups? Have there been changes in recent years, particularly in response to the opioid epidemic?
    c. What state policy changes do you think would be necessary to improve treatment for substance use disorders in your state? What groups are advocating for policy changes to improve treatment for people with substance use disorders?
11. Review the downloadable case about Willow's transition. What protections would Willow have in your state to ensure that her transition-related health care can be paid for with

insurance? Would it be different if she had private coverage, CHIP, or Medicaid? Also, what resources can you find in your community for health care for Willow? Are there ample providers with expertise with transgender adolescents? What efforts are underway to improve the capacity of the health care system to meet these youths' needs?

12. You remember from earlier chapters that framing and messaging are important parts of the claims-making process. Consider one of the issues you care about through the lens of social determinants of health. Looking at media coverage of the topic, is it framed as a health issue? For example, is there coverage discussing child maltreatment as a threat to public health? Or lack of public transportation? If so, who is making these claims, and how effective are they? If not, why do you think that is, and what difference do you think it could make?

CHAPTER 11

Policies and Programs for Older Adults

Age is opportunity, no less than youth itself.

Henry Wadsworth Longfellow

IN THE MEDIA, IN PUBLIC POLICY DEBATES, and perhaps in our own conversations, we encounter messages about the roles older adults play in society. Many of these messages depict older people as dependent, idle, or entitled. Hopefully, you know a variety of older adults and have witnessed first-hand how they have contributed and continue to contribute to your own life and to their communities, so you can counter such negative stereotypes. If not, consider ways to increase the age diversity of your social circle. Engagement with people at different ages can help you become more familiar with experiences at all stages of life. Such encounters can also provide opportunities to reflect on your own aging self. Social workers who see older people as integral parts of our society, rather than a distant "other," are committed to advocating for policies that build on older adults' capacities. As is true in other populations, strengths-based social policy development begins with listening to the voices of diverse groups and understanding their goals and needs.

This chapter will help you understand the opportunities and challenges older adults face and their implications for people of all ages. Social workers understand interdependence and what it means for how policies aimed at one group—children, young adults, or older adults— shape the experiences of other groups. For example, health care, education, and employment policies that have shaped your life thus far will have great influence on the outcomes you experience in later life, while, in fundamental ways, the well-being of the entire society is connected to how well our policy structures support older adults.

Do you think "old age" begins at age 50, when people often receive an invitation to membership in AARP? Or at 60 when people become eligible for services through the **Older Americans Act (OAA)**? Or at 65, the age at which most people become eligible for Medicare, or at 67, when most young people today can expect to become eligible for full Social Security retirement benefits? Take time to consider at what age you will start thinking of yourself as "old" and the forces that have influenced these beliefs. In a Pew Research Center study, Americans aged 18 to 29 reported that they believed that the average person becomes "old" when they turn 60.

Middle-aged respondents said that old age begins closer to 70, and people age 65 and older responded that the average person becomes "old" at 74 (Pew Research Center, 2009).

For many people, beliefs about when they will feel "old" are influenced at least in part by assumptions about life expectancy. The assumption that aging means decline and poor health can be a deadly self-fulfilling prophecy, but many people today can expect to live to a healthy old age, particularly when community supports and investments facilitate those outcomes. Consider what sorts of policies you want in place as you age into your 80s and beyond. How long do you expect to live? While factors such as income, occupation, geography, and race drive disparities in life expectancy, men who are now 25 can expect, on average, to live to be 82; 25-year-old women can expect to live to be 86 (Social Security Administration [SSA], 2019c). Fully half of children born in developed countries today will live to age 100 (Gratton & Scott, 2016). Depending on the definition of "old" being used, then, people may be categorized as old for over a third or even over half of their lives. Crucially, just as a child aged four has different strengths and needs than a child aged 15, even though policies often consider both part of the same "child" population, an age category that can include people from 50 to 119 contains adults with extremely diverse needs and capacities. Exhibit 11.1 gives a glimpse into this diversity.

In addition to differences by age, older adults are diverse in terms of gender, race, ethnicity, and other dimensions that influence their outcomes. As illustrated in Exhibit 11.2, a person's likelihood of living to a certain age differs according to race and ethnicity as well as gender. In some cases, these differences stem from social determinants across the lifespan, including those that shape income and poverty status. Other differences appear paradoxical and, then, may

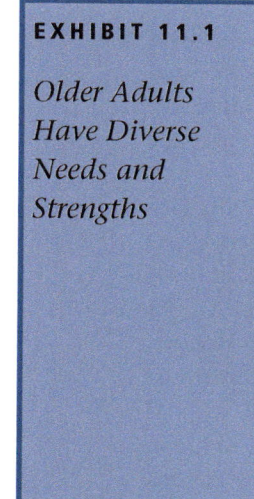

EXHIBIT 11.1

Older Adults Have Diverse Needs and Strengths

Source: Shutterstock

EXHIBIT 11.2

Life Expectancy at Birth, by Gender and Race

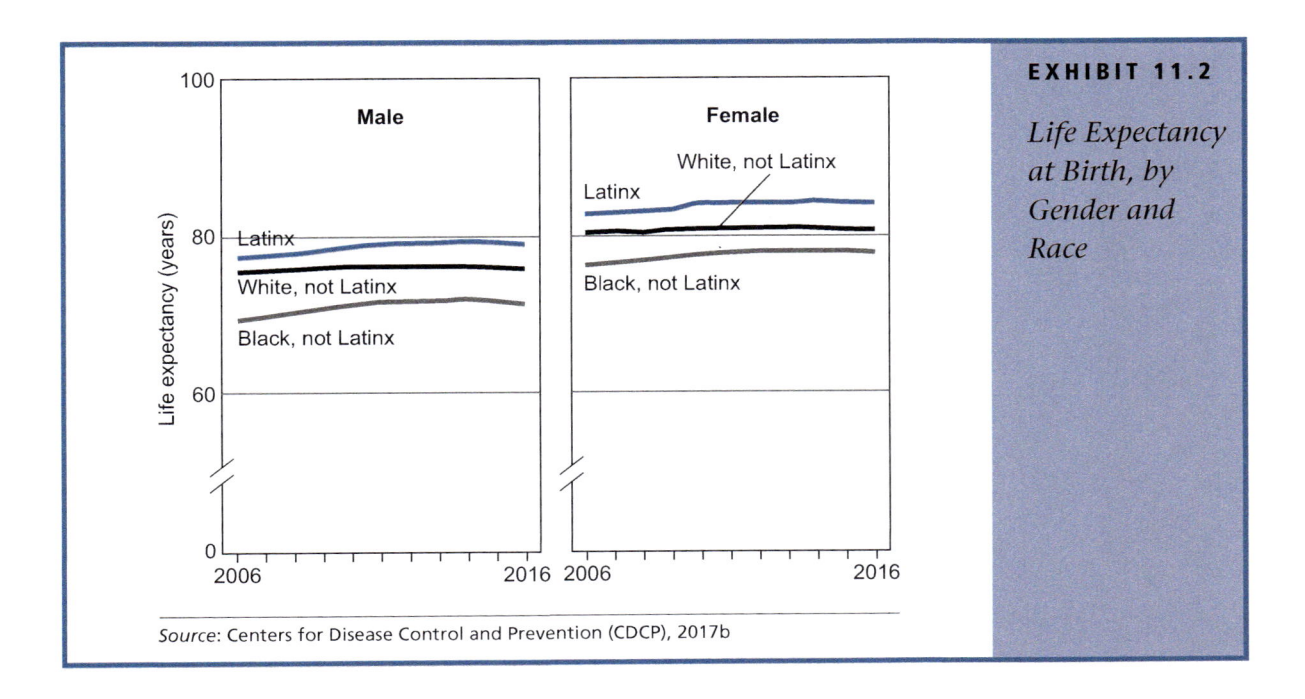

[Chart showing life expectancy (years) from 2006 to 2016 for Male and Female, with lines for Latinx, White not Latinx, and Black not Latinx]

Source: Centers for Disease Control and Prevention (CDCP), 2017b

point to ways to counter the effects of disadvantages on older adults' outcomes. For example, researchers hypothesize that Latinx individuals' health habits and strong social networks help explain their longer life expectancies, despite greater incidence of poverty (Scommegna, 2013). This is an example of how incorporating diverse populations' strengths into policy analysis and development may reveal promising avenues for intervention.

Policies responding to older adults should be flexible and robust enough to meet the needs of this diverse population. Indeed, we need policies that not only provide for *current* needs but also build on strengths and lay a strong foundation for the future. Attaining the age of 65, 75, and increasingly even 100 is a testament to the strengths of older adults. On the societal level, these gains are also policy successes to be celebrated. While the dramatic gains in life expectancy at birth within the past century, depicted in Exhibit 11.3, vary by race and gender, these trends demonstrate the positive effects of social policies, particularly in sanitation, workplace safety, child labor, and preventative health. The resulting dramatic drop in childhood death rates is a major driver of increased life expectancy at birth. Further, for those who survive child and young adult death risks, life expectancy is even higher than at birth. The rewards of survival should not be poverty, loneliness, premature institutionalization, or societal resentment. Rather, to understand the issues associated with aging from the strengths perspective, we need to focus not only on its challenges, but also on the goals people have for their later lives and the resources individuals need to age well. Further, because older adults have a lifetime of experience, a solution-focused approach that asks service users to propose workable strategies is particularly applicable with older adults.

Kahana and Kahana (1996), prominent scholars in the aging field, define **aging well** as a comprehensive and holistic process in which older adults continuously adapt themselves

EXHIBIT 11.3

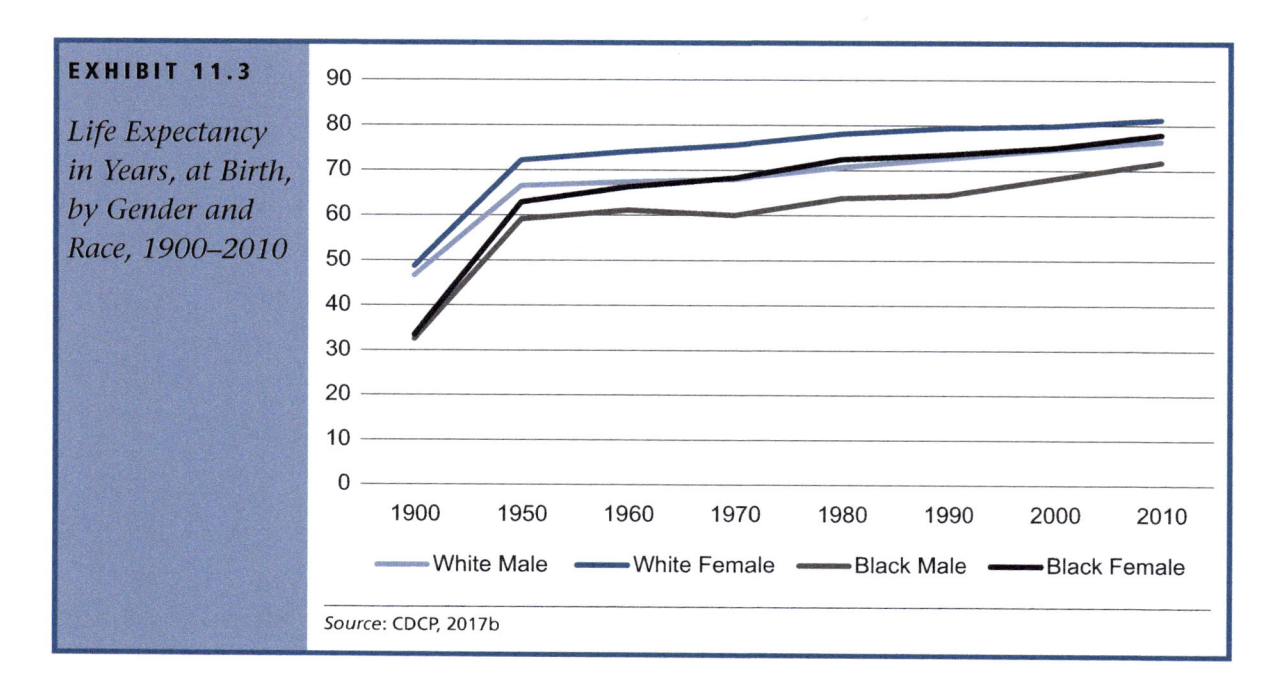

Life Expectancy in Years, at Birth, by Gender and Race, 1900–2010

— White Male — White Female — Black Male — Black Female

Source: CDCP, 2017b

and their environment to respond to the challenges of aging. According to this framework, aging well is possible when we (1) minimize the negative effects of losses often associated with aging—in areas such as employment and physical health—and (2) maximize the benefits that accompany a long life, such as the wisdom that comes from years of surmounting obstacles. The ecological perspective, which recognizes the influence of relationships and transactions among the older adult, other people, and the environment, supports definitions of aging well that emphasize social integration and engagement.

Focusing on what older adults want to do can enable them to use the diversity of resources they possess to create and pursue their own visions of aging well. In turn, these older adults' journeys can positively influence their communities. For example, an older adult may have the time to work part-time for the city parks and recreation department, tending flowers in a park or coaching children's sports teams. Additionally, if laws prohibiting age discrimination are enforced, older adults can take part in meaningful, productive activities far into advanced age. Carefully crafted social policies can help older adults overcome barriers in the environment that limit their autonomy. Resources such as adequate public transportation can facilitate paid work and other activities older adults find meaningful, like spending time with friends and family. The older adult depicted in Exhibit 11.4 is enjoying the interdependence of generations and her ability to make positive contributions to the life of a child. With necessary supports, such positive outcomes are possible for all older people. This chapter provides an overview of key policy issues that directly affect older adults and explores policy strategies that promote economic security, health, and social engagement, toward the goal of "aging well."

Before 1870, most U.S. workers were employed on farms and most people worked as long as they possibly could, before then relying primarily on their families to support them. However,

EXHIBIT 11.4

Generations Intertwined

Credit: Rosemary Chapin

in the late nineteenth and early twentieth centuries, industrialization spread rapidly, and families became much more mobile. Traditional supports for older people were disappearing as longevity was increasing, but social programs to fill these gaps were slow to develop. Although private charities, community organizations, and local governments did provide some relief for destitute and disabled older adults, there were few public social programs for older adults prior to the 1930s.

POLICY AND PROGRAM RESPONSES

In response to changing demographics and economic and social contexts, public and private institutions developed policies and programs to help older adults meet their needs—particularly in the areas of income support, health, and social engagement. While these policies have changed considerably over time, tracing some of this history can help social workers understand the origins and rationales for some of the approaches they encounter in their practice with older adults still today.

Economic Security in Later Life

While many older adults today are in the labor force, older Americans' economic security depends in large part on the availability and adequacy of income supports that provide sufficient resources to meet their financial needs as they transition from full-time work. For most older adults, the most important of these income supports are private or public retirement programs, such as pensions and employer-based investment accounts, for which older adults accrue eligibility based on their employment history, and public retirement programs, particularly Social Security.

Private Retirement Programs In 1875, the American Express Company established the first private pension plan in the United States. Within a short time, some banking, utility, railroad, and manufacturing companies also started offering pensions to their employees (Pension Benefit Guaranty Corporation [PBGC], 2009). Most of these early pension plans provided **defined benefit plans** that paid a specific amount every month if the retired person had worked the required number of years. These early plans were funded entirely by employers (PBGC, 2009). However, only a fraction of U.S. employees (mostly non-Latinx White men) worked in jobs covered by such plans. Scholars and advocates trace the roots of today's racial wealth gap—where White households have net worth nearly $240,000 greater than that of Black households—to inequities in wealth-building systems such as these (Traub et al., 2016).

Public Retirement Programs By the early 1900s, many states and municipalities had established retirement programs for their employees. In addition, by that time many European countries had developed publicly supported retirement systems. For example, in 1899, Chancellor Otto von Bismarck established a state retirement system in Germany that provided benefits for retired workers aged 65 and older.

During the first half of the twentieth century, the ideas that people should leave the workforce at a certain age and that public benefits should subsidize their retirement gained wider support. Industrialization, advances in medicine, and the problem of surplus labor during economic downturns contributed to political support for retirement policy. In the United States, the Great Depression was a particularly hard time, as many elders lost their homes, farms, and life savings. Jobs were in short supply, which increased public support for policies to push older adults out of the workforce. Often, children moved away to pursue opportunities and therefore could not be counted on to support their parents. Given these conditions, social movements gained momentum, exerting strong political pressure on the federal government to enact old-age insurance (Axinn & Stern, 2001). Like the Townsend Movement discussed in Chapter 3, the **Ham and Eggs Movement**, catalyzed in the 1930s, pressed for weekly pensions for unemployed Californians age 50 and older. The movement's rallying cry was "$30 every Thursday," reflecting a commitment to providing subsistence-level support to older adults who were no longer in the workforce (SSA, 2007). Although some of the policies this group championed were based on dubious economics, this was the first time in U.S. history that elders organized as a voting bloc to support legislation. Lending credence to the idea of "policy windows" (Kingdon, 2003), it was the confluence of ideology, economic cycles, and social mobilization that made possible the enactment of watershed legislation such as the Social Security Act of 1935, which established a federal public retirement system now known as Old-Age, Survivors, and Disability Insurance (OASDI).

Changes to Job-Specific Pension Programs The number of people with job-specific pensions increased markedly among private sector workers between 1950 and 1980. The 1974 **Employee**

Retirement Income Security Act (ERISA) created the Pension Benefit Guaranty Corporation and was the first comprehensive effort to regulate private pensions. ERISA covers health as well as pension benefits in qualified plans. We examine ERISA in more detail later in this chapter.

In the 1980s, the trend toward more private employers offering job-specific pensions reversed itself. Many companies eliminated or cut their pension programs and/or switched from defined benefit pensions to defined contribution plans (Munnell, Aubry, & Muldoon, 2008). A **defined contribution plan** is one in which employers contribute a certain amount to a retirement account that the employee then invests in company-approved investment options. Unlike defined benefit plans, defined contribution plans do not guarantee a specific amount of retirement income. Because participation in defined contribution plans is usually voluntary and often requires employee contributions before employers will contribute, employees are also less likely to participate in these plans than in the mandatory defined benefit plans they replace. In 2016, only 56 percent of households had any employer-sponsored retirement account through a current or previous workplace (St. Louis Federal Reserve Bank, 2018). Asset accumulation is sparse, even among those who are saving. The median household has only $1,100 in their retirement account, while those earning less than median income have no or negligible retirement assets. Even relatively high-earning households at the 70th percentile hold only about $40,000 in retirement accounts (St. Louis Federal Reserve Bank, 2018). Clearly, these assets are unlikely to be adequate to sustain people for extended periods if they stop working. This realization is likely motivating the two-thirds of workers who report expecting to continue to work after they turn 65 (Pew Research Center, 2018a). Many workers today anticipate working as long as they are able, even if they do not actually desire to stay in the labor force that long.

The financing of retirement is not only largely inadequate, it is also highly inequitable. While many Americans are concluding that they cannot afford to stop working in later life or to pursue interests and goals that require some level of financial security, the most advantaged households earning at the 95th percentile hold more than $612,000 in retirement accounts (St. Louis Federal Reserve Bank, 2018). Additionally, retirement saving seems to compound; while only 20 percent of those without employer-sponsored retirement accounts are saving for retirement through other vehicles, such as an Individual Retirement Account (IRA), almost 40 percent of households with employer-sponsored retirement plans also have assets in independent vehicles. These privileged workers are the "winners" in today's risk-shifted landscape, while the 35 percent of U.S. households who do not participate in any retirement savings plan are left out of the wealth building on which their futures largely depend.

As Exhibit 11.5 illustrates, in 2018, more than half of private-sector workers had access only to a defined contribution retirement plan through their employer. Further, only 77 percent of all full-time workers in the private sector had access to *any* employment-based retirement plan, meaning that these workers' incomes in retirement are likely to depend largely—if not entirely—on Social Security benefits. Even when people have employer-provided retirement plans and participate in them, they may be inadequate sources of economic security. Compared to those with defined benefit plans, employees in defined contribution plans are more vulnerable to fluctuations in the market that may diminish their assets. Fewer than half of the people who have job-specific pensions have worked enough years to be fully vested in their plans and hence entitled to their pensions, and few private pensions provide an income

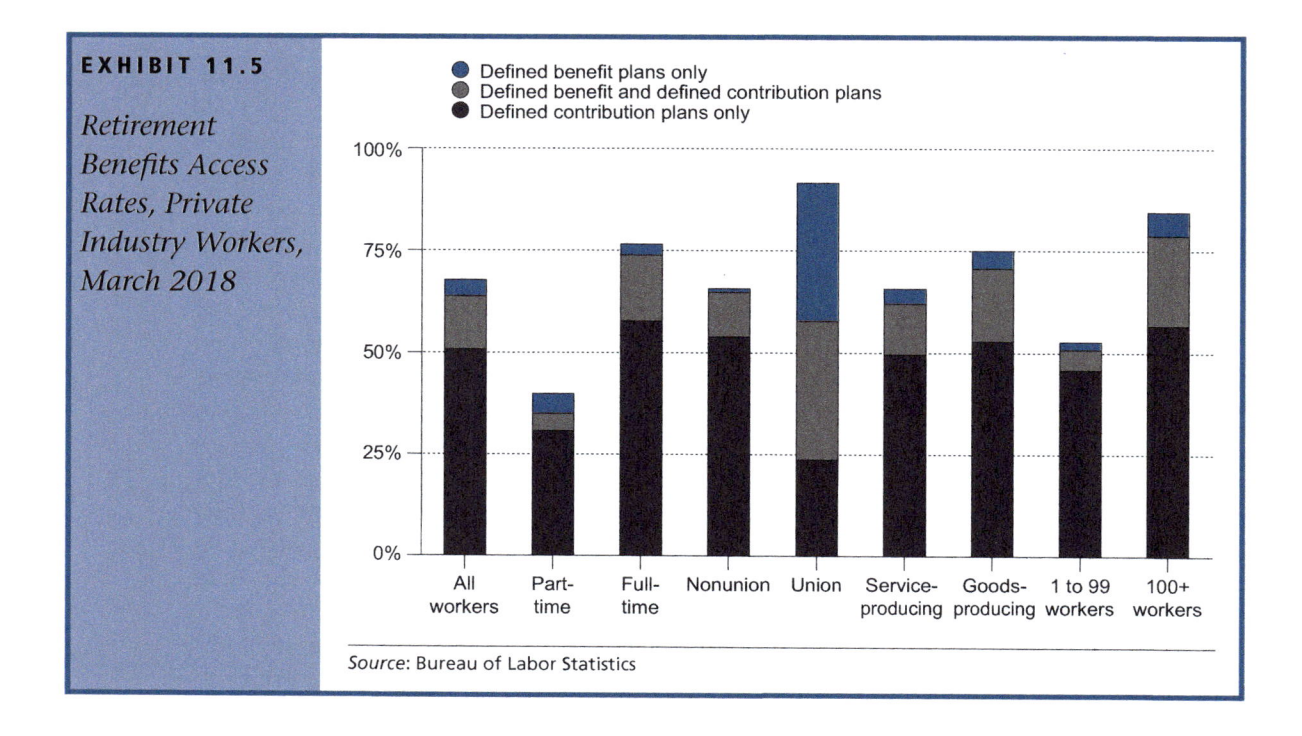

EXHIBIT 11.5

Retirement Benefits Access Rates, Private Industry Workers, March 2018

- Defined benefit plans only
- Defined benefit and defined contribution plans
- Defined contribution plans only

Source: Bureau of Labor Statistics

replacement rate adequate for retirement. Finally, most job-specific pension plans do not provide cost-of-living increases. Collectively, the differences between defined benefit and defined contribution retirement plans suggest that the latter are inferior tools in pursuit of financially sound retirement policy.

Pensions at Risk In addition to the potential of asset loss due to fluctuations in investment value, pensions are often underfunded by employers. This increases the risk that money will not be there for workers when they retire. In 2018, pensions were underfunded even among the largest corporations, with assets sufficient to meet just 84 percent of expected liabilities (Miller, 2019). To close this gap, employers often take steps that further shift risk to employees. For example, some offer lump-sum payments to vested workers rather than the promised monthly benefit, while others transfer assets to an annuity, which removes protection by the Pension Benefit Guaranty Corporation (Miller, 2019). Accelerating the trend toward defined contribution plans, companies with underfunded pensions are closing their plans to new participants and shifting benefits to defined contribution approaches. Even in the public sector where more defined benefit plans are still in place, some plans are dangerously underfunded. In 2016, public pensions in at least ten states were less than 60 percent funded—a far direr accounting than Social Security's finances (Pew Charitable Trusts, 2018). Only four states' systems were 90 percent or more funded (Pew Charitable Trusts, 2018). Teachers in public schools, first responders, and social workers in public departments are counting on these now-troubled plans to support them in retirement.

During the first decade of the twenty-first century, President George W. Bush attempted to retool Social Security so that it would resemble a defined contribution plan. Bush proposed that a portion of workers' Federal Insurance Contributions Act (FICA) taxes be diverted into private accounts, which workers could then invest, with the potential for market gains and losses. These proposals to at least partially privatize Social Security promoted yet more risk-shifting, here from the federal government to individuals. Although Bush's initiatives to privatize Social Security faltered, these ideas continue to be part of the discussion about Social Security reform.

While perhaps most urgent for those approaching retirement age, retirement security is not only an issue of concern to older adults. Younger workers also face substantial risks and experience considerable anxiety as they contemplate retirement. The Federal Reserve Board (2018) found that confidence about income prospects in retirement was greatest for the oldest cohorts, while Generation X and, especially, young Millennials, are the most concerned about their retirement futures. And, with income in retirement increasingly depending on households' own financial preparations, younger Americans have reason to be worried. These generations will live longer than previous cohorts but have fewer institutional supports to secure their financial futures (Gale, 2019). In 2014, median net worth for those ages 35 to 44 was $21,870; for those ages 45 to 54, it was $33,940 (U.S. Census Bureau, 2018f). Sixty-six percent of Millennials have nothing saved for retirement (Brown, 2018). Changes in the labor market mean that younger workers will likely work for many different companies and in contingent and informal arrangements—trends that may keep them from accruing any employer-provided retirement benefits.

Additionally, squeezed by high student debt and stagnant wages, many young workers have insufficient personal savings to cover short-term needs. Surveys of Millennials have found that as many as 60 percent could not cover a $1,000 emergency from their own savings. As a result, workers with retirement plans may have to make premature withdrawals from those accounts, further jeopardizing their financial futures. Importantly, however, if they have sufficient work history, these young people will receive some retirement income from Social Security. Indeed, while polls find Millennials and other younger workers worried that Social Security will not be there for them when they retire, OASDI's social insurance is a far more certain pillar of income support than defined contribution or individual retirement accounts. However, Social Security was designed not to be individuals' only support in retirement, but rather as one source of income that, when combined with others—principally employer pensions and personal savings—would provide adequate income in later life. With inadequate resources to supplement Social Security, large proportions of Americans will be unable to maintain their current standard of living in retirement (Commission on Retirement Security and Personal Savings, 2016).

Supplemental Security Income for Older Adults   In 1974, Congress again amended the Social Security Act to create the Supplemental Security Income (SSI) program. Unlike OASDI, SSI is not public insurance, and benefits do not depend on work history or marital status. Instead, as a means-tested public benefit, people must be extremely poor and possess very few assets to qualify for SSI. Over 2.2 million older adults receive SSI; the average monthly benefit is $446 (SSA, 2018e).

In November 2018, 1,272,000 older adults received benefits through both OASDI and SSI. This means that their benefit from OASDI was so low that they were still in poverty. Additionally, approximately 995,000 older adults received only SSI, meaning that neither they nor their spouse worked enough years in a job where they contributed to OASDI (SSA, 2018e). Women make up the majority of beneficiaries for old-age assistance under SSI, largely because of inequities they experience within OASDI, employer-provided retirement plans, and the overall labor market. SSI receipt increases with age, as older adults exhaust their assets. Based on the Supplemental Poverty Measure, almost 19 percent of adults age 80 and older, compared to 12.3 percent of those 65 to 69 years old, live in poverty (Cubanski et al., 2018). Further, while many low-income older adults receive SSI, the SSI benefit is so low that many who receive it are still in poverty. The Social Security Administration administers SSI, which is funded through general tax revenues, not through the payroll and self-employment taxes that finance Social Security.

Policies to Provide Health Care and Support Social Engagement

Many of the other major public programs that aid older adults were not established until 30 years after the 1935 Social Security Act. With the passage of Medicare, Medicaid, and the OAA, 1965 was a banner year for legislation for older people. As discussed in the previous chapter, Medicare is a health insurance program for older adults and people with disabilities, and Medicaid is a means-tested health insurance program for people who have low incomes. Medicare provides eligible older adults with coverage for inpatient hospital care. Older adults may pay an additional premium to purchase optional Medicare coverage for outpatient and doctors' services and may also opt into coverage for prescription drugs. Medicaid is the primary payment source for nursing facility care. Because access to health care is an essential component of aging well, social workers must be familiar with the resources Medicaid and Medicare provide, gaps that may persist, and how elders can navigate these programs to secure the health care they need.

In 1965 Congress also passed the OAA. The law was designed to improve the coordination of planning and programs for older adults and to support elders' efforts to remain in the community, even when they need long-term care. Although the OAA has never been adequately funded, it has facilitated the development of vital local programs to support older adults' well-being. With the passage of OASDI, Medicare, Medicaid, and the OAA, the United States established policies in the crucial arenas of older adults' economic security, health care, and social engagement.

The National Institute on Aging In 1974, the National Institute on Aging (NIA) was established to conduct research and provide training related to the aging process and the needs of an aging population. The NIA funds scientific research, technological development, and other innovation designed to improve quality of life for older adults. For example, the NIA has primary responsibility for research involving Alzheimer's disease. If a cure or even more effective treatment for this devastating disease could be found, health care savings—as well as improvement in the lives of older adults and their caregivers—would be profound. You can learn more about the NIA's current and past research initiatives on their website at **www.nia.nih.gov**.

Mental Health Services The 1975 amendments to the Community Mental Health Act, in combination with Medicare and Medicaid, made it possible for a greater number of older adults to receive mental health services (Tice & Perkins, 1996). In addition, funds provided by the OAA and services made available through some senior centers and community mental health centers helped increase availability of mental health care for older adults. However, older adults are still particularly underserved. Inadequate access continues for several reasons, including those specific to older adults as well as barriers that plague access to mental health care for Americans of all ages. These barriers include:

- inadequate training of mental health providers to meet the specific needs of older adults;
- reluctance on the part of many community mental health centers to perform outreach to older adults;
- lack of parity in mental health reimbursement, which can make mental health care unaffordable;
- misinformation about the efficacy of mental health treatment for older adults' needs; and
- elders' own stigma about receiving mental health services.

Suicide rates among older adults, particularly older men, are a serious concern. The most tragic consequence of mental health crises, suicide is an urgent mental health priority. Additionally, unmet mental health needs are system-wide concerns in aging policy. Older adults who have untreated or inadequately treated mental illness are more likely to need more costly levels of care. Treatment of mental health concerns in older adults can be very effective, but substantial changes are needed in how mental health professionals and the systems in which they work respond to older adults.

Long-Term Care While many older adults will never need formal **long-term care (LTC)**, all are at risk of requiring it. Although a chronic physical or mental disability that necessitates LTC may occur at any age, the older we become, the more likely it is that such a disability will develop or worsen. An anticipated 52 percent of today's 65-year-olds will develop a disability that requires LTC services (Favreault & Dey, 2015). Because they live longer, women are more likely to need LTC—and for longer periods—than men. On average, however, only 14 percent of today's older adults are expected to need LTC for five years or more (Favreault & Dey, 2015). LTC includes many types of medical and social services for people with disabilities or chronic illness. In addition to institutional care, LTC also includes home care services and unpaid help from informal caregivers (Fox-Grage et al., 2001). One component of LTC, **home- and community-based services**, typically are defined as services and supports that assist individuals to continue to live within their communities. Personal care, assistance with chores, nutritional programs, night support, and transportation are examples of home- and community-based services (Kane, Kane, & Ladd, 1998).

Before the 1980s, the primary option for formal LTC services was nursing facility care—formerly, the only LTC covered by Medicaid. However, in 1981, the Medicaid Home- and Community-Based Services (HCBS) waiver program was established as part of the Social Security Act. The HCBS waiver program gives states the authority to waive certain Medicaid regulations and to offer additional services not otherwise available through their Medicaid programs. The Medicaid HCBS waiver recognizes that many people at risk of being institutionalized can be served in their communities at a cost that is no higher and may even be lower than that of institutional care. Since many older adults admitted to long-term facilities as private-pay residents will eventually become eligible for Medicaid, diverting people who could be served in their homes saves public resources.

HCBS spending has grown more rapidly than institutional expenditures for the past three decades, such that, in fiscal year (FY) 2016, HCBS accounted for 57 percent of Medicaid LTC spending (Musumeci, Chidambaram, & O'Malley Watts, 2019). However, compared to younger people with disabilities, HCBS is less often an LTC option for older adults. Additionally, as is increasingly true in Medicaid, there are tremendous variations in HCBS among states. In Mississippi, 27 percent of Medicaid LTC spending goes to HCBS; in Oregon, the figure is 81 percent (Eiken et al., 2018).

Despite the appeal of home- and community-based services and their potential for improved outcomes at lower cost, nursing facilities remain a mainstay of the LTC system, especially for older adults. Social workers who are employed in nursing facilities witness the challenges these institutions face and the critical role they play. The Nursing Home Reform Act, which was part of the Omnibus Budget Reconciliation Act of 1987, provided for reforms including in staff training, survey and certification procedures, pre-admission screening, and annual reviews for people with mental illness. It also mandated that nursing facility residents have access to ombudspersons when they require protection and/or advocacy. Quality of nursing facilities is extremely uneven. The first comprehensive revisions to nursing home regulations in decades were issued in 2016, with implementation of some components still being contested. Efforts to reform nursing home care continue, but the Trump Administration's scrutiny of Obama-era regulatory changes may weaken even the current protections for nursing home residents, widely regarded as inadequate.

Finally, any discussion of LTC policy would be incomplete without careful attention to the role of family caregivers in providing informal (unpaid) LTC services. Most older adults in need of LTC depend completely on family members and friends. Further, most people who receive formal LTC services continue to receive informal assistance from their social networks. In 2015, almost 40 million Americans were caring for an adult; about half the time, this is care provided to an elderly parent or parent-in-law (National Alliance for Caregiving [NAC] & AARP, 2015). Most caregivers are female, reflecting both the fact that women more frequently care for an elderly spouse and that caregiving falls disproportionately on women of any age. The median age of a family caregiver was 49, but 10 percent of caregivers are themselves older than 75 (NAC & AARP, 2015). Although informal caregivers will continue to be the major source of care for older adults, few family members are able to provide adequate support. These gaps can result in poorer health outcomes for older adults with disabilities or chronic health conditions. Further, when older adults must supplement informal care with purchased services, those who do not have the resources to pay for care suffer. These gaps can also result in greater demand for publicly funded services. Crucially, this provision of informal care often comes at considerable cost to the caregiver as well. The current economic cost, in foregone earnings, of unpaid family caregiving to older adults is about $67 billion; by 2050, this figure is expected to double, to at least $132 billion (Mudrazija, 2019). Clearly, this is an area where families and older adults themselves still need additional supports.

Prescription Drug Policy   Although recent changes closed the "donut hole" and made the 2003 Medicare Prescription Drug Improvement and Modernization Act easier to navigate, older adults and their families may still have difficulty understanding the costs and benefits of insurance plans. However, State Health Insurance Assistance Programs (SHIPs) can help older adults and social workers understand publicly funded health care programs. SHIP is a national program created as part of the Omnibus Budget Reconciliation Act of 1990. The Act authorized grants to states to provide Medicare recipients and their families with free counseling and assistance on a wide range of Medicare and Medicaid matters. This program relies heavily on trained volunteers. To find out where older adults in your state can access these services, visit the SHIP National Network at **www.shiptacenter.org**.

Shortage of Gerontologically Trained Professionals   A variety of federal, state, and foundation initiatives have been implemented to help close the gap between the needs of the aging Baby Boomer generation and the current supply of physicians, nurses, social workers, and other professionals who have gerontological expertise. However, there is still a critical need to increase incentives for students interested in practice with older adults, particularly in rural areas. Social workers equipped for strengths-based practice in aging communities will be positioned to make positive contributions to older adult populations and the overall field, while also advancing their own career prospects.

DEMOGRAPHICS AND FUTURE POLICY IMPERATIVES

In 2016, there were almost 50 million adults age 65 or older in the United States, and they made up about 15 percent of the population (U.S. Census Bureau, 2018g). That number is expected to reach 94.7 million, or 23.5 percent of the population, by 2060 (U.S. Census Bureau, 2018g). Already in 2018, an estimated 16 percent of the population was 65 or older, and trends are moving in the direction of population aging (U.S. Census Bureau, 2019a). More than 80 percent of U.S. counties had older median ages than in 2010, reflecting more rapid growth in older adult than child populations (U.S. Census Bureau, 2019a). In the future, although the number of children will not decline, the ratio of children to older adults will decrease markedly, with older adults expected to outnumber children for the first time in 2035. Additionally, the representation of the oldest older adults will increase; globally, the population of people older than 100 is expected to exceed 3.7 million in 2050, compared to only 95,000 in 1990 (Stepler, 2016a). As the individuals who comprise the older adult population change, so too will this population's expectations and needs. Demographics such as these have a powerful effect on public policy demands, including the size of the workforce, the need for health and social services, and societal attitudes. For example, although proportionately more families are caring for older adults than ever before and will undoubtedly continue to do so, in future generations there will be proportionately fewer adult children to provide informal care for more older relatives. Thus, we can expect that the need for formal care will increase.

Advances in medicine, technology, and public health policy have contributed to increased adult life expectancy. As shown in Exhibit 11.6, men who survive to age 65 can expect to live an average of 19.2 more years (to 84.2), approximately six years longer than in 1950. Women who survive to 65 will live on average about 21.6 years (to 87), about 6.6 years longer than in 1950 (Commission on Retirement Security and Personal Savings, 2016). On average, the life expectancy of people who survive to age 85 is 93 years for women and 91.2 years for men. However, while a 25 percent decline in African-American mortality between 1999 and 2015 has helped to shrink the racial gap in life expectancy, disparities persist (CDCP, 2017d), as do racial disparities in years of healthy functioning. Specifically, increases in longevity have been accompanied by postponed disability for Whites more than for Black older adults. Today, Black older women are especially disadvantaged in terms of the proportion of years expected to be lived without disability (Freedman & Spillman, 2016).

Despite significant historical gains, life expectancy at age 65 in the United States is lower than that of many other industrialized nations. For example, in 2013, women aged 65 in France could expect to live on average 23.6 more years; in Japan they could expect to live 24 more years (Organisation for Economic Co-operation and Development [OECD], 2016). Nonetheless, the number of people in the United States who are 85 and over is growing rapidly. Many older adults 85+ have no disabilities, while others have various functional limitations. There is great diversity even among the very old.

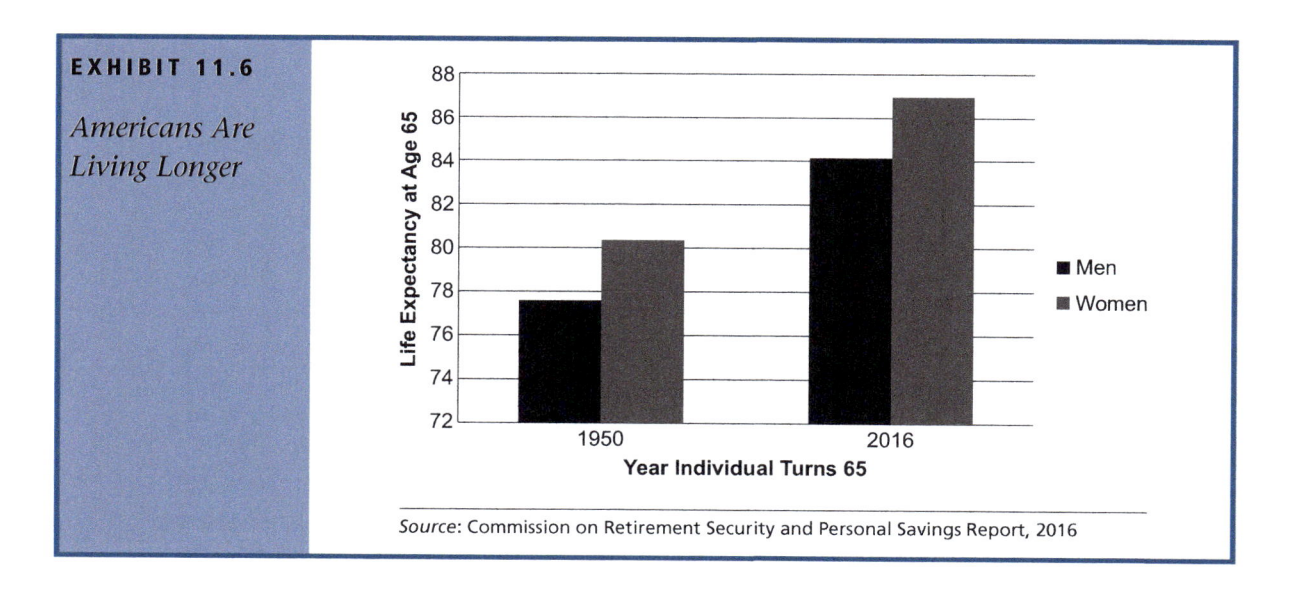

EXHIBIT 11.6

Americans Are Living Longer

Source: Commission on Retirement Security and Personal Savings Report, 2016

EXHIBIT 11.7

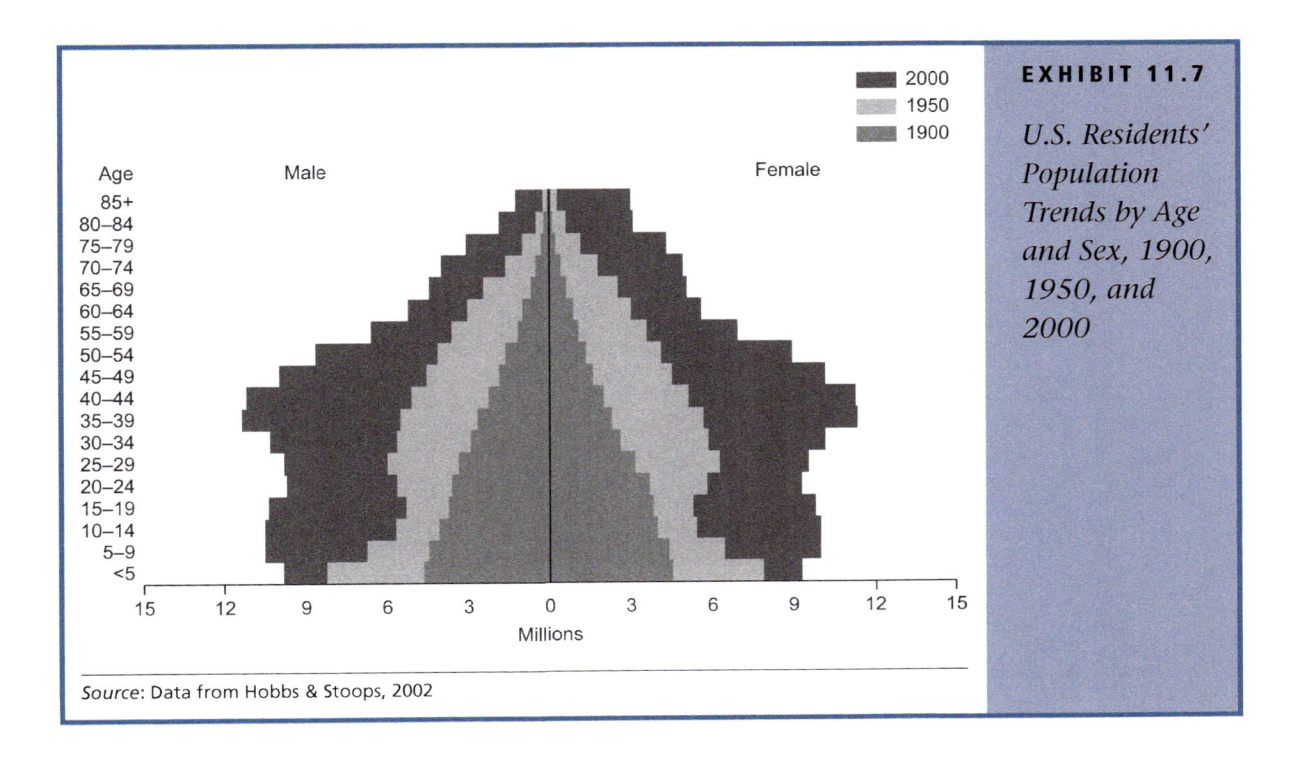

U.S. Residents' Population Trends by Age and Sex, 1900, 1950, and 2000

Source: Data from Hobbs & Stoops, 2002

Exhibit 11.7 shows how U.S. demographics changed between 1900 and 2000. Note that the population in 1900 resembles a pyramid, with many children and comparatively fewer adults. In 1950, the Baby Boom was just beginning, so the under-five age group was markedly larger than the cohort of children born in the 1930s and early 1940s. By 2000, people born during the Baby Boom were in their middle years. The oldest were in their 50s, and the youngest were in their 30s. You can see there is a bulge in the population in those age groups.

Now look at Exhibit 11.8. In this chart, the U.S. population distribution is changing shape. Although children continue to be born and young immigrants continue to arrive, more people are living to older adulthood. The population age 65 and over is increasing—especially among the oldest in that cohort. And, as projected and depicted, given improvements in health care and technology that translate into reduced mortality, the large generations following the Baby Boomers can expect to live even longer. The 85+ population is projected to increase from 6.2 million in 2014 to 14.6 million in 2040 (Administration on Aging, 2015) and to more than 18.2 million by 2060.

These charts also indicate that women outnumber men in the older adult population. This disparity becomes even more pronounced after age 85, with women making up 71 percent of the population. When you consider those aged 100 and over, 85 percent are women. This is an area where demographics are outpacing research and practice. Although many more people are now living to be 85 and older, little analysis has yet been focused on understanding how

EXHIBIT 11.8

U.S. Population by Age and Sex, 2012 and 2060

2012 Population = 314 million
2060 Population = 420 million

Source: U.S. Census Bureau

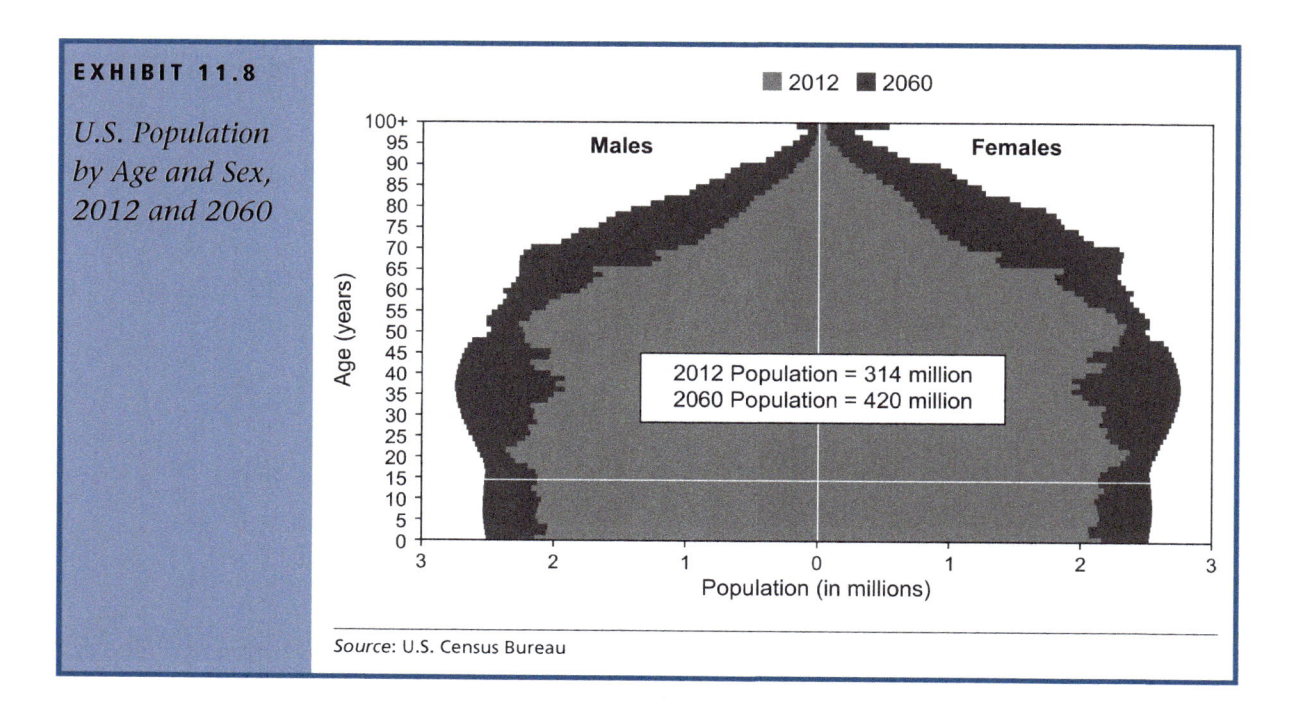

policies differentially affect the oldest Americans. Few practitioners in any profession are specially trained to assess the strengths, needs, and goals of those nearing a full century of life.

In addition to changes in age distribution, the ethnic and racial composition of the older-adult population is also changing, paralleling our diversifying society. In 2012, 79.3 percent of Americans age 65 and older were non-Latinx White; by 2050, this proportion will have fallen to 60.9 percent (Ortman, Velkoff, & Hogan, 2014). This future older adult population will be 12.3 percent African American, 7.1 percent Asian, and 18.4 percent Latinx (Ortman et al., 2014). While the oldest cohort will be whiter than the rest of the population, by 2050, one in five Americans age 85+ will be people of color (Ortman et al., 2014).

While the percentage of older adults who are considered members of "minority" racial or ethnic groups will increase to 39.1 percent by 2050 (Ortman et al., 2014), diversity among younger generations will be much greater. By way of comparison, by the 2020 Census, more than half of the nation's children are expected to be Black, Asian, Native American, and/or Latinx (U.S. Census Bureau, 2015). As a result, an increasingly racially and ethnically pluralistic cohort of younger people will be called on to care for, work alongside, and live in community with an elder population that will remain predominantly White. Becoming familiar with the changes depicted here will help you understand and anticipate the challenges our society will face in the coming years.

In addition to growing racial and ethnic diversity, LGBTQ+ elders; people with developmental disabilities; immigrants and refugees; and older people in prisons will also constitute a larger percentage of the older-adult population in the future. For example, by 2030, there will be an estimated seven million LGBTQ+ people in the United States over age 50. As described in Chapter 7, LGBTQ+ Americans often experience individual and institutional discrimination; as these individuals age and consider their needs and options, many express concerns about how well-equipped health care providers, senior services, and other resources are to provide culturally competent assistance (AARP Research, 2018). Social policy aimed at older adults must be intersectional and account for the unique needs of elders whose gender, racial, sexual, and other identities influence their experiences of aging. Policy outcomes must be scrutinized for differential effect.

Poverty and Aging in the Community

If we hope to enable older adults to age in place, we need to address issues of poverty and inequities in service delivery. While, as described in Chapter 8, older adults have lower poverty rates than other age cohorts, poverty is still a reality for many older Americans. Further, while 9.2 percent of older adults lived below the official poverty line in 2017, this figure is more than 14 percent when measured by the Supplemental Poverty Measure, which tries to account more accurately for older adults' actual needs (Cubanski et al., 2018). Remember from Chapter 8 that the official poverty line is particularly inadequate for older adults, since people 65 and older must have lower incomes than younger people to be considered "poor." In 2017, a person under age 65 who earned less than $12,752 was considered poor, but someone 65 or older had to earn less than $11,756 to be considered in poverty. This disparity reflects the assumption that older people spend less on food and other necessities. This formula ignores older people's high housing and health care costs, as well as special dietary needs related to chronic conditions such as diabetes and hypertension. If the same standard were used for older adults as for the rest of the population, the poverty rate for older adults would be higher. Even as defined today, more than 30 percent of older adults lived below 200 percent of the official line, still a low income from which to attempt to live securely in later life.

Official poverty measures also fail to adequately account for geographic differences in experiences of poverty. While costs of living are often higher in urban areas, older adults in rural areas are poorer than their peers in urban communities. Rural older adults also have higher levels of chronic disease and greater likelihood of dying a preventable death. Older people are a larger percentage of the rural population than in urban areas. In many communities, older residents' desire to age in place prevents more rapid population loss and provides essential stability in a context of dramatic change. Importantly, while health care shortages and gaps in institutional supports are acute in many rural areas and make it harder for many older adults to meet their needs, some rural communities are finding ways to leverage strong social ties and existing organizational resources to confront the challenges of living in poverty in later life.

In communities of any size, poverty rates increase with age; those 85 and older, particularly women, have higher rates of poverty than the overall 65+ population. Above all, however, poverty statistics for older adults illustrate the potential for public policy to positively affect individual and group well-being. Were it not for Social Security, the official poverty rate for older adults would top 40 percent (Center on Budget and Policy Priorities [CBPP], 2018c). Instead, Social Security efficiently and effectively keeps millions of older adults out of poverty every year—in many cases, for the rest of their lives.

Voting Patterns of Older Adults

Although older adults were only 42 percent of the population of eligible American voters in 2016, their high rates of voter registration and, especially, turnout, earn them political power that often exceeds their demographic and economic might. Exhibit 11.9 shows that, while the large and vocal Millennial generation is a growing political force, its voter turnout rates still lag those of older adults.

Although older adults are diverse politically, as in other dimensions, analysis of voting patterns and self-reported ideology reveals some broad trends that shed light on older adults' political preferences and possible future political realignments, as the makeup of the U.S. electorate shifts. While Americans of all ages are more likely today to report liberal views on same-sex marriage, compared to previous decades, on many issues, older adults express more conservative views than do younger voters, particularly Millennials (Pew Research Center, 2018b). Although the gaps depicted in Exhibit 11.10 can be partially explained by the ethnic and racial diversity of younger cohorts and the greater likelihood that these diverse groups express more liberal views, older adults are more consistently conservative than other voters. However, because the elder population is heterogeneous in ways that may influence how they look at social policy, it is naive to expect that they will support the same priorities. Encouragingly, majorities of Americans of all ages believe that the government is not doing enough to help older people (Pew Research Center, 2018c); as these convictions are asserted in the electoral arena, more policymakers may elevate elder issues on the political agenda.

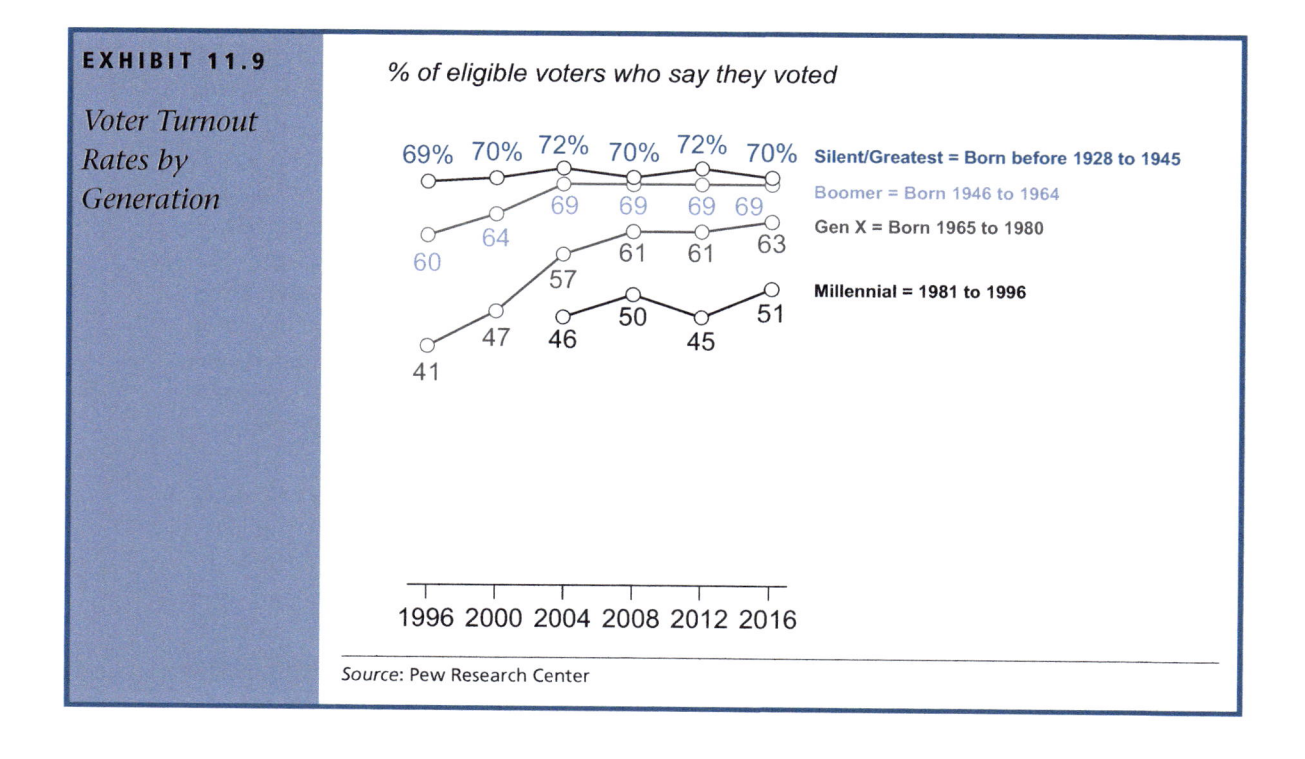

EXHIBIT 11.9

Voter Turnout Rates by Generation

% of eligible voters who say they voted

Year	Silent/Greatest	Boomer	Gen X	Millennial
1996	69%	60	41	—
2000	70%	64	47	—
2004	72%	69	57	—
2008	70%	69	61	46
2012	72%	69	61	50
2016	70%	69	63	51

Silent/Greatest = Born before 1928 to 1945
Boomer = Born 1946 to 1964
Gen X = Born 1965 to 1980
Millennial = 1981 to 1996

Source: Pew Research Center

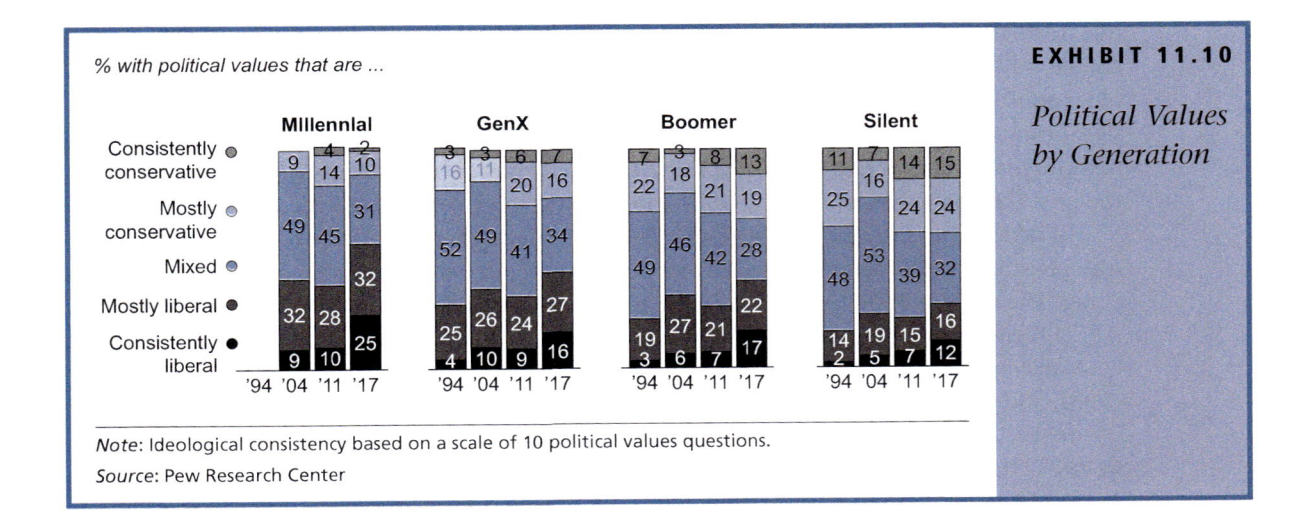

EXHIBIT 11.10

Political Values by Generation

% with political values that are ...

[Bar chart showing political values across Millennial, GenX, Boomer, and Silent generations for years '94, '04, '11, '17, with categories: Consistently conservative, Mostly conservative, Mixed, Mostly liberal, Consistently liberal]

Millennial:
- '94: 9, 49, 32, 9 (with 4 consistently conservative)
- '04: 14, 45, 28, 10 (with 2 consistently conservative)
- '11: 10, 31, 32, 25
- '17: —

GenX:
- '94: 3, 16, 52, 25, 4
- '04: 3, 11, 49, 26, 10
- '11: 6, 20, 41, 24, 9
- '17: 7, 16, 34, 27, 16

Boomer:
- '94: 7, 22, 49, 19, 3
- '04: 3, 18, 46, 27, 6
- '11: 8, 21, 42, 21, 7
- '17: 13, 19, 28, 22, 17

Silent:
- '94: 11, 25, 48, 14, 2
- '04: 7, 16, 53, 19, 5
- '11: 14, 24, 39, 15, 7
- '17: 15, 24, 32, 16, 12

Note: Ideological consistency based on a scale of 10 political values questions.
Source: Pew Research Center

MAJOR POLICIES AND PROGRAMS FOR OLDER ADULTS

To a considerable extent, all U.S. social policy can be considered "aging policy." Child welfare policy in particular, has a major influence on outcomes for older adults; when children and families have the supports they need to facilitate healthy development to adulthood, people are much more likely to thrive as they continue to age. How well we help people develop their capacities, achieve their goals, and amplify their strengths throughout the lifespan influences the quality of their later lives, arguably more than any policy aimed specifically at the needs of older adults. Here, then, we consider only two major policies that influence the lives of older adults: the Older Americans Act of 1965 and the Employee Retirement Income Security Act of 1974. This section concludes with discussion of policy initiatives in other areas that affect older adults' lives, including long-term care and elder abuse prevention.

The Older Americans Act

Congress passed the Older Americans Act (OAA) (Public Law 89-73) in 1965 to reduce the fragmentation in public services for older adults and generate additional resources to assist them. The OAA created the **Administration on Aging (AOA)**, a federal agency housed in the U.S. Department of Health and Human Services (USDHHS) that coordinates the implementation of the Act and heightens awareness of aging concerns.

In 2012, the AOA became part of the newly created federal *Administration for Community Living (ACL)* within the USDHHS. The ACL brings together into a single entity the AOA, the Administration on Disabilities, and the National Institute on Disability, Independent Living, and Rehabilitation Research. The ACL works with states, tribes, businesses, nonprofit organizations, universities, and families to help people of all ages with disabilities to continue to live in their homes and to be full participants in their communities. Some have criticized this change as a distortion of the original purpose, which aimed specifically to address the needs of older adults. Although many older adults have disabilities, many of those who do not still face significant barriers, such as discrimination in the workplace, lack of inclusion in community planning, and insufficient support for charting new roles as they age. Narrowing the focus to the physical challenges of aging could create yet another barrier to seniors' goal of aging well.

In addition to creating the AOA, the OAA also made grants available to states for community planning and programs as well as for research, demonstration, and training initiatives on aging. The OAA provides monies for services such as case management, in-home personal care and chore assistance, senior centers, meal programs, transportation, and legal assistance. The OAA also supports health promotion and disease prevention, services targeted to low-income elders, and advocacy initiatives such as the LTC ombudsperson program.

In 1972, the OAA was expanded to include a national nutrition program for older adults. In 1973, the OAA Comprehensive Services Amendments established local Area Agencies on Aging (AAAs) and created an employment program for low-income older adults. In addition, the amendments provided grants to local community agencies for multipurpose senior centers. The Older Americans Act Amendments of 2000 created the **National Family Caregiver Support Program**, which helps sustain caregivers and guards against social isolation. Beginning in 2003, the AOA has been working with the Centers for Medicare and Medicaid Services (CMS) to develop Aging and Disability Resource Centers (ADRCs) across the country to integrate aging and disability services. The intent is that the ACL and ADRCs can catalyze attention to community inclusion both for older adults and people with disabilities.

State agencies provide oversight for local AAAs, which are responsible for identifying local needs. With an aim of promoting social engagement and enhancing independent living, AAAs plan and fund services, which they may either deliver themselves or contract with private entities to deliver. The OAA is financed by general federal tax revenues, with state and local monies often used to provide additional funding. This results in wide variation in the availability of services from state to state and community to community. Programs funded through the OAA are not entitlements; consequently, money for these programs often runs out. The original intent was that OAA-funded services would be available to people aged 60 and older, regardless of income. However, funding shortages have necessitated rationing approaches. When services are rationed based on income, older people who hover just above the poverty line often fall through the cracks—ineligible for public services but seldom able to afford private replacements. Rationing also undermines widespread support for the program, particularly among those seniors most likely to vote.

In 2016, nearly five years after its official expiration, President Obama signed the reauthorization of the OAA. Reauthorization included a small funding increase, better coordination of information and referral services, and increased attention to elder abuse. It allowed nursing home ombudspersons to serve facility residents of all ages and broadened the scope of the Act to serve people of any age with disabilities. The reauthorization also made technical assistance available for modernizing multipurpose senior centers. Modernization is crucial for attracting a new generation of older adults. Beyond referrals, low-cost meals, help with taxes, a chance to socialize, and transportation, today's senior centers can offer services including job training,

> **EXHIBIT 11.11**
>
> *Older Americans Act (OAA), 1965*
>
> | | |
> |---|---|
> | Policy goals | To create a comprehensive, coordinated service network for older adults. |
> | Benefits or services provided | Planning, coordination, and services, which may include transportation, outreach, case management, in-home care, legal assistance, congregate and home-delivered meals, and the National Family Caregiver Support Program. |
> | Eligibility rules | Age 60 and over. Priority is given to low-income elders, elders of color, and older adults living in rural areas. |
> | Service delivery system | The federal Administration on Aging coordinates overall implementation. State agencies oversee local Area Agencies on Aging, which deliver services directly or through contracts with private agencies. |
> | Financing | Federally funded by general tax revenue. |

physical fitness, health and safety screenings, technology classes, intergenerational activities, opportunities for meaningful volunteer work, and general support for older adults as they reinvent retirement. It is time again for reauthorization of the OAA. Funding for this crucial initiative is currently 20 percent below the 2000 level, while the population aged 60 and over has increased more than 40 percent in the same period. See Exhibit 11.11 for a summary of the OAA.

The Employee Retirement Income Security Act

The Employee Retirement Income Security Act (ERISA) (Public Law 93-406), enacted in 1974, was the first comprehensive effort to regulate the private pension system. ERISA defines how long a person can be required to work before becoming eligible to participate in a private pension plan, to accumulate benefits, and to be **vested**, that is, to have a non-forfeitable right to those benefits. ERISA also requires plan sponsors to provide adequate funding for the plan and guarantees payment of certain benefits if an insured plan is terminated.

Created by ERISA, the Pension Benefit Guaranty Corporation (PBGC) insures defined benefit pension plans by guaranteeing benefits, but only up to specified legal limits. This means that some workers will not get their full pensions if their company underfunds their pension program and the PBGC becomes involved. The PBGC is funded through insurance premiums paid by employers, investments, and assets recovered from terminated plans. As described earlier, weaknesses in some of the plans that the PBGC insures have fueled concerns about the corporation's capacity to fund promised benefits. See Exhibit 11.12 for a summary of the Act.

The Pension Protection Act of 2006 modified ERISA and required that employers significantly increase funding for defined benefit plans. The Act increased limits for contributions to IRAs and 401(k)s and made permanent the Saver's Credit, which is a tax credit for retirement

EXHIBIT 11.12 *Employee Retirement Income Security Act (ERISA), 1974*	Policy goals	To regulate private pensions by setting minimum standards and providing limited pension guarantees.
	Benefits or services provided	Established minimum standards for participation, vesting, benefit accrual, and funding in qualified programs. Ensures payments to employees who have met the time requirements for non-forfeiture.
	Eligibility rules	Participants in employer-provided defined benefit pension plans covered by the Act, who meet time requirements for full participation in the plan.
	Service delivery system	Benefits paid through the Pension Benefit Guaranty Corporation (PBGC). Federal oversight by the Labor Department's Employee Benefits Security Administration and the Internal Revenue Service.
	Financing	The PBGC is funded by insurance premiums paid by employers, investments, and recovered assets from terminated plans.

savings that benefits people with low to moderate incomes. However, it did not reverse the trend of "risk-shifting" in retirement benefit structures, which leaves so many older adults vulnerable to uncertain economic futures.

The PBGC insures both multi-employer and single-employer pension plans. Multi-employer pension plans result from collective bargaining agreements with labor unions and two or more employers. The Multiemployer Pension Reform Act of 2014 allows cuts to multiemployer pensions if the plan is projected to run out of money, in which case workers will not get promised pension amounts (U.S. Department of the Treasury, 2016). The PBGC's multiemployer program remains likely to use up its assets by the end of 2025 (PBGC, 2017). Single-employer plans are in comparatively better shape.

No CLASS: Loss of the Long-Term Care Provisions of the Affordable Care Act

When originally passed in 2010, the Community Living Assistance Services and Supports (CLASS) provisions of the ACA created a voluntary national insurance program to provide cash benefits to people with serious disabilities. However, the Obama Administration withdrew support for CLASS because of concerns that, without substantial changes, the premiums would be far too expensive for most buyers and the program may be financially unsustainable. In 2013, as part of a budget deal, Congress repealed CLASS and authorized a new national commission to develop a plan for better financing and delivery of LTC services. However, the commission was unable to reach a consensus. Currently, people in need of LTC are regularly impoverished by its high costs. In the absence of federal policy progress, some states are innovating LTC options.

In 2019, Washington passed the nation's first LTC benefit program (Bunis, 2019). Other states, including Minnesota and Hawaii, are also forging new initiatives. Additionally, some advocates have proposed tax policy changes to allow assets in tax-preferential retirement accounts to be used for LTC costs or premiums, although many caution that this could exacerbate the inadequacies in people's retirement savings (Winegar, 2016). At the state and federal levels, advocacy groups will continue to push for legislation to increase access to LTC and make it affordable.

The Elder Justice Act and the Patient Safety and Abuse Prevention Act

Elder abuse is mistreatment of an older adult that results in harm or loss. It may take many forms, including physical, emotional, or sexual abuse; financial exploitation; neglect (either self-neglect or neglect by a caretaker); and abandonment. The National Center for Elder Abuse concedes that the true prevalence of elder abuse is unknown, as elders rarely self-report and signs are often missed due to professionals' lack of training in detection. However, a literature review finds prevalence of approximately 10 percent, considering all forms of mistreatment (Lachs & Pillemer, 2015).

Some older adults are at greater risk of abuse. Risk factors include dementia (Quinn & Benson, 2012), lack of social support, previous experience of trauma (Acierno et al., 2010), and functional impairment (Friedman et al., 2015). Older women are more likely to be victims (Laumann, Leitsch, & Waite, 2008), and perpetrators are more commonly male—usually adult children, spouses, or other relatives (Lachs & Pillemer, 2015). Older women who are victims of domestic violence may be particularly wary of reporting abuse for fear of being served not in a domestic violence shelter but in a LTC facility, which could lead to loss of their home. Elder abuse rates are increasing, particularly among men (Logan et al., 2019). Increases in financial exploitation and rapid growth in the older adult population fuel greater need for Adult Protective Services (APS). However, funding is inadequate; some states have even cut funding. More resources and greater national urgency to prevent elder abuse are badly needed.

The Elder Justice Act and the Patient Safety and Abuse Prevention Act were both part of the ACA. The main provisions of the Elder Justice Act include funding for APS, grants to support the Long-Term Care Ombudsman Program, and the establishment of an Elder Justice Coordinating Council. Although the legislation was to include funding for more APS caseworkers, this funding has been slow to materialize. Similarly, the Patient Safety and Abuse Prevention Act required criminal background checks for persons seeking employment in nursing facilities and other LTC facilities, but little funding has been appropriated to enforce the provision.

Indeed, this is a pattern with legislation to combat elder abuse. In October 2017, President Trump signed the Elder Abuse Prevention and Prosecution Act, which increased the federal government's focus on preventing and punishing elder abuse and exploitation. It required several actions across multiple government agencies, including designation of Elder Justice Coordinators in each federal judicial district and in the Federal Trade Commission, publication of Department of Justice and USDHHS data on elder abuse investigations, and increased penalties for convictions of interstate fraud where the victim is elderly. However, no additional money accompanied the law, leading advocates to worry that its objectives will be difficult to achieve.

> **EXHIBIT 11.13**
>
> *Advocates for Children and Elders Join Forces*
>
> Field instructors and social work students used their policy practice skills to improve the lives of older adults. Their state had consolidated call centers for reporting child and adult abuse due to budget cuts. When someone called to report abuse, it was common to have to leave a message. After doing research, consulting with colleagues, and attending a coalition meeting where they brought up this problem, social workers contacted the Silver-Haired Legislature (an advocacy group made up of older adults) and the AARP chapter, shared what they had learned, and asked if these organizations would be interested in collaborating to improve this dysfunctional system. They got media coverage for the issue and contacted a legislator who helped build an intergenerational coalition to press for additional funding in this critical area.

The advocates described in Exhibit 11.13 focused their efforts on the need for funding to ensure that critical interventions are adequately funded.

The issue of elder abuse clearly remains on the political agenda, although the emphasis on financial exploitation can obscure the serious threat of physical and other forms of maltreatment. In 2018, the Senior Safe Act was included in a bipartisan banking reform package signed by President Trump. The measure allows financial institutions to report suspected financial exploitation of older adults without fear of retaliatory lawsuits, as long as they have trained their employees in how to detect suspicious activity. For more information on policies and programs to combat elder abuse, go to the website of the National Center on Elder Abuse at the AOA at **ncea.acl.gov**.

EVALUATING POLICIES AND PROGRAMS FOR OLDER ADULTS

Policy for older adults should build on the assets and resources that have supported them throughout their lives, while providing a foundation on which they can construct a satisfying final chapter. Social workers informed by the strengths perspective understand that many of the same policy structures that work for older adults are also in the best interests of younger people. Social policy is not a zero-sum game. Everyone wins when more people have what they need for healthy, rewarding lives. Toward this ideal, the remaining sections of this chapter focus on identifying needed strengths-based policy changes in the areas of economic security, health care, and social engagement. We begin by examining the social contexts in which people grow old. Diversity in life experiences greatly influences the lives of older adults. Older adults who were poor all their lives, who were denied educational and employment opportunities, and who received inadequate health care bring that legacy of poverty and discrimination to their later years. At the same time, strong ties to family, friends, church, and community, created and nurtured over a lifetime, may continue to provide older adults with needed support. The life of the older adult depicted in Exhibit 11.14 likely evidences both of those threads—challenge and triumph. Policy that aims to respond to her needs should reflect both as well, building on strengths and accounting for difficulty.

EXHIBIT 11.14

Native American Elder

Credit: iStock

When we consider needed policy reforms for older adults, we must be careful not to equate "strengths" with independence. Although independence is a core American value, it is largely an illusion. Most people experience intersecting periods of both independence and interdependence. Even those who pride themselves on being "self-made" acknowledge the considerable role that others—as well as public policy investments—play in their success. Family and community relationships are intergenerational and interdependent: parents, grandparents, and community members care for children; friends and neighbors form "families of choice"; and grown children care for their parents and other relatives. Interdependence is the glue that holds society together—a strength, not a weakness. Discussing this interdependence—particularly the contributions that older adults can and often do make to younger people and to the larger society—helps us reframe relationships by emphasizing their reciprocal nature.

There are many community-based organizations that provide opportunities for Americans from different generations to come together for common purposes. More than 10,000 volunteers, many of whom are retired older adults, mentor entrepreneurs, most of whom are women, through SCORE (www.score.org). The mentoring has tangible economic benefits, as mentored entrepreneurs created 61,534 jobs in 2017. Some intergenerational programming receives public investment. The Corporation for National Service, for example, manages the Retired and Senior Volunteer Program and Senior Corps, which utilize older adult volunteers in service to children, elders, and community organizations around the country. Our society needs to develop more policies and programs that build links and promote generational interdependence, while highlighting the strengths of both young and old people.

Focusing on reciprocity in relationships will become increasingly important during the next 20 to 30 years because of changes in family structures and the needs of older adults. As informal supports are the backbone of the U.S. system of caring for older adults—and will likely continue to be—we will need policies and programs that provide resources such as elder care at the worksite, increased respite care, and training to improve caregivers' abilities. Additionally, lower birth rates, geographic distance, and high divorce rates mean that few families are able to provide adequate support for aging relatives. As more couples delay family formation, when they have children, their parents will on average be older, may be less able to help care for grandchildren, and may themselves need greater care. When middle-aged people care for young children and aging parents at the same time, these adults are known as the *sandwich generation*, and they confront stresses associated with these dual demands. Increasingly, then, formal support will be necessary to complement informal resources.

Economic Security

In previous chapters we discussed the provisions of OASDI, the mainstay of economic security for older adults in this country. Popularly known as Social Security, this program is often described as one leg of the three-legged stool that supports retirement, along with individual savings and job-specific pensions. However, as described, both private savings and job-specific pensions are insufficient and inequitable. To compensate for these inadequacies, people refer to a fourth leg that supports people in old age: work. More older Americans are working than at any time since the turn of the twentieth century, and today's older workers are spending more time on the job than their peers did in previous years. In 2016, almost 19 percent of Americans 65 and older reported working full- or part-time. As Exhibit 11.15 illustrates,

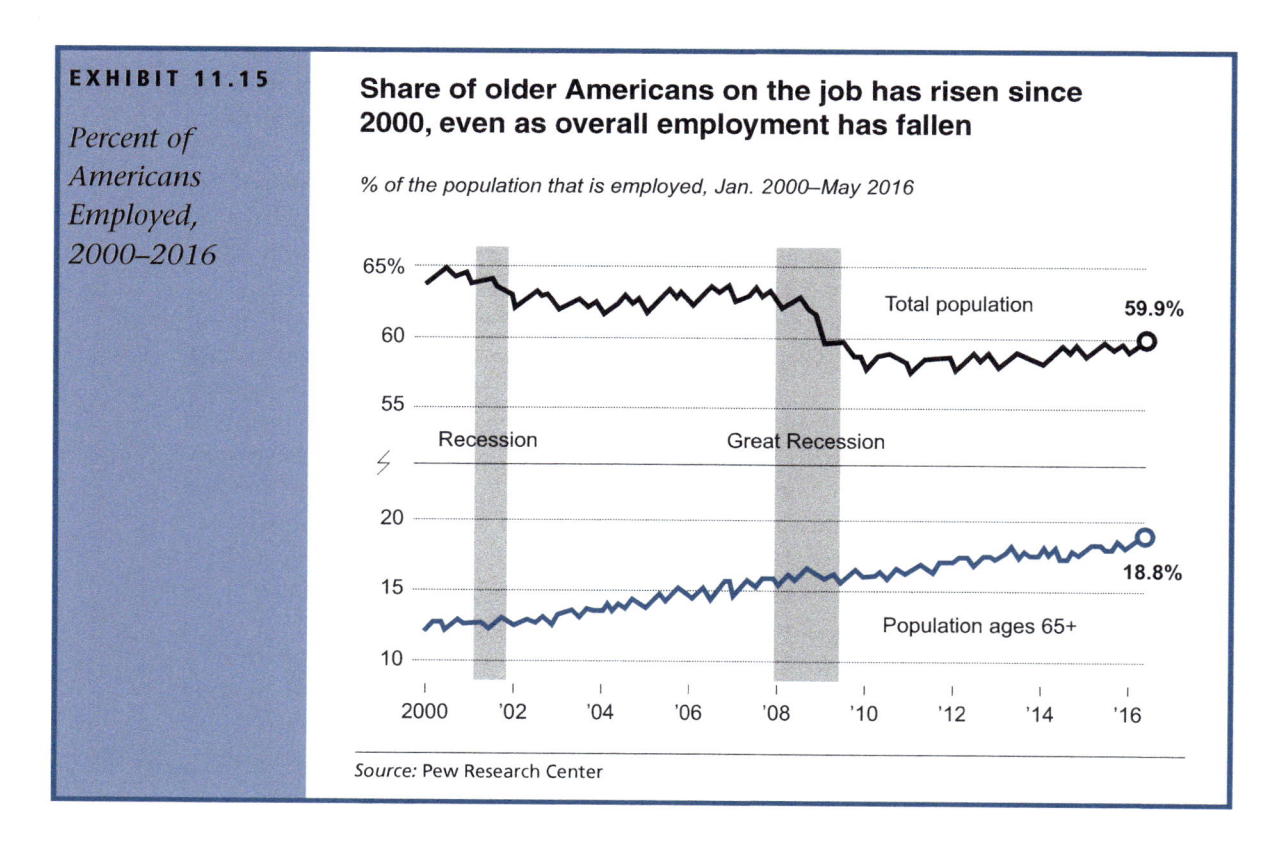

EXHIBIT 11.15

Percent of Americans Employed, 2000–2016

Share of older Americans on the job has risen since 2000, even as overall employment has fallen

% of the population that is employed, Jan. 2000–May 2016

Total population: **59.9%**

Population ages 65+: **18.8%**

Recession; Great Recession

Source: Pew Research Center

this reflects a steady increase, even as employment rates have fallen in the rest of the population. And many older adults who are not working would like to; in May 2018, the labor force participation rate of older adults without disabilities—including those working and those actively seeking work—was nearly 25 percent (U.S. Bureau of Labor Statistics, 2018a). Of course, staying on the job or returning to work is possible only (1) when elders do not suffer serious disabilities, which are more common in old age and which disproportionately affect elders of color, and (2) when jobs are available and extended to older adults in a non-discriminatory manner.

Exhibit 11.16 presents income sources for older adults by income quintiles. Social Security is the major income source for people in the first three quintiles. This exhibit also illustrates disparities in other sources of income, such as assets and pensions.

Social Security keeps many people out of poverty and is particularly vital for some groups of older adults. In 2017, 51.7 percent of African-American older adults and 46.1 percent of Latinx elders would have been poor without Social Security (Romig, 2018). In recognition of its transformative role as a pillar of economic security in the increasingly uncertain U.S. economy, support for preserving Social Security is high among both older adults and many younger people. Nearly nine in ten Americans say Social Security is more important than ever to ensure that

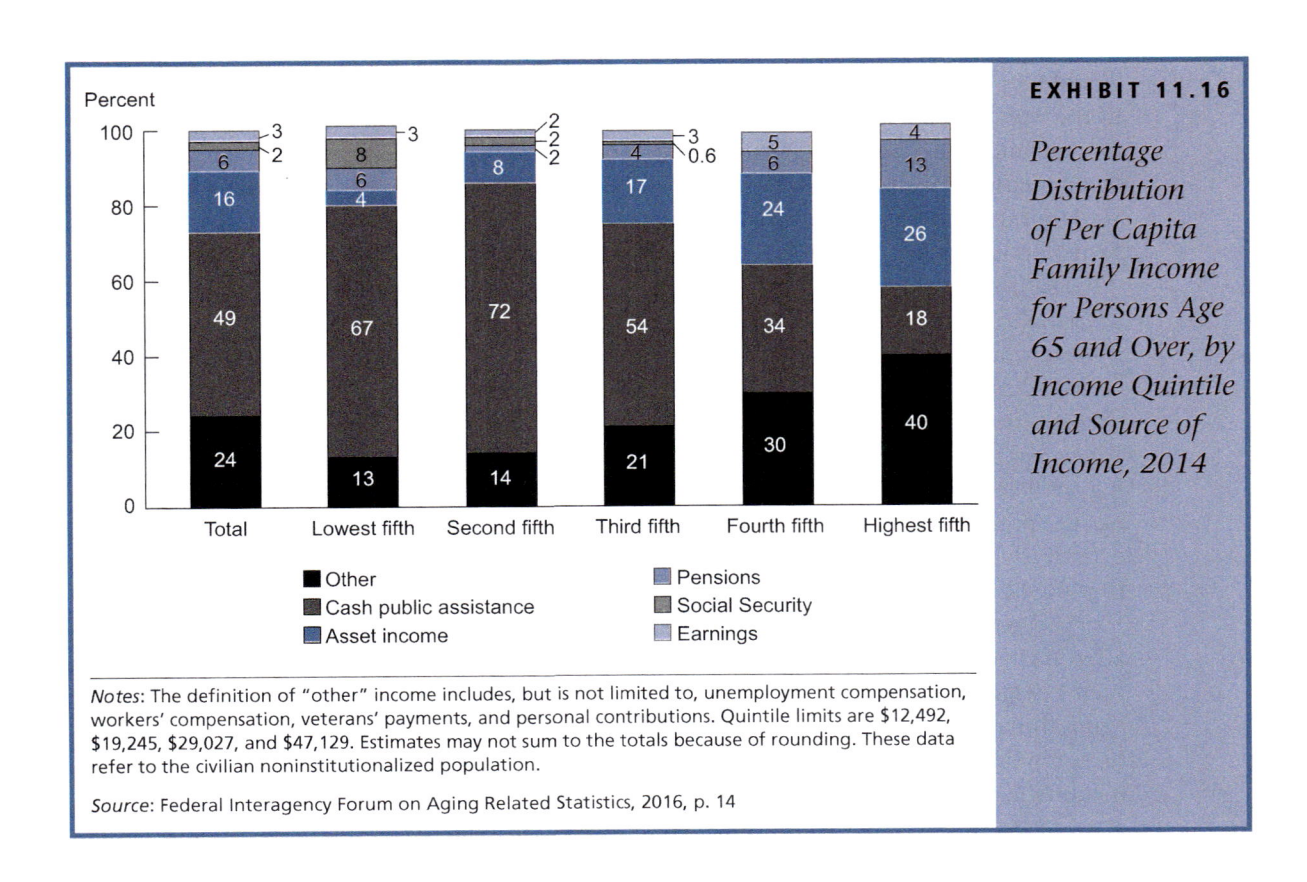

EXHIBIT 11.16

Percentage Distribution of Per Capita Family Income for Persons Age 65 and Over, by Income Quintile and Source of Income, 2014

Source	Total	Lowest fifth	Second fifth	Third fifth	Fourth fifth	Highest fifth
Other	3	3	2	3	5	4
Pensions	2	—	2	—	—	—
Cash public assistance	6	8	2	4	6	13
Asset income	16	6	8	17	24	26
Social Security	49	67	72	54	34	18
Earnings	24	13	14	21	30	40
(Earnings row small value)	—	4	—	0.6	—	—

Notes: The definition of "other" income includes, but is not limited to, unemployment compensation, workers' compensation, veterans' payments, and personal contributions. Quintile limits are $12,492, $19,245, $29,027, and $47,129. Estimates may not sum to the totals because of rounding. These data refer to the civilian noninstitutionalized population.

Source: Federal Interagency Forum on Aging Related Statistics, 2016, p. 14

retirees have a dependable income (Walker, Reno, & Bethell, 2014). In addition to understanding that Social Security provides the only guaranteed source of retirement income that most of them will ever have, young workers also value the security of knowing that their parents and grandparents have adequate and stable income. In the 2018 midterm elections, 66 percent of voters were more likely to support candidates who advocated expanding Social Security benefits (Public Policy Polling, 2018).

In 2014, the National Academy of Social Insurance conducted a large multigenerational survey. Survey responses indicated that 68 percent of young people were not confident about the future of Social Security. However, far from abandoning the concept of social insurance, respondents expressed strong support for policy approaches that increase revenues, pay for benefit improvements, and eliminate the projected funding gap (Walker et al., 2014). Further, after respondents received accurate information about steps that could be taken to preserve Social Security, their confidence in the system improved. Social workers and other advocates committed to improving economic security among older adults should look for ways to leverage this public support to secure reforms that will keep OASDI financially solvent for the long term. This objective is especially imperative given demographic pressures and the shakiness of the other sources of income in retirement.

In addition to OASDI reform, one strategy for improving the economic status of older adults with low incomes is to change the SSI program. For example, raising SSI benefits to 110 percent of the federal poverty line (FPL) and lowering the age of eligibility from 65 to 62 would help a great many older adults escape deep poverty. However, because of inadequacies in the way the United States defines poverty, elders at 110 percent of the FPL still have very low incomes. Additionally, barriers to accessing benefits, such as complex forms and insufficient staffing, need to be addressed. Many older adults who likely are eligible for SSI never apply for it. More low-income older adults also need to be informed about the Supplemental Nutrition Assistance Program (SNAP), the Low-Income Housing Energy Assistance Program (LIHEAP), and programs such as Low-Income Subsidies for Medicare.

Finally, we should enact policies that support access to employment for older adults who want to work. One such policy is **phased retirement**, in which an individual reduces the hours worked during the years leading up to retirement. Other initiatives include creating more part-time positions and strictly enforcing laws that prohibit age discrimination in hiring and layoffs. Today, researchers and practitioners are placing greater emphasis on productive aging, including involvement in paid work, caregiving, and volunteering. However, a productivity focus has the potential to further disadvantage those whose accumulated life strains make engaging extensively in productive activities difficult. In contrast, discussions of *aging well* can encompass the needs and contributions of all older adults.

The twenty-first century will be unique in that four or five generations of families may be alive at the same time. Therefore, we need to evaluate all policies and proposals carefully for their intergenerational impacts. Overemphasis on the negative economic impact of population aging threatens to exacerbate conflicts between young and old. For example, public expenditures for elders that outpace spending on programs for children could be used as evidence of inequitable treatment of young people. Critics may then propose cuts in spending on elders as a "remedy" to this alleged injustice. These arguments typically overlook several vital points.

First, comparisons of spending on children and older adults often focus on federal spending and ignore state and local spending, which distorts the analysis, as most investment in children's development comes in the form of state and local appropriations for public education. Second, any comparison of growth in spending must consider per capita, rather than aggregate, spending, given substantial increases in the size of the older adult population. Further, differences in the cohorts complicate comparisons. Children comprise a group made up of people 18 and under, while the older-adult age group spans more than 30 years; it is unsurprising, then, that spending over the longer period would be greater. Also, benefits such as the Earned Income Tax Credit and the Child Tax Credit, which are designed to support families with children, are delivered through the tax code and therefore usually omitted as "spending." Finally, the growth in spending on older adults is largely due to uncontrolled growth in health care costs. It is no surprise that, in general, children require less health care than older adults, but here the focus should be on finding ways to control costs while ensuring effective care for all generations. In sum, then, the fundamental importance of intergenerational solidarity needs to be underscored in policy decisions. There is little indication of a crowding-out effect (Brady, 2009). Instead, countries willing and able to spend on one group typically also have progressive policies to help the other.

Replacing the pejorative concept of an "aging crisis," attention to longevity economics helps increase awareness of the many opportunities to leverage the advantages of an aging society. As is also often the case for immigrants, the dominant narrative may ignore the positive economic impact of older adults' activities as both producers and consumers. Many older adults have substantial buying power due to earlier savings and pensions. These contributions are particularly valuable in certain geographies and some industries, where older adults' consumer preferences are driving innovation and their expenditures are bolstering local economies (Gerontological Society of America [GSA], 2018). Older adults often provide increased community stability as they support young families and shore up housing markets and health care systems. Unlike workers who may lose their jobs, older adults typically have stable sources of income via monthly pensions and Social Security checks that can sustain a community during times of high unemployment. Older workers are driving positive changes in workplace cultures and contributing to practices that will benefit everyone. As volunteers, civic leaders, and treasured community members, older adults make contributions that are difficult to quantify but nonetheless highly valuable, particularly as the United States contends with challenges on many fronts. Social workers should take a perspective that emphasizes building on the strengths and capacities of all people.

Significantly, the moral obligation of one generation to another can be combined with enlightened self-interest to craft policies that support the multigenerational families of the future. Because the cohort of children born during the Great Depression is smaller than previous cohorts, the ranks of the oldest old (85+) will not begin to swell until 2030. The last of the Baby Boomers will not reach 65 until 2029 or 85 until 2049. This gives policymakers some time to adopt innovative approaches to deal with coming demographic and social shifts. Further, many Baby Boomers and their families are eager to participate in planning and implementing policy changes. Approaches that emphasize their strengths and contributions will increase the likelihood that we enact effective policy responses to our changing society.

Health Care

Rising health care costs create a heavy burden for all of us. Even when they receive Medicare benefits, many older adults have very high expenses for deductibles, co-pays, premiums for additional insurance, and expenses that Medicare does not cover. It is in long-term care (LTC) that older adults are most vulnerable.

Long-Term Care There are few policy structures that provide much protection for older adults in need of LTC. Although private LTC insurance is touted as an initiative that helps older adults meet these needs, only a small proportion of older adults can afford to pay the premiums over the course of the many years before they need the service. Although only 2.5 percent of older Americans reside in a nursing facility on any given day (Harris-Kojetin et al., 2016), an estimated 56 percent will need at least one night of nursing facility care and 5 percent will need long stays costing $47,000 or more (Hurd, Michaud, & Rohwedder, 2017). While aging should not be equated with disability, disabilities do increase with age. The average age of nursing facility residents is well over 80; in 2014, 41.6 percent of nursing home residents were 85 or older (Harris-Kojetin et al., 2016). Medicaid, the public program that pays for the majority of LTC, is available only to people with very low incomes and few financial assets. High LTC costs can rapidly impoverish middle-income and low-income elders. According to the 2018 Genworth Cost of Care Survey, the annual median cost for nursing facility care was over $100,000 for a private room and over $89,000 for a semi-private room. Further, although spouses remaining in the community no longer have to completely impoverish themselves before getting help with nursing home bills, as was the case prior to 1988, they still must "spend down" income, typically to 150 percent of the federal poverty line, in order for a spouse with a disability to be eligible for Medicaid LTC services.

Elders will increasingly demand LTC options that maximize choice, incorporate evolving technologies, and innovate promising models and service delivery options (Sloane, Zimmerman, & D'Souza, 2014). In the process, these developments will reshape the LTC landscape. To maximize both quality of life and cost-effectiveness, there needs to be much more emphasis on home- and community-based services within LTC policy. Alliances between disability rights groups and the aging community allow for freer exchange of ideas and may result in a stronger LTC system and more home- and community-based options for all people with disabilities. While states have expanded HCBS waivers to reduce expenditures and to provide alternatives to institutionalization, more than 173,000 people were on waiting lists for aged or aged/disabled waivers in 2016 (Kaiser Family Foundation [KFF], 2016c). Clearly, there is room to shift more LTC spending toward community-based approaches. As an option that affirms older adults' own priorities, home- and community-based LTC is strengths-based. Surveys have consistently found that more than 60 percent of older adults would prefer to stay in their own homes and have someone care for them there if they became unable to live on their own (Stepler, 2016b). This is another example, then, where listening to people's goals for their lives steers policy in a direction more cost-efficient and, ultimately, effective.

Contrary to public perception, research indicates that many older adults rely on public community-based LTC services for a limited period, often following an acute care episode such as a stroke or a broken hip. Then the older adult may stop needing these services but remain in the community (Chapin et al., 2009). However, if that person stays in a nursing home, costs for their care are much higher and could well continue for the rest of their lives. Older adults often have difficulty transitioning from nursing facilities back into their communities. They may have lost their home during their facility stay; may no longer drive; and/or may lack the funds, energy, and knowledge of resources necessary to arrange for needed services. We need to prioritize policies to ensure the nursing facility does not become a permanent residence for older adults who want to return to the community and could do so with support.

Long-term care reform must include more than innovating financing mechanisms and pivoting toward community-based care. For older adults who must have care in a nursing facility, the culture change movement is working to transform the nursing home environment to make the physical and organizational structures of nursing facilities less institutional. Begun as a grassroots movement to catalyze more person-centered care, the facility culture-change movement has been furthered by facilities' innovations to secure competitive advantage (Sloane et al., 2014), supportive regulations from the Centers for Medicare and Medicaid Services (CMS, 2006), and a research agenda that has documented, among other outcomes, improvements in residents' quality of life and facilities' staff turnover rates (Koren, 2010; Zimmerman, Shier, & Saliba, 2014). Different facilities have different concepts of culture change, with some radically redesigning the space so that it resembles a home and others giving residents more autonomy within a still-institutional structure. Cost-effective public policies that integrate the facility into the community and create a more home-like environment should be supported, particularly as they can improve outcomes for older adults regardless of where they live. Additionally, higher minimum standards for nursing staff are needed to improve the quality of care provided in nursing facilities, even with the recognition that this will raise costs.

Some states have implemented Medicaid consumer-directed service models that give people the option of directing their own LTC. While consumers have more choice with these options, they also assume more responsibility. In evaluating these developments, it is important to be mindful of the potential for risk-shifting, if the focus shifts from funding needed services to giving people a capped amount to spend.

Mental Health Policies and programs to address mental health are vital to improving overall well-being, helping older adults remain in the community, and reducing health care costs, including those for LTC. Effectively responding to older adults' mental health needs will require first countering the stigma associated with mental illness. Depression in older adults is *not* a normal part of aging. When older adults do suffer from depression, they often are reluctant to talk about it. The current health care system exacerbates these barriers. Primary care physicians often overlook depression in older adults. As discussed in Chapter 10, mental health treatment is often inaccessible and unaffordable. Further, many mental health centers do little to reach out to older adults. Exhibit 11.17 illustrates the percentage of the adult population age 51 and over that has clinical depression.

The 2008 Medicare Improvement for Patients and Providers Act achieved some progress in making mental health services for older adults more affordable. This Act reduced co-pays incrementally for Medicare's outpatient mental health services. However, as discussed earlier,

EXHIBIT 11.17

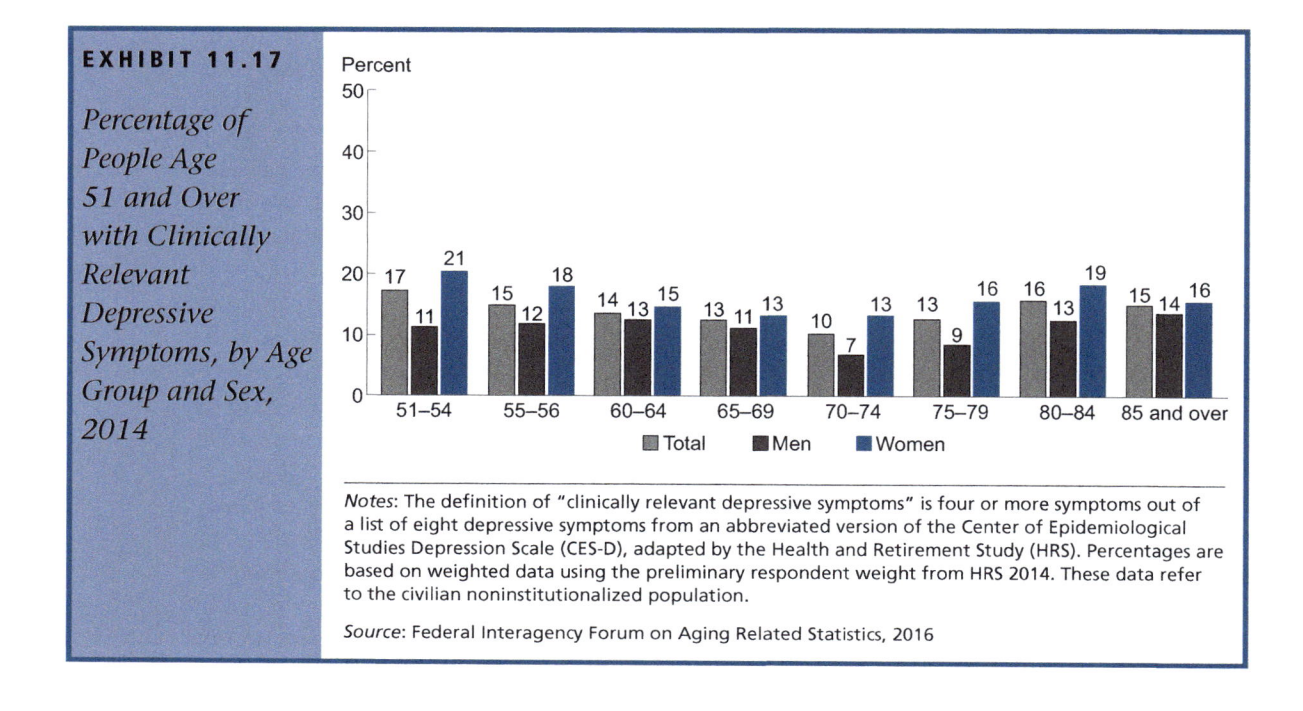

Percentage of People Age 51 and Over with Clinically Relevant Depressive Symptoms, by Age Group and Sex, 2014

Age Group	Total	Men	Women
51–54	17	11	21
55–56	15	12	18
60–64	14	13	15
65–69	13	11	13
70–74	10	7	13
75–79	13	9	13
80–84	16	13	19
85 and over	15	14	16

Notes: The definition of "clinically relevant depressive symptoms" is four or more symptoms out of a list of eight depressive symptoms from an abbreviated version of the Center of Epidemiological Studies Depression Scale (CES-D), adapted by the Health and Retirement Study (HRS). Percentages are based on weighted data using the preliminary respondent weight from HRS 2014. These data refer to the civilian noninstitutionalized population.

Source: Federal Interagency Forum on Aging Related Statistics, 2016

trained clinicians to provide these services are in very short supply. The American Geriatrics Society estimates that by 2030, there will only be about 1,650 geriatric psychiatrists in the United States—less than one per 6,000 estimated older adults with mental health or substance use disorders (Bartels & Naslund, 2013). This need for mental health providers is particularly acute in rural areas and among racial and ethnic groups generally underserved. The mental health system is insufficient for people of all ages and particularly failing older adults.

End-of-Life Planning Although it is not always honored, all people in the United States have the right to make known their wishes for end-of-life care by signing two basic documents: (1) a living will that states the desired treatment, and (2) a durable power of attorney for health care decisions, which allows a person to designate an individual to make those decisions once they can no longer do so. In 2010, President Obama issued the memorandum *Respecting the Rights of Hospital Patients to Receive Visitors and to Designate Surrogate Decision Makers for Medical Emergencies*, which directed hospitals to follow patients' advance directives. This memorandum reaffirmed the responsibility of hospitals to follow patients' wishes regarding end-of-life care. At the agency level, policies and programs need to be designed so that they consider cultural differences in end-of-life preferences.

Most older people in the United States die outside their homes, in nursing homes or hospitals. As more older adults seek to retain control of their care even to the end of life, use of hospice services is growing. **Hospice care** is an approach to end-of-life care that focuses on comfort and alleviation of pain rather than treatment of illness. In 2016, 48 percent of

Medicare beneficiaries who died received at least one day of hospice care and were enrolled in hospice care at the time of their death (National Hospice and Palliative Care Organization [NHPCO], 2017). Almost 60 percent of these Medicare hospice patients were women, and about 64 percent were 80 years old or older (NHPCO, 2017).

A few states have passed "death with dignity" legislation. These laws make it possible for adults who are mentally competent and terminally ill to make a voluntary request and then obtain a prescription medication that will hasten their death. As of 2018, seven states allowed such an option for their residents—six by statute (California, Colorado, Hawaii, Oregon, Vermont, and Washington) and one by court decision (Montana). The National Association of Social Workers (NASW) supports the decision of terminally ill patients to hasten death (NASW, 2015k). However, some advocates for people with disabilities oppose such policies, believing that they devalue the lives of those with seriously disabling conditions. You will want to consider the ethical dimensions of this issue, including individuals' right to self-determination and the importance of sending strengths-based messages about the potential for a fulfilling life even with terminal illness.

Social Engagement

Social engagement—including opportunities to make choices in how and when to participate, build relationships, set goals, and work to attain them—is integral to aging well. We can gain insight into the kinds of policies needed to support aging well by examining research that can inform effective policy initiatives in this area (Baltes & Baltes, 1990; Kahana & Kahana, 1996; Nelson-Becker, Chapin, & Fast, 2013).

Social exchange theory helps us understand the importance of social engagement in the lives of older adults (Dowd, 1980). This theory uses the economic metaphor of *exchange* to explain social interaction among older adults. In general, people develop social relationships because they find them mutually rewarding. However, aging often involves decreasing social, political, and economic power due to changes in the person's economic, psychological, and employment statuses. At the same time, people who have invested considerably in others throughout their lives may be able to draw upon additional resources from those who feel the need to reciprocate. These individuals have built social capital within a strong social network.

Many theories of aging well are used to describe older adults' adaptation and coping based on stress models. It is important for researchers and policymakers to think in terms of the *process* of aging well instead of concentrating attention primarily on the physical and psychological *outcomes* of aging. For example, Baltes and Baltes (1990) describe "aging well" in terms of *selective optimization with compensation*. That is, older adults who age well adapt to changing physical and cognitive limitations by concentrating on high-priority areas. Further, the strengths perspective helps us recognize the potential for older adults to set new goals. Our understanding of the aging process is changing rapidly. Social workers' practice with older adults should reflect these new discoveries.

Changes in longevity, the reality that many older adults must continue to work, and the realization that our aging society cannot afford to lose the productivity of the large older adult population are propelling a new vision of successful aging. This vision focuses on the roles older adults are called upon to play as key participants in their own process of aging well, based on their competencies, resilience, and life experiences. For example, due to institutional sexism and relationship dynamics within individual families, some older women are confronted with the task of taking control of their lives for the first time. When older women have support in this transition, their capacity for self-determination is affirmed. Further, over time, such women may help to reshape gender norms, including for younger generations.

Policies to support elders' capacity for self-determination are critical to helping them age well even when their life conditions may necessitate more emphasis on interdependence. Self-determination and interdependence are not mutually exclusive. For example, an elder could choose to turn to their family for advice and care. The family may recommend that the elder consider a nursing facility. However, the elder's right to choose should be preserved to the extent that their cognitive abilities allow. Social work values compel us to provide support for client self-determination, particularly with vulnerable and underserved populations.

Theoretical work on social exchange sheds light on the relationship between social resources and social engagement. Sexism, racism, and ageism continue to be barriers to policies and practices that support aging well. We know the older adult population of the future will be larger, older, and more diverse. If older adults are to have the opportunity to age well, social policies will need to fully embrace the strengths people bring to later life. Policies that address economic security, health care, and opportunities for social engagement will need to be continually evaluated for differences in effectiveness across these diverse groups.

Next Step: Supporting Long, Healthy Lives

Although many people are now living longer than in the past, as explained in Chapter 10, overall life expectancy fell again in 2017 for the third straight year (Murphy et al., 2018). Health promotion and disease prevention efforts may help increase life expectancy and, importantly, extend *healthy* life expectancy. New policies are needed to address issues such as lack of access to healthy food choices in low-income areas. Such initiatives can help increase the number of older adults who experience a healthy old age while also controlling health care costs. Additionally, research has highlighted healthy nutrition, regular exercise, and amelioration of psychosocial stress and major depressive episodes as strategies that may prevent dementia (Rakesh et al., 2017)—estimated to afflict almost 14 percent of the population age 71 and older (Plassman et al., 2007). Although a variety of factors contribute to the onset of dementia, including genetic factors and head trauma, increasing evidence suggests that what is good for your heart is good for your brain. A strengths-based agenda for helping elders to age well must include more research into the link between social isolation, depression, and dementia; more attention to the approaches that science suggests may prevent dementia; and increased investment in building dementia-friendly communities. Businesses that have received education about how to effectively respond to people with dementia can support caregivers who are trying to help older adults remain safely in the community. Senior centers and other community agencies could be more proactive in getting older adults involved in health and wellness programs. In some areas, initiatives designed to build on older adults' strengths to reduce depression and help maintain overall health have been successfully implemented (Chapin et al., 2013). Peer models to utilize older adults to support other elders could enhance the well-being of individuals with different strengths and needs. Policy could scale these interventions to meet the challenges anticipated in the future.

As older adult populations are growing, more places around the country are becoming **naturally occurring retirement communities (NORCs)**—or could become NORCs with necessary policy changes and supports. Broadly defined as communities where individuals either remain or move when they retire, NORCs embody many of the strengths-based investments older adults need to thrive: opportunities for social interaction, intergenerational connection, and infrastructure that facilitates healthy activities. Research has demonstrated that transforming physical spaces into conduits of individual and population health can improve health, promote feelings of well-being, and enhance older adults' lives, for considerably less cost than age-segregated institutional approaches (Masotti et al., 2006).

Next Step: Promoting Economic Security in Later Life

The Commission on Retirement Security and Personal Savings (2016) concluded what many Americans already know or are quickly learning: most people are not saving enough to have a secure retirement. While the 2018 Employee Benefit Retirement Institute (EBRI) Confidence Survey found that 64 percent of workers age 25 and older and 71 percent of those 55+ are at least somewhat confident of their financial prospects in retirement, there is evidence that this self-professed assurance may reflect how little Americans understand about what retirement security will really require in today's risk-shifted environment (EBRI, 2018a). That same survey found that only 38 percent of workers had reviewed their expected Social Security benefits and only 29 percent have estimated their expenses in retirement (EBRI, 2018b). Half of those nearing retirement admit they do not know how much they should have saved or what it will mean if they fall short. Especially when compared to research documenting Americans' actual financial preparedness for retirement, these findings reveal the fallacy of expecting people to assume the risk for their own lifelong financial security—exactly the conclusion that prompted the establishment of OASDI and the rise of employer-based retirement benefits.

While people who earn very high incomes or are otherwise economically advantaged are often able to navigate the risky landscape of retirement financing, other Americans struggle to do so. Factors that make adequate saving difficult include:

- lack of access to workplace retirement savings plans;
- markedly lower retirement plan participation when people are not automatically enrolled;
- insufficient personal savings for short-term needs, which too often leads individuals to raid their retirement savings; and
- inadequate knowledge of basic personal finance.

Given projected life expectancies, many people are at risk of outliving their retirement savings. This reality should be understood within the overall context of employment volatility, low personal savings rates, high levels of consumer debt—particularly student borrowing—and risk shifting in arenas such as health care. As was the case in the 1930s, ensuring that the last years of Americans' lives are free from deprivation and financial anxiety will require a reinvestment in social insurance. In addition, there are ways to make the prospect of retirement saving fairer and more successful. For example, requiring employers to offer and automatically enroll employees in a retirement plan could dramatically increase participation rates (Clark & Young, 2018). Some existing policy tools, such as the Saver's Credit, could be improved, and an initial public match might encourage younger workers to begin saving for retirement early. As described in Chapter 8, exempting at least some assets from means tests for public benefit programs could facilitate saving by lower-income households. Finally, efforts to address Americans' financial insecurity all along the lifespan are essential to helping more people reach retirement age in good financial shape.

Shoring up OASDI and improving its benefit structure must be central components of any policy to improve older adults' financial well-being. As discussed earlier, policy alternatives considered for Social Security's future include cutting benefits, raising taxes, limiting eligibility, or some combination of all three. Each of these alternatives will increase the burden on some groups. For example, cutting benefits will most negatively impact low-income older adults, particularly very old women. Many people already receive small benefits. Even for those who retire at full retirement age (66, until 2020) and have maximum taxable earnings for at least 35 years, the maximum monthly benefit is only $2,687 per month. Conversely, raising taxes on retirement benefits for higher-income older adults could generate additional revenues without destroying the universal, insurance-based approach, although it could erode some political support for OASDI by shifting it closer to a means-tested program. Lawmakers could increase payroll taxes (FICA) and require high-income taxpayers to pay FICA on all earned income. Another option is to raise the age at which an individual becomes eligible for full benefits to 68, 69, or even 70. Additionally, the age when people can receive reduced benefits, often referred to as taking early retirement, could be raised beyond 62. Such an approach, however, would further penalize people of color, who have shorter life expectancies, as well as those who need to leave the job market to serve as caregivers or because they are experiencing disabilities.

Nonetheless, policymakers could add additional incentives to OASDI to encourage people to work longer and could mount more robust campaigns to publicize the significant benefit increases for people who do so. Because even rhetorical changes can influence behavior, referring to early retirement as "reduced benefit age" could help focus attention on the significant lifelong reduction in benefits for those who opt to take benefits before reaching full retirement age.

For social workers and other concerned groups, there is some consensus around necessary improvements to Social Security. These include:

- implementing a minimum benefit as a less stigmatizing way to keep low-paid workers out of poverty in later life;

- providing earnings credits for people who take time out of the paid workforce to care for a child or family member; and

- increasing benefits to widowers when a spouse dies.

As explained in Chapter 8, if enacted soon, relatively minor adjustments can keep OASDI solvent well beyond current projections. However, the longer reform is delayed, the greater the changes that will be necessary.

Developing a Strengths-Based Agenda

How can we chart a policy agenda that helps build on the strengths of older adults so that the years after 65, 85, or even 100 are good years to be alive? To craft new policies that support aging well for a diverse population of older adults, strengths perspective policy principles direct us to engage older adults and their families in defining common interests and determining how best to build on their strengths, overcome barriers, and garner needed resources. Older adults in all economic, racial, ethnic, and social groups should also be integrally involved in evaluating policy outcomes. Policies that combat injustice benefit disadvantaged groups broadly, across the lifespan, and in mutually reinforcing ways. Policies that diminish the rates of poverty among young people will likely improve their health in later life. Initiatives such as living wage campaigns and expanded job training can reduce poverty for all ages; because they help people access better job opportunities, they are also key to aging well. To implement a strengths-based agenda, we need to build coalitions that can more equitably redistribute wealth; when our national assets are shared fairly, both children and older adults will be more secure. We need to ensure that a safety net that largely depends on employers still works in the increasingly temporary and irregular labor markets of the future. We must commit ourselves to the policies that will redeem the social contract on which the nation's strides in improving financial, social, and physical well-being—while imperfect, incomplete, and certainly inequitable—have been founded (Scanlon & Friedline, 2016).

Many organizations are working to forge coalitions among generations. These include groups formed to advocate for Social Security and Medicare and the politically active Generations United, which works to promote intergenerational policies, such as those that support grandparents raising their grandchildren and that develop intergenerational community spaces. You can learn more about some of their efforts and view proposals for policy reforms that older adults support at the Medicare Rights Center (**www.medicarerights.org**) and Generations United (**www.gu.org**) websites.

It is essential that we challenge biases that devalue older adults. Supporting older people's strengths so that they can remain active and contributing members of the community, rather than narrowly focusing on traditional services, will be an important component of planning for, responding to, and reaping the potential gains of the elder boom. The social work values of self-determination and social justice are basic to strengths-based policy practice and can guide the development of needed policies and programs as the nation prepares for the opportunities and challenges we face.

Creating Needed Infrastructure

Efforts are underway at the agency, local, state, and federal levels to create the infrastructure necessary for continued social engagement for older adults, including those with disabilities. For example, communities are designing age-sensitive infrastructures so that older adults with impaired mobility can have access to places such as churches, restaurants, and public buildings. In some communities, universal housing codes that enhance accessibility in residential construction are receiving greater support. Some policymakers are even enacting policies that require all new construction to conform to these codes. Other public entities are considering how to create an environment that works for all ages. For example, many state transportation departments have realized the importance of testing the visibility of road-sign paint with 65-year-old drivers, rather than just young people, so that older adults can continue driving safely. At the agency level, organizations that provide services in a variety of arenas—sexual and domestic violence, developmental disabilities, affordable housing, addictions, homelessness, and veterans' services—are considering how their current approaches may fail to equitably serve older adults, and how changes could improve their ability to meet these potential clients' needs.

Local and state aging agencies continue to implement promising initiatives that support the strengths of families, such as the National Family Caregiver Support Program. In addition to developing strategies to more equitably recognize the contributions of unpaid caregivers in public pension systems, we need to institutionalize best practices in caregiver supports, including flexible employer policies and innovative use of technology for caregiver training and peer connection. Finally, we need to develop and implement individualized caregiver assessment tools that help us to identify the unique needs of caregivers who may be any age, gender, economic status, race, or ethnicity.

Given the well-publicized growth in the older adult population, public planning for transportation, building, recreation, and other future needs should explicitly incorporate attention to how these plans will impact older adults. Social workers must insist on this inclusion.

CONCLUSION

Reciprocity between young and old people provides the mutual support upon which both groups rely. Today, more older adults than ever have the possibility of aging well. The challenge is to craft policies that are equitable and acceptable to young and old alike. The social work profession has the necessary value base and practice orientation to lead efforts to craft effective policies and provide services for older adults. While relatively few social workers report specializing in the aging field, at least 75 percent of social workers are likely to practice with older adults and their families in some capacity (Pace, 2014). Although philanthropic initiatives and some public policy investments have sought to induce more students and new professionals to focus on underserved populations, including older adults, the already large gap in the number of social workers with the gerontological preparation needed to serve this population is growing. Armed with your knowledge of the contexts in which today's older adults struggle or thrive, you can play a critical role in charting social policy for our nation's future and your own.

MAIN POINTS

- Policies and programs for older adults should promote "aging well," understood as the process of minimizing the losses associated with aging by adapting to the challenges and maximizing the benefits of long life.

- Economic security, health care, and social engagement are three areas addressed in key policies for older adults, including Old-Age, Survivors, and Disability Insurance (OASDI), Medicare, Medicaid, and the Older Americans Act (OAA).

- Long-term care (LTC) refers to medical and social services provided to people with disabilities or chronic illnesses. LTC occurs in many settings, including nursing facilities, unpaid care by informal caregivers, and formal home- and community-based services. Informal unpaid caregivers still provide the majority of LTC, although changes in demographics, family composition, and the economy strain this reliance on informal supports.

- Congress enacted the OAA to support planning and to coordinate services for older adults. Services financed through the OAA include in-home care, legal assistance, senior centers, meal programs, and other supports.

- Compared to previous cohorts, older adults today comprise a larger percentage of the entire population. These trends are projected to continue. The Baby Boom generation will continue to greatly impact policy as the United States decides how to meet the needs and leverage the strengths of a larger, older, and more diverse population.

- The Employee Retirement Income Security Act (ERISA), passed in 1974, was the first federal legislation to regulate private pensions. The Act set minimum standards for participation, vesting, funding, and benefit accrual in qualified job-specific pensions. ERISA established the Pension Benefit Guaranty Corporation to insure certain defined benefit pension plans.

- Public insurance programs such as OASDI, public assistance programs such as Supplemental Security Income (SSI), and private resources such as job-specific pensions and private savings contribute to the economic security of older adults. As many employment-based pension systems have disappeared or have shifted risk to individuals, there is greater likelihood that vulnerable seniors will experience deprivation.

- Additionally, as the economic supports on which older adults rely are increasingly insufficient to meet their needs, a growing number of older adults are working at part- and full-time jobs. While paid employment can provide valuable social engagement opportunities and crucial financial resources, persistent age-related discrimination and the reality of health challenges make the labor market a difficult landscape for many elders.

- Policy reforms to remove barriers to productive work for older adults must be carefully planned lest the emphasis on productive aging contribute to marginalizing older adults whose physical or other limitations prevent such work.

- Long-term financial solvency of OASDI needs to be the focus of political decisions. Making changes now, such as increasing payroll taxes and the taxable income limit, decreasing benefits, or increasing the age of eligibility for retirement benefits, will enable the program to provide full benefits beyond 2034. Social workers should encourage policymakers to evaluate the equity and adequacy of these options.

- SSI is a federal income supplement program, not social insurance. Increasing SSI benefits is one option for addressing the needs of low-income older adults.

- The current push in LTC is for community tenure, with the establishment of home- and community-based services, use of nursing homes for short-term rehabilitation, and hospice services that serve people dying at home.

- When the OAA—originally passed in 1965—was last reauthorized in 2016, some services were expanded to include people of any age with disabilities.

- While most older adults will never need extensive stays in LTC facilities, development of financially sustainable options for LTC is still an urgent policy priority. Congress repealed the CLASS provisions of the Affordable Care Act. This means there is still a gaping LTC hole in health care protection, which threatens to impoverish many Americans.

- Proposals to increase personal retirement savings include requiring employers to establish retirement plans, auto-enrolling workers in employer-matched plans, matching savers' contributions, making plans portable, and providing financial education about the importance of saving for retirement.

- Such efforts to help people prepare for retirement should not obscure the need to recalibrate risk-sharing arrangements. Our retreat from social insurance principles has left more older adults vulnerable and increased economic insecurity across the lifespan.

- Arguments about inequitable spending on children compared to spending on older adults often overlook state and local spending on children and focus on aggregate, rather than per-person, spending. Uncontrolled health care spending that negatively affects all age groups is also a major driver of projected increases in spending on older adults.

- There is a large and growing need for social workers with specialization in aging.

- Strengths-perspective policy principles can help to chart a policy agenda informed by the needs and goals of an increasingly diverse older adult population and younger generations.

EXERCISES

1. Test your knowledge about aging with the online Aging Quiz at **aging.umkc.edu/quiz** (Breytspraak & Badura, 2015). How did you do? What were you surprised to learn? What do you think has shaped your beliefs about aging? How can you increase your knowledge about aging in preparation for effective practice with older adults?

2. Go to the Sanchez case at **www.routledgesw.com/cases**. Think about what you have learned about the family and the supports available to them.
   a. As they age, how do you think the needs of Hector and Celia Sanchez might differ from those of their peers who are not immigrants?
   b. How do you think the family and community supports available to Mr. and Mrs. Sanchez may differ from other older adults'?
3. Go to the Washburn case at **www.routledgesw.com/cases**. Strengths-based social policy analysis and development focus on giving a voice to clients. Although you cannot talk to Mrs. Washburn, imagine yourself in her situation and try to answer these questions from her perspective.
   a. What needs and concerns might Mrs. Washburn voice?
   b. What might Mrs. Washburn say are her goals for "aging well"?
   c. What do you think Mrs. Washburn would like to see implemented in terms of additional policies and programs? Identify three things. How might she become involved in trying to realize those changes?
4. What strengths in Carla Washburn's community could a social worker build on when attempting to meet the needs of elders and others in the community? How might activation of these strengths have positive ripple effects for younger community members?
5. Sometimes social workers admit homeless older adults who have disabilities to nursing facilities because they feel that at least in these facilities, people will have food and shelter.
   a. Thinking about Riverton and what homeless older adults may be experiencing there, do you think this service strategy is in the best interest of older adults?
   b. Do you think it is cost-effective? Do you think it is consistent with the strengths perspective?
   c. Can you think of a more effective strategy? What policy changes might be needed to create alternative options?
6. In small groups, discuss the policy implications of the demographic changes this country will undergo between now and 2060.
   a. Approaching from a strengths perspective, list three positive aspects of these changes. Explore how policy changes could build on these positive aspects.
   b. List three challenges associated with these changes. Explore what policy responses may be needed to confront these challenges.
7. Older adults are seldom adequately consulted when a community such as Hudson City does disaster planning, even though they may experience particular risks in such a disaster.
   a. What steps would need to be taken to change this fact? Who would need to take them? How might stereotypes about aging interfere with a community's need to fully include older adults in the disaster planning process?
   b. See if you can find out if/how disaster planning in your community considers the needs of older adults, particularly those who also have disabilities. List some strategies that might help to more completely include these groups.

c. How are older adults involved in responding to natural disasters in your community or those nearby? In many places, older adults make up the core volunteer base of disaster response efforts. What lessons could these experiences provide to inform other groups' consideration of older adults' potential contributions?
8. Visit your nearest senior center. Find out how the center is funded. What services does the center provide, and who is eligible to receive them? (If you do not have a senior center nearby, find out how far away the closest such resource is. What do older adults do without a local senior center? What difference might it make if they had this resource?)
   a. How old is the average participant?
   b. Do you think the senior center will need to change if it is to attract future cohorts of older adults? If so, what policy and program changes would you suggest?
   c. Are there any intergenerational aspects to programming? What opportunities for intergenerational programming do you see?
   d. Is the senior center involved in any policy advocacy? What issues is it championing? How does it engage older adults in these efforts?
9. Interview an older adult. Ask their opinion on issues that concern you—for example, student debt or funding for public education. Older adults are also stakeholders in these issues. Where do they get information about these issues? Do they consult the same sources you do?
   a. Do the older adult's views of these subjects differ from yours? If so, how?
   b. Why do you think they hold these views?
10. Although the role of the social worker in the Brickville case is primarily focused on work with youths, consider how older adults can be engaged to help the youths of the community and to promote community well-being.
    a. How could older adults be involved in building youths' leadership skills?
    b. What roles might older adults play in improving community safety?
    c. What strategies could you use to help residents young and old identify common goals and begin to work together? How would you go about recruiting both groups? What potential barriers to this approach can you identify, and how would you transcend them?
11. Media shape our beliefs about a variety of social policy issues. Review at least three broadcast media stories (on television, online, or on the radio) that discuss aging. What is the specific issue highlighted? What messages about aging is this coverage advancing? How might messages like these shape policy debates?
    a. Whose voices are represented? Are older adults themselves featured, or are other people talking *about* older adults?
    b. How might you use stories you hear from older adults in direct practice settings to counter negative messages about aging? How could changing these narratives help social workers advocate for more effective policies for older clients?
12. Go to the AARP website and use the Strengthen Social Security Tool to determine how you would close the Social Security funding gap. The tool allows you to adjust the benefits people receive and/or the contributions they make while working. You can see how those

changes impact future solvency and the benefits you and your clients will rely on in old age. Policymakers must make these kinds of difficult trade-offs if they are to close the projected funding shortfall.
a. What choices did you make? What was the hardest to decide?
b. Did any of your choices surprise you? Which ones and why?
c. How might putting yourself in policymakers' shoes help you to be a more effective advocate for the positions you support and, most importantly, for your clients' needs?

CHAPTER 12

The Future

EXHIBIT 12.1

Marchers at Global Climate March in Washington, DC

Source: Shutterstock/Rena Schild

BECAUSE NO ONE HAS AN ACCURATE CRYSTAL BALL, it might seem unwise to try to foretell the future. Certainly, some important events in the recent past have appeared to take observers by surprise, often with dramatic—and sometimes dire—consequences for social workers and those we serve. Many people failed to anticipate crucial political events in 2016, including Britain's vote to exit the European Union and Donald Trump's election. Some major natural disasters have unfolded with relatively little advance notice; even when technology reveals a coming disaster, it can be impossible to know exactly where, how, and whom it will affect most. And, although we now have greater clarity about warning signs that were missed (Fernandez & Nikolsko-Rzhevskyy, 2011), the Great Recession that followed the collapse of U.S. housing and financial markets was apparent to many people only in hindsight. These forecasting failures do not mean people were not trying. The world today is a forecasting context some describe as "wicked"—rapidly changing and unpredictable, where the past provides little preparation for the future (Epstein, 2019, p. 53). This reality makes forecasting more difficult and raises the stakes on the need to consider and critically analyze diverging claims about where we are headed.

Although predicting the future is uncertain work, we now know more about the biases that can lead us astray. For example, many polls leading up to the 2016 election overlooked the significance of those who did not respond to inquiries (Mercer, Deane, & McGeeney, 2016). Analysts failed to consider the extent to which these unheard Americans would support the candidate who promised to restore their position in the political landscape, and many pundits seemed eager to look for evidence that would support their preferred outcome. Whenever we try to figure out what the future holds, there is a risk that we will seek information that confirms our own beliefs, instead of systematically interrogating our assumptions. As we try to understand a changing future, social workers must guard against these tendencies.

Contemplating the future and what we expect from it is not merely an intellectual exercise. Beliefs about the future and what it might hold are central to the actions we take. For example, when rainy weather is forecast, we grab an umbrella. This action then influences our outcomes; those who prepared for rain will be less bothered by it than those caught in a downpour. In the social policy arena, when we anticipate a coming demographic or economic change, we are better positioned to take actions that will help us successfully navigate these currents. Because policy and programs are enacted to influence the future and must work within the context as it evolves, your policy practice will require you to be attuned to predictions about future conditions. As Macarov (1991) has pointed out, without forecasting, there is no freedom of decision. To make sound choices, you must have some image of what the future options are and some sense of the impact of your choices and how their consequences may reverberate.

This chapter outlines some of the forces shaping the future of social policy. It presents predictions about the future, highlights where predictions vary or even compete, and encourages social work students to think critically about how social work will be affected by likely future developments. In this chapter, we also discuss strategies for understanding why certain forecasts are made and for interpreting potential future scenarios. Importantly, as in the rest of this text, our vision for the future looks through the lens of strengths, particularly the strengths of client groups. As we evaluate the validity of different claims about the future, we assess the extent to which they incorporate clients' experiences and aspirations. We consider how taking different paths can build on clients' strengths or, conversely, impair clients' chances to meet their goals.

Today, we are inundated with dire warnings about the future: our communities are threatened by demographic changes and economic insecurity, our economy and social safety net are imperiled, our politics are irreparably polarized, our fates are controlled by technological forces, our natural environment is damaged beyond repair. Polls suggest that Americans are largely pessimistic about where the nation is headed, in terms of widening inequality, deteriorating environmental conditions, and political polarization; further, many people fear our institutions and leaders are unprepared to steer in the right direction (Parker, Morin, & Horowitz, 2019). These apocalyptic warnings contrast with suspiciously euphoric predictions about the bright future that awaits us: technology will solve our problems, economic growth will improve everyone's quality of life, a particular elected official will deliver us to a better tomorrow. We see the ways predictions can influence how people think and feel, and we know that catalyzing momentum for forward progress on the issues that concern us begins with articulating a vision of what is possible for our shared futures.

If we are to advance a realistic but strengths-based view of where we stand and where we might go, we must somehow evaluate these claims, chart a course for ourselves, and decide how best to help those we serve. Here, we examine a set of guidelines for analyzing forecasts that will help you make sense of the myriad and often conflicting predictions you will be asked to consider in the coming years. Then, we explore major trends that are expected to influence future social policy and possible ways strengths-based policy could respond. Finally, you are challenged to use this information to develop the foresight that can help improve policies and, ultimately, outcomes for your clients. You can draw on the strengths-based approach to policy development to move from challenges to goals. In the process, you can build individual and community capacity and help people secure the resources they need for full economic and social inclusion—and a prosperous and healthy future.

GUIDELINES FOR UNDERSTANDING FUTURE FORECASTS

We can more clearly understand forecasts if we consider the motivations of those who make them, the assumptions on which they are based, and the contexts in which they are made. Quick Guide 8 provides a set of guidelines you can use to understand why people make forecasts, whether they are likely to be accurate, and how they might influence future actions, including policymaking. As you become familiar with these guidelines and begin to use them to analyze forecasts you encounter, you will be better able to identify which forecasts are not credible, which ones should be heeded, and how to influence people's understanding of and response to forecasts about our shared future. You can also develop your skills to chart an alternative course when a particular forecast could have negative consequences for the clients you serve.

QUICK GUIDE 8   Understanding Future Forecasts

1. Analyze the purpose:
   - social mobilization, to encourage people to be prepared for the future being forecast;
   - system replacement;
   - enhancement of a specific professional group; and/or
   - collective learning and adaptation.
2. Assess the underlying assumptions animating the forecast and the credibility of source information.
3. Consider the influence of current socioeconomic conditions.
4. Do not expect the numbers to speak for themselves.
5. Assess the extent to which surprise events have been anticipated.

Analyze the Purpose

When you examine assertions about the future, consider first the perspectives of those making the forecast, including the reasons why they are trying to predict the future. People make forecasts for many reasons, including to activate people to prepare for a particular future, to encourage investment in systems viewed as inadequate to meet future needs, to enhance the status of a particular group or profession, and/or to facilitate collective learning and adaptation, in advance of changing realities. While some of these motivations are more noble than others, all represent potential distortions of the forecast and should, then, be critically analyzed.

Social mobilization refers to efforts to encourage large groups of people to prepare themselves for the future. Education reformers use forecasts about the changing labor market to induce changes in what students are taught and how schools are evaluated. Social workers use forecasts about the growing older adult population to urge policymakers to invest in supports for elders. Scientists and advocates use data about the warming planet to spur more urgent action. Forecasts are such a potent tool for social mobilization that the forecasts themselves can become a target. For example, the Trump Administration ordered government agencies to stop reporting on the future effects of climate change (Davenport & Landler, 2019); without public data to present a picture of what the earth could look like by the end of the century if trends are not reversed, forecasting itself is imperiled.

People pressing for system replacement are trying to demonstrate that unless a system is fundamentally changed or replaced, it will be unable to deal adequately with future conditions. In some cases, they may fear that even a system that has functioned well up to this point may be headed for failure due to changing demands and/or expectations. While some have other intentions, analysts and advocates forecasting insolvency in entitlement programs such as Social Security and Medicare are largely motivated by a desire to shore up these systems. Similarly, several prominent voices are highlighting the need to ensure that infrastructure systems, including bridges and the energy grid, are strong enough to withstand internal pressures and external threats.

People who believe future conditions will make their professional group more important will want to publicize that forecast. This could explain some individuals' assertions that their technological developments will play key roles in reshaping our lives; certainly, today's technology innovators enjoy prestige and influence, largely because their products are seen as integral to our future. Similarly, financial planners' forecasts about retirement seldom include proposals for strengthening social insurance systems or facilitating older adults' success in the labor force. Instead, their vision of financial security in later life largely hinges on individuals amassing enough in personal assets—with the assistance of their profession—to finance years of leisure.

People also make forecasts to foster collective learning and adaptation. Much of the forecasting related to ways automation will transform the U.S. labor market aims to catalyze adaptation. On the individual level, people are encouraged to seek out and prepare themselves for "robot-proof" jobs or to learn how to successfully work alongside artificial intelligence systems, while policymakers explore ways to help communities deal with being displaced by machines.

Although learning and adaptation often prompt change in response to a forecast, unlike social mobilization, these motivations emphasize information dissemination and individual response rather than collective organizing for broad-scale social change.

To illustrate how forecasts can affect different constituencies, consider predictions about the social work labor force. For example, one claim is that the number of jobs for social workers will grow by about 16 percent between 2016 and 2026 (U.S. Bureau of Labor Statistics, 2017b). The need for gerontological social workers is predicted to increase particularly quickly. If social work education does not change to prepare more social workers to work with older adults, the profession will not be able to provide services to those who need them. Additionally, the profession's ability to capitalize on the growth may be compromised if new social workers are not prepared for the available jobs. Other professions may fill perceived gaps and, in the process, elevate their own stature. Indeed, many long-term care facilities already employ non-social workers to provide direct services and administer programs. In response to forecasts, social work education is adding coursework in aging, offering scholarships to students who intend to work in gerontology, and developing initiatives designed to increase social workers' aptitude and enthusiasm for work with older adults. This example illustrates three purposes of claims about the future: system replacement, social mobilization, and professional enhancement.

To orient yourself to competing claims about the future and sharpen your ability to evaluate various projections, try to find forecasts in the popular press and from analysts. Investigate the backgrounds of the people making these forecasts and consider which of the motivations outlined above might have fueled them. Ask yourself, "What is the purpose of this forecast?" As we have discussed previously, people construct reality based on their own points of view. A forecast is such a construction, projected to deal with a possible future reality. Awareness of the ways differing purposes bias predictions can augment your understanding of the forecast. For example, whose interests are served by forecasts that predict that fewer young people will want to buy homes and will instead want a range of rental housing options? How might such predictions benefit some groups, such as developers of rental housing and people with resources to rent luxury apartments, while disadvantaging others, including families of color who need assistance to buy a home and build wealth? Similarly, what would motivate different professions to make competing predictions about the future of our natural environment? Who might want to predict that climate change will devastate coastal communities, and who has an interest in claiming that technological advances will prevent climate disaster? Understanding different stakeholders' reasons for making predictions does not necessarily tell you how credible these predictions are, nor what their implications would be for your clients. However, analyzing predictions with a critical eye will increase your ability to accurately assess and appropriately respond to various visions of what the future may hold.

Assess Underlying Assumptions and the Credibility of Source Information

After you have analyzed the purposes of forecasts and the interests of those making them, carefully consider the sources on which they rely and the credibility of these sources.

One prominent example of a credible source on which many forecasts are based is U.S. Census Bureau population projections. The term **population projection** refers to the number of people who are expected to be in a given group in a specific year. Population projections are based on underlying assumptions. Demographers who make population projections start with a set of characteristics in a population for a base year. They then apply different assumptions about the amount, direction, and rate of change that could be experienced by that population in ensuing years. For example, to create a population projection of the number of women over 40 in 2030, demographers could begin with the number of women over 20 in 2010 (a base census year) and then apply assumptions about how many women would either die or migrate in or out of the country over the next 20 years.

The U.S. Census Bureau uses a **cohort-component method** for developing projections. This method follows each cohort of people of the same age across time. It bases population projections on assumptions about trends that affect population growth. The U.S. Census Bureau collects data on net migration—the balance of people entering and leaving a population. It also relies on National Center for Health Statistics data on mortality—the rate of death for each age group, generally considered separately for men and women, and by race—and fertility—the rate of births, generally considered separately by age group and race. The projected population in a given year, then, can be calculated by adding the net population increase (births minus deaths, plus net in-migration) to the population in the base year. Birth, death, and migration rates are influenced by long-term trends (changing attitudes about parenting and family size, population trajectories in other countries) and by unanticipated events (epidemics, crop failures, economic and political crises). Policy changes in areas such as immigration, family planning, and financial support can also induce changes in birth, death, and migration rates, with implications for future population. To attempt to account for these forces, the U.S. Census Bureau creates a range of projections. Each range is based on different sets of assumptions, some of which may be in error. For example, in 2013 researchers at the Max Planck Institute for Demographic Research asserted that the assumptions the U.S. Census Bureau used to estimate future fertility rates failed to capture the changing pattern of delayed childbearing. In 2018, the U.S. fertility rate hit a 40-year low, largely confirming the trends in women waiting until they are older to have children. Other, less-anticipated trends also slowed U.S. population growth, including rising mortality levels in some populations and some reductions in migration. Other population projections have been even more flawed. A 1970 book vividly titled *The Population Bomb* predicted worldwide starvation and prompted panic about overpopulation (Ehrlich, 1970). Simultaneously, technology increased agricultural output and population growth started a long deceleration; as a result, the crisis predicted never materialized, although global population pressures today intensify environmental threats. These examples illustrate how social norms, public policies, and economic conditions all influence behavior and events. When population projections fail to take those shifts into account, forecasts are less accurate.

There is nothing inherently wrong with basing predictions largely on assumptions. However, it is vital that you examine those assumptions before accepting a forecast as an accurate portrayal of the future. For example, policymakers who want to cut cash assistance and other safety-net investments may predict that these policies will lead more people to get and keep jobs. If this prediction is accurate, such cuts are easier to justify; fewer people will need assistance.

However, the assumption that work requirements will reduce the need for financial support is questionable; indeed, years of experience with such policies reveal that many families suffer when their futures do not unfold as promised and they cannot secure a job paying a living wage (Heinrich, 2014). Today, demographic and economic constraints and shifting social norms are fueling a push to view future older people as healthy and capable of self-support. While these projections may lead to policies that facilitate more active engagement of older adults, they may also be used as rationale for cutting supports on which vulnerable older adults depend.

To consider another example, think about how people talk about the potential of technology to counter environmental challenges. Policies that ignore or even exacerbate the threats posed by global climate change are easier for policymakers to tout—and for people to accept—when it is predicted that technology will be capable of mitigating the worst consequences. There are a series of assumptions embedded in these claims—about technological capacity and the pace of its development, the scale of climate threat, and the extent to which those most adversely affected by climate change will be able to access and utilize such technologies. Allowing ourselves to be consoled by comforting predictions without rigorously examining the assumptions on which they rest is irresponsible. It increases the likelihood that we find ourselves unprepared for the future that awaits.

Even though people may try to persuade you to the contrary, numbers do not speak for themselves. They must be interpreted. For example, the fact that a smaller share of the future U.S. population will be non-Latinx White than in the past does not necessarily mean formerly "minority" communities will enjoy the privilege that being in the "majority" would connote. Factors other than sheer population size determine political and economic power, and it is not yet certain how the U.S. landscape will be reshaped as it becomes more pluralistic. We cannot assume that groups that have been disadvantaged through decades—even centuries—of inequity will automatically experience better outcomes as they occupy a larger share of the population. Instead, projections of growth in the Latinx population and among communities of color should underscore the importance of policies to level the playing field. A critical consideration of these forecasts rejects naïve assumptions that size equals influence, to instead call for policies that facilitate asset accumulation, educational attainment, and political empowerment as investments in the well-being of our increasingly diverse population.

Similarly, some projections of future dependency ratios assume that the population age 65 and older represents the number of people incapable of working. However, many older adults can and do work, and more will if public policy supports this choice. Finally, advocates who use the total number of foreign-born individuals in the United States to argue for further restrictions in immigration present an assumption that continued immigration at the current rate would be disastrous. However, a larger percentage of the U.S. population was foreign-born in 1890 (15 percent) than in 2017 (13.7 percent), and history does not suggest that this earlier immigration was detrimental to the country (Lopez, Bialik, & Radford, 2018).

We can emphasize or downplay different interpretations of projections depending on the future we want to portray. We can present portrayals of the future that incite fear—as do many who oppose immigration and growing diversity—or to excite people about future possibilities—as in the case of some technological advances. We can pivot from discussions of public costs associated with population aging to focus on the strengths of older adults and policy options for maximizing their choices and leveraging their contributions (Gerontological Society of America [GSA], 2018). We can talk about high levels of immigration as a problem we need to address or as an enduring part of our national fabric and a testament to the allure of the United States as a land of opportunity. Diverging assumptions about the future lead to very different conclusions about the kinds of policies social workers should support today—for our tomorrow.

Strengths-based social workers can engage in reframing discussion of the future. For example, instead of allowing discussion of the aging of our society to be framed as a "tsunami," social workers can celebrate the advances that have made longer life expectancy possible. Instead of acquiescing to political rhetoric about the "threat" immigrants pose, social workers can promote integration within communities. Instead of echoing alarms about increasing automation and the ways in which it will disrupt people's work lives, social workers can reflect on the gains past technological developments have delivered to human well-being. We can then use careful analysis of the projected impact of technology to push for investments in a robust and revitalized social safety net, ready to meet the challenges of the future, and ensure that people can reap the fruits of future technological advances.

In evaluating forecasts, a final consideration is the extent to which the person making a prediction acknowledges surprise events that could influence its accuracy. For example, the events of September 11, 2001, sparked an economic downturn and greater U.S. involvement in global conflict. While in retrospect, many observers believe that the United States should have been more prepared for a catastrophic terrorist attack, it is certainly difficult to imagine how we could have entirely predicted the events and their consequences. Similarly, the Great Recession unexpectedly changed our economic outlook. These events significantly affected the accuracy of earlier forecasts about economic trends during the first decade of the twenty-first century. Such surprises are not rare anomalies. Scholars who study forecasts have found that events experts considered "impossible" occur 15 percent of the time, while those they deemed "sure things" failed to materialize even more frequently (Tetlock, 2016). Even if analysts do not alert people that surprise events may dramatically change the accuracy of their projections, it is incumbent on observers to consider that possibility. Think about surprise events you have seen in your lifetime and unlikely events you can imagine. How might they affect future forecasts? Consider the extent to which policy changes might affect the likelihood of these events, as well as whether they can truly be considered "unforeseen" by an adept forecaster. Think about how expected future changes, including in demographics and social norms, will be affected by less anticipated events, and about how the changing nature of information and communication has altered what it means to be "surprised" by the future.

Although nobody can anticipate and consider all future scenarios, social policy practitioners should attempt to account for the most likely events. For example, demographers and policymakers attempting to anticipate future Medicare and Medicaid costs can create alternative scenarios based on events that may affect future costs of care, as well as rates of disability. Current approaches allow factoring in likely possibilities such as breakthroughs in disease prevention. When they craft these forecasts, analysts should consider the possible impact of such factors as more stringent anti-smoking campaigns, Baby Boomers' greater participation in exercise programs, Affordable Care Act investments in preventative care, and possible advances in the treatment of Alzheimer's disease or cancer. Planners in the private sector also consider the likelihood of such alternative scenarios when they make decisions regarding future investments in long-term care (LTC) facilities and housing options that will help seniors age in place. Savvy planners in all areas of the economy make similar calculations. Today, scientists can model the potential effects of climate change so that real estate developers, farmers, architects, and other constituencies can account for future scenarios. Analysts can predict the extent to which still undeveloped technologies will disrupt the working lives of people in different industries and how women and men may be differently affected (Hegewisch, Childers, & Hartmann, 2019). Of course, there is no guarantee that the future will come to pass as these predictions suggest. What is certain is that analyzing the best available information to consider what the future may look like and how we can deal with it will result in better future outcomes than aimlessly drifting toward an unknown shore.

THINKING ABOUT THE FUTURE USING A VALUES-BASED LENS: THE STRENGTHS APPROACH

While the guidelines discussed above can help us analyze the accuracy of a forecast, accuracy is not the only criterion that should drive social workers' evaluation. Additionally, from a strengths perspective, forecasts should always be evaluated to gauge whether they are based on a deficit view or whether they provide a foundation for building on people's strengths. For example, not very long ago, a common prediction was that people with disabilities would spend their lives in institutions. This forecast was based on the assumption that this population was totally dependent on others. In turn, this prediction contributed to social policies that failed to invest in the capacities of people with disabilities, including those that put far more resources into residential care than into community-based services. As a result, this prediction became a sort of self-fulfilling prophecy—until people living with disabilities challenged the assumptions on which these forecasts were based, to chart their own futures. Similarly, decades of policies and practices that assumed women and girls were uninterested in careers in science and math depressed their representation in these fields, until pioneers asserted their own vision for their futures.

It is also important to consider how well forecasters really understand the current conditions in which they are rooting their projections. Just as the U.S. Census Bureau uses a base year to craft its population projections, so too do forecasters anticipating future developments in technology, economics, or social relationships need a comprehensive and accurate picture of what those areas look like today. Too often, biases and injustices reduce the extent to which some groups' perspectives are accounted for in forecasts. For example, people who make forecasts about the future needs of Latinx individuals must pay attention to the life conditions, strengths, and goals of these individuals today, including the diversity within this population. If they do so, they will not overlook such vital information as the rate of entry of Latinas into the full-time workforce, dramatic increases in Latinx college enrollment, and the growth of Latinx populations in suburban communities. These are important factors in forecasting needs such as childcare, diverse college completion supports, and culturally competent service providers in suburban social service agencies. Understanding these trends and how they may evolve is essential for making accurate forecasts. For example, Latinx birth rates and overall U.S. population growth may be altered by Latinas' labor force participation, and social attitudes about immigration may change as the Latinx population diffuses to new communities.

Values rooted in the National Association of Social Workers (NASW) Code of Ethics underpin the strengths approach—today and as we contemplate the future. Social workers must carefully consider the interplay of professional values, societal goals, and political realities when they evaluate future scenarios. In the face of uncertainty, professional values such as commitment to social justice offer an anchor that social workers can use when considering future policies. For example, we might favor spending more money on children because children experience higher poverty rates than other cohorts. However, forecasts used to support such policy changes must be carefully crafted, lest we lend unintentional support to those who would pit the needs of children against those of older adults.

FACTORS THAT WILL SHAPE FUTURE SOCIAL POLICIES

Armed with these insights into understanding forecasts, we turn now to major factors that are likely to influence future social policy: increasing racial and ethnic diversity, medical and technological advances, automation and the changing nature of work, political realignments, and climate change. In this section, we analyze these factors and how they are already affecting the lives of those we serve. We then consider what their effects on policy might be and the kinds of policies social workers should urge in response.

Population Growth and Shifts

In 2019, the U.S. population exceeded 328 million, and the world population exceeded 7.5 billion (U.S. Census Bureau, 2019b). The U.S. Census Bureau projects that by 2060, the U.S. population will exceed 417 million (Colby & Ortman, 2015). The United Nations projections put the global population at more than 9.7 billion people in 2050 and more than 11 billion by 2100 (United Nations, 2017). As Exhibit 12.2 illustrates, although the rate of population growth projected over the next century is a fraction of the rate of the past 100 years, the world population will continue to grow. Most of this projected growth will be concentrated in Africa and Asia, the population of which will account for more than 80 percent of the world's population by 2100 (United Nations, 2017).

It took thousands of years for the world population to reach one billion people, only 124 years to reach two billion, and only 12 years to add a billion people between 1999 and 2011. The rate of global population growth peaked in 1962 and 1963. Researchers have identified several possible reasons for slower global population growth rates today and, as projected, in the future: increased access to education for women and girls, greater availability of contraceptives, growing expectation that children will survive to adulthood, lack of adequate supports such as affordable childcare and paid family leave for working parents, and an increase in the number of deaths due to an aging population. Additionally, cataclysmic disasters and economic depressions can also influence population growth rates, particularly in the parts of the globe especially vulnerable to such events.

EXHIBIT 12.2

World Population Growth, 1750–2100

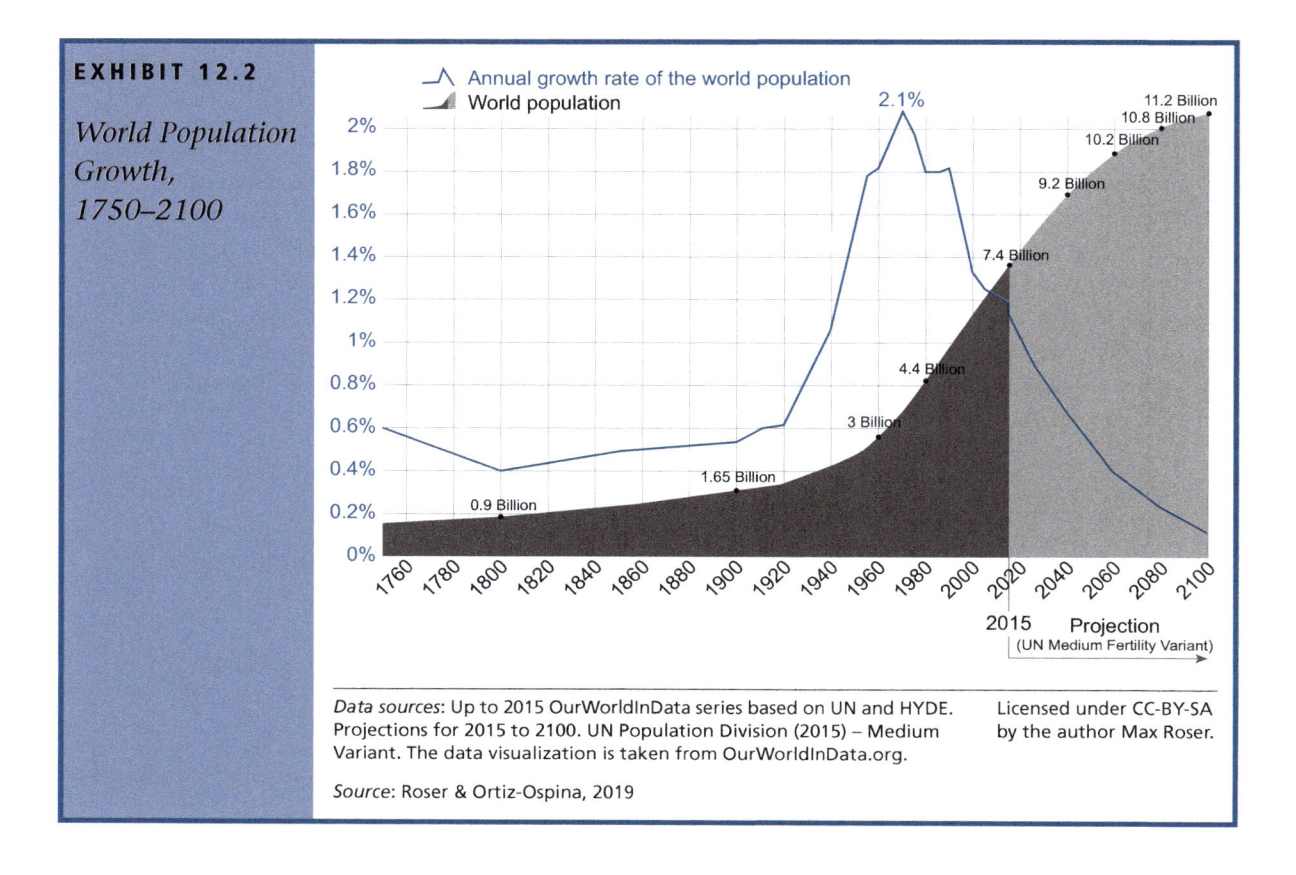

Data sources: Up to 2015 OurWorldInData series based on UN and HYDE. Projections for 2015 to 2100. UN Population Division (2015) – Medium Variant. The data visualization is taken from OurWorldInData.org. Licensed under CC-BY-SA by the author Max Roser.

Source: Roser & Ortiz-Ospina, 2019

As described above, the two major factors driving a country's population growth are fertility and net migration. In the United States, the rate of births per 1,000 people fell to a 30-year low in 2018, to considerably below the rate required for a generation to reproduce itself (called the **replacement rate**). Although the total number of births rose slightly, as the population of women at childbearing age increased, fertility rates fell (Martin, Hamilton, & Osterman, 2018). Importantly, while fertility rates are largely influenced by social and cultural factors, including attitudes about age of family formation and women's roles, there is evidence that public policy also influences these seemingly personal decisions. Specifically, by reducing the financial and psychological toll of early childrearing, more generous paid family leave policies can increase fertility rates (Olivetti & Petrongolo, 2017). This analysis suggests that the U.S. failure to provide such supports may be contributing to declining fertility rates. In the United States, only 41 percent of workers between ages 20 and 54 have a child at home today, down from more than 60 percent in 1968 (Van Dam, 2019). Crucially, this is not because more parents are staying home with their children; the share of parents who are in the labor force has been stable in these decades. Instead, more American workers are foregoing parenthood. These trends are contributing to growing political momentum for investments in policies that respond to the needs of young, would-be parents. These dynamics illustrate how policy developments, demographic changes, and changing predictions about the future can interact, with implications for individuals and the larger society.

Including net immigration and the share of births that are to foreign-born women, foreign-born individuals are projected to account for most of population growth in the United States for at least the next 40 years (Colby & Ortman, 2015). As a result, a larger proportion of the future U.S. population will be made up of people of color and Latinx individuals. These population shifts have important implications for the distribution of political and economic power and will require that social workers consider how policy changes can best adapt to and leverage these changing demographics. Further, as described in Chapter 11, the percentage of children is expected to remain stable through 2030, while the percentage of older adults is expected to grow (Colby & Ortman, 2015). By 2060, approximately 20 percent of the U.S. population will be younger than 18, almost a quarter will be 65 and older, and less than 60 percent will be adults between 18 and 64 (Colby & Ortman, 2015). Exhibit 12.3

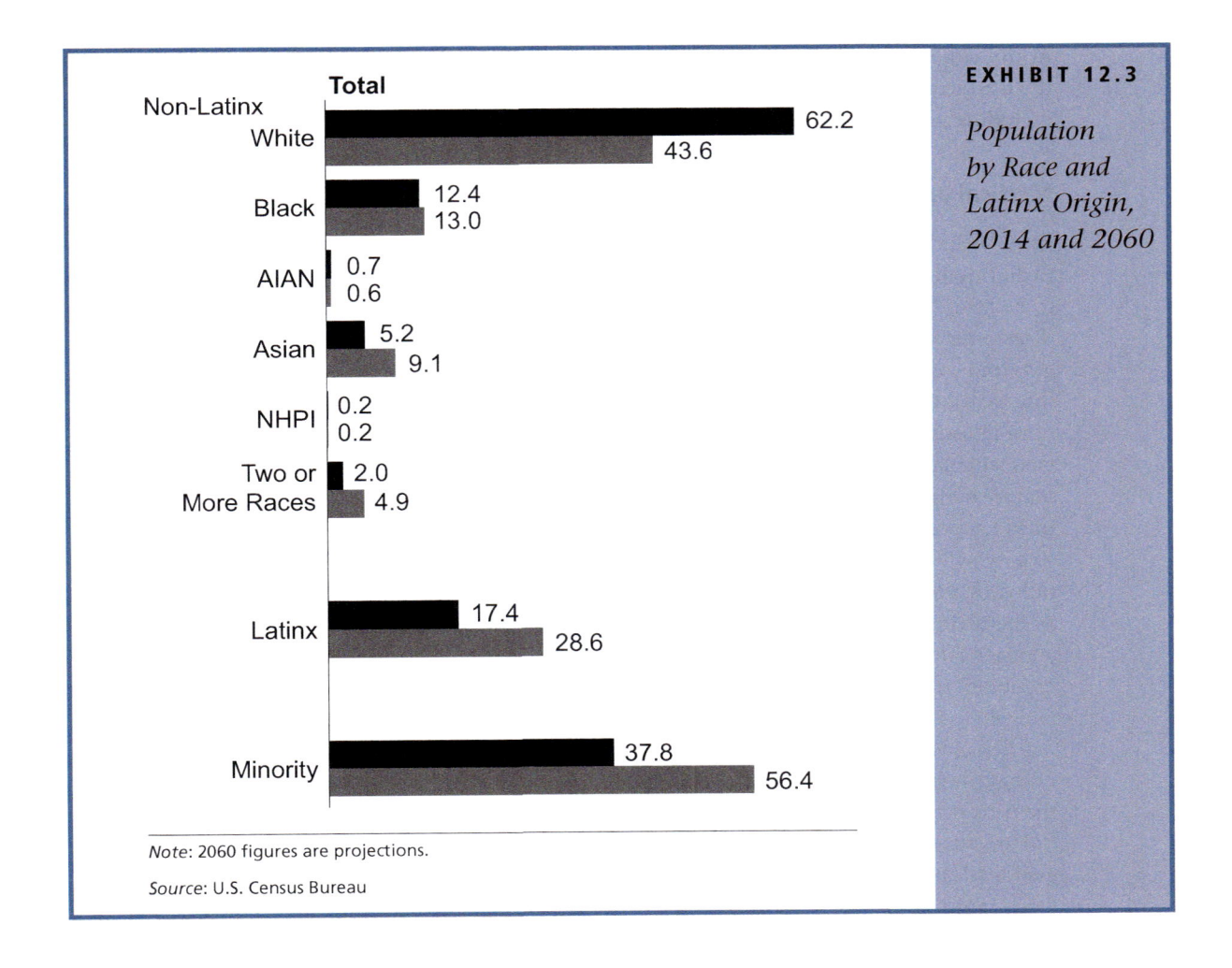

EXHIBIT 12.3

Population by Race and Latinx Origin, 2014 and 2060

Total

Group	2014	2060
Non-Latinx White	62.2	43.6
Black	12.4	13.0
AIAN	0.7	0.6
Asian	5.2	9.1
NHPI	0.2	0.2
Two or More Races	2.0	4.9
Latinx	17.4	28.6
Minority	37.8	56.4

Note: 2060 figures are projections.

Source: U.S. Census Bureau

illustrates projected increases in the proportion of the population of different racial and ethnic groups, between 2014 and 2060. As depicted, no group will make up a majority by the middle of this century (U.S. Census Bureau, 2012). Examining these population projections underscores the importance of enacting social policies that meet the needs and build on the strengths of a population that will be larger, older, and more diverse. As we consider our coming future, the core social work aims of empowering people, facilitating healthy communities, and supporting collective well-being are clear national imperatives.

While more than half of Latinx individuals are native-born U.S. citizens, immigration has significantly contributed to growth in the U.S. Latinx population. Immigration rates provide a good example of the interconnection of different forecasts. For example, because the U.S. Latinx population has a younger median age and higher birth rate than non-Latinx Whites, as well as a high rate of labor force participation, growth in this population is a significant factor in keeping Social Security solvent. Latinx workers play particularly important roles in the current and future economies in areas—geographies and industries—where they make up a larger share of the labor force, such as the American Southwest and the health and dependent care sectors. At the same time, the growing prominence of Latinx individuals, families, and communities in the U.S. economy, political system, and culture has also contributed to anti-immigrant backlash, including policies with effects that ripple throughout society.

Medical and Technological Advances

Medical and technological advances are fundamentally reshaping many aspects of American life, including how long life itself can be expected to last, as well as how we think, what we believe to be "true" (Manjoo, 2008), and even what it means to be "human" (Bess, 2016). Advances in disease detection and prevention, development of adaptive technologies, research into the origins and consequences of health problems, innovations in genetic and reproductive science, and interventions for those with chronic conditions are altering many people's lives. These changes have already affected the provision of social work services, and new technologies not yet discovered will likely bring additional changes. Applications derived from genetic research could lead to major changes in reproduction, organ replacement, and treatment, leading not only to increases in life expectancy but also to dramatic changes in disability rates (Gore, 2013). However, our society will continue to wrestle with complex ethical issues related to utilization of medical technologies. For example, research involving early embryonic human–animal chimeras could lead to life-saving medical breakthroughs, but these scientific possibilities also raise crucial questions about the definition of humanity, our responsibility to other creatures, and the limits of technical capability (Hyun et al., 2007). As such research proceeds, policymakers must decide how to regulate what is allowable and how to enforce the limits they impose.

Social workers have already encountered ethical quandaries related to evolving medical technology, including in the domain of assisted reproduction, where disputes about parenthood and the intrusion of profit motive have threatened the well-being of various stakeholders. New medical advances provide more alternatives for reproduction, but they also create opportunities for exploitation. While poor women's fertility has been contested throughout history, new technologies bring new risks. The same groups historically pressured to limit their reproduction may now feel compelled to provide children for childless people, through coerced surrogacy or other mechanisms (Peng, 2013). Additionally, children may struggle to gain access to their own genetic and parentage information when they were conceived using certain technologies. Popular media regularly features stories of adults whose stories of their own ancestry were upended by genetic testing that revealed shockingly different origins.

Breakthroughs in genetic research may create life-saving innovations, but these technical feats raise new issues, including agonizing choices for expectant parents contemplating their child's future with a difficult diagnosis, as well as the trade-offs associated with finding out that one has a serious condition oneself. Social workers will likely be at the center of many controversies, helping clients navigate options and make medical decisions, but also pushing policymakers and health care providers to prioritize the values of self-determination, respect for the dignity and worth of all, and the primacy of client concerns. For example, future social workers may have to help a client decide whether to attempt a new genetic therapy that could prevent their future children from inheriting certain conditions, while being careful to frame these choices from a strengths perspective. Without such a commitment, people living with disabilities may feel that their experiences are being pathologized or even "erased" (Boardman, Young, & Griffiths, 2017). Social workers will also need to attend to issues of social justice and equity, given the risks that promising medical advances will be available only to those with the economic, social, and political resources to secure them. If targeted cancer therapies, early diagnostic tools, and adaptive technologies are distributed as unevenly as today's health care resources are, the march of progress will bring greater inequality, with life or death consequences.

Scientific advances in medical research and treatment are not the only ways technological development will change our shared future. As you may have witnessed in your own life or in your social work practice, advances in information technology have transformed the ways people communicate, access information, learn new skills, exchange resources, investigate options, and conduct business. Ours is a society in technological flux. This context has implications for the way we approach daily tasks. It is also reshaping our culture and exacting new demands from our institutions. While information is more readily available than ever before imagined, the "truth" may be obscured by technologies that can seamlessly alter videos and voices and allow people to avoid interacting with those who hold opposing views. Artificial intelligence is transforming industries from customer service to higher education to health care, but it is not clear whether these technologies will foster the social bonds possible through human connection, nor whether such automated approaches will equitably meet the needs of marginalized constituencies. And, while social work is among the professions least likely to experience significant displacement due to automation, social workers are now adjusting to ways technologies are altering practice. Electronic communication has changed how social workers provide services, educate practitioners, manage agencies, influence policy, and conduct research (NASW, 2015l). These shifts will likely accelerate in the future. Further, technology is altering not just how social workers practice, but also the issues with which the profession contends. Social workers are helping clients deal with anxieties catalyzed or exacerbated by the ubiquity of social media (Seabrook, Kern, & Rickard, 2016). Those who work with survivors of intimate partner violence grapple with the rise in online stalking and the devastating effects of "revenge porn," even as policymakers struggle to keep up with evolving threats. Today's social work students may not be able to imagine completing case documentation without electronic devices, navigating to home visits without a Global Positioning System, or keeping up with co-workers without email. Tomorrow's social workers will likely find online therapy, virtual client contacts, and the use of digital applications for catalyzing social movements just as indispensable.

While in 2018, only 70 percent of Americans said that the Internet has been "mostly good" for society (Smith, 2018), from a strengths perspective, there are reasons to be encouraged by the proliferation of digital technology. Human rights advocates are partnering with law enforcement to use artificial intelligence to combat human trafficking (Rosenberg, 2019) and using sophisticated digital tools to analyze incidents of police violence (Anzilotti, 2019). Social workers, too, are incorporating digital techniques into their work. Technology can reach underserved communities, provide greater equity for those isolated by geography or language, and reduce the stigma associated with seeking help. Social workers may use videoconferencing and other tools to provide cost-effective interventions to a larger client base (Barak & Grohol, 2011), and there is evidence to support the efficacy and acceptability of telemedicine in mental health (Bashshur et al., 2016). Gaming and virtual reality applications can help clients prepare for difficult challenges. For example, some corrections systems are utilizing virtual reality to equip offenders for successful reentry (Teng, Hodge, & Gordon, 2019). There are many mobile apps that allow people struggling with mental or physical illnesses to chart their symptoms. A clinician can use these applications to detect patterns and work with the client to develop more effective responses. While these innovations are promising, social workers must critically analyze the potential implications of new technologies for the well-being of individual clients and the larger society. Our practice should include advocating for policies that can steer us through the still-uncertain future. As an example of the cautions, clients' consultation of online sources before approaching a provider gives people more control over their treatment but also raises concerns about the veracity of information, particularly as many people have difficulty identifying erroneous health information online (Kortum, Edwards, & Richards-Kortum, 2008).

The key point for social workers considering the evolving future, then, is that advances in technology provide challenges as well as opportunities. Issues of privacy and confidentiality are becoming more critical as more personal health and financial information is stored in computer databases. Unauthorized use of data and hacking compromise privacy; over time, these breaches may erode people's confidence in providers and willingness to disclose personal information. There are other ethical considerations to explore, as well. Increasingly fluid lines between client and practitioner can blur boundaries. Clients may be vulnerable to undue influence from pharmaceutical companies, self-help marketers, or other powerful actors, particularly when they are desperately seeking answers. On a macro level, we have seen how social media can disseminate hateful messages with greater speed and ease and may, then, increase the risk of violence. As countries, including the United States, grapple with how to balance ideals of free exchange of information with the imperative of preventing harm, rapidly shifting technologies complicate this already complex task.

Deciding how to deploy available technology is not the only issue policymakers and practitioners face. As in all of U.S. society, the digital landscape is characterized by inequality. In 2018, 11 percent of American adults did not use the Internet, including nearly 20 percent of those earning less than $30,000 per year and almost a quarter of those in rural areas (Anderson,

Perrin, & Jiang, 2018). People who face cultural, linguistic, and disability-related barriers may also lack access to computers and/or to high-speed Internet, which limits their ability to participate in a digital society. This divide keeps people from benefiting from technological innovations in social work interventions and limits opportunities to find employment, receive adequate health care, communicate with powerful entities, and even receive a comprehensive education. In anticipation of an increasingly digital future, the NASW endorses policies that ensure that all people in all communities have access to crucial technology (NASW, 2015l).

Occupational Automation

Our daily lives have been changed so dramatically by technology that they might be virtually unrecognizable to previous generations. In many cases, our transportation, communication, and entertainment options did not exist just several years ago. However, it is in the arena of work where technological change is poised to most profoundly alter Americans' experiences, including in ways we are still struggling to predict or even understand. Assuredly, technological innovation has always been crucial to economic progress, from the earliest human developments to more recent breakthroughs. While this history suggests that the advances many forecast could bring benefits to American workers and consumers, this will not happen without policies that prepare for the changes and attend to their consequences. The current moment seems particularly critical; if previous developments are any indication, even huge changes often penetrate the labor market gradually, at least potentially giving policymakers and others time to adapt (Cass, 2018). There are some signs of willingness to assume this responsibility, including a Trump Administration executive order on artificial intelligence, which sought to increase access to federal data for informing artificial intelligence systems, enhance digital infrastructure, provide financial support for research, and improve workforce development (West, 2019). To ensure that the United States can take full advantage of the opportunities artificial intelligence could present, such steps must be followed with policy implementation and robust investment. Social workers can play important roles in marshalling the political will to ensure the nation will greet the new day equipped for success.

Although estimates vary somewhat, between 38 and 47 percent of U.S. workers have a high probability of seeing their jobs at least partially automated over the next 20 years (Frey & Osborne, 2013). Even where jobs are not entirely replaced by machines, humans will be responsible for an increasingly small share of the tasks—transforming work experiences even for those whose job titles are unchanged (Muro, Maxim, & Whiton, 2019). As technology becomes more sophisticated, the range of jobs robots or other applications can perform grows. As a result, industries impacted by coming waves of automation include not only manufacturing, which has already been transformed by automated processes, but also transportation, data management, and retail. Self-driving vehicles may replace many taxi drivers and truckers, computers may make many office workers unnecessary, and robots may dominate the sales and customer service sectors that currently employ millions. At previous points in history, we have seen technology change the workplace. As described in Chapters 2 and 3, the introduction of machines into agriculture and manufacturing allowed people to produce more, more quickly. These trends contributed to greater prosperity but also intensified inequality, as those who owned the

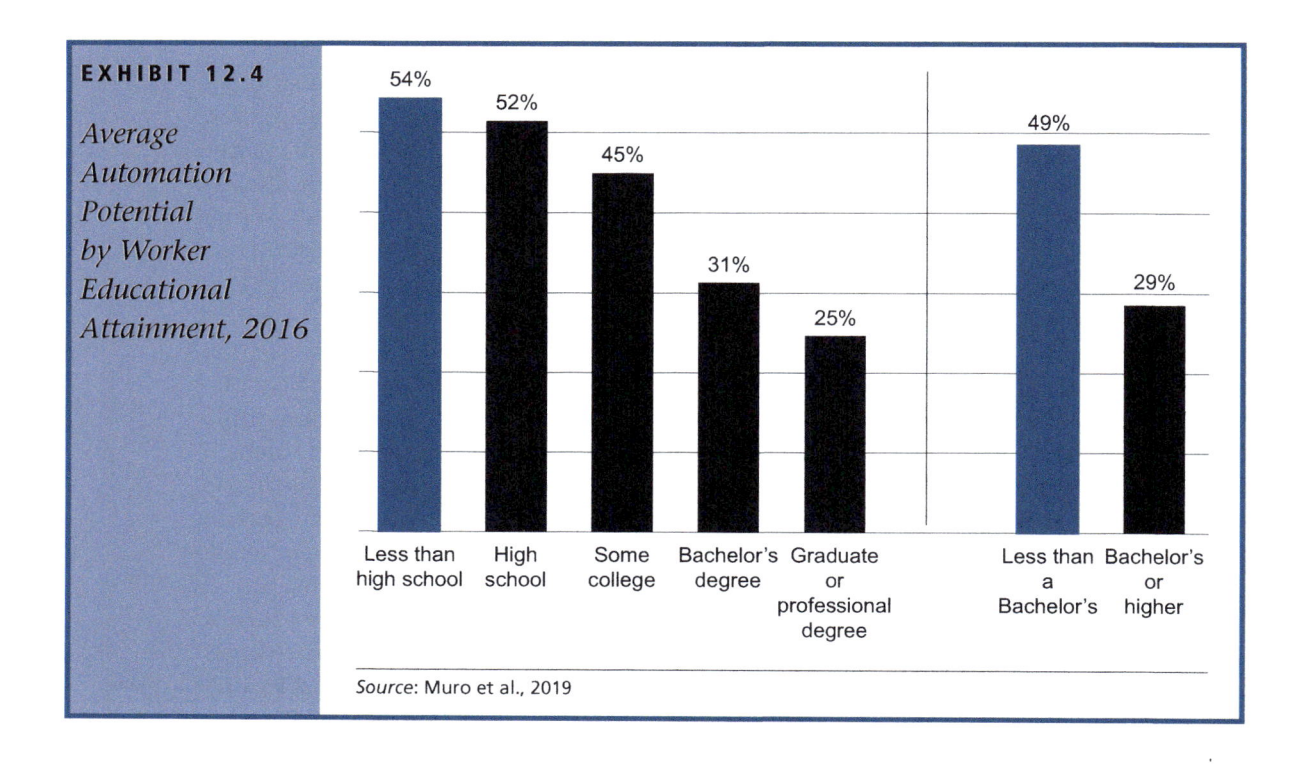

EXHIBIT 12.4

Average Automation Potential by Worker Educational Attainment, 2016

Category	Percentage
Less than high school	54%
High school	52%
Some college	45%
Bachelor's degree	31%
Graduate or professional degree	25%
Less than a Bachelor's	49%
Bachelor's or higher	29%

Source: Muro et al., 2019

---

methods of production profited the most. So too today, those among the first to understand and capitalize on technological progress are best-positioned to seize its spoils. Workers whose advanced educations prepare them for jobs complemented, rather than replaced, by technology will likely see their wages increased and their living standards improve, as technology increases productivity and its rewards—but only for some (Graetz & Michaels, 2015; Muro et al., 2019). Conversely, Exhibit 12.4 illustrates that Americans with less educational attainment are the most vulnerable to technological displacement at work.

As automation contributes to more rapid innovation and greater opportunities for some people to accumulate the resulting wealth, increasingly sophisticated technology is expected to exacerbate economic and political divides. Individuals in smaller metropolitan areas and isolated rural communities are particularly exposed to automation's effects on jobs. Although, theoretically, digital technologies should be "borderless," local economies hollowed out by trends in recent decades are less resilient to the coming restructuring. Manufacturing workers who have struggled to retrain and pivot to new opportunities when their jobs in the textile or automobile industries disappeared are among those facing the greatest challenges to successful transition. Further, in most of the country, men, people of color, and younger workers are concentrated in occupations and industries particularly vulnerable to automation: production, food service, and construction. For these reasons, many are concerned about the economic, political, and social implications of a larger number of Americans who may be unable to find a place for themselves in the evolving U.S. labor market.

Various forces are competing to predict not only the future of workplace automation, but also its likely consequences. As described at the beginning of the chapter, these forecasters have differing motivations. For example, those responsible for and profiting from technological innovation are among those expressing optimism about how robots will improve productivity and quality of life (West, 2018), while advocates for low-wage workers mostly take a darker view, fearing that digital agents will render entire occupations obsolete and result in "vast increases in income inequality, masses of people who are effectively unemployable, and breakdowns in the social order" (Smith & Anderson, 2014). Some forecasters argue that people in most industries will be able to adapt their jobs to accommodate new technologies and are focusing their efforts on investing in the skills required to succeed in the new labor market. Others are trying to capitalize on this moment to pivot from the concept of "work" as we have known it for most of modern history.

Social workers have important roles to play in helping people navigate the restructuring of work, at the individual and societal levels. Even fairly upbeat prognoses about the coming "robot age" acknowledge that work tasks will be changed by automation. Analyses suggest that 60 percent of jobs could have up to 30 percent of their functions eliminated using currently available technologies (Manyika et al., 2017), even if fewer than 10 percent of occupations will be ceded entirely to robots (Arntz, Gregory, & Zierahn, 2016). These types of shifts may not result in mass unemployment, but they will surely require people to become adept at using technology as part of their work, which will mean additional education and training. As is the case during most substantial changes, the effects of greater automation will likely be psychological as well as functional. Employment disruption can erode people's sense of control over their daily realities and provoke anxiety and growing unhappiness (Pearlman, 2015). Further, technological change may also mean that American workers—many of whom are already in tenuous positions in the ascendance of the flexible but precarious jobs of the sharing economy—are increasingly seen as expendable. In the future, those who push for higher wages, better benefits, or greater job security may risk being replaced by someone else—or by a machine. Today, the United States spends less than almost every other industrialized nation on "active labor market policies" that help workers train and match for jobs—and less than we used to (Maxim & Muro, 2019). If Americans are to experience technological advances as exciting, rather than merely threatening, these priorities will have to change. Finally, some question whether our definition of prosperity should be reconsidered, to emphasize people's need for dignity and productivity as important national priorities (Cass, 2018). Social workers need to be part of the conversation about what work means, why it matters, and the kinds of human activities that should not be automated, even if technology makes it possible to do so.

Global Political Realignments

Political shifts may be the most difficult to forecast. While population shifts can be seen well in the future and medical and technological advances follow relatively predictable paths from initial appearance to incorporation as part of the "new normal," political developments can sometimes seem to come out of nowhere. That is perhaps truer than ever today, as Americans' political futures are affected not only by our own domestic context, but also by conditions, events, and actors in other countries. However, while the speed with which such developments travel and the extent to which they ripple have intensified with greater global integration, currents in other countries have always influenced U.S. policy. Early founders brought social policy ideas and movements with them, immigrants' ingenuity and sacrifice fueled national economic development, and slaves' labor subsidized the country's foundation. In the last century, growing economic, political, and social integration seemed to "shrink the world," such that Americans' fortunes were tied nearly as closely to events in Brussels or Beijing as to Baltimore or Brooklyn. As people increasingly came to perceive that their futures and fortunes depended on faraway actors and unaccountable global corporations, there has been a backlash against economic globalization as practiced in the modern age. As described in Chapter 4, the resulting economic nationalism has reverberated in the political landscapes of Europe, South America, and the United States. This anti-globalist sentiment has not, however, changed the reality of global connectedness. While some may resent this fact, our fates are still linked to those of people around the world. As strengths-based social workers, our challenge is to advance strengths-based visions of global integration.

Globalization and the interdependence it fosters have created opportunities for growth and development. At the same time, however, companies' ability to travel the globe in pursuit of needed labor has pitted workers against each other, destabilized industries, and allowed corporations to disavow responsibility to the citizens of a particular nation. Transnational corporations have successfully advocated for social welfare systems in many countries to be restructured, with the stated goal of making the economy more competitive. These forces and their consequences encourage a resurgence of narrowly defined national economic interests. Of course, this overlooks the fact that a healthy and well-educated population is essential to economic prosperity. As social workers attempting to understand where global economies might be headed, we must focus on people's lived experiences and listen authentically and empathically. We must critique the approach to globalization often practiced by the world's most powerful economic actors, identify alternative paths that build on the capacities of people around the world, and articulate a vision of democratic global cooperation that places the needs of people at the center of decision-making—regardless of the nation they call home.

Additionally, as people from different backgrounds come into close contact, particularly as refugee flows increase dramatically, religious and cultural conflicts are becoming more visible, virulent, and even violent. People in many parts of the world have yet to find ways of accommodating diversity by peaceful means. Extremists have exploited anxiety about changing demographics to advance racist and xenophobic ideologies. And global competition for natural resources—expected to increase as the world population grows and resources are depleted—can create tension. This can result in people drawing ever-tighter circles around those with whom they identify and are willing to share. The resulting tribalism makes it difficult for many to find common cause with those that differ from themselves in any way.

However, even as prevailing political winds lead people—especially some powerful leaders—to retreat from global alliances, the world undeniably faces challenges no nation can address in a vacuum. Indeed, some of the greatest needs of the United States are those with which other nations have already contended, including population aging and concerns about the sustainability of retirement supports. Other challenges—including climate change and terrorism—can only be resolved through concerted collective action. The concept of growing similarity in the challenges countries face and the policies they enact is known as **convergence**. Sources of policy convergence include borrowing of policy ideas from other countries, as the United States did in crafting the Social Security Act. Similar policies in different countries can also develop independently in response to parallel domestic problems or pressures—rising sea levels, for example, or restrictions on immigration as war and disaster increase migrant flows.

Politics in the United States and elsewhere are increasingly polarized. The same technologies that have facilitated transmission of innovations and perspectives from around the world are, today, diffusing ideas of nationalism and resistance to "foreign interference." In this political context, strengths-based social workers have important roles to play in helping people to see the potential from cross-national cooperation. Crucially, social workers must also attend to the urgent needs of many in anti-globalization camps. In many cases and for many constituencies, diverging views on globalization reflect the reality that current arrangements create winners and losers, with the gap between the two growing. As illustration, in the United States, the 53 largest metropolitan areas have seen more than 96 percent of population growth and 74 percent of employment gains since 2014, while smaller cities and rural areas have lost ground (Muro & Whiton, 2018). There is a growing divide, in other words, not just along lines of partisanship, but between communities profiting in the economy of the future and those who long to return to a more secure past. As their futures grow increasingly precarious, those left out of the promises of progress understandably search for something—and someone—to blame.

Our ability to meet future challenges will depend in large part on how we can leverage a global pool of knowledge while elevating the experiences of those who have been on the losing end of the changes wrought by globalization. Across many social policy domains, there are critical lessons to be learned from other nations' journeys. Disadvantaged Americans could potentially benefit from importation of ideas such as European experiments with universal basic income and paid family leave. Anti-poverty policy here could be strengthened by examining Latin American innovations in **conditional cash transfers**, which pay poor families in cash when they participate in services that build their human capital. Our domestic need for policies that advance longevity economics could be well-served by considering Japanese efforts to support older adults in the workforce. U.S. states pursuing parental leave are learning from other nations' efforts and considering ways to ensure that fathers will equitably participate. Similarly, the U.S. broad-based approach to higher education, which encourages widespread access to institutions of varying degrees of selectivity, has informed international education policy, spurring some nations to reduce their reliance on "tracking" students in favor of more democratic educational opportunities. We can best address many of the challenges that will shape our future through global collaboration.

Policymakers and advocates for social justice should reject attempts to retreat from worldwide partnerships. As described in Chapter 10, we cannot hope to counter the spread of infectious disease without global cooperation. Similarly, security threats in one part of the world can imperil Americans' safety; global events continue to underscore the ways that regional conflicts can spill over. To be effective in the global response to these growing challenges, social workers will need to draw on our values of inclusion, cultural humility, diversity, and respect for the dignity of others. We can rely on our cross-cultural competence and skills in consensus-building. We will have allies in communities around the globe, who continue to work toward a more equitable, healthy, and prosperous world. Workers in Chicago, Buenos Aires, and elsewhere have borrowed radical tactics to occupy factories to protest growing automation. Scientists and public health workers have shared approaches to combating infectious disease and have even collaborated on research and pooled funding across national boundaries. What we need is a new consensus that supports tackling common worldwide problems—together—and that places strengths at the center of a capacity-building approach to confronting our future.

Climate Change and Environmental Justice

To most scientists (Oreskes, 2004), many farmers (Niles et al., 2013), and a growing number of people living in affected communities (Kennedy, 2018), the reality of climate change is undeniable. The planet's average surface temperature has risen about 1.62 degrees Fahrenheit since the late nineteenth century, a change scientists attribute largely to increased carbon dioxide and other human-made emissions into the atmosphere (National Oceanic and Atmospheric Administration [NOAA], 2019). These global temperatures are forecast to continue to rise (Intergovernmental Panel on Climate Change, 2018), with resulting consequences including warming and rising seas, shrinking ice and snow cover, greater likelihood of extreme weather (Harvey, 2018), and acidification of the oceans (National Aeronautics and Space Administration [NASA], 2019). Although there are some uncertainties about the pace of climate change, the mitigating effects of developing technology and changing policy, and the way that unpredictable elements such as natural disasters will unfold, these forecasts—based on extensive collection and rigorous analysis of scientific data—are more certain than those made in many other areas.

Even before the future arrives, we are already witnessing climate change effects on property destruction, economic growth, and human well-being. The Union of Concerned Scientists (2018) forecasts that more than $136 billion in property will be threatened by chronic flooding—due to rising sea levels and increasingly intense rainstorms—by 2045. People will lose their homes. Roads, bridges, and power plants will be threatened, with dire consequences for individuals, communities, and the economy. Again, some of these effects are already unfolding; severe flooding in Midwestern states in 2019 caused more than $3 billion in damage to states previously thought to be among the "safest" from climate change. In a typical year, federal spending on disaster relief is more than ten times greater than a generation ago, even controlling for inflation (Stein & Van Dam, 2019). This is the "new normal," whether we're ready for it or not.

While everyone will be affected by climate change, the disadvantaged populations with whom social workers most concern ourselves are particularly adversely affected (U.S. Global Change Research Group, 2018). Low-income households are less able to afford modifications that make their homes resistant to storms that are increasing in frequency and intensity. In disasters such as hurricanes, tornadoes, and wildfires, these populations are disproportionately hurt and killed, as they are less able to move out of harm's way. Inequality intensifies post-disaster (National Public Radio, 2019). Older adults and individuals with disabilities are more adversely affected by higher temperatures, particularly when they cannot afford to sufficiently cool their homes. Around the world, people living in poverty struggle with food prices driven up by agricultural pressures and grapple with water shortages that threaten their livelihoods and their health. Drought has contributed to unprecedented suicides in India (Carleton, 2017) and mental health crises among farmers in Australia, and it is those already vulnerable who are most at risk.

While climate change is the most urgent and potentially catastrophic environmental crisis facing the planet, social workers must also attend to other environmental issues that cast a shadow over our future, including pollution, deforestation, depletion of other natural resources, and loss of biodiversity. Children exposed to high levels of mercury and lead experience higher rates of developmental disabilities. Poor air quality contributes to severe respiratory problems, and, particularly in North America, low-income children are most adversely affected (Hajat, Hsia, & O'Neill, 2015). Exposure to air pollution can even harm children's brain development before birth (Perera et al., 2006). High levels of toxins threaten health, particularly for those least protected from these dangers. People living in poverty and communities of color are more likely to be victimized by unsafe environmental practices, as illustrated dramatically and tragically in the crisis over lead contamination in the municipal water supply of Flint, Michigan, a largely African-American community in which approximately 40 percent of residents have low incomes (Martinez, 2016).

In recognition of the importance of these issues and the profession's need to contribute to addressing them (Dominelli, 2013), the Council on Social Work Education (CSWE) elevated environmental justice as a core competency that students must be prepared to advance, alongside social and economic justice. More social work programs are increasing their course and field content on environmental justice, and more social workers are engaging in environmental advocacy. Social work practitioners and students have protested government inaction in the face of climate change and provided on-the-ground assistance to survivors of disasters. They have pushed for environmentally responsible policies at the local, state, and federal government levels, including energy-efficiency building standards, tax credits for clean fuel development, increased penalties for polluters, and requirements that residents' interests are considered in the construction of industrial or waste facilities. While meeting our environmental challenges will require broad-based collaboration, social workers can play key roles in catalyzing efforts to safeguard our future.

Social workers understand, moreover, that the future of environmental justice is global. People in many communities continue to forge transnational grassroots organizations to address shared environmental concerns. For instance, indigenous groups from the United States and Canada are joining together to oppose threats to tribal water resources affected by policies across borders. The Tohono O'odham Nation, which straddles the United States and Mexico, has opposed President Trump's proposed border wall as an unnatural and harmful division. In March 2019, students across 123 different countries took part in a coordinated global school walkout and other actions to protest inaction on climate change. Scientists alarmed by the Trump Administration's withdrawal from the Paris Climate Accord continue to work with their counterparts in other countries, albeit outside of official government channels (Mathieson, 2018). Labor organizations have united displaced workers in the United States with the laborers in Central America who now work for the same companies, so that they can collectively agitate for fair labor practices and stronger environmental protections. Supported by researchers, advocates, and community-based organizations, farmers around the world are exchanging ideas, technologies, and even seeds as they seek to adapt to the new conditions that result from climate change. If these collaborations are to be supported, replicated, and continually adapted, every country will need policies that encourage global exchange and invest in individual and collective capacity. Whether working with a family reeling from a climate-related natural disaster, a community seeking to improve its water and air quality, or a global collective elevating environmental justice on the world stage, social workers can contribute work from strengths toward a healthier and more sustainable future.

The State of the Future Index

One tool to help us consider the future from a global perspective is the State of the Future Index (SOFI). The SOFI is constructed with key variables and forecasts that, in the aggregate, provide insight about the future. The SOFI is designed to show direction and intensity of change and to identify responsible factors. Developed in 2000 as part of the Millennium Project of the United Nations, the SOFI was last updated in 2017. Exhibit 12.5 traces net progress on key indicators over the past few decades and projects trends for the coming years.

The 2017 SOFI cites considerable progress on key measures of human well-being across the globe. The world has made strides in reducing poverty, child mortality, and undernourishment (Glenn & Florescu, 2017). Today, more countries are defined as politically "free," and the world has realized gains in educational attainment, literacy, energy-efficiency, political representation of women, availability of physicians, availability of clean water, and life expectancy (Glenn & Florescu, 2017). However, while the world is "winning" in more areas than we are losing, the SOFI underscores serious future risks. The areas where we are making the least progress, or even

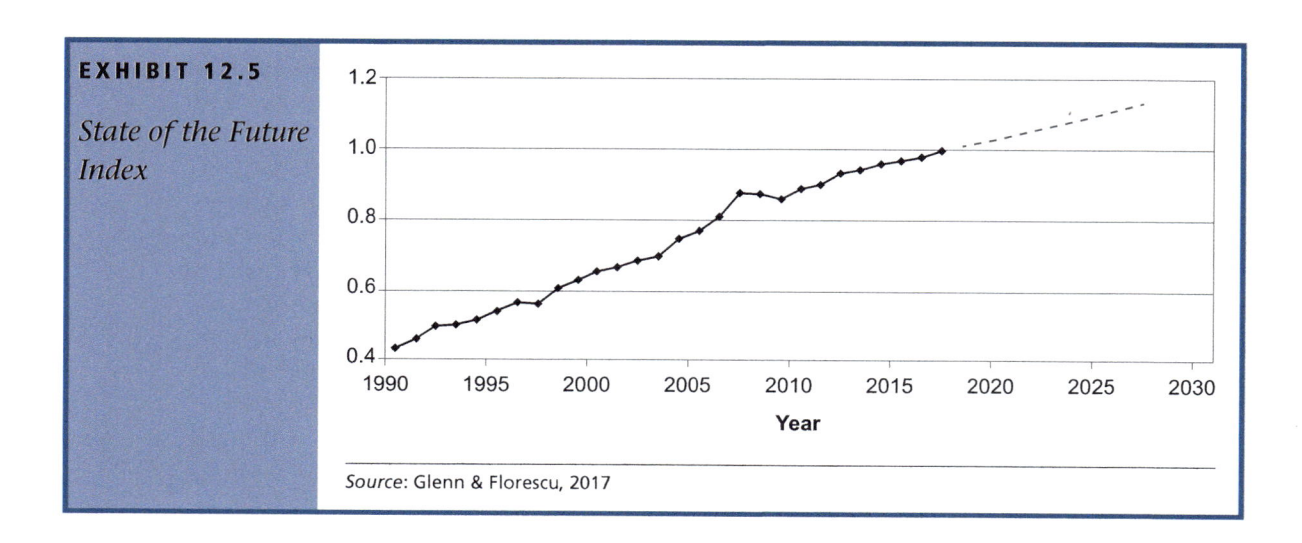

EXHIBIT 12.5

State of the Future Index

Source: Glenn & Florescu, 2017

moving in the wrong direction, have high stakes. These include carbon emissions, loss of forest land and biocapacity, social unrest and the spread of conflict and terrorism, growing unemployment, and widening income inequality (Glenn & Florescu, 2017).

The danger in combining many variables into a single index is that detail is lost, as progress in one area can obscure declines in another. Variables differ in importance and should be weighted accordingly. Additionally, the construction of a composite measure can minimize the experiences the numbers represent. For example, while global poverty has declined remarkably, life is undeniably difficult for the estimated 600 million people living in extreme poverty around the world (Chandy & Gertz, 2011). Their harsh realities should not be lost in a celebration of aggregate progress. Nonetheless, this approach does provide a way of thinking about the relationship among variables and how changes in one indicator could ripple into other domains. For example, if a policy is enacted that increases enrollment in secondary education, is there a corresponding change in poverty rates, unemployment, or infant mortality? Could reductions in poverty reduce social unrest? How might environmental degradation stall economic progress? The SOFI can help us think through the impact of proposed policy changes, make nation-to-nation comparisons, and consider parallels in experiences in different parts of the world. You can find more information on SOFI and other efforts to anticipate and respond to global challenges at the Millennium Project site at **www.millennium-project.org**.

FUTURE POLICY DIRECTIONS

As we have seen, demographic trends, technological advances, the economic and social changes that accompany increasing globalization, and growing threats to the natural environment will influence future social policies. This text has provided numerous examples of how, in the wake of earlier changes, the government created social policies to protect the general public and address the needs of specific populations. For example, when economic changes necessitated a more skilled workforce, policy invested in expanded educational access. As a generation of military service members returned from World War II and needed housing and educational opportunities to catalyze their own prosperity and national economic development, policies provided affordable mortgages and financial aid for college. As science revealed more about the health effects of new manufacturing processes, the United States developed policies to protect people from pollutants. This text has also highlighted examples of when U.S. social policy failed to adequately respond to changing conditions. Unaffordable and unavailable childcare is a legacy of insufficient adjustment to the rise in households where all adults are working. The financial hardship and compromised health experienced by older adults without adequate long-term care is an indictment of the nation's failure to provide sufficient public supports to compensate for informal care family members are not able to provide. While the past does not necessarily preview the future, these dynamics may contribute to future social policy. We need to continually advocate for policies better equipped to support equitable, sustainable, and prosperous futures.

Policies are often designed to quell unrest and preserve the interests of capitalism during periods of rapid change. This is a potent motivation in our current age, as analysts, political leaders, and people around the world question whether capitalism can still deliver on the promise of a better future (Reeves, 2019). Ideology—the beliefs that guide a group—will also continue to shape policy responses to future trends. For example, U.S. society has been divided between those who believe that government contributes to the creation of social problems and those who believe government can be a force for good. These lines, too, are shifting; in recent years, even among idealistic young people, Americans are less likely to see government as the solution to problems (Giridharadas, 2018). Admittedly, as this text has described, there are ample cases of policies that made problems worse. However, just as surely, social workers cannot afford to give up on the idea that the power of the U.S. government should be leveraged to improve our future. Toward that end, we now consider future social policy directions that could more effectively support social work's vision of enhanced well-being; greater equity; and social, economic, and environmental justice.

The Future of Work

Given that U.S. social policies have consistently emphasized individualism, personal responsibility, and a strong work ethic, particularly for people in poverty, we can expect that future policies will likely continue to emphasize attachment to the workforce. Thus, if a safety net is to survive, it will quite likely be at least somewhat work-based. However, advocates of a work-based safety net will need to consider the impact of changes in economic structures, including how automation will reshape what it means to be "employed," whether the U.S. education system is currently structured to equip individuals to perform adequately in the evolving economy, and the increasing importance of assets—in addition to income—in determining well-being. Above all, if the safety net is to remain largely work-linked, the United States needs policies of full employment, both nationally and with specific emphasis on those regions where jobs are least secure and lowest-paid (Muro et al., 2019). As we consider the future we want and the policies required to construct it, these visions must address the needs of Americans with few viable employment prospects in the present.

Workplace policies that provide the support necessary for mothers and fathers to succeed in their dual roles as parents and employees will be vital to the well-being of families, children, and society. Generous family leave and flexible work schedules will be crucial. Universal, affordable, high-quality childcare is capacity-building, as investment in early childhood development can help close gaps between low-income children and their peers and result in increased opportunities for success. While supports for working families are particularly urgent for those with lower incomes, inadequate childcare is an issue that cuts across economic and partisan divides and may have political appeal even in this divisive age. Across ideological barriers, 89 percent of voters support policy to make early childhood education more available and affordable (First Five Years Fund, 2017). Workplace policy also needs to recognize the intergenerational nature of the family by providing additional supports for workers who care for older relatives. Intergenerational families from diverse backgrounds must have a voice in the development of employment and family policies. Without attention to these issues, policies may inadvertently undermine the functioning and development of the diverse families of the future.

Working caregivers are not the only people who need new policy approaches to succeed in the changing workplace. In 2017, more than 10 percent of the U.S. workforce was in a "nonstandard" job arrangement, typically temporary or independent contractor work (National Employment Law Project [NELP], 2018). While the sharing economy has given birth to new ways of earning income as people turn their homes, cars, and "free time" into instruments of income generation, these arrangements often carry high costs for workers' ability to accrue retirement and health benefits, as well as for health and well-being, particularly given the higher incidence of occupational hazards and the stresses of unpredictable schedules and earnings. Women and workers of color are overrepresented in these nonstandard jobs and, then, are among those most in need of new social safety nets and protections to accompany them in the workforce.

Consider how you have seen the employment landscape change in your lifetime and what public social policies will be necessary to support the future workforce. Due to globalization, these changes to what it means to "work" or "have a job" are not unique to the United States. Across the countries that are part of the Organisation of Cooperation and Development (OECD), one in six workers are self-employed. While this underscores the extent to which global economic forces are outmatching national policy apparatuses, it also creates opportunities for convergence in the construction of new supports to meet the needs of workers in the future.

Countries have sought to ensure workers' well-being through a variety of approaches that can inform social policy in the United States. Some have made retirement and health benefits more universal and less dependent on attachment to the formal workforce. Some have emphasized employment security, rather than job security, by providing robust social insurance that can buffer people from the shocks of frequent job changes—what some have called "flexicurity" (Cass, 2018, p. 150). Some have layered voluntary protections that allow workers to access public systems to supplement work-based supports—somewhat analogous to the health insurance marketplaces created by the ACA. Some countries have redefined "unemployment" so part-time, freelance, or seasonal workers have some income protection during fluctuations. And a few nations have found that these policy efforts have had the effect of slowing the shift to nonstandard employment, as companies see less financial incentive to adjust employment terms if they cannot evade social responsibilities by doing so (OECD, 2018). When these policies reflect understanding of workers' concerns and the hopes they have for their futures, they are promisingly strengths-based.

However, convergence works in many directions—not always in ways that move toward social work values. Some countries are cutting back on the social safety net as economic woes increase. Many saw Great Britain's departure from the European Union as a particularly dramatic example of turning inward in the face of economic and social change. There are lessons here for social workers in the United States seeking to protect our less-developed but still crucial social safety net. Americans need to understand the ways in which economic, health, educational, and environmental investments translate to tangible gains in their own lives, and they need to feel that they have a voice in policy development and reform, particularly in a time of great uncertainty. The "submerged state" (Mettler, 2010) needs to be made more visible. Social workers must ensure that people see public programs that provide for older adults, people with disabilities, unemployed workers, and children as strengthening our economy. Further, these programs can be reconfigured to build on people's capacities. For example, many people with disabilities and older adults would welcome support to help them succeed in the labor market, and this emphasis may also reduce their need for cash assistance. Given the scope and scale of the challenges we face, we cannot afford to overlook or undercount anyone's strengths.

There are key policy domains that need to be shored up if a work-based safety net is to be viable in the labor market of the future: government policy to harness the power of technology for elevating human well-being; lifelong investment in human capital; commitment to helping individuals and industries adjust to technological and demographic change; and creation of an asset-based foundation of financial security (Muro et al., 2019). Seen through this lens, tangible policy priorities can be knitted together into a package that makes the future seem less frightening—less a chaotic mechanized frontier or new global order, and more the resetting of social arrangements for a new age.

Wages, Jobs, and Retirement Even before the full effects of projected automation are felt, many people have experienced years of wage stagnation, manufacturing jobs have largely disappeared in some areas, families' finances are unstable, and guaranteed retirement pensions are becoming much rarer. In the future, efforts to increase economic security across the lifespan will become more complex. However, there also are promising approaches. A revitalized organized labor movement could enhance workers' bargaining power. Toward this end, 2018 was the biggest year for U.S. labor protests in a generation, as more than 485,000 teachers and workers in other industries used collective strategies to win tangible improvements in wages and working conditions. In August 2018, Americans were twice as likely to approve than disapprove of labor unions and more likely to want organized labor to have greater, rather than less, influence over public policy (Gallup, 2018). In times of change, people search for institutions that can help steer through shifting currents to a secure future.

Gaining ground within a challenging context will require change on multiple fronts and deployment of multiple strategies. Improving women's wages—by ending wage discrimination and providing universal childcare—is central to improving children's economic security. Because employers increasingly expect workers to assume responsibility for managing their guaranteed contribution retirement programs, access to comprehensive and clear financial education is crucial, particularly for women and people of color who have traditionally had more limited opportunities to gain experience with investing. Policies that provide retirement savings options beyond those linked to formal employment can facilitate asset accumulation by people with different work arrangements. We need to pursue redistributive policies that provide fair chances for those disadvantaged to claim their rightful share of what this country has to offer. Progressive tax policy proposals, including an expanded Earned Income Tax Credit and refundable credits to facilitate wealth-building, could improve households' economic positions. Smarter and stronger worker adjustment programs could help those whose jobs were displaced by global trade and/or technology find places to thrive in the changing economy (Brainard, 2008). The education system should be retooled to prepare people to succeed in the workforce alongside robots. This includes cultivating social and emotional competency—humans' greatest competitive advantage—among young people, making post-secondary education affordable for all, and creating and financing alternative degree paths. These innovations should be attuned to the demographic trends that will occur in tandem, including growing shares of the future labor force for whom English is a second language.

A new paradigm is developing, whereby retirement is considered a process marked by successive decisions, not a single and irreversible event. More companies and individuals are embracing alternatives to the "40 years of 40-hour work weeks until retirement" conception of work life. Such alternatives include part-time positions, job sharing, and phased retirement. We need to design policies that support this kind of workplace flexibility while protecting health and retirement benefits and adequately meeting the needs of those whose disabilities or family responsibilities prevent them from working later in life. Such policies also benefit younger people who are trying to juggle the responsibilities of work and dependent care. Finally, given the increasing numbers of people who will work in multiple countries over a lifetime, there is a need for global steps to ensure stability and transferability of income and health supports. Developing such policies does not require the creation of a world government; rather, what is needed are intergovernmental vehicles that align with global structures and build on the core idea that countries can benefit by cooperating with certain common rules.

Health

Advances in medical technology have enabled us to map our genes, artificially prolong life, and pursue alternative options for reproduction. As described above, social workers must contend with the ethical dilemmas surrounding the human impacts of these advances. The Genetic Information Non-Discrimination Act of 2008 offers Americans some protection from discrimination based on their genetic information in both health insurance and employment, and the ACA strengthened this protection. Nonetheless, social workers often will be on the front lines in health care and other settings, making sure that individuals' rights are protected and that these technologies can be benevolent forces in people's lives, rather than tools of oppression. Social workers will be called on to advance a vision of health policy that builds people's capacity for productive, meaningful, satisfying lives, and that distributes the gains medical technologies have made possible fairly and responsibly.

Information Technology and Privacy

Technological advances have the potential to increase efficiency of data collection and analysis and to reduce the burden on clients; however, confidentiality and privacy must also be guarded. As high-profile data breaches of private and government servers have underscored, we must be wary about the extent to which information stored is truly protected from compromise. Further, when new technology is implemented, we need to advocate for policies that emphasize clients' ownership of their own information. Today, falsifying information is easier than ever, and many client groups may be particularly vulnerable to fraudulent production and use of data. Social workers, too, may find ourselves targeted by "deep fake" videos or other malevolent technologies that misrepresent our work. Our agencies and professional associations must strive to anticipate and prepare for these potentialities. If we are to successfully navigate the rapidly changing landscape of the future, social workers must be informed and critical consumers and defenders of information—ours, our clients', and other actors'.

Devolution and the Geography of Opportunity

While the United States has always had a federal system that reserves some powers explicitly for state governments, many advances in securing individual rights and promoting well-being have been won through expanding action of the federal government. In recent years, devolution of responsibilities in many critical arenas has intensified geographic inequity. As described in previous chapters, policies related to income support, child welfare, juvenile justice, and health care can vary dramatically depending on the state where one lives. Technological changes, demographic shifts, and political polarization can be expected to exacerbate these effects. Increasingly, then, how Americans experience social policy may depend largely on where they live. Already, some communities are fairly effective engines of upward mobility, creating pathways that allow families to improve their standard of living, while other communities experience stagnation and multiple dimensions of loss.

Today, there are stark divides between communities in the outcomes they produce and, then, the experiences of people who call them home. Typical household income in the wealthiest 20 percent of counties is more than twice that in the poorest 20 percent. Poverty rates are three times higher in these struggling places than in the most prosperous, and life expectancy is six years longer in the top 20 percent of counties than in the bottom (Nunn et al., 2018). Adding to these dynamics are diverging policy decisions, largely fueled by differences in ideology. To cite just a few examples, some states are expanding reproductive rights while others are severely restricting them. Some states have expanded Medicaid and moved in the direction of universal health care, while others have used waivers to make public health programs more limited and punitive. Some states are experimenting with paid family leave, while in others, only a fraction of eligible households get any childcare assistance at all. There is much discussion of the political polarization between "red" and "blue" regions and the distance that divides people by partisan affiliation, degree of religiosity, and other indicators. Social workers' policy analysis and the visual depiction of figures like the exhibit reveal profound differences not just in how people feel or what they believe, but also in the outcomes they experience and the chances they have to anticipate a brighter future. Social workers must confront our future as a collective one, seeking policies that work for people no matter where they live and that avoid pitting communities' interests against each other. Strengths-based policy practitioners understand that we can have both local responsiveness and distributive justice. As we face our future, social workers can ensure that people's voices are heard in the policymaking process and affirm everyone's right to share in the fruits of our national gains.

Today, devolution is further amplified by the trend toward privatization—the shifting of responsibility from government (at any level) to private entities. As discussed in previous chapters, privatization is not a new phenomenon. Private organizations have played important roles in education, health care, and social services since the origins of our social welfare system. This trend toward privatization continues, with some new arenas subject to privatization and private actors playing ever-larger roles in some sectors. Two particularly notable examples are corrections and higher education. While obviously different in purpose and scope, both have seen dramatic shifts in the direction of private—particularly for-profit—prominence, with some disturbing consequences for the client groups social workers serve. Between 2000 and 2016, the number of people housed in private prisons increased five times faster than the total prison population (Carson, 2018). Because promised cost savings seldom materialize, private prisons may reduce staff salaries and cut other corners to be profitable. Further, as some states depend particularly heavily on private correctional institutions, the use of private prisons exacerbates inequity among different states. While nonprofit colleges and universities have long been part of the landscape, the shift to for-profit institutions has attracted the attention of policymakers, social workers, and education advocates. Measured according to student loan burden, completion rates, and return on degree, outcomes at many of these institutions are concerning; specifically, there is evidence that low-income or otherwise disadvantaged students are particularly ill-served by these profit-minded institutions (Gelbgiser, 2018).

Despite these complications, pluralism, as reflected in public–private partnerships and the sharing of obligations among local, state, and federal governments, is often the favored response to public challenges. It also sustains nonprofit organizations and a commercial welfare industry. Further, privately provided services are often more acceptable to people who believe in less government. It is unlikely, then, that we will return to public provision of services that have been privatized, even if privatized services do not prove to be more cost-effective, equitable, or efficacious. As a result, for the foreseeable future, policymakers and many social work advocates will focus on making privatized approaches work.

This will require attention to the government responsibility for oversight and regulatory enforcement, as well as engagement in policy practice that mobilizes constituencies to insist on accountability and transparency in these systems. Privatization initiatives promoted on the basis of cost-effectiveness should be monitored to see if they actually reduce costs. Turning even more public funds over to private entities without evidence of improved outcomes must be contested. Further, social workers will need to challenge a narrow metric of efficiency to press for service delivery options that are more expensive when they show greater potential for positive outcomes. Finally, the rights of social workers and other professionals providing services within these privatized systems must be protected. Compared to public institutions, private entities often have fewer safeguards to ensure whistleblowers can expose unsafe, unwise, or unethical practices. However, as recent revelations in the national political landscape have underscored, ensuring that courageous and principled actors can expose issues to public scrutiny is essential. As service delivery systems evolve, social workers must be vigilant to hold privatized arrangements to the high standards client groups deserve.

Environmental and Climate Justice

Social workers appreciate the importance of the person-in-environment fit in the helping process. Policies that will help maintain a healthy environment are critical to attaining and maintaining an adequate quality of life for all. Social workers' policy analysis should include attention to sustainability, so that we avoid compromising future health and well-being for

> **EXHIBIT 12.6**
>
> *Majority of Americans Favor Protecting the Environment, Even at Risk of Curbing Economic Growth*
>
> With which one of these statements about the environment and the economy do you most agree – protection of the environment should be given priority, even at the risk of curbing economic growth (or) economic growth should be given priority, even if the environment suffers to some extent?
>
> ■ % Environment   ■ % Economic growth
>
> % Environment values: 61 (1984), 71 (1991), 62 (1997), 70 (2000), 55, 54, 50, 56, 57 (2018)
> % Economic growth values: 28, 19, 32, 23, 37, 36, 41, 35, 35
>
> GALLUP
>
> *Source:* Polling by Gallup (Newport, 2018b)

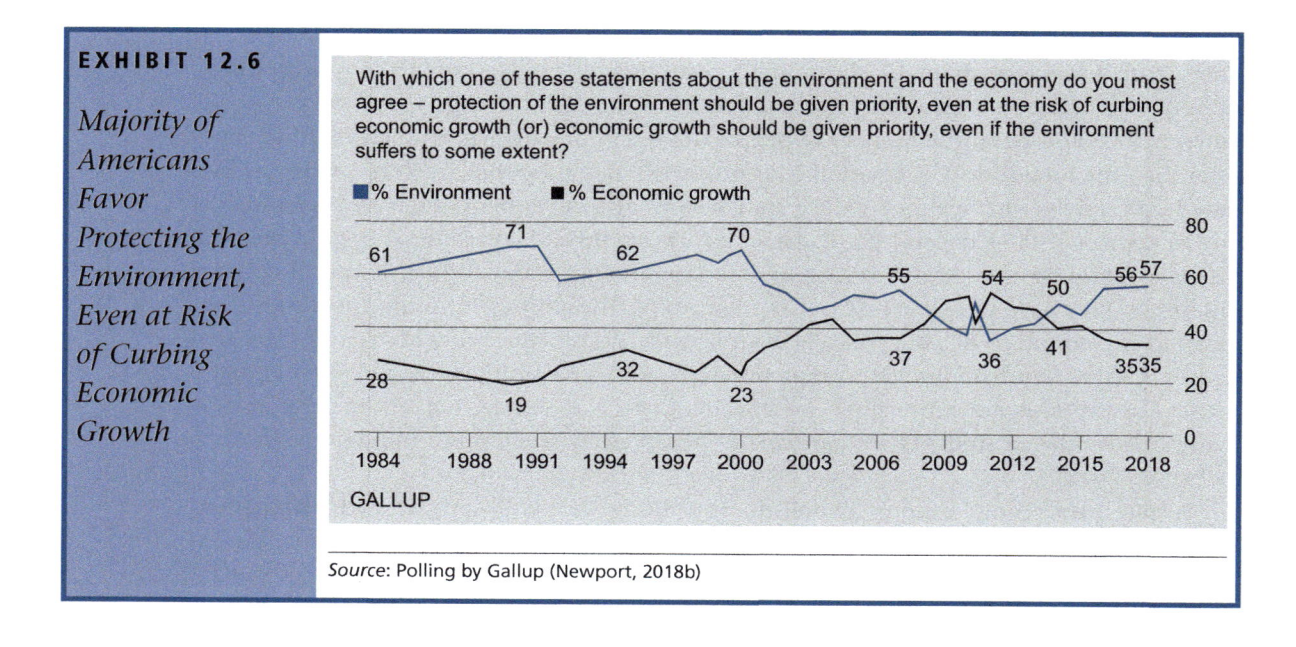

short-term gains. This is particularly crucial in the arena of economic development, where the lure of job creation can often obscure the real, long-term costs of environmental degradation. As Exhibit 12.6 shows, a majority of Americans now prioritize environmental protection, even at the cost of slowed economic growth. However, these preferences were reversed during the Great Recession, when rejuvenating the economic engine was a primary imperative. This suggests that emphasis on environmental preservation may vary somewhat with economic cycles. Of course, these aims are not necessarily opposed. Strengths-based social workers can be part of movements to invest in "green jobs" that present opportunities for both economic growth and environmental stewardship. Indeed, such approaches will be increasingly important in the future.

Social workers must also be alert to cases of environmental injustice, including diverting needed water and other natural resources to more powerful communities. In our role as activist clinicians, it is important that we consider environmental factors when assessing clients' needs and that we challenge policies that damage clients' physical environments. As we confront the existential threat of global climate change, social workers need to be attentive to the unequal burdens climate change imposes on vulnerable populations. Climate changes will impact food security, migration, disease, and the need for disaster relief (Achstatter, 2014). Because social workers are deeply involved in all these areas, as a profession and as individual practitioners, we must work for climate justice. A first step is to educate social workers about the impact of climate change on our practice. We then need to help build the networks and infrastructure necessary for collective action. Social workers should also be part of discussions about ways to slow the damaging effects of climate change. Some communities are changing zoning requirements to prohibit construction in expanding floodplains; others are investing in stronger water and sanitation systems that can withstand projected strains. Policies to protect the environment will be effective only if the public agencies charged with enforcing them are adequately funded. Social workers can advocate for changes in federal policies related to disaster relief, flood insurance, and climate study, as well as for state and local policies that take an explicit environmental justice approach. Additionally, social work agencies can become more environmentally responsible in purchasing, travel, and other decisions, to reduce the profession's environmental footprint and to model sustainability. To learn more about examples of climate-resilient community development, visit the website of the Natural Resources Defense Council at **www.nrdc.org/issues/climate-resilience**.

Using the Electoral Process

As in the past, future social policy will be largely determined by electoral realities and changing public pressures. Tomorrow's electorate will be reshaped by changing demographics, including growing diversity and population aging. Technological advances will change how political activism is pursued and will alter some of the issues contested—privacy and freedom of expression, for example, and use of resources to counter environmental destruction. For example, more than four in five voters—across political affiliations—report they are more concerned about climate change than in the past (Deeg et al., 2019). Policymakers will be compelled to respond. Some future interactions of changing conditions and shifting politics are yet uncertain. The changing nature of work may contribute to resurgent labor politics or result in a growing and increasingly disillusioned "idle" class. Long-contested issues, such as reproductive rights, are being redrawn as medical technology advances and court precedents shift. Political parties will be forced to contend with global political realignments and geographic divisions within the United States. Population shifts will alter the makeup of U.S. society in ways that will then be codified and commodified following the 2020 Census. As these changes contribute to realignments in social, economic, and political structures, nearly everything about our electoral process may be up for reconsideration, from the way we engage in elections, to who gets to participate and on what terms, to what issues will be at stake. Importantly, social workers do not have to just cross our fingers and hope the future unfolds in ways that reflect our values and respond to our clients' needs. We can actively help shape what is to come.

The key to a more equitable future is for people who believe in such a vision to participate in crafting it. The NASW regularly develops policy statements outlining the organization's support for a wide variety of needed policy changes. If these policies are to be implemented, more social workers must engage in electoral politics and help elect candidates—including social workers themselves—who will support needed changes. In 2018, the NASW produced resources designed to encourage social workers' electoral participation, using the message that *Voting is Social Work*. In the future, the profession must give increased attention and support to the work of the NASW's Political Action for Candidate Election (PACE) and to other strategies to influence national and state policies. To learn more about ways in which social workers are involved in policy deliberation, visit the website of the Social Work Policy Institute at **www.socialworkpolicy.org**.

More immediately, if you are a U.S. citizen, you can register to vote—if you are not already registered—and encourage your friends and colleagues to vote. Bring up issues of social justice and engage in debate. Volunteer for election protection efforts to ensure that every American's vote is counted. See if you can integrate nonpartisan voter registration information into your organization's intake process and advocate internally to dedicate resources to nonpartisan Get-Out-the-Vote and voter education efforts. Contact your elected officials regularly to share your concerns about policy directions. Consider doing some policy-related research for your policymakers. For example, an MSW student who is committed to increasing voter turnout is researching the possibility of reducing the voting age to 16. Such policies have already been adopted in other countries and could make it possible to conduct more meaningful voter education in high schools in the future.

Try to find an issue or a candidate that arouses your passion, and then try not to lose heart when a campaign flounders or a policy you endorse does not produce all the outcomes you had hoped. Social workers should resist the impulse—so prevalent today—to oversimplify challenges and identify a single, "fix-all" approach. Trained to think critically and see connections, we recognize that no one policy will change behavior, reduce structural barriers, and solve all our troubles. Instead, as you take steps toward the future, remember what you learned about history and consider how discouraged advocates of abolition and women's suffrage must have become at points in their struggles. Look at issues intersectionally, connect with allies working on other concerns, discover where you have common cause, and seek solidarity in your shared struggles.

When forces seem arrayed against our values and progress appears elusive, there is a tendency to view this moment as an especially difficult time. Strengths-based social workers can be important reminders—including for social work colleagues—of the ways our profession has overcome other hard times, as well as the bright spots that suggest potential promise. Instead of being surprised or discouraged by opposition, prepare for it. Use the tools you have learned to address backlash, protect effective programs, and continue to press for a more just social contract. Social work practice, at its core, relies on the use of skills and relationships to effect significant changes that improve people's lives. Social policy advocacy is another arena in which to manifest this mission. Your education and value base equip you to shape social policy currents, which will, in turn, create a more supportive context for your work with clients.

THE STRENGTHS PERSPECTIVE IN A NEW ERA

Effective social work practice requires "searching the environment for forces that enhance or suppress human possibilities and life chances and attending to those through community building, resource development, and acquisition" (Saleebey, 2013, p. 295). Doing this work in a way that emphasizes client self-determination and possibility is at the heart of the strengths approach. Asking client groups what solutions they suggest can uncover new ideas and potentially energize clients' involvement. By creating opportunities for policymakers to listen to these constituencies from the beginning of the policy development process and explicitly focusing on outcomes important to these groups, social workers can help policymakers craft future strengths-based policy. This work can also challenge views of the future that are deficit-focused, so that future policy reflects clients' realities. We need social work values in the policy debate, elevating the dignity and worth of all people and advancing effective policy responses that build on people's strengths and work toward their goals.

CHARTING A NEW AGENDA: SOCIAL WORK GRAND CHALLENGES

We have been considering societal factors that will likely affect our future and how social work can provide leadership in charting a policy agenda that promotes social and economic justice. At this point in your social work education, you may have encountered another prominent effort to help the profession not only prepare for the coming future, but actively chart future policy consistent with social work values and priorities: The Social Work Grand Challenges. These 12 challenges were selected because they are important and broadly compelling, connect to intervention possibilities that social workers and partners could deliver, and represent areas amenable to meaningful and measurable change within ten years (American Academy of Social Work and Social Welfare, 2016). This social agenda centers on improving individual and family well-being, strengthening the social fabric, and helping create a more just society. The Grand Challenges are listed in Exhibit 12.7. Those who outlined this ambitious agenda for our profession recognized that current capacity is insufficient to meet these future challenges. Therefore, these Grand Challenges are for you. Pick the ones you are passionate about. Connect with social work scholars and practitioners working in these areas. Build on what you have learned about policy practice and what you are learning through your work with clients. Chart your future as a change agent and, in the process, change the future of our profession, our society, and our world.

EXHIBIT 12.7

Social Work Grand Challenges

- ensure healthy development for all youth;
- close the health gap;
- stop family violence;
- advance long and productive lives;
- eradicate social isolation;
- end homelessness;
- create social responses to a changing environment;
- harness technology for social good;
- promote smart decarceration;
- reduce extreme economic inequality;
- build financial capability for all; and
- achieve equal opportunity and justice.

CONCLUSION

To make decisions in the present, we need an image of a future worth seeking. We also need some guidance on how to get there. The synthesis of careful data analysis, constituency involvement, and reliance on professional values enables us to sketch an image of the future that energizes our efforts to craft effective policy. Think about how you can listen to your clients and interact in a way that supports their hopes for the future. Consider how you can support them in becoming engaged in crafting more effective programs. There are multiple ways for you to develop and demonstrate skills in change leadership, starting with your field placements. For example, as part of your field placement plan, you can participate in collaborative efforts to identify and implement needed changes in your agency and community.

As you listen to predictions about the future, analyze the motivations of the predictor. Some forces issue "prophecies" for the future they are actively trying to create, so that they can then capitalize on that future (Giridharadas, 2018). However, you will approach forecasting with a different motivation. You can articulate a strengths-based vision that builds on our shared values of opportunity and fairness. Armed with beginning skills in policy practice and, hopefully, inspired to bring your intelligence and creativity to bear on the big challenges we face, you can help develop and implement policies and programs that promote inclusion and make it possible for more people to achieve their dreams. Take time to celebrate any victories you achieve. Celebration of progress is central to the strengths approach. We wish you well in this exciting work to create a better future for our clients and ourselves.

MAIN POINTS

- A framework for understanding future forecasts draws attention to the following components: purpose, underlying assumptions and credibility of sources, influence of current socioeconomic conditions, interpretation of numbers or data, and anticipation of surprise events.

- When thinking about the future from the strengths perspective, take into account the life conditions, strengths, and goals of those for whom predictions are being made. Anchor your thinking about future policies and their potential impacts in the social work Code of Ethics.

- The population of the United States is expected to increase in the next 50 years because of fertility rates and net immigration. However, the rate of growth will decrease, owing to the greater age of the population and subsequent number of deaths, declining birth rates, and other factors.

- The U.S. population will become more ethnically and racially diverse, resulting in a pluralistic society that will require a commensurately responsive and empowering policy landscape.

- In addition to increases in population size and diversity, other forces will exert pressures on social policy and change how people experience the future. Among the most prominent are medical and technological advances, which are already changing life expectancy and the provision of health services, including within social work.

- Automation is changing the nature of work in the United States and around the globe. More occupations and individuals will be affected by automation in the coming years, with yet unknown effects on economic well-being and overall quality of life.

- Given U.S. values and preferences, we can expect future social policy to continue to emphasize attachment to the workforce. This raises the specter of gaps in supports as people's relationships to their jobs change, particularly with increasing automation and non-standard employment. Global efforts will be necessary to ensure retirement security and health care for an increasingly mobile and temporary workforce.

- Family-friendly workplace policies are needed to support workers as parents, caregivers for older relatives, and employees.

- Political realignments are both resulting from and contributing to other changes. Backlash to globalization is altering people's willingness to participate in international alliances, even as we contend with increasingly global challenges.

- Depletion of natural resources and climate change will shape the future, including individual and community health.

- Social work system reformers should carefully evaluate the benefits and limitations of privatization of publicly funded social services, so that future funding and oversight can be tailored to deliver adequate services.

- Social workers need to participate effectively in electoral politics to implement policies that promote the well-being of individuals, particularly client groups. We can do this by voting, organizing, debating, running for office, campaigning, donating, lobbying, and conducting policy-related research.

- The Grand Challenges for Social Work represent areas where meaningful and measurable change can be made within ten years.

EXERCISES

1. The Sanchez family is personally experiencing the impact of immigration policies. Go to the American Immigration Council (**www.americanimmigrationcouncil.org**) and examine the latest immigration policy reforms being proposed.
   a. What roles might the Sanchez family play in pushing for positive immigration policy? How could you support them, as their social worker?

b. What "surprise" events might occur that could influence the likelihood of comprehensive immigration reform? How could a social work policy practitioner anticipate and prepare for these potential events?

c. Consider the policy debates about immigration that have been prominently profiled in media coverage, including separation of families at the border and proposed changes to public charge rules. How might a family like the Sanchez family have experienced the media coverage of these policies and proposals?

2. As is evident in Riverton, homelessness exists in wealthy nations as well as in poor countries. Various governments attend to this problem differently. Do an online search to find out how different governments define, prioritize, and address this problem.

   a. What can we learn from other countries about policies and programs that would help address homelessness in Riverton?

   b. What differences between the United States and other countries might influence the effectiveness of a specific policy or program developed in another country to address homelessness if we tried to adopt it in Riverton?

3. Imagine it is ten years from now and write down a personal goal you hope you will have achieved. Now write down a goal for a change in social policy you think can be achieved in the next ten years. Be ready to discuss your social policy ideas with your classmates.

4. What do you think are the benefits and drawbacks of allowing 16-year-olds to vote?

   a. Are you for or against such a policy change? Why?

   b. Do you think we might have more policies that address the needs of children if younger people could vote?

   c. What other policies could have an impact on voter participation? Which approaches do you think would be most valuable? How could these policy changes impact future social policy?

5. The RAINN case provides an example of how technology may alter delivery of social services. Thinking about the clients with whom you work or clients served in an agency with which you are familiar, how could they be served using online resources?

   a. What barriers might they face as more services are provided online?

   b. What strategies could help these people receive the services and benefits they need in the face of these changes?

6. Experts believe that we will face more frequent and more severe natural disasters in the future due to climate change. As we face this future, consider what disaster-related policies would have helped residents of Hudson City prior to the disaster. How should such disaster prevention and relief policies take into account the experiences of marginalized populations?

   a. Look at media coverage related to a recent natural disaster to examine some of the effects on different individuals and constituencies. Whose voices are included in this coverage? What questions do you have about how particular groups were impacted?

   b. Pick a social service agency in your community and find out how it has prepared for disasters. What policies are in place to make sure clients are safe and continue to receive vital services and benefits?

   c. What additional plans and policies should the agency consider putting in place? Go to **www.fema.gov/plan** for ideas.

7. Think of your practicum agency, a social work agency where you have volunteered, or another organization that provides services. How well prepared is this organization, in your assessment, for the changes in population diversity and age demographics discussed in this chapter? What changes might it need to make to improve its chances of accommodating these shifts?
8. Community development initiatives present an opportunity to think about the future infrastructure needs of a city or town. Consider the Brickville case.
    a. Identify some factors that planners should consider to ensure environmental sustainability. What potential impact would the plan you envision have on the residents of Brickville?
    b. What about accommodations for an aging population? What would be beneficial?
    c. What are your ideas about how community design can support better health outcomes and a higher quality of life for all residents?
9. Social workers can improve their ability to understand, interpret, and make predictions by becoming more informed consumers of predictions about the future. Review some analysis about what has made recent predictions (related to weather forecasts, electoral outcomes, or economic trends) more or less accurate. What do these analyses suggest about threats to prediction accuracy? How can you use this knowledge to (a) make your own predictions more accurate and (b) critically assess others' predictions?

Afterword

As this fifth edition goes to press, the United States Congress is locked in a bitter battle. Following explosive revelations from a whistleblower inside the Administration, weeks of public and closed-door testimony, and an official finding by the Intelligence Committee that the President abused the power of his office to solicit political help from a foreign power and to obstruct the inquiry into his actions (Shear, 2019), Donald Trump has become only the third president in U.S. history to be impeached by the U.S. House of Representatives. Today, his removal from office by the U.S. Senate appears unlikely, but, as Chapter 12 underscores, these types of political events are notoriously difficult to forecast. We cannot know with any precision what Congress will do, how voters will react, or what the future might hold.

How are social work students and policy practitioners to navigate the current political landscape? The American electorate is sharply divided about whether the President's actions constitute impeachable offenses. Some people have eagerly followed every twist in the impeachment drama—a group roughly evenly split between those hoping for vindication of the President and those watching for his undoing. Other Americans have been repulsed by the partisan wrangling and by salacious details about redacted transcripts and secret envoys. A majority of Americans disapprove of how both President Trump and Democrats have handled the hearings, and fewer than half report following the live hearings at all (Salvanto et al., 2019). We, too, find it hard to stomach the personal attacks and difficult to follow the sequence of events. And so, we understand the temptation to avert one's eyes.

However, all the possible outcomes of the investigation and impeachment processes hold ominous implications for social workers and the clients we serve. This makes our attention imperative. First, the allegations of influence peddling and political manipulation threaten to confirm Americans' worst suspicions about government and policymaking. If the nation turns away even more completely from public institutions as solutions to our problems, the consequences will be far-reaching and even longer-lasting than the seemingly endless swirl of controversies that have surrounded this president. Indeed, if Congress excuses attempts to manipulate U.S. elections, Americans could take that as evidence that fears of rigged elections are more reality than conspiracy theory. In an era when most Americans—of all ideological persuasions—already feel the political deck is stacked against them, reinforcing beliefs that powerful actors can get away with blatant distortion and global subterfuge would make it even harder for social workers to enthusiastically answer skeptics' questions about whether their votes really matter. Finally, even those who do not give up on politics entirely may be nonetheless distracted from other urgent concerns by the nonstop impeachment coverage, which drowns out other headlines. This could result in more lost ground for social workers and our clients, regardless of the ultimate outcome for the president. The chapters in this text underscore the opportunity cost of a myopic focus on any single concern. While impeachment and its consequences may alter the balance of power and ripple throughout our electoral system, it is not the only—nor, in many cases, the strongest—force shaping Americans' lives. Additionally, what happens in the domains of immigration, reproductive rights, child welfare, criminal justice, and health care determine people's opportunities and outcomes, and policy in these arenas seldom reflects clients' strengths and goals. While strengths-based policy practice obviously must encompass efforts to identify and support elected officials whose values align with our profession's and to insist that voters' voices are not overridden by corrupt dealings, social workers cannot afford to abandon our efforts on other policy fronts, while the impeachment process grinds on.

As Chapters 2 and 3 remind us, there are lessons from history that can inform our actions today. While the political eras and precise circumstances are different, the aftermath of other presidential scandals and partisan impasses gives credence to the fear that the greatest loser in impeachment may be government itself and, by extension, those whose fortunes largely depend on intervention by a robust public sector. Many trace the decline of public trust in government to the investigation of then-President Nixon (Hardy, 2015). Of particular relevance for the current moment, although that disgraced president was a Republican, in many ways Democrats have struggled the most against the anti-government sentiment the scandal unleashed (Zelizer, 2014). This legacy is seen in some of the policy debates detailed in this text, including the backlash against the Affordable Care Act as "government takeover" of health care and congressional failure to reach compromise to ensure Social Security solvency or safeguard elections against foreign interference. While government is surely not the solution to all the social problems social workers and our clients face, it is just as surely more difficult to contemplate the construction of an equitable, sustainable, and vibrant future—the vision toward which strengths-based social workers aim—if public actors are considered largely unworthy of our trust. Further, as Chapter 7 emphasizes, since active exercise of voting rights is the bedrock on which other policy victories are constructed, retreat from civic engagement could preclude advances for years to come.

While we cannot know all the ramifications of this impeachment, then, we can see the tasks social work policy practitioners confront in this moment. For strengths-based social workers like us, politics has always been about the potential to more equitably distribute resources, center the realities of those otherwise overlooked, and leverage collective power to tangibly improve people's lives. To have a meaningful chance to pursue this vision, we must do what social workers in every practice domain excel at: simultaneously attend to multiple tasks. We decry the machinations and maneuvering that subvert the potential of our democratic process. We affirm the value of our public institutions and insist on Americans' right to craft our own political futures. And, at the same time, we commit ourselves to remaining focused on the core challenges of policy practice from a strengths perspective: to align policy objectives with clients' goals, catalyze movements for social justice both inside and outside government channels, and chart a vision of inclusive, progressive, policymaking capable of capturing the attention of a disillusioned public and animating an agenda worthy of public trust. This text is designed to equip the next generation of strengths-based social workers for those challenges.

References

AARP Research. (2018, March). *Maintaining dignity: Understanding and responding to the needs of older LGBT Americans*. Retrieved from: www.aarp.org/content/dam/aarp/research/surveys_statistics/life-leisure/2018/maintaining-dignity-lgbt.doi.10.26419%252Fres.00217.001.pdf

Abramovitz, M. (1996). *Regulating the lives of women: Social welfare policy from colonial times to the present* (rev. ed.). Boston, MA: South End Press.

Abramovitz, M. (2001). Everyone is still on welfare: The role of redistribution in social policy. *Social Work, 46*(4), 297–308.

Achstatter, L. C. (2014). Climate change: Threats to social welfare and social justice requiring social work intervention. *21st Century Social Justice, 1*(1). Retrieved from: http://fordham.bepress.com/swjournal/vol1/iss1/4

Acierno, R., Hernandez, M. A., Amstadter, A. B., Resnick, H. S., Steve, K., Muzzy, W., & Kilpatrick, D. G. (2010). Prevalence and correlates of emotional, physical, sexual, and financial abuse and potential neglect in the United States: The National Elder Mistreatment Study. *American Journal of Public Health, 100*(2), 292–297.

ACLU. (2018, May). *Neglect and abuse of unaccompanied immigrant children by U.S. Customs and Border Protection*. Retrieved from: www.dropbox.com/s/lplnnufjbwci0xn/CBP%20Report%20ACLU_IHRC%205.23%20FINAL.pdf?dl=0

Adams, G. (2018). *A historic boost to child care funding means states can start to realize the potential of the Child Care and Development Block Grant*. Washington, DC: The Urban Institute. Retrieved from: www.urban.org/urban-wire/historic-boost-child-care-funding-means-states-can-start-realize-potential-child-care-and-development-block-grant

Adamson, B. J. S., Cohen, A. B., Estevez, M., Magee, K., Williams, E., Gross, C. P., Meropol, N. J., & Davidoff, A. F. (2019). Affordable Care Act (ACA) Medicaid expansion impact on racial disparities in time to cancer treatment. *Journal of Clinical Oncology, 37*(18), LBA1.

Adarand Constructors v. Peña, 515 U.S.C. 200 (1995). Retrieved from: http://caselaw.lp.findlaw.com/scripts/getcase.pl?court=us&vol=000&invol=v10252

Adler, L. (2001). The meaning of permanence: A critical analysis of the Adoption and Safe Families Act of 1997. *President and Fellows of Harvard College Harvard Journal on Legislation, 38*(1), 1–38.

Administration for Children and Families (ACF). (2012, March 15). *TANF work requirements and state strategies to fulfill them*. Retrieved from: www.acf.hhs.gov/programs/opre/resource/tanf-work-requirements-and-state-strategies-to-fulfill-them

Administration on Aging. (2015). *Profile of older Americans: 2015*. Retrieved from: www.aoa.acl.gov/Aging_Statistics/Profile/2015/2.aspx

Adoptive Couple v. Baby Girl, 570 U.S. 637 (2013).

Agency for Healthcare Research and Quality. (2016). *2015 National Healthcare Quality and Disparities Report*. Retrieved from: www.ahrq.gov/research/findings/nhqrdr/nhqdr15/index.html

Agiesta, J., Luhby, T., & Sparks, G. (November 7, 2018). Exit polls: This election is about Donald Trump. *CNN*. Retrieved from: www.cnn.com/2018/11/06/politics/2018-exit-poll-results/index.html

Ahsan, N. (1996). The Family Preservation and Support Services Programs. *The Future of Children, 6*(3), 157–160.

Akee, R. (2019, March 12). *How does measuring poverty and welfare affect American Indian children?* Washington,

DC: Brookings Institution. Retrieved from: **www.brookings.edu/blog/up-front/2019/03/12/how-does-measuring-poverty-and-welfare-affect-american-indian-children/?utm_campaign=Brookings%20Brief&utm_source=hs_email&utm_medium=email&utm_content=70720162**

Alegeus. (2018). *Alegeus 2018 HSA participant profile*. Retrieved from: **http://info.alegeus.com/rs/798-TAC-188/images/2018_HSA_Participant_Profile_Report.pdf**

Alesina, A., & La Ferrara, E. (2005) Preferences for redistribution in the land of opportunities. *Journal of Public Economics, 89*(5–6), 897–931.

Allard, P., & Young, M. C. (2002). Prosecuting juveniles in adult court: The practitioner's perspective. *Journal of Forensic Psychology Practice, 2*(2), 65–78.

American Academy of Child and Adolescent Psychiatry. (1975). *Policy statement: Placement of American Indian children*. Retrieved from: **www.aacap.org/aacap/policy_statements/1975/Placement_of_American_Indian_Children.aspx**

American Academy of Social Work and Social Welfare. (2016). *Grand challenges for social work: Draft policy briefs announced*. Retrieved from: **http://aaswsw.org/news/grand-challenges-for-social-work-draft-policy-briefs**

Americans with Disabilities Act of 1990, Pub. L. No. 101-336, 104 Stat. 328. Retrieved from: **www.ada.gov/pubs/ada.htm**

Anapol, A. (2018). Poll: *Nearly half of Millennial Democrats identify as socialist or democratic socialist*. The Hill. Retrieved from: **https://thehill.com/homenews/campaign/409877-poll-nearly-half-of-millennial-democrats-identify-as-socialist-or**

Anderson, B. W. (1986). *Understanding the Old Testament* (4th ed.). Englewood Cliffs, NJ: Prentice Hall.

Anderson, C. (2018). *One person, no vote: How voter suppression is destroying our democracy*. New York, NY: Bloomsbury Publishing.

Anderson, M., Perrin, A., & Jiang, J. (2018). *11% of Americans don't use the Internet. Who are they?* Washington, DC: Pew Research Center. Retrieved from: **www.pewresearch.org/fact-tank/2018/03/05/some-americans-dont-use-the-internet-who-are-they/**

Annie E. Casey Foundation. (2018). *National Kids Count data book*. Baltimore, MD: Author. Retrieved from **www.aecf.org/m/resourcedoc/aecf-2018kidscountdatabook-2018.pdf**

Anti-Defamation League. (2017). *Audit of anti-Semitic incidents: 2017 year in review*. Retrieved from: **www.adl.org/resources/reports/2017-audit-of-anti-semitic-incidents**

Anzilotti, E. (2019, April 16). This platform wants to fix the disturbing lack of data on police violence. *Fast Company*. Retrieved from: **www.fastcompany.com/90335499/this-platform-wants-to-fix-the-disturbing-lack-of-data-on-police-violence**

Arntz, M., Gregory, T., & Zierahn, U. (2016). The risk of automation for jobs in OECD Countries: A comparative analysis. *OECD Social, Employment and Migration Working Papers*, No. 189. Paris: OECD Publishing.

Austin, L. T. (1993). *Babies for sale: The Tennessee Children's Home adoption scandal*. New York, NY: Praeger.

Axinn, J., & Stern, M. J. (2001). *Social welfare: A history of the American response to need* (5th ed.). Boston, MA: Allyn & Bacon.

Bailey, M. S., & Hemmeter, J. (2010). *Characteristics of noninstitutionalized DI and SSI program participants, 2010 update*. Retrieved from: **www.ssa.gov/policy/docs/rsnotes/rsn2014-02.html**

Bailey, R. (1994). The other side of slavery: Black labor, cotton, and textile industrialization in Great Britain and the United States. *Agricultural History, 68*(2), 35–50.

Baltes, P. B., & Baltes, M. M. (1990). Psychological perspectives on successful aging: The model of selective optimization with compensation. In P. B. Baltes & M. M. Baltes (Eds.), *Successful aging: Perspectives from the behavioral sciences* (pp. 1–34). Cambridge: Cambridge University Press.

Banerjee, M. (2002). Voicing realities and recommending reform in PRWORA. *Social Work, 47*(3), 315–358.

Barak, A., & Grohol, J. (2011). Current and future trends in Internet-supported mental health interventions. *Journal of Technology in Human Services, 29*, 155–196.

Barch, D., Pagliaccio, D., Belden, A., Harms, M. P., Gaffrey, M., Sylvester, C. M., Tillman, R., & Luby, J. (2015). Effect of hippocampal and amygdala connectivity on the relationship between preschool poverty and school-age depression. *The American Journal of Psychiatry, 173*(6), 625–634.

Barker, R. (1999). *Milestones in the development of social work and social welfare.* Washington, DC: NASW Press.

Barker, R. (2003). *The social work dictionary* (5th ed.). Washington, DC: NASW Press.

Barker, R. (2014). *The social work dictionary* (6th ed.). Washington, DC: NASW Press.

Barnes, R., & Lamothe, D. (2019, January 22). Supreme Court allows Trump restrictions on transgender troops in military to go into effect as legal battle continues. *Washington Post.* Retrieved from: www.washingtonpost.com/politics/courts_law/supreme-court-allows-trump-restrictions-on-transgender-troops-in-military-to-go-into-effect-as-legal-battle-continues/2019/01/22

Barnett, J. C., & Berchick, E. R. (2017). *Health insurance coverage in the United States: 2016.* Washington, DC: U.S. Census Bureau. Retrieved from: www.census.gov/content/dam/Census/library/publications/2017/.../p60-260.pdf

Bartels, L. (2002). *Economic inequality and political representation.* New York, NY: Russell Sage Foundation. Retrieved from: www.russellsage.org/sites/all/files/u4/Bartels_Economic%20Inequality%20%26%20Political%20Representation.pdf

Bartels, S. J., & Naslund, J. A. (2013). The underside of the silver tsunami: Older adults and mental health care. *New England Journal of Medicine, 368,* 6.

Bashshur, R. L., Shannon, G. W., Bashshur, N., & Yellowlees, P. M. (2016). The empirical evidence for telemedicine interventions in mental disorders. *Telemedicine Journal and e-Health: The Official Journal of the American Telemedicine Association, 22*(2), 87–113.

Bastian, J. & Michelmore, K. (2018). The long-term impact of the Earned Income Tax Credit on children's education and employment outcomes. *Journal of Labor Economics, 36*(4), 1127–1163.

Bauer, L., Parsons, J., & Shambaugh, J. (2019). *How do work requirement waivers help SNAP respond to a recession?* Washington, DC: The Brookings Institution. Retrieved from: www.brookings.edu/research/how-do-work-requirement-waivers-help-snap-respond-to-a-recession/

Baughman, R. A. (2012). *The effects of state EITC expansion on children's health: The Carsey Institute at the Scholars' Repository, paper 168.* Retrieved from: http://scholars.unh.edu/carsey/168

Bazelon Center. (2018). *Mental health systems.* Retrieved from: www.bazelon.org/our-work/mental-health-systems/

Bell, T., & Romano, E. (2015). Permanency and safety among children in foster family and kinship care: A scoping review. *Trauma, Violence, & Abuse, 18*(3), 268–286.

Bell, W. (1987). *Contemporary social welfare* (2nd ed.). New York: Macmillan.

Belsky, J., Steinberg, L. D., Houts, R. M., Friedman, S. L., DeHart, G., Cauffman, E., & Susman, E. (2007). Family rearing antecedents of pubertal timing. *Child Development, 78,* 1302–1321.

Berchick, E., Barnet, J., & Upton, R. (2019). *Health insurance coverage in the United States: 2018.* Washington, DC: U.S. Census Bureau. Retrieved from: www.census.gov/library/publications/2019/demo/p60-267.html

Berchick, E. R., Hood, E., & Barnett, J. C. (2018). *Health insurance coverage in the United States: 2017.* U.S. Government Printing Office, Washington, DC. Retrieved from: www.census.gov/content/dam/Census/library/publications/2018/demo/p60-264.pdf

Bertram, E. (2011). Democratic divisions in the 1960s and the road to welfare reform. *Political Science Quarterly, 126,* 579–610.

Bess, M. (2016). *Our grandchildren redesigned: Life in the bioengineered society of the near future.* Boston, MA: Beacon Press.

Bhatt, C., & Beck-Sague, C. (2018). Medicaid expansion and infant mortality in the United States. *American Journal of Public Health, 108*(4), e1–e3.

Blackman, K. (2018). *Opioid policy trends continue in 2018 legislative sessions.* Washington, DC: National Conference of State Legislatures. Retrieved from: www.ncsl.org/blog/2018/09/12/opioid-policy-trends-continue-in-2018-legislative-sessions.aspx

Blank, R., & Burau, V. (2010). *Comparative health policy* (3rd ed.). New York: Palgrave Macmillan.

Blau, J., & Abramovitz, M. (2007). *The dynamics of social welfare policy* (2nd ed.). New York: Oxford University Press.

BMJ. (2018). US life expectancy falls for third year in a row. *BMJ, 363*. doi: **https://doi.org/10.1136/bmj.k5118**

Boardman, F. K., Young, P. J., & Griffiths, F. E. (2017). Impairment experiences, identity and attitudes towards genetic screening: The views of people with spinal muscular atrophy. *Journal of Genetic Counseling, 27*(1), 69–84.

Boaz, D. (2018, October 25). Young people like "socialism," but do they know what it is? *National Review*. Retrieved from: **www.cato.org/publications/commentary/young-people-socialism-do-they-know-what-it**.

Borenstein, S., & Forster, N. (2019, June 18). U.S. air quality is slipping after years of improvement. *Associated Press*. Retrieved from: **www.apnews.com/d3515b79af1246d08f7978f026c9092b**

Bowditch, C. (1993). Getting rid of troublemakers: High school disciplinary procedures and the production of dropouts. *Social Problems, 40*, 493–507.

Bowling, B., Newman, D., White, C., Wood, A., & Coustasse, A. (2017). Provider reimbursement following the Affordable Care Act. *Business & Health Administration Proceedings*, 168–175.

Bradlee, B. (2018). *The forgotten: How the people of one Pennsylvania county elected Donald Trump and changed America*. New York, NY: Little, Brown and Company.

Bradley, E. H., & Taylor, L. (2013). *The American health care paradox: Why spending more is getting us less*. New York, NY: Public Affairs.

Brady, D. (2009). *Rich democracies, poor people: How politics explains poverty*. New York, NY: Oxford University Press.

Brainard, L. (2008). *New economy safety net: A Proposal to enhance worker adjustment programs*. Washington, DC: Brookings Institution. Retrieved from: **www.brookings.edu/articles/new-economy-safety-net-a-proposal-to-enhance-worker-adjustment-programs/**

Bramlett, M. D., Radel, L. F., & Chow, K. (2017). Health and well-being of children in kinship care: Findings from the National Survey of Children in Nonparental Care. *Child Welfare, 95*(3), 41–60.

Brenan, M. (2018). *Record-high 75% of Americans say immigration is good thing*. Washington, DC: Gallup. Retrieved from: **https://news.gallup.com/poll/235793/record-high-americans-say-immigration-good-thing.aspx**

Brennan Center for Justice. (2019). *New voting restrictions in America*. Retrieved from: **www.brennancenter.org/new-voting-restrictions-america**

Breytspraak, L., & Badura, L. (2015). *Facts on aging quiz* (revised; based on Palmore (1977; 1981)). Retrieved from: **https://aging.umkc.edu/quiz/**

Briar-Lawson, K. (2014). Building the social work workforce: Saving lives and families. *Advances in Social Work, 15*(1), 21–33.

Briar-Lawson, K., Naccarato, T., & Drews, J. (2009). Child and family welfare policies and services. In J. Midgley & M. Livermore (Eds.), *The handbook of social policy* (2nd ed., pp. 315–335). Thousand Oaks, CA: Sage Publications.

Brill, S. (2015). *America's bitter pill: Money, politics, backroom deals, and the fight to fix our broken healthcare system*. New York, NY: Random House.

Brissett-Chapman, S. (1995). Child abuse and neglect: Direct practice. In R. L. Edwards & J. G. Hopps (Eds.), *Encyclopedia of social work* (19th ed.; pp. 353–366). Alexandria, VA: National Association of Social Workers.

Broome, B. (April 2018). Amid the opioid epidemic, White means victim, Black means addict. *The Guardian*. Retrieved from: **www.theguardian.com/us-news/2018/apr/28/opioid-epidemic-selects-white-victim-black-addict**

Brown v. Board of Education of Topeka, 347 U.S. 483 (1954). Retrieved from: **http://caselaw.lp.findlaw.com/scripts/getcase.pl?court=us&vol=347&invol=483**.

Brown, J. (2018). *Millennials and retirement: Already falling short*. Washington, DC: National Institute on Retirement Security. Retrieved from: **www.nirsonline.org/wp-content/uploads/2018/02/Millennials-Report-1.pdf**

Brown, R. (2005, April 29). Billboards criticize Biden's violence law. *The News Journal*. Cited in *Frequently asked questions about VAWA and gender*. National Task Force to End Sexual and Domestic Violence Against Women. Retrieved from: **www.ncdsv.org/images/FAQ_VAWA%20and%20Gender.pdf**

Brown-Iannuzzi, J. L., Lundberg, K. B., Kay, A. C., & Payne, B. K. (2015). Subjective status shapes political preferences. *Psychological Science, 26*(1), 15–26.

Buck v. Bell, 274 U.S. 200 (1927).

Bruner, C. (2002). *A stitch in time: Calculating the costs of school un-readiness*. Washington, DC: The Finance Project.

Bumpus, J. A. (2014). *Transracial adoption: Racial identity, resilience, and self-esteem of African American adoptees*. Retrieved from: http://aura.antioch.edu/etds/101

Bunis, D. (2019, May 14). *Washington State enacts public long-term care insurance*. Washington, DC: AARP. Retrieved from: www.aarp.org/politics-society/advocacy/info-2019/washington-long-term-care-law.html

Bunting, L., Davidson, G., McCartan, C., Hanratty, J., Bywaters, P., Mason, W., & Steils, N. (2018). The association between child maltreatment and adult poverty: A systematic review of longitudinal research. *Child Abuse and Neglect, 77*, 121–133.

Burchinal, P., Kainz, K., Cai, K., Tout, K., Zaslow, M., Martinez-Beck, I., & Rathgeb, C. (2009). *Early care and education quality and child outcomes*. Washington, DC: Administration of Children and Families, Office of Planning, Research, and Evaluation. Retrieved from: www.acf.hhs.gov/sites/default/files/opre/early_ed_qual.pdf

Burd-Sharps, S., & Rasch, R. (2015). *Impact of the US housing crisis on the racial wealth gap across generations*. Washington, DC: Social Sciences Research Council. Retrieved from: www.aclu.org/sites/default/files/field_document/discrimlend_final.pdf

Burns, E. (1965). Where welfare falls short. *The Public Interest, 1*, 1–138.

Burnside, A., & Floyd, I. (2019, January 22). *TANF benefits remain low despite increases in some states*. Washington, DC: Center on Budget and Policy Priorities. Retrieved from: www.cbpp.org/research/family-income-support/tanf-benefits-remain-low-despite-recent-increases-in-some-states

Burrell, S., & Warboys, L. (2000). *Special education and the juvenile justice system*. Washington, DC: Office of Juvenile Justice and Delinquency Prevention. Retrieved from: www.ncjrs.gov/pdffiles1/ojjdp/179359.pdf

Burton, A., Peters, R. A., Wengle, E., Elmendorf, C., & Aarons, J. (2018). *What explains 2018's marketplace enrollment rates?* Washington, DC: Urban Institute. Retrieved from: www.urban.org/sites/default/files/publication/98650/marketplace2018_2001877.pdf

Bush, G. W. (January 20, 2005). *Second inaugural address*. Retrieved from: www.npr.org/templates/story/story.php?storyId=4460172

Butler, J. (2019). *How safe is the schoolhouse? An analysis of state seclusion and restraint laws and policies*. Autism National Committee. Retrieved from: www.autcom.org/pdf/HowSafeSchoolhouse.pdf

Cain, P. A. (1993). Litigating for lesbian and gay rights: A legal history. *Virginia Law Review, 79*, 1551–1642.

California v. Bakke, 483 U.S. 265 (1978). Retrieved from: http://caselaw.lp.findlaw.com/cgi-bin/getcase.pl?court=us&vol=438&invol=265

Campaign for Youth Justice. (2018). *FY 2018 omnibus bill signed into law*. Retrieved from: www.campaignforyouthjustice.org/news/cfyj-news-press-releases/item/fy-2018-omnibus-bill-signed-into-law

Canada Revenue Agency. (2018). *Canada child benefit*. Retrieved from: www.canada.ca/en/revenue-agency/services/forms-publications/publications/t4114/canada-child-benefit.html#cctb

Cancian, M., & Meyer, D. (2018). *How a child support assurance program could help low-income families*. Washington, DC: American Enterprise Institute. Retrieved from: www.aei.org/publication/can-child-support-assurance-help-low-income-families/

Canda, E. R. (2002). Wisdom from the Confucian classics for spiritually sensitive social welfare. *Currents: New Scholarship in the Human Services, 1*(1), 1–11. Retrieved from: www.ucalgary.ca/currents/files/currents/v1n1_canda2.pdf

Cannon, J. (Ed.) (1997). *The Oxford companion to British history*. New York, NY: Oxford University Press.

Carcasson, M. (2006). Ending welfare as we know it: President Clinton and the rhetorical transformation of the anti-welfare culture. *Rhetoric and Public Affairs, 9*(4), 655–692.

Carey, L. A. (2007). Teaching macro practice, *Journal of Teaching in Social Work, 27*(1–2), 61–71.

Carleton, T. A. (2017). Crop-damaging temperatures raise suicide in India. *Proceedings of the National Academy of Sciences,114*(33), 8746–8751.

Carlino, G. (2017). *Did the fiscal stimulus work?* Philadelphia, PA: Federal Reserve Bank. Retrieved from: **www.philadelphiafed.org/-/media/research-and-data/publications/economic-insights/2017/q1/eiq117_did-the-fiscal-stimulus-work.pdf?la=en**

Carlson, S., Neuberger, Z., & Rosenbaum, D. (2017). *WIC participation and costs are stable*. Washington, DC: Center on Budget and Policy Priorities (CBPP). Retrieved from: **www.cbpp.org/research/food-assistance/wic-participation-and-costs-are-stable#_ftnref12**

Carlton-LaNey, I. (1999). African American social work pioneers' response to need. *Social Work, 44*(4), 311–321.

Carson, E. A. (2018). *Prisoners in 2016*. United States Department of Justice: Bureau of Justice Statistics. Retrieved from: **www.bjs.gov/index.cfm?ty=pbdetail&iid=6187**

Case, A., & Deaton, A. (2015). Rising morbidity and mortality in midlife among White non-Hispanic Americans in the 21st century. *Proceeding of the National Academy of Sciences of the United States of America, 112*(49), 15078–15083.

Casey Family Programs. (2015). *Placement patterns for American Indian children involved with child welfare*. Baltimore, MD: Author. Retrieved from: **https://caseyfamilypro-wpengine.netdna-ssl.com/media/NSCAW-Placement-Patterns-Brief.pdf**

Cass, O. (2018). *The once and future worker: A vision for the renewal of work in America*. New York, NY: Encounter Books.

Cauchi, R. (2018). *State laws and actions challenging certain health reforms*. Washington, DC: National Conference of State Legislatures. Retrieved from: **www.ncsl.org/research/health/state-laws-and-actions-challenging-ppaca.aspx**

Cawley, J., Schroeder, M., & Simon, K. I. (2006). How did welfare reform affect the health insurance coverage of women and children? *Health Services Research, 41*(2), 486–506.

Center on Budget and Policy Priorities (CBPP). (2016, August 16). *Policy basics: Introduction to Medicaid*. Retrieved from: **www.cbpp.org/research/health/policy-basics-introduction-to-medicaid**

Center on Budget and Policy Priorities (CBPP). (2018a). *Chart book: The legacy of the great recession*. Retrieved from: **www.cbpp.org/research/economy/chart-book-the-legacy-of-the-great-recession**

Center on Budget and Policy Priorities (CBPP). (2018b). *Top ten facts about Social Security*. Retrieved from: **www.cbpp.org/research/social-security/policy-basics-top-ten-facts-about-social-security**

Center on Budget and Policy Priorities (CBPP). (2018c). *Policy basics: The Earned Income Tax Credit*. Retrieved from: **www.cbpp.org/research/federal-tax/policy-basics-the-earned-income-tax-credit**

Center on Budget and Policy Priorities (CBPP). (2019). *Policy basics: Federal tax expenditures*. Washington, DC: Author. Available at: **www.cbpp.org/research/federal-tax/policy-basics-federal-tax-expenditures**

Centers for Disease Control and Prevention (CDCP). (2013). *Social determinants of health*. Retrieved from: **www.cdc.gov/socialdeterminants**

Centers for Disease Control and Prevention (CDCP). (2016a). *Sexual identity, sex of sexual contacts, and health-risk behaviors among students in grades 9–12: Youth risk behavior surveillance*. Atlanta, GA: U.S. Department of Health and Human Services.

Centers for Disease Control and Prevention (CDCP). (2016b). National Center for Health Statistics. *Adolescent health*. Retrieved from: **www.cdc.gov/nchs/fastats/adolescent-health.htm**

Centers for Disease Control and Prevention (CDCP). (2016c). *More young children with ADHD could benefit from behavior therapy*. Retrieved from: **www.cdc.gov/media/releases/2016/p0503-children-ADHD.html**

Centers for Disease Control and Prevention (CDCP). (2017a). *Leading causes of death by age group*. Retrieved from: **www.cdc.gov/injury/images/lc-charts/leading_causes_of_death_by_age_group_2017_1100w850h.jpg**

Centers for Disease Control and Prevention (CDCP). (2017b). *Life expectancy at birth, by race, gender, and Hispanic origin: United States, 2006-2016*. Retrieved from: **www.cdc.gov/nchs/data/hus/2017/fig01.pdf**

Centers for Disease Control and Prevention (CDCP). (2017c). *Why it matters: the pandemic threat*. Retrieved from: **www.cdc.gov/globalhealth/**

healthprotection/fieldupdates/winter-2017/why-it-matters.html

Centers for Disease Control and Prevention (CDCP). (2017d). *Vital signs: racial disparities in age-specific mortality among Blacks or African Americans: United States, 1999–2015.* Retrieved from: **www.cdc.gov/mmwr/volumes/66/wr/mm6617e1.htm?s_cid=mm6617e1_w**

Centers for Disease Control and Prevention (CDCP). (2018a). *Health 2017, with a special feature on mortality.* Retrieved from: **www.cdc.gov/nchs/data/hus/hus17.pdf**

Centers for Disease Control and Prevention (CDCP). (2018b). *Provisional drug overdose data.* Retrieved from: **www.cdc.gov/nchs/nvss/vsrr/drug-overdose-data.htm**

Centers for Disease Control and Prevention (CDCP). (2019a). *Pregnancy-related deaths.* Retrieved from: **www.cdc.gov/vitalsigns/maternal-deaths**

Centers for Disease Control and Prevention (CDCP). (2019b). *WISQARS fatal injury data visualization.* Retrieved from: **https://wisqars-viz.cdc.gov:8006/**

Centers for Medicare and Medicaid Services (CMS) (2006). *Nursing home culture change regulatory compliance questions and answers.* Retrieved from: **www.cms.gov/Medicare/Provider-Enrollment-and-Certification/SurveyCertificationGenInfo/downloads/SCLetter07-07.pdf**

Centers for Medicare and Medicaid Services (CMS). (2010). *The Mental Health Parity and Addiction Equity Act.* Retrieved from: **www.cms.gov/CCIIO/Programs-and-Initiatives/Other-Insurance-Protections/mhpaea_factsheet.html**

Centers for Medicare and Medicaid Services (CMS). (2013). *Your Medicare coverage.* Retrieved from: **www.medicare.gov/coverage/your-medicare-coverage.html**

Centers for Medicare and Medicaid Services (CMS). (2015). *Women's health.* Retrieved from: **www.medicaid.gov/medicaid-50th-anniversary/women/women.html**

Centers for Medicare and Medicaid Services (CMS). (2016). *Quality payment program: Delivery system reform, Medicare payment reform, and MACRA.* Retrieved from: **www.cms.gov/Medicare/Quality-Initiatives-Patient-Assessment-Instruments/Value-Based-Programs/MACRA-MIPS-and-APMs/MACRA-MIPS-and-APMs.html**

Centers for Medicare and Medicaid Services (CMS). (2017). *National health expenditure fact sheet.* Retrieved from: **www.cms.gov/research-statistics-data-and-systems/statistics-trends-and-reports/nationalhealthexpenddata/nhe-fact-sheet.html**

Centers for Medicare and Medicaid Services (CMS). (2018a). *Medicaid and CHIP enrollment data: October 2018.* Retrieved from: **www.medicaid.gov/medicaid/program-information/medicaid-and-chip-enrollment-data/report-highlights/index.html**

Centers for Medicare and Medicaid Services (CMS). (2018b). *CMS fast facts.* Retrieved from: **www.cms.gov/research-statistics-data-and-systems/statistics-trends-and-reports/cms-fast-facts/index.html**

Centers for Medicare and Medicaid Services (CMS). (2018c). *Contract year (CY) 2020 Medicare Advantage and Part D drug pricing proposed rule (CMS-4180-P).* Retrieved from: **www.cms.gov/newsroom/fact-sheets/contract-year-cy-2020-medicare-advantage-and-part-d-drug-pricing-proposed-rule-cms-4180-p**

Centers for Medicaid and Medicare Services (CMS). (2019a) *2019 annual report of the Boards of Trustees of the Federal Hospital Insurance and Federal Supplementary Medical Insurance Trust Funds.* Retrieved from: **www.cms.gov/Research-Statistics-Data-and-Systems/Statistics-Trends-and-Reports/ReportsTrustFunds/Downloads/TR2019.pdf**

Centers for Medicare and Medicaid Services (CMS). (2019b). *Health insurance exchanges: 2019 open enrollment report.* Retrieved from: **www.cms.gov/newsroom/fact-sheets/health-insurance-exchanges-2019-open-enrollment-report**

Central Intelligence Agency (CIA). (2017). *World factbook.* Retrieved from: **www.cia.gov/library/publications/the-world-factbook/rankorder/2091rank.html**

Chait, N., & Glied, S. (2018). Promoting Prevention Under the Affordable Care Act. *Annual Review of Public Health, 39*, 507–524.

Chambers, D. E. (2000). *Social policy and social programs: A method for the practical public policy analyst* (3rd ed.). Boston, MA: Allyn & Bacon.

Chambers, D., & Bonk, J. F. (2013). *Social policy and social programs: A method for the practical public policy analyst* (6th ed.). Boston, MA: Allyn & Bacon/Pearson.

Chandy, L., & Gertz, G. (2011). *Poverty in numbers: The changing state of global poverty from 2005 to 2015.* Washington, DC: The Brookings Institution.

Chapin, R. (1995). Social policy development: The strengths perspective. *Social Work, 40*(4), 506–514.

Chapin, R., Baca, B., Macmillan, K., Rachlin, R., & Zimmerman, M. (2009). Residential outcomes for nursing facility applicants who have been diverted: Where are they five years later? *The Gerontologist, 49*(1), 46–56.

Chapin, R., & Cox, E. (2001). Changing the paradigm: Strengths-based and empowerment-oriented social work with frail elders. *Journal of Gerontological Social Work, 6*(3/4), 165–180.

Chapin, R., Sergeant, J. F., Landry, S. T., Leedahl, S. N., Rachlin, R., Koenig, T. L., & Graham, A. (2013). Reclaiming joy: Pilot evaluation of a mental health peer support program for Medicaid waiver recipients. *The Gerontologist, 53*(2), 345–352.

Charles, E., et al. (2017). Impact of Medicaid expansion on cardiac surgery volume and outcomes. *The Annals of Thoracic Surgery, 104*, 1251–1258. Retrieved from: **http://www.annalsthoracicsurgery.org/article/S0003-4975(17)30552-0/pdf**

Cherokee Nation v. Georgia, 30 U.S. 1 (1831). Retrieved from: **http://caselaw.lp.findlaw.com/scripts/getcase.pl?court=us&vol=30&invol=**

Chetty, R., Friedman, J. N., & Rockoff, J. (2011). *New evidence on the long-term impacts of tax credits.* Cambridge, MA: National Bureau of Economic Research. Retrieved from: **www.irs.gov/pub/irs-soi/11rpchettyfriedmanrockoff.pdf**

Chetty, R., Grusky, D., Hell, M., Hendren, N., Manduca, R., & Narang, J. (2016). *The fading American Dream: Trends in absolute income mobility since 1940.* NBER Working Paper No. 22910. Cambridge, MA: National Bureau of Economic Research. Retrieved from **www.nber.org/papers/w22910.pdf**

Chetty, R., Hendren, N., & Katz, L. (2016). The effects of exposure to better neighborhoods on children: New evidence from the Moving to Opportunity Project. *American Economic Review, 106*(4). Retrieved from: **https://scholar.harvard.edu/hendren/publications/effects-exposure-better-neighborhoods-children-new-evidence-moving-opportunity**

Chetty, R., Hendren, N., Jones, M., & Porter, S. (2018). *Race and economic opportunity in the United States: An intergenerational perspective.* Prepared for U.S. Census Bureau. Retrieved from: **www.equality-of-opportunity.org/assets/documents/race_paper.pdf**

Chetty, R., Hendren, N., Kline, P., & Saez, E. (2014). *Where is the land of opportunity? The geography of intergenerational mobility in the United States.* Stanford, CA: Stanford University, Equality of Opportunity Project. Retrieved from: **www.equality-of-opportunity.org/assets/documents/mobility_geo.pdf**

Child Abuse Prevention and Treatment Act, 42 U.S.C. 5106 § (1974).

Child Trends. (2018). *Racial and ethnic composition of the child population.* Retrieved from **www.childtrends.org/indicators/racial-and-ethnic-composition-of-the-child-population**

Child Welfare Information Gateway. (2012). *How the child welfare system works.* Washington, DC: U.S. Department of Health and Human Services, Children's Bureau.

Child Welfare Information Gateway. (2016). *Child welfare information gateway.* Retrieved from: **www.childwelfare.gov**

Child Welfare Information Gateway. (2017). *Foster care statistics 2016.* Washington, DC: U.S. Department of Health and Human Services, Children's Bureau.

Childcare Aware. (2017). *Parents and the high cost of child care.* Arlington, VA: Author. Retrieved from: **http://usa.childcareaware.org/wp-content/uploads/2017/12/2017_CCA_High_Cost_Report_FINAL.pdf**

Children's Bureau. (2018). *The adoption and foster care analysis and reporting system report.* Retrieved from: **www.acf.hhs.gov/sites/default/files/cb/afcarsreport25.pdf**

Children's Defense Fund. (2010). *Fostering connections to success and increasing adoptions act summary.* Retrieved from: **www.childrensdefense.org/library/data/FCSIAA-detailed-summary.pdf**

Children's Defense Fund. (2012). *The state of America's children, 2012 handbook.* Washington, DC:

Children's Defense Fund. Retrieved from: www.childrensdefense.org/library/data/soac-2012-handbook.pdf

Children's Defense Fund. (2018, September). *Child poverty in America 2017: State analysis.* Retrieved from: www.childrensdefense.org/wp-content/uploads/2018/09/Child-Poverty-in-America-2017-State-Fact-Sheet.pdf

Citizens United v. Federal Election Commission, 558 U.S. 310 (2010).

Clark, J. W., & Young, J. A. (2018). *Automatic enrollment: The power of the default.* Vanguard. Retrieved from: https://institutional.vanguard.com/iam/pdf/CIRAE.pdf

Clark, K., Esch, C., & Delvac, G. (2016). How welfare money funds college scholarships. *Marketplace.* Retrieved from: www.marketplace.org/2016/06/09/wealth-poverty/how-welfare-money-funds-college-scholarships

Clark, P., & Slack, P. (1976). *English towns in transition: 1500–1700.* New York, NY: Oxford University Press.

Claxton, M., & Hansen, R. (2004). Working poor suffer under Bush tax cuts. *The Detroit News.*

Coates, T. (2017, October). The first White president. *The Atlantic.* Retrieved from: www.theatlantic.com/magazine/archive/2017/10/the-first-white-president-ta-nehisi-coates/537909/

Coibion, O., Gorodnichenko, Y., & Koustas, D. (2013). *Amerisclerosis? The puzzle of rising U.S. unemployment persistence.* Brookings Papers on Economic Activity. Retrieved from: www.brookings.edu/wp-content/uploads/2016/07/2013b_coibion_unemployment_persistence.pdf

Colburn, G., & Allen, R. (2016). Rent burden and the Great Recession in the USA. *Urban Studies*, 1–18. Retrieved from: www.hhh.umn.edu/sites/hhh.umn.edu/files/rent_burden_report.pdf

Colby, S. L., & Ortman, J. M. (2015). *Projections of the size and composition of the U.S. population: 2014 to 2060.* U.S. Census Bureau. Retrieved from: www.census.gov/content/dam/Census/library/publications/2015/demo/p25-1143.pdf

Coley, R. J., & Baker, B. (2013, July). *Poverty and education: Finding the way forward.* Retrieved from: www.ets.org/s/research/pdf/poverty_and_education_report.pdf

Coll, B. (1972). Public assistance in the United States: Colonial times to 1860. In E. W. Martin (Ed.), *Comparative development in social welfare* (pp. 128–158). London: Allen & Unwin.

Collins, J. W., David, R. J., Handler, A., Wall, S., & Andes, S. (2004). Very low birthweight in African American infants: The role of maternal exposure to interpersonal racial discrimination. *American Journal of Public Health, 94*(12), 2132–2138.

Collins, S. R., Gunia, M. Z., Doty, M. M., & Bhupal, H. K. (2018, May 1). First look at health insurance coverage in 2018 finds ACA gains beginning to reverse: Findings from the Commonwealth Fund Affordable Care Act Tracking Survey, Feb.–Mar. 2018. *To the Point* (blog), Commonwealth Fund.

Commager, H. (Ed.) (1958). *Documents of American history* (6th ed.). New York, NY: Appleton Century-Crofts.

Commission on Retirement Security and Personal Savings. (2016). *Securing our financial future: Report of the Commission on Retirement Security and Personal Savings.* Retrieved from: http://cdn.bipartisanpolicy.org/wp-content/uploads/2016/06/BPC-Retirement-Security-Report.pdf

Committee on Ways and Means. (2000). *2000 green book.* Washington, DC: U.S. Government Printing Office.

Commonwealth Fund. (2017). *International profiles of health care systems.* Retrieved from: www.commonwealthfund.org/publications/fund-reports/2017/may/international-profiles-health-care-systems

Congressional Budget Office (CBO). (2017a). *H.R. 1628, the Better Care Reconciliation Act of 2017: An amendment in the nature of a substitute.* Retrieved from: www.cbo.gov/publication/52941

Congressional Budget Office (CBO). (2017b). *Repealing the individual health insurance mandate: An updated estimate.* Washington, DC. November.

Congressional Budget Office (CBO). (2018a, January). *The budget and economic outlook: 2018 to 2028.* Retrieved from: www.cbo.gov/publication/53766

Congressional Budget Office (CBO). (2018b). *Veteran's benefit programs.* Retrieved from: www.cbo.gov/publication/45615

Congressional Budget Office (CBO). (2018c). *Exploring the growth of Medicaid managed care.* Retrieved from: www.cbo.gov/publication/54235

Congressional Budget Office (CBO). (2019a). *Effects of the partial shutdown ending January 2019.* Retrieved from: www.cbo.gov/system/files?file=2019-01/54937-PartialShutdownEffects.pdf

Congressional Budget Office (CBO). (2019b, January). *The budget and economic outlook: 2019 to 2029.* Retrieved from: www.cbo.gov/publication/54918

Cook, B. L., & Alegría, M. (2011). Racial-ethnic disparities in substance abuse treatment: The role of criminal history and socioeconomic status. *Psychiatric Services (Washington, DC), 62*(11), 1273–1281.

Cooper, J. L. (2008). *Toward a better behavioral health system for children, youth, and their families.* National Center for Children in Poverty. Retrieved from: www.nccp.org/publications/pub_804.html

Corporation for Enterprise Development (CFED). (2009). *American dream demonstration.* Retrieved from: https://cfed.org/assets/pdfs/American_Dream_Demonstration.pdf

Costamagna, F. (2016). Restricting access to social benefits and the lasting legacy of the Brexit debate. *EuVisions.* Turin, Italy: Centro Einaudi. Retrieved from: www.euvisions.eu/restricting-access-to-social-benefits-and-the-lasting-legacy-of-the-brexit-debate/

Council on Social Work Education (2015). *Educational Policy and Accreditation Standards.* Washington, DC: Author. Retrieved from: www.cswe.org/Accreditation/Standards-and-Policies/2015-EPAS.

Council on State Governments. (2016). *State welfare reforms: TANF time limits by the numbers.* Lexington, KY: Author. Retrieved from: http://knowledgecenter.csg.org/kc/content/state-welfare-reforms-tanf-time-limits-numbers

Cramer, K. (2016). *The politics of resentment: Rural consciousness in Wisconsin and the rise of Scott Walker.* Chicago, IL: University of Chicago Press.

Cramer, R., O'Brien, R., Cooper, D., & Luengo-Prado, M. (2009, November). *A penny saved is mobility earned: Advancing economic mobility through savings.* Economic Mobility Project. Retrieved from: www.pewtrusts.org/~/media/legacy/uploadedfiles/pcs_assets/2009/empsavingsreportpdf.pdf

Crenshaw, K. (1989). Demarginalizing the intersection of race and sex: A Black feminist critique of antidiscrimination doctrine, feminist theory, and antiracist politics. *University of Chicago Legal Forum, 139*–167.

Cubanski, J., Damico, A., & Neuman, T. (2018). *Medicare Part D: A first look at prescription drug plans in 2019.* Kaiser Family Foundation. Retrieved from: www.kff.org/medicare/issue-brief/medicare-part-d-a-first-look-at-prescription-drug-plans-in-2019/

Cubanski, J., & Neuman, T. (2018). *The facts on Medicare spending and financing.* Kaiser Family Foundation. Retrieved from: http://kff.org/medicare/issue-brief/the-facts-on-medicare-spending-and-financing

Cubanski, J., Orgera, D., Damico, A., & Neuman, T. (2018). *How many seniors are living in poverty? National and state estimates under the official and supplemental poverty measures in 2016.* Kaiser Family Foundation. Retrieved from: http://files.kff.org/attachment/Data-Note-How-Many-Seniors-Are-Living-in-Poverty-National-and-State-Estimates-Under-the-Official-and-Supplemental-Poverty-Measures-in-2016

Cummings, J. R., Wen, H., & Ko, M. (2016). Decline in public substance use disorder treatment centers most serious in counties with high shares of Black residents. *Health Affairs (Project Hope), 35*(6), 1036–1044.

Curtis, M. A., Garlington, S., & Schottenfeld, L. S. (2013). Alcohol, drug, and criminal history restrictions in public housing. *Cityscape: A Journal of Policy Development and Research, 15*(3).

Dahl, G. B., & Lochner, L. (2010). *The impact of family income on child achievement: Evidence from the Earned Income Tax Credit.* CIBC Working Paper, No. 2010-5. London, Ontario: The University of Western Ontario, CIBC Centre for Human Capital and Productivity.

Daly, M. C., & Bengali, L. (2014, May 5). Is it still worth going to college? *Federal Reserve Bank of San Francisco.* Retrieved from: www.frbsf.org/economic-research/publications/economic-letter/2014/may/is-college-worth-it-education-tuition-wages

D'Andrade, A. C. (2009). The differential effects of concurrent planning practice elements on reunification and adoption. *Research on Social Work Practice, 19*(4), 446–459.

Darwin, C. (1859). *On the origin of species by means of natural selection, or, the preservation of favoured races in the struggle for life*. London: J. Murray.

Davenport, C., & Landler, M. (2019, May 27). Trump Administration hardens its attack on climate science. *New York Times*. Retrieved from: **www.nytimes.com/2019/05/27/us/politics/trump-climate-science.html?login=email&auth=login-email**

Davis, A. (1984). *Spearheads for reform*. New Brunswick, NJ: Rutgers University Press.

Dawson, L., Kates, J., & Damico, A. (2018). *The Affordable Care Act and insurance coverage changes by sexual orientation*. Kaiser Family Foundation. Retrieved from: **www.kff.org/disparities-policy/issue-brief/the-affordable-care-act-and-insurance-coverage-changes-by-sexual-orientation/**

Day, P. (2000). Social policy from colonial times to the Civil War. In J. Midgley, M. Tracy, & M. Livermore (Eds.), *The handbook of social policy* (pp. 85–96). Thousand Oaks, CA: Sage Publications.

Day, P. (2009). *A new history of social welfare* (6th ed.). Boston, MA: Pearson.

Dedon, L. (2018). *Using emergency declarations to address the opioid epidemic*. Washington, DC: National Governors Association. Retrieved from: **www.nga.org/wp-content/uploads/2018/09/09-11-18-Issue-Brief-HSPS-Opioids-and-Emergency-Declarations.pdf**

Deeg, K., Lyon, E., Leiserowitz, A., Maibach, E., & Marlon, J. (2019). *Who is changing their mind about global warming and why?* New Haven, CT: Yale Program on Climate Change Communication. Retrieved from: **https://climatecommunication.yale.edu/publications/who-is-changing-their-mind-about-global-warming-and-why/**

Delgadillo, L. M. (2015). Using Individual Development Accounts (IDAs) to sustain homeownership and foster financial skills, practices, and self-efficacy. *Journal of Family and Consumer Sciences, 107*(3), 18–26.

DeLoria, P. J. (1993). The twentieth century and beyond. In B. Ballantine & I. Ballantine (Eds.), *The Native Americans: An illustrated history* (pp. 384–465). Atlanta, GA: Turner Publishing.

DeNavas-Walt, C., & Proctor, B. (2015). *Income and poverty in the United States: 2014*. Washington, DC: U.S. Bureau of the Census.

Desilver, D. (2018, August 7). *For most U.S. workers, real wages have barely budged in decades*. Washington, DC: Pew Research Center. Retrieved from: **www.pewresearch.org/fact-tank/2018/08/07/for-most-us-workers-real-wages-have-barely-budged-for-decades/**

DeWitt, L. (2003). *Brief history*. Social Security Administration Historian's Office. Retrieved from: **www.ssa.gov/history/briefhistory3.html**

Dimock, M., Kiley, J., Keeter, S., Doherty, C., & Tyson, A. (2014). *Beyond red vs. blue: The political typology*. The Pew Research Center for the People & the Press. Retrieved from **www.people-press.org/files/2014/06/6-26-14-Political-Typology-release1.pdf**

DiNitto, D. M., & Johnson, D. H. (2016). *Social welfare: Politics and public policy*. Boston, MA: Pearson.

Division of Facilities Compliance and Recovery. (2016). *The Hill–Burton Free Care Program*. Retrieved from: **www.hrsa.gov/gethealthcare/affordable/hillburton/hillburton.pdf**

Dolgoff, R., & Feldstein, D. (2013). *Understanding social welfare: A search for social justice*. New York, NY: Pearson.

Dominelli, L. (2013). Environmental justice. *International Journal of Social Welfare, 22*, 431–439.

Dowd, J. (1980). Aging as exchange: A preface to theory. In J. Quadagno (Ed.), *Aging, the individual, and society* (pp. 103–121). New York: St. Martin's Press.

Dowell, D., Haegerich, T., & Chou, R. (2019). No shortcuts to safer opioid prescribing. *New England Journal of Medicine, 380*, 2285–2287.

Downs, S. W., Costin, L. B., & McFadden, E. J. (1996). *Child welfare and family services: Policies and practice*. White Plains, NY: Longman.

Drake, B., & Pandey, S. (1996). Understanding the relationship between neighborhood poverty and specific types of child maltreatment, *Child Abuse & Neglect, 20*(11), 1003–1018.

Dred Scott v. Sandford, 60 U.S. 393 (1857). Retrieved from: **http://caselaw.lp.findlaw.com/scripts/getcase.pl?court=us&vol=6&invol=393**

Drew, E. (1996). *Showdown: The struggle between the Gingrich Congress and the Clinton White House*. New York, NY: Simon & Schuster.

Dripps, D. A. (1996). A new era for gay rights? *Trial, 32*(9), 18–21.

Drought, K. E., & Heintz, R. D. (2017). *New Hampshire Supreme Court: Children's SSI is not income for the whole family*. Chicago, IL: Sargent Shriver Center on Poverty Law. Retrieved from: **www.povertylaw.org/clearinghouse/stories/drought**

Dunkle, R. E., Ingersoll-Dayton, B., & Chadiha, L. A. (2015). Support for and from aging mothers whose adult daughters are seriously mentally ill. *Journal of Gerontological Social Work, 58*(6), 590–612.

Dushi, I., Iams, H. M., & Trenkamp, B. (2017). The importance of Social Security benefits to the income of the aged population. *Social Security Bulletin, 77*(2).

Easterling, D., & McDuffee, L. (2018). Social determinants of health: How are health conversion foundations using their resources to create change? *Health Affairs*. Retrieved from: **www.healthaffairs.org/do/10.1377/hblog20180313.6738/full/**

Economist Intelligence Unit. (2018). *Democracy index 2018*. Retrieved from: **www.eiu.com/Handlers/WhitepaperHandler.ashx?fi=Democracy_Index_2018.pdf&mode=wp&campaignid=Democracy2018**

Edelman, P. (2017). *Not a crime to be poor: The criminalization of poverty in America*. New York, NY: The New Press.

Edin, K., & Shaefer, L. (2016). *$2.00 a day: Living on almost nothing in America*. New York, NY: Mariner Books.

Education for All Handicapped Children Act of 1975, Public Law 94-142, S. 6. Retrieved from: **www.gpo.gov/fdsys/pkg/STATUTE-89/pdf/STATUTE-89-Pg773.pdf**

Edwards, K., & Mason, L. M. (2003). *State policy trends for individual development accounts in the United States: 1993–2003*. St. Louis, MO: Center for Social Development.

Ehrenfreund, M. (2017). Kansas Republicans raise taxes, ending their GOP governor's 'real live experiment' in conservative policy. *Washington Post*. Retrieved from: **www.washingtonpost.com/news/wonk/wp/2017/06/07/kansas-republicans-raise-taxes-rebuking-their-gop-governors-real-live-experiment-in-conservative-policy**

Ehrlich, P. (1970). *The population bomb*. New York, NY: Ballantine Books.

Eiken, S., Sredl, K., Burwell, B., & Amos, A. (2018, May). *Medicaid expenditures for long-term services and supports in FY 2016*. Retrieved from: **www.medicaid.gov/medicaid/ltss/downloads/reports-and-evaluations/ltssexpenditures2016.pdf**

Eikenberry, A. M., & Kluver, J. D. (2004). The marketization of the nonprofit sector: Civil society at risk? *Public Administration Review, 64*(2).

Elk v. Wilkins, 112 U.S. 94 (1884). Retrieved from: **http://supreme.justia.com/us/112/94/case.html**

Ellen, I. G., & Dastrup, S. (2012). *Housing and the Great Recession*. Russell Sage Foundation and Stanford Center on Poverty. Retrieved from: **https://furmancenter.org/files/publications/HousingandtheGreatRecession.pdf**

Elliott, D. E., Bjelajac, P., Fallot, R. D., Markoff, L. S., & Reed, B. G. (2005). Trauma-informed or trauma-denied: Principles and implementation of trauma-informed services for women. *Journal of Community Psychology, 33*(4), 461–477.

Elliott, W. (2013). Small-dollar children's savings accounts and children's college outcomes. *Children and Youth Services Review, 35*(3), 572–585.

Elliott, W., Jung, H., & Friedline, T. (2011). Raising math scores among children in low-wealth households: Potential benefit of children's school savings. *Journal of Income Distribution, 20*(2), 72–91.

Elliott, W., Kite, B., O'Brien, M., Lewis, M., & Palmer, A. (2016). *Initial elementary education finding from Promise Indiana's children's savings account program*.

Lawrence, KS: University of Kansas, Center on Assets, Education, and Inclusion.

Elliott, W., & Lewis, M. (2018). *Making education work for the poor: The potential of children's savings accounts*. New York, NY: Oxford University Press.

Ellis, R. (2003). *Impacting social policy: A practitioner's guide to analysis and action*. Pacific Grove, CA: Thomson/Brooks Cole.

Ellis, R. P., & McGuire, T. G. (1996). Hospital response to prospective payment: Moral hazard, selection, and practice-style effects. *Journal of Health Economics, 15*, 257–277.

Ellis, W., & Dietz, W. H. (2017). A new framework for addressing adverse childhood and community experiences: The building community resilience model. *Academic Pediatrics, 17*(7), S86–S93.

Elperin, J., & Dennis, B. (2019, January 24). Civil penalties for polluters dropped dramatically in Trump's first two years, analysis shows. *Washington Post*. Retrieved from: www.washingtonpost.com/national/health-science/civil-penalties-for-polluters-dropped-dramatically-in-trumps-first-two-years-analysis-shows/2019/01/24/

Emmons, W. R., & Noeth, B. J. (2015). Why didn't higher education protect Hispanic and Black wealth? *Federal Reserve Bank of St. Louis in the Balance, 12*. Retrieved from: www.stlouisfed.org/~/media/publications/in-the-balance/images/issue_12/itb_august_2015.pdf

Employment Benefit Retirement Institute (EBRI). (2018a). *2018 retirement confidence survey*. Retrieved from: www.ebri.org/docs/default-source/rcs/1_2018rcs_report_v5mgachecked.pdf?sfvrsn=e2e9302f_2

Employment Benefit Retirement Institute (EBRI). (2018b). *Current population survey: Issues continue for retirement plan participation and retiree income estimates*. Retrieved from: www.ebri.org/retirement/publications/issue-briefs/content/current-population-survey-issues-continue-for-retirement-plan-participation-and-retiree-income-estimates

Eneliko v. Dreyfuss, No. 2:11-cv-0312 (2011).

Epperson, M. W., & Pettus-Davis, C. (2015). *Smart decarceration: Guiding concepts for an era of criminal justice transformation (CSD Working Paper No. 15-53)*. St. Louis, MO: Washington University, Center for Social Development.

Epstein, D. (2019). *Range: Why generalists triumph in a specialized world*. New York, NY: Riverhead Books.

Equal Employment Opportunity Commission. (1999). *Milestones in the history of the U.S. Equal Employment Opportunity Commission*. Retrieved from: www.eeoc.gov/eeoc/history/35th/milestones/index.html

Esping-Andersen, G. (2002). *Why we need a new welfare state*. New York, NY: Oxford University Press.

Estrada, R., & Marksamer, J. (2006). Lesbian, gay, bisexual, and transgender young people in state custody: Making the child welfare and juvenile justice systems safe for all youth through litigation, advocacy, and education. *Temple Law Review, 79*(2).

Ettlinger, M., & Linden, M. (2012). *The failure of supply-side economics*. Washington, DC: Center for American Progress. Retrieved from: www.americanprogress.org/issues/economy/news/2012/08/01/11998/the-failure-of-supply-side-economics/

Evans-Campbell, T., & Campbell, C. (2011). Indigenist oppression and resistance in Indian child welfare: reclaiming our children. In J. H. Schiele (Ed.), *Social welfare policy: Regulation and resistance among People of Color*. Los Angeles, CA: Sage Publications.

Evans-Campbell, T., Walters, K. L., Pearson, C. R., & Campbell, C. D. (2012). Indian boarding school experience, substance use, and mental health among urban two-spirit American Indian/Alaska natives. *The American Journal of Drug and Alcohol Abuse, 38*(5), 421–427.

Every Student Succeeds Act of 2015, Public Law 114-95 § 114 S. 1177 (2015).

Faderman, L. (2015). *The gay revolution: The story of the struggle*. New York, NY: Simon & Schuster.

Faragher, J. (1990). *The encyclopedia of colonial and revolutionary America*. New York, NY: Facts on File.

Faust, D. G. (2009). *This republic of suffering: Death and the American Civil War*. New York, NY: Vintage.

Favreault, M., & Dey, J. (2015). *Long-term services and supports for older Americans: Risks and financing research brief*. Washington, DC: Office of the Assistant Secretary for Planning and Evaluation, US Department of Health and Human Services. Retrieved from: **https://aspe.hhs.gov/basic-report/long-term-services-and-supports-older-americans-risks-and-financing-research-brief**

Federal Bureau of Investigation. (2018). *2017 hate crime statistics*. Retrieved from: **https://ucr.fbi.gov/hate-crime/2017**

Federal Interagency Forum on Aging Related Statistics. (2016). *Older Americans 2016 indicators of well-being*. Retrieved from: **https://agingstats.gov/**

Federal Reserve Board. (2018). *How worried are Americans about retirement?* Retrieved from: **www.stlouisfed.org/on-the-economy/2018/march/worried-americans-retirement**

Fehr, R., Cox, C., Levitt, L., & Claxton, G. (2019). *How affordable are 2019 ACA premiums for middle-income people?* Kaiser Family Foundation. Retrieved from: **www.kff.org/health-reform/issue-brief/how-affordable-are-2019-aca-premiums-for-middle-income-people/**

Fernandez, A., & Nikolsko-Rzhevskyy, A. (2011). *Forecasting the end of the global recession: Did we miss the early signs?* Dallas, TX: Federal Reserve Bank of Dallas. Retrieved from: **www.dallasfed.org/institute/~/media/documents/research/staff/staff1101.pdf**

Fichtner, J., & Dutta-Gupta, I. (2017, April). Reforming the earned income tax credit could be a bipartisan victory for Trump. *The Hill*. Retrieved from: **https://thehill.com/blogs/pundits-blog/economy-budget/327666-reforming-earned-income-tax-credit-could-be-a-bipartisan**

Finkelstein, A., Taubman, S., Wright, B., Bernstein, M., Gruber, J., Newhouse, J. P., Allen, H., & Baicker, K., The Oregon Health Study Group. (2011). The Oregon health insurance experiment evidence from the first year. *NBER Working Paper Series*. Retrieved from: **www.nber.org/papers/w17190.pdf**

First Five Years Fund. (2017). *2017 national poll*. Retrieved from: **www.ffyf.org/2017-poll/**

Fischer, G. (1992). The development and history of the poverty thresholds. *Social Security Bulletin, 55*(4), 3–14.

Fisher v. University of Texas, 570 U.S. (2013)

Flores, A. (2017). *How the U.S. Hispanic population is changing*. Washington, DC: Pew Research Center. Retrieved from: **www.pewresearch.org/fact-tank/2017/09/18/how-the-u-s-hispanic-population-is-changing/**

Foner, P. S. (1950). *The life and writings of Frederick Douglass, Volume II Pre-Civil War Decade 1850–1860*. New York, NY: International Publishers Co., Inc.

Fontenot, K., Semega, J., & Kollar, M. (2018, September). *Income and poverty in the United States: 2017*. Washington, DC: U.S. Census Bureau. Retrieved from: **www.census.gov/library/publications/2018/demo/p60-263.html**

Food and Nutrition Service. (2009). Retrieved from: **www.fns.usda.gov**.

Food Research and Action Center. (2017). *Community eligibility continues to grow in the 2016–2017 school year*. Washington, DC: Author. Retrieved from: **www.frac.org/wp-content/uploads/CEP-Report_Final_Links_032317.pdf**

Foote, C. L., & Ryan, R. W. (2015). Labor-market polarization over the business cycle. *NBER Macroeconomics Annual, 29*(1), 371–413.

Fowler, K. A., Dahlberg, L. L., Haileyesus, T., Gutierrez, C., & Bacon, S. (2017). Childhood firearm injuries in the United States. *Pediatrics*. Retrieved from: **http://pediatrics.aappublications.org/content/pediatrics/early/2017/06/15/peds.2016-3486.full.pdf**

Fox, L. (2018). *The supplemental poverty measure: 2017*. Washington, DC: U.S. Census Bureau. Retrieved from: **www.census.gov/library/publications/2018/demo/p60-265.html**

Fox, L. E., Wimer, C., Garfinkel, I., Kaushal, N., & Waldfogel, J. (2015). Waging war on poverty: Poverty trends using a historical supplemental poverty measure. *Journal of Policy Analysis and Management, 34*(3), 567–592.

Fox, N. A., & Hane, A. A. (2008). Studying the biology of human attachment. In J. Cassidy & P. R. Shaver (Eds.), *Handbook of attachment: Theory, research, and clinical applications* (2nd ed., pp. 217–240). New York: Guilford Press.

Fox-Grage, W., Folkemer, D., Burwell, B., & Horahan, K. (2001). *Community-based long-term care*. Denver, CO: National Conference of State Legislatures.

Frasch, K. M., & Brooks, D. (2003). Normative development in transracial adoptive families: An integration of the literature and implications for the construction of a theoretical framework. *Families in Society: The Journal of Contemporary Human Services, 84*(2), 201–212.

Frazier, E. F. (1962). *Black bourgeoisie*. New York, NY: Collier Books.

Freedman, V. A., & Spillman, B. C. (2016). Active life expectancy in the older US population, 1982–2011: Differences between Blacks and Whites persisted. *Health Affairs (Project Hope), 35*(8), 1351–1358.

Frey, C. B., & Osborne, M. (2013). *The future of employment: How Susceptible are jobs to computerisation?* Oxford University. Retrieved from: www.oxfordmartin.ox.ac.uk/downloads/academic/The_Future_of_Employment.pdf

Frey, W. (2019a). *As Americans spread out, immigration plays a crucial role in local population growth*. Washington, DC: The Brookings Institution. Retrieved from: www.brookings.edu/research/as-americans-spread-out-immigration-plays-a-crucial-role-in-local-population-growth/

Frey, W. (2019b). *Less than half of U.S. children under 15 are White, Census shows*. Washington, DC: The Brookings Institution. Retrieved from: www.brookings.edu/research/less-than-half-of-us-children-under-15-are-white-census-shows/.

Friedan, B. (1963). *The feminine mystique*. New York: Norton.

Friedman, B., Santos, E. J., Liebel, D. V., Russ, A. J., & Conwell, Y. (2015). Longitudinal prevalence and correlates of elder mistreatment among older adults receiving home visiting nursing. *Journal of Elder Abuse and Neglect, 27*(1), 34–64.

Fukui, S., Goscha, R., Rapp, C., Mabry, A., Liddy, P., & Marty, D. (2012). Strengths model case management fidelity scores and client outcomes. *Psychiatric Services, 63*, 708–710.

Fukuyama, F. (2018). *Identity: The demand for dignity and the politics of resentment*. New York, NY: Farrar, Straus and Giroux.

Gale, W. (2019, March 20). *Are the kids alright? Saving and wealth accumulation among the Millennial generation*. Washington, DC: Brookings Institution. Retrieved from: www.brookings.edu/blog/up-front/2019/03/20/are-the-kids-alright-saving-and-wealth-accumulation-among-the-millennial-generation/

Gale, W., Gelfond, H., Krupkin, A., Mazur, M. J., & Toder, E. (2018). *Effects of the tax cuts and Jobs Act: A preliminary analysis*. Washington, DC: Tax Policy Center, Urban Institute and Brookings Institution. Retrieved from: www.brookings.edu/wp-content/uploads/2018/06/ES_20180608_tcja_summary_paper_final.pdf

Gale, W., & Krupkin, A. (2019, March 13). *Did the tax cuts and Jobs Act pay for itself in 2018?* Washington, DC: Tax Policy Center, Urban Institute and Brookings Institution. Retrieved from: www.taxpolicycenter.org/taxvox/did-tax-cuts-and-jobs-act-pay-itself-2018

Gallup. (2018). *Labor unions*. Retrieved from: https://news.gallup.com/poll/12751/labor-unions.aspx

Garfield, I., McLanahan, S., & Wimer, C. (2016). *Children of the Great Recession*. New York, NY: Russell Sage.

Garfield, R., Damico, A., & Orgera, K. (2018). *The coverage gap: Uninsured poor adults in states that do not expand Medicaid*. Kaiser Family Foundation. Retrieved from: www.kff.org/medicaid/issue-brief/the-coverage-gap-uninsured-poor-adults-in-states-that-do-not-expand-medicaid/

Garfield, R., Hinton, E., Cornachione, E., & Hall, C. (2018). *Medicaid managed care plans and access to care: Results from the Kaiser Family Foundation 2017 Survey of Medicaid Managed Care Plans*. Kaiser Family Foundation. Retrieved from: www.kff.org/medicaid/report/medicaid-managed-care-plans-and-access-to-care-results-from-the-kaiser-family-foundation-2017-survey-of-medicaid-managed-care-plans/

Geertz, C. (1973). *The interpretation of cultures*. New York, NY: Basic Books.

Geiger, A. (2017). *Many minority students go to schools where at least half of their peers are their race or ethnicity*. Washington, DC: Pew Research Centers. Retrieved from: www.pewresearch.org/fact-tank/2017/10/25/many-minority-students-go-to-schools-where-at-least-half-of-their-peers-are-their-race-or-ethnicity/

Gelbgiser, D. (2018). College for all, degrees for few: For-profit colleges and socioeconomic differences in degree attainment. *Social Forces, 96*(4), 1785–1824.

Genty, P. (2003). Damage to family relationships as a collateral consequence of parental incarceration. *Fordham Urban Law Journal, 1671.* Retrieved from: https://ir.lawnet.fordham.edu/ulj/vol30/iss5/6

Genworth Financial. (2018). *Cost of care survey.* Retrieved from: www.genworth.com/aging-and-you/finances/cost-of-care.html

Georgetown University Health Policy Institute. (2018). *Administration stops risk adjustment payments to insurers: Another sabotage?* Retrieved from: https://ccf.georgetown.edu/2018/07/11/administration-stops-risk-adjustment-payments-to-insurers-another-act-of-sabotage/

Gergen, K. (1999). *An invitation to social construction.* Thousand Oaks, CA: Sage Publications.

Germain, C. (1991). *Human behavior in the social environment: An ecological view.* New York, NY: Columbia University Press.

Gerontological Society of America (GSA). (2018). *Longevity economics: Leveraging the advantages of an aging society.* Retrieved from: www.geron.org/programs-services/alliances-and-multi-stakeholder-collaborations/longevity-economics

Gershoff, E. T., & Font, S. A. (2016). Corporal punishment in U.S. public schools: Prevalence, disparities in use, and status in state and federal policy. *Social Policy Report, 30,* 1.

Gilbert, N. (2002). *Transformation of the welfare state: The silent surrender of public responsibility.* New York, NY: Oxford University Press.

Gilbert, N., & Terrell, P. (2013). *Dimensions of social welfare policy* (8th ed.). Boston, MA: Allyn & Bacon.

Ginther, D., & Johnson-Motoyama, M. (2017, December). *Do state TANF Policies affect child abuse and neglect?* Presentation at Childhood Poverty and the Kansas Child Welfare Crisis. Lawrence, KS: University of Kansas. Retrieved from: www.dcf.ks.gov/Agency/CWSTF/Documents/Protective%20Services%20and%20Family%20Preservation/2018-04-20/KU_ChildabuseTANFKU2017mj%2012182017.pdf

Giridharadas, A. (2018). *Winners take all: The elite charade of changing the world.* New York, NY: Knopf.

Gleckman, H. (2018). *The TCJA Shifted the benefits of tax expenditures to higher-income households.* Washington, DC: Tax Policy Center. Retrieved from: www.taxpolicycenter.org/taxvox/tcja-shifted-benefits-tax-expenditures-higher-income-households

Glenn, J., & Florescu, E. (2017). *State of the future V.* Retrieved from: www.millennium-project.org/state-of-the-future-version-19-0/.

Godofsky, J., van Horn, C., & Zukin, C. (2010). *American workers assess an economic disaster.* New Brunswick, NJ: John J. Heldrich Center for Workforce Development, Rutgers.

Goldberg v. Kelly, 397 U.S. 254 (1970).

Goldstein, A. (2019). A job-scarce town struggles with Arkansas' first-in-nation Medicaid work rules. *Washington Post.* Retrieved from: www.washingtonpost.com/national/health-science/a-job-scarce-town-struggles-with-arkansass-first-in-nation-medicaid-work-rules/2019/03/26

Goodkind, N. (2018, October 16). Mitch McConnell calls for Social Security, Medicare, Medicaid cuts after passing tax cuts, massive defense spending. *Newsweek.* Retrieved from: www.newsweek.com/deficit-budget-tax-plan-social-security-medicaid-medicare-entitlement-1172941

Gordon, L. (1998). How welfare became a dirty word. *New Global Development: Journal of International and Comparative Social Welfare, 14,* 1–14.

Gordon, T. (2012). *State and local budgets and the Great Recession.* Washington, DC: The Brookings Institution. Retrieved from: www.brookings.edu/articles/state-and-local-budgets-and-the-great-recession/

Gore, A. (2013). *The future: Six drivers of global change.* New York, NY: Random House.

Gorin, S. H. (2010). The Patient Protection and Affordable Care Act, cost control, and the battle for health care reform. *Health & Social Work, 35*(3), 163–166.

Gorin, S., & Moniz, C. (2017). Health and mental health policy. In M. Reisch, (Ed.), *Social policy and social justice.* Thousand Oaks, CA: Sage Publications.

Graetz, G., & Michaels, G. (2015). *Robots at work.* London: Centre for Economic Performance. Retrieved from: http://cep.lse.ac.uk/pubs/download/dp1335.pdf

Graham v. Florida, 560 U.S. 48 (2010).

Grall, T. (2018). *Custodial mothers and fathers and their child support: 2015*. Washington, DC: U.S. Census Bureau. Retrieved from: www.census.gov/content/dam/Census/library/publications/2018/demo/P60-262.pdf

Gramlich, J. (2017). *Nearly half of Americans have a family member or close friend who's been addicted to drugs*. Washington, DC: Pew Research Center. Retrieved from: www.pewresearch.org/fact-tank/2017/10/26/nearly-half-of-americans-have-a-family-member-or-close-friend-whos-been-addicted-to-drugs/

Gratton, L., & Scott, A. (2016). *The 100-year life: Living and working in an age of longevity*. London: Bloomsbury.

Gratz v. Bollinger, 539 U.S. 244 (2003). Retrieved from: http://caselaw.lp.findlaw.com/scripts/getcase.pl?court=us&vol=000&invol=02-516

Green, E. L., Benner, K., & Pear, R. (2018, October 21). "Transgender" could be defined out of existence in the Trump Administration. *New York Times*. Retrieved from: www.nytimes.com/2018/10/21/us/politics/transgender-trump-administration-sex-definition.html

Greenstein, R., Kogan, R., & Horton, E. (2018). *Low-income programs not driving nation's long-term fiscal problems*. Washington, DC: Center on Budget and Policy Priorities. Retrieved from: www.cbpp.org/research/long-term-fiscal-challenges/low-income-programs-not-driving-nations-long-term-fiscal

Greenstone, M., & Looney, A. (2013). *The lasting effects of the Great Recession: Six million missing workers and a new economic normal*. Washington, DC: The Brookings Institution. Retrieved from: www.brookings.edu/blog/jobs/2013/09/12/the-lasting-effects-of-the-great-recession-six-million-missing-workers-and-a-new-economic-normal/

Griffith, K., Evans, L., & Bor, J. (2017). The Affordable Care Act reduced socioeconomic disparities in health care access. *Health Affairs, 36*(8). Retrieved from: www.healthaffairs.org/doi/abs/10.1377/hlthaff.2017.0083

Grinstead, M. L., Mauldin, T., Sabia, J. J., Koonce, J., & Palmer, L. (2011). Saving for success: Financial education and savings goal achievement in Individual Development Accounts. *Journal of Financial Counseling and Planning, 22*(2), 28–40.

Gross v. FBL Financial, Inc., 557 U.S. (2009). Retrieved from: http://caselaw.lp.findlaw.com/cgi-bin/getcase.pl?court=us&navby=case&vol=000&invol=08-441

Grutter v. Bollinger, 539 U.S. 306 (2003). Retrieved from: http://caselaw.lp.findlaw.com/scripts/getcase.pl?court=us&vol=000&invol=02-241

Gumbel, A. (September 23, 2015). Junípero Serra's brutal story in spotlight as pope prepares for canonisation. *The Guardian*. Retrieved from: www.theguardian.com/world/2015/sep/23/pope-francis-junipero-serra-sainthood-washington-california

Guttmacher Institute. (2016). *The last five years account for more than one-quarter of all abortion restrictions enacted since Roe*. Retrieved from: www.guttmacher.org/article/2016/01/last-five-years-account-more-one-quarter-all-abortion-restrictions-enacted-roe

Guy, G. P., Zhang, K., Schieber, L. Z., Young, R., & Dowell, D. (2019). County-level opioid prescribing in the United States, 2015 and 2017. *JAMA Internal Medicine*. doi:10.1001/jamainternmed.2018.6989

Guyer, J., Heberlein, M., & Alker, J. (2011). CHIP: Not a model for a Medicaid block grant. Georgetown University Health Policy Institute. Retrieved from: https://ccf.georgetown.edu/wp-content/uploads/2012/03/Federal%20medicaid%20policy_CHIP-not-a-model-for-block-grant.pdf

Hacker, J. (2002). *The divided welfare state*. New York, NY: Cambridge University Press.

Hacker, J. (2006). *The great risk-shift: The assault on jobs, families, health care, and retirement*. New York, NY: Oxford University Press.

Hadland, S. E., Rivera-Aguirre, A., Marshall, B. D. L., & Cerdá, M. (2019) Association of pharmaceutical industry marketing of opioid products with mortality from opioid-related overdoses. *JAMA Network Open, 2*(1), e186007.

Hager, E., & Flagg, A. (2018). *How incarcerated parents are losing their children forever*. New York, NY: The Marshall Project. Retrieved from: www.themarshallproject.org/2018/12/03/how-incarcerated-parents-are-losing-their-children-forever?ref=hp-1-100

Hahn, R. A., Barnett, W. S., Knopf, J. A., et al. (2016). Early childhood education to promote health equity: A community guide systematic review. *Journal of Public Health Management and Practice, 22*(5), E1–E8.

Hair, N. L., Hanson, J. L., Wolfe, B. L., & Pollak, S. D. (2015). Association of child poverty, brain development, and academic achievement. *JAMA Pediatrics, 169*(9), 822–829.

Hajat, A., Hsia, C., & O'Neill, M.S. (2015). Socioeconomic disparities and air pollution exposure: A global review. *Current Environmental Health Reports, 2*(4), 440–450.

Hall, C., & Tolbert, J. (2018). *Health care and the candidates in the 2018 midterm elections: Key issues and races.* Kaiser Family Foundation. Retrieved from: **www.kff.org/health-reform/issue-brief/health-care-and-the-candidates-in-the-2018-midterm-elections-key-issues-and-races/**

Hamilton, D., & Darity, W. A., Jr. (2010). Can "baby bonds" eliminate the racial wealth gap in putative post-racial America? *Review of Black Political Economy, 37*(3–4), 207–216.

Hamilton, E., Samek, D. R., Keyes, M., McGue, M. K., & Iacono, W.G. (2015). Identity development in a transracial environment: Racial/ethnic minority adoptees in Minnesota, *Adoption Quarterly,18*(3), 217–233.

Hardy, M. (2015). Watergate scandal: public distrust of government begins. Federal Times. Available at: **https://www.federaltimes.com/smr/50-years-federal-times/2015/12/01/watergate-scandal-public-distrust-of-government-begins/**.

Harkness, J., & Newman, S. J. (2005). Housing affordability and children's well-being: Evidence from the national survey of America's families. *Housing Policy Debate,16*(2), 223–255.

Harrington, M. (1962). *The other America: Poverty in the United States.* New York: Macmillan.

Harris-Kojetin, L., Sengupta, M., Park-Lee, E., Valverde, R., Caffrey, C., Rome, V., & Lendon, J. (2016). Long-term care providers and services users in the United States: Data from the National Study of Long-Term Care Providers. *Vital Health Statistics, 3*(38), x–xii, 1–105, 2013–2014.

Hartig, H., & Doherty, C. (2018). *More in U.S. see drug addiction, college affordability and sexism as "very big" national problems.* Washington, DC: Pew Research Center. Retrieved from: **www.pewresearch.org/fact-tank/2018/10/22/more-in-u-s-see-drug-addiction-college-affordability-and-sexism-as-very-big-national-problems/**

Harvard T. H. Chan School of Public Health. (2019). *Life in rural America.* Retrieved from: **www.hsph.harvard.edu/horp/life-in-rural-america**

Harvey, C. (2018). Scientists can now blame individual natural disasters on climate change. *Scientific American.* Retrieved from: **www.scientificamerican.com/article/scientists-can-now-blame-individual-natural-disasters-on-climate-change/**

Harvey, D. (2005). *A brief history of neoliberalism.* Oxford, UK: Oxford University Press.

Haspel, M., & Knotts, H. (2005). Location, location, location: Precinct placement and the costs of voting. *The Journal of Politics, 67*(2), 560–573.

Hays, E. M. (1989). *Prayers for the planetary pilgrim.* Leavenworth, KS: Forest of Peace Publishing.

Health Affairs. (2018). Inside the Trump Administration's proposed Medicaid managed care rule. Retrieved from: **www.healthaffairs.org/do/10.1377/hblog20181204.187478/full/**.

HEARTH Act, 42 U.S.C. §1143 2009P. L. 111-22 Cite McKinney-Vento Homeless Assistance Act, 42 U.S.C. § 11301 et seq. (1987).

Hegewisch, A., Childers, C., & Hartmann, H. (2019). *Women, automation, and the future of work.* Washington, DC: Institute for Women's Policy Research. Retrieved from: **https://iwpr.org/publications/women-automation-future-of-work/**

Heinrich, C. (2014). Parents' employment and children's wellbeing. *Future of Children, 24*(1), 121–146.

Hempstead, K. (2018). *Coverage declines may slow health care spending growth.* Robert Wood Johnson Foundation. Retrieved from: **www.rwjf.org/en/library/research/2018/03/slowdown-in-spending-growth.html**

Hendrick v. Department of Health & Human Services, 145 A.3d 1055 (2016).

Henry, M., Mahathey, A., Morrill, T., Robinson, A., Shivji, A., & Watt, R. (2018). *The 2018 Annual Homeless Assessment Report (AHAR) to Congress.* Washington, DC: U.S. Department of Housing and Urban Development. Retrieved from: **www.**

hudexchange.info/resources/documents/2018-AHAR-Part-1.pdf

Herbst, C. M., & Tekin, E. (2010). *The impact of child care subsidies on child well-being: Evidence from geographic variation in the distance to social service agencies.* National Bureau of Economics Research. Retrieved from: www.nber.org/papers/w16250

Hershbein, B., & Kahn, L. B. (2018). Do recessions accelerate routine-biased technological change? Evidence from vacancy postings. *American Economic Review, 108*(7), 1737–1772.

Hill, K. (2008). A strengths-based framework for social policy: Barriers and possibilities. *Journal of Policy Practice, 7*(2–3), 106–121.

Hill, H. A., Elam-Evans, L. D., Yankey, D., Singleton, J. A., & Kang, Y. (2018). Vaccination coverage among children aged 19–35 months—United States, 2017. *MMWR Morbidity Mortality Weekly Report, 67*, 1123–1128.

Hine, R., & Faragher, J. (2000). *The American West: A new interpretive history*. New Haven, CT: Yale University Press.

Hinkle, H., & Levinson-Waldman, R. (2018, July 30). *The Abolish ICE Movement explained.* New York, NY: Brennan Center for Justice. Retrieved from: www.brennancenter.org/blog/abolish-ice-movement-explained

Hobbs, F., & Stoops, N. (2002). *Demographic trends in the 20th century: Census 2000 Special Reports.* Washington, DC: U.S. Government Printing Office. Retrieved from: www.census.gov/prod/2002pubs/censr-4.pdf

Hochschild, A. R. (2018). *Strangers in their own land: Anger and mourning on the American right.* New York, NY: The New Press.

Hoefer, R. (2019). *Advocacy practice for social justice.* New York, NY: Oxford University Press.

Hoffman, S. D. (2008). *Kids having kids: Economic costs and social consequences of teen pregnancy.* Washington, DC: The Urban Institute Press.

Hofstadter, R. (1963). *The Progressive Movement, 1900–1915.* Englewood Cliffs, NJ: Prentice-Hall.

Hoge, E., Bickham, D., & Canton, J. (2017). Digital media, anxiety, and depression in children. *Pediatrics, 140*(2), S76–S80.

Holahan, J., Buttgens, M., & Dorn, S. (2013). *The cost of not expanding Medicaid.* Kaiser Family Foundation. Retrieved from: www.kff.org/medicaid/report/the-cost-of-not-expanding-medicaid/

Hollinger, J. (1998). *A guide to the Multiethnic Placement Act of 1994 as amended by the Interethnic Adoption Provisions of 1996.* Washington, DC: American Bar Association Center on Children and the Law, National Resource Center on Legal and Court Issues.

Hooyman, N. R. (1994). Diversity and populations at risk: Women. In F. G. Reamer (Ed.), *The foundations of social work knowledge* (pp. 309–345). New York, NY: Columbia University Press.

Horn, W. (2001). *Wedding bell blues: Marriage and welfare reform.* Washington, DC: The Brookings Institution. Retrieved from: www.brookings.edu/articles/wedding-bell-blues-marriage-and-welfare-reform/

Hoynes, H., Miller, D., & Simon, D. (2015). Income, the Earned Income Tax Credit, and infant health. *American Economic Journal: Economic Policy, 7*(1), 172–211.

Hsueh, J., Alderson, D. P., Lundquist, E., Michalopoulos, C., Gubits, D., David Fein, D., & Knox, V. (2012). *OPRE Report 2012–11. The supporting healthy marriage evaluation: Early impacts on low-income families.* Washington, DC: Office of Planning, Research and Evaluation, Administration for Children and Families, U.S. Department of Health and Human Services.

Huang, C. (2015, September 16). *Working-family tax credits lift millions out of poverty.* Center on Budget and Policy Priorities. Retrieved from: www.cbpp.org/blog/working-family-tax-credits-lift-millions-out-of-poverty

Huang, J., Kim, Y., & Sherraden, M. (2017). Material hardship and children's social-emotional development: Testing mitigating effects of Child Development Accounts in a randomized experiment. *Child: Care, Health and Development, 43*(1), 89–96.

Huang, J., Sherraden, M., Kim, Y., & Clancy, M. (2014). Effects of Child Development Accounts on early social-emotional development: An experimental test. *JAMA Pediatrics, 168*(3), 265–271.

Hudson, D. M. (1998). *Along racial lines: Consequences of the 1965 Voting Rights Act.* New York, NY: Peter Lang.

Huelsman, M. (2015). *The debt divide: The racial and class bias behind the "new normal" of student borrowing.* Retrieved from: www.demos.org/publication/debt-divide-racial-and-class-bias-behind-new-normal-student-borrowing.

Human Rights Watch. (2018a). *Violence against the transgender community in 2018.* Washington, DC: Author. Retrieved from: www.hrc.org/resources/violence-against-the-transgender-community-in-2018

Human Rights Watch. (2018b). *All we want is equality.* Washington, DC: Author. Retrieved from: www.hrw.org/report/2018/02/19/all-we-want-equality/religious-exemptions-and-discrimination-against-lgbt-people

Hurd, M. D., Michaud, P-C., & Rohwedder, S. (2017). Lifetime nursing home use. *Proceedings of the National Academy of Sciences, 114*(37), 9838–9842.

Huseman, J., & Waldman, A. (2017, June 15). Trump Administration quietly rolls back civil rights efforts across federal government. *ProPublica.* Retrieved from: www.propublica.org/article/trump-administration-rolls-back-civil-rights-efforts-federal-government

Hymowitz, C., & Weissman, M. (1980). *A history of women in America.* New York, NY: Bantam Books.

Hyun, I., Taylor, P., Testa, G., Dickens, B., Jung, K. W., McNab, A., Robertson, J., Skene, L., & Zoloth, L. (2007). Ethical standards for human-to-animal chimera experiments in stem cell research. *Cell Stem Cell, 1*(2), 159–163.

Institute for Women's Policy Research. (2018). *Pay equity and discrimination.* Retrieved from: https://iwpr.org/issue/employment-education-economic-change/pay-equity-discrimination/

Intergovernmental Panel on Climate Change. (2018). Summary for policymakers. In V. Masson-Delmotte et al. (Eds.), *Global Warming of 1.5°C. An IPCC special report on the impacts of global warming of 1.5°C above pre-industrial levels and related global greenhouse gas emission pathways, in the context of strengthening the global response to the threat of climate change, sustainable development, and efforts to eradicate poverty.* Geneva, Switzerland: World Meteorological Organization.

Internal Revenue Service (IRS). (2018). *2018 EITC income limits, maximum credit amount and tax law updates.* Retrieved from: www.irs.gov/credits-deductions/individuals/earned-income-tax-credit/eitc-income-limits-maximum-credit-amounts-next-year

Irons, J. (2009). *Economic scarring: The long-term impacts of the recession.* Washington, DC: Economic Policy Institute. Retrieved from: www.epi.org/publication/bp243/

Isaacs, J. B., Lou, C., Hahn, H., Hong, A., Quakenbush, C., & Steuerle, C. E. (2018). *Kids' share 2017: Report on federal expenditures on children through 2017 and future projections.* Urban Institute. Retrieved from: www.urban.org/research/publication/kids-share-2018-report-federal-expenditures-children-through-2017-and-future-projections

Issa, P., & Zedlewski, S. R. (2011). *Poverty among older Americans: 2009.* Urban Institute. Retrieved from: www.urban.org/UploadedPDF/412296-Poverty-Among-OlderAmericans.pdf

Ivkovic, A. F. (2016). Limitations of the GDP as a measure of progress and well-being. *Review of Contemporary Business, Entrepreneurship, and Economic Issues, 29*(1).

Jan, T. (October 2, 2019). Civil rights groups slam Comcast for trying to weaken a key protection against racial discrimination. *Washington Post.* Retrieved from: www.washingtonpost.com/business/2019/10/02/civil-rights-groups-slam-comcast-trying-weaken-key-protection-against-racial-discrimination/

Jansson, B. (2013). *Becoming an effective policy advocate: From policy practice to social justice* (7th ed.). Belmont, CA: Brooks/Cole.

Johnson, L. (2018, December). JJDPA reauthorization passes Congress after 16 years. *Juvenile Justice Information Exchange.* Retrieved from: https://jjie.org/2018/12/13/jjdpa-reauthorization-passes-congress-after-16-years/

Johnson, R. (2005). A taxonomy of measurement objectives for policy impact analysis. *Policy Studies Journal, 2*(3), 201–208.

Joint Center for Housing Studies at Harvard University. (2017). *Rental affordability.* Retrieved from: www.jchs.harvard.edu/sites/default/files/05_harvard_jchs_americas_rental_housing_2017.pdf

Joint Center for Housing Studies at Harvard University. (2018). *The state of the nation's housing:*

2018. Retrieved from: www.jchs.harvard.edu/sites/default/files/Harvard_JCHS_State_of_the_Nations_Housing_2018.pdf

Joint Committee on Taxation. (2017, November). *Macroeconomic analysis of the "Tax Cut and Jobs Act" as ordered reported by the Senate Committee on Finance on November 16, 2017* (JCX-61-17). Retrieved from: www.jct.gov

Joint Committee on Taxation. (2018, October). *Estimates of federal tax expenditures for fiscal years 2018–2022* (JCX-81-18). Retrieved from: www.jct.gov/publications.html?id=5148&func=startdown

Jones, B. (2019). *Majority of Americans continue to say immigrants strengthen the U.S.* Washington, DC: Pew Research Center. Retrieved from: www.pewresearch.org/fact-tank/2019/01/31/majority-of-americans-continue-to-say-immigrants-strengthen-the-u-s/

Jones, J. (2018). *Americans' identification as independents back up in 2017*. Washington, DC: Gallup. Retrieved from: https://news.gallup.com/poll/225056/americans-identification-independents-back-2017.aspx

Jones, R., Cox, D., & Navarro-Rivera, J. (2014). *Economic insecurity, rising inequality, and doubts about the future: Findings from the 2014 American Values Survey*. Washington, DC: Public Religion Research Institute. Retrieved from: www.prri.org/wp-content/uploads/2014/09/AVS-web.pdf

Juffer, F., & van IJzendoorn, M. H. (2007). Adoptees do not lack self-esteem: A meta-analysis of studies on self-esteem of transracial, international, and domestic adoptees. *Psychological Bulletin, 133*(6), 1067–1083.

Kahana, E., & Kahana, B. (1996). Conceptual and empirical advances in understanding aging well through proactive adaptation. In V. L. Bengtson (Ed.), *Adulthood and aging: Research on continuities and discontinuities* (pp. 18–40). New York, NY: Springer.

Kaiser Family Foundation (KFF). (2012, August 1). *A guide to the Supreme Court's decision on the ACA's Medicaid expansion*. Retrieved from: http://kff.org/health-reform/issue-brief/a-guide-to-the-supreme-courts-decision

Kaiser Family Foundation (KFF). (2013). *Policy options to sustain Medicare for the future*. Retrieved from: www.kff.org/medicare/report/policy-options-to-sustain-medicare-for-the-future/view/print/

Kaiser Family Foundation (KFF). (2015). *The Medicare Part D prescription drug benefit*. Retrieved from: http://kff.org/medicare/fact-sheet/the-medicare-prescription-drug-benefit-fact-sheet

Kaiser Family Foundation (KFF). (2016a). *Infant mortality rate (deaths per 1,000 live births) by race/ethnicity*. Retrieved from: http://kff.org/other/state-indicator/infant-mortality-rate-by-race-ethnicity

Kaiser Family Foundation (KFF). (2016b). *Births financed by Medicaid*. Retrieved from: www.kff.org/medicaid/state-indicator/births-financed-by-medicaid

Kaiser Family Foundation (KFF). (2016c). *Waiting list enrollment for Medicaid Section 1915(c) home and community-based services waivers*. Retrieved from: www.kff.org/health-reform/state-indicator/waiting-lists-for-hcbs-waivers

Kaiser Family Foundation (KFF). (2017). *Medicaid's role in nursing home care*. Retrieved from: www.kff.org/infographic/medicaids-role-in-nursing-home-care/

Kaiser Family Foundation (KFF). (2018a). *Two-thirds of Americans don't want the Supreme Court to overturn Roe v. Wade*. Retrieved from: www.kff.org/health-reform/press-release/poll-two-thirds-of-americans-dont-want-the-supreme-court-to-overturn-roe-v-wade/

Kaiser Family Foundation (KFF). (2018b). *Employer health benefits survey*. Retrieved from: www.kff.org/health-costs/report/2018-employer-health-benefits-survey/

Kaiser Family Foundation (KFF). (2018c). *Medicaid managed care market tracker*. www.kff.org/data-collection/medicaid-managed-care-market-tracker/

Kaiser Family Foundation (KFF). (2018d). *Federal and state Medicaid spending*. Retrieved from: http://kff.org/medicaid/state-indicator/federalstate-share-of-spending

Kaiser Family Foundation (KFF). (2018e). *Where are states today? Medicaid and CHIP eligibility levels for adults, children, and pregnant women*. Retrieved from: http://kff.org/medicaid/fact-sheet/where-are-states-today-medicaid-and-chip

Kaiser Family Foundation (KFF). (2018f). *Total monthly Medicaid and CHIP enrollment*. Retrieved from: www.kff.org/health-reform/state-indicator/total-monthly-medicaid-and-chip-enrollment

Kaiser Family Foundation (KFF). (2019). *Medicaid waiver tracker*. Retrieved from: www.kff.org/medicaid/issue-brief/medicaid-waiver-tracker-approved-and-pending-section-1115-waivers-by-state/#Table5

Kamal, R., Semanskee, A., Long, M., Claxton, G., & Levitt, L. (2017). *How the loss of cost-sharing subsidy payments is affecting 2018 premiums*. Kaiser Family Foundation. Retrieved from: www.kff.org/health-reform/issue-brief/how-the-loss-of-cost-sharing-subsidy-payments-is-affecting-2018-premiums/

Kane, R., Kane, R., & Ladd, R. (1998). *The heart of long-term care*. New York, NY: Oxford University Press.

Kangas, S., Jauhisinen, S., Simaninen, M., & Yikanno, M. (2019). *The basic income experiment 2017–2018 in Finland: Preliminary results*. Helsinki, Finland: Ministry of Social Affairs and Health. Retrieved from: http://julkaisut.valtioneuvosto.fi/bitstream/handle/10024/161361/Report_The%20Basic%20Income%20Experiment%202020172018%20in%20Finland.pdf?sequence=1&isAllowed=y

Kansas Action for Children. (2001). *The Kansas child welfare system: Where are we? Where should we be going?* Topeka: Author.

Katz, M. (2008). *The price of citizenship*. Philadelphia, PA: University of Pennsylvania Press.

Katznelson, I. (2005). *When affirmative action was White: An untold history of racial inequality in twentieth-century America*. New York, NY: W.W. Norton.

Kellner, D. (2004). The media and social problems. In G. Ritzer (ed.), *Handbook of social problems: A comparative international perspective* (pp. 209–225). Thousand Oaks, CA: Sage Publications.

Kennedy, B. (2018). *Most Americans say climate change affects their local community*. Washington, DC: Pew Research Center. Retrieved from: www.pewresearch.org/fact-tank/2018/05/16/most-americans-say-climate-change-affects-their-local-community-including-two-thirds-living-near-coast/

Kenney, C. (1981). New look to grants. *Boston Globe*, p. 1. Retrieved from: http://proquest.umi.com

Keynes, J. M. (1936). *The general theory of employment, interest and money*. New Delhi: Atlantic.

Kids Count. (2018). Baltimore, MD: Annie E. Casey Foundation.

Kingdon, J. (2003). *Agendas, alternative, and public policies* (2nd ed.). New York, NY: Addison-Wesley Educational Publishers.

Kinsey, A. C. (1948). *Sexual behavior in the human male*. Philadelphia: W. B. Saunders.

Kirzinger, A., Wu, B., Munana, C., & Brodie, M. (2018). *Kaiser health tracking poll—late summer 2018: The election, pre-existing conditions, and surprises on medical bills*. Retrieved from: www.kff.org/health-costs/poll-finding/kaiser-health-tracking-poll-late-summer-2018-the-election-pre-existing-conditions-and-surprises-on-medical-bills/

Knappman, E., Christianson, S., & Paddock, L. (Eds.) (2002). *Great American trials* (2nd ed., Vols. *1–2*). Detroit, MI: Gale Group.

Ko, S. J., Ford, J. D., Kassam-Adams, N., Berkowitz, S. J., Wilson, C., Wong, M., Breymer, M., & Layne C. M. (2008). Creating trauma-informed systems: Child welfare, education, first responders, health care, juvenile justice. *Professional Psychology: Research & Practice, 39*, 396–404.

Kochanek, K. D., Murphy, S. L., Xu, J. Q., & Arias, E. (2017). *Mortality in the United States, 2016*. NCHS Data Brief, no 293. Hyattsville, MD: National Center for Health Statistics.

Kolodner, M. (2015). Black students are being shut out of top public colleges. *Huffington Post*. Retrieved from: www.huffingtonpost.com/entry/black-students-are-being-shutout-of-top-public-colleges_us_56703e08e4b0e292150f40c4

Koren, M. J. (2010). Person-centered care for nursing home residents: The culture-change movement. *Health Affairs, 29*(2).

Kortum, P, Edwards, C, & Richards-Kortum, R. (2008). The impact of inaccurate internet health information in a secondary school learning environment. *Journal of Medical Internet Research, 10*(2), e17.

Kretzmann, J., & McKnight, J. (1993). *Building communities from the inside out: A path toward finding and mobilizing a community's assets*. Evanston, IL: Institute for Policy Research, Northwestern University.

Kutler, S. I. (Ed.) (2003). *Dictionary of American history* (3rd ed., Vols. *1–10*). New York, NY: Charles Scribner's Sons.

Lachs, M., & Pillemer, K. (2015). Elder abuse. *New England Journal of Medicine, 373*, 1947–1956.

Lafleur, J.-M., & Mescoli, E. (2018). Creating undocumented EU migrants through welfare: A conceptualization of undeserving and precarious citizenship. *Sociology, 52*(3), 480–496.

Laumann, E., Leitsch, S., & Waite, L. (2008). Elder mistreatment in the United States: Prevalence estimates from a nationally representative study. *The Journals of Gerontology Series B, Psychological Sciences and Social Sciences, 63*(4), S248–S254.

Lawrence, J. C. (2014). ASFA in the age of mass incarceration: Go to prison—lose your child. *William Mitchell Law Review, 40*(3), Article 5.

Leachman, M., Masterson, K., & Figueroa, E. (2017). *A punishing decade for school funding*. Washington, DC: Center on Budget and Policy Priorities (CBPP). Retrieved from: **www.cbpp.org/research/state-budget-and-tax/a-punishing-decade-for-school-funding**

Levin, E. (2014, January). *Federal policy brief: Upside down—tax incentives to save and build wealth*. Corporation for Enterprise Development. Retrieved from: **http://cfed.org/blog/inclusiveeconomy/expand_economic_opportunity_by_turning_upside-down_tax_programs_right-side_up**

Linden, M., & Ettlinger, M. (2011). *The Bush tax cuts are the disaster that keeps on giving*. Washington, DC: Center for American Progress. Retrieved from: **www.americanprogress.org/issues/economy/news/2011/06/07/9785/the-bush-tax-cuts-are-the-disaster-that-keeps-on-giving/**

Link, A., & Catton, W. (1967). *American epoch: A history of the United States since the 1890s. Vol. 1: 1897–1920* (3rd ed.). New York, NY: Alfred A. Knopf.

Lipnic, V. A. (2018). *The state of age discrimination and older workers in the U.S. 50 years after the Age Discrimination in Employment Act (ADEA)*. Washington, DC: U.S. Equal Employment Opportunity Commission. Retrieved from: **www.eeoc.gov/eeoc/history/adea50th/report.cfm**

Lipsitz, G. (2006). *The possessive investment in Whiteness: How White people profit from identity politics*. Philadelphia, PA: Temple University.

Lipsky, M. (1980). Street-level bureaucrats as policymakers. In M. Lipsky (Ed.), *Street-level bureaucracy: Dilemmas of the individual in public services* (pp. 13–25). New York, NY: Russell Sage Foundation.

Livingston, G. (2018). *About one-third of U.S. children living with an unmarried parent*. Pew Research Center. Retrieved from: **www.pewresearch.org/fact-tank/2018/04/27/about-one-third-of-u-s-children-are-living-with-an-unmarried-parent/**

Loehrer, A., et al. (2018). Association of the Affordable Care Act Medicaid expansion with access to and quality of care for surgical conditions. *Journal of the American Medical Association Surgery*. Retrieved from: **https://jamanetwork.com/journals/jamasurgery/article-abstract/2670459?redirect=true**

Loeske, D. (1995). Writing rights: The "homeless mentally ill" and involuntary hospitalization. In J. Best (Ed.), *Images of issues* (pp. 261–286). New York, NY: Aldine De Gruyter.

Logan, J. E., Haileyesus, T., Ertl, A., Rostad, W. L., & Herbst, J. H. (2019, April 5). Nonfatal assaults and homicides among adults aged ≥60 years—United States, 2002–2016. *Morbidity and Mortality Weekly Report, 68*, 297–302. Retrieved from: **www.cdc.gov/mmwr/volumes/68/wr/mm6813a1.htm**

Lopez, G. (2016). Southern states have closed down at least 868 polling places for the 2016 election. *Vox*. Retrieved from: **www.vox.com/policy-and-politics/2016/11/4/13501120/vote-polling-places-election-2016**

Lopez, G., Bialik, K., & Radford, J. (2018). *Key facts about U.S. immigrants*. Washington, DC: Pew Research Center. Retrieved from: **www.pewresearch.org/fact-tank/2018/11/30/key-findings-about-u-s-immigrants/**

Lopez, G., Ruiz, N.G., & Patten, E. (2017). *Key facts about Asian Americans, a diverse and growing population*. Washington, DC: Pew Research Center. Retrieved from: **www.pewresearch.org/fact-tank/2017/09/08/key-facts-about-asian-americans/**

Lopez, M. H., Gonzalez-Barrera, A., & Krogstad, J. M. (2018). *More Latinos have serious concerns about their place in America under Trump*. Washington, DC: Pew Research Center. Retrieved from: **www.pewhispanic.org/2018/10/25/more-latinos-have-serious-concerns-about-their-place-in-america-under-trump/**

Lowe, T. B. (2006). Nineteenth century review of mental health care for African Americans: A legacy of service and policy barriers. *Journal of Sociology & Social Welfare, 33*(4), 29–51.

Lowell, J. S. (1890). The economic and moral effects of public outdoor relief. In *Proceedings of the National Conference of Charities and Corrections* (pp. 81–91). Madison, WI: Midland.

Lowrey, A. (2018). *Give people money: How a Universal Basic Income would end poverty, revolutionize work, and remake the world.* New York, NY: Random House.

Lubrano, A. (2013, May 20). Private charity no match for federal poverty aid, experts say. *Seattle Times.* Retrieved from: **www.seattletimes.com/nation-world/private-charity-no-match-for-federal-poverty-aid-experts-say/**

Luby, J., Belden, A., Botteron, K., Marrus, N., Harms, M. P., Babb, C., Nishino, T., & Barch, D. (2013). The effects of poverty on childhood brain development: The mediating effect of caregiving and stressful life events. *JAMA Pediatrics, 167*(12), 1135–1142.

Lundquist, E., Hsueh, J., Lowenstein, A., Faucetta, K., Gubits, D., Michalopoulos, C., & Knox, V. (2014). *A family-strengthening program for low-income families: Final impacts from the supporting healthy marriage evaluation.* OPRE Report 2014-09A. Washington, DC: Office of Planning, Research and Evaluation, Administration for Children and Families, U.S. Department of Health and Human Services.

Macarov, D. (1991). *Certain change: Social work practice in the future.* Silver Spring, MD: NASW.

Madowitz, M., Rowell, A., & Hamm, A. (2016). *Calculating the hidden cost of interrupting a career for child care.* Washington, DC: Center for American Progress. Retrieved from: **www.americanprogress.org/issues/early-childhood/reports/2016/06/21/139731/calculating-the-hidden-cost-of-interrupting-a-career-for-childcare/**

Mani, A., Mullainathan, S., Shafir, E., & Zhao, J. (2013). Poverty impedes cognitive function. *Science, 341,* 976.

Manjoo, F. (2008). *True enough: Learning to live in a post-fact society.* Hoboken, NJ: Wiley.

Manyika, J., Lund, S., Chui, M., Bughin, M., Woetzel, J., Batra, P., Ko, R., & Sanghui, S. (2017). *Jobs lost, jobs gained: Workforce transitions in a time of automation.* McKinsey Global Institute. Retrieved from: **www.mckinsey.com/~/media/mckinsey/featured%20insights/Future%20of%20Organizations/What%20the%20future%20of%20work%20will%20mean%20for%20jobs%20skills%20and%20wages/MGI-Jobs-Lost-Jobs-Gained-Report-December-6-2017.ashx**

Mapping Police Violence. (2018). *2017 police violence report.* Retrieved from: **https://policeviolencereport.org/**

Marmot, M., & Brunner, E. (2005). Cohort profile: The Whitehall II study. *International Journal of Epidemiology, 34*(2), 251–256.

Marr, C., & Huang, Y. (2019). *Childless adults are lone group taxed into poverty.* Washington, DC: Center on Budget and Policy Priorities. Retrieved from: **www.cbpp.org/research/federal-tax/childless-adults-are-lone-group-taxed-into-poverty**

Marshall, T. H. (1950). *Citizenship and social class, and other essays.* Cambridge: Cambridge University Press.

Martin, J. A., Hamilton, B. E., & Osterman, M. J. (2018). *Births in the United States, 2017.* NCHS Data Brief, no 318. Hyattsville, MD: National Center for Health Statistics.

Martin, J. A., Hamilton, B. E., Osterman, M. J., Driscoll, A. K., & Drake, P. (2018). *Births: Final data for 2016.* Hyattsville, MD: National Center for Health Statistics. Retrieved from: **www.cdc.gov/nchs/pressroom/sosmap/teen-births/teenbirths.htm**

Martin, P., Kelly, N., Kahana, B., Kahana, E., Willcox, B., Willcox, D., & Poon, L. (2014). Defining successful aging: A tangle or elusive concept? *The Gerontologist, 55*(1), 14–25.

Martinez, M. (2016). Flint, Michigan: Did race and poverty factor into water crisis. *CNN.* Retrieved from: **www.cnn.com/2016/01/26/us/flint-michigan-water-crisis-race-poverty**

Marty, D., & Chapin, R. (2000). The legislative tenets of client's right to treatment in the least restrictive environment and freedom from harm: Implications for community providers. *Community Mental Health Journal, 36*(6), 545–556.

Masotti, P. J., Fick, R., Johnson-Masotti, A., & MacLeod, S. (2006). Healthy naturally occurring retirement communities: A low-cost approach to facilitating healthy aging. *American Journal of Public Health, 96*(7), 1164–1170.

Matheson, L. (1996). The politics of the Indian Child Welfare Act. *Social Work, 41*(2), 232–235.

Mathieson, K. (2018, December 3). The "climate diaspora" trying to save the Paris Agreement from Trump. *The Guardian*. Retrieved from: www.theguardian.com/environment/2018/dec/03/save-paris-climate-agreement-from-trump

Mattis, J. (2018, February 22). *Memorandum for the President*. Washington, DC: U.S. Department of Defense. Retrieved from: https://media.defense.gov/2018/Mar/23/2001894037/-1/-1/0/MILITARY-SERVICE-BY-TRANSGENDER-INDIVIDUALS.PDF

Max Planck Institute for Demographic Research. (2013, March 21). *Lifetime fertility on the rise*. Retrieved from: www.mpg.de/7042238/Demography

Maxfield, M. (2013). *The effects of the Earned Income Tax Credit on child achievement and long-term educational attainment*. Retrieved from: https://msu.edu/~maxfie17/20131114%20Maxfield%20EITC%20Child%20Education.pdf

Maxim, R., & Muro, M. (2019). *Automation and AI will disrupt the American labor force. Here's how we can help workers*. Washington, DC: Brookings Institution. Retrieved from: www.brookings.edu/blog/the-avenue/2019/02/25/automation-and-ai-will-disrupt-the-american-labor-force-heres-how-we-can-protect-workers/

Maxwell, A., & Shields, T. (2017). *The impact of "modern sexism" on the 2016 presidential election*. Fayetteville, AR: Diane D. Blair Center of Southern Politics & Society. Retrieved from: https://blaircenter.uark.edu/the-impact-of-modern-sexism/

Mazzara, A., & Sard, B. (2018). *Chart book: Employment and earnings for households receiving federal rental assistance*. Washington, DC: Center on Budget and Policy Priorities. Retrieved from: www.cbpp.org/research/housing/chart-book-employment-and-earnings-for-households-receiving-federal-rental

McCall, D.N., Eckenrode, J., & Olds, D.L. (2009). Home visiting for the prevention of child maltreatment: Lessons learned during the past 20 years. *Pediatric Clinics of North America, 56*(2), 389–403.

McCance-Katz, E. (2017). *Testimony on addressing the opioid crisis in America: Prevention, treatment, and recovery before the Senate subcommittee*. Washington, DC: National Institutes of Health. Retrieved from: www.nih.gov/about-nih/who-we-are/nih-director/testimony-addressing-opioid-crisis-america-prevention-treatment-recovery-before-senate-subcommittee

McCarthy, J. (2018, May 23). *Two in three Americans support same-sex marriage*. Washington, DC: Gallup. Retrieved from: https://news.gallup.com/poll/234866/two-three-americans-support-sex-marriage.aspx

McCarty, N., Poole, K. T., & Rosenthal, H. (2016). *Polarized America: The dance of ideology and unequal riches*. Cambridge, MA: MIT Press.

McGuire, T. G., Newhouse, J. P., & Sinaiko, A. D. (2011). An economic history of Medicare part C. *The Milbank Quarterly, 89*(2), 289–332.

McInnis-Dittrich, K. (1994). *Integrating social welfare policy and social work practice*. Pacific Grove, CA: Brooks/Cole.

McKay, C., Pollack, E., & Fitzpayne, A. (2018, January). *Modernizing unemployment insurance for the changing nature of work*. Washington, DC: Aspen Institute. Retrieved from: https://assets.aspeninstitute.org/content/uploads/2018/01/Modernizing-Unemployment-Insurance_Report_Aspen-Future-of-Work.pdf?_ga=2.202914001.1514270250.1544034334-722155863.1544034334.

McKinney–Vento Homeless Assistance Act, 42 U.S.C. § 11301 et seq. (1987).

McKee-Ryan, F. M., Song, Z., Wanberg, C. R., & Kinicki, A. J. (2005). Psychological and physical well-being during unemployment: A meta-analytic study. *Journal of Applied Psychology, 90*(1), 53–76.

McKernan, M. S., Ratcliffe, C., Steuerle, E., & Zhang, S. (2014, April). *Impact of the great recession and beyond disparities in wealth building by generation and race*. Washington, DC: Urban Institute. Retrieved from: www.urban.org/sites/default/files/alfresco/publication-pdfs/413102-Impact-of-the-Great-Recession-and-Beyond.PDF

McMillen, J. C., Morris, L. A., & Sherraden, M. (2004). Ending social work's grudge match: Problems versus strengths. *Muskie School of Public Service, 5*.

McPhail, B. A. (2003). A feminist policy analysis framework: Through a gendered lens. *The Social Policy Journal, 2*(3), 39–61.

Meckler, L., & Barrett, D. (2019, January 3). Trump administration considers rollback of anti-discrimination rules. *Washington Post.* Retrieved from: www.washingtonpost.com/local/education/trump-administration-considers-rollback-of-anti-discrimination-rules/2019/01/02/

Meckler, L., & Svrluga, S. (2019, January 30). Nearly 100,000 comments on Betsy DeVos' plan to overhaul rules on sexual assault. *Washington Post.* Retrieved from: https://www.washingtonpost.com/local/education/nearly-100000-comments-on-betsy-devoss-plan-to-overhaul-rules-on-sexual-assault-probes/2019/01/30

Melnick, S. (2019). *The Department of Education's proposed sexual harassment rules: Looking beyond the rhetoric.* Washington, DC: The Brookings Institution. Retrieved from: www.brookings.edu/blog/brown-center-chalkboard/2019/01/24/the-department-of-educations-proposed-sexual-harassment-rules-looking-beyond-the-rhetoric

Mercer, A., Deane, C., & McGeeney, K. (2016). *Why 2016 election polls missed their mark.* Washington, DC: Pew Research Center. Retrieved from: www.pewresearch.org/fact-tank/2016/11/09/why-2016-election-polls-missed-their-mark/

Mettler, S. (2010). Reconstituting the submerged state: The challenges of social policy reform in the Obama era. *Perspectives on Politics, 8*(3), 803–824.

Metzler, M., Merrick, M. T., Klevens, J., Ports, K. A., & Ford, D. C. (2017). Adverse childhood experiences and life opportunities: Shifting the narrative. *Children and Youth Services Review, 72,* 141–149.

Middleman, R., & Goldberg-Wood, G. (1990). *Skills for direct practice in social work.* New York, NY: Columbia University Press.

Midgley, J. (2009). Social development and social work: Towards global dialogue. In H. G. Homfeldt & C. Reutlinger (Eds.), *Sociale Arbeit und Sociale Entwicklung* (pp. 12–24). Berlin: Scheiner Verlag.

Midgley, J. (2012). The institutional approach to social policy. In J. Midgley, M. Tracy, & M. Livermore (Eds.), *The handbook of social policy* (pp. 365–375). Thousand Oaks, CA: Sage Publications.

Midgley, J. (2014). Austerity versus stimulus: Theoretical perspectives and policy implications. *Journal of Sociology and Social Welfare, 41*(2), 11–32.

Midgley, J., & Sherraden, M. (2009). The social development perspective in social policy. In J. Midgley & M. Livermore (Eds.), *The handbook of social policy* (2nd ed., pp. 279–294). Thousand Oaks, CA: Sage Publications.

Mildred, J. (2003). Claimsmakers in the child sexual abuse "wars": Who are they and what do they want? *Journal of Social Work, 48*(4), 492–503.

Miller v. Alabama, 567 U.S. 460 (2012).

Miller, K. (2010). *Myth vs. fact: Keeping All Students Safe Act.* Retrieved from: http://edlabor.house.gov/blog/2010/02/myth-vs-fact-preventing-harmfu.shtml

Miller, S. (2019). *Corporate pensions plans hit hard in 2018.* Retrieved from: www.shrm.org/resourcesandtools/hr-topics/benefits/pages/corporate-pension-plans-hit-hard.aspx

Mizrahi, T., & Davis, L. (Eds.) (2008). *Encyclopedia of social work* (20th ed.). Washington, DC: National Association of Social Workers and Oxford University Press.

Moffitt, R. (1993). Welfare reform: An economist's perspective. *Yale Law & Policy Review, 11*(1), 1–61.

Monitz, C., & Gorin, S. (2003). *Health and heath care policy: A social work perspective.* Boston, MA: Allyn & Bacon.

Movement Advancement Project. (February 2017). *Mapping transgender equality in the United States.* Retrieved from: www.lgbtmap.org/mapping-trans-equality

Moynihan, D. P. (1973). *The politics of a guaranteed income: The Nixon Administration and the family assistance plan.* New York, NY: Vintage Books.

Mudde, C., & Kaltwasser, C. R. (2017). *Populism: A very short introduction.* New York, NY: Oxford University Press.

Mudrazija, S. (2019). Work-related opportunity costs of providing unpaid family care in 2013 and 2050. *Health Affairs, 38*(6), 1003–1010.

Munnell, A., Aubry, J., & Muldoon, D. (2008). *The financial crisis and private defined benefit plans.* Center for Retirement Research at Boston College. Retrieved from: http://crr.bc.edu/briefs/the-financial-crisis-and-private-defined-benefit-plans/

Muro, M., Maxim, R., & Whiton, J. (2019). *Automation and artificial intelligence: How machines are affecting people and places*. Washington, DC: Brookings Institution. Retrieved from: **www.brookings.edu/wp-content/uploads/2019/01/2019.01_BrookingsMetro_Automation-AI_Report_Muro-Maxim-Whiton-FINAL-version.pdf**

Muro, M., & Whiton, J. (2018). *Geographic gaps are widening while U.S. economic growth increases*. Washington, DC: Brookings Institution. Retrieved from: **www.brookings.edu/blog/the-avenue/2018/01/22/uneven-growth/**

Murphey, D., Guzman, L., & Torres, A. (2014). *America's Hispanic children: Gaining ground, looking forward*. Child Trends Hispanic Institute. Retrieved from: **www.childtrends.org/wp-content/uploads/2014/09/2014-38AmericaHispanicChildren.pdf**

Murphy, S. L., Xu, J. Q., Kochanek, K. D., & Arias, E. (2018). *Mortality in the United States, 2017*. NCHS Data Brief, no 328. Hyattsville, MD: National Center for Health Statistics.

Mustillo, S., Krieger, N., Gunderson, E. P., Sidney, S., McCreath, H., & Kiefe, C. I. (2004). Self-reported experiences of racial discrimination and Black-White differences in preterm and low-birthweight deliveries: The CARDIA Study. *American Journal of Public Health, 94*(12), 2125–2131.

Musumeci, M. B., Chidambaram, P., & O'Malley Watts, M. (2019). *Medicaid home and community-based services enrollment and spending*. Kaiser Family Foundation. Retrieved from: **www.kff.org/report-section/medicaid-home-and-community-based-services-enrollment-and-spending-issue-brief/**

Mutz, D. (2018). Status threat, not economic hardship, explains the 2016 presidential vote. *Proceedings of the National Academy of Sciences USA, 115*, E4330–E4339.

Nabokov, P. (1993). Long threads. In B. Ballantine & I. Ballantine (Eds.), *Native Americans: An illustrated history* (pp. 301–383). Atlanta, GA: Turner Publishing.

Nash, G. B., Jeffrey, R. J., Howe, J. R., Frederick, P. J., Davis, A. D., & Winkler, A. M. (2004). *The American people: Creating a nation and a society* (6th ed.). New York, NY: Pearson/Longman.

National Academies of Sciences, Engineering, and Medicine (2019). *A roadmap to reducing child poverty*. Washington, DC: The National Academies Press.

National Aeronautics and Space Administration (NASA). (2019). *Climate change: How do we know?* Washington, DC: Author. Retrieved from: **https://climate.nasa.gov/evidence/**

National Alliance for Caregiving (NAC) and AARP. (2015). *Caregiving in the U.S.* Retrieved from: **www.caregiving.org/wp-content/uploads/2015/05/2015_CaregivingintheUS_Executive-Summary-June-4_WEB.pdf**

National Alliance on Mental Illness (NAMI). (2015a). *State mental health legislation 2015: Trends, themes, and effective practices*. Retrieved from: **www.nami.org/About-NAMI/Publications-Reports/Public-Policy-Reports/State-Mental-Health-Legislation-2015/NAMI-StateMentalHealthLegislation2015.pdf**

National Alliance on Mental Illness (NAMI). (2015b). *Jailing people with mental illness*. Retrieved from: **www.nami.org/Learn-More/Public-Policy/Jailing-People-with-Mental-Illness**

National Alliance on Mental Illness (NAMI). (2018). *NAMI celebrates mental health victories in federal funding bill*. Retrieved from: **www.nami.org/Press-Media/Press-Releases/2018/NAMI-Celebrates-Mental-Health-Victories-in-Federal**

National Alliance to End Homelessness. (2009). *HEARTH Act section-by-section analysis*. Retrieved from: **www.endhomelessness.org/content/article/detail/2385**

National Association of Social Workers (NASW). (1973). *Standards for social service manpower*. Washington, DC: NASW Press.

National Association of Social Workers (NASW). (2003). People with disabilities. In *Social work speaks: National Association of Social Workers policy statements, 2003–2006* (6th ed., pp. 270–275). Washington, DC: NASW Press.

National Association of Social Workers (NASW). (2009). Affirmative action. In *Social work speaks: National Association of Social Workers policy statements, 2009–2012* (8th ed., pp. 22–28). Washington, DC: NASW Press.

National Association of Social Workers (NASW). (2012a). *Building on progressive priorities: Sustaining our nation's safety net*. Retrieved from: **www.naswdc.org/advocacy/2012%20NASW%20Obama%20Document.pdf**

National Association of Social Workers (NASW). (2012b). Child abuse and neglect. In *Social work speaks: National Association of Social Workers policy statements, 2012–2014* (9th ed., pp. 43–49). Washington, DC: NASW Press.

National Association of Social Workers (NASW). (2015a). Transgender and gender identity issues. In *Social work speaks: National Association of Social Workers policy statements, 2015–2017* (10th ed., pp. 302–310). Washington, DC: NASW Press.

National Association of Social Workers (NASW). (2015b). Lesbian, gay, and bisexual issues. In *Social work speaks: National Association of Social Workers policy statements, 2015–2017* (10th ed., pp. 198–206). Washington, DC: NASW Press.

National Association of Social Workers (NASW). (2015c). Affirmative action. In *Social work speaks: National Association of Social Workers policy statements, 2015–2017* (10th ed., pp. 21–25). Washington, DC: NASW Press.

National Association of Social Workers (NASW). (2015d). Immigrants and refugees. In *Social work speaks: National Association of Social Workers policy statements, 2015–2017* (10th ed., pp. 176–181). Washington, DC: NASW Press.

National Association of Social Workers (NASW). (2015e). Civil liberties and justice. In *Social work speaks: National Association of Social Workers policy statements, 2015–2017* (10th ed., pp. 42–46). Washington, DC: NASW Press.

National Association of Social Workers. (NASW). (2015f). Poverty and economic justice. In *Social work speaks: National Association of Social Workers policy statements, 2015–2017* (10th ed., pp. 235–239). Washington, DC: NASW Press.

National Association of Social Workers (NASW). (2015g). Juvenile justice and delinquency prevention. In *Social work speaks: National Association of Social Workers policy statements, 2015–2017* (10th ed., pp. 188–193). Washington, DC: NASW Press.

National Association of Social Workers (NASW). (2015h). Child abuse and neglect. In *Social work speaks: National Association of Social Workers policy statements, 2015–2017* (10th ed., pp. 32–38). Washington, DC: NASW Press.

National Association of Social Workers (NASW). (2015i). School violence. In *Social work speaks: National Association of Social Workers policy statements, 2015–2017* (10th ed., pp. 271–274). Washington, DC: NASW Press.

National Association of Social Workers (NASW). (2015j). Child welfare workforce. In *Social work speaks: National Association of Social Workers policy statements, 2015–2017* (10th ed., pp. 39–41). Washington. DC: NASW Press.

National Association of Social Workers (NASW). (2015k). End-of-life decision making and care. In *Social work speaks: National Association of Social Workers policy statements, 2015–2017* (10th ed., pp. 101–107). Washington, DC: NASW Press.

National Association of Social Workers (NASW). (2015l). Technology and social work. In *Social work speaks: National Association of Social Workers policy statements, 2015–2017* (10th ed., pp. 298–301). Washington, DC: NASW Press.

National Association of Social Workers (NASW). (2016) *NASW social work pioneers*. Retrieved from: **www.naswfoundation.org/pioneers/h/height.htm**

National Association of Social Workers (NASW). (2017a). *Code of ethics*. Washington, DC: NASW. Retrieved from: **www.socialworkers.org**

National Association of Social Workers. (NASW). (2017b). *NASW strongly opposes legislation to repeal the Affordable Care Act*. Retrieved from: **www.socialworkers.org/News/News-Releases/ID/151/NASW-strongly-opposes-House-legislation-to-repeal-the-Affordable-Care-Act**

National Association of Social Workers (NASW). (2018a). *Social work speaks* (11th ed.) Washington, DC: NASW Press.

National Association of Social Workers (NASW). (2018b). *Family First Prevention Services Act sets to improve outcomes for vulnerable children*. Retrieved from: **www.socialworkers.org/practice/child-welfare/family-first-prevention-services-act**

National Association of Social Workers (NASW). (2019). *NASW calls for end to federal government shutdown*. Retrieved from: **www.socialworker.com/blogs/social-work-news/nasw-calls-for-end-to-federal-government-shutdown/**

National Campaign to Prevent Teen and Unplanned Pregnancy. (2016). *Making the case: For wanted and welcomed pregnancy. Retrieved from: http://thenationalcampaign.org/why-it-matters

National Center for Education Statistics. (2019). *Indicator 15: Retention, suspension, and expulsion.* Retrieved from: https://nces.ed.gov/programs/raceindicators/indicator_rda.asp

National Center for Juvenile Justice and Mental Health. (2006). *Mental health counts.* Retrieved from: www.ncmhjj.com/resources/juvenile-mental-health-courts-emerging-strategy/

National Conference of State Legislatures. (2016). *Teen pregnancy prevention.* Retrieved from: www.ncsl.org/research/health/teen-pregnancy-prevention.aspx

National Conference of State Legislatures. (2017). *Child support pass-through and disregard policies for public assistance recipients.* Retrieved from: http://www.ncsl.org/research/human-services/state-policy-pass-through-disregard-child-support.aspx

National Conference of State Legislatures. (2018a). *SNAP work requirements fact sheet.* Retrieved from: www.ncsl.org/research/human-services/snap-work-requirements-fact-sheet.aspx

National Conference of State Legislatures. (2018b). *Tax credits for working families: The Earned Income Tax Credit.* Retrieved from: www.ncsl.org/research/labor-and-employment/earned-income-tax-credits-for-working-families.aspx

National Conference of State Legislatures. (2018c). *Health finance issues.* Retrieved from: www.ncsl.org/research/health/health-finance-issues.aspx

National Council on Disability. (2012, September 27). *Rocking the cradle: Ensuring the rights of parents with disabilities and their children.* Retrieved from: www.ncd.gov/publications/2012/Sep272012

National Drug Intelligence Center. (2011). *National drug threat assessment.* Washington, DC: U.S. Department of Justice.

National Employment Law Project (NELP). (2018). *America's nonstandard workforce faces wage, benefit penalties, according to US data.* Retrieved from: www.nelp.org/news-releases/americas-nonstandard-workforce-faces-wage-benefit-penalties-according-us-data/

National Hospice and Palliative Care Organization (NHPCO). (2017). *Facts and figures: Hospice care in America.* Retrieved from: www.nhpco.org/sites/default/files/public/Statistics_Research/2017_Facts_Figures.pdf

National Institute on Aging. (2019). *What is long-term care?* Washington, DC: National Institutes of Health. Retrieved from: www.nia.nih.gov/health/what-long-term-care

National Juvenile Justice and Delinquency Prevention Coalition (NJJDPC). (2013). *Promoting safe communities: Recommendations for the administration. Opportunities for juvenile justice & delinquency prevention reform.* Retrieved from: http://promotesafecommunities.org/images/pdfs/NJJDPC_RecstoCongress_03122013_web.pdf

National Juvenile Justice and Delinquency Prevention Coalition (NJJDPC). (2015). *Promoting safe communities: Recommendations for the administration 2015–2016.* Retrieved from: http://promotesafecommunities.org/recommendations/administration

National Juvenile Justice Network. (2016). *Keep youth out of adult courts, jails, and prisons.* Retrieved from: www.njjn.org/about-us/keep-youth-out-of-adult-prisons

National Kidney Foundation (2018). NKF concerned about proposed changes to Medicare Part D. Retrieved from: www.kidney.org/news/nkf-concerned-about-proposed-changes-to-medicare-part-d

National Low-Income Housing Coalition. (2016). *The long wait home.* Retrieved from: https://nlihc.org/sites/default/files/HousingSpotlight_6-1_int.pdf

National Oceanic and Atmospheric Administration (NOAA). (2019). *Global climate change indicators.* Washington, DC: Author. Retrieved from: www.ncdc.noaa.gov/monitoring-references/faq/indicators.php

National Public Radio (NPR). (2019, March 5). *How federal disaster money favors the rich.* Retrieved from: www.npr.org/templates/transcript/transcript.php?storyId=688786177

National Urban League. (2018). *2018 state of Black America.* Retrieved from: www.ncbw-qcmc.org/

uploads/1/0/2/9/.../nul-soba2018-executive_summary.pdf

National Women's Law Center. (2018). *National snapshot: Poverty among women and families, 2018.* Retrieved from: https://nwlc.org/resources/national-snapshot-poverty-among-women-families-2018/

NCD Risk Factor Collaboration (NCD-RisC). (2019). *Rising rural body-mass index is the main driver of the global obesity epidemic in adults. Nature.* doi:10.1038/s41586-019-1171-x

Neighbors, H.W., Jackson, J.S., Campbell, L., & Williams, D. (1989). The influence of racial factors on psychiatric diagnosis: A review and suggestions for research. *Community Mental Health Journal, 25*(4).

Nelson-Becker, H., Chapin, R., & Fast, B. (2013). The strengths model with older adults: Critical practice components. In D. Saleebey (Ed.), *The strengths perspective in social work practice*. White Plains, NY: Longman.

Neubeck, K. J., & Cazenave, N. (2001). *Welfare racism: Playing the race card against America's poor.* New York, NY: Routledge.

Newport, F. (2018a). *Democrats more positive about socialism than capitalism.* Washington, DC: Gallup. Retrieved from: https://news.gallup.com/poll/240725/democrats-positive-socialism-capitalism.aspx

Newport, F. (2018b). *Americans want government to do more on environment.* Washington, DC: Gallup. Retrieved from: https://news.gallup.com/poll/232007/americans-want-government-more-environment.aspx

Nicholson, H., & Gruwell, A. (2018). *Lowering health insurance costs with reinsurance.* Washington, DC: National Conference of State Legislatures. Retrieved from: www.ncsl.org/research/health/lowering-health-insurance-costs-with-reinsurance.aspx

Niles, M. T., Lubell, M., Haden, V. R., & Jackson, L. (2013). *Farmers' climate change attitudes: Past, present and future perspectives.* Davis, CA: Center for Environmental Policy and Behavior. Retrieved from: https://policyinstitute.ucdavis.edu/wp-content/uploads/2013-07-24_Yolo_Climate_Attitudes_Policy_Brief_FINAL_2.pdf

Nissen, L. (2006). Bringing strengths-based philosophy to life in juvenile justice. *Reclaiming Children and Youth, 15*(1), 40–46.

Norton, M. I., & Ariely, D. (2011). Building a better America—one wealth quintile at a time. *Perspectives on Psychological Science, 6*(1), 9–12.

Norton, M. I., & Sommers, S. R. (2011). Whites see racism as a zero-sum game that they are now losing. *Perspectives on Psychological Science, 6*(3), 215–218.

NPR/Marist. (2018). *NPR/Marist poll results September 2018: Election security.* Retrieved from: http://maristpoll.marist.edu/?page_id=42883

Nunn, R., Parsons, J., & Shambaugh, J. (2018). *The geography of prosperity.* Washington, DC: The Brookings Institution. Retrieved from: www.hamiltonproject.org/assets/files/PBP_FramingChapter_compressed_20190307.pdf

Nunn, R., Parsons, J., & Shambaugh, J. (2019a). *Nine facts about state and local policy.* Washington, DC: The Brookings Institution. Retrieved from: www.brookings.edu/research/nine-facts-about-state-and-local-policy/

Nunn, R., Parsons, J., & Shambaugh, J. (2019b). *How difficult is it to find a job?* Washington, DC: The Brookings Institution. Retrieved from: www.brookings.edu/blog/up-front/2019/05/02/how-difficult-is-it-to-find-a-job/

Obergefell et al. v. Hodges, Director, Ohio Department of Health, et al. 576 U. S. (2015).

O'Connor, J. (1973). *The fiscal crisis of the state.* New York, NY: Saint Martin's Press.

Office of Juvenile Justice and Delinquency Prevention (OJJDP). (2011). *Final plan for fiscal year 2011.* Retrieved from: www.gpo.gov/fdsys/pkg/FR-2011-07-08/html/2011-17186.htm

Office of Juvenile Justice and Delinquency Prevention (OJJDP). (2018). *OJJDP statistical briefing book.* Retrieved from: www.ojjdp.gov/ojstatbb/crime/JAR_Display.asp?ID=qa05200

Oko, J. (2006). Evaluating alternative approaches to social work: A critical review of the strengths perspective. *Families in Society, 87*(4), 601–611.

Oliphant, B. (2017). *Prescription drug abuse increasingly seen as a major U.S. public health problem.* Washington, DC: Pew Research Center. Retrieved from:

www.pewresearch.org/fact-tank/2017/11/15/prescription-drug-abuse-increasingly-seen-as-a-major-u-s-public-health-problem/

Olivetti, C., & Petrongolo, B. (2017). The economic consequences of family policies: Lessons from a century of legislation in high-income countries. *Journal of Economic Perspectives, 31*(1), 205–230.

Ollove, M. (2015). *New efforts to keep the mentally ill out of jail*. The Pew Charitable Trusts. Retrieved from: www.pewtrusts.org/en/research-and-analysis/blogs/stateline/2015/5/19/new-efforts-to-keep-the-mentally-ill-out-of-jail

Olmstead v. L. C., 527 U.S. 581 (1999). Retrieved from: http://caselaw.lp.findlaw.com/scripts/getcase.pl?court=us&vol=000&invol=98-536

Olsen, K. (1999). *Daily life in 18th-century England*. Westport, CT: Greenwood Press.

Olshansky, S. J., Antonucci, T., Berkman, L., Binstock, R. H., Boersch-Supan, A., Cacioppo, J. T., Cames, B. A., Carstensen, L. L., Fried, L. P., Goldman, D. P., Jackson, J., Kohli, M., Rother, J., Zheng, Y., Rowe, R. (2012). Differences in life expectancy due to race and educational differences are widening, and many may not catch up. *Health Affairs, 31*, 1803–1813.

Oltmanns, T. F., & Emery, R. E. (1995). *Abnormal psychology*. Englewood Cliffs, NJ: Prentice Hall.

Organisation for Economic Co-operation and Development (OECD). (2016). *Life expectancy at 65*. Retrieved from: https://data.oecd.org/healthstat/life-expectancy-at-65.htm

Organisation for Economic Co-operation and Development (OECD). (2018). *The future of social protection: What works for non-standard workers? Policy brief on the future of work*. Retrieved from: www.oecd.org/employment/future-of-social-protection.pdf

Organisation for Economic Co-operation and Development (OECD). (2019a). *Social expenditure report: 2019*. Retrieved from: www.oecd.org/social/expenditure.htm

Organisation for Economic Co-operation and Development (OECD). (2019b). *Health spending (indicator)*. doi:10.1787/8643de7e-en

Oreskes, N. (2004). The scientific consensus on climate change. *Science, 1686*.

Ortman, J. M., Velkoff, V. A., & Hogan, H. (2014). *An aging nation: The older population in the United States*. United States Census Bureau. Retrieved from: www.census.gov/prod/2014pubs/p25-1140.pdf

Oxford Poverty and Human Development Initiative. (2018). *Global Multidimensional Poverty Index (MPI): 2018*. Retrieved from: https://ophi.org.uk/multidimensional-poverty-index/global-mpi-2018

Pace, P. R. (2014). Need for geriatric social work grows. *National Association of Social Work News, 59*(2). Retrieved from: www.socialworkers.org/pubs/news/2014/02/geriatric-social-work.asp

Papanicolas, I., Woskie, L. R., & Jha, A. K. (2018). Health care spending in the United States and other high-income countries. *Journal of the American Medical Association, 319*(10), 1024–1039.

Park, E., & Broaddus, M. (2012). *Lower-than-expected Medicare drug costs mostly reflect lower enrollment and slower overall price drug price increases, not reliance on private plans*. Washington, DC: Center on Budget and Policy Priorities. Retrieved from: www.cbpp.org/research/lower-than-expected-medicare-drug-costs-mostly-reflect-lower-enrollment-and-slowing-of

Parker, K., Morin, R., & Horowitz, J.M. (2019). *Looking to the future, public sees an America in decline on many fronts*. Washington, DC: Pew Research Center. Retrieved from: www.pewsocialtrends.org/2019/03/21/public-sees-an-america-in-decline-on-many-fronts/

Patterson, J. T. (1996). *Great expectations: The United States, 1945–1974*. New York, NY: Oxford University Press.

Payne, K. (2017). *The broken ladder: How inequality affects the way we think, live, and die*. New York, NY: Viking.

Pavetti, L. (2018). *TANF studies show work requirement proposals for other programs would harm millions, do little to increase work*. Washington, DC: Center on Budget and Policy Priorities (CBPP). Retrieved from: www.cbpp.org/research/recent-report-on-tanfs-responsiveness-to-the-recession-has-serious-flaws

Pear, R. (1986, February 5). Reagan seeks welfare plan to free poor from government dependency. *New York Times*. Retrieved from: **www.nytimes.com/1986/02/05/us/reagan-seeks-welfare-plan-to-free-poor-from-government-dependency.html**

Pearlman, J. (2015). The consequences of job displacement for health: Moderating influences of economic conditions and educational attainment. *Social Science Research, 52*, 570–587.

Peng, L. (2013). Surrogate mothers: An exploration of the empirical and the normative. *American University Journal of Gender Social Policy and Law, 21*(3), 555–582.

Pension Benefit Guaranty Corporation (PBGC). (2009). *History of Pension Benefit Guaranty Corporation*. Retrieved from: **www.pbgc.gov/about/who-we-are/pg/history-of-pbgc.html**

Pension Benefit Guaranty Corporation (PBGC). (2017). *Projections report*. Retrieved from: **www.pbgc.gov/about/projections-report**

Perera, F. P., Rauh, V., Whyatt, R. M., Tsai, W. Y., Tang, D., Diaz, D., Hoepner, L., Barr, D., Tu, Y. H., Camann, D., and Kinney, P. (2006). Effect of prenatal exposure to airborne polycyclic aromatic hydrocarbons on neurodevelopment in the first 3 years of life among inner-city children. *Environmental Health Perspectives, 114*(8).

Perrin, J. M., Houtrow, A., Kelleher, K., Hoagwood, K., Stein, R.E.K., & Zima, B. (2016). Supplemental security income benefits for mental disorders. *Pediatrics, 138*(1).

Perron, R. (July 2018). *The Value of Experience Study*. Washington, DC: AARP. Retrieved from: **www.aarp.org/research/topics/economics/info-2018/multicultural-work-jobs.html**

Peterson-Kaiser Health System Tracker. (2017). Per enrollee spending growth has slowed recently for all major payers. Retrieved from: **www.healthsystemtracker.org/chart-collection/u-s-spending-healthcare-changed-time/#item-per-enrollee-spending-growth-has-slowed-recently-for-all-major-payers_2017**

Petr, C. G. (2004). *Social work with children and their families: Pragmatic foundations* (2nd ed.). New York, NY: Oxford University Press.

Pettit, B., & Sykes, B. (2017). *State of the union 2017: Incarceration*. Stanford, CA: Stanford Center on Poverty and Inequality. Retrieved from: **www.themarshallproject.org/documents/4316517-Pettit-Sykes-2017-incarceration-report**

Pew Charitable Trusts. (2012). *Pursuing the American dream: Economic mobility across generations*. Retrieved from: **www.pewtrusts.org/~/media/legacy/uploadedfiles/pcs_assets/2012/pursuingamericandreampdf.pdf**

Pew Charitable Trusts. (2013). *Moving on up: Why do some Americans leave the bottom of the economic ladder, but not others?* Retrieved from: **www.pewtrusts.org/~/media/assets/2013/11/01/movingonuppdf.pdf**

Pew Charitable Trusts. (2015a). *States' recovery from Great Recession is slow and uneven*. Retrieved from: **www.pewtrusts.org/en/research-and-analysis/articles/2014/09/state-fiscal-recovery-from-great-recession-is-slow-and-uneven**

Pew Charitable Trusts. (2015b). *The role of emergency savings in family financial security: What resources do families have for financial emergencies?* Retrieved from: **www.pewtrusts.org/-/media/assets/2018/04/rent-burden_report_v2.pdf**

Pew Charitable Trusts. (2018). *The state pension funding gap*. Retrieved from: **www.pewtrusts.org/en/research-and-analysis/issue-briefs/2018/04/the-state-pension-funding-gap-2016**

Pew Research Center. (2009). *Growing old in America: Expectations vs. reality*. Retrieved from: **www.pewsocialtrends.org/2009/06/29/growing-old-in-america-expectations-vs-reality**

Pew Research Center. (2015). *The changing religious landscape*. Retrieved from: **www.pewforum.org/2015/05/12/americas-changing-religious-landscape**

Pew Research Center. (2017). *Latinos and the Trump Administration*. Retrieved from: **www.pewhispanic.org/2017/02/23/latino-priorities-for-the-trump-administration-and-congress-in-2017/**

Pew Research Center. (2018a). *When do Americans plan to retire?* Retrieved from: **www.pewtrusts.org/en/research-and-analysis/issue-briefs/2018/11/when-do-americans-plan-to-retire**

Pew Research Center. (2018b). *The generation gap in American politics*. Retrieved from: www.people-press.org/2018/03/01/the-generation-gap-in-american-politics/

Pew Research Center. (2018c). *Majorities say government does too little for older people, the poor and the middle class*. Retrieved from: www.people-press.org/2018/01/30/majorities-say-government-does-too-little-for-older-people-the-poor-and-the-middle-class/

Pew Research Center. (2019a). *Political independents: Who they are, what they think*. Retrieved from: www.people-press.org/2019/03/14/political-independents-who-they-are-what-they-think/

Pew Research Center. (2019b). *Public trust in government: 1958–2019*. Retrieved from: www.people-press.org/2019/04/11/public-trust-in-government-1958-2019/

Pfeffer, F. T., Danziger, S., & Schoeni, R. F. (2013). Wealth disparities before and after the Great Recession. *The Annals of the American Academy of Political and Social Science, 650*(1), 98–123.

Phillips, K. W. (2014, October 1). How diversity makes us smarter. *Scientific America*. Retrieved from: www.scientificamerican.com/article/how-diversity-makes-us-smarter

Piketty, T. (2014). *Capital in the twenty-first century*. Cambridge MA: Belknap Press of Harvard University Press.

Piven, F. F., & Cloward, R. A. (1971). *Regulating the poor: The functions of public welfare*. New York, NY: Pantheon.

Plassman, B. L., Langa, K. M., Fisher, G. G., Heeringa, S. G., Weir, D. R., Ofstedal, M. B., Burke, J. R., Hurd, M. D., Potter, G. G., Rodgers, W. L., Steffens, D. C., Willis, R. J., & Wallace, R. B. (2007). Prevalence of dementia in the United States: The aging, demographics, and memory study. *Neuroepidemiology, 29*, 125–132.

Plessy v. Ferguson, 163 U.S. 537 (1896). Retrieved from: http://caselaw.lp.findlaw.com/scripts/getcase.pl?court=us&vol=163&invol=537

Poirier, J. M., Fisher, S. K., Hunt, R. A., & Bearse, M. (2014). *A guide for understanding, supporting, and affirming LGBTQI2-S children, youth, and families*. Washington, DC: American Institutes for Research.

Politico. (2017, November 29). Full video of playbook interview with Senator Marco Rubio. Retrieved from: www.politico.com/video/2017/11/29/full-video-of-playbook-interview-sen-marco-rubio-064454#t=21m45s

Pollard, W. L. (1995). Civil rights. In R. L. Edwards & J. G. Hopps (Eds.), *Encyclopedia of social work* (19th ed., pp. 494–502). New York, NY: NASW Press.

Popple, P. (1995). Social work profession: History. In R. L. Edwards & J. G. Hopps (Eds.), *Encyclopedia of social work* (19th ed., pp. 2282–2292). Washington, DC: NASW Press.

Popple, P. R., & Leighninger, L. (2012). *The policy-based profession: An introduction to social welfare policy analysis for social workers* (8th ed.). New York, NY: Pearson.

Postrel, V. I. (1988, May 20). Religious rights: A matter of property. *Wall Street Journal*, p. 1.

Poutre, A., Rorrison, J., & Voight, M. (2017). *Limited means, limited options*. Washington, DC: Institute for Higher Education Policy.

Prosperity Now. (2018). *Asset limits in public benefit programs*. Retrieved from: http://scorecard.prosperitynow.org/reports#report-policy-brief

Prosperity Now. (2019). *Asset poverty rate*. Retrieved from: https://scorecard.prosperitynow.org/data-by-issue#finance/outcome/asset-poverty-rate

Provine, D. (2007). *Unequal under law: Race in the war on drugs*. Chicago, IL: University of Chicago Press.

Pryke, S. (2012). Economic nationalism: Theory, history and prospects. *Global Policy, 3*, 281–291.

Public Policy Polling. (2018). *National survey results: March 2018*. Retrieved from: https://socialsecurityworks.org/wp-content/uploads/2018/03/Nat-Social-Security-March-18-2-Results.pdf

Putnam-Walkerly, K., & Russell, E. (2016, September 15). What the heck does "equity" mean? *Stanford Social Innovation Review*. Retrieved from: https://ssir.org/articles/entry/what_the_heck_does_equity_mean

Quadagno, J. (1999). *Aging and the life course: An introduction to social gerontology*. Boston, MA: McGraw-Hill.

Quadagno, J. (2000). Promoting civil rights through the welfare state: How Medicare integrated southern hospitals. *Social Problems, 47*(1), 68–69.

Quigley, W. (1996a). Five hundred years of English Poor Laws, 1349–1834: Regulating the working and nonworking poor. *Akron Law Review, 30*(1), 73–128.

Quigley, W. (1996b). Work or starve: Regulation of the poor in colonial America. *University of San Francisco Law Review, 31*, 35–83.

Quinn, M. (2016). Baltimore takes a broader view of public health. *Governing*. Retrieved from: www.governing.com/topics/health-human-services/gov-baltimore-health-commissioner-leana-wen.html

Quinn, K., & Benson, W. (2012). The states' elder abuse victim services: a system in search of support. *Generations, 36*(3), 66–71.

Radel, L., Baldwin, M., Crouse, G., Ghertner, R., & Waters, A. (2018). *Substance use, the opioid epidemic, and the child welfare system: Key findings from a mixed methods study*. Washington, DC: U.S. Department of Health and Human Services. Retrieved from: https://aspe.hhs.gov/system/files/pdf/258836/SubstanceUseChildWelfareOverview.pdf

Raffaele-Mendez, L. M. (2003). Predictors of suspension and negative school outcomes: A longitudinal investigation. In J. Wald & D. J. Losen (Eds.), *New directions for youth development: Vol. 99. Deconstructing the school-to-prison pipeline* (pp. 17–34). San Francisco, CA: Jossey-Bass.

Rape Abuse and Incest National Network (RAINN). (2016). *Victims of sexual assault violence: statistics*. Retrieved from: https://rainn.org/get-information/statistics/sexual-assault-victims

Rakesh, G., Szabo, S. T., Alexopoulos, G. S., & Zannas, A. S. (2017). Strategies for dementia prevention: Latest evidence and implications. *Therapeutic Advances in Chronic Disease, 8*(8–9), 121–136.

Rank, M. R., & Hirschl, T .A. (2015). The likelihood of experiencing relative poverty over the life course. *PLoS One, 10*(7), e0133513.

Rapp, C., Pettus, C., & Goscha, R. (2006). Principles of strengths-based policy. *Journal of Policy Practice, 5*(4), 3–18.

Ratcliffe, C., & Kalish, E. (2017). *Escaping poverty: Predictors of persistently poor children's economic success*. Washington, DC: The Urban Institute. Retrieved from: www.urban.org/sites/default/files/publication/90321/escaping-poverty.pdf

Ratcliffe, C., McKernan, S., Wheaton, L., Kalish, E., Ruggles, C., Armstrong, S., & Oberlin, C. (2016). *Asset limits, SNAP participation, and financial stability*. Washington, DC: Urban Institute.

Rauscher, E. (2014). *Culture of mobility: Parental behaviors and the intergenerational transmission of poverty*. Lawrence, KS: Center on Assets, Education, and Inclusion.

Reed, K., Stansfield, A., Wehner, M., & Zarzycki, C. (2018). *The human influence on Hurricane Florence*. Stony Brook, NY: Stony Brook University. Retrieved from: https://cpb-us-e1.wpmucdn.com/you.stonybrook.edu/dist/4/945/files/2018/09/climate_change_Florence_0911201800Z_final-262u19i.pdf

Reeves, R. (2019, June 5). *Capitalism used to promise a better future. Can it still do that?* Washington, DC: The Brookings Institution. Retrieved from: www.brookings.edu/opinions/capitalism-used-to-promise-a-better-future-can-it-still-do-that/

Reflective Democracy. (2017). *Research summary*. Retrieved from: https://wholeads.us/wp-content/uploads/2018/09/reflective-democracy-2017-research-summary.pdf

Reflective Democracy. (2018). *Rising tide?* Retrieved from: https://wholeads.us/2018-report/

Regents of the University of California v. Bakke, 438 US 265 (1978).

Reich, D. (2018). *Trump budget would cut non-defense programs deeply in 2019 and beyond*. Washington, DC: Center on Budget and Policy Priorities. Retrieved from: www.cbpp.org/research/federal-budget/trump-budget-would-cut-non-defense-programs-deeply-in-2019-and-beyond

Reich, R. (2015). The political roots of widening inequality. *The American Prospect*. Retrieved from: https://prospect.org/power/political-roots-widening-inequality/

Reid, P. N. (1995). Social welfare history. In R. L. Edwards & J. G. Hopps (Eds.), *Encyclopedia of social work* (19th ed., pp. 2006–2225). Washington, DC: NASW Press.

Reid, T. R. (2009). *The healing of America: A global quest for better, cheaper and fairer healthcare.* New York, NY: Penguin Press.

Reisch, M. (2000). Social policy and the great society. In J. Midgley, M. Tracy, & M. Livermore (Eds.), *The handbook of social policy* (pp. 127–142). Thousand Oaks, CA: Sage Publications.

Reisch, M. (2017a) U.S. social policy and social welfare: A critical historical review. In M. Reisch (Ed.), *Social policy and social justice.* Thousand Oaks, CA: Sage Publications.

Reisch, M. (2017b). U.S. social policy in a turbulent environment. In M. Reisch (Ed.), *Social policy and social justice.* Thousand Oaks, CA: Sage Publications.

Reynolds, A. J., Temple, J. A., Ou, S. R., Arteaga, I. A., & White, B. A. B. (2011). School-based early childhood education and age-28 well-being: Effects of timing, dosage, and subgroups. *American Association for the Advancement of Science, 333*(6040), 360–364.

Richmond, M. (1917). *Social diagnosis.* New York, NY: Russell Sage Foundation.

Roberts, P. C. (1988). Supply-side economics: Theory and results. *Public Interest, 93.* Retrieved from: **www.nationalaffairs.com/public_interest/detail/supply-sideeconomicstheory-and-results**

Roe v. Wade, 410 U.S. 113 (1973).

Roll, S. P., Davison, G., Grinstein-Weiss, M., Despard, M. R., & Bufe, S. (2018). *Refund to savings 2015–2016: Field experiments to promote tax-time saving in low- and moderate-income households* (CSD Research Report No. 18-28). St. Louis, MO: Washington University, Center for Social Development.

Romer v. Evans, U.S. C 517 U.S. 620. (1996). Retrieved from: **http://caselaw.lp.findlaw.com.cgi-bin/getcase.pl?court=us&vol=000&invol=u10179**

Romich, J. L., Simmelink, J., & Holt, S. D. (2007). When working harder does not pay: Low-income working families, tax liabilities, and benefit reductions. *Families in Society, 88*(3), 418–426.

Romig, K. (2018). *Social Security lifts more Americans out of poverty than any other program.* Washington, DC: Center on Budget and Policy Priorities. Retrieved from: **www.cbpp.org/research/social-security/social-security-lifts-more-americans-above-poverty-than-any-other-program**

Roose, R., Roets, G., & Schiettecat, T. (2014). Implementing a strengths perspective in child welfare and protection: A challenge not to be taken lightly. *European Journal of Social Work, 17*(1), 3–17.

Roper v. Simmons, 125 S.Ct. 1183 (2005); *543 U.S.* (2005). Retrieved from: **www.refworld.org/cases,USSCT,42d7a1f34.html**

Rosenberg, T. (2019, April 9). A.I. joins the campaign against sex trafficking. *New York Times.* Retrieved from: **www.nytimes.com/2019/04/09/opinion/ai-joins-the-campaign-against-sex-trafficking.html**

Roser, M., & Ortiz-Ospina, E. (2019). *World population growth.* Retrieved from: **https://ourworldindata.org/world-population-growth**

Rovner, J. (2016). *Racial disparities in youth commitments and arrests. The Sentencing Project.* Retrieved from: **www.sentencingproject.org/publications/racial-disparities-in-youth-commitments-and-arrests**

Rovner, J. (2018). *Juvenile life without parole: An overview. The Sentencing Project.* Available: **www.sentencingproject.org/publications/juvenile-life-without-parole/**

Rowe-Finkbeiner, K. (2018). *Keep marching: How every woman can take action and change our world.* New York, NY: Hachette Books.

Rowse, A. L. (1950). *The England of Elizabeth.* New York, NY: Macmillan.

Rudowitz, R., Hinton, E., & Antonisse, L. (2018). *Medicaid enrollment and spending growth: FY2018 and FY2019.* Kaiser Family Foundation. Retrieved from: **www.kff.org/medicaid/issue-brief/medicaid-enrollment-spending-growth-fy-2018-2019/**

Ryan, C. L., & Bauman, K. (2016). *Educational attainment in the United States: 2015.* U.S Census Bureau. Retrieved from: **www.census.gov/content/dam/Census/library/publications/2016/demo/p20-578.pdf**

Ryan, L. (2013). *No more delays Mr. President: Appoint the nation's next Juvenile Justice Chief.* Retrieved from: **http://jjie.org/no-more-delays-mr-president-appoint-nations-next-juvenile-justice-chief**

Ryan, P. (2012). In Kettl, D. (2014). Paul Ryan declares war on poverty. *Governing.* Retrieved from: **www.governing.com/columns/washington-watch/gov-paul-ryan-poverty-war.html**

Sacks, J. J., Gonzales, K. R., Bouchery, E. E., Tomedi, L. E., & Brewer, R. D. (2015). 2010 national and state costs of excessive alcohol consumption. *American Journal of Preventive Medicine, 49*(5), e73–e79.

Saleebey, D. (Ed.) (1992). Introduction: Power in the people. In D. Saleebey (Ed.), *The strengths perspective in social work practice* (pp. 3–17). New York, NY: Longman.

Saleebey, D. (2013). *The strengths perspective in social work practice* (6th ed.). Boston, MA: Pearson.

Salvanto, A., de Pinto, J., Backus, F., & Khanna, K. (2019, November 12). Poll finds negative views of Democrats' and Trump's handling of impeachment inquiry. *CBS News*. Available at: **https://www.cbsnews.com/news/trump-impeachment-americans-hold-negative-views-democrats-trumps-handling-impeachment-inquiry-latest-cbs-news-poll/**.

Samaan, R. A. (2000). The influences of race, ethnicity, and poverty on the mental health of children. *Journal of Health Care for the Poor and Underserved, 11*(1), 100–110.

Samimi, P., & Jenatabadi, H. S. (2014). Globalization and economic growth: Empirical evidence on the role of complementarities. *PloS One, 9*(4), e87824.

Savage, C. (2017, August 1). Justice Department to take on affirmative action in college admissions. *New York Times*. Retrieved from: **www.nytimes.com/2017/08/01/us/politics/trump-affirmative-action-universities.html**

Sawhill, I. & Thomas, A. (2005). For love and money? The impact of family structure on family income. *The Future of Children, 15*(2), 57–74.

Sawyer, W. (2018). *Youth confinement: The whole pie*. Washington, DC: Prison Policy Initiative. Retrieved from: **www.prisonpolicy.org/reports/youth2018.html**

Scanlon, E., & Friedline, T. (2016, April 12). *More than a dream: A new social contract for the 21st century*. Speech presented at Hall Center for the Humanities Conference Hall, Lawrence, KS.

Schaefer, S. A., Kreader, J. L. & Collins, A. M. (2010). *Parent employment and the use of child care subsidies*. Research Connections Research Brief. New York, NY: National Center for Children in Policy.

Schick, A. (with LoStracco, F.). (2000). *The federal budget: Politics, policy, process* (rev. ed.). Washington, DC: Brookings Institution Press.

Schoen, C., Davis, K., & Willink, A. (2017). *Medicare beneficiaries' high out-of-pocket costs: cost burdens by income and health status*. Commonwealth Fund. Retrieved from: **www.commonwealthfund.org/sites/default/files/documents/___media_files_publications_issue_brief_2017_may_schoen_medicare_cost_burden_ib_v2.pdf**

Schott, L., & Hill, M. (2015). *State general assistance programs are weakening despite increased need*. Retrieved from: **www.cbpp.org/research/family-income-support/state-general-assistance-programs-are-weakening-despite-increased**

Schreiner, M., Clancy, M., & Sherraden, M. (2002). *Saving performance in the American Dream demonstration: A national demonstration of individual development accounts*. St. Louis, MO: Center for Social Development. Retrieved from: **www.microfinance.com/English/Papers/IDAs_in_ADD_Final_Report.pdf**

Schulte, B., & Durana, A. (2016). *The New America care report*. Washington, DC: New America. Retrieved from: **www.newamerica.org/better-life-lab/policy-papers/new-america-care-report/**

Schwab, R. (2018, July 26). *Coverage that (doesn't) count: How the short-term, limited duration rule could lead to underinsurance*. Georgetown University Health Policy Institute. Retrieved from: **http://chirblog.org/coverage-doesnt-count-short-term-limited-duration-rule-lead-underinsurance/**

Scommegna, P. (2013). *Exploring the paradox of U.S. Hispanics' longer life expectancy*. Washington, DC: Population Reference Bureau. Retrieved from: **www.prb.org/us-hispanics-life-expectancy/**

Seabrook, E. M., Kern, M. L., & Rickard, N. S. (2016). Social networking sites, depression, and anxiety: A systematic review. *JMIR Mental Health, 3*(4), e50.

Semet, A., Persily, N., & Ansolabehere, S. (2014). *Bush v. Gore* in the American mind: Reflections and survey results on the tenth anniversary of the decision ending the 2000 election controversy. In R. Michael Alvarez and B. Grofman (Eds.), *Election reform in the United States: The state of reform after Bush v. Gore*. Cambridge, UK: Cambridge University Press.

Sen, A. (1999). *Development as freedom*. New York, NY: Anchor.

Sentencing Project. (2013). *Report of the Sentencing Project to the United Nations Human Rights Committee: Regarding racial disparities in the United States criminal justice system*. Retrieved from **http://sentencingproject.org/wp-content/uploads/2015/12/Race-and-Justice-Shadow-Report-ICCPR.pdf**

Sharkey, P. (2013). *Stuck in place: Urban neighborhoods and the end of progress toward racial equality*. Chicago, IL: University of Chicago Press.

Shear, M. (2019). Key Takeaways from the House Intelligence Committee's Impeachment Report. *New York Times*. Available at: **https://www.nytimes.com/2019/12/03/us/politics/key-takeaways-impeachment-report.html**.

Shelby County v. Holder, 570 U.S. 529 (2013).

Sherraden, M. (1991). *Assets and the poor: A new American welfare policy*. Armonk, NY: M.E. Sharpe.

Sherraden, M. (2000). From research to policy: Lessons from individual development accounts. *Journal of Consumer Affairs, 34*(2), 159–181.

Sherraden, M. S., Slosar, B., & Sherraden, M. (2002). Innovation in social policy: Collaborative policy advocacy. *Social Work, 47*(3), 209–223.

Shoag, D. (2019). *Removing barriers to accessing high-productivity places*. Washington, DC: The Hamilton Project. Retrieved from: **www.brookings.edu/wp-content/uploads/2019/01/Shoag_PP_web_20190128.pdf**

Shonkoff, J. P., Garner, A. S., Siegel, B. S., Dobbins, M. I., Earls, M. F., McGuinn, L., & Wood, D. L. (2012). The lifelong effects of early childhood adversity and toxic stress. *Pediatrics, 129*(1), 232–246.

Shook, J. J., & Goodkind, S. A. (2009). Racial disproportionality in juvenile justice: The interaction of race and geography in pretrial detention for violent and serious offenses. *Race and Social Problems, 1*, 257.

Short, K. (2012, November). *The research supplemental poverty measure: 2011*. Retrieved from: **www.census.gov/prod/2012pubs/p60-244.pdf**

Singhal, A., Tien, Y-Y., & Hsia, R. Y. (2016). Racial-ethnic disparities in opioid prescriptions at emergency department visits for conditions commonly associated with prescription drug abuse. *PLoS One, 11*(8), e0159224.

Singman, J. (1995). *Daily life in Elizabethan England*. Westport, CT: Greenwood Press.

Skiba, R. J., & Rausch, M. K. (2006). Zero tolerance, suspension, and expulsion: Questions of equity and effectiveness. In C. M. Evertson & C. S. Weinstein (Eds.), *Handbook of classroom management: Research, practice, and contemporary issues* (pp. 1063–1089). Mahwah, NJ: Erlbaum.

Skocpol, T. (1993). America's first social security system: The expansion of benefits for Civil War veterans. *Political Science Quarterly, 108*(1), 85–116.

Sloane, P. D., Zimmerman, S., & D'Souza, M. F. (2014). What will long-term care be like in 2040? *North Carolina Medical Journal, 75*(5).

Smeeding, T. (2012). *Income, wealth, and debt and the Great Recession*. Stanford, CA: Stanford Center on Poverty and Inequality.

Smith, A. (2018). *Declining majority of online adults say the Internet has been good for society*. Washington, DC: Pew Research Center. Retrieved from: **www.pewinternet.org/2018/04/30/declining-majority-of-online-adults-say-the-internet-has-been-good-for-society/**

Smith, A., & Anderson, A. (2014). *AI, robots, and the future of jobs*. Washington, DC: Pew Research Center. Retrieved from: **www.pewinternet.org/2014/08/06/future-of-jobs/**

Smith, C., & Chandy, L. (2014). *How poor are America's poorest? U.S. $2 a day poverty in a global context*. Washington, DC: The Brookings Institution. Retrieved from: **www.brookings.edu/research/how-poor-are-americas-poorest-u-s-2-a-day-poverty-in-a-global-context/**

Smith, I. Z., Bentley-Edwards, K. L., El-Amin, S., & Darity, W. Jr. (2018). *Fighting at birth: Eradicating the Black–White infant mortality gap*. Duke University's Samuel DuBois Cook Center on Social Equity and Insight Center for Community Economic Development.

Smith, S. (2017). *Public remains divided over role of government in financial regulation*. Washington, DC: Pew Research Center. Retrieved from: **www.pewresearch.org/fact-tank/2017/03/02/**

public-remains-divided-over-role-of-government-in-financial-regulation/

Smock, P. J., Manning, W. D., & Gupta, S. (1999). The effect of marriage and divorce on women's economic well-being. *American Sociological Review, 64*(6), 794–812.

Social Security Administration (SSA). (2007). *A brief history of social security*. Retrieved from: www.ssa.gov/history/briefhistory3.html

Social Security Administration (SSA). (2013). *Number of credits to be eligible for Social Security retirement benefits*. Retrieved from: http://ssa-custhelp.ssa.gov/app/answers/detail/a_id/356/kw/Eligibility%20for%20OASDI%20benefits

Social Security Administration (SSA). (2018a). *Fast facts about Social Security*. Retrieved from: www.ssa.gov/policy/docs/chartbooks/fast_facts/index.html

Social Security Administration (SSA). (2018b). *Benefits planner: Social Security credits*. Retrieved from: www.ssa.gov/planners/credits.html

Social Security Administration (SSA). (2018c, October). *Monthly statistical snapshot, October 2018*. Retrieved from: www.ssa.gov/policy/docs/quickfacts/stat_snapshot

Social Security Administration (SSA). (2018d). *Spotlight on resources*. Retrieved from: www.ssa.gov/ssi/spotlights/spot-resources.htm

Social Security Administration (SSA). (2018e). *SSI federal payment amounts for 2019*. Retrieved from: www.ssa.gov/oact/cola/SSI.html

Social Security Administration (SSA) (2018f). *Supplemental Security Income recipients*. Retrieved from: www.ssa.gov/policy/docs/quickfacts/stat_snapshot/

Social Security Administration (SSA) (2019a). *Monthly statistical snapshot*. Retrieved from: www.ssa.gov/policy/docs/quickfacts/stat_snapshot/

Social Security Administration (SSA). (2019b). *The 2019 annual report of the Board of Trustees of the Federal Old-Age and Survivors Insurance and Federal Disability Insurance Trust Funds*. Retrieved from: www.ssa.gov/oact/TR/2019/index.html

Social Security Administration (SSA). (2019c). *Life expectancy calculator*. Retrieved from: www.ssa.gov/cgi-bin/longevity.cgi

Solomon-Fears, C. (2016). *Child support: An overview of Census Bureau data on recipients*. Washington, DC: Congressional Research Service. Report to U.S. House Committee on Ways and Means. Retrieved from: https://greenbook-waysandmeans.house.gov/sites/greenbook.waysandmeans.house.gov/files

Sommeiller, E., & Price, M. (2018). *The new gilded age*. Washington, DC: Economic Policy Institute. Retrieved from: www.epi.org/publication/the-new-gilded-age-income-inequality-in-the-u-s-by-state-metropolitan-area-and-county/

Soni, A., Hendryx, M., & Simon, K. (2017). Medicaid expansion under the Affordable Care Act and insurance coverage in rural and urban areas. *The Journal of Rural Health*. Retrieved from: http://onlinelibrary.wiley.com/doi/10.1111/jrh.12234/full

Sonnega, A., Robinson, K., & Levy, H. (2016). Home and community-based service and other senior service use: Prevalence and characteristics in a national sample. *Home Health Care Services Quarterly, 36*(1), 16–28.

Spano, R. (2000). Creating the context for the analysis of social policies: Understanding the historical context. In D. Chambers (Ed.), *Social policy and social programs: A method for the practical public policy analyst* (pp. 31–45). Boston, MA: Allyn & Bacon.

Sparer, M. (2012, September). *Medicaid managed care: Costs, access, and quality of care*. Retrieved from: www.rwjf.org/content/dam/farm/reports/reports/2012/rwjf401106

Specht, H., & Courtney, M. (1994). *Unfaithful angels: How social work has abandoned its mission*. New York, NY: The Free Press.

Sroufe, L. A., Egeland, B., Carlson, E. A., & Collins, W. A. (2005). *The development of the person. The Minnesota study of risk and adaptation from birth to adulthood*. New York, NY: Guilford Press.

St. Louis Federal Reserve Bank. (2018). *Many Americans still lack retirement savings*. Retrieved from: www.stlouisfed.org/publications/regional-economist/first-quarter-2018/many-americans-still-lack-retirement-savings

Stancil, W. (2018, March 14). School segregation is not a myth. *The Atlantic*. Retrieved from: **www.theatlantic.com/education/archive/2018/03/school-segregation-is-not-a-myth/555614/**

Stanger-Hall, K. F., & Hall, D. W. (2011). Abstinence-only education and teen pregnancy rates: Why we need comprehensive sex education in the U.S. *PLoS One, 6*(10), e24658.

Statistics Canada. (2019). *Canadian income survey, 2017*. Retrieved from: **www150.statcan.gc.ca/n1/daily-quotidien/190226/dq190226b-eng.htm**

Steckel, R. H. (1979). Slave mortality: Analysis of evidence from plantation records. *Social Science History, 3*(3/4), 86–114.

Steckel, R. H. (1986). A dreadful childhood: The excess mortality of American slaves. *Social Science History, 10*(4), 427–465.

Stegelin, D. (2004). Early childhood education. In F. P. Schargel & J. Smink (Eds.), *Helping students graduate: A strategic approach to dropout prevention* (pp. 115–123). Larchmont, NY: Eye on Education.

Stein, J., & Van Dam, A. (2019). Taxpayer spending on U.S. disaster fund explodes amid climate change, population trends. *Washington Post*. Retrieved from: **www.washingtonpost.com/us-policy/2019/04/22/taxpayer-spending-us-disaster-fund-explodes-amid-climate-change-population-trends/?utm_term=.011a210711e6**

Stepler, R. (2016a). *World's centenarian population projected to grow eightfold by 2050*. Retrieved from: **www.pewresearch.org/fact-tank/2016/04/21/worlds-centenarian-population-projected-to-grow-eightfold-by-2050/?utm_campaign=2019-02-01+ATF+pilot+Living+Longer&utm_medium=email&utm_source=Pew**

Stepler, R. (2016b). *Smaller share of women ages 65 and older are living alone*. Washington, DC: Pew Research Center. Retrieved from: **www.pewsocialtrends.org/2016/02/18/smaller-share-of-women-ages-65-and-older-are-living-alone/**

Stokes, B. (2018). *Americans, like many in other advanced economies, not convinced of trade's benefits*. Washington, DC: Pew Research Center. Retrieved from: **www.pewglobal.org/2018/09/26/americans-like-many-in-other-advanced-economies-not-convinced-of-trades-benefits/**

Substance Abuse and Mental Health Services Administration (SAMHSA). (2010). *About SAMSHA*. Retrieved from: **www.samhsa.gov/about**

Substance Abuse and Mental Health Services Administration (SAMHSA). (2014). *Projections of national expenditures for treatment of mental and substance use disorders, 2010–2020*. HHS Publication No. SMA-14-4883. Rockville, MD: Substance Abuse and Mental Health Services Administration.

Substance Abuse and Mental Health Services Administration (SAMHSA). (2017). *Treatment Episode Data Set (TEDS): 2005–2015. National admissions to substance abuse treatment services*. BHSIS Series S-91, HHS Publication No. (SMA) 17-5037. Rockville, MD: Substance Abuse and Mental Health Services Administration, Center for Behavioral Health Statistics and Quality.

Substance Abuse and Mental Health Services Administration (SAMHSA). (2018). *Key substance use and mental health indicators in the United States: Results from the 2017 National Survey on Drug Use and Health* (HHS Publication No. SMA 18-5068, NSDUH Series H-53). Rockville, MD: Center for Behavioral Health Statistics and Quality, Substance Abuse and Mental Health Services Administration. Retrieved from: **www.samhsa.gov/data/**

Sung, S., Simpson, J. A., Griskevicius, V., Kuo, S. I.-C., Schlomer, G. L., & Belsky, J. (2016). Secure infant–mother attachment buffers the effect of early-life stress on age of menarche. *Psychological Science, 27*(5), 667–674.

Sunstein, C. (2004). *The second Bill of Rights: FDR's unfinished revolution—and why we need it more than ever*. New York, NY: Basic Books.

Swatos, W. (Ed.) (1998). *Encyclopedia of religion and society*. Walnut Creek, CA: AltaMira Press.

Taylor, J. (1997). Niches and practice: Extending the ecological perspective. In D. Saleebey (Ed.), *The strengths perspective in social work practice* (2nd ed., pp. 217–227). New York, NY: Longman.

Temple University (2018). *Involuntary outpatient commitment laws*. Philadelphia, PA: Policy Surveillance Project. Retrieved from: **http://lawatlas.org/**

datasets/involuntary-outpatient-commitment-1442865639

Teng, Q., Hodge, M., & Gordon, E. (2019). *Participatory design of a virtual reality-based reentry training with a women's prison*. Extended Abstracts of the Conference on Computer Human Interactions.

Tetlock, P.E. (2016). *Superforecasting: The art and science of prediction*. New York, NY: Broadway Books.

Thakrar, A. P., Forrest, A. D., Maltenfort, M. G., & Forrest, C. B. (2018). Child mortality in the U.S. and 19 OECD comparator nations: A 50-year time-trend analysis. *Health Affairs, 37*(1), 140–149.

Thomas, J. T., & Wilson, M. (2018). *The color of juvenile transfer: Policy and practice recommendations*. Washington, DC: National Association of Social Workers and Campaign for Youth Justice. Retrieved from: **www.socialworkers.org/LinkClick.aspx?fileticket=30n7g-nwam8%3d&portalid=0**

Thomhave, K. (2018, October 3). The battle over TANF family cap intensifies. *Spotlight on Poverty*. Retrieved from: **https://spotlightonpoverty.org/spotlight-exclusives/battle-over-tanf-family-cap-intensifies/**

Thompson, F. J., Gusmano, M. K., & Shinohara, S. (2018). Trump and the Affordable Care Act: Congressional repeal efforts, executive federalism, and program durability. *Publius: The Journal of Federalism, 48*(3), 396–424.

Thompson, T. R. (2016). Can rehabilitative programs reduce the recidivism of juvenile offenders? *Electronic Theses, Projects, and Dissertations*, Paper 278.

Tice, C., & Perkins, K. (1996). *Mental health issues and aging*. Pacific Grove, CA: Brooks/Cole.

Tice, C., & Perkins, K. (2002). *The faces of social policy: A strengths perspective*. Pacific Grove, CA: Wadsworth Group, Brooks/Cole.

Title IX Education Amendments. (1972). *20 U.S.C. Section 1681–1688*. Retrieved from: **www.dol.gov/oasam/regs/statutes/titleix.htm**

Titmuss, R. M. (1974). *Social policy: An introduction*. New York, NY: Pantheon Books.

Towle, C. (1987). *Common human needs*. Silver Spring, MD: National Association of Social Workers. (Original work published 1945.)

Trattner, W. (1999). *From poor law to welfare state: A history of social welfare in America* (6th ed.). New York, NY: The Free Press.

Traub, A., Ruetschlin, C., Sullivan, L., Meschede, T., Dietrich, L., & Shapiro, T. (2016). *The racial wealth gap: Why policy matters*. Demos and the Institute for Assets and Social Policy. Retrieved from: **www.demos.org/publication/racial-wealth-gap-why-policy-matters**

Treatment Advocacy Center. (2018). *Homelessness increases among individuals with serious mental illness*. Retrieved from: **www.treatmentadvocacycenter.org/fixing-the-system/features-and-news/3965-research-weekly-homelessness-increases-among-individuals-with-serious-mental-illness**

Treuer, D. (2019). *The heartbeat of Wounded Knee: Native America from 1890 to the present*. New York, NY: Random House/Penguin.

Truffer, C., Wolfe, C., & Rennie, K. (2017). *2016 actuarial report on the financial outlook for Medicaid*. Office of the Actuary, Centers for Medicare & Medicaid Services, and the Department of Health & Human Services. Retrieved from: **www.cms.gov/Research-Statistics-Data-and-Systems/Research/ActuarialStudies/Downloads/MedicaidReport2016.pdf**

Tucker-Drob, E. M., & Bates, T. C. (2015). Large cross-national difference in gene × socioeconomic status interaction on intelligence. *Psychological Science, 27*(2), 138–149.

Turner, J. B., & Turner, R. J. (2004). Physical disability, unemployment, and mental health. *Rehabilitation Psychology, 49*(3), 241–249.

Turner, M. A., Santos, R., Levy, D. K., Wissoker, D. A., Aranda, C., & Pitingolo, R. (2013). *Housing discrimination against racial and ethnic minorities 2012: Full report*. Retrieved from: **www.huduser.org/portal/Publications/pdf/HUD-514_HDS2012.pdf**

Tuzeman, D. (2018). *Why are prime-age men vanishing from the labor force?* Kansas City, MO: Federal Reserve Bank of Kansas City. Retrieved from: **www.kansascityfed.org/~/media/files/publicat/econrev/econrevarchive/2018/1q18tuzemen.pdf**

Union of Concerned Scientists. (2018). *Underwater: Chronic floods, rising seas, and the implications for U.S. coastal real estate*. Cambridge, MA: Author.

Retrieved from: www.ucsusa.org/global-warming/global-warming-impacts/sea-level-rise-chronic-floods-and-us-coastal-real-estate-implications

United Nations. (2017). *World population prospects: The 2017 revision, key findings and advance tables*. Working Paper No. ESA/P/WP/248. UN Department of Economic and Social Affairs, Population Division. Retrieved from: https://population.un.org/wpp/Publications/Files/WPP2017_KeyFindings.pdf

United States v. Windsor, 570 U.S. 744 (2013).

Urban Institute. (2017). *Nine charts about wealth inequality in America*. Washington, DC: Author. Retrieved from: https://apps.urban.org/features/wealth-inequality-charts/

U.S. Bureau of Labor Statistics. (2017a). *Total health care employment*. Bureau of Labor Statistics, State Occupational Employment Statistics Survey. Retrieved from www.bls.gov/oes/tables.htm

U.S. Bureau of Labor Statistics. (2017b). *Occupational outlook handbook: Social workers*. Retrieved from: www.bls.gov/ooh/community-and-social-service/social-workers.htm

U.S. Bureau of Labor Statistics. (2018a). Labor force statistics from the Current Population Survey. Retrieved from: www.bls.gov/web/empsit/cpsee_e16.htm

U.S. Bureau of Labor Statistics. (2018b). *Civilian labor force participation rate: With no disability, 65 years and over*. Retrieved from: https://fred.stlouisfed.org/series/LNU01375379

U.S. Census Bureau. (2009). *Poverty thresholds by size of family and number of children*. Retrieved from: www.census.gov/hhes/www/poverty/threshld.html

U.S. Census Bureau. (2012). *2012 national population projections: Summary tables—Table 1*. Retrieved from: www.census.gov/population/projections/data/national/2012/summarytables.html

U.S. Census Bureau (2015). *Quick facts*. Retrieved from: www.census.gov/quickfacts/table/PST045215/00

U.S. Census Bureau. (2016). *World population: 1950–2050*. Retrieved from: www.census.gov/population/international/data/idb/worldpopgraph.php

U.S. Census Bureau. (2017). *Educational attainment in the United States: 2017*. Washington, DC: Author. Retrieved from: www.census.gov/data/tables/2017/demo/education-attainment/cps-detailed-tables.html

U.S. Census Bureau. (2018a). *Selected economic characteristics for the civilian noninstitutionalized population by disability status*. Washington, DC: Author. Retrieved from: https://factfinder.census.gov

U.S. Census Bureau. (2018b). *Asian and Pacific Islander population in the United States*. Washington, DC: Author. Retrieved from: www.census.gov/library/visualizations/2018/comm/api.html.html

U.S. Census Bureau. (2018c). *Historical poverty thresholds*. Retrieved from: www.census.gov/data/tables/time-series/demo/income-poverty/historical-poverty-thresholds.html

U.S. Census Bureau. (2018d). *Historical poverty tables: People and families*. Retrieved from: www.census.gov/data/tables/time-series/demo/income-poverty/historical-poverty-people.html

U.S. Census Bureau. (2018e). *An aging nation: Projected number of children and older adults*. Retrieved from: www.census.gov/library/visualizations/2018/comm/historic-first.html

U.S. Census Bureau. (2018f). *Wealth, asset ownership, and debt of households: 2014*. Retrieved from: www.census.gov/data/tables/2014/demo/wealth/wealth-asset-ownership.html

U.S. Census Bureau. (2018g). *Older people projected to outnumber children for first time in U.S. history*. Retrieved from: www.census.gov/newsroom/press-releases/2018/cb18-41-population-projections.html

U.S. Census Bureau. (2019a). *Population estimates show aging across race groups differs*. Retrieved from: www.census.gov/newsroom/press-releases/2019/estimates-characteristics.html

U.S. Census Bureau. (2019b). *Population clock*. Accessed July 10, 2019. Retrieved from: www.census.gov/popclock/

U.S. Department of Agriculture (USDA). (2016, March 11). *SNAP Policy on non-citizen eligibility*. Retrieved from: www.fns.usda.gov/snap/snap-policy-non-citizen-eligibility

U.S. Department of Agriculture (USDA). (2017). *National and state-level estimates of Special Supplemental Nutrition Program for Women, Infants, and

Children (WIC) eligibles and program reach in 2014, and updated estimates for 2005–2013. Retrieved from: www.fns.usda.gov/wic/national-state-level-estimates-wic-eligibles-program-reach-2014-and-updated-estimates-2005-2013

U.S. Department of Agriculture (USDA). (2018a). *Program information report*. Retrieved from: https://fns-prod.azureedge.net/sites/default/files/datastatistics/keydata-july-2018_0.pdf

U.S. Department of Agriculture (USDA). (2018b). *Am I eligible for SNAP?* Retrieved from: www.fns.usda.gov/snap/eligibility

U.S. Department of Agriculture (USDA). (2018c). *Frequently asked questions about WIC?* Retrieved from: www.fns.usda.gov/wic/frequently-asked-questions-about-wic

U.S. Department of Agriculture (USDA). (2018d). *WIC monthly data*. Retrieved from: https://fns-prod.azureedge.net/sites/default/files/pd/37WIC_Monthly.pdf

U.S. Department of Defense. (2019). *Annual report on sexual assault in the military*. Retrieved from: www.sapr.mil/sites/default/files/DoD_Annual_Report_on_Sexual_Assault_in_the_Military.pdf

U.S. Department of Education. (2017). *FY 2018 budget request: Student financial assistance*. Retrieved from www2.ed.gov/about/overview/budget/budget18/justifications/o-sfa.pdf

U.S. Department of Health and Human Services (USDHHS). (2017). *Trends in teen pregnancy and childbearing*. Washington, DC: Office of Adolescent Health. Retrieved from: www.hhs.gov/ash/oah/adolescent-development/reproductive-health-and-teen-pregnancy/teen-pregnancy-and-childbearing/trends/index.html

U.S. Department of Health and Human Services (USDHHS). (2018a). *FY 2017 federal TANF and state MOE financial data*. Retrieved from: www.acf.hhs.gov/sites/default/files/ofa/tanf_financial_data_fy_2017_81518.pdf

U.S. Department of Health and Human Services (USDHHS). (2018b). *Child maltreatment 2016*. Retrieved from: www.acf.hhs.gov/sites/default/files/cb/cm2016.pdf#page=20

U.S. Department of Health and Human Services (USDHHS). (2018c). *Foster care statistics 2016*. Retrieved from: www.childwelfare.gov/pubPDFs/foster.pdf

U.S. Department of Health and Human Services (USDHHS). (2019). *Poverty guidelines*. Retrieved from: https://aspe.hhs.gov/2019-poverty-guidelines

U.S. Department of Housing and Urban Development (HUD). (2018). *Picture of subsidized households: 2018*. Retrieved from: www.huduser.gov/portal/datasets/assthsg.html

U.S. Department of Justice. (2000). *Introduction to federal voting rights laws*. Retrieved from: www.usdoj.gov/crt/voting/intro/intro_b.htm

U.S. Department of Labor. (2012, December 10). *Unemployment insurance*. Retrieved from: http://workforcesecurity.doleta.gov/unemploy/uitaxtopic.asp

U.S. Department of Labor. (2019, March 21). Unemployment insurance weekly claims. Retrieved from: www.dol.gov/ui/data.pdf

U.S. Department of the Treasury. (2016). *The Kline–Miller Multiemployer Pension Reform Act of 2014*. Retrieved from: www.treasury.gov/services/Pages/Benefit-Suspensions.aspx

U.S. Department of Veterans' Affairs. (2013). *Compensation*. Retrieved from: www.benefits.va.gov/COMPENSATION/index.asp

U.S. Department of Veterans' Affairs. (2018a). *Veterans compensation benefit rate tables – effective 12/1/18*. Retrieved from: www.benefits.va.gov/compensation/resources_comp01.asp

U.S. Department of Veterans' Affairs. (2018b). *PTSD: National Center for PTSD*. Retrieved from: www.ptsd.va.gov/understand/common/common_veterans.asp

U.S. Department of Veterans' Affairs. (2018c). *Critical deficiencies at the Washington, DC VA Medical Center*. Retrieved from: www.va.gov/oig/pubs/vaoig-17-02644-130.pdf

U.S. Global Change Research Group (USGCRP). (2018). *Impacts, risks, and adaptation in the United States: Fourth National Climate Assessment, Volume II*. U.S. Global Change Research Program, Washington, DC: Author.

U.S. Government Accountability Office (USGAO). (2012). *Concerns remain about appropriate services for children in Medicaid and foster care*. Retrieved from: **www.gao.gov/assets/660/650716.pdf**

U.S. Government Accountability Office (USGAO). (2017). *HHS has taken steps to support states' oversight of psychotropic medications, but additional assistance could further collaboration*. Retrieved from: **www.gao.gov/assets/690/681916.pdf**

U.S. Government Accountability Office (USGAO). (2018). *Status of public health emergency authorities*. Retrieved from: **www.gao.gov/products/GAO-18-685R**

U.S. House Committee on Ways and Means. (2016). Child welfare. In *Green book*. Retrieved from: **https://greenbook-waysandmeans.house.gov/2016-green-book/chapter-11-child-welfare**

Van Dam, A. (2019, February 26). Working parents are an endangered species: That's why Democrats are talking child care. *Washington Post*. Retrieved from: **www.washingtonpost.com/us-policy/2019/02/26/working-parents-are-an-endangered-species-thats-why-democrats-are-talking-child-care/?utm_term=.f552db593acb**

V.R. v. Ohl, No. 3:98-cv-1176 (1999).

W. Haywood Burns Institute for Justice, Fairness, and Equity. (2017). *Unbalanced juvenile justice*. Retrieved from: **www.burnsinstitute.org/tag/data-map/**

Waldfogel, J. (2000). Economic dimensions of social welfare policy. In J. Midgley, M. Tracy, & M. Livermore (Eds.), *The handbook of social policy* (pp. 27–40). Thousand Oaks, CA: Sage Publications.

Walker, D. B. (1987). Evaluating Reagan federalism. *New England Journal of Public Policy, 3*(2), Article 4.

Walker, E. A., Reno, V., & Bethell, T. N. (2014). Americans make hard choices on social security: A survey with trade-off analysis. *National Academy of Social Insurance*. Retrieved from: **www.nasi.org/sites/default/files/research/Americans_Make_Hard_Choices_on_Social_Security.pdf**

Wall Street Journal. (January 17, 2018). 37 ways Donald Trump has remade the rules for business. Retrieved from: **www.wsj.com/articles/how-donald-trump-has-remade-the-rules-for-business-1516190400**

Wan, L. (1999). Parents killing parents: Creating a presumption of unfitness. *Albany Law Review, 63*(1), 333–359.

Washington Post-ABC News. (2019, April 22–25). Frustrations with economic and political system, and how Americans' weigh Trump's agenda ahead of 2020 election. Retrieved from: **www.washingtonpost.com/page/2010-2019/WashingtonPost/2019/04/29/National-Politics/Polling/release_549.xml**

Weaver, R. D., & Campbell, D. (2015). Fresh start: A meta-analysis of aftercare programs for juvenile offenders. *Research on Social Work Practice, 25*(2), 201–212.

Weick, A. (1986). The philosophical context of a health model of social work. *Social Casework, 67*(9), 551–559.

Weimer, D., & Vining, A. R. (1999). *Policy analysis: Concepts and practice* (3rd ed.). Upper Saddle River, NJ: Prentice Hall.

Weiss, E. (2016). *Housing access for people with criminal records*. Washington, DC: National Low-Income Housing Coalition. Retrieved from: **https://nlihc.org/sites/default/files/2016AG_Chapter_6-6.pdf**

Weiss, R. J. (1997). *"We want jobs": A history of affirmative action*. New York, NY: Garland Press.

West, D. M. (2018). *The future of work: Robots, AI, and automation*. Washington, DC: Brookings Institution Press.

West, D. M. (2019). *Assessing Trump's artificial intelligence executive order*. Washington, DC: The Brookings Institution. Retrieved from: **www.brookings.edu/blog/techtank/2019/02/12/assessing-trumps-artificial-intelligence-executive-order/**

Wexler, R. (2018). *Don't believe the hype. The Family First Act is a step backwards for child welfare finance reform*. Washington, DC: National Coalition for Child Protection Reform. Social Justice Solutions. Retrieved from: **www.socialjusticesolutions.org/2018/02/15/dont-believe-hype-family-first-act-step-backwards-child-welfare-finance-reform/**

Wheaton, L., & Sorenson, E. (2007). *The potential impact of increasing child support payments to TANF families*. Urban Institute. Retrieved from: **www.urban.org/UploadedPDF/411595_child_support.pdf**

Wheeler, R. (August 27, 2018). *Trump has reshaped the judiciary but not as much as you might think*. Washington, DC: The Brookings Institution. Retrieved from: **www.brookings.edu/blog/fixgov/2018/08/27/trump-has-reshaped-the-judiciary-but-not-as-much-as-you-might-think/**

White House. (2016). *Presidential memorandum: Mental health and substance use disorder parity task force.* Retrieved from: **www.whitehouse.gov/the-press-office/2016/03/29/presidential-memorandum-mental-health-and-substance-use-disorder-parity**

White Hughto, J. M., Rose, A. J., Pachankis, J. E., & Reisner, S. L. (2017). Barriers to gender transition-related healthcare: Identifying underserved transgender adults in Massachusetts. *Transgender Health, 2*(1), 107–118.

Whitehurst, G. J. R. (2017). *Why the federal government should subsidize childcare and how to pay for it*. Washington, DC: The Brookings Institution. Retrieved from: **www.brookings.edu/research/why-the-federal-government-should-subsidize-childcare-and-how-to-pay-for-it/**

Wilensky, H. L., & Lebeaux, C. N. (1965). *Industrial society and social welfare: The impact of industrialization on the supply and organization of social welfare services in the United States*. New York, NY: The Free Press.

Wilkinson, R., & Pickett, K. (2009). *The spirit level: Why more equal societies almost always do better*. London: Penguin.

Williams, T. (2000). *The Homestead Act: A major asset-building policy in American history*. St. Louis, MO: Center for Social Development, Washington University.

Williams, T. (2003). *Asset building as a response to wealth inequality: Implications from the Homestead Act*. St. Louis, MO: Center for Social Development, Washington University. Retrieved from: **https://csd.wustl.edu/Publications/Documents/WP03-05.pdf**

Williamson, A. (2018). *Impact KCK assessment: Reducing Student homelessness through collective impact.* Kansas City, MO: University of Missouri-Kansas City. Retrieved from: **https://bloch.umkc.edu/wp-content/uploads/2019/02/Impact-KCK-Assessment.pdf**

Wiltz, T. (2015). *Should states tell welfare recipients how to spend their benefits?* Stateline: Pew Charitable Trusts. Retrieved from: **www.pewtrusts.org/en/research-and-analysis/blogs/stateline/2015/4/24/should-states-tell-welfare-recipients-how-to-spend-their-benefits**

Wiltz, T. (2016). *Drug addiction epidemic creates crisis in foster care*. Stateline: Pew Charitable Trusts. Retrieved from: **www.pewtrusts.org/en/research-and-analysis/blogs/stateline/2016/10/07/drug-addiction-epidemic-creates-crisis-in-foster-care**

Winegar, M. (2016). Innovative ideas in LTC insurance. *Long-Term Care News*. Retrieved from: **www.soa.org/Library/Newsletters/Long-Term-Care/2016/august/ltc-2016-iss-42-winegar.aspx**

Winokur, M., et al. (2015). Systematic review of kinship care effects on safety, permanency, and well-being outcomes. *Research on Social Work Practice*. Retrieved from: **http://journals.sagepub.com/doi/abs/10.1177/1049731515620843**

Wolff, E. N. (2017). *Household wealth trends in the United States, 1962 to 2016: Has middle class wealth recovered?* NBER Working Papers 24085, National Bureau of Economic Research, Inc.

Workman, S., & Jessen-Howard, S. (2018). *Understanding the true cost of child care for infants and toddlers*. Washington, DC: Center for American Progress. Retrieved from: **www.americanprogress.org/issues/early-childhood/reports/2018/11/15/460970/understanding-true-cost-child-care-infants-toddlers/**

World Bank. (2018a). *Mortality rate, infant*. Retrieved from: **https://data.worldbank.org/indicator/SP.DYN.IMRT.IN**

World Bank. (2018b). *Life expectancy at birth: 2017*. Retrieved from: **https://data.worldbank.org/indicator/sp.dyn.le00.in**

World Health Organization. (2018). *Density of physicians*. Retrieved from: **http://gamapserver.who.int/gho/interactive_charts/health_workforce/PhysiciansDensity_Total/atlas.html**

Wright, M., Molloy, M., & Lockhart, K. (2018). Parkland students vs the NRA: Has the powerful US gun lobby met its match in Generation Snapchat? *The Telegraph*. Retrieved from: **www.telegraph.co.uk/news/2018/02/26/parkland-students-vs-nra-has-powerful-us-gun-lobby-met-match/**

Yadama, G., & Sherraden, M. (1996). Effect of assets on attitudes and behaviors: Advance test of a social policy proposal. *Social Work Research, 20*, 3–11.

Yagan, D. (2018). *Employment hysteresis from the Great Recession.* Berkeley, CA: National Bureau of Economic Research. Retrieved from: https://eml.berkeley.edu/~yagan/Hysteresis.pdf

York, E. (2019). *Evaluating education tax provisions.* Washington, DC: Tax Foundation. Retrieved from: https://files.taxfoundation.org/20190219152812/Tax-Foundation-FF637.pdf

Young, N., & Gardner, S. (2003). *A preliminary review of alcohol and other drug issues in the states' children and family service reviews and program improvement plans.* Retrieved from: www.ncsacw.samhsa.gov/files/SummaryofCFSRs.pdf

Zelizer, J. (2014). Distrustful Americans still live in an age of Watergate. CNN. Available at: http://www.cnn.com/2014/07/07/opinion/zelizer-watergate-politics/.

Zengerle, J. (August 22, 2018). How the Trump Administration is remaking the courts. *New York Times.* Retrieved from: www.nytimes.com/2018/08/22/magazine/trump-remaking-courts-judiciary.html

Zerbe, R., & McCurdy, H. (2000). The end of market failure. *Regulation, 23*(2), 10–14.

Zhan, M. (2003). *Saving outcomes of single mothers in Individual Development Accounts.* St. Louis, MO: Center for Social Development.

Zimmerman, S., Shier, V., & Saliba, D. (2014). Transforming nursing home culture: Evidence for practice and policy. *The Gerontologist, 54*(1), S1–S5,

Zinn, A. (2009). Foster family characteristics, kinship, and permanence. *Social Services Review, 83*, 185–219.

Zinshteyn, M. (2017). Who benefits from New York's free college plan? *Hechinger News.* Retrieved from: http://hechingerreport.org/benefits-new-yorks-free-college-plan/

Zong, J., Ruiz Soto, A. G., Bataloya, J. Gelatt, J., & Capps, R. (2017, November). *A profile of current DACA recipients by education, industry, and occupation.* Washington, DC: Migration Policy Institute. Retrieved from: www.migrationpolicy.org/research/profile-current-daca-recipients-education-industry-and-occupation

Zucman, G. (2019). *Global wealth inequality.* Cambridge, MA: National Bureau of Economic Research. Retrieved from: http://papers.nber.org/tmp/38195-w25462.pdf

Glossary/Index

Note: page references in italics indicate Exhibits and Quick Guides. Entries in italics refer to court decisions.

AACWA *see* Adoption Assistance and Child Welfare Act (AACWA) (1980)
abortion 74, 83, 111, 134, 174, 230–31
absolute poverty: a measure of who is poor whereby the government determines an objective income level threshold or *poverty line*. 259–60; *see also* poverty
ACA *see* Affordable Care Act (ACA) (2010)
accountable health communities model 409
action plans: a tool that details steps you will take in planning and implementing your action strategy. 193–97, *194*, *195*; Sample Action Plan *198–203*
Adarand Constructors v. Peña (1995) 238
Addams, Jane 44, *45*, 46, 55, 312
adequacy: the ability of social welfare programs to sufficiently meet public needs. 127–33, *128*, *129*, *130*, *132*
Administration for Community Living (ACL): a federal agency created in 2012, that works with states, tribes, businesses, nonprofit organizations, universities, and families to help people of all ages with disabilities to continue to live in their homes and to be full participants in their communities. 433–34
Administration on Aging (AOA): a federal agency housed in the Department of Health and Human Services (USDHHS) that coordinates the implementation of the OAA and heightens awareness of aging concerns. 433
Adoption and Safe Families Act (ASFA) (1997) 329–31, *331*, 339–40
Adoption Assistance and Child Welfare Act (AACWA) (1980) 326, *326*, 329
adoptions: and Fostering Connections to Success and Increasing Adoptions Act (2008) 325, 333; and Indian Child Welfare Act (ICWA) (1978) 324–25; and Multi-Ethnic Placement Act (MEPA) (1994) 327–29, *328*; privatization of 348
Adoptive Couple v. Baby Girl (2013) 324–25

advance directive: a document or statement by patients specifying choices for medical treatment or designating a person to make those choices should the patient be unable to do so. 228, 361
advocacy: in the context of social work policy practice, the act of publicly supporting actions that will improve policies and programs that impact our clients. 7
AFDC *see* Aid to Families with Dependent Children (AFDC)
affirmative action: a general term that refers to policies and programs designed to compensate for discrimination against marginalized groups such as women and people of color. 77–78, 237–39, *238*
Affordable Care Act (ACA) (2010) 364–69, *366*; and Barack Obama 88, *88*, 89, 365; contraceptive coverage in 231; efforts to overturn/undermine 92, 176, 366–68, 400; financing and cost-control issues 387–88, *388*; health issues unaddressed by 368–69; and long-term care 436–37; and Maternal, Infant, and Early Childhood Home Visiting Program (MIECHV) 344–45; and mental health 400–1; and privacy rights 485; and social workers 407; Supreme Court Decision on (2012) 365
African Americans: and adoption 329; and child welfare system 329, 339; and civil rights movement 63–66, *64*, *65*; civil rights of 212–14, *215*; during Civil War era 41; employment of 62; and Freedmen's Bureau 41; Jim Crow laws 42, 63, 64–66; and the juvenile justice system 319; and law enforcement 282, 319, 339; and mental health system 389; mothers' pensions 49; and OASDI 295–96; population projection of 314; post-Independence treatment of 34–36, *35–36*; poverty rates of 270, 283, 295, 299, 315, *315*, 479; and Prohibition 51; during Reconstruction 41; slavery 32–33, 40–41; as social workers 47; voting rights 40–41; *see also* civil rights; discrimination

I-1

GLOSSARY/INDEX

Age Discrimination in Employment Act (ADEA) (1967) 227
ageism: discrimination based on age, usually directed towards older adults, but often towards children as well. 206–7; compassionate 228; and health care costs 400; and mandatory retirement 227
agencies, economic contexts of 135–38
agenda: "the list of subjects or problems to which government officials, and people outside of government closely associated with those officials, are paying some serious attention at any given time" (Kingdon, 2003, p. 3). 174–75, 185–86, *185*
aging in the community 431
aging well: a comprehensive and holistic process in which older adults adapt themselves and their environment to respond actively to the challenges of aging (Kahana & Kahana, 1996). 417–18, 442
AIDS/HIV 403, *404*
Aid to Dependent Children (ADC) 58
Aid to Families with Dependent Children (AFDC) 58–59, 69, 80–81, 83, 118, 155, 163, 271, 272
Alcatraz protest 75, *76*
almshouses: institutions for poor people supported by private funds and typically reserved for the "worthy poor," particularly the elderly. 30, 32
American Health Care Act (AHCA) (2017) 367
American Indian Movement (AIM) 75, 214
American Indians *see* Native Americans
American Recovery and Reinvestment Act (ARRA) (2009) 87, 267
American Red Cross 54–55
American Revolution 33
Americans with Disabilities Act (ADA) (1990) 9, *81*, 81–82, 224, 231–32, *241*
analysis *see* policy analysis
appropriations: the actual allocation of money to be spent on different programs. 119
Area Agencies on Aging (AAAs) 434
Area Redevelopment Act (1961) 69
ARRA *see* American Recovery and Reinvestment Act (ARRA) (2009)
ASFA *see* Adoption and Safe Families Act (ASFA) (1997)
Asian Americans *219*, 219–20, 232–33
asset-based policies and programs 299–301, *304*
asset poverty: measured by examining the extent to which people lack sufficient assets to continue to meet their basic needs during temporary hard times. 299
automation, occupational 473–75, *474*

Bakke, Allan 238
baseline data: data collected to understand the condition of the target group prior to an intervention. 191
Basic Income Grant (BIG) 73, 301–3
"bathroom bills" 223–24
Battered Immigrant Women's Protection Act (2000) 242
"benefit cliff" 292
benefits and services 159–60; cost-effectiveness and outcomes 164; eligibility rules 160–61; financing 163–64; service delivery systems 161–63, *162*
Better Care Reconciliation Act (BCRA) 367
BIA *see* Bureau of Indian Affairs (BIA)
BIG *see* Basic Income Grant (BIG)
Bill of Rights 211
Bipartisan Budget Act (2018) 331, 350
birth rates 217, 341, *342*, 467, 470
Black Lives Matter 213
Black power 72
block grants: funds made available by the federal government where much of the decision-making authority regarding how the money is to be spent is allocated to the states (Kenney, 1981). 81, 271–75, 382–83, 394–95
Brace, Charles Loring 43–44
Bracero Program 66
Bridges, Ruby *206*
Brill, Steven 405
Brown, Michael 213
Brown v. Board of Education of Topeka (1954) 63–64, 212
Buck v. Bell (1927) 391
Buddhism 23
budget allocation issues 120–21, *121*
Bureau of Indian Affairs (BIA) 36, 75
Bush, George H. W. 81–82, *82*
Bush, George W. 84–86, 110, 114, 224, 423
Bush v. Gore (2000) 84
Byrd, James, Jr. 243–44

campaign spending 89
Canada Child Benefit 311
capacity building approach: policies and programs that focus on strengthening the skills, competencies, and abilities of people and on helping them secure the resources they need for full economic and social inclusion. 63
capacity building state: focuses on strengthening the skills and competencies of people and on helping

them secure the resources and support needed for full economic and social inclusion. 108
capitalism 47, 105–6, 108, 110, 481–82
capitated approach: a strategy for providing health care in which an HMO or managed care provider is expected to provide all elements of health care covered in the enrollee's contract in return for a fixed payment per enrollee. 362
CAPTA *see* Child Abuse Prevention and Treatment Act (CAPTA) (1974)
CARA *see* Comprehensive Addiction and Recovery Act (CARA) (2016)
Carmichael, Stokely 72
Carter, Jimmy 74
case advocacy: advocacy that focuses on helping a particular client navigate existing systems. 46–47
categorical grants: funds made available by the federal government, which strictly stipulates how the monies could be spent for specific programs. 81
Catt, Carrie Chapman 55
causal theory 152–53
Centers for Medicare and Medicaid Services (CMS) 228, 381
Chafee Foster Care Independent Living Act (1999) 333
Chaney, James 65
Charity Organization Society (COS) 21, 42, 44, 46
Chavez, Cesar 67, 210, *210*
Cherokee Nation v. Georgia (1831) 37, 41, 214
Child Abuse Prevention and Treatment Act (CAPTA) (1974) 74, 321–22, *322*
Child and Dependent Care Tax Credit 344
Child and Family Services Improvement Act (2006) 327
child care 262
Child Care Development Block Grant (CCDBG) 343–44
Child Development Accounts (CDAs) 300–1
child labor *50*, 50–51
child maltreatment: "serious harm (neglect, physical abuse, sexual abuse, and emotional abuse or neglect) caused to children by parents or primary caregivers, such as extended family members or babysitters" (Child Abuse Prevention and Treatment Act, 1974). 315–18, 331, 340
Child Nutrition Act 5, 7
Child Protective Services (CPS) 310, 316
children: anti-poverty policy 297–98, *298*; with disabilities 239–40, *240*; evaluating policies and programs for 337–48, *338*; health insurance 382–84, *383*, *384*; history of programs protecting 312; and mental health 401–2; poverty rates 270, 292, 298, 315, *315*, 467; safety and family rights 339–45, *342*; with special needs 335–36; in the U.S. today 312–20, *313*, *314*, *315*; *see also* child welfare system; juvenile justice system
Children's Aid Society (CAS) 43, *43*
Children's Bureau 50, 57
Children's Health Insurance Program (CHIP) 370, 382–84, *383*, *384*
Children's Health Insurance Programs Reauthorization Act (CHIPRA) (2009) 383, *383*
Children's Savings Accounts (CSAs) 137, 300–1, 306
child-saving movement 42–44
Child Support Enforcement (CSE) program 333–35
Child Tax Credit (CTC) 288, *289*
child welfare system 309–52; and African Americans 329, 339; evaluating policies and programs 337–48, *338*; family reunification 340–41; history and background 50–51, 312; impact of poverty rates on 315–16; major policies and programs 320–36; and Native Americans 76–77; overview of 316–17; privatization of 342–43; programs (quick guide) *336–37*; role of social workers in 348; strategies to improve 343–45; from the strengths perspective 339; and teen pregnancy 341–42, *342*; transition services 332–33, *338*; *see also* juvenile justice system
Christianity 23, 24
citizenship 41, 94
Citizens United v. Federal Election Commission (2012) 89
Civilian Conservation Corps (CCC) 56
civil rights: legally enforceable protections that prevent the government, other entities, or individuals from arbitrarily abusing others. 205–57; of African Americans 63–66, *64*, *65*, 212–14, *215*; agency analysis (quick guide) *251*; of Asian Americans 219–20; background and history 205–11, *206*, *207–8*, *209*, *210*; and the Constitution 33–34; indicators of continued injustice *207–8*; of Latinx communities 66–67, *67*, 216–19; of LGBTQ+ individuals 68, 82, 220–24, *221*; major policies and programs 232–44; and Medicare, Medicaid 361; of Native Americans 75–77, *76*, 214–16; next steps 247–51; ongoing challenges 244–47; of people with disabilities 224–25, *225*; of people with mental illness 225–28; and regulatory retreat 93; of women 74, 228–32, *229*; *see also* African Americans
Civil Rights Act (1964) 66, 77–78, 233–34, *234*
Civil Rights Act (1991) 81, 233
Civil Rights Restoration Act (1987) 233
Civil War era 40–42

Civil Works Administration (CWA) 56
claims-making: work done by concerned individuals and groups to make the case to policymakers, key actors, and the public at large that resources should be allocated to meet a recognized need. 10–11; assumptions embedded in 155–56; bases of 154–55; groups involved in *173*, 173–74; and legislative agenda 174–75
class advocacy: advocacy that focuses on helping groups of clients and communities who have similar needs. 47
classical conservatives: advocate preservation of personal wealth, private ownership, and a *laissez-faire* approach to economics. 111
Clayton Antitrust Act (1914) 47
client groups: the population that is the primary focus of a social policy or program. 3; identifying and defining target 183–84, *184*; supporting 195
client outcomes, evaluating policy based on 189–91
client perspectives: identifying policy that includes 187; incorporating 159
clients: the recipient of the direct service or benefits a social worker provides. 3; expanding role of 10
climate change 90, 93, 113, 478–80, 488–90, *488*
Clinton, Bill 82–84
Clinton, Hillary 90, 112
Cloward, Richard 72
Coates, Ta-Nehisi 213
cohort-component method 463
communitarians: emphasize responsibility to community and advance a political philosophy that seeks a middle ground between liberal and conservative traditions. 112
community action programs (CAPs) 70
Community Living Assistance Services and Supports (CLASS) provision 436–37
community mental health 391–93
Comprehensive Addiction and Recovery Act (CARA) (2016) 321
concurrent planning: provides states with the option of working on an alternative plan for children receiving protective services even while attempting reunification (Adler, 2001). 329–30
conditional cash transfers: cash payments to poor families when they participate in services that build human capital (e.g., enrolling their children in early childhood programs). 477
conflict theory 247–48
Confucianism 23
consensus, achieving 176

conservatives 111–12
Constitution: 13th Amendment 41; 14th Amendment 41, 63, 64, 222; 15th Amendment 41; 16th Amendment 49; 18th Amendment 51; 19th Amendment 49, 55; 24th Amendment 66; Bill of Rights 211; and civil rights 33–34, 211; Equal Rights Amendment (ERA) 55–56, 74; *see also* civil rights
Consumer Price Index (CPI) 261, 262, 295
consumer-side economics *see* Keynesian economics
contraception 56, 144, 231, 367
Contract with America 83–84
convergence: the growing similarity in challenges countries face and policies they enact. 477
cost-benefit analysis 189
cost-effectiveness 164
Council on Social Work Education (CSWE) 479
countercyclical programs: programs that always grow to meet rising need during economic downturns. 120
Curtis, Lois 224, *225*

Dakota Access pipeline 216
Daughters of Bilitis 68
Dawes Act (1887) 37, 214
death with dignity 447
decision agenda 174
deep poverty 71, 270, 276, 442
de facto segregation: segregation caused due to social practices, political acts, or economic circumstances, not by explicit laws. 245
Defense of Marriage Act (DOMA) (1996) 222
Deferred Action for Childhood Arrivals (DACA) (2017) 94, 246–47
Deferred Action for Parental Accountability (DAPA) 246–47
Deficit Reduction Act (DRA) (2005) 273
defined benefit plans: pension plans under which the retiree is paid a specific amount every month if the retired person has worked the required number of years. 420
defined contribution plans: pension plans whereby employers contribute to a retirement account that the employee can then invest in company-approved fund options. Unlike defined benefit plans, defined contribution plans do not guarantee a specific retirement income. 421
deinstitutionalization: providing community-based services for people who were formerly served in institutions. 68, 81, 391–94
demand-side economics *see* Keynesian economics

Democratic Leadership Council (DLC) 82
Democratic Party 33, 41, 82–84, 109, 112
democratic socialism: posits that because capitalism is predicated on the pursuit of individual self-interest and profit, it inevitably increases social inequality and cannot be relied on to advance the public good. 110, 112
demogrant 73
Developmentally Disabled Assistance and Bill of Rights (2000) 224
devolution: transfer of responsibility for social welfare from the federal government to the states. 79, 80–82, *82*, 486–88
diagnosis-related groups 362
disabilities, people with: Americans with Disabilities Act (ADA) (1990) 9, *81*, 81–82, 224, 231–32, *241*; children 239–40, *240*; civil rights of 224–25, *225*; and Medicaid 83; and Medicare 83, 85; *Olmstead* ruling for 224, *225*; and special education 240, 335; strengths perspective view of 8–9; Supplemental Security Income (SSI) program 285; Ticket to Work and Work Incentives Improvement Act (1999) 83
disability insurance 59, 263–64, 286, 393
discretionary spending: all the spending authorized by the 13 appropriation bills that are passed each year by Congress, including funding for national defense, transportation, educational and social programs, agriculture, and general operation of the government. 117–18, *118*, 121, *121*
discrimination: against African Americans 51, 212–14, *215*; against Asian Americans 219–20; employment 77–78, 82, 227; Genetic Information Non-Discrimination Act (2008) 485; against immigrants 38–39, 94–95; against Latinx communities 210, *211*, 216–19; against LGBTQ+ individuals 220–24, *221*; and mothers' pensions 49; against Native Americans 214–16; and "neutral" policies 248–49; against older adults 226–28, 400; against people with disabilities 224–25, *225*; against people with mental illness 225–26; and Prohibition enforcement 51; reverse discrimination 78; structural discrimination 209; against women 69, 228–32, *229*, 484; *see also* racism
disenfranchised groups 211–32, *215*, 219, *221*, *225*, *229*
diversity 6, 248
divorce rates 440
Dix, Dorothea 39–40, 391
Domenici, Pete 364
domestic violence *see* family violence

"Don't Ask, Don't Tell" policy 223
Douglass, Frederick 32
Dred Scott v. Sandford (1857) 34
drug abuse *see* substance use disorders
dual assessment: the act of examining clients' needs and goals as well as the policies and programs that either help or create barriers to the achievement of their goals. 7, 167
dual eligible: individuals who are simultaneously eligible for both Medicare and Medicaid coverage. 381

Earned Income Tax Credit (EITC) 73, 119, 125, 180, 262, 287–89, *289*
Ebola virus 403
ecological perspective: in social work, this perspective focuses on the ways in which people and their environment influence, change, and shape each other (Germain, 1991). 181–82, 270–71, 418
economic context: context of social policy that focuses on the production, distribution, and use of resources. 99; affecting social policy 100–3; of agencies 135–38; influences on the social welfare system 104–16; schools of thought 108–10
economic efficiency 102, 127
economic justice: an ideal condition in which all members of society have sufficient opportunities to obtain material resources necessary to survive and fulfill their potential. 99
economic mobility 128
economic nationalism: the practice of using policy to bolster and protect national economies in the context of world economic markets. 113
Economic Opportunity Act (1964) 70
economic security 419–24, *422*, *440*, 440–43, *441*, 449–51
economics *see* democratic socialism; Keynesian economics; supply-side economics
education: and affirmative action 77–78; for children with special needs 240, 335; as protective factor 346; segregation 63–64; zero-tolerance policies 218, 346; *see also* public schools
Education for All Handicapped Children Act (1975) 224, 239–40, *240*
elder abuse: mistreatment of an older adult that results in harm or loss. 437
Elder Abuse Prevention and Prosecution Act (2017) 437
Elder Justice Act 437–38, *438*

elderly adults *see* older adults
electoral processes 489–90
eligibility rules 160–61, 381
Elk v. Wilkins (1884) 41
Emanuel African Methodist Episcopal Church (Charleston, SC) 213
Employee Retirement Income Security Act (ERISA) (1974): the first comprehensive effort to regulate private pensions. 420–21, 435–36, *436*
employment: and affirmative action 77–78; of African Americans 62; and benefits, as tied to 273–77; discrimination 77–78, 82, 227; future of 482–85; job-specific pension programs, changes to 420–21; occupational automation 473–75, *474*; unemployment insurance 266–68, *268*; welfare-to-work (WTW) 277; of women 59–62, *61*; workers' compensation 268–69, *269*
empowerment 11, 247–48, 290
enabling niches: environments that provide resources to help people meet their needs. 182
enabling state: one where public benefits are provided in order to help people be more productive workers. 108
end-of-life planning 446–47
English Poor Laws *see* Poor Laws
entitlement program: government programs for which all people who meet the eligibility requirements legally qualify. 117, 263
entrapping niches: environments with barriers that prevent people from filling their needs. 182
environmental justice 478–80, 487–90, *488*
Environmental Protection Agency 93
Equal Employment Opportunity Commission (EEOC) 222
Equality Index 250
equality *vs.* equity *209*
Equal Pay Act (1963) 69, 228
Equal Rights Amendment (ERA) 55, 74
equity 6, 103
Every Student Succeeds Act (2015) 336
executive branch: the division of federal government that includes the president, the vice-president, the cabinet, the president's advisers, and all the offices and agencies that serve the president. 114

Fair Employment Practices Commission (FEPC) 62
faith-based initiatives 25–26, 85
Family and Medical Leave Act (FMLA) (1993) 83
family assistance 72–73
Family Assistance Plan (FAP) 72–73

Family First Prevention Services Act (FFPSA) (2018) 331–32, *332*
family leave 83
Family Preservation and Support Services: encourage the development of cohesive, community-based, family-centered supports that involve collaboration between child welfare workers and other service providers, toward the goal of safe, nurturing home environments. 327
family reunification 340–41
family rights 339–45, *342*
family violence 145
Family Voices 337–38
federal budget and spending 117–21, *118*, *119*, *121*
federal debt 119–20
federal deficit *119*, 119–20
Federal Emergency Relief Administration (FERA) 57
Federal Insurance Contribution Act (FICA) 123, 265, 296
federal judiciary 93–94
fee-for-service systems: systems that provide payment for specific services rendered. 361
feminization of poverty: the disproportionately high number of women who are living in poverty. 230
fertility rates 313, 463, 468
fiscal conservatives: prioritize reducing government spending and the federal debt. 111
fiscal impact statement: estimate prepared by a government agency that predicts how legislation would affect public finances. 189
fiscal policy: policy designed to regulate the economy by increasing or decreasing spending and taxes in response to economic conditions. 109
Fisher v. University of Texas (2013) 238
Food Stamp Act (1964) 71
Food Stamp Program *see* Supplemental Nutrition Assistance Program (SNAP)
Ford, Gerald 73, 74
foster care system 183, 326–33, 340–41, 401; transition services 332–33, *338*
Fostering Connections to Success and Increasing Adoptions Act (2008) 325, 333
Freedmen's Bureau 41
Friedan, Betty 74
Friedman, Milton 109
Full Employment and Balanced Growth Act (1978) 74
"full-family sanctions" 274
funding: evaluating 134; federal budget and spending policies 117–21, *118*, *119*, *121*; from private sector 133–34; public *vs.* private 34; state budgets and spending policies 121–22; tax strategies 123–26,

124, 125; see also economic context; social welfare expenditures
funding cuts 85–86, 91, 122, 321, 392, 404, *406*, 436
future forecasts *458*, 458–96; and devolution 486–87; and electoral processes 489–90; employment 473–75, *474*, 482–85; environment and climate change 90, 93, 113, 478–80, 487–89, *488*; global political realignments 475–78; guidelines for understanding *460*, 460–62; health care 485; information technology and privacy 485–86; medical/technological advances 470–73; older adults 427–33, *428*, *429*, *430*; policy directions 481–91; population growth and shifts 467–70, *468*, *469*; social work Grand Challenges 491–92, *491*; State of the Future Index (SOFI) *480*, 480–81; and strengths perspective 466–67, 490

Gadsden Purchase (1853) 38
gag rules 83
gender identity: a person's internal sense of belonging to the categories of "male," "female," "both," or "neither." 220–24, *221*
General Assistance (GA) 286–87, *287*
general tax revenue 58, 118, 280, 381, 424
Genetic Information Non-Discrimination Act (2008) 485
geography of opportunity 486–87
GI Bill of Rights (1944) 62–63, 79
Gingrich, Newt 83
Global Gender Gap Index 228
globalization: the economic, political, and social integration of the world's nations. ramifications of 135–38; and social development 137–38
global political realignments 475–78
Goldberg v. Kelly (1970) 161
government, branches of 114–16, *116*
Graham v. Florida (2010) 320
Gratz v. Bollinger (1998) 238
Great Depression 50, 56–58
Great Recession 85–87, 109, 264
Great Society initiatives 70
gross domestic product (GDP): the total monetary value of all goods and services produced in a country annually. 117
Gross v. FBL Financial, Inc. (2009) 227
Grutter v. Bollinger (1998) 238

Hacker, Jacob 79
Ham and Eggs movement: a movement that pressed for weekly pensions for unemployed Californians age 50 and older. 420

Harding, Warren G. 56
Harrington, Michael 69
Hatch Act (1939) 196
hate crimes 243–44, *244*
Head Start 70
health, strategies to promote 406–7
health care 353–414, *354*; and civil rights 361; costs of 359–64, 368, 400; current state of, in the U.S. *354*, 354–69, *358*; evaluating 397–404, *398*; federal involvement in, growing 360–61; finance and cost control, background on 361–64; future directions of 485; and immigrants 357, 372; major policies and programs 369–88; for older adults 400, 424–27, 444–47, *446*; reforms 83, 88, *88*, 364, 404–9; single-payer health care plan 365; *see also* Affordable Care Act (ACA) (2010); Medicaid; Medicare; mental health policies and programs
Health Care and Education Affordability Reconciliation Act 88, 353, 364–65, 406
Health Insurance Portability and Accountability Act (HIPAA) (1996) 364
health maintenance organizations (HMOs): provide health care for each member enrolled in its system in return for an amount, per person, decided in advance by insurers. 364
Health Savings Accounts (HSAs) 363–64
Health Security Act (1994) 83
Height, Dorothy I. 66
Helping Families Save Their Home Act (2009) 148–49
heterosexism: discrimination against people who are LGBTQ+, based on their sexual orientation or gender identity. 206
Hill–Burton Act (1946) 360
Hispanics/Latinos *see* Latinx
historical context 21–52; colonial- to progressive-era social policies 31–50; and current policy, framework for linking *25*, 25–27; English poor laws 27–30; and genesis of social welfare policy 22–25
HIV/AIDS 403, *404*
Holocaust 62
home and community based services (HCBS): services and supports that assist individuals to continue to live within their communities. 425–27
HOME Investment Partnership programs 284
Homeless Emergency Assistance and Rapid Transition to Housing (HEARTH) Act (2013) 148–53, 155, 164
homelessness 8, 10, 141–42, 283; *see also* housing programs; rapid rehousing
Homestead Act (1862) 42
homophobia 221, 243

Hoover, Herbert 56
Hopkins, Harry 57, *57*
horizontal equity: equal distribution of resources to people irrespective of factors such as demographics, location, and socioeconomic status. 103
hospice care: an approach to end-of-life care that focuses on comfort and alleviating pain rather than treating illness. 446
housing programs *162*, 162–63, 281–82
Huerta, Dolores 67, *67*, 210
Hull House 44, *45*, 46
human capital: productive capacity, which can be enhanced through programs such as education, health care, and job training. 109
human trafficking 472

ideology 152
immigrants: children of 314; discrimination against 38–39, 94–95; and the education system *168–69*; and health care 357, 372; ineligibility for services/programs 279, 286, 372; and law enforcement 246, 282; and Medicaid 372; older adults 443; and the Personal Responsibility and Work Opportunity Reconciliation Act (PRWORA) (1996) 84
immigration 27–28; during Civil War era 34–40, *35–36*, *38*, *40*; Obama Administration policy on 89; during Progressive era 51; Trump Administration policies on 94–95, 101, 217–18, 246–47, 479
Immigration and Nationality Act (1965) 219
incarceration 212, 232, 393–94; *see also* juvenile justice system
inclusion: educating children with disabilities in classrooms with their peers without disabilities. 240
income distribution 127–29, *128*
income-support policies and programs 262–63; and anti-poverty policy 297–303; evaluation of 290–97; quick guide to *304*; selective programs 270–89; universal programs 263–70
income tax: corporate income tax 91; Earned Income Tax Credit (EITC) 73, 119, 125, 180, 262, 287–89, *289*; negative income tax 72; overview of 123; as progressive tax strategy 49
indentured servitude 32–33
independent living transition services 332–33
Independent Payment Advisory Board (IPAB) 387
Indian Appropriation Act (1851) 37
Indian Child Welfare Act (ICWA) (1978) 76–77, 323–25, *324*, *325*, 328
Indian Health Service (IHS) 357
Indian Removal Act (1830) 36–37
Indian Reorganization Act (1934) 75
Indian Self-Determination and Education Assistance Act (1975) 214
Individual Development Accounts (IDAs) 300
individual responsibility 79–80
Individual Retirement Accounts (IRAs) 300
Individuals with Disabilities Education Act (IDEA) (1990) 188, 240
industrialization 105, 419
industrialization-welfare hypothesis: emphasizes industrialization as a significant factor in the development of the welfare state. 105
inequality *see* income inequality
infant mortality rates 133, 315, 369, 409
information technology 485–86
infrastructure 451–52
institutional approach: asserts that government should ensure that everyone's basic needs are met as a right of membership in advanced economies. 31, 103–4
intellectual disabilities 68
intersectionality: the interrelation or intersection of forms of oppression such as race and gender, which can create interdependent systems of disadvantage and discrimination. 66, 207
Involuntary Outpatient Commitments (IOCs) 392
Islam 22–23, 94; *see also* Muslims

Jackson, Andrew 37
Japanese Americans 62
Jefferson, Thomas 33
Jim Crow laws: laws that legally separated Blacks and Whites in public areas and institutions, including schools, restaurants, theaters, hospitals, and parks. 42, 63, 64–66
jobs *see* employment
Johnson, Lyndon B. 69, 70, 234
Judaism 22
judicial branch: the division of government comprising the court system. Both federal and state judiciaries include a supreme court, a court of appeals, and courts of original jurisdiction 115
Juvenile Justice and Delinquency Prevention Act (JJDPA) (1974) 322–23, *323*
juvenile justice system 317–20, *319*, *320*; child welfare programs *336–37*; major policies and programs affecting 320–36; programs (quick guide) *336–37*; from the strengths perspective 345–47; *see also* child welfare system

Kavanaugh, Brett 93, 232
Keating-Owen Child Labor Act (1916) 51
Keeping Children and Families Safe Act (2003) 321
Kelley, Florence 46
Kennedy, John F. 65, 68, 69, 258
Keynes, John Maynard 56, 109
Keynesian economics: (also referred to as demand-side economics): an economic school of thought that supports government intervention to help stimulate and regulate the economy. 109, 113
King, Coretta Scott *210*
King, Martin Luther, Jr. 64, 66–67, 72
King, Rodney 81
Kinsey, Alfred 68
kinship care: child living with relatives without a parent present in the home. 340
Ku Klux Klan 41, 51

latent goals: goals that are not typically publicized because it would be difficult to achieve a consensus to support these goals, or the goals would not be considered socially acceptable. 158–59
Lathrop, Julia 50
Latinas, mothers' pensions 49
Latinx, as term 20n1
Latinx communities: children in foster care 328; and civil rights 66–67, *67*; discrimination against 210, *211*, 216–19; future projections for 464, 466–67, 469, *469*; in juvenile justice system 319; and OASDI 295–96; poverty rates of 270, 292; and territory in the southwest 37–38
Ledbetter, Lilly 229, *229*, 243–44, *244*
Ledbetter v. Goodyear Tire & Rubber Co. 229
legislative agenda 174–75
legislative branch: the division of government charged with passing legislation. At the federal level and in most states, it consists of two chambers. 115
legislative process 115–16, *116*
lesbian, gay, bisexual, transgender, questioning (LGBTQ+) individuals: civil rights of 68, 82, 220–24, *221*; in juvenile justice system 319–20; older adults 430–31
Lewis, John 65, *65*
LGBTQ+ *see* lesbian, gay, bisexual, transgender, queer (LGBTQ+) individuals
liberalism: a political philosophy that endorses individual freedom and advocates government intervention to ensure an adequate minimum living condition for all people 109, 111–12

liberals: believe in an active government role in achieving a just society. 111–12
libertarians: advocate unrestricted liberty and posit that government grows at the expense of individual freedom. 112
licensure 78
life expectancy 265, 355, 359, 416–17, *417*, *418*, 428, *428*, 448, 486
Lilly Ledbetter Fair Pay Act (2009) 229, *229*, 243, *244*
Lincoln, Abraham 40
living wage: the income necessary to live adequately within a given community. 292
local responsibility: a principle that mandates that each locality should be responsible for helping only its own residents. 28
long-term care (LTC): services designed to meet a person's health or personal care needs, to help them live as independently and safely as possible when they can no longer perform everyday activities on their own (National Institute on Aging, 2019). 425–27, 436–37, 444–45
Lowell, Josephine Shaw 21, 44
Low-Income Housing Tax Credits 284

macro-level practice: practice that involves intervening in large systems and that may affect policies and practices at the agency, local, state, national, and global levels. 7
maintenance of capitalism hypothesis: contends that the welfare state specifically encourages capitalism by providing some assistance in order to reduce the pressure for radical political and economic restructuring. 105–6
"maintenance of effort" (MOE) 271
Malcolm X 72
male privilege: societal advantages and rights that accrue to individuals identified as male. 249
managed care: a health care system under which the insurer controls the person's health care. 362; and Medicaid 374–76; and mental health 394–95, *395*
mandatory spending: government spending directed toward individuals and institutions that are legally entitled to it. 117–18, *118*, 120–21, *121*
manifest goals: publicly stated goals. 158–59
Manning, Leah Katherine Hicks 76, *77*
Manpower Development Training Act (MDTA) (1962) 69
March on Washington movement 62, 81, *215*
market failure: a "circumstance in which the pursuit of private interest does not lead to an efficient

use of society's resources or a fair distribution of society's goods" (Weimer & Vining, 1999, p. 41). 102
marketplace economy: people exchange goods and services to meet their needs. 100
Marshall and Titmuss hypotheses 106
Martin, Trayvon 213
Maternal, Infant, and Early Childhood Home Visiting Program (MIECHV) 344–45
maternalistic approaches 49–50
Mattachine Society 68
Matthew Shepard and James Byrd, Jr. Hate Crimes Prevention Act (2009) 243–44, *244*
McKinney, Stewart B. *147*
McKinney–Vento Homeless Assistance Act (1987) 147–49, *148*, 155, 158, 160, 162, 164
means testing: a method of determining eligibility for benefits based on the applicant's financial circumstances, usually focused on income. 71, 104
Meat Inspection Act (1906) 49
median income 282–83, 421
Medicaid: a health care program for certain categories of people with very low incomes, jointly funded by the federal and state governments. 369–77, *375*; and children 370, *370*; and civil rights 361; eligibility for 161, 180; establishment of 70–71; and family leave 83; and health care access *376*, 376–77; and health reforms *407*, 407–8, *408*; and managed care 374–76; mandatory and optional coverage 371; and people with disabilities 83; and the Personal Responsibility and Work Opportunity Reconciliation Act (PRWORA) (1996) 371–72; policy changes to 188; waivers and variations among states 372–74, *373*
Medicaid Home- and Community-Based Waivers 80
medical advances 470–73
medical model 8, 46
Medical Savings Accounts (MSAs) 364
Medicare: a national government health insurance program for people 65 or older who are eligible for Social Security and for certain categories of younger people with disabilities. *377*, 377–80; challenges for *399*, 399–400; and civil rights 361; and the conservative agenda 78, 85; cost debate on 400; enrollment *380*, 381; establishment of 70–71; and family leave 83; financing 120, 380–82, 465; and people with disabilities 83, 85; and the private sector 85, 161; reforms 188, 405, 461
Medicare Access and CHIP Reauthorization Act (MACRA) (2015) 382, 383

Medicare Improvement for Patients and Providers Act (2008) 445
Medicare Part A, Hospital Insurance (HI) 377–78
Medicare Part B 378
Medicare Part C (Medicare Advantage) 378
Medicare Part D 85, 378–79
Medicare Trust Funds 382
Mental Health Act (1946) 63
Mental Health Bill of Rights Act (2011) 224
Mental Health Parity Act (1996) 226, 364
mental health policies and programs: and block grants 81; and children 401–2; and civil rights 68, 225–26; community-based 391–93; and deinstitutionalization 391–93; history and background of 391–94; incarceration of people with mental illness 393–94; major 388–97, *390*; managed care and 394–95, *395*; for older adults 425, 445–46, *446*; parity and concerns for specific populations 400–2; prevalence of mental health issues *390*; promoting more effective care *406*, 406–9, *407*, *408*; reform 39–40; and substance use disorders 395–97, *396*; veterans' 401
Mental Health Systems Act (1980) 392
mental hygiene movement 391
Mentally Ill Offender Treatment and Crime Reduction Act (MIOTCRA) (2018) 393–94
Mental Retardation Community Mental Health Centers Construction Act (1963 and 1965) 68, 394, *395*
Me Too movement 231–32
mezzo-level practice: practice that may involve work with groups and neighborhoods. 7
micro-level practice: practice that focuses on engaging clients at the individual level. 7
Midgley, James 104–5
Miller v. Alabama (2012) 320
minimum wage 84, 292–93
monetarism: theory that posits that stable economic growth is best promoted by controlling the amount of money circulating in the economy to match the capacity for productive growth. 109
Montgomery bus boycott 64
morals tests 49
mothers' pensions 49–50
Mott, Lucretia 55
Moving to Opportunity 283–84, *284*
Moynihan, Daniel Patrick 72
Multidimensional Poverty Index (MPI) 303
Multi-Ethnic Placement Act (MEPA) (1994) 327–29, *328*
Muslims 85, 89, 94

National Alliance on Mental Illness (NAMI) 17
National American Woman Suffrage Association (NAWSA) 55
National Association for the Advancement of Colored People (NAACP) 49, 63, 213
National Association of Black Social Workers (NABSW) 328
National Association of Colored Women's Clubs (NACWC) 47
National Association of Social Workers (NASW) 3, 16, 74, 92, 192, 221, 247, 249–50, 318, 348; Code of Ethics 3, 6, 16, 78, 167, 181, 205, 221, 247; *Policy Statement on Juvenile Justice and Delinquency Prevention* 347
National Committee on Lesbian, Gay, Bisexual, and Transgender Issues (NCLGBTI) 221
National Conference of Charities and Correction 46
National Congress of American Indians (NCAI) 75
National Family Caregiver Support Program: an AOA program to help sustain caregivers and guard against social isolation. 434
National Farm Workers Association 67
National Institute of Mental Health (NIMH): part of the National Institute of Health in the Department of Health and Human Services; the federal agency primarily responsible for research on mental and behavioral disorders. 63, 391
National Institute on Aging (NIA) 424
National Organization for Women (NOW) 74
National Social Work Exchange 46
National Urban League 49, 250
National Women's Political Caucus 66
Native Americans: and child welfare 76–77, 316; and civil rights 75–77, *76*, 214–16; during Civil War era 36–37, *38*; colonial-era policy 31–34; Homestead Act (1862) 42; Indian Child Welfare Act (ICWA) (1978) 76–77, 323–25, *324*, *325*, 328; Indian Health Service (IHS) 357; Indian Removal Act (1830) 36–37; Indian Reorganization Act (1934) 75; Indian Self-Determination and Education Assistance Act (1975) 214; and Medicaid 248–49; militancy and sovereignty 75–76, *76*, 216; mothers' pensions 49; and population forecasts 314; poverty rates of 292; during Reconstruction 41; spiritual traditions 23; termination and relocation policies 75
naturally occurring retirement communities (NORCs): communities where individuals either remain or move when they retire, and where people have opportunities and resources to facilitate social engagement and health. 449

need: the gap between an existing condition and some societal standard or required condition. 2
needs determination: defining 144–45; defining and documenting 147–52, *148*; groups involved in *173*, 173–74; and making claims 172–75, *173*; as shaping policy 146–47; and strengths perspective 146–47
negative income tax 72
neglect: the failure of caregivers to provide for basic needs such as nutrition, shelter, emotional care, and supervision. 316
neoliberals 111
"neutral" policies 248–49
New Deal 56–60, 74, 75, 109
"New Democrats" 82–84
New Federalism 80–82, *82*, 393
New Frontier programs 69–70
Nixon, Richard 72–73, 75
NORCs *see* naturally occurring retirement communities (NORCs)
normalization: a policy whereby schools endeavor to create an environment for children with disabilities similar to that experienced by other children. 335
nursing home care 71, 370, 426
Nursing Home Reform Act (1987) 426

Obama, Barack: and the Affordable Care Act (2010) 365; and Dakota Access pipeline 216; economic and political influences on policies 113–14; and family formation initiatives 273; and the Homeless Emergency Assistance and Rapid Transition to Housing (HEARTH) Act (2009) 148; and immigration policy 246; and Keynesian economics 109; and LGBTQ+ civil rights 224; and the *Olmstead* ruling for people with disabilities 224, *225*; social policies of 86–90, *88*; on social welfare 54; *see also* Affordable Care Act (2010)
Obergefell v. Hodges (2015) 222–23
Office of Management Budget (OMB) 117, 261
Old-Age, Survivors, and Disability Insurance (OASDI): benefits of 263–66, *264*, *266*; establishment of 58, 102; and people of color 295–96; and Poor Laws 30; and poverty 59; as regressive and progressive 296; solvency and reform of 296–97, 442, 450–51; and SSI 423, 424; and strengths perspective 294–97; and women 294–95
Old Age and Survivors' Insurance (OASI) 59
Old Age Insurance (OAI) 59
older adults 415–57, *416*, *417*, *418*, *419*; civil rights of 226–28; Community Living Assistance Services and Supports (CLASS) provisions 436–37;

demographics and future policy for 427–33, *428, 429, 430*; and economic security *440*, 440–43, *441*, 449–51; Elder Justice Act 437–38, *438*; Employee Retirement Income Security Act (ERISA) (1974) 420–21, 435–36, *436*; end-of-life planning 446–47; evaluating policies and programs for 438–52, *439*; gerontological professionals, shortage of 427; health care policies 424–27, 444–47, *446*; healthy lives of, supporting 448–49; infrastructure for 451–52; life expectancy rates *417, 418, 428*; long-term care (LTC) 425–27, 436–37, 444–45; major policies and programs for 433–38; and mental health 425, 445–46, *446*; National Institute on Aging (NIA) 424; pension programs, job-specific 420–23, *422*; policy and program responses 419–27; and poverty 431; prescription drug policy for 427; retirement programs for 420; social engagement policies 424–27, 447–48; strength-based agenda, development of 451; Supplemental Security Income (SSI) program 73, 80, *285*, 285–86, *286*, 423–24; voting patterns of *432*, 432–33, *433*

Older Americans Act (OAA) (1965): a federal law passed in 1965 designed to improve the coordination of programs for older adults that support their efforts to remain in the community. 71, 415, 424, 433–35, *435*

Older Workers Benefit Protection Act (OWBPA) (1990) 227

Olmstead v. L.C. (1999) 224–25, *225*, 226

Omnibus Budget Reconciliation Act (OBRA) (1981) 80–82, *81, 82*, 426

opioid epidemic 188, 228, 323, 396–97, 402

opportunity cost: loss of potential gain from other policy alternatives when one policy approach is chosen. 177

opposition 194–95

Organisation for Economic Co-operation and Development (OECD) 131

orphan trains 43–44

Orshansky, Mollie 260

outcomes: and cost-effectiveness 164; evaluating 180; evaluating policies based on 189–91

outdoor relief: aid provided to people in their homes or other non-institutional settings. 30

overpopulation 463

overservice 361, 362

pandemics: epidemics that occur across large regions. 403–4, *404*

Parks, Rosa 64, *64*

participatory action research: research that occurs when practitioners, researchers, and people in groups under study collaborate to conduct research to contribute to social action. 186

Patient-Centered Outcomes Research Institute (PCORI) 387

Patient Protection and Affordable Care Act (2010) *see* Affordable Care Act (ACA) (2010)

Patient Safety and Abuse Prevention Act 437–38, *438*

Patients' Self-Determination Act (1990) 227–28

PATRIOT Act 174, 246

Paul Wellstone and Pete Domenici Mental Health Parity and Addiction Equity Act (2008) 364, 400

Pay Check Fairness Act 228–30

payment bundling: an approach where insurance providers pay hospitals and physicians a lump sum for an episode of care rather than paying separately for each service. 363

payroll tax: taxes that your employer deducts from your pay and sends to the government 58, 123

Pell Grants 124

Pension Benefit Guaranty Corporation (PBGC) 435–36

pension programs 420–23, *422*

Pension Protection Act (2006) 435

Perkins, Frances 57, *60*

Perkins, K. 34

Personal Responsibility and Work Opportunity Reconciliation Act (PRWORA) (1996) 83–84, 273–74, 277, 371–72

phased retirement: an approach whereby an individual reduces the hours worked during the years leading up to retirement. 442

philanthropy 34

Pierce, Franklin 39–40

Piketty, Thomas 129

Piven, Frances 72

Planned Parenthood 56

Plessy v. Ferguson (1896) 42, 63

pluralism 108–9, 487

polarization 486

policy analysis framework 156–64, *157*; benefits/services provided 159–60; cost-effectiveness and outcomes 164; eligibility rules 160–61; financing 163–64; fundamentals 141–45; overview (quick guide) *171*; and policy goals and objectives *157*, 157–59; service delivery systems 161–63, *162*

policy development: the process by which policies are created and implemented to meet identified needs. 167–204; action plans 193–97, *194, 195, 198–203*; ecological perspective 181–82; research and practice 182–91; sample action plan (quick guide) *198–203*; seeking support *192*, 192–93, *193*; social workers' role in 181–82; steps in 170–80; "workability" of alternatives 177–79

policy entrepreneurship: actions to take advantage of opportunities to influence policy outcomes (Kingdon, 2003). 167

policy goal: a statement of the desired human condition or social environment that is expected to result from implementation of a policy. *157*, 157–59; crafting *175*, 175–76; locating 158; manifest and latent 158–59; negotiating 187

policy impact analysis 190

policymakers 195–96

policy objectives: specific statements that operationalize desired results and provide detail about services and outcomes on which programs are evaluated. 158

policy practice: "professional efforts to influence the development, enactment, implementation, modification, or assessment of social policies, primarily to ensure social justice and equal access to basic social goods" (Barker, 2003, p. 330). 6; and clients 183–84, *184*, 187, 189–91; connecting social work values to 15; developing abilities for 15–17, *17*; ecological perspective 181–82; feasibility of ideas 188–89; and policymakers' agendas *185*, 185–86; and social workers' views 184–85; and social work values 6–7; and strengths perspective 9–13, *11*; *see also* **macro-level practice; mezzo-level practice; micro-level practice; social policy(ies)**

Political Action for Candidate Election (PACE) 192–93

political activism: actions taken to influence the outcome of elections or government decisions. 193, *193*, 196–97

political capital 113

political context: context of social policy that focuses on the pursuit and exercise of power in public affairs. 99

poor, the: colonial-era America 31–32; religious views on 22–23; "worthy" *vs.* "unworthy" 24, 29–31, 43, 59, 134, 152; *see also* poverty

Poor Laws 27–30, *29*, 84

population projection: the number of people who are expected to be in a given group in a specific year. 27–28, 314, 463, 467–70, *468*, *469*

populists: claim to represent the unified "will of the people," in opposition to an enemy, according to a view that sees society as separated into two groups—the "pure people" and the "corrupt elite." 112–13

poverty: absolute poverty 259–60; alternative measures 262; anti-poverty policy 297–303; anti-poverty social work practice 303–5; asset poverty 299; child welfare, impact on 315–16; deep poverty 71, 270, 276, 442; definitions of 259–62; feminization of 230; global context 303; guidelines on 261; and Latinx communities 270, 292; and Native Americans 292; and older adults 431; and the Poor Law 28; rates of 270, 292, 298, 315, *315*, 467; relative poverty 260; Roadmap to Reducing Child Poverty 297–98, *298*; and Social Darwinism 24; and universal-basic income 301–3; War on Poverty initiatives 69–72

poverty guidelines 261

poverty line/threshold: a yearly cash income threshold determined by the federal government and used to classify individuals or families as poor; also described as the *poverty index* or *level*. 259, 260–61

poverty rates 67, 71, 73, 81, 85, 230, 260, 262, 290, *291*, 295, 299, 303, 311, 315–16, 431, 481; child 270, 292, 298, 315, *315*, 467

preschool 177–78, 189, 311, 404

privacy 485–86

privatization: the practice of transferring ownership or control from government to private enterprise. 79–80; of child welfare system 342–43; and faith-based initiatives 85; of foster care and adoptions 348; and Medicare 85, 161; retirement programs 420; role of private sector 133–34

privilege 249

Progressive Era 46, 47–51, *48*, *50*, 112

progressive taxes: taxes that require people with higher incomes to pay higher rates or proportions of their income, compared to lower-income taxpayers. 123

Prohibition 51

Promoting Safe and Stable Families (PSSF) (1997) 327

prospective payment: a reimbursement strategy whereby the insurer determines ahead of time the average cost for a procedure in a previous year and then sets an amount they will pay the provider for the service—before treatment is provided. 362

protected classes: people who are members of specified groups, including women; any group that shares a common race, religion, color, or national origin; people over 40; and people with physical or mental disabilities. 250

Protestant work ethic 24
PRWORA *see* Personal Responsibility and Work Opportunity Reconciliation Act (PRWORA) (1996)
public housing 281–82
public institutions 39
public opinion 46, 95, 101, 186
public retirement programs 420
purchase-of-service (POS) contracting: the government contracts with private entities to provide services rather than providing services directly (Petr, 2004). 342
Pure Food and Drug Act (1906) 49

racism: prejudice or discrimination directed against someone of a different race based on the belief that one's own race is superior. 206; and African American social workers 47; and Fair Employment Practices Commission (FEPC) 62; and Jim Crow laws 42, 63, 64–66; *see also* discrimination
Randolph, A. Philip 62
Rank, Mark 270
Rankin, Jeanette 55
rapid rehousing *162*, 162–63
Reagan, Ronald 54, 62, 78–81, 109, 233, 393
reality, alternative views on 145
Reconstruction 41
redistributive process 120
Regents of the University of California, The, v. Bakke (1978) 238
regressive taxes: taxes that require people with lower incomes to pay higher rates or proportions of their income, compared to higher-income taxpayers. 123
regulatory policies 100–1
regulatory retreat 92–93
relative poverty: a measure of poverty influenced heavily by societal standards, whereby a threshold of income is determined that will allow people to afford what is generally considered to be an adequate standard of living at a given time and place. 260
religious and spiritual traditions 22–23
religious institutions 25–26
replacement rate 468
Republican Party 36, 41, 111, 112
residual approach: posits that government should intervene only when the family, religious institutions, the marketplace, and other private entities are unable to adequately meet needs. 31, 103–4
retirement programs 300, 420–21, 435–36, *436*, 442, 449, 484–85

retrospective payment: a reimbursement strategy whereby the provider submits a bill after services have been rendered and the insurer then reimburses the provider. 361
reverse discrimination: discrimination against the dominant group due to policies designed to redress discrimination against minority groups. 78
Richmond, Mary 46, 54
Roadmap to Reducing Child Poverty (National Academies of Sciences, Engineering and Medicine) 297–98, *298*
Roe v. Wade (1973) 74, 230
Romer v. Evans (1996) 221
Roosevelt, Franklin D. 54, 56, 58, 62, 74, 258, 364
Roosevelt, Theodore 47–49
Roper v. Simmons (2005) 320
Ross, John 37
Ryan, Paul 21, 405
Ryan White Comprehensive AIDS Resources Emergency (CARE) Act (1999) 403, *404*

Sagastume, Rob *168–69*
sales taxes 87, 123
same-sex marriage 90, 222–23
sandwich generation 440
Sanger, Margaret 56
Santon, Elizabeth Cady 55
"scientific charity" 44
secondary labor market: the segment of the economy made up of the lowest-paying jobs, disproportionately held by women and people of color. 245
segregation: de facto 245; housing 93; Jim Crow laws 42, 63, 64–66; school 63–64
selective programs: base eligibility on the satisfaction of parameters such as income, diagnosis, or geographic residence. 103, 270–89; Earned Income Tax Credit (EITC) 287–89, *289*; General Assistance (GA) 286–87, *287*; non-cash programs 277–84, *279*, *280*, *284*; Supplemental Security Income (SSI) program *285*, 285–86, *286*; Temporary Assistance for Needy Families (TANF) 271–77, *274*, *275*, *276*
self-determination: people's ability to control their own destiny. 6
Self Employment Contributions Act (SECA) 286
self-help organizations 35
Senior Safe Act (2018) 438
September 11, 2001, attacks 84, 156, 174, 246, 465
serious mental illness (SMI) 389
service delivery systems 161–63, *162*

Servicemen's Readjustment Act (1944) 62–63
Settlement House Movement 42, 44–46
sexism: discrimination based on gender. 206; and Equal Pay Act (1963) 69, 228; and Equal Rights Amendment (ERA) 55, 74; and *Ledbetter v. Goodyear Tire & Rubber Co.* 229; and older women 448; towards women in politics 90; *see also* women
sexual harassment 145, *229*, 231–32; Me Too movement 231–32
sexual orientation: a person's emotional, sexual, and/or relational attraction to others (Poirier et al., 2014). 220–24, *221*
sexual violence 207, 231–32
Shelby County v. Holder (2013) 237
Shepherd, Matthew 243–44
Sherraden, Michael 299
"should statements" 152
single-payer health care plan: a system under which government pays for all health care. 365
Sitting Bull 309
slavery 32–33, 40–41
smart decarceration: policies to substantially reduce the incarcerated population and redress social disparities among the incarcerated while maximizing safety and societal well-being (Epperson & Pettus-Davis, 2015). 212
SNAP *see* Supplemental Nutrition Assistance Program (SNAP)
social class 409
social conditions 142–43
social conscience hypothesis: contends that human beings' innate, altruistic concerns for others have led to the creation of the welfare state. 106
social conservatives: oppose the expansion of personal liberty and assert traditional beliefs about the family, religion, and the role of women. 111
social constructionist approach: posits that our explanations of all human interactions—including social problems—are based on views of reality that are socially and personally constructed (Geertz, 1973; Gergen, 1999). 144; to family violence 145; needs and problems, defining using 144–45; to teenage pregnancy 144
social contract: understanding that governs people's expectations of what core benefits government will provide as part of societal membership. 79
social control 22, 26, 46, 105, 151, 317
Social Darwinism: a philosophy that applied Darwin's theory of evolution based on natural selection to human societies (Day, 2009). 24, 44

social determinants of health: "the circumstances in which people are born, grow up, live, work, and age, as well as the systems put in place to deal with illness" (CDCP, 2013). 354–55
social development approach: an approach that seeks to harmonize economic development with social welfare policy by redistributing resources in ways that promote economic growth (Midgley & Sherraden, 2009). 137–38
social engagement 424–27, 447–48
social enterprises: organizations that address unmet needs or solve social or environmental problems through market-driven approaches. 133
social exchange theory: proposes that social behavior is the result of exchanges, the purpose of which is to maximize benefits and minimize cost or loss. 447–48
Social Gospel 24
social insurance 47
social justice: the equitable distribution of societal resources to all people, as well as equity and fairness in the social, economic, and political spheres. 2, 6, 211–32, *215*, *219*, *221*, *225*, *229*
social media 194, *195*
social mobilization 461
social niches: the environmental habitat of people, including the resources they utilize and the people with which they associate" (Taylor, 1997). 182
social policy(ies): the laws, rules, and regulations that govern the benefits and services provided by governmental and private organizations to assist people in meeting their needs. 1–2; of colonial era 31–34; connecting to personal experience 7; enacting 179–80; English Poor Laws' influence on 30; evaluating, based on outcomes 189–91; faith-based origins of 22–24; framework for linking history and current policy 25, 25–27; how context affects 100–3; implementing 179–80; implications for understanding 113–14; "neutral" policies 248–49; during Progressive era 47–51; as shaped by needs definition 146–47; social workers' responsibility for 6–7; and social work practice 4–7, *5*, 15; strengths-based *vs.* problem-centered approaches *12*; strengths perspective approach to 8–15; *see also* **policy practice**
social problems: concerns about the quality of life of large groups of people that are either held as a broad consensus among a population or voiced by social and economic elites (Chambers & Bonk, 2013). 2, 147–56; causal theories 152–53;

claims-making 154–56; defining and documenting problems/needs 147–52, *148*; and ideologies/values 152; and social conditions 142–43

social programs: the specified set of activities designed to solve social problems and/or meet human needs. 5; adequacy of 127–33, *128*, *129*, *130*, *132*; impetus for 101–3; reforms 73–74

Social Security Act (1935) 58–59, 69–70, 74, 107

Social Security Disability Insurance (SSDI) 286, 393

Social Security Trust Fund 120

social welfare: a nation's system of programs, benefits, and services that help people meet those social, economic, educational, and health needs fundamental to the maintenance of society. 3; colonial-era 31; conflicting historical views on 24–25; genesis of 22–25; impact of 290–91, *291*; institutional approach to 31, 103–4; public and private components of 34; residual approach to 31, 103–4; "welfare", as term 107

social welfare expenditures: all spending necessary to sustain core social welfare programs. adequacy of 127–31; current U.S. 126–34; federal budgets 117–21, *118*, *119*, *121*; nature of 126–27; state budgets 121–22; of U.S., *vs.* other countries 131–33, *132*; *see also* funding; **tax expenditures**

social work: "the professional activity of helping individuals, groups or communities to enhance or restore their capacity for social functioning and creating societal conditions favorable to this goal" (NASW, 1973, p. 4). 3–8; Grand Challenges 491, *491*; origins of modern 42–47, *43*, *45*; practice of, and social policy 4–6, *5*; as profession 46–47, 57, 78; and the strengths perspective 8–15, *11*; values of 6–7, 15, 466–67

social workers: African American 47, 328; and personal experience, connecting policy to 7; perspectives of, examining 184–85; responsibility for policy practice 6–7; role of, in child welfare system 348; role of, in civil rights struggles 249–51; role of, in policy development 181–82; and social policy, relationship between 5; *see also* National Association of Social Workers (NASW)

Society for the Prevention of Cruelty to Children 44, 312

solutions-focused approaches: approaches that ask people to identify the outcomes they want for themselves, their families, and their communities. 16

Southern Christian Leadership Conference (SCLC) 64, 66

special education 240, 335–36

special needs, children with 335–36

Special Supplement Nutrition Program for Women, Infants, and Children (WIC) 5, 157–58, 280–81

Speenhamland System 28–29, 30

spiritual traditions 22–23

stakeholders 16, 135, 173, 175, 176, 179, 187, 194

Stanton, Elizabeth Cady 55

Starr, Helen Gates 44, 45

state budget and spending policies 121–22

State Children's Health Insurance Program (SCHIP) 84, 382, 383

State Comprehensive Mental Health Services Plan Act (1986) 394–95, *395*

State Health Insurance Assistance Programs (SHIPs) 427

State of the Future Index (SOFI) *480*, 480–81

Stonewall Riots 68, 220–21

"story banks" 186

"street-level bureaucracy" 161

strengths perspective: a philosophical approach to social work that posits that the goals, strengths, and resources of people and their environment, rather than their problems and pathologies, should be the central focus of the helping process (Saleebey, 1992). 8–15; benefits of 13–14; cautions regarding 14–15; and children protection policy 339; developing policy practice abilities 15–17, *17*; and economic nationalism 113; for future policy 466–67, 490; and GI Bill 63; and juvenile justice 345–47; and needs determination 146–47; and OASDI 294–97; and older adults 451; and policy development 176; and policy practice 9–11; principles of *11*, 11–13; *vs.* problem-centered approach (quick guide) *12*; and settlement house movement 46; and social development approach 137; and TANF 291–94

structural discrimination: entrenched societal practices that favor one group over another. 209

Substance Abuse and Mental Health Services Administration (SAMHSA): a federal agency established in 1992 whose purpose is to improve the lives of people with or at risk of mental and substance use disorders. 395–97

substance use disorders 395–97, *396*, 402–3

suffrage *see* voting rights

Supplemental Nutrition Assistance Program (SNAP) 71, 119, 163, 218, 261, 262, 278–80, *279*, *280*

Supplemental Poverty Measure (SPM) 262

Supplemental Security Income (SSI) program 73, 80, *285*, 285–86, *286*, 423–24

supply-side economics 80, *86*, 109–10
Support for Patients and Communities Act (2018) *396*
Supporting Healthy Marriages (SHM) program 273

TANF *see* Temporary Assistance for Needy Families (TANF)
Taxas v. Azar 368
tax credits 73; Child and Dependent Care Tax Credit 344; Child Tax Credit (CTC) 288, *289*; Earned Income Tax Credit (EITC) 73, 119, 125, 180, 262, 287–89, *289*; Low-Income Housing Tax Credits 284
tax cuts 80, 85–86, 91
Tax Cuts and Jobs Act (TCJA) (2017) 91, 125, 134, 367, 368, 405
tax expenditures: taxes that are not collected from particular groups, in order to assist them in obtaining goods and services such as housing, health care, and education. 123–26, *124*, *125*; *see also* **income tax**
tax increases 83
tax strategies 123–26, *124*, *125*
Taylor, Jim 181–82
technological advances 470–73
teenage pregnancy 144, 153, 341–42, *342*
Temperance Movement 51
Temporary Assistance for Needy Families (TANF) 30, 271–77, *274*; *vs.* AFDC 83–84; and Child Support Enforcement (CSE) program 334; and drug-testing requirement 172; family formation goals 273; and the federal budget 119, 164; goals of 272–73; history and development of 272; and Medicaid 372; and poverty 261, 274–77, *275*, *276*; reforming 293–94; *vs.* SNAP 279–80, *280*; state spending on 275, *276*; from the strengths perspective 291–94; work requirements and sanctions 273–77
tenant-based rental assistance program 282–84, *284*
terrorism 477, 481
Ticket to Work and Work Incentives Improvement Act (1999) 83
Towle, Charlotte 57
Townsend Movement 58, 156
"Trail of Broken Treaties" caravan 75
Trail of Tears 37
transaction costs: all costs incurred during government interventions including financial, economic, personal, and environmental costs. 102
transgender individuals: an umbrella term for people whose gender, gender identity, or expression of gender is in some way different from social norms for their assigned birth sex. 220–24, *221*

transporting niches: environments where people can get the help they need to move out of entrapping niches. 182
Treaty of Guadalupe and Hidalgo (1848) 37
tribal sovereignty: the right of Native peoples to self-govern, determine tribal membership, regulate tribal business and domestic relations, and manage tribal property. 214
Tribal Supreme Court Project 216
"trickle down" economics 110
Truman, Harry S. 364
Trump, Donald 91–95; and abortions 230; and Affordable Care Act (ACA) (2010) 366–67; and climate change 461; and consent decrees 250; and Dakota Access pipeline 216; and Deferred Action for Childhood Arrivals (DACA) (2017) 246–47; and Elder Abuse Prevention and Prosecution Act (2017) 437; and federal judiciary, reshaping of 93–94; immigration policies 94–95, 101, 217–18, 246–47, 479; and LGBTQ+ civil rights 223, 224; and Medicare Part D 378–79; nationalistic policies, impact of 111, 136; and nursing homes 426; and occupational automation 473; and official poverty guidelines 262; and opioid epidemic 188, 396; and racism 213; regulatory retreat of 90, 92–93; and Senior Safe Act (2018) 438; and sexual violence 232; and SNAP 278; and social workers 406; tax cuts 110; and voting restrictions 235; and wealth inequality 130; and younger voters 110
"trust busting" 47
Tubman, Harriet 35–36

unanticipated consequences: unexpected events that result from the implementation of a policy. 180
underinsured: people whose insurance coverage is inadequate to provide affordable access to necessary health care. 356
underservice 362
unemployment insurance 266–68, *268*
United Farm Workers (UFW) 67
United Nations Convention on the Rights of the Child 339
United States v. Windsor (2013) 222
Universal Basic Income (UBI) 73, 301–3
universal programs: serve everyone in a broad category. 103, 263–70; Old-Age, Survivors, and Disability Insurance (OASDI) 263–66, *264*, *266*; unemployment insurance 266–68, *268*; veterans' benefits 269–70; workers' compensation 268–69, *269*; *see also* specific programs

upside-down welfare state 127, 299–300
urbanization 39
Urban League 70
U.S. Department of Agriculture (USDA) *175*
U.S. Department of Health and Human Services (USDHHS) poverty guidelines 261
U.S. Department of Housing and Urban Development (HUD) 282–83
U.S. Public Health Service 34

Vento, Bruce F. *148*
vertical equity: redistribution of resources to people who possess fewer resources or have more severe needs, to help equalize conditions. 103
vested: to have a non-forfeitable right to pensions or other retirement benefits. 435
veterans: in colonial-era America 34; mental health issues 401
veterans' benefits 269–70
victim blaming: the devaluing act of holding a person experiencing a problem primarily responsible for the problem, instead of also considering other causal factors. 14
Violence Against Women Act (1994) 231
Violence Against Women Act (2005) 242–43, *243*
Violence Against Women Act (2013) 242–43
Violence Against Women Act grants 92
Volstead Act (1919) 51
Volunteers in Service to America (VISTA) 70
voting patterns 432, *432*
voting rights: for African Americans 40–41; new restrictions on 235–36, *236*; *Shelby County v. Holder* (2013) 237; for women 41, 49, *55*, 55–56
Voting Rights Act (1965) 234–37, *235*, *236*

wage discrimination 69, 228, 484
War on Poverty initiatives 69–72; Great Society programs 70; Medicare and Medicaid 70–71; New Frontier programs 69–70; successes and failures 71–72
Watergate scandal 74
water shortages 479
wealth inequality *129*, 129–31, *130*
Weick, Ann 407
welfare pluralists: believe that society benefits when a variety of private groups as well as various levels of government participate in the provision of social welfare services. 132
Welfare Rights Movements 69
welfare rolls 69
welfare system *see* social welfare
welfare-to-work (WTW) grants 277
Wellstone, Paul 364
Whitehall Studies 408–9
white privilege: societal advantages and rights that accrue to individuals identified as White. 249
Whole Woman's Health v. Hellerstedt 230
WIC *see* Special Supplement Nutrition Program for Women, Infants, and Children (WIC)
Wilson, Woodrow 55
windows of opportunity: moments when policymakers' attention has been captured by external events, such that advocates may find a more receptive audience for their proposals. 174
women: as caregivers 426; and civil rights 66, 74, 228–32, *229*; and contraception 56, 144, 231, 367; and elder abuse 437; end-of-life planning for 447; and life expectancy 425, 428, *428*, 429; and mothers' pensions 49–50; and OASDI 294–95, 450; and poverty 230, 271, 431; sexual harassment 145, *229*, 231–32; sexual violence 207, 231–32; social activists 49–50, 51; social engagement of 429, 448; and SSI program 424; voting rights 41, 49, *55*, 55–56; wage discrimination 69, 228, 484; "welfare mothers" 155; women of colour, and intersectionality 246; in the workforce 59–62, *61*, 483; *see also* sexism
workers' compensation 268–69, *269*
workhouses: publicly funded establishments in which large numbers of laborers were brought together to perform some type of work and sometimes to receive job training. 29, *29*, 32
Works Progress Administration (WPA) 56
World War I 54–55
World War II 59–62, *61*

Young, Whitney, Jr. 70, *215*

zero tolerance 218, 346
Zika virus 403

9780367357054